READER'S DIGEST

A Garden for all Seasons

READER'S DIGEST

A Garden for all
Seasons

THE READER'S DIGEST ASSOCIATION, INC.

PLEASANTVILLE, NEW YORK • MONTREAL

A GARDEN FOR ALL SEASONS
was edited and designed by The Reader's Digest Association Limited, London

First Edition Copyright © 1991
The Reader's Digest Association Limited, Berkeley Square House, Berkeley Square, London W1X 6AB
Copyright © 1991
Reader's Digest Association Far East Limited
Philippines Copyright 1991
Reader's Digest Association Far East Limited

Printed in Belgium
ISBN 0-89577-380-5

Reader's Digest Fund for the Blind is publisher of the Large-Type Edition of *Reader's Digest*.
For subscription information about this magazine, please contact Reader's Digest Fund for the Blind,
Inc., Dept. 250, Pleasantville, N.Y. 10570.

COVER ILLUSTRATION
The continuity of the seasons in the garden is represented in SPRING by *Narcissus* 'Jack Snipe',
Anemone blanda and the grape hyacinth *Muscari armeniacum*; in SUMMER by *Rosa* 'Graham Thomas';
in AUTUMN by *Rosa rugosa* hips and the fluffy seed heads of *Clematis tangutica*;
and in WINTER by the white and gold flowers of *Helleborus niger*.

Acknowledgments

*The publishers wish to express their gratitude
to the following people for their major contributions to the book:*

CONSULTANT EDITOR
John Kelly

CONSULTANT PLANTSMAN
Kenneth A. Beckett

MAJOR CONTRIBUTORS

John Bond	Dr James Morison
Nigel Colborn	Bill Nelmes
Fred Downham	Philip Swindells
Jim Gardiner	Jane Taylor
Duncan Lowe	Ray Waite

ARTISTS

Sophie Allington	Kevin Dean	Brenda Katté	Sally Smith
Julie Banyard	Shirley Felts	Nicki Kemball	Gill Tomblin
Leonora Box	Sarah Fox-Davies	Roy Knipe	Barbara Walker
Wendy Bramall	Helen Haywood	Jane Reynolds	Ann Winterbotham

STILL-LIFE PHOTOGRAPHERS
Laurie Evans
Jacqui Hurst
Martin Langfield

*Many other people and organisations assisted in the preparation of this book.
The publishers would like to thank the following for their help:*

Peter Atkinson	Nicholas Hall	Lyn Randall
R.C. Balfour	Ann and David	Mary Robinson
Kathleen Beard	Hitchcock	Tony Russell
Andrew Boyton	Brenda Hyatt	Lady Christine
Graham Clarke	Donald Maginnis	Skelmersdale
Michael Cox	Gerald Mann	Jennifer Trehane
Stephen Craven	Neville Martin	Dirk van Klaveren
Nicholas Freed	Reg Perryman	John Walkers
Lt Col J.K. Grapes	Paul Picton	Ronald Whitehouse

GARDENS AND NURSERIES

Aylett Nurseries, St Albans · Garden of the Rose, St Albans · Royal Horticultural Society's Garden, Wisley
Savill Garden, Windsor · Springfields Horticultural Society, Spalding · Trehane Nursery, Dorset
Wansdyke Nursery, Wiltshire · Westonbirt Arboretum, Gloucestershire · Whitehouse Ivies, Essex

Contents

ABOUT THIS BOOK

THE GLORIES OF THE ENGLISH GARDEN – its splendid flower beds and borders, and its elegant arrangements of trees, turf, and shrubs – should be a tremendous inspiration to American gardeners. Yet too often we feel only envy and discouragement. Anything will grow in that mild British climate, we complain, and the English have a special knack with plants. The plain facts are, though, that the British climate isn't better, it's just different, and English gardeners don't owe their success to any inborn talent. Instead, they achieve it through the skillful application of a handful of basic principles. That's what you'll find in the pages ahead, the rule book by which the English cultivate their stunning success.

A landscape that's beautiful year-round is the English gardener's ideal, and the key to this lies in a judicious choice of plants. This book makes the selection process easy with its four seasonal plant catalogues. Each of these provides an overview of what that season can offer, with detailed descriptions of the plants themselves and how to grow them. Within each season, the plants are divided according to their horticultural category – trees, shrubs, perennials, etc – and are listed in alphabetical order under their botanical names. Common names are given in every relevant entry and in the main index.

Many of the plants, in addition to their main season of bloom, offer a second flush of flowers, a glowing crop of fruit, or an arresting winter profile. Some, the true all-season plants that always enhance a landscape's beauty, are the framework of the English garden, and these have a section of their own.

Continuity is also essential to a pleasing horticultural display, and scattered through the plant catalogues are features on 'Bridging the Seasons'. Here you'll find suggestions on how plants, or combinations of plants, can bridge the lulls between the different seasonal peaks of color and bloom. Other features concentrate on specialized planting themes, such as rock or water gardens, that add emphasis to your garden's all-season framework.

Some plant groups can bewilder with their huge number of species and cultivars, but the photographic features here will sort them out by presenting the gardener with a select portrait gallery of the very best. Most of the species in the book are grown in America, although certain British cultivars may not easily be found on this side of the Atlantic. If a particular cultivar appeals to you and you can't find it, browse through your garden center or scan a seed catalogue to find an American cultivar similar in color, shape, and growth habit. If you decide that only the British cultivar will do, obtain a British seed catalogue; gardening magazines usually have ads telling you where to write for one.

In any case, instructions for the use and care of a plant apply to the species as a whole, not its myriad cultivars. A section at the back of the text explains cultural techniques in detail, and includes a season-by-season guide to the tasks that keep the garden looking good throughout the year. Closing the book is a plant selector, a guide to plants adapted to your particular garden conditions.

Differences between the British and North American climates mean that, unless you live in the Pacific Northwest, you probably can't transplant an English garden intact. Throughout most of our North, the colder winters would take a toll of the more tender English plants, and the hardiest ones often won't tolerate the hotter summers of the South. But even if you can't have the whole plant catalogue, you can learn the secrets of the English gardener. And with them, you can make your American garden just as splendid.

THE GARDEN YEAR

No DOUBT King Charles II was feeling a certain proprietary interest when he described the British climate as 'The best in the world.' In his kingdom, he explained, 'A man can enjoy outdoor exercise on all but five days of the year.' And, he might have added, a gardener can grow an extraordinary collection of plants from every corner of the globe on the same half acre.

North Americans, by contrast, tend to take pride in the extremes of their local weather. Where an Englishman boasts of his climate's mildness, a West Texan tells stories of summer heat and the length and severity of droughts, a Vermonter jokes about the spring that came (and went) on Wednesday, and a Minnesotan retails anecdotes about winters that never end. The fact is that climate may vary from subtropical to genuinely arctic, depending on where you live within the continental United States and Canada. As a result, gardeners here are much better advised to study what flora is best adapted to their region rather than concentrating on the simply foreign and rare.

But if there are notable points of difference between the British and North American climates, we can still learn much from British gardeners. The basic cycle of seasons is the same, and in both lands, it is the changes in temperature, day length and precipitation that waken plants from dormancy, set them flowering, and then cause them to stop. How the weather varies from day to day determines everything from the blooming of the day lily to the population of aphids on a rose stem. An understanding of this natural interplay is essential everywhere to horticultural success. And British gardeners, at least the best of them, are masters of this kind of lore.

For it is British gardeners' close, keen observation of the daily weather that enables them to work in partnership with nature, rather than against it, and to achieve stunning results.

Studying the changes that come with the year's progress, however, will do more than help you become a better grower; it will also increase your success as a designer. This book is about creating a garden that changes with the moods of the seasons. To accomplish that, you must first understand the seasons themselves.

SHEER SIZE provides the most obvious reason for America's smorgasbord of climates and the dramatic extremes of our seasons. The continental United States (the 48 conterminous states) stretches across more than 20 degrees of latitude. When Canada and Alaska are included in the reckoning, you are dealing with a land mass that runs all the way from the Arctic Circle to within a hundred miles or so of the Tropic of Cancer.

To grasp the extreme variation that occurs within this area, you need only look at the Plant Hardiness Zone Map developed by the United States Department of Agriculture. This document divides this country by each region's average annual minimum temperature into eleven separate climate zones. In Zone 11, which includes coastal areas of the Hawaiian Islands and Southern California, temperatures drop only to 40°F during the average winter, while in Zone 1, central Alaska, temperatures more than 50°F below zero are normal. Familiarity with this map is essential to successful gardening, since it is the standard reference nurserymen use in specifying the winter-hardiness of different plants.

Distance from the equator plays the primary role in determining the relative warmth of a region, but as the USDA map shows, other factors affect climate as well. Since the oceans do not change temperature as quickly as the land, they help to moderate temperatures in coastal regions, curbing both winter lows and summer highs. This phenomenon has given the tip of the Alaskan peninsula – washed by warm Pacific currents – a climate no colder than much of Virginia.

In general, it is the regions remote from the oceanic influence that experience the greatest seasonal variations between summer and winter, and the most abrupt transitions. So, for example, Montana has registered the lowest winter temperature in the continental US (−70°F). But it has also recorded a high of 117°F, and a record-setting rise of 34°F in just seven minutes, on a December day when the thermometer rose from −5°F to 75°F, melting 30 inches of snow.

Altitude also takes a hand in determining the severity of the seasons; on average, temperatures drop 3°–4°F with a climb of 1000 feet, so that a mountain peak 2500 feet tall may belong to a different climate zone than the surrounding plain. In addition, mountains help set patterns of rainfall. By forcing sea breezes upward and chilling them, the coastal ranges of the Pacific states condense their moisture as rainfall. As a result, along the northwest coast, rainfall in some places reaches 150 inches a year; yet immediately to the east of the mountains lie some of our driest deserts.

Every geographical region of North America has a distinctive pattern of rainfall. Through the northeastern and north central states of the US, precipitation is abundant year-round, though usually peaking in early summer. On the south Florida plain, in contrast, winter is normally a dry season, yet in Arizona this, together with late summer, is when the state receives most of its meager allotment of precipitation.

THE SEASONS

The four seasons are generally demarcated into groups of months, but the seasons are inclined to topple into one another, and in reality the boundaries are not nearly so clear cut. What determines the seasons is the sun's position in relation to the Earth, which affects temperature and the length of daylight. But because the sun's heat and light are affected by winds, clouds, and the circulation of air about the globe, the weather often behaves unseasonably; this may have a considerable influence on the conditions for plant growth and the length of the growing season.

SPRING – MARCH APRIL MAY

Spring is generally acknowledged as the time when Earth wakes from its winter lethargy, and growing things begin to stir in the ground. According to the calendar, it all begins on March 21, when the sun's position is such that day and night are of approximately equal length. Through most of the country, temperature is the stimulus: it climbs to around 43°F, and the soil becomes sufficiently warm for growth to begin. This temperature may be reached early in February in the South and might be delayed until May in northern New England. In

Spring's arrival is evinced more in the blossoming of shrubs and trees, such as the magnificent yulan tree, *Magnolia denudata*, than in anything else. (Photo: Beckett Picture Library)

Summer's colorful bounty is captured in this generous planting of *Campanula persicifolia*, delphiniums, geraniums, and pink sweet williams. (Photo: Eric Crichton; Barnsley House, Glos.)

the most southerly regions, however, where winters are mild, it is moisture from spring rains that sets growth in motion. Amid all the swelling buds, though, it is important to remember that even in the mid-South a late frost may blast tender seedlings.

SUMMER – JUNE JULY AUGUST

Both the beginning and the highlight of this season is June 21, known traditionally as Midsummer Day. It possesses the greatest length of daylight, some 16 hours in the northern states and 24 hours in Fairbanks, Alaska. The average temperature ranges widely from region to region, with a daily high of 105°F in Phoenix, Arizona through July, and

75°F in Seattle, Washington. The highest temperatures are usually in mid-August, and in the hottest areas, such as the Gulf Coast and Southern California, intense heat may temporarily halt plant growth. In many areas, especially the arid West, rainfall decreases dramatically in summer, though in the Southeast and Southwest, late summer brings the year's heaviest storms.

AUTUMN – SEPTEMBER OCTOBER NOVEMBER

Early September is often a golden extension of summer, but as the days shorten, so the warmth of the sun decreases, and the temperature differential between North and South becomes much more pronounced than it was in August. High pressure

AUTUMN foliage brings a last great blaze of color to the garden, particularly among maples, which can glow like fire even in the dullest weather or as dusk falls. (Photo: Tania Midgley)

WINTER blizzards may lay the garden flat, but there are still many joys to be found outdoors, among them the frosted berries of this *Cotoneaster lacteus*. (Photo: Eric Crichton)

often brings calm, sunny days but they can be followed by still, cloudless nights attended by early morning frosts to plague the gardener, especially in the upland areas of the North. By the middle of October, much of the North will have experienced the first ground frost of the oncoming winter, and wise gardeners will look to their geraniums. In the South, however, the cooler weather brings renewed growth and a second flush of blossoms that is nearly the equal of spring's. Even in the North, autumn is one of the garden's finest seasons – and, according to some experts, more beautiful in North America than anywhere else in the world. This is a time for admiring the russets and golds of ornamental grasses gone to seed, the scarlet of

berries, and the vivid palette of the changing foliage. Chrysanthemums, asters, and many other perennial flowers choose this season for their floral display, making cheerful the Indian summer that seems a heaven-sent time for propagating plants and for general garden maintenance. With its moderate temperatures and gentle sunshine, this is also an excellent time of year for planting everything from grass-seed to roses.

WINTER – DECEMBER JANUARY FEBRUARY

Not really the dead season in the garden, for it is a time to plan and, when weather permits, to prepare plots new and old for next spring and summer. December can be bitterly cold, especially in the

northern Great Plains – the average daily minimum drops to 13.5°F in Omaha, Nebraska by year's end. But in the South, winter is more often a month of squally winds and rains, interspersed with periods of surprising gentleness, and on the West Coast, winter is a period of moderate temperatures (Los Angeles hardly drops below 45°F, even in January) and abundant precipitation. In the deep snowpack that builds up in the mountains – one area of Washington *averages* more than 500 inches annually – nature stores the moisture that will nurture spring's growth. Despite the optimism engendered by lengthening days, January is apt to bring the coldest weather of the year. Southerly winds in late February can sometimes bring a warm spell and a thaw, tempting gardeners to believe that winter is over. But ignore such blandishments; except in the extreme south and west, the month still has numerous shots in store.

HOW THE SEASONS AND ELEMENTS AFFECT PLANT GROWTH

Plants need light, heat, air and water to grow. In these northerly latitudes, most summer-flowering plants, also known as long-day plants, bloom when the daylight lasts 12 hours or more. Spring and autumn-flowering plants, called short-day plants, require less light, while a third category, day-neutral plants, are independent of day length – pansies, daisies and wallflowers, for example, whose growth is solely dependent on temperature.

The number of daylight hours is dictated by the angle at which the sunlight reaches the Earth, so varies according to season and geographical position. Since sunlight provides the energy essential for plant growth, many plants have developed the ability to turn their leaves towards the sun in order to capture as much light as possible. If the light is too bright they simply turn their edge towards the sun.

Shade-dwelling plants – ferns like *Polystichum* and *Dryopteris*, for example, have developed larger, thinner leaves to entrap more of the available light.

But they can adapt to different light intensities, and will survive in full sun in the north as long as they are kept moist. They may look less impressive, however, because in full sun their leaf colour may change to a paler green and the tissues may thicken up. Sun-loving plants, conversely, will not grow well in deep shade.

TEMPERATURE

Together with day length, temperature is critical in determining the time a plant takes to go through its life cycle of germination, leaf growth, stem elongation, flowering, and fruiting. Although plants can survive extreme temperatures while dormant, they are active only within a limited temperature range, which varies according to species. Typically, most plant growth occurs between about 43°F and 86°F. The warmer it is in early spring, the earlier most species will begin to grow and the earlier they will flower. If temperatures are too low over a long period, a plant may not have time to flower or bear fruit at all. On the other hand, temperatures higher than about 86°F can be damaging to plants native to temperate climates.

Plants have adapted in different ways to keep cool or warm. Many alpines, for instance, have adapted against wind by forming a cushion of low-growing leaves which also help them to keep warm and moist. The complete effects of temperature on a plant must also include the way other organisms are affected by it. The best temperature for its seed germination, for example, will be just in advance of the temperature that activates the soil fungi that attack the seed, while successful fruiting depends on the right air temperature to bring forth and activate pollinating insects at flowering time.

CHILLING AND FROSTS

Although a study of average temperatures can be a useful guide to plant performance, gardeners are often taken unaware by late frosts or unexpected drops in temperature that destroy buds and blooms on early flowering shrubs, or kill newly planted seedlings. Many plants grown in summer are of subtropical origin, and these especially can be chilled and injured by day temperatures lower than 50°F. The symptoms of chilling are wilting, inhibited growth, or even the death of leaves or

On the Pacific Coast, warm, moist air carried by prevailing westerly winds, cools and condenses as rainfall when it reaches the coastal mountains; if you live on the lee side you can expect less rain, and sunnier summers.

stems. If the cool temperatures are not prolonged, or not too severe, the plant may recover. There are two types of frost – air frost and ground frost. Ground frosts are more frequent, but air frosts are more damaging because they are colder. They usually occur on still, cold nights when the soil surface cools and there is no air movement to clear the freezing air gathering around plants. Frosts can strike in all but the mildest parts of the country at any time of the year.

Some locations, termed frost hollows, are particularly prone to frosts. These can occur on any sloping ground but they are more likely to be a worse problem on north-facing slopes. They can also be found where the cool air drains down into a valley, or where cold air is trapped against a fence or thick hedge, for example.

How much a frost affects plants depends on its severity and duration, and on the stage of development the plants have reached. They are damaged when the water between the cells freezes and the crystals of ice so formed puncture the cell walls. Half-hardy species can be killed outright, or lose many leaves, in a single sharp overnight frost of no less than four degrees Fahrenheit below freezing if the plant has not been hardened off – gradually adjusted to cooler temperatures. Temperate perennial and biennial plants adjust naturally as autumn approaches, but even these are damaged by late spring or early autumn frosts, when new growth is still tender and has not had time to acclimatise.

Frosts at the right time of the year, when plants have hardened and are dormant, are actually a good thing. They help to break up the surface of heavy soils and kill weed seedlings and insect pests close to the surface. Several types of overwintering aphids and other insect pests are killed by temperatures around 19°F, so in the following spring, only their overwintering eggs will hatch. In the northern states and Canada, conditions are generally cold enough to kill overwintering aphids, which is why stock plants of raspberry, for example, can be grown there without risk of their developing the virus spread by these creatures.

FROST-CONSCIOUS PLANTING

In avoiding frost damage, a prime consideration is deciding when to plant outdoors. If gardeners play safe by planting out late in the season, the plants may not be left with sufficient time to mature. This is particularly the case in northern and upland areas where the frost-free season is short anyway. One method of deciding when to plant out, is to study the first and last frost dates locally for previous seasons, then to pick a date when there is a 70 per cent chance that there will be no more frosts. This is likely to be successful in seven years out of ten, and even if frost does occur, it is unlikely to be severe, and plants can be given protection against it. To do this, double-wrap light plastic sheeting around tender plants; protect shrubs with dry leaves, straw or plastic sheeting mounted on a frame of chicken wire or canes.

WATER

Plants continually draw water from the soil through their roots – a well-stocked border has several miles of root for every square yard of ground. The job is done by the very finest white roots, covered with microscopic hairs. It is these root hairs that remove water from the soil, which must be damp and open enough to allow them to establish themselves and provide the 'piped supply' of moisture for the plant. When a plant is moved, the number and distribution of the roots in the soil is disrupted, which makes the plants vulnerable to temporary dehydration. Large plants and shrubs can take weeks, or even months, to re-establish the necessary water-supply system.

Without sufficient water, a plant reacts by closing its leaf pores, and eventually wilts. Wilting is not always permanent, but there is a point beyond which a plant cannot recover, even if its water supply is restored. A plant's performance is affected by drought long before it shows obvious signs of wilting, however, and expanding buds, leaves, flowers and fruit can be held back or damaged. The more plants there are in a flowerbed, and the more leaves and stems a plant has, the greater the demand for water. A large tree can use up to 10 gallons of water an hour on a clear summer day. Although a lot of this is taken up from deeper layers of soil than used by neighbouring plants, it will dry out the soil to some extent. Hedges also dry out the soil and limit the amount of rain reaching other plants on their lee sides.

Plants lose water by evaporation as the leaf pores open to let in carbon dioxide from the air. The moisture must be constantly replaced through their root systems, though bright sunshine and a drying wind can make this a losing race. Some plants conserve water better than others. Plants native to dry places – broom for example – tend to have small leaves, which lowers evaporation.

If you live on a slope, especially a north-facing one: beware! On clear, still nights, cold air flows downhill into frost hollows in valleys or can become trapped behind a fence or wall.

YOUR GARDEN'S MICROCLIMATE

The USDA plant hardiness zone map (see page 11) gives a general idea of climate and an indication of what will grow in various regions of the country, but conditions can differ considerably even within a fairly restricted neighborhood. Local climate is affected by distance from the sea, the height and lie of the land, and other factors. Although you cannot change the weather, you can do something about its effect on your garden.

You can make it more sheltered, for example, and make the best use of its slopes, shade or suntraps in deciding what to plant where, bearing in mind that plants grow best in conditions of temperature, soil and moisture that are as similar as possible to those found in their native habitat.

ASPECT AND EXPOSURE

The sun is to the south at midday, and air temperature is warmer in the afternoon, so a south-west-facing garden is the warmest. A sheltered spot between two walls facing south-west and south-east is suitable for tender plants, because the walls capture and reflect the sun's rays during the warmest part of the day.

Land sloping towards the sun gets the most heat because of the angle at which the rays meet the surface – on flat land (or land sloping away from the sun), the rays are spread over a wider area and are less intense. East-facing slopes warm up quickest on summer mornings. A north-facing garden gets the least hours of sunshine, so is generally more suitable for shade-loving plants.

An exposed garden will be cooler by day, windier, and less productive than one sheltered by fences, hedges, buildings, trees, or the lie of the land. Town gardens are warmer than those in open country. Shelter from the wind is generally beneficial because it stops the plants being buffeted and reduces the effects of wind-chill. Shelter can also make for higher temperatures because it prevents the sun's heat being dissipated. Hedges make the best shelter. Fences can create turbulence some distance downwind, because they deflect the wind rather than reduce it. A hedge absorbs some of the wind's energy, and lets some air through to the lee side, so creating less turbulence.

Too much shelter, however, may stop rain reaching plants, and turn gardens into frost pockets. North-facing slopes, for instance, have a particular problem when the sun leaves them and the ground begins to cool. The cold air, being denser, flows downhill. If the flow is obstructed by a building, fence, thick hedge or bank, the cold air builds up into a layer, creating a frost hollow.

All Seasons

T HE COMFORTING thing about the march of the seasons through the garden is its inevitability, and the assurance that with the cycle of the planet we will again be greeted by the plants we cherished – a little more mature, and a little closer to the roles envisaged for them. That the inevitability seems more so in Britain than elsewhere is due to the islands' climate. Though not much admired by foreigners – the Roman historian Tacitus called it 'always objectionable, with frequent rains and mists, but there is no extreme cold' – it is perfectly designed for all-seasons cultivation.

The seasons come and go, and with them spring's golden glow of daffodils, summer's rich parade of roses and lilies, and autumn's leafy glories. But year-long there remains the steadfast band of old friends that hold the garden together; tall evergreens for stature, shapely bushes for punctuation, deciduous plants chosen for their autumnal hues. Foliage, in fact, is the pivot on which the garden turns, providing leaves for emphasis, for contrast and for framing seasonal groups.

The seasons change but the beauty of plants like holly, pyracantha and euonymus is constant.

All Seasons
SHRUBS

Shrubs are one of the most important of the permanent elements in the all-seasons garden. They range from hardy, diminutive, hugging the ground alpines to plants that may reach the dimensions of small trees. Their woody stems and twiggy bushiness of character can often be used to give form and shape to the garden, even if they are bare of leaves in the winter. Other backbone shrubs contribute evergreen or everchanging foliage colour interest, and a passing panoply of flowers.

Camellia

The most famous camellia of all, *Camellia sinensis*, bears small white flowers, but is cultivated solely for its leaves – the source of our national beverage, tea. Leaves are also prized in the garden camellias, their dark, polished surfaces catching light throughout the year.

The delicate hues and oriental beauty of the flowers belie the hardiness of camellias. Although early flushes can be damaged by frost, each bush bears a profusion of buds ready to take over time and time again – between November and May, depending on the cultivar. The blooms of some cultivars, especially those of *C. japonica*, fade on the bush, but with those of other species they 'shatter', their petals falling gently to decorate the ground beneath with a colourful carpet.

Camellia japonica 'Adolphe Audusson' blooms do not need deadheading; instead of fading on the bush, the petals simply fall gently to the ground.

Two plants with magnificent foliage – a dark, lustrous ivy and a *Camellia japonica* cultivar – come together for a polished year-round display.

Underplant camellias with hardy fuchsias such as 'Alice Hoffman', to add interest during summer.

The height of camellias varies with soil and climatic conditions. A dense, bushy form, such as *C. × williamsii* 'Inspiration', may reach 8ft at most in 20 years. But other, more vigorous varieties may reach 15ft in the same period in ideal conditions.

COLOUR THROUGH THE YEAR

Classic companions in acid soil – and a large garden – are rhododendrons. Select cultivars whose flowering will precede or follow on from the gorgeous camellia display, such as the early flowering *Rhododendron* 'Praecox' (February-March), or the late-flowering *R.* 'Fabia' (June) and 'Windlesham Scarlet' (May-June). Another evergreen companion, whose rich blue blossom would follow on from early to mid-season camellias, is the lowish, mound-forming *Ceanothus thyrsiflorus* 'Repens'.

On a smaller scale, camellias can make a glamorous backdrop for a seasonal succession of flowering bulbs, from autumn and winter-flowering snowdrops (*Galanthus*) to *Narcissus* cultivars, and *Eranthis hyemalis* in shades of cream and gold, and the bright blue *Scilla sibirica* of spring. The Himalayan cowslip (*Primula florindae*), *Veratrum nigrum* and *Meconopsis × sheldonii* will all flourish in the light shade around the camellia and contribute colour until summer. At a higher level, the leaves of *Acer palmatum* and *A. p.* 'Senkaki' would provide contrasting foliage, especially with their flaming autumn colours, while the brilliant red twigs of 'Senkaki' would illuminate the winter months.

CULTIVATION

Camellias are not as lime-sensitive as rhododendrons, but do need a lightish, neutral to acid soil, enriched with humus for moisture retention, and regular mulching with organic

Camellia japonica 'Contessa Lavinia Maggi' is a bold, upright shrub with large, round leaves, and has a long display of raspberry ripple blooms.

matter. The flowers are liable to wind damage, so select a reasonably sheltered position. In general plant in semi-shade in the South and full sun in the Midlands and North. *C. × williamsii* varieties, such as 'Donation', are more likely to flower well in the north of England and Scotland than *C. japonica*.

Deadhead faded blooms, taking care not to damage the young buds, but leave the blooms that shatter naturally. Prune any long whippy young growths in February, and trim trained plants after flowering.

Propagate by taking a few semi-hardwood cuttings in August and placing them in a mixture of peat and sand in a closed cold frame or heated propagator. Pot the following spring and grow on under cover until large enough to plant out.

Camellia 'Leonard Messel' is hardy enough to produce a reliable abundance of peony-like flowers even in the north of Britain. It is partnered here with another evergreen, the dwarf, wide-spreading *Cotoneaster* 'Skogholm', which will give a rewarding display of large, coral-red berries in autumn.

Polished performance by lustrous camellias

In Victorian times, the oriental glamour of camellias was confined to heated conservatories. But there are many splendid varieties that, with careful siting, will flourish even in the north outdoors. The camellias' dark, lustrous foliage bestows richness on the garden's all-season framework, and in spring, as one flush of exquisite blooms fades, a host of plump buds is waiting to take over. If you can, plant two or three bushes with overlapping flowering periods together, to extend the display.

Photographed in early March at Trehane Nursery, Wimborne, Dorset.

Camellia × *williamsii* 'Freedom Bell'
Dense, small-leaved, twiggy bush suitable for small garden. Best March-April.

Camellia × *williamsii* 'Freestyle'
Very hardy, slow-growing, and very dense foliage; ideal for small garden. Best March-April.

Camellia × *williamsii* 'Joan Trehane'
Open and upright growth; flowers weather well. Best April-June.

Camellia × *williamsii* 'Bow Bells'
Slow-growing, dense bush with small leaves; long, profuse flowering until late spring. Best February-March.

Camellia × *williamsii* 'Jury's Yellow'
Particularly glossy, dense, bushy foliage; very free-flowering. Best April-May.

Camellia japonica 'C.M. Hovey'
Fairly vigorous, tends to be wider than its height. Best March-April.

Camellia × williamsii
'Inspiration'
Very hardy, with upright,
dense, bushy habit.
Best March-May.

Camellia japonica
'Ruddigore'
Bushy growth,
bronze young foliage.
Best April-May.

Camellia × williamsii
'Donation'
Very hardy and free-flowering;
prune to curb vigour.
Best March-May.

Camellia × williamsii
'Bridal Gown'
Weathers better than most
whites; upright and bushy
once it is over 3ft high.
Best April-May.

Camellia japonica 'Primavera'
Bushy growth, downward-curving leaves;
blooms weather well for a white.
Best April-May.

Camellia × williamsii
'Anticipation'
Compact, bushy and upright
in form with dark, glossy leaves.
Best April-May.

Camellia japonica
'Victor Emmanuel'
Toothed, rounded leaves
on twiggy bush. Best March-April.

Camellia japonica
'Commander Mulroy'
Particularly glossy, dense foliage
of upright, bushy habit.
Best March-April.

Choisya ternata and Saxifraga × urbium both have excellent all-season foliage, and in spring coincide in a foam of complementary blossom.

Choisya ternata

MEXICAN ORANGE BLOSSOM

Height 6ft · *Spread* 6-8ft
Best All year

An asset to any garden, though it may be damaged in cold areas in severe winters, Mexican orange blossom forms a bushy dome of rich, glossy, evergreen leaves, each with three leaflets. Crush a leaf and it gives off a strong, pungent scent. In spring and early summer, the green dome is adorned with clusters of sweetly scented white flowers, and often a few more appear intermittently until autumn.

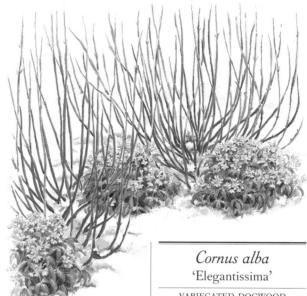

Hellebores grouped among stems of *Cornus alba* 'Elegantissima' evoke a fairytale landscape.

The cultivar 'Sundance', is a golden-leaved form.

Mexican orange blossom's bold foliage blends well with that of the evergreen perennial *Helleborus argutifolius*, which has larger, apple-green leaves of a similar shape. It also looks good in company with *Yucca filamentosa*, which has sword-shaped leaves. For follow-on, *Ceanothus* 'Delight' planted behind the orange blossom provides small, bright blue flowers against dark leaves in May.

CULTIVATION Plant in April or May in any well-drained soil, preferably in a sunny, sheltered position. No pruning needed. Propagate in late summer from semi-hardwood cuttings placed in a cold frame.

Cornus alba
'Elegantissima'

VARIEGATED DOGWOOD

Height 8-10ft · *Spread* 10ft
Best All year

The dogwood forms a picturesque thicket of upright, red-barked stems which can bring a bright show of colour to the garden throughout winter, and look particularly striking against a background of snow. In spring and summer, the leaves, margined and mottled with white, provide another startling display, especially if introducing a touch of light to a shady spot. The shrub really works for its place in the garden, for in autumn the leaves turn shades of yellow and red, setting off bunches of white, blue-tinged October berries.

For an unforgettable display, plant *Clematis viticella* to trail among the dogwood's stems. The nodding, blue-purple flowers of the clematis, which bloom from July to September,

The summer foliage of *Cornus alba* 'Elegantissima' is a perfect setting for luminous white delphiniums.

look like bright butterflies among the dogwood leaves. An underplanting of the snowdrop *Galanthus elwesii*, which bears green-tinged flowers in January and February, makes an effective contrast to the dogwood's red winter stems. The snowdrop bulbs also benefit from the shrub's shade in summer.

CULTIVATION Plant in autumn or spring in any moist, fertile soil, in sun or partial shade. No pruning is necessary, but in alternate years hard pruning of old stems in spring will provide better-coloured winter stems, since it is the current season's shoots that show the most red. Propagate by taking hardwood cuttings in autumn, and rooting them in a cold frame.

As autumn advances, *Cornus alba* 'Spaethii' foliage softens to pale gold with a hint of rose, to contrast with the bold red stems within.

The autumnal glow of *Cornus alba* 'Elegantissima' is enhanced by the gilded density of *Thuja occidentalis* 'Rheingold' and darker conifers behind. In the foreground, *Cedrus deodora* 'Pendula' and *Vinca major* 'Variegata' make a sea of gold and green, splendidly broken by an island of dark, leathery-leaved *Viburnum davidii*.

Cornus alba 'Spaethii'

GOLDEN VARIEGATED DOGWOOD

Height 7ft · *Spread* 7ft
Best All year

In the summer months, the big, bright gold and green variegated leaves of this superb dogwood make a rich combination with the upstanding, red stems beneath. Early in the season, there are also small clusters of white flowers – the precursors of bunches of white, blue-tinged berries that ripen around October. In autumn, too, the leaves turn to pale gold, and after they have fallen the stark, vivid red stems are left to provide winter colour.

For a brilliant summer display, allow red, orange and yellow nasturtiums to trail through the dogwood stems. In autumn, the shrub makes a good background for white-flowered forms of *Anemone* × *hybrida*. Alternatively, you could plant a succession of crocuses to contrast with the bare stems, such as autumn-flowering *Crocus speciosus* followed by *C. tommasinianus* 'Whitewell Purple' and *C. vernus* in spring.

CULTIVATION Plant in autumn or spring in any soil, in sun or shade. No pruning is necessary, but in alternate springs a cut back to within a few inches of the ground will provide better-coloured winter stems, as it is the current season's shoots that are the most vividly coloured. Propagate by taking hardwood cuttings in autumn, and rooting them in a cold frame.

On a mature *Euonymus fortunei* 'Silver Queen' the white margins are very prominent. The tiny flowers appear in early summer.

Euonymus fortunei
'Silver Queen'

Height 2-3ft · *Spread* 3-4ft
Best All year

The newly opened leaves of this evergreen euonymus are rich creamy-yellow, but mature to bright green with a broad creamy-white margin. It makes a compact shrub in a border, but against a wall will climb slowly to 8-9ft high. It thrives well in shade, so is good for brightening up a north wall or a shady corner under trees. The small, green-white flowers are borne in May and June on adult plants. *Euonymus fortunei* 'Emerald 'n' Gold' is similar but smaller, with a yellow-margined leaf that takes on subtle pink tints as winter begins to assert itself.

The dark, evergreen, finger-like leaves of *Helleborus foetidus* make a splendid contrast with

Dense *Euonymus fortunei* 'Emerald 'n' Gold' is a low-growing evergreen shrub that makes a good backing for border plants.

the euonymus leaves. Plant a drift of *Scilla mischtschenkoana* nearby to provide a splash of pale blue flowers in winter, and dog's-tooth violet (*Erythronium dens-canis*) to follow on with pink flowers in April and May. CULTIVATION Plant in spring in any soil, in sun or shade. In a dry place, such as under trees, use a mulch and keep the shrub well watered. No pruning is necessary. Propagate by taking half-ripe cuttings in late summer; root in a cold frame.

In a late summer scene of shrewdly planned gaiety, two clumps of *Euonymus fortunei* 'Silver Queen' add their silvery glow to a border highlighted by the delicately pink and white flushed blooms of *Anemone × hybrida* 'September Charm'. Against the window, the foliage of spring-flowering *Chaenomeles × superba*, its leaves paling as autumn approaches, provides a subtle background, contrasting with the deep green leaves of a hellebore in the foreground.

The rich green and gold of *Euonymus japonicus* 'Ovatus Aureus' makes an effective companion to an underplanting of summer pansies.

The snow-white spring flowers of *Hebe pinguifolia* 'Pagei' create a dense covering for a low wall.

Euonymus japonicus
'Ovatus Aureus'

EVERGREEN SPINDLE

Height 8-10ft · *Spread* 6-8ft
Best All year

One of the commonest of the evergreen spindles, this handsome shrub has oval leaves marked with a broad margin of rich yellow. It can be used very effectively to provide a rich golden effect at the back of a mixed border. The leaves tend to revert to green with only a vestige of yellow if given too much shade, and the shrub has gained a bad reputation for losing leaf variegation through being too much overshadowed in Victorian-style shrubberies and public parks.

Plant the shrub behind Mexican orange blossom (*Choisya ternata*) for foliage contrast, and for a white and gold theme in spring, when the 'orange blossom' bears scented white flowers. The beautiful, pink-shooted, deciduous shrub *Exochorda giraldii* 'Wilsonii' will augment the theme in May with sprays of starry white flowers.

CULTIVATION Plant in autumn or spring – spring is best in a cold garden. Any well-drained soil is suitable – *Euonymus japonicus* will flourish in coastal areas. Site it in full sun to bring out the colour variegation. Prune in February as necessary for general shaping, and remove any shoots with leaves that are totally green. Propagate from cuttings in late summer, rooted in a propagator or cold frame.

Fatsia japonica

Height 8ft · *Spread* 8ft
Best All year

The fatsia's huge, glossy leaves are the largest of any evergreen shrub grown outdoors in these northern climes.

Throughout the year, their strongly shaped outlines can transform a shady corner into a striking focal point of the garden. In autumn the fatsia bears large-branched clusters of round-headed white flowers

With its giant, glossy leaves and pompon flower heads, *Fatsia japonica* draws attention to itself in an otherwise dull corner of a garden.

rather like those of an ivy but much more decorative. These are followed by pea-sized black berries, arranged in spherical clusters.

An even more impressive architectural plant feature can be created by combining the fatsia with other evergreens of different character, such as *Sarcococca hookeriana digyna* and *Helleborus foetidus*. Together, they would make a deep green backdrop for the spring-flowering *Pulmonaria angustifolia* and the long, tubular summer flowers of *Symphytum × uplandicum* 'Variegatum'.

CULTIVATION Plant in spring or autumn, in almost any soil. If sheltered from rainfall beneath trees they may need watering and mulching. If the plant gets leggy cut back hard, but do not prune otherwise. Propagate by seed in spring. *Fatsia japonica* is not hardy in northern and eastern Scotland.

Hebe pinguifolia
'Pagei'

Height 3-6in · *Spread* 2-3ft
Best All year

The spreading mats of tiny blue-grey leaves hug the ground, and look most effective tumbling over a low, sunny wall. The foliage maintains its silvery appearance throughout the year, and in late spring small white flowers add extra sparkle. To make the most of hebe's silver tones, associate it with grey-leaved plants – the spring-flowering *Pulmonaria saccharata*, for example, with its silver-white mottled leaves, and the aromatic shrub *Caryopteris × clandonensis* 'Arthur Simmonds' which has grey-green foliage and blue flowers in summer.

The yellow-splashed leaves of *Ilex × altaclarensis* 'Lawsoniana' may revert to green.

In spring, *Ilex × altaclarensis* 'Golden King' spreads its gilded leaves above a pretty, naturalised scattering of blue and white bluebells.

Shiny leaves and heavy, rich clusters of berries are features of *Ilex × altaclarensis* 'Wilsonii'.

The flowers of *Kalmia latifolia* look like sugar icing and have conspicuous deep pink stamens.

The laurel-like leaves of *Kalmia latifolia* set off the deep pink flowers of the variety 'Ostbo Red'.

(*Hebe pinguifolia* cont)
CULTIVATION A position in sun and well-drained soil will promote dense, bushy growth and well-coloured foliage. No pruning is necessary, but cut back in April if growth becomes straggly. Propagate in autumn from semi-ripe cuttings planted in a peat and sand mixture then placed in a cold frame.

Ilex × altaclarensis 'Golden King'

HOLLY

Height 12ft · *Spread* 8ft
Best All year

Despite its name, this gilded holly is female. With a male cultivar such as 'Silver Queen' nearby, it will bear a glowing crop of orange berries in early autumn that deepen to red by winter. 'Golden King' is a vigorous hybrid that develops into a fine pyramid-shaped feature for a lawn or a wide border with a little judicious pruning of any wayward branches. Other hybrids include 'Lawsoniana' (orange-red berries) and the larger 'Wilsonii'.

A group of *Salix alba* 'Britzensis', with bright orange winter stems, planted near the holly will create a spectacular display of rich, warm colours when these are most needed, and underplanting with *Narcissus* 'February Gold' and *Eranthis hyemalis* would continue a golden theme into spring.
CULTIVATION Plant at any time in any reasonably well-drained soil. Prune in April to keep in good shape. Propagate by cuttings in autumn in a cold frame.

Kalmia latifolia

CALICO BUSH

Height 6-8ft · *Spread* 6-8ft
Best All year, particularly June

Place this slow-growing evergreen where its glossy leaves can catch the light. The leaves are sometimes edged with an attractive brownish-purple and in early summer make a splendid background for masses of sugar-icing pink flowers like open parasols. The resemblance of the petals to crimped calico has given the plant its American common name. The variety 'Ostbo Red' is a deeper pink.

Kalmia latifolia is an excellent foliage plant for use as an isolated specimen, but it also goes well with rhododendrons and shrub roses. The brilliant red shoots of *Pieris* 'Forest Flame' would precede the kalmia flowers, and *Buddleia alternifolia* would continue a flowering display into July.
CULTIVATION Calico bushes require moist but well-drained acid soil with plenty of leaf mould or composted bark added at planting time. They tolerate dappled shade but flower best in full sun as long as the soil is kept moist. No pruning is needed. Propagate by layering shoots of the current season in late summer, or by half-ripe cuttings taken in August and placed in a compost of peat and sand in a shaded cold frame.

Lavendula angustifolia 'Hidcote' makes a compact bush, ideal for edging paths and borders.

Clematis 'Jackmanii Superba' (left) has been trained to completely conceal an old tree stump, and its stems with their enormous blooms trail through a wide border of *Lavendula angustifolia*. The effect in an informal garden is one of spontaneity and charm that will last from July until the dying days of September.

Lavandula angustifolia

OLD ENGLISH LAVENDER

Height 2ft · *Spread* 2ft
Best All year, particularly
July-August

Fragrant old English lavender, though it actually originates from the warm Mediterranean regions, is a favourite in both cottage gardens and the grounds of stately homes. Its spikes of pale blue, red-tinged flowers appear in July and August, and aromatic scent wafts from its tiny, oblong, silver-grey leaves for most of the year.

Lavender makes a good edging plant for paths and borders, and can be grown as a compact bush or for a dwarf hedge. The cultivar 'Hidcote' has the deepest lavender colour and the smallest size. There are also a number of white and pink-flowered cultivars.

A border of lavender is a fine complement to shrub roses. To continue the colour theme through half the year, plant lavender in company with tulips for a bright spring display, which could then be followed in early summer by the white, pink or purple flowers of one of the species or hybrids of the evergreen shrub *Cistus*. From July all the way through to September the white-flowered *Phlox* 'Fuji-yama' would make an excellent bedmate, when supported by the stately lemon flowers of *Hemerocallis citrina* that open in the evening, or the red-apricot tinged blooms and broad, handsome leaves of *H. fulva*.

CULTIVATION Plant in spring in any well-drained soil and in full sun to bring out the plant's scent and keep it compact. Clip the lavender after flowering to maintain a good shape. Take semi-hardwood cuttings in September and October and root them in a cold frame. The plants are best discarded or replaced after five or six years, as they grow leggy with age.

Mahonia japonica flowers from November through to spring.

When its flowers have gone, *M. japonica* bears grape-like berries that turn purple by early summer.

Mahonia japonica

Height 6-8ft · *Spread* 6-8ft
Best All year,
but especially in winter

Forming a bold mass of glossy greenery, *Mahonia japonica* is a widespreading shrub with large evergreen leaves made up of pairs of leaflets along each leaf stem. It looks impressive on its own, it fits in well with other distinctive foliage plants, and it will flourish in dry, shady places. A few weeks before Christmas the long, pendulous sprays of pale yellow flowers open in clusters, and last until March. The flowers have a delicious scent reminiscent of lily of the valley. Occasionally, the shrub produces a leaf or two with brilliant autumnal colour.

Let orange lilies, such as the elegant *Lilium superbum*, glow against the stately green of *M. japonica* in summer, after the flaming red shoots of nearby *Pieris* 'Forest Flame' have turned pink, then white and then green. *Hydrangea macrophylla* 'Mariesii' placed nearby will show off its shell-pink or blue lacecap flowers in summer and well into autumn. Alternatively, grow *M. japonica* on its own as a specimen shrub.

CULTIVATION Plant in April-May in any well-drained soil in sun or, preferably, partial shade. The shrub will tolerate lime. Work in some composted bark when planting, and a handful or two of a general fertiliser – especially if the site is under overhanging trees. Pruning is necessary only when the plant gets lanky or out of hand.

Propagate by leaf-bud cuttings, with a shortened leaf and 1in of stem inserted in a heated propagator in February. Maintain humidity until rooting has occurred. *M. japonica* is a reliable shrub; once established, it will need little attention.

Mahonia japonica, with its pendulous, lemon-yellow racemes, is seen here on a winter's day with erect-flowered *M.* 'Winter Sun', a handsome cultivar of *M. × media*, *M. japonica* being one of the parents of the hybrid.

BRIDGING THE SEASONS WITH *Mahonia*

WITH THEIR shiny, leathery, evergreen leaves, cheerful yellow flowers and dark fruits covered in a white, waxy bloom, mahonias are among the greatest ornaments of the cold-weather garden. There are two grown here – *Mahonia japonica* and *M.* 'Winter Sun', for the shrewd tortoise-and-hare reason that 'Winter Sun' makes a big, brilliant show of fragrant, upright flower spikes that begins in midwinter and lasts for about a month. *M. japonica*, on the other hand, may flower from October onward into spring.

When the main show is over, the late spring and summer dress of handsome, dark foliage can be used as a background to play games with colours, and even with the perspective of the garden. A big underplanting of light blue against the dark green has a distancing effect, apparently lengthening the garden.

In late spring, the mahonia's leaves make a backdrop for a drift of blue forget-me-nots (*Myosotis*).

Late summer continues the blue theme with a planting of *Agapanthus campanulatus* in the foreground.

Magnificent shuttlecocks of brilliant golden-yellow flower spikes brighten the end of the year when *Mahonia × media* blooms.

Pernettya mucronata 'Alba' bears small white fruits in winter.

Mahonia × media

Height 7-10ft · *Spread* 5-8ft
Best All year, particularly November and December

A tall, splendid upright shrub with ruffs of huge leaves that have a bold midrib and rows of spiny, dark green leaflets. It is a hybrid between *Mahonia japonica* and *M. lomariifolia*, and is available in several forms, such as 'Charity', 'Buckland' and 'Winter Sun'. Long, unscented racemes of yellow flowers form in clusters at the tips of the stems in late autumn, and grow on into early winter.

Grow these shrubs in conjunction with deciduous azaleas, whose flamboyant colours will stand out against the mahonia like jewels in a green-lined tray. Their brilliant red autumn leaves are a daring foil for the deep evergreen of the mahonia. The large, veined, blue-green leaves of *Hosta sieboldiana* 'Elegans' also provide a striking contrast, and in addition lavender flowers in July and August. CULTIVATION Plant in April or May in any well-drained soil, in sun or partial shade. Propagate by leaf-bud cuttings in a heated propagator in February.

Pernettya mucronata

Height 3ft · *Spread* 3ft
Best All year, especially autumn and winter

One of the best berry-bearing shrubs, *Pernettya mucronata* has large clusters of marble-sized berries throughout autumn and winter, and birds do not seem to like them. Berry colours vary from white to pink, to red and purple and to most shades in between, so it is best to buy plants while they are in fruit. Plant them in drifts of various colours, and include one or two certified male plants to ensure cross-pollination. The shrub is dark, dense and twiggy, with small, prickly tipped, glossy green leaves on reddish stems, and bears an abundance of tiny white heath-like flowers in May and June.

The pernettya goes well with heathers such as *Erica carnea* 'Myretoun Ruby', which has flowers throughout winter and early spring. The purple-red flowers of *E. erigena* (syn *E. mediterranea*) 'Brightness' carry on until June, and blend with the pernettya's red stems.
CULTIVATION Plant in a sunny site, in autumn or winter in mild weather, and in acid soil with plenty of leaf mould and composted bark. No pruning is necessary. Set plants in groups of three or five to assist pollination and to ensure fruiting. Propagate by division in spring, or take cuttings of side shoots in July/August and root in a closed frame or propagator.

Candy-floss clusters of pink and white flowers weigh down the stems of *Pyracantha* 'Mohave' in spring.

As welcome in the garden as the bird it is named after, *Photinia × fraseri* 'Red Robin' is a fiery harbinger of spring and summer.

Come autumn, *Pyracantha* 'Mohave' goes into its second act, with a grand finale of ruby-red berries.

Photinia × fraseri
'Red Robin'

Height 8-10ft · *Spread* 8ft
Best Spring to autumn

A fine display of long, gleaming leaves makes the photinia a cheerful shrub throughout the year. 'Red Robin' is a hybrid, the result of crossing *Photinia glabra* with *P. serrulata*, which in spring is transformed into a mass of flaming colour as brilliant red new leaves appear. The effect is similar to that of a pieris, but the photinia does not need acid soil. New red leaves continue to form until midsummer, gradually darkening to mid-green as they age. There are small white flowers, too, in late spring, followed by red or black berry-like fruits.

As an effective combination, *Pulmonaria angustifolia* could be planted beneath the photinia for its sky-blue and pink spring flowers, with *Phlox paniculata* varieties for bright summer colour. Once the photinia shrub has reached a mature size, it could support a clematis hybrid, such as 'Henryi', which has large white flowers in early summer and again in autumn.
CULTIVATION Plant in autumn or spring in any fertile soil, adding general fertiliser and some organic matter. No pruning is necessary. Propagate by taking semi-hardwood cuttings in summer placed in a propagator, or by hardwood cuttings placed in a cold frame in autumn.

When winter comes, *Pyracantha rogersiana* 'Flava' comes into its own with its bright berries and glossy leaves.

Pyracantha
Hybrids

FIRETHORN

Height 12ft · *Spread* 12ft
Best September-December

Even on the darkest winter days, the berries of the superb firethorn will glow like the embers of an autumn bonfire. Though magnificent in all its forms, it excels itself with *Pyracantha* 'Orange Glow', a vigorous and free-fruiting Dutch-raised hybrid whose clusters of brilliant orange berries festoon the bushy, evergreen stems from September through to spring. Close behind in the peerless stakes comes the American hybrid 'Mohave', a red-berried beauty that bears its berries from mid-August onwards, and follows its winter display with sprays of scented, pink and white flowers.

The needle-sharp spines of pyracantha ensure it is ideal for hedging; it will also look good as a free-standing shrub against a north or east-facing wall or as a specimen in the open. In company with other shrubs, try it as a backdrop to *Abeliophyllum distichum*, whose pink-tinged white flowers will show up well against the glossy green foliage, or the deservedly popular *Hamamelis mollis* (Chinese witch hazel) with its red-flushed pale yellow flowers.
CULTIVATION Plant in autumn or spring in any well-drained soil. Add some composted bark to improve the soil, and a sprinkling of compound fertiliser. The shrub is susceptible to fireblight and its fruits to scab, but 'Mohave' is resistant. For hedging, plant 15-24in apart. Provide trellis or wires for support for a wall-trained plant. Prune back the long growths after flowering. Propagate by half-ripe cuttings in July or August, rooted in a heated frame.

BRIDGING THE SEASONS
WITH
Pyracantha

CHOCOLATE-BOX MAKERS, manufacturers of greetings-cards and expatriates are alike agreed that there are few symbols more English than a cottage with roses round the door. No one feels nearly so wistful about pyracantha, but mingle it with roses, and you create a threshold that is a home thought from abroad enshrined and encapsulated.

The principal rose in this instance is the climbing *Rosa* 'Emily Gray', which produces clusters of semidouble flowers the colour of new chamois leather in early summer. Unfortunately, its flowering season is not long, so it is reinforced here with some shrub roses and by *Pyracantha* 'Mohave', which puts on a froth of hawthorn-like blossoms at the same time that 'Emily Gray' is in flower.

In early autumn, or even in late August, the pyracantha produces a wealth of berries whose colour is more reminiscent of New, rather than Olde, England – with some justice, since *P.* 'Mohave' is an American hybrid. The splendidly clear, orange-red display continues all through autumn and winter into March; for the last few weeks of the show, you might accompany it with tall daffodils. Their colour would set off the berries admirably. 🌿

Personality changes are imparted by seasonal dress. That for summer (top) is based upon the rose 'Emily Gray' and *Pyracantha* 'Mohave', which also decrees the autumnal fashion of red berries.

The evergreen *Rhamnus alaternus* 'Argenteovariegata' has red berries in autumn.

Rhamnus alaternus
'Argenteovariegata'

Height 10ft · *Spread* 8ft
Best All year

'Tall and handsome' well describes this splendid evergreen, with its pale green leaves edged with a creamy-white margin, tiny yellow-green flowers in spring and, after a hot summer, a host of red berries in autumn. It comes from the Mediterranean region originally, and so thrives best in a warm, sheltered position; in cold areas place it against a wall.

'Argenteovariegata' is best contrasted with foliage plants of different shapes, such as *Yucca filamentosa* whose pointed narrow leaves have given it the common name 'Adam's needle', and *Cortaderia selloana* 'Pumila' – a compact pampas grass – with its bomb-burst of rush-like leaves and feathery autumn plumes. For spring colour it would be hard to better the

31

Rhamnus alaternus 'Argenteo-variegata' is a rewarding evergreen that thrives even in seaside areas.

(*Rhamnus alaternus* cont) ever-popular tulip; 'Golden Apeldoorn', for example, would provide a display of white and gold. In summer, you could let *Rhamnus alaternus* sparkle with the brilliant scarlet flowers of *Tropaeolum speciosum* scrambling in its branches.

CULTIVATION Plant in spring in any well-drained soil. Pruning is not necessary, but remove any branches that have reverted to green, otherwise the whole shrub may eventually lose its creamy variegation. Propagate by taking semi-ripe cuttings in late summer, and allowing them to root in a warm propagator.

Rhododendron

A rhododendron in full bloom is a glorious, but relatively short-lived, sight. The strong, dark foliage, however, can be enjoyed all year and enlisted too, to play a major role in the garden's all-season structure.

The genus *Rhododendron* encompasses a great variety of plants, ranging from shrublets an inch or two high to giants with leaves nearly 2ft long. The genus also includes azaleas (see pages 100-101), which were originally classified separately. The choice is enormous, and a selection has therefore been made among the medium-sized species and their hybrids.

NOT JUST A PRETTY FLOWER

Most of the rhododendrons have elegant, funnel-shaped flowers in a wonderful range of fantasy colours. They are carried in trusses at the ends of the previous year's young growth – as the growing season draws to an end, the buds have already formed and overwinter before swelling into bloom in spring. If you have the space, it is worth combining the early *Rhododendron cinnabarinum* with later-flowering cultivars for a succession of spring colour. The mature leaves have a solidity of colour which provides a perfect foil for the exotic spring blooms. But they often have other attributes too; the undersurface of *R. yakushimanum* leaves are brushed with bronze fur, the texture of suede. And the young leaves, which appear after the flowers have gone, can provide an arresting early summer dis-

One of the first rhododendrons to flower – sometimes as early as February – is the compact hybrid *Rhododendron* 'Praecox'.

play as bright green or silver spearheads emerge boldly from collars of darker mature foliage. The related *R.* 'Golden Torch' and *R.* 'Hydon Dawn' have glossy leaves that are dusted with a silver-grey sheen.

GARDENS GREAT AND SMALL

A large garden is not essential for growing rhododendrons. The modern compact hybrids, such as 'Hydon Dawn', 'Golden Torch' and 'Dreamland', are derived from the Japanese species *R. yakushimanum*, and were bred especially for small gardens. Though modest in stature they successfully marry hardiness with the handsome foliage of the parent species.

As long as their shade requirements are met, the

A *Rhododendron cinnabarinum* hybrid – a medium to large shrub – joins bluebells for a late spring rhapsody in blue and pink.

smaller rhododendrons can take centre stage in a group of other acid-soil lovers such as heathers. Alternatively, to create a simple but satisfying woodland theme, mix hardy ferns – say *Asplenium scolopendrium* or *Dryopteris filix-mas* – with shade-tolerant bulbs such as snowdrops (*Galanthus elwesii* and *G. nivalis* hybrids), a bright gold carpet of winter aconites (*Eranthis hyemalis*), and an

informal planting of *Narcissus* cultivars, *Primula denticulata* or Regal polyanthus strains.

CULTIVATION

Plant during spring or autumn in well-drained, ordinary but acid garden soil. Mulch each year with a 1-2in layer of organic matter, which should be spread rather than forked in to avoid damaging the roots just beneath the surface. The site

In early summer, shuttlecocks of young *Rhododendron yakushimanum* leaves thrust forth from the mature foliage of the previous year's growth.

Dryopteris ferns soften the transition from the vigorous hybrid *Rhododendron* 'Bagshot Ruby' to the neat *R. yakushimanum*, in a woodland glade-style setting.

should be partially shaded, especially from early morning sun, yet away from surface-rooting trees such as birches and sycamores. The plants can be transplanted at almost any stage of their development with success, but never at a greater depth than the original planting. Deadhead by pinching off the faded blooms. Propagate by layering in spring or by taking semi-hardwood cuttings during summer and early autumn. Place the cuttings in a warm propagator in a mixture of two parts peat to one part of sand, and pot up in a peat-based compost under a cold frame the following spring.

A bright shock of dwarf rhododendron cultivars uplifts this mature shrub border in spring. Later, the rhododendron foliage provides a welcome foil to the yellow summer flowers of the ever-grey *Senecio* 'Sunshine' and the autumn reds and golds of *Amelanchier lamarckii* behind.

All-season aristocrats of acid soils

Rhododendrons reign supreme as the backbone plants
for acid soils. The handsome foliage gives stature,
dignity and shape to the garden throughout the year, and the lush
abundance of their spring blooms is breathtaking. By combining
two or more cultivars with different flowering periods,
the splendour of rhododendrons in spring
can be extended over three months.

Painted from plants at The Savill and Valley Gardens,
Windsor Great Park, Berkshire, in early May.

Rhododendron 'Vanessa Pastel'
Compact habit.
Height 6½ft. Spread 6½ft. Best May.

Rhododendron 'Brocade'
Compact with neat, rounded leaves.
Height 6½ft. Spread 5ft. Best early May.

Rhododendron 'St Tudy'
Small leaves on well-clothed shrub.
Height 6½ft. Spread 6½ft. Best April.

Rhododendron 'Sennocke'
Good, dark, compact foliage.
Height 6½ft. Spread 6½ft.
Best April-May.

Rhododendron 'Loder's White'
Large, dome-shaped shrub.
Height 10ft. Spread 8ft. Best May.

Rhododendron 'Pink Pebble'
Compact form with tiny, rounded,
very dark green leaves.
Height 5ft. Spread 5ft.
Best April.

Rhododendron concatenans
Compact form with striking,
small bluish leaves.
Height 5ft. Spread 5ft. Best April.

Rhododendron 'Fabia'
Dense foliage.
Height 6½ft.
Spread 6½ft.
Best late May.

Rhododendron 'Hydon Dawn'
Profuse flowering, well-clothed shrub.
Height 5ft. Spread 5ft.
Best May.

Rhododendron
yakushimanum
Compact dome, fine foliage.
Height 5ft. Spread 5ft. Best May.

35

The pale lavender flowers of *Rosmarinus officinalis* are borne on erect stems in spring.

Rosmarinus officinalis

Height 3-4ft · *Spread* 3-4ft
Best April-June

Shakespeare may have had his own Elizabethan garden in mind when he wrote: 'There's rosemary, that's for remembrance.' For centuries *Rosmarinus officinalis,* commonly called rosemary, has been a garden favourite, and rightly so with its masses of flowers bursting upon the spring scene and continuing to appear sporadically until September. There are several varieties, and two are worthy of special note; 'Benenden Blue' with strongly scented leaves and bright blue flowers, and 'Miss Jessop's Upright' which, as its name implies, is an erect form which may grow to 6ft. Its flowers are pale lavender and it, too, has

Exochorda racemosa (top left) and *Phalaris arundinacea* (top right) provide a backing of summer green for the blue-grey of *Ruta graveolens*.

leaves that are strongly aromatic, especially when crushed.

Both varieties need a sunny, sheltered position, and so will go well with other sun-loving plants. 'Benenden Blue' will make an excellent combination with the gold-striped leaves of *Hakonechloa macra* 'Aureola' in summer. For ground cover between the shrubs, a carpet of *Allium moly* with its heads of yellow flowers will provide a display of summer sunshine.

'Miss Jessop's Upright' could be used to establish a Mediterranean corner of the garden, with yellow *Sternbergia lutea*, pale pink *Ceanothus* × 'Perle Rose' and bright blue *Caryopteris* × *clandonensis* 'Arthur Simmonds' to echo the sky.
CULTIVATION Plant in spring in well-drained soil and in a warm, sunny position. Propagate by cuttings in late summer. Cut out dead growth and shorten straggly shoots in March.

The decorative, white-splashed leaves of *Salvia officinalis* 'Tricolor' are tinged with shades of pink.

Ruta graveolens
'Jackman's Blue'

RUE

Height 2-3ft · *Spread* 2-3ft
Best All year

The striking, compact foliage of 'Jackman's Blue', with its evergreen blue-grey leaves, makes a splendid edging for a border. In early summer, mustard-yellow flowers appear which, not being particularly attractive, should be removed so as not to detract from the full, vivid beauty of the fern-like leaves.

The glossy evergreen foliage and sweetly scented white flowers of *Choisya ternata* will make a good backing in the border in spring. *Cornus alba* 'Elegantissima' could be used for summer colour. Apart from its red stems, it has bright white variegated leaves which would show off the rue's blue-grey leaves very well. A group of autumn crocuses, such as the

The distinctive green and gold leaf markings of *Salvia officinalis* 'Icterina' form irregular patterns.

lilac *Colchicum autumnale* and its white cultivar 'Album', would round off the season's colour display nicely.
CULTIVATION Plant in spring in any well-drained soil in a sunny position. Propagate by cuttings early in autumn in a cold frame, then pot on or plant out the following spring.

Salvia officinalis

COMMON SAGE

Height 2ft · *Spread* 3-4ft
Best May-October

Though usually grown in a herb or kitchen garden, the hardy, evergreen sage is well worth promoting to the border, where its grey-green leaves make it a fine companion for cultivars that have other leaf colours. *Salvia officinalis* 'Icterina', for example, has green and gold variegated leaves; the young leaves and stems of 'Purpurascens' are suffused with purple,

Asters add a pink flush to the border in late summer, while the brick-red of *Sedum* 'Autumn Joy' contrasts with a purple-tinged *Salvia officinalis* 'Purpurascens' and the silver-grey of *Artemisia ludoviciana*.

The yellow button flowers of *Santolina chamaecyparissus* form a dense, long-lasting mound in July.

Santolina chamaecyparissus insularis has more feathery leaves than *S. chamaecyparissus*.

while the grey-green leaves of 'Tricolor' are splashed with pink and white.

All the cultivars go well with other foliage plants, such as the spring-flowering *Euphorbia characias wulfenii*. Its florets of yellow-green would blend nicely with the golden foliage of 'Icterina'. Then, in a nearby sunny patch, you could establish 'Tricolor' alongside a clump of *Festuca glauca*, the dwarf blue-grey grass.

CULTIVATION Plant in spring in a well-drained soil, enriched with well-rotted compost, in full sun. Shorten any straggly branches in spring. Propagate by cuttings in early October in a cold frame, and plant out in late spring.

Santolina chamaecyparissus
(syn *S. incana*)

COTTON LAVENDER

Height 1½-2ft · *Spread* 1½-2ft
Best July

Plant a number of these charming little shrubs along the front of a border or in a rock garden, where their woolly, silvery leaves will quite quickly form a series of small, dense mounds that can in time unite into a miniature hedge. Lemon-coloured, mushroom-shaped flowers, half an inch across, are produced in July, standing above the evergreen foliage on long, erect stalks so slender as to be almost invisible.

The mounds look particularly well around a rose bed, lending a delightfully old-fashioned air and, of course, foliage colour when the rose stems are bare. You could also alternate cotton lavender with old English lavender, *Lavandula officinalis*, along the border to combine grey-blue flower spikes with the lemon-yellow ones in summer, and year-round fragrance as well.

Santolina chamaecyparissus insularis (syn *S. neapolitana*) also forms a mound of grey foliage, but the leaves are longer and more feathery.

CULTIVATION Plant in autumn or spring, in full sun and in ordinary moist, but well-drained soil. After flowering, dead-head the stems immediately.

For hedges, set the plants 12-15in apart. Pinch out the growing points once or twice during the first years. The plants can be clipped to shape during summer, but this will prevent flowering. During the following spring, prune mature plants back to the old wood. Propagate from semi-hardwood cuttings, 2-3in long, in late summer and insert them in a compost of equal parts of peat and sand.

A frosting of snow lends a Yuletide air to the holly-like berries of *Skimmia japonica*.

Skimmia japonica 'Rubella' flower buds and snowdrops make a charming winter display.

As well as providing ground cover, *Vinca major* can be trained to conceal unsightly objects such as the base of a drainpipe.

Skimmia japonica

Height 3-5ft · *Spread* 3-5ft
Best April, May, Autumn

Skimmia japonica originated in Japan and has been known in Britain since the 19th century, when many plants from the Far East were introduced by botanical explorers. Its aromatic, glossy foliage will brighten the drabbest days of the year, and there are many other benefits too – rich spring blossoms of creamy-white flowers, followed in some forms by berries that glow like rubies among the handsome evergreen leaves.

The male form 'Rubella' does not develop fruit, but its leaves are faintly rimmed with crimson in cold weather. In late autumn and winter it bears clusters of blood-red buds that burst into white, red-anthered flowers in early spring.

'Rubella' grows into an upright, dense shrub, up to 4ft in height. It would make a fine mate for *S.* × 'Foremanii', a female form of more spreading stature, which needs a male companion to ensure a splendid show of large, round scarlet berries in autumn. *S. japonica reevesiana* is self-sufficient, needing no male form to produce its matt red berries in

Clusters of pale flowers follow the vivid red buds of *Skimmia japonica* 'Rubella' in spring.

autumn. It reaches a height and spread of about 3ft.

Any of the skimmias will go well with a twiggy shrub like *Corylopsis pauciflora*, with its pendulous racemes of lemon-yellow flowers in April. The fiery *Euphorbia griffithii* 'Fireglow' or the golden-yellow flowers of *Hypericum* 'Hidcote' would contrast well, too, and continue flowering into the summer months. Any spaces around the shrubs could be filled

with the purple, white, blue or pink forms of *Geranium sylvaticum*, or the bold, heart-shaped leaves of *Bergenia* × 'Silberlicht'.

Try smaller companions with the lower-growing *S. japonica reevesiana*, such as *Daphne mezereum* or perhaps *Sarcococca hookeriana digyna*, both of which flower between February and April. *Berberis thunbergii* 'Atropurpurea Nana', with its rich, purple-red leaves, and an evergreen carpet of *Waldsteinia ternata*, splashed with yellow flowers, would continue colour into summer.

CULTIVATION Plant whenever the weather is suitable in autumn or spring in any humus-rich soil, in

sun or light shade. Propagate by semi-ripe cuttings in early autumn, or by seed taken from the ripe berries in September and sown in John Innes seed compost in a cold frame.

Vinca major

GREATER PERIWINKLE

Height 1-2ft · *Spread* Indefinite
Best April-June

It is said that in the Middle Ages a garland of periwinkle was used to crown the heads of those condemned to the gallows, though why this charming little flower should be so used is a

The trailing stems of *Vinca major* 'Variegata' make a decorative edging for a low stone wall.

The wayward *Vinca minor* comes into its own in a wayward garden. Here spring comes to life with 'Variegata' lapping the foot of a wild cherry and the fragrant pink blooms of honesty taking centre stage, with a stately rhododendron ready to enter left in June.

mystery. From March to June, and usually again in autumn, this spreading shrub with its bright blue flowers will form a luxurious carpet, which over the years will grow and grow and grow. Its arching stems root at their tips, covering the ground with glossy, evergreen leaves, which in the form of the slightly less vigorous *Vinca major* 'Variegata' are variegated pale green with a cream margin. Its flowers are pale purple-blue.

Such a fast-spreading plant will go well in shrub or mixed borders, or in a wild garden. Try it also as ground cover around obliging *Lonicera fragrantissima,* the honeysuckle whose

scented cream flowers appear in late winter, and when they have faded the rose-red flowers of *Kalmia latifolia* 'Clementine Churchill', appearing in June, will contrast well with the vinca's glossy leaves.

In autumn the periwinkle can be used in association with bulbs such as colchicums and

the autumn-flowering crocuses (*Crocus speciosus, C. medius* and *C. kotschyanus*). These produce sheaves of flowers like goblets and, because they have no foliage, are sometimes called naked ladies. A ground covering of periwinkle will conceal such immodesty, and provide a backcloth for these colourful plants.

CULTIVATION Plant in spring or autumn in any well-drained garden soil, in sun or partial shade. Propagate by semihardwood cuttings, taken in early autumn or spring, in a cold frame, or by division any time from early autumn to midspring and replanted in permanent sites.

Vinca minor

LESSER PERIWINKLE

Height 4-6in · *Spread* Indefinite
Best April-June

Though its flowers and leaves are smaller than the greater periwinkle's, *Vinca minor* is

The majestically named *Vinca minor* 'Alba Variegata' has white flowers and greeny-gold leaves.

The blue flowers of *Vinca minor* are about 1in across, only a little smaller than those of *V. major*.

The deep purple 'Atropurpurea' is one of the many varieties of *Vinca minor*.

All Seasons
TREES

THE IMPACT of trees on a garden planted for all-season interest is greater than that provided by any other group of plants. Trees provide the garden framework, set the scene, and determine the degree of light and shade. A mixture of deciduous and evergreen trees will achieve a balanced overall effect, the evergreens providing year-round foliage and the deciduous trees contributing variety with the changes they bring to each season. Some all-seasons trees remain the same through the year, lending stability and form to the garden; others meet each new season's challenge with a display of blossom, foliage, fruit or bark to delight the eye.

Amelanchier lamarckii

SNOWY MESPILUS, JUNEBERRY

Height 10-15ft *Spread* 10-15ft
Best April-May, October

Every year, without fail, the hardy and reliable amelanchier gives two fine performances. First, in spring, comes a brief but breathtaking snowfall of starry white flowers set in clusters against unfurling leaves of soft coppery-purple that glisten in the sun. A grand finale comes in autumn, when the slender branches are bedecked in foliage of flaming oranges and reds.

The cultivar 'Ballerina' is a more prolific flowerer than the

Few trees can compete with the fiery autumn brilliance of *Amelanchier lamarckii*, one of the best specimen trees for a large garden.

(*Vinca minor* cont)
also as vigorous, but with a neater and denser spreading habit. Moreover, it offers a wide range of colours in its many varieties. These include 'Alba', white; 'Albo-plena', a double white; 'Atropurpurea', purple; 'Burgundy', like the wine; 'La Grave', blue-purple and 'Multi-plex', double plum-purple.

Any of these will provide spectacular ground cover in spring, especially if strategically planted to contrast with the evergreen leaves of *Fatsia japonica* and *Helleborus foetidus*, which also has green flowers. Then follow up the hellebores with the star-like, deep plum flowers of *Astrantia major* 'Rubra' for a sombre glow.

CULTIVATION Plant between autumn and spring in well-drained soil. Propagate by division in winter or spring.

species, but puts on a less dramatic autumn show.

The amelanchier can be grown as a tree or as a handsome, multi-stemmed shrub, that takes centre stage among winter and spring-flowering heathers such as *Erica carnea*, *E. × darleyensis* and *E. mediterranea*. Or try the golden-scaled male fern *Dryopteris affinis* and the rosy flowered *Bergenia cordifolia* for arresting shapes and fine winter colour.

CULTIVATION Plant between autumn and spring in well-drained soil, ideally neutral to acid, in full sun. Propagate from seed sown in summer, in pots of John Innes seed compost placed in a cold frame, or by separating and replanting rooted suckers between autumn and spring.

The spring display of *Amelanchier lamarckii* (right), with its flowers like snow on the boughs, makes a perfect backdrop for the rose-pink of a flowering currant.

The cinnamon-coloured bark and winter flowers of *Arbutus* × *andrachnoides* make it invaluable in the year-round garden.

Arbutus × *andrachnoides*

HYBRID STRAWBERRY TREE

Height 15-30ft
Spread 10-15ft
Best October-March

You need a reasonable amount of space to do justice to this magnificent evergreen. It is moderately fast-growing, soon displaying all the glory of its maturity in the smooth, rich cinnamon-red branches and lustrous leaf. The bark flakes off to expose a paler skin beneath. The strawberry-like fruits are edible but tasteless; they hang like bright Christmas baubles, ripening to deep orange as sprays of ivory flowers appear between autumn and spring.

Tree heathers such as *Erica arborea* 'Estrella Gold', *E. australis* and *E. lusitanica* would make compatible bedfellows, with the stunning white winter stems of *Cornus alba* or *Rubus cockburnianus* nearby.

Stature and shape, bark and glossy foliage combine to make the strawberry tree a fine showpiece.

CULTIVATION Plant in autumn or spring in any well-drained garden soil. It is a hardy tree, and tolerant of most conditions, but will grow best in full sun with some shelter from cold winds. In severe winters, leaves and stem tips may be browned or killed. Propagate by taking semi-hardwood cuttings in August or September.

Creating an unusual colour contrast, the little urn-shaped flowers of *Arbutus unedo* appear at the same time as the previous year's fruits ripen.

Arbutus unedo

KILLARNEY STRAWBERRY TREE

Height 10-20ft · *Spread* 10-20ft
Best October-January

The mild south-west tip of Ireland and the Mediterranean are the natural homes of this strawberry tree. Less vigorous and, as it ages, more gnarled in its form than *Arbutus × andrachnoides,* its outer bark peels to expose a smooth, deep brown surface beneath, rather like that of eucalyptus, and its evergreen leaves are equally handsome. The round, pimpled fruits that dangle among the glossy, bay-like foliage in shades of yellow, orange and red, are edible, but look a good deal better than they taste. They coincide with the clusters of white or pinkish autumn flowers reminiscent of the tiny bells of lily of the valley.

As with *A. × andrachnoides,* heathers are ideal companions. Those that display gold-orange or red foliage from late summer to spring, like *Calluna vulgaris* 'Wickwar Flame', 'Robert Chapman' and 'Gold Haze', contrast particularly well, combined with *Erica vagans* cultivars for summer flowers.

CULTIVATION Plant in autumn or spring; although an ericaceous plant and happiest in a neutral to acid soil, it is lime-tolerant. *A. unedo* is hardy enough to withstand high winds in coastal areas, but grows best in full sun with some degree of shelter. Propagate by taking semi-hardwood cuttings in July.

Chamaecyparis and other dwarf conifers

Dwarf conifers are backbone trees on a small scale. As the plants around them flourish or fade with the seasons, they are constant, lending structure and depth of colour to the plot in every season of the year.

Some dwarf forms, such as *Pinus pumila,* occur naturally. Others were developed by the propagation of dwarf mutant growths on branches of large-growing kinds, or from dwarf mutations in developing seeds.

Although the tallest of the selection, *Juniperus communis* 'Sentinel' may reach 4ft in ten years in ideal conditions, it is slender, and will not be out of place in a small-scale planting.

Choose different varieties for an interesting range of foliage texture – from the soft, feathery effect of the small-leaved *Chamaecyparis thyoides* 'Ericoides' to the spiky *Pinus leucodermis* 'Schmidtii' and *Picea pungens* 'Globosa'. Or let the rich gold-green of *C. pisifera* 'Filifera Golden Mop', and the golden highlights of *C. lawsoniana* 'Treasure' contribute colour to the winter scene. Their golds and the rusty tinges of *C. thyoides* are heightened by cold winter temperatures.

PLANT COMPANIONS

The dwarf conifers are often swamped in a mixed border, but make interesting features in an island bed or rock garden, or as container plants in paved areas. They associate particularly well with dwarf rhododendrons, small hostas, grasses and ferns. In acid soil, conifers can be the strong, vertical points that add emphasis to a year-round display of heathers such as *Erica tetralix* 'Alba Mollis', *E. vagans* cultivars, and *Calluna vulgaris* (see pages 376-377). Winter and spring-flowering heathers *E. carnea* and *E. × darleyensis* would also be good companions on alkaline soil. A succession of some of the larger-flowering bulbs could be grown around the conifers, or even push up through the branches of prostrate forms such as *Juniperus communis* 'Green Carpet'. *Narcissus* 'February Gold' or 'Tete-a-Tete', and the robust snowdrop *Galanthus elwesii* would add colour in winter and spring, followed by the ornamental onions *Allium moly* and *A. neapolitanum* in summer. The greyish foliage of *Caryopteris × clandonensis* and *Salix lanata* would make a delicate foil to the dense conifer foliage.

CULTIVATION

Plant container-grown dwarf conifers at any time of the year as long as they can be kept well watered during dry periods. The soil should be well drained and reasonably fertile – add peat or leaf mould to sandy or clay soils. The conifers will thrive in an open position or partial shade, but the golden varieties need full sun to show their best colours. Little pruning is necessary; any vigorous vertical shoots from the horizontal

In this miniature winter landscape, created in a sink, a well-chosen mixture of dwarf conifers lend authority to a collection of through-season rock plants that include picea, houseleek, saxifrage and *Galanthus elwesii.*

forms should be removed, and some forms may need a light annual trim to keep them compact and reduce the risk of branches being damaged by heavy rain or snowfall. Any extra-strong shoots must be removed totally, or they may revert and swamp the dwarf parent. Propagate by taking cuttings in early autumn and placing them in a cold frame,

A bed of dwarf and slow-growing conifers, in shades of blue, green and gold, combine with heathers to bring a sense of cool relief to the garden in the heat of late summer.

although some genera, such as *Picea*, *Abies* and *Pinus*, do not always take successfully. Try dipping the stems of *Pinus* in hot water before you insert them in the rooting compost.

A cheerful mauve sea of spring-flowering *Anemone blanda* washes around dark columns of slow-growing *Juniperus communis* 'Compressa'.

Dwarf conifers contribute vertical interest, strength of form, and a hint of sobriety to the gay colours of a summer rock garden.

Chamaecyparis thyoides
'Ericoides'
Four-year specimen;
annual growth 1½-2in.
Red male flowers
in spring.

Picea glauca albertiana
'Conica'
Four-year specimen;
annual growth 2½in.

Chamaecyparis lawsoniana
'Snow White'
Three-year specimen;
annual growth 4in.

Chamaecyparis lawsoniana
'Ellwood's Pillar'
Four-year specimen;
annual growth 6in.

Abies balsamea 'Nana'
Four-year specimen; annual growth 1-1½in.

Picea pungens 'Globosa'
Five-year specimen;
annual growth 2-2½in.

Chamaecyparis lawsoniana
'Pygmaea Argentea'
Seven-year specimen; annual growth 1½in.

Impact on a small scale

Dwarf conifers have dense evergreen foliage
that adds strength and body to small-scale planting schemes
in rock and heather gardens or raised beds. They can be planted in
tubs as patio features, to add substance to more frivolous annuals and
bulbs, or provide welcome contrast to the bright colours of a mixed
border. Rather than let one miniature tree stand on its own
as a solitary punctuation mark, take advantage of the
shapes, colours and textures of different cultivars,
and try incorporating two or three in a composition
of year-round character and interest.

Photographed at a private collection in February.

Juniperus communis
'Sentinel'
Five-year specimen;
annual growth 2½in.

Chamaecyparis lawsoniana
'Treasure'
Four-year specimen;
annual growth 3in.

Juniperus communis
'Compressa'
Seven-year specimen;
annual growth 1in.

Juniperus squamata 'Blue Star'
Four-year specimen; annual growth 3½in.

Juniperus communis 'Green Carpet'
Four-year specimen; annual spread 4in.

Chamaecyparis pisifera
'Filifera Golden Mop'
Four-year specimen; annual growth 3in.

Pinus leucodermis 'Schmidtii'
Seven-year specimen;
annual growth ½-1in.

Chamaecyparis lawsoniana
'Minima Aurea'
Three-year specimen;
annual growth 1½in.

Shades of purple tinge the lower foliage of *Cryptomeria japonica* as autumn arrives, blending with a liquidambar in the background.

The mottled bark of the mature snow gum is its outstanding feature in autumn.

The golf ball-like flower heads of *Echinops* (globe thistle) are seen here growing through the branches of *Eucalyptus gunnii*.

Cryptomeria japonica 'Elegans'

JAPANESE RED CEDAR

Height 8-10ft · *Spread* 7-10ft
Best November-April

There is a touch of melancholy beauty about this cryptomeria, with its dense soft foliage drooping in deeply shadowed layers. The foliage subtly changes tone with the seasons, as the fresh, blue-green growth of summer gradually merges into a winter haze of bronze and purple. The Japanese red cedar is moderately vigorous in growth, needing space to show itself to its best effect. It can be grown as a single, roughly cone-shaped, specimen tree, or be encouraged instead to develop as a widely spreading, arching form by cutting out the leading stems. *Cryptomeria japonica* 'Elegans Aurea' is a slower-growing variety with bright green foliage that intensifies to golden-green in winter.

Handsome, white-stemmed birches or, on a more modest scale, the ornamental brambles *Rubus cockburnianus* and *R. biflorus* would contrast superbly with the dense cryptomeria foliage, while the ground-hugging *Juniperus* × *media* 'Gold Coast' could make a further contribution of strong shape and colour.

CULTIVATION Plant container-grown trees at any time of year in firm, moisture-retentive soil. A sunny position that is not too exposed will produce the healthiest growth. Propagate by cuttings in autumn.

Eucalyptus

GUM TREE

Height 25-45ft · *Spread* 10-20ft
Best All year

Sit in the shade of a eucalyptus on a hot summer's day, and be charmed by the gentle rustle of its aromatic evergreen leaves, by its graceful openness of habit and by its smooth, creamy bark. Although gum trees are native to Australia and Tasmania, there are, nevertheless, quite a number of species that are sufficiently hardy to survive in British gardens.

If you want to fill a gap in a planting scheme quickly, the fast-growing cider gum (*Eucalyptus gunnii*) could be a solution. But beware, if it is left unchecked, the tree can attain a height of 60ft or more with remarkable rapidity. The cider gum's young leaves are silvery blue-green discs that are replaced by grey-green lances in maturity. The bark of young branches is a creamy-brown, turning to dark cinnamon then to soft grey-brown with age. The youthful character may be retained, and the tree's vigour bridled, by annual pruning.

The cabbage gum *E. pauciflora*, and alpine snow gum, *E. p. niphophila*, grow more slowly, reaching about 30ft in 20 years. They usually form single-stemmed trees whose bark flakes off to give a painting-by-numbers effect of browns and pinks, soft greys, greens and silver. All the gums carry clusters of fluffy flowers in early or late summer; these are followed by bunches of inedible, hard-shelled, fruits – 'gum nuts'.

For companions to accompany the eucalyptus, choose other sun-loving plants which enjoy the same conditions. Try the low-growing *Ceanothus thyrsiflorus* 'Repens' or rock roses (*Cistus*).

CULTIVATION Buy plants about 6-12in tall. Plant in early summer in a sheltered, sunny position in moderately rich, slightly acid or neutral soil which should be well drained but kept moist until the plant is well established. Cut back to 18in in early spring one year after planting if the young tree has outgrown its root system and fallen over.

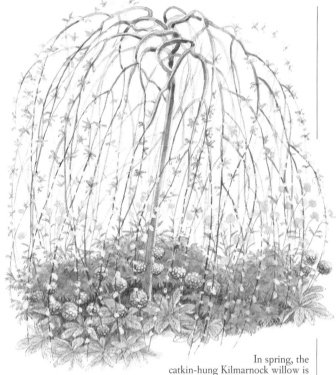

When fully grown, the graceful *Pyrus salicifolia* 'Pendula' needs a clear space to show off its many talents, not the least of which is the magnificent spring display of soft, creamy-white flowers and silver-grey foliage.

In spring, the catkin-hung Kilmarnock willow is supported by some trollius and primulas.

Pyrus salicifolia
'Pendula'

WILLOW-LEAVED PEAR

Height 8-14ft · *Spread* 6-10ft
Best April-October

Elegant, softly coloured and willowy at all times, this ornamental pear has a different mood for every season. As the silver-furred leaves push open along the weeping branches in early spring, there are red-tipped flower buds too, opening to small clusters of white blossom. The summer profile is soft and cool, clothed in long, narrow, silver-grey leaves, and the muted leaf tones of autumn are decorated by tiny green, pear-shaped but tasteless fruit.

If possible, plant the pyrus near water, where the gentle movement of its pendant branches can be reflected.

Beneath the shelter of the tree, plant bright, early flowering *Primula denticulata* or *P. rosea*. Alternatively, the oranges and yellows of *Euphorbia griffithii* and *E. epithymoides*, could introduce more colour in spring, and blue *Clematis macropetala* climb through the branches just as the pear is coming into leaf.

CULTIVATION Plant at any time between autumn and spring in any reasonably well-drained soil in full sun. Add an annual mulch in spring in the early years. Propagate from seed in late winter or early spring.

Salix caprea
'Kilmarnock'

KILMARNOCK WILLOW

Height 4-8ft · *Spread* 3-6ft
Best February-April

The Kilmarnock willow, also known as 'Pendula', has all the character of the big weeping willows, but is small, neat and perfectly tailored for the small garden. The tracery of the bare winter profile is replaced by a spring display of silky, silver catkins that become gilded with pollen. The leaves that follow are quite big in relation to the size of the tree, greyish in colour and slightly wrinkled. Personable enough to give stature to the smallest of garden ponds, or become a focal point in a patch of lawn, bed or border, the willow could shelter a carpet of yellow winter aconites (*Eranthis hyemalis*), followed by a colourful mix of red, blue and white strains of *Primula denticulata*, and the globe flower, *Trollius × hybridus*.

CULTIVATION Plant between autumn and spring in rich, moist soil and in a sunny position.

Soft, silky catkins with bright golden pollen stems are borne by the male *Salix caprea* in spring.

Two heads are better than one when two specimens of *Sorbus* 'Joseph Rock' stand side by side.

Sorbus
'Joseph Rock'

Height 20-30ft · *Spread* 10-15ft
Best September-December

Neat and slender of bearing, this cultivated mountain ash, or rowan, makes a striking silhouette in the winter garden. The rewards for the rest of the year are more ostentatious, with sprays of delicate white blossom in early summer, and refreshing bright green leaves made up of neat ranks of leaflets. As the summer deepens, heavy clusters of creamy-yellow, bead-like berries take on a glorious amber hue, and the leaves begin to assume their

The branches of *Sorbus scalaris* drip with scarlet berries in late summer.

extraordinary autumn livery of crimson, scarlet and purple.

The dark, glossy green of rhododendrons – such as the compact *Rhododendron yakushimanum* and its hybrids – provide a strong contrast to the rowan's lightness of character as long as the soil is acid. Alternatively, the huge white flower heads of *Hydrangea paniculata* 'Grandiflora' would peak just before the late summer and autumn glory of berry and leaf on the sorbus.

CULTIVATION Plant in autumn or spring in well-drained soil in a sunny position. Propagation is not for the amateur – it involves budding or grafting; easier to buy a new tree.

Sorbus scalaris

FERN-LEAVED ROWAN

Height 15-20ft · *Spread* 10-20ft
Best October-December

The Chinese rowan is shorter and broader than *Sorbus* 'Joseph Rock', but has an equally

impressive parade of seasonal glories. In late spring, clusters of creamy blossom are set in profusion against the young fern-like foliage. The summer leaves are rich dark green, with a slight gloss that gives them a lasting fresh look. Flamboyant bunches of small scarlet berries bridge the changeover from summer to autumn foliage, when the leaves turn yellow, then gold and red, and finally fall in early winter.

A rewarding year-round display can be achieved by planting low-growing evergreen shrubs around the sorbus – try *Skimmia japonica reevesiana,* with its red autumn berries, or *Sarcococca hookeriana digyna*, with scented, pale pink winter flowers. Colour could be added in spring by planting narcissus cultivars, *Anemone blanda* and *Crocus tommasinianus*.

CULTIVATION Plant any time in autumn or spring in any well-drained soil in a sunny position. Propagate by taking seeds from berries in October. Plant in seed compost under a cold frame.

There are plenty of young buds waiting to follow on when the elegant flowers of *Stuartia pseudocamellia* appear in summer.

After its serene spring and summer display, the boisterous transformation of *Stuartia pseudocamellia* in autumn is startlingly dramatic.

Stuartia pseudocamellia

Height 15-25ft · *Spread* 8-15ft
Best July-August, and October

A sunburst of flowers resembling camellias is just one of the attractive features that helps to put this fairly slow-growing Japanese tree into a class of its own. The individual blooms, satiny and white with gold centres, are short-lived, but as the first ones begin to fade, there are many fat, round buds nearby, preparing to carry the pageant forward into late summer. When this is over, the

handsome foliage gradually assumes shades of red and crimson to give a long and rewarding autumn display.

Even though the tree is deciduous, its loss of leaf in autumn does not reduce its appeal throughout the year, for its smooth bark peels in winter to create a mottled, pastel pattern of rust, grey and cream.

A stuartia can be planted as a centrepiece among groups of prostrate shrubs, either evergreen or deciduous. The neat, evergreen *Rhododendron williamsianum*, with its leaves of shining chocolate bronze turning to dark green and grey, and

In winter, the peeling bark of *Stuartia pseudocamellia* reveals a trunk like mottled marble.

bell-shaped flowers of the softest pink, would make a gracious and suitably ostentatious companion. As heralds for the stuartia's blooms, employ the white, scented flowers of *Osmanthus delavayi* that appear in April.

CULTIVATION Plant during autumn or early spring in moist but well-drained, acid to neutral soil. Ideally, the site should be in dappled shade, but full sun is acceptable providing the soil is kept moist. Propagate by softwood cuttings in early summer.

Trachycarpus fortunei
(syn *T. excelsa*)

CHUSAN PALM

Height 5-12ft · *Spread* 4-8ft
Best May-September

Giant fans of pleated fronds waving above a thick, palm trunk are more suggestive of a tropic isle than a British garden. Yet the Chusan is surprisingly hardy and, given some protection from wind-battering, is

A Chusan palm, with its echoes of the East, makes an eye-catching all-year specimen for a lawn when grown in a sheltered position.

happy even in such chilly parts of the realm as Northumbria. In particularly favoured spots in the Isle of Wight, say, or the West Country, it can grow to around 30-40ft or more; but in most places it is hardly likely to exceed a quarter of that height. However, the broad fans of evergreen leaves, up to 4ft across, are extremely impressive; moreover, in a warm May and June, a mature tree will produce 2ft long, drooping panicles of small, yellow flowers.

If the palm is not to seem incongruous in its temperate surroundings, its companions must be chosen with care. The strong shapes of yuccas and phormiums would add conviction to a pseudo-tropical scheme, while bedding plants like begonias, *Lavatera* 'Silver Cup' and African daisies (*Osteospermum ecklonis*), brilliant blue and white, might also contribute a hint of faraway places.

CULTIVATION Plant in late spring in any ordinary, well-drained garden soil in a warm, sheltered position. Propagate by seed sown in spring, or by detaching suckers in late spring.

All Seasons
PERENNIALS

PERENNIALS ARE non-woody plants that live for several years. They may be herbaceous, in which case they die down every year in winter, or they can be evergreen. The perennials which contribute most to a garden for all seasons are those which are evergreen, or that keep their leaves for the greater part of the year. Evergreen phormiums, for instance, are year-round plants, while hellebores – including the Christmas rose *Helleborus niger* – whose leaves are evident for much of the year, are important features at ground level.

Ajuga reptans

BUGLE

Height 8-12in
Planting distance 1-1½ft
Best April-August

A partially evergreen mat of foliage makes bugle an ideal ground-cover plant, and in late spring it sounds off with deep blue flower spikes. There are several forms, 'Burgundy Glow' being the brightest with its leaves splashed and stippled with cream, pink, purple and green. 'Variegata' is more subdued, but still has a nice show of cream-tinged leaves, while 'Purpurea' makes a vigorous mat of deep purple-bronze foliage, as also does blue-flowered 'Braunherz'.

The bronze and purple forms go well with orange and yellow

Ajuga reptans 'Variegata' puts on a summer show of blue, backed by cream-tinged leaves.

Even before its flowers appear in spring, *Ajuga reptans* 'Burgundy Glow' bears handsome foliage.

flowers, such as *Geum × borisii* or *Erigeron aurantiacus*. Blue-grey foliage, especially the grasses of *Festuca glauca* or *Helictotrichon sempervirens*, will go well with dark ajuga leaves. A pleasing effect can also be achieved by planting snowdrops and low-growing narcissus bulbs under ajuga; they will push through the dark mat of leaves in spring and will not harm the plant.

CULTIVATION Plant in ordinary soil in sun or light shade. Propagate by dividing the plants and replanting.

BRIDGING THE SEASONS
WITH
Ajuga reptans

THERE ARE few corners of the garden that cannot be recruited to add continuing grace to the whole. Take, for instance, that dampish, shady corner, beloved of toads, at the foot of the rockery. Without disturbing the amphibians, you can easily lighten the gloom with some shade-loving, ground-covering plants, and one of the best for such a situation is *Ajuga reptans* 'Atropurpurea'. Well established in the moist soil, in early summer it raises its blue-purple spikes above a bed of dark, bronze-purple leaves. These mingle well with the shapely foliage of *Alchemilla erythropoda*, which enjoys the same kind of conditions and comes into flower about the same time. In the midst of the ajugas are the leaves and last remaining flowers of the native primrose *Primula vulgaris*. Filling the background farther up the slope, and therefore in a drier, sunny situation, is the dwarf shrub *Helianthemum* 'Wisley Primrose', just coming into bud.

A few weeks later, in high summer, IT IS the helianthemum, a plant always welcome for its soft yellow colouring, that grabs attention. The tiny flowers of the alchemilla are still in evidence, and go well with the helianthemum.

In winter, the site is occupied by foliage, principally that of helianthemum, primrose and ajuga. From late winter onwards, the primrose flowers glow against the ajuga's purple background. 🌱

SPRING There can be few better ways to see the dying winter out than to dress a sombre corner in the bright gold of *Primula vulgaris* – our native primrose – and the imperial purple of *Ajuga reptans* foliage.

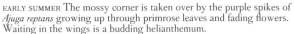
EARLY SUMMER The mossy corner is taken over by the purple spikes of *Ajuga reptans* growing up through primrose leaves and fading flowers. Waiting in the wings is a budding helianthemum.

HIGH SUMMER With its two-tone yellow flowers, the dwarf shrub *Helianthemum* 'Wisley Primrose' rings an echo of the flowers of spring. Though past their best, the ajugas still make a definite contribution.

Given free rein, *Alchemilla mollis* will run riot, as here where its summer sprays of lime-green flowers have almost taken over a brick-paved pathway, and the only concession to formality is the potted clipped box bush.

In late summer and autumn, drumstick heads of scarlet berries appear on *Arum italicum* 'Pictum'.

The magnificently veined leaves of *Arum italicum* 'Pictum' in spring are like giant tropical butterflies.

Alchemilla mollis

LADY'S MANTLE

Height 1-1½ft
Planting distance 2ft
Best April-November

After a light summer shower or in the early morning dew, the broad, seven-lobed leaves of alchemilla seem to be decked with pearls – just one of the charming characteristics of a plant whose free-seeding habit can be put to good use in borders or on terraces and patios. Sprays of lime-green flowers in intricately branched heads appear in early summer and last for weeks.

The handsome foliage of lady's mantle goes well with just about anything, and is particularly effective spreading beneath rose bushes. Alternatively, its strong foliage will give substance to a border set with delicate dianthus or columbines. On a patio or terrace, plant lady's mantle and allow it to spread among the paving, interspersing it with violets.

Arum italicum
'Pictum'

Height 1-1½ft
Planting distance 1-1½ft
Best September-June

Foliage of bright green, spear-shaped leaves, strongly veined with cream, arrives in autumn and stays fresh through winter and spring. Then the creamy-green hood-like spathes, up to 1ft long, with their upright spikes appear, similar to the lords and ladies seen growing wild in woodlands. They are followed by scarlet berries in autumn. Sadly this flash of brilliance may be all too brief, as birds can make short work of the berries.

Arum italicum 'Pictum' is ideal for growing at the front of shrub and mixed borders and beneath trees. It will admirably set off many lovely spring flowers which have disappointing foliage. The black iris *Hermodactylus tuberosus* and grape hyacinths, for example, will both benefit from a nearby show of the spiky leaves, as will the later-flowering violas.

CULTIVATION Plant in shade or sun from midsummer to early autumn, in fertile soil that does not dry out rapidly. Container-grown plants can be planted at any time. Propagate by seed; collect the berries before the birds do, wash off the fleshy parts and sow straight away.

CULTIVATION Plant sometime between autumn and spring, in a moist but well-drained soil and in a sunny or partially shaded position. Support with twiggy sticks. Cut back the stems to 1in after flowering. Propagate by seed sown in seed compost in a cold frame during early spring, or by division in mild winter periods.

BRIDGING THE SEASONS IN A *City Garden*

Leaf form and colour plus the odd floral blaze, can coax drama even out of a tucked-away corner in a tiny garden. The marbled, wavy-edged leaves are those of *Arum italicum* 'Pictum', which emerge from the ground in autumn, ride handsomely through the winter and now, in early May, await the arrival of the plant's creamy flower spikes that are cupped in curved spathes of palest green. Even more striking is the young foliage of *Hosta fortunei* 'Albopicta', whose primrose spears are edged with pale green. Shortly before the lilac flower trumpets appear the leaves fade to a primrose shade and the green margins darken. The backdrop is a tree peony *Paeonia lutea*, which produces single yellow flowers with a lily fragrance in June; while the foreground is occupied by *Saxifrage umbrosa primuloides*, a rich pink version of London pride. Despite the proprietary emotions the plant arouses in Londoners, the name in fact perpetuates that of Messrs London and Wise, the plantsmen who developed the first hybrid in the 18th century. All the same, the crowd of pink stars looks very well in a city garden and does much to flatter the surrounding foliage.

In July, the floral show is ended by the hosta, which sends up spires of lilac trumpets. From then on, the attention is once more centred upon foliage. That of the London pride consists of rosettes of leaves, and the tree peony has darkened. The hosta has grown larger and gone through still another metamorphosis; each leaf now shows two tones of green. Richer and rarer is the change that has overtaken the arum. Between June and September its leaves and flowers disappear entirely, and in their place are bright orange-red berry spikes like lollipops that signal their presence all over the garden. ❧

In spring, this rich association for a small garden shows the marbled leaves of *Arum italicum*, the yellow foliage of *Hosta fortunei* 'Albopicta' and the spiky leaves of a tree peony. The pink flowers belong to *Saxifraga umbrosa primuloides*.

By autumn, the association has changed. The hosta's leaves are now two-tone green, and all that can be seen of the arum are its red seed spikes.

Ruffled and pleated fronds add to the interest of *Asplenium scolopendrium* 'Undulatum'.

Asplenium scolopendrium

(syn *Phyllitis scolopendrium*)

HART'S-TONGUE FERN

Height 1-2ft
Planting distance 2ft
Best All year

The bright green fronds of the hart's tongue will lighten shady places in the garden and, being evergreen, will do so all year round. The fertile fronds are covered with a rusty down, which disappears as they mature and is followed by rows of spore cases forming a chevron-like pattern along the length of the undersides. There are several interesting forms from which to choose; 'Crispum Nobile' and 'Undulatum' have ruffled fronds, and 'Cristatum' has odd tufts or crests growing at the tips.

The plant provides good company for spring-flowering

The new spring shoots of hart's-tongue fern are curled at the tip before opening out fully.

woodlanders, such as bluebells or the evergreen *Helleborus foetidus* with its purple-rimmed yellow-green flowers. A shady rock garden will also benefit from a show of hart's-tongue alongside, say, *Viola labradorica* 'Purpurea' or *Waldsteinia ternata*. *Asplenium scolopendrium* will also look well among others of its kind.

CULTIVATION Plant in any moist but well-drained ordinary soil

The glossy foliage of *Bergenia cordifolia* makes a fine path edging, and creates a lush summer setting for a pink bush rose and delphiniums.

during autumn or spring, in a shady place or partial sun. Propagate by division in early spring, or by sowing spores in spring or late summer.

Bergenia

Height 1-1½ft
Planting distance 1½-2ft
Best All year

Bergenias are excellent for ground cover, and especially *Bergenia cordifolia* whose large leaves, crinkled at the edges, contrast well with spiky or feathery foliage and will provide a lush effect in a border, or will soften the outlines of a

The white and pink bell-shaped flowers of the bergenia hybrid 'Silberlicht' appear in April.

terrace or patio. Its large clusters of pink flowers appear from March until June, when their reddish stems will have lengthened to a foot or more.

In autumn, the leaves of *Bergenia* 'Sunningdale' take on the appearance of burnished copper.

Besides making excellent ground cover, there are several hybrids of special merit. One of them, 'Ballawley', has sprays of crimson-purple flowers rising

The tightly packed, interwoven fronds of *Blechnum penna-marina* make a splendid deep-pile carpet.

From summer to autumn, *B. penna-marina* displays tall, purple-brown spore-bearing fronds.

(*Bergenia* cont)
above the foliage. These last well into summer. 'Abendglut', meaning 'evening glow', and whose deep magenta bells appear almost phosphorescent at sunset, is another charmer, as are the white flowered 'Silberlicht' and 'Bressingham White'.
CULTIVATION Plant well-rooted plants from autumn to spring in any soil, in sun or partial shade. Propagate by division during autumn or spring.

Blechnum
penna-marina

Height 4-10in
Planting distance 1-3ft
Best All year

Add a touch of glamour to the garden with this lush fern from south of the equator; from temperate South America, Australia and New Zealand. Its fronds, attractively shaped and rough to the touch, seldom grow taller than 8in and will develop into a splendid spreading carpet of deep green. In summer the taller, fertile fronds are darkest purple-brown.

Blechnum penna-marina will make excellent ground cover around shrubs, so let it scramble around the feet of *Buddleia davidii*, a daphne or a forsythia, or any other shrubs whose stems tend to be bare at the base. Or set it in company with some of the tall-growing perennials such as acanthus, digitalis, phlox or kniphofia (red-hot poker) for contrasts of form.
CULTIVATION Plant in spring in neutral to acid soil treated with peat or leaf mould, and in a moist and sheltered site. Propagate by division in spring.

THE POINT ABOUT a planting such as this, is that apart from a few things that pop up and down in spring and autumn, most of the plants remain throughout the year, each standing firm at its post and each interacting with the rest in their seasonal garb. The effect is one of casual, trouble-free elegance and therefore naturally requires a good deal of planning and a large number of ingredients to make it work.

Standing tall at the centre is a crab apple, *Malus* 'Golden Hornet', which has white flowers in May and yellow fruits in autumn that remain long after the foliage has departed. Surrounding it is *Bergenia purpurascens* 'Ballawley', with its strange, leathery leaves. Patches of red stand out against the dark green at any time of year, before the first frosts turn them beetroot and mahogany and roll the leaf margins inwards. Vivid magenta flowers stand above the leaves in spring.

To camera right is *Euonymus fortunei* 'Emerald 'n' Gold', whose foliage is an astonishing green, gold and pink before it fades to a more modest bronze in winter. Among the background crowd scene from this angle is a well-shaped young tree of *Juniperus chinensis* 'Stricta', a specimen of the conical *Picea glauca albertiana* 'Conica', and a couple of berberis; *Berberis thunbergii* 'Atropurpurea Nana' and *B. verruculosa*. All these make their presence felt throughout the year, though like *B. thunbergii*, which is purple-red in spring and summer and brilliant crimson in autumn, they may fulfil different roles as the months go by.

Other plants, due to size or habit, show only for a brief space in the passage of the seasons, yet have a bold statement to make. Take, for instance, the dwarf *Picea pungens* 'Globosa', whose intense, silvery-blue foliage can only be seen properly as its surroundings die back in autumn. Or the red, yellow and crimson *Saxifraga moschata* hybrids that pick up the note set by the bergenia in spring. Each plant in fact has a carefully orchestrated part to play in a scheme whose subtlety would have delighted even that Edwardian doyenne of gardeners, Miss Gertrude Jekyll. ❧

Touched by frost, the leaves of *Bergenia purpurascens* 'Ballawley' curl under. Yet even in winter, the association it commands is impressive.

In spring, the bergenia leaves have regained their proper stance and are supplemented by brilliant magenta flowers. About them are evergreen trees and shrubs in their fresh livery.

Autumn gradually turns the bergenia leaves to red and those of *Euonymus fortunei* 'Emerald 'n' Gold' to bronze. But it also reveals the glorious silver foliage of *Picea pungens* 'Globosa'.

A moist and sunny pondside position brings out the brilliant gold summer tones and fountain-like form of *Carex elata* 'Aurea' to perfection.

Carex elata
'Aurea'
(syn *C. stricta* 'Aurea')

BOWLES' GOLDEN SEDGE

Height 1½-2ft
Planting distance 1½-2ft
Best April-October

The arching, golden leaves, striped with subtle shades of lime-green, make this sedge perfect for highlighting a border or an informal part of the garden. In early summer, if sited in a moist, well-lit area, the gold is intense, taking on greener tones as the year advances. The sedge comes into its own when joining flowering plants that benefit from its display. Try it with *Trollius* hybrids, whose bright yellow flowers in spring will be enhanced by the golden foliage, or with *Rodgersia pinnata* 'Superba' or *R. podophylla*, both of which have green and bronze foliage and flower throughout June and July.

CULTIVATION Plant in moist, ordinary soil from autumn to spring. Propagate by dividing clumps in spring.

Cortaderia selloana

PAMPAS GRASS

Height 8ft · *Planting distance* 6ft
Best August-October

The pampas grass is a giant of a plant. Fortunately, the height refers to the joyous feathered plumes that rear up from a fountain of narrow leaves, whose tips trail the ground. The plumes appear in autumn, and can be cut when the days draw in for indoor decoration. The cultivar 'Sunningdale Silver' has large, loose plumes; 'Rendatleri' has pink plumes that reach a height of 10ft.

Although there is a dwarf form, 'Pumila', that grows to 5-6ft, it takes a big garden to accommodate more than one pampas grass. Look instead at

The stately silvered plumes of *Cortaderia selloana* wave over a regal planting that combines purple *Berberis thunbergii* 'Atropurpurea Nana' with the gilded foliage of *Fuchsia magellanica* 'Aurea'.

other grasses, such as *Miscanthus sinensis*, or let the silvered feathers illuminate a background screen of conifers. *Cortaderia richardii* is a related species with less dense clumps of leaves and earlier, arching plumes, but it needs the mild climate of the south-west and western coasts to thrive.

Low, evergreen shrubs, like *Juniperus squamata*, or the deciduous smoke tree, *Cotinus coggygria* 'Royal Purple', would also make fine companions.

CULTIVATION Plant in mid-spring in any well-drained, fertile soil in a sunny, reasonably sheltered site. Wear thick gloves when removing the dead leaves in spring; they have edges like razors. Propagate by dividing clumps in mid-spring.

Dryopteris affinis
(syn *D. borreri*)

GOLDEN-SCALED MALE FERN

Height 2-4ft
Planting distance 3ft
Best April-December

In April the green fronds of this stately British fern begin to emerge. They grow erect on

The graceful *Dryopteris affinis* softens many a planting scheme.

their golden-scaled stems to form a giant shuttlecock shape that stays fresh-looking until late autumn – and longer in a mild winter. The ultimate height depends on how rich and moist the soil is, and the intensity of light.

A wild garden is the best place for a group of dryopteris, where they can combine with other ferns to consort with lilies, meconopsis or hellebores. The refreshing green foliage makes a perfect foil for the soft blue of *Meconopsis betonicifolia*. Later, as the fronds darken, they could provide a soft backdrop for the yellow, strongly scented *Lilium pyrenaicum*. In a small garden a single fern will make a graceful companion for a shrub rose such as the pink 'Felicia', or form the backcloth to a mixed group of hostas.

CULTIVATION Plant during spring in fertile, moisture-retentive soil in a shady position. Propagate by lifting and dividing clumps in spring.

Euphorbia characias is forceful even in winter; here its bold character is softened by snowdrops and *Helleborus orientalis* hybrids.

Euphorbia characias

Height 4ft · *Planting distance* 4ft
Best February-June

In midwinter, the bright green, petal-like leaf bracts of this delightful plant appear and open to reveal tiny brown flowers at their hearts. In tightly clustered columns at the heads of tall stems, they contrast handsomely with whorls of narrow, grey-green leaves. The sub-species *Euphorbia characias wulfenii* has broader spikes of yellowish-green flowers with citrus-yellow centres. Both can make valuable contributions to indoor flower arrangements.

The assertive colours and foliage of *Euphorbia characias wulfenii* add shape and character to a mixed planting scheme. In this late spring scene, the flowers and foliage are complemented by the strong lines of a tall bearded iris cultivar and a busy foreground of *Hebe pinguifolia*, *Phlox subulata* and *Viola labradorica* 'Purpurea'.

While *E. characias* puts on a good display in winter, its long flowering season makes it a fine companion for spring and summer blooms too. Scarlet *Tulipa sprengeri* and *Anemone fulgens*, though both shorter, would make striking companions. Later, the euphorbia could join such strong characters of the mixed summer border as the golden *Rudbeckia* 'Goldsturm', *Sedum spectabile*, with its broad flower heads of long-lasting value, or brightly coloured *Phlox paniculata* cultivars. Despite its size, *E. characias* imparts an olde-worlde air grown between paving stones, providing it is placed where there is not too much traffic.
CULTIVATION Plant between autumn and mid-spring in a sunny position in any ordinary well-drained soil. Cut the flowered stems to ground level in July for a fresh autumn show of foliage. Sow seed in a cold frame during early spring and transplant seedlings in autumn.

FOR LONG-LASTING opulence, it would be hard to beat this jewel-box of an association that immediately suggests an extravagance at the garden centre, or horticultural friends who are generous with cuttings. Actually, the centrepiece is not especially grand, except in the rolling syllables of its name, *Euphorbia characias wulfenii*, and in the unbelievable brightness of its yellow-green spring flowers. Now, in May, they are just beginning to darken, but this, if anything, helps to emphasise the rich colours round about. Below the pink flecks of *Endymion hispanicus* 'Rose Queen' are the crimson bells of *Rhododendron forrestii*, a low, mat-forming species with deeply veined, evergreen, leathery leaves that make an excellent foil for surrounding plants. To the euphorbia's right are the lobe-tipped, chestnut-like leaves of *Rodgersia podophylla* backed by a brilliant deciduous azalea. This is set off in turn by the feathery, bronze-red foliage of the Japanese maple *Acer palmatum* 'Dissectum Atropurpureum'. The background consists of the red form of *Enkianthus campanulatus* in full flower and *Cornus kousa chinensis*, still with a month to go before it produces its annual flamboyance of white and purple-green flower clusters.

Summer is the time too when the *Rodgersia podophylla* puts on its cream flowers against the darkening leaves in the vicinity, though the euphorbias are still distinguished by their comparatively lighter grey-green. It is the panoply produced by the first frosts, though, that really takes the breath away. The heart of the matter is the euphorbias, now in their smart new livery of bright blue-grey foliage that has formed through the summer, with the evergreen rhododendron leaves before. They serve to extol the surrounding foliage even higher; the rich bronze of the broad rodgersia leaves, the singing scarlet and yellow of the azalea, the crimson shades of the acer, and the yellow and red of the enkianthus. 🐟

SPRING The richness of this gathering is more suggestive of silks and velvets than mere foliage. Pinning it together are the endearing bottle-brush shapes of *Euphorbia characias wulfenii* with its intricate, lime-green flowers.

AUTUMN The season of mist and mellow fruitfulness was seldom better advertised than by this same gathering of rodgersia, azalea and Japanese maple in autumn dress. Euphorbias and a rhododendron give them emphasis.

Highlighted by frost, the foliage of *Festuca glauca* handsomely punctuates the garden in winter.

In June, arching sprays of astilbe are neatly enhanced by the blue-grey flowers of *Festuca glauca*.

Festuca glauca

BLUE FESCUE

Height 9-12in
Planting distance 9in
Best All year

The small, neat tussocks of blue fescue are a pleasing shade of blue-grey, as are the flower stems which turn pale fawn as they age among a cascade of thin, cylindrical leaf blades.

Festuca glauca provides attractive blocks of colour in a formal flowerbed or border, where it contrasts well with deep purple foliage, such as that of *Ajuga reptans* 'Atropurpurea'. Any mauve, purple or pink flowers such as *Geranium* 'Russell Prichard', dianthus and *Echinacea purpurea* will also be enhanced by its presence. In a more random display, individual tussocks can be dotted about in the border front or in a gravel garden, where they will

provide evergreen colour.
CULTIVATION Plant in autumn or spring in a sunny position, in light, well-drained soil. Cut back by about two-thirds in July for fresh autumn growth. Propagate by division in spring.

Hakonechloa macra

'Aureola'

Height 1ft
Planting distance 1-1½ft
Best April-December

This colourful grass, one of the most graceful in cultivation, comes from Japan, where its beauty is highly prized. 'Aureola' has rich, golden suffusions, and there is a jaunty cream and yellow striped form, 'Albo-aurea'. During spring and summer the showy leaves, six inches long and half an inch wide, are arranged on alternate sides of thin stems that bow under their weight. By autumn,

Hakonechloa macra takes the eye to a summer association that includes *Lamium maculatum* 'Aureum', *Juniperus chinensis* 'Pyramidalis', *Hypericum androsaemum* and the seed heads of *Allium albopilosum*.

In Japan, *Hakonechloa macra* is valued for its grace of form. But in Western gardens it also pleases with its exotic air, especially in autumn when, as seen here, it occasionally produces feathery flower plumes on its stems.

As courtly in appearance as it is in its behaviour, *Helictotrichon sempervirens* spreads its steely-blue, graceful stems in the summer sun.

The muted hues of *Helleborus atrorubens* might almost have been borrowed from an old print.

(*Hakonechloa macra* cont) some of the stems will have feathery flowers at their ends.

It requires little imagination to see that *Hakonechloa macra* will make a splendid contribution to several parts of the garden. At the feet of shrubs, in an ornamental tub, or spilling over onto a pathway, its arching habit gives it immense charm.
CULTIVATION Plant in spring in moist, fertile soil. Propagate by division in spring.

Helictotrichon sempervirens

PERENNIAL OAT

Height 3-4ft
Planting distance 3ft
Best All year

Helictotrichon has been called a 'safe grass' and a grass with perfect manners. Which means that it can be planted in almost any company and will not invade or trouble its neighbours. And what a handsome fellow it is, with its arching grey-green foliage forming an evergreen tussock, and lofty erect stems bearing oat-like sage-green flowers that turn to the colour of parchment as summer advances.

Because of its neat habit and relatively small size it makes a good alternative to such giants as cortaderia and miscanthus. As a single specimen it will command attention, but will also look well in a group of perennials. Spring and autumn-flowering bulbs can come and go – the foliage of colchicums, for example, will make a pleasing contrast in May, and their lilac flowers will gleam like jewels among the grey grass in September. Or for a stronger contrast, try the purple foliage

Crisp and entirely in keeping with winter are the cool, clear flowers of *Helleborus argutifolius*.

and purple-pink flowers of *Sedum* 'Vera Jameson'.
CULTIVATION Plant in spring in any soil in a sunny site. Propagate by division in spring.

Helleborus argutifolius makes a fine summer foliage show with subtly contrasting alchemillas and salvias.

Helleborus argutifolius

(syn *H. lividus corsicus*)

CORSICAN HELLEBORE

Height 2ft · *Planting distance* 3ft
Best December-March

Sprays of apple-green flowers, up to two inches across, burst forth from the Corsican hellebore's clusters of buds in midwinter. The delicate shades are nicely matched by the foliage, which by now will have aged to lustrous deep green.

The pink or carmine flowers of *Cyclamen coum* make demure companions at the hellebore's feet. Behind it, *Chimonanthus praecox* (winter sweet), a shrub with yellow and purple winter

flowers, or *Hamamelis mollis* (witch hazel), will complete the winter display. In spring, try red tulips, especially the fairly late-flowering *Tulipa sprengeri*, for a vivid contrast to the hellebore's foliage.
CULTIVATION Plant in autumn in partial shade and in deep, well-drained but moist soil. Once planted, do not disturb. Propagate by division.

Helleborus atrorubens

Height 1ft · *Planting distance* 3ft
Best December-July

In the sombre days of winter, when most of the garden sleeps, along comes *Helleborus atrorubens*, a form of *H. orientalis*, with all the beauty and elegance of a spring or summer flower. The deeply bronzed foliage appears just before Christmas, and soon after the flowers

Despite its inelegant common name, *Helleborus foetidus* is one of the most attractive and useful of winter-flowering plants, especially when it lights dark corners with its pale green bells, delicately touched with maroon.

Though *Helleborus lividus* is too delicate for all but the balmiest counties, it has been able to pass on its rosy-green hue to its tougher offspring, *H. × sternii* 'Boughton Beauty', here adding grace to a spring border.

appear – deep plum-purple, up to two inches across and with yellow anthers. And they stay for months, still playing their part when spring bulbs have come and gone.

The rich, dark shades of *H. atrorubens* are a perfect foil for brightly coloured daffodils, hyacinths, crocuses or tulips. Or they can be mixed with their own kind, such as the white-flowered *H. niger* and *H. orientalis* for shades of crimson, pink and white. Such a mixture would look well planted among pink or white-flowering shrubs, like skimmia or pieris, or even among some early flowering rhododendrons and camellias.

CULTIVATION Plant and increase as for *Helleborus argutifolius*.

Helleborus foetidus

STINKING HELLEBORE, SETTERWORT

Height 1½-2ft
Planting distance 2ft
Best Late winter

Don't be put off by its common name – normally stinking hellebore is no more odiferous than many other garden plants, and its winter flowers are as attractive as those of any of its cousins; however, its leaves do smell when crushed. When the pale, curved flower stems begin to emerge in February they contrast nicely with the dark green foliage, and soon have flowers shaped like soft, green rounded bells, brushed with maroon at their tips. A fine cultivar is 'Wester Flisk', with reddish leaf stems and flowers.

The winter-flowering shrubs *Mahonia japonica* or *Daphne mezereum* will be enhanced by a sprinkling of *Helleborus foetidus* around them. Its evergreen foliage in a perennial border will set off early herbaceous plants such as *Lunaria rediviva* (perennial honesty) and the spring pea *Lathyrus vernus*.

CULTIVATION Plant and increase as for *Helleborus argutifolius*.

Helleborus lividus

Height 1½ft · *Planting distance* 2ft
Best Early spring

In contrast to *Helleborus foetidus*, this is one of the few scented hellebores, and is certainly one of the most beautiful with its grey-marbled foliage of deepest green, reddish stems and sprays of green flowers with purplish-pink overtones. It is, unfortunately, not fully hardy and can be grown only in the warmest parts of the country. However, it is an attractive plant and worth a try.

Because of its tenderness, *H. lividus* needs a sheltered garden, and can be placed in a walled border alongside phormiums, *Amaryllis belladonna* or *Nerine bowdenii*. Elsewhere, go for one of the tougher hybrids, such as *H. × sternii* 'Boughton Beauty', in which an even more purple-tinted flower is matched with better toleration of cold.

CULTIVATION Plant and increase as for *Helleborus argutifolius*.

In a mild winter, the flowers of the Christmas rose, *Helleborus niger*, may well bloom in December.

Helleborus niger

CHRISTMAS ROSE

Height 1ft
Planting distance 1½ft
Best January-April

In the winter garden the flowers of *Helleborus niger* shine like stars, their white faces lit up by golden stamens at their centre. They appear in late December and last until March. When the flowers have gone, the leathery evergreen leaves still make a pleasing background for other, smaller plants.

To make the most of the Christmas rose's seasonal display, set it among evergreen shrubs such as *Viburnum davidii* or *Sarcococca confusa*. It will look good beside a display of red berries too, holly for example, or *Iris foetidissima*. In early spring, pulmonarias and scillas will make a magnificent show of blue and white with Christmas roses.

CULTIVATION Plant and propagate as for *Helleborus argutifolius*.

Helleborus orientalis hybrids and the yellow-green flowers of *H. foetidus* are the mainstays of this glorious spring gathering in a lightly shaded woodland setting; the handsome hellebore leaves, wedge-shaped and lance-like respectively, remain to grace the scene long after the flowers have gone.

Helleborus orientalis
Hybrids

LENTEN ROSE

Height 1½ft
Planting distance 2ft
Best December-April

One thing it would be hard to give up during Lent is the joy of seeing the Lenten rose putting on its spring exhibition. Colours range from white through pink to purple and near-black, and the flowers may be shaped like bowls or saucers, whose sepals are spotted or streaked with combinations of soft green, dark pink or purple. Broad, dark green leaves appear after the plant has flowered, and stay throughout the year, lending emphasis to summer's hues.

Lenten roses look good anywhere in the garden, but a mixed border will get off to a particularly good start if they are planted among snowdrops and bright yellow winter aconites. This makes a hard act to follow, but try *Brunnera macrophylla*, with its clusters of blue flowers in May and June.

CULTIVATION Plant and propagate as for *Helleborus argutifolius*.

A rich purple form of *Helleborus orientalis* – but this variable plant can also be found in shades of crimson, white and pink.

Handsome *Iris unguicularis* 'Mary Barnard' is an excellent flower to cut for indoors.

Iris unguicularis cretensis has finer leaves and smaller blooms than the type and its cultivars.

Iris unguicularis

ALGERIAN IRIS

Height 9-12in
Planting distance 1½-2ft
Best November-May

There are many forms of *Iris unguicularis*, all of which produce lovely winter blooms around 2½-3in across, and dark green blades of leaves all year round. Given a summer baking, some strains can start flowering from as early as November and continue through until March,

but after a poor summer, others may not bloom until February. 'Walter Butt', with pale, silvery-lavender flowers, is one of the most prolific bloomers; 'Alba' and 'Bowles White' are off-white, but the former is more difficult to establish. One of the most striking of the unguicularis group is 'Mary Barnard', which bears dark purple-blue flowers with yellow markings from February. There is also a dwarf form, 'Oxford Dwarf', which has grassy foliage and neat, dark blue flowers that are useful in arrangements.

The plants need careful placing to see them at their best. Try putting them alongside the kaffir lily, *Schizostylis coccinea* 'Major', whose deep red, star-shaped flowers appear in autumn – *I. unguicularis* could then take over to provide colour until spring. Mellowed stone or red-brick walls would make a fine background for such a combination.

CULTIVATION Plant clumps 1in deep in spring, in a hot, sunny position, such as against a south-facing wall. Any well-drained soil is suitable. Propagate by division in spring.

Phalaris arundinacea 'Picta' spreads quickly and easily among shrubs to form a bamboo-like thicket.

Phalaris arundinacea
'Picta'

GARDENER'S GARTERS

Height 2-4ft
Planting distance 2-4ft
Best Summer

Gardener's garters is a magnificent grass, but can be a tyrant if planted in permanently moist soil. Growing to 3ft or more, its pink, green and white striped blades could take over a border and smother everything in their wake. But set among shrubs,

The forceful profile of *Phormium tenax* makes a strong-bodied feature among the more gentle contours of most shrubs and perennials.

where it can rampage to its heart's content, it can look superb. If it is planted in drier positions, near tall, thirsty trees, for example, its vigour will be curbed and it will provide useful ground cover.

The dark green of laurels, and the sombre foliage of rhododendrons after the flowers have faded, can be brightened by the white-striped grass throughout the summer and autumn months. For a stunning all-year effect, and contrast in form and colour, grow it with *Phormium tenax* 'Purpureum'.

CULTIVATION Plant between autumn and mid-spring in ordinary, well-drained soil. *Phalaris arundinacea* is a tenacious grass, but it will usually succumb to selective weedkillers if it becomes too invasive. Propagate by taking up rooted pieces and replanting.

Phormium tenax

NEW ZEALAND FLAX

Height 6-10ft
Planting distance 6ft
Best All year

Phormium tenax is a tall and elegant native of New Zealand. The bold, greyish-green foliage stands erect, like a bristle of sword blades, at 5ft or more, and the summer stems towering above bear 2in long, dull red flowers. Later the fruits develop as conspicuous, upstanding pods. Cultivars include 'Purpureum' which has leaves suffused with reddish-purple and pods that range from copper-red to green. 'Variegatum' has green and yellow striped leaves. *P. cookianum* is smaller and more compact than *P. tenax*, growing to 5ft and forming a

The flamboyant *Phormium* hybrid cultivar 'Dazzler' is partnered with another New Zealand native, *Pittosporum tenuifolium* 'Variegatum'.

Introduce a cool oriental quality to the garden with the elegant bamboo *Pleioblastus viridistriatus*.

A harmonious woodland effect is created by planting the magnificent fern *Polystichum setiferum* in front of a dark-leaved rhododendron.

(*Phormium tenax* cont)
thick, wide-spreading clump of arching sword-like leaves.

There are several good colour forms, including 'Yellow Wave' with leaves broadly marked in yellow and cream, and 'Tricolor' (stripes of red, yellow and green).

The spiky foliage of the phormiums is useful for off-setting the more rounded shapes of neighbouring shrubs. The reddish forms go well in deciduous shrubberies where spring-flowering species need an extra boost of interest in summer. For interesting harmonies, try *Acer palmatum* near *P. t.* 'Purpureum', or place *P. t.* 'Variegatum' near blue hydrangeas. Alternatively, partner alongside other plants with arresting foliage, such as *Euphorbia characias*.

CULTIVATION Plant in mid to late spring in ordinary, moisture-retentive soil in a warm and

The pale foliage of *Phormium cookianum* 'Cream Delight' is uplifted by a dark background.

sunny position. The plants are susceptible to severe frosts, so protect the base with straw in winter. Remove any damaged leaves in spring, and dead flower stems in early autumn. Propagate by division in spring.

Pleioblastus viridistriatus

(syn *Arundinaria viridistriata*)

BAMBOO

Height 3-5ft
Planting distance 3-5ft
Best April-December

Most bamboos grow to a considerable height, but this one is better mannered than its relatives and will not dominate the garden. It is just as grand, however, with thin canes that are purplish in sun and green in shade. The lance-shaped leaves are yellow, with dark green stripes that give an overall appearance of greenish-gold.

One of the joys of bamboos is their graceful movement when caught by a breeze, creating subtle colour changes like shot silk. So site this plant in an open space, but sheltered from the

most severe winds. Daubs of blue from *Aquilegia* 'Hensol Harebell' or the later-flowering caryopteris will heighten the impact of the golden leaves. Or try it near the regal tones of *Acer palmatum* 'Atropurpureum' or *Prunus × cistena*.

CULTIVATION Plant in ordinary moist garden soil in late spring. Cut weather-damaged stems back to ground level in early spring. Propagate by division in spring – the roots will need chopping through with a spade.

Polystichum setiferum

SOFT SHIELD FERN

Height 1-2ft
Planting distance 3ft
Best All year

Polystichum setiferum has all the qualities of a classic fern. Its low, arching, feathery fronds retain their refreshing green all

The young fronds of the soft shield fern *Polystichum setiferum* 'Divisilobum' unfurl in spring.

winter. The fronds of the cultivar 'Divisilobum' are even more finely divided than those of the species, and arch when young. Similar to *Polystichum setiferum*, but less hardy, is the hard shield fern, *P. aculeatum*.

Either fern looks splendid in a partly shaded border combined with flowering plants

Pulmonaria angustifolia carpets the ground with its blue flowers in early spring, then with its handsome leaves for long afterwards.

such as *Nicotiana* cultivars. *P. setiferum* will also grow, if there is enough moisture, in paving that is not in full sun all day. The graceful foliage can be emphasised by placing the fern beneath a deciduous tree with shapely, solid-leaved plants such as pulmonarias, hostas or bergenias nearby.
CULTIVATION Plant in mid-spring in light shade, in any moist but well-drained soil. Propagate by division, setting the new plants in soil to which leaf mould or peat has been added.

High among the manifold charms of *Pulmonaria angustifolia* is the surprise of its tender pink buds opening to flowers of rich blue.

Pulmonaria saccharata is grown for the mottled leaves that inspired its common name of lungwort.

Pulmonaria angustifolia

NARROW-LEAVED LUNGWORT

Height 9in
Planting distance 1½ft
Best March-July

Sprays of bell-shaped flowers have a gem-like quality against the dark foliage. Narrow leaves, brushed with fine down beneath, develop into luscious ground cover after the flowers have gone. The forms 'Munstead' and 'Azurea' have deeper blue flowers.

Pulmonarias are natural woodlanders, and make lasting low-level companions when planted beneath later-flowering shrubs such as *Exochorda × macrantha* or buddleias.
CULTIVATION Plant in autumn in sun or light shade, in well-drained, humus-rich soil. Propagate by division in spring.

Underplant pulmonaria with tulips for coinciding spring flowers. The lungwort's leaves take over later.

Pulmonaria saccharata

LUNGWORT

Height 1ft
Planting distance 1½ft
Best February-October

Few plants offer such perfect combinations of decorative foliage and beautiful flowers as *Pulmonaria saccharata*. The broad, silver-blotched leaves are a fine foil for the masses of flowers that appear in early spring, and are virtually evergreen. The flowers open pink and change to sky-blue before they fade. A mixed range of cultivars will give a long display of colour. Recommended forms include *P. saccharata* 'Sissinghurst White', 'Cambridge Blue', the deeper blue 'Highdown' and the pink 'Margery Fish'. *P. rubra* has given rise to 'Bowles Red' and 'Redstart', which often flowers in January.

Informality is the best plan for lungworts; plant them at random, most especially among shrubs, where they will make handsome ground cover, or mix them with daffodils. In time they will seed and hybridise freely, with interesting results.
CULTIVATION Plant and propagate as for *Pulmonaria angustifolia*.

Justly named 'foam flower', *Tiarella cordifolia* makes a fine set of footlights for a blue chorus of *Endymion hispanicus*, and a backdrop of rhododendrons and deciduous azaleas.

In autumn, the bronze markings on the tiarellas' maple-like, evergreen leaves become more pronounced, making a fitting foreground for the luminous scarlet and gold of the azaleas.

BRIDGING THE SEASONS
IN A
Woodland Glade

It was baron Ferdinand de Rothschild who is said to have confided that no garden, however small, should have less than four acres of woodland. Should you be in a position to share this view, then you could not use a corner of the boscage in a happier manner than to dress it for late spring in the most characteristic colours of the season's palette. And, as a matter of fact, the ingredients could also be used to enliven a so far neglected corner of a much more modest garden.

The white is that of the North American foam flower *Tiarella cordifolia* that spreads out on surface runners to form a dense carpet of flower spikes – actually masses and masses of branching panicles, each bearing a cloud of tiny white flowers in May. It is backed by several ranks of *Endymion hispanicus*, a sturdy, old-fashioned standby for this time of year, whose leaves and flowers are broader than those of its relative, the English bluebell, but will naturalise just as readily and persist, if undisturbed, for decades. Their colour is echoed by that of the last flowers of *Rhododendron* 'Blue Chip', which comes out in April, and complemented by the cream and yellow of two deciduous azaleas. They are backed by a Portugal laurel, *Prunus lusitanica*, which has attractive dark green, glossy leaves, smaller than those of common laurel and with red stalks. It is equally happy being left to develop into a handsome, smallish tree or used to form a hedge.

Summer is a time of contrasting greens – those of the rhododendrons and the maple-like leaves of the tiarella – the only other note being provided by the creamy, hawthorn-scented flowers of the Portugal laurel; they are followed by red fruits that gradually turn dark purple. Drama, however, returns in the autumn when the bronzy-brown markings along the veins of the tiarella leaves become more pronounced, and the foliage of the azaleas, touched by frost, flares to brilliant scarlet and orange.

Rhododendron, tiarellas and the Portugal laurel are all evergreen, so even when the autumnal show dies away there is a fine mixture of leaf form and colours to take the corner through the winter and to provide, from the tiarellas at ground level to the top of the rhododendron, a most efficient windbreak and fantastical battlements when snow falls.

There is an icy coolness about the delicate flowers of *Tiarella cordifolia* that appear in May and June.

Yucca filamentosa 'Variegata' is a distinctive plant with its white-edged leaves.

In America the yucca's tall columns of creamy bell-shaped flowers are called 'candles of the Lord', and the sword-like leaves and arching outer ones of *Yucca recurvifolia* make a splendid 'candleholder'.

Tiarella cordifolia

Height 6-10in
Planting distance 1-1½ft
Best All year

The downy, heart-shaped leaves, turning in autumn from soft green to bronze, and the feathery off-white flowers of *Tiarella cordifolia* make it an excellent ground-cover plant, but one for the chorus line rather than centre stage.

Among trees or below a north-facing wall they can be used to unify a planting scheme, especially with a background of rhododendrons, small willows or any shrubs that will thrive in cool conditions. Good companions would be Solomon's seal, Turk's-cap lilies and fragrant lily of the valley.

CULTIVATION Plant in autumn or spring in moisture-retentive soil. Propagate by division in autumn or spring.

Yucca filamentosa

Height 4ft · *Spread* 3-4ft
Best All year

The erect, sword-like leaves of *Yucca filamentosa* make it a striking plant ideal for grouping with others that are similarly bold. It forms a dense clump, with the outer leaves spreading, and from this arise flower spikes up to 6ft tall. In midsummer they make an impressive display, with hanging, 3in long, creamy-white blooms. There is also a variegated form, *Y. f.* 'Variegata', its leaves striped and margined with white.

Such a distinctive plant needs distinctive companions, such as the bold grass *Stipa gigantea* with plumes similar to those of pampas grass, and the semi-prostrate *Juniperus media* 'Gold Coast'. They could be grouped at the front of a border, or as an isolated display on a paved terrace or patio.

CULTIVATION Plant in spring or autumn in any well-drained soil, in a sunny but sheltered position. Propagate by division in spring or by root cuttings.

Yucca recurvifolia

Height 6-8ft · *Spread* 6ft
Best All year

Long, tapering leaves are a distinctive feature of *Yucca recurvifolia*, and all but the central cluster are attractively bent. This makes a distinctive base for the tall flower stem and its creamy-white flowers, borne in late summer.

In a mixed border, backed by bamboo or a clipped yew hedge, *Y. recurvifolia* will blend well with tulips such as 'Apricot Beauty' and 'Orange Monarch', which could be followed by a summer grouping of the blue *Eryngium planum* and *Echinops ritro*, and continued a long way into autumn with *Agapanthus* 'Headbourne Hybrids'.

CULTIVATION Plant and cultivate as for *Y. filamentosa*.

All Seasons
ALPINES

STRICTLY SPEAKING, an alpine is a plant that is adapted to growing above the tree line on a mountain. In the garden, however, alpines are held to embrace virtually any plant that looks right in a rock garden, in raised beds, and trough and sink gardens. Although small in stature, they can play an important part in the garden for all seasons if treated in groups rather than as individual plants. Each member of the planting group can then show its flowers and foliage effects in turn throughout the year, to create a changing focus of colour.

In summer, *Acaena* 'Blue Haze' lives up to its name with a brilliant display of blue-grey foliage.

Reddish-brown seed heads in autumn contrast vividly with the distinctive foliage of 'Blue Haze'.

In midsummer the scarlet seed heads of *Acaena microphylla* are like stars from a firework display.

The mustard-yellow flowers of *Achillea tomentosa*, 3in across, are at their best in midsummer.

Acaena
'Blue Haze'

Height 3-4in
Planting distance 1½-2ft
Best All year

The acaenas are grown principally for the beauty of their evergreen glaucous foliage and summer to autumn fruit heads. The cultivar 'Blue Haze' is among the best for the pronounced blue-grey hue of its leaves, like those of a tiny mountain ash in form and with stalks of a rich mahogany. It is often used as ground cover because it spreads rapidly, but in a good situation it can be very vigorous and a threat to slow-growing, more restrained neighbours.

The small button flower heads are unspectacular but they develop later into burr-like seed heads, resembling miniature sea urchins with glossy, russet spines. The soft-toned mat of foliage makes a perfect carpet for blue-flowered bulbs, such as April-flowering *Scilla sibirica* 'Spring Beauty'.

CULTIVATION Plant in any neutral or slightly acid, light soil. Avoid heavily shaded areas. Propagate in spring or autumn by division.

Acaena microphylla

Height 1-2in
Planting distance 1½-2ft
Best All year

Small is beautiful in the case of this New Zealand species. It forms an evergreen mat of bronze leaves, sometimes grey shaded beneath. Insignificant flower heads appear in summer, but are soon replaced by the prettiest seed heads of all the acaenas, less spiny than most, with soft burrs of translucent scarlet. *Acaena novae zelandiae* has rich, bright green leaves, larger than those of *Acaena microphylla*, and its burrs are of a more muted purplish hue.

A. microphylla behaves like a midget bramble, and its effect is heightened if you let it creep around warm brown stones or over the amber of a gravel path. If a few self-rooted shoots are inserted in a little sandy soil between the paving of a patio or terrace, they will form runnels of bronze between the slabs.

CULTIVATION No particular soil preparation is necessary, but a light soil and some sun produces the best results. Acaenas may not succeed in strongly limy soils but will grow in chalky soils. Propagate as for the hybrid *A.* 'Blue Haze'.

Achillea tomentosa

Height 6in
Planting distance 10in
Best June-August

The densely packed, bright yellow flower heads of *Achillea tomentosa* will bring a splash of sunshine to a border or rock garden on even the dullest midsummer day. The feathery, evergreen leaves make a dense mat, and their fine, downy covering gives them a silvery-grey hue.

If there is a sunny patch or dappled shade nearby, plant the spot with *Ornithogalum nutans* (Star of Bethlehem) for its translucent, green and white flowers. Close by, but in a sunny space, *Crocus medius* should grow happily, and its lilac-purple blooms will appear in November, before its leaves have developed.

CULTIVATION Plant in a sunny spot, or in light shade, between October and March, in ordinary, well-drained, but moisture-retentive soil. Propagate by taking softwood cuttings in late summer, or by division and immediate replanting of a few young shoots in early autumn.

The domes of the pink-flowered *Armeria juniperifolia* and a *Sedum spathulifolium* 'Cape Blanco' sparkle like jewelled cushions.

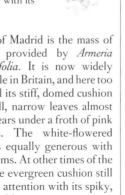

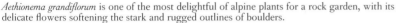

Aethionema grandiflorum is one of the most delightful of alpine plants for a rock garden, with its delicate flowers softening the stark and rugged outlines of boulders.

The sea pink, often a cliff-hanger in its native habitat, is not an invasive plant and is therefore ideal for setting in rock-garden crevices.

Aethionema grandiflorum

Height 9-12in
Planting distance 1-1½ft
Best May-July

Though a native of the Mediterranean, the large-flowered and evergreen *Aethionema grandiflorum* is surprisingly hardy in our cooler, wetter gardens. Many closely growing stems rise from the rootstock to create an upstanding, wiry bushlet with grey-green, needle-like leaves. Between May and July, the foliage is complemented by a profusion of delicate pink four-petalled flowers. Frosts may cut back the stems, but fresh growth will make good the loss the following spring.

The plant thrives in a warm limestone terrain; as semper-vivums enjoy much the same conditions, they make an interesting companion planting.

The hybrid *A*. 'Warley Rose' produces flowers of a richer pink than *A. grandiflorum*, while *A*. 'Warley Rubra' is a strong crimson-magenta.

CULTIVATION Plant between autumn and spring, or at any time if the plant is containerised, in a warm, sunny place where the soil is not too fertile. Propagate from softwood cuttings in midsummer.

Armeria juniperifolia

Height 2-3in
Planting distance 6-9in
Best May-June

One of the most eagerly awaited harbingers of spring in the Sierra de Guadarrama to the north of Madrid is the mass of colour provided by *Armeria juniperifolia*. It is now widely available in Britain, and here too in April its stiff, domed cushion of small, narrow leaves almost disappears under a froth of pink flowers. The white-flowered form is equally generous with its blooms. At other times of the year the evergreen cushion still attracts attention with its spiky, clustered leaves.

In light soils, young plants placed about a foot apart along the edge of a sunny bed or path will eventually join up to form a weed-proof edging that will contribute much to the garden throughout the year. Both in and out of flower the plant makes a good strong contrast to silver-leaved prostrate plants such as *Sedum spathulifolium* 'Cape Blanco' or *Thymus × citriodorus* 'Silver Queen'.

CULTIVATION Plant in spring or autumn in a crevice, wall, pavement or trough – a limy soil will cause no problems.

Armeria maritima

SEA PINK, SEA THRIFT

Height 6-12in
Planting distance 1ft
Best May-June

Clinging as doggedly to the cliffs as the barnacles below, sea thrift can be seen spreading drifts of pink flowers around Britain's coasts as summer approaches. Each dense tuffet of long, thin, evergreen leaves sends up tough, wiry stalks carrying tight heads of flowers. Their colour can vary from plant to plant, ranging from raspberry pink through lilac tints, to white. And even after they have died, the dead heads are decorative. They remain, like crisp tissue paper, long after the colour has faded from them.

Because sea thrift spreads so little, it is ideal for trough

The early summer show of *Armeria maritima* 'Bloodstone'.

One form of *Aubrieta deltoidea* 'Variegata' in early summer.

Dryas × suendermannii flowers for many weeks in summer.

The soft silver-grey hummock of *Euryops acraeus* is seen at its best against a background of dark green foliage plants.

(*Armeria maritima* cont)
gardens and other similar large containers. It makes a perfect bedfellow for *Dryas × suendermannii* and helianthemums.
CULTIVATION Plant in ordinary soil in a sunny position during spring or autumn. Propagate by taking semi-hardwood cuttings in mid or late summer or by division in early spring.

Aubrieta deltoidea
'Variegata'

Height 4-6in
Planting distance 1½-2ft
Best May-June

Dozens of colour forms of aubrietia are offered by nurseries and garden centres. *Aubrieta deltoidea* 'Variegata' is available in two, equally attractive, violet-purple flowered forms, but the permanently variegated leaves give an extra sparkle through the months after the flowers have faded.

The darker, second form of *Aubrieta deltoidea* 'Variegata'.

'Variegata Argentea' has leaves edged with cream, while 'Variegata Aurea' is trimmed with golden-yellow. Both are neat, prostrate plants.
For a really spectacular show of flowers, try growing *A. deltoidea* on sunny banks and walls where there is poor soil. The plant does well in most situations with plenty of sun, and tolerates poor, light soil. If it is grown in open ground, it can

be underplanted with tulips – for example 'Red Riding Hood' or 'Stresa' – to prolong the splash of intense colour.
CULTIVATION Plant in autumn. Clip back with shears after flowering to promote compact growth and plenty of bloom in the following year. Propagate by cuttings or division in spring or by layering between early spring and autumn.

Dryas × suendermannii

Height 4-8in
Planting distance 1½-2ft
Best May-July

Splaying its hoary, chestnut-coloured stems hard against the ground or among rocks, *Dryas × suendermannii* is one of the best mat-forming alpine plants. The scalloped, evergreen leaves, held close to the stems, occasionally twist to show a silver-white reverse.

For weeks from late spring onwards there is a parade of flowers, each opening from a yellow bud to a shallow chalice of eight or more overlapping, creamy-white petals that surround a golden button of crowded stamens. As the flowers fade, their stalks double in height to carry silky whorls of seeds which last until late summer and grow in beauty as they age, almost outshining the flowers.
The mat of leafy stems is not too greedy for an underplanting of dwarf bulbs – *Crocus vernus* would be suitable.
CULTIVATION Plant in mid-autumn or early spring in any soil. Dryas will thrive in a gravel path or between paving stones on a patio or terrace; it flourishes in sun and is resistant to drought. It is a long-lived plant and needs up to a square yard of space for its eventual sprawl. Propagate by taking self-rooted stems and growing these on as rooted cuttings.

Euryops acraeus

Height 10-12in
Planting distance 15-18in
Best June-July

Though most other members of the genus are tender, *Euryops acraeus* is much hardier and is regularly grown outside everywhere in Britain. It is one of the finest miniature shrubs for silver foliage, with a bushy, upright habit. The strap-shaped evergreen leaves are enhanced by a metallic sheen and sprout from the rising stems in 'bottle-brush' clusters. The shrub's rounded dome of silver uplifts any dull patches in a winter garden. In late spring to early summer the foliage is studded with rich yellow, daisy-like flowers that rise among fresh growth of blue-grey shoots.
The year-round sparkle of this shrub can brighten plants which are rather sombre when out of flower, such as *Phlox*

The flowers of *Euryops acraeus* are a generous early summer bonus.

The bright lemon summer flowers of *Hypericum olympicum* 'Citrinum' are set off by a delicate, pink *Geranium sanguineum* 'Splendens'.

douglasii or *Sternbergia lutea*. Alternatively, it could provide a cooling influence to a fiery, fragrant display of purple-red *Cyclamen purpurescens*.

CULTIVATION Plant in early to mid-spring in gritty soil in full sun; the plant will not thrive in cold, wet sites and loses its silver lustre if grown in shade. To propagate, take softwood cuttings in mid to late summer, or take hardwood cuttings in early autumn.

Globularia cordifolia

Height 2-4in
Planting distance 10in
Best June-July

The natural home of *Globularia cordifolia* is among rocks on the lower slopes of the Pyrenees and the Alps. On the flat, its mat-forming habit makes it a good subject for planting in pavements and stone walls.

The plant's colours are

Globularia cordifolia in summer bears stemless flowers set tightly in a mat of evergreen leaves like fancy pins in a pincushion.

restrained. Dark evergreen leaves crowd close to the ground, while in early summer, Wedgwood-blue flowers, like little drumsticks with fluffy heads, rise out of the foliage.

These characteristics are in harmony with an association with *Tulipa tarda*. In early spring, the open, white and yellow stars of the tulip would stand a few inches above the dark green carpet of globularia.

An underplanting of *Crocus kotschyanus* would extend the gentle colour theme after the globularia's summer flowers and seed heads, into autumn.

CULTIVATION Plant in mid-autumn or mid-spring, in any soil in a sunny position. Shade will cause lax, leafy growth and poor flowering. Propagate by division in early spring or take cuttings of semi-hardwood shoots in midsummer.

Hypericum olympicum flowers cluster above soft foliage.

Hypericum olympicum

Height 10-12in
Planting distance 1ft
Best July-August

Although *Hypericum olympicum* is one of the smallest plants of the hypericum genus – which encompasses the plants commonly known as St John's worts – its flowering display can compete easily with the finest of its larger relatives.

Wiry stems, clothed with

small grey-green leaves, rise each spring from the shrub's woody rootstock. This soft foliage provides a perfect foil, in mid to late summer, for the dramatically large, golden-yellow flowers with prominent stamens.

The softness and colouring of *H. olympicum* make a beautiful contrast in summer with the bold, sword-like leaves and rich royal-blue heads of *Iris xiphioides*. To create a link through the seasons, plant a couple of dwarf conifers alongside, for instance *Chamaecyparis obtusa* 'Nana Compacta', with dense, bright green foliage, or that joy of small rockeries, the neat, blue-green *Juniperus communis* 'Compressa'.

CULTIVATION Plant during early spring or autumn in a relatively poor soil. The site should be open but sheltered from the coldest winds; avoid shade and badly drained soil. Propagate by softwood cuttings in mid-summer, or by seed in spring.

BRIDGING
THE SEASONS
IN A
White Corner

IT'S MAY, with all the botanical exuberance that the month conjures up. The scene is that most gracious of settings, a bed in a terrace of lichen-clad stone, but a white corner is a very effective device for almost any background, from Sissinghurst to cottage border. At this time, the centrepiece is the spreading, evergreen *Iberis sempervirens* 'Snowflake', which creates a pure white mat that lasts through to July. Reinforcements are provided by the broad, vividly white-margined leaves of *Hosta crispula* and a tall, graceful group of *Tulipa* 'Purissima', whose lovely cream flowers open to the sun.

By late summer, the iberis flowers have gone and the tulips have been lifted. They have been standing over a number of *Galtonia candicans* bulbs, which have now produced their tall spires of white hyacinth-like flowers. These are given emphasis by lilac hostas.

In autumn, all the flowers of summer have departed, the leaves of the hosta are dying back, and beside them the foliage of the iberis makes an evergreen hummock. Around the hosta, however, a good solid planting of *Galanthus nivalis reginae-olgae*, earliest of snowdrops, raises nodding white bells in October, well before the leaves appear. They are interspersed with another layer of bulbs, those of *G. n.* 'Atkinsii', a most graceful snowdrop that, like the snows themselves, will carry the white theme into January. 🌺

When others are attempting to impress with bright colours, it's cool to cut a dash with a white border. Pre-eminent in May is the dazzling white of *Iberis sempervirens*, noticeable as the brightest red. Here it draws the eye to the white-margined leaves of hostas and a group of cream tulips.

In late summer, the tulips have been lifted or have died back. The sombre foliage of the iberis now serves as a background for the tall white blooms of *Galtonia candicans*, and the only colour in the scheme is the pale purple trumpets of the hostas.

Iberis sempervirens 'Snowflake' seen in full dress for early summer.

Indifferent to stony soil, shade and low temperatures, *Saxifraga × haagii* will warm the least hospitable of corners at the least joyous time of year.

Though past its flowering peak in May, the foliage of *Saxifraga apiculata* still makes a comfortable bed for the blooms of the spring gentian *Gentiana verna*.

Iberis sempervirens
'Snowflake'

CANDYTUFT

Height 6-9in · *Spread* 1½-2ft
Best May-July

The all-year attractiveness of this dwarf shrub's deep green hummock of leaves places 'Snowflake' among those plants that really give value for money over many months. It can be used in the rock garden, or around the edge of the herbaceous border as a useful filler whose dark foliage will serve to point up lighter plants

When in flower, 'Snowflake' is irresistible. In May, the whole plant disappears under a pure white cap of flower heads, jostling for space and lasting for weeks.

Usually long-lived, it needs room to spread but it does not become invasive. 'Snowflake' can be associated with fairly strong growers. For example, if

Small green hillocks of *Saxifraga apiculata* 'Alba', crowned by white stars, would make a fine edging to a naturalised planting of spring bulbs.

planted a yard or so in front of the May-flowering Warminster broom (*Cytisus × praecox*) it will emphasise the acid yellow of the broom's flowers, and its own whiteness will be intensified.
CULTIVATION Plant in late autumn in any well-drained soil and in a sunny position. Propagate from softwood cuttings taken in midsummer.

Saxifraga

CUSHION OR KABSCHIA GROUP

Height 4-6in
Planting distance 9-15in
Best February-April

The kabschia saxifrages are the earliest to flower, and some are bold enough in character to

have a telling effect in planting schemes away from the rock garden. The easiest of all to grow is *Saxifraga apiculata*, and its hummocky, apple-green foliage would look well edging a pathway. There are two colour forms, a fresh primrose yellow and 'Alba', a pure white, both of which bloom profusely in spring.

The hybrid *S. × haagii*, equally trouble-free, forms a low, spreading cushion of bright green leaf rosettes which are less tightly packed than most kabschias. Its buttercup-yellow flowers appear in March.

If you have room for only one saxifrage, try *S. burserana*. It can live for years, slowly expanding into tight cushions of blue-grey leaves and never failing to bloom in early spring. 'Brookside' has large, white saucer-shaped flowers. The intense blue of our native spring gentian, *Gentiana verna*, would certainly make an excellent foil.

Plant *S. apiculata* with other loosely spreading plants such as *Polygonum vacciniifolium*, which trails beautifully over walls, and *Helianthemum nummularium*. Both will flower later in the year. Alternatively, introduce vertical interest with nearby dwarf alliums such as *Allium moly* or *A. mairei*. The dark, bronzed leaves of *Dianthus alpinus* 'Joan's Blood' would complement the foliage of *S. × haagii* and follow on with a show of intense red flowers.
CULTIVATION Plant in autumn in any light soil, though 'Brookside' will thrive better in an equal mixture of limestone chippings and potting compost, topped with a layer of stone chippings. The situation should be north-facing or in shade, since a day's strong sun in summer will blight the plants forever. The site should also be well-drained, for prolonged damp can be equally fatal. To propagate them, separate single rosettes in early summer and place in damp, coarse sand.

The flowers of silver-leaved *Saxifraga cochlearis* stand about 8in high on branched stems.

A cascade of *Saxifraga callosa* and a *Penstemon pinifolius* brighten the grey stones and pebbles of a rock garden.

Dense mounds of *Saxifraga* 'Pearly King' merge with the crimson 'Ballawley Guardsman' – both are mossy saxifrage cultivars.

Saxifraga

MOSSY GROUP

Height 2-3in
Planting distance 8in
Best April-May

The 'mossies' possess a delicacy that belies their strong constitution. Their springy, emerald-green foliage grows thickly in compact, dome-shaped buns that in late summer and autumn are often tinted bronze and yellow. The evergreen leaves are larger and softer than those of the kabschia saxifrages. Massed, saucer-shaped flowers rise above the green carpet to create a coloured haze in mid to late spring.

The species *Saxifraga moschata* has subdued those rather creamy flowers that enhance the Pyrenees and the Alps. Among the host of garden varieties developed from it are 'Fairy', a compact, late flowerer with white blooms on 6in stems, 'Peter Pan' with carmine flowers and 'Flowers of Sulphur', a flatter and more spreading plant in habit, with pale, yellow blooms.

Though mossies are rampant in some conditions, you might with caution combine them with silver-leaved and kabschia saxifrages. Their different flowering periods will create an evergreen tapestry of green, gold and silver foliage throughout the year, and a sequence of flowers from Christmas until well into early summer.

CULTIVATION Plant during late winter and early spring in dappled shade and in light, moist soil. Propagate by detaching the rosettes and setting them singly in moist sand during midsummer.

Saxifraga

SILVER-LEAVED GROUP

Height 1ft
Planting distance 1ft
Best June-July

It is their large rosettes of frosty foliage combined with voluminous sprays of white flowers that help to make the silver-leaved saxifrages into major stars of the rock garden.

The king of the silver saxifrages is *Saxifraga longifolia*, which has narrow leaves of dazzling silver leaves and in maturity, after three years or so, splendid, arching plumes of white flowers. *S. callosa*, though smaller, is equally attractive, with rosettes of strap-shaped leaves edged with lime, and bright, starry, white flowers. The milk-white flowers of *S. cochlearis* are more delicate than those of *S. callosa*, and are borne on mahogany-coloured stems.

Grown in limy soil it is the most heavily silvered of the entire group. Plant these last two saxifrages together for a wonderful, evergreen foliage display in the rock garden.

As for *S. longifolia*, let it cascade from a container, or over a wall, perhaps with *Phlox douglasii* and *P. subulata* nearby for their lavender and pink flowers. *S. callosa* is best suited to a wall crevice, where its plumes will go well with the reddish-brown tints of *Sempervivum tectorum*. Because of its dwarf, slow-growing habit, associate *S. cochlearis* with non-invasive plants such as *Armeria juniperifolia*, which bears bright pink, stemless flowers in May.

CULTIVATION Plant in spring or autumn in stony, well-drained, preferably limy soil, with a covering of stone chippings. Propagate by detaching young rosettes in midsummer, and rooting them in moist sand. Plant them out in spring.

A cotton lavender and dwarf conifer hold centre stage in a rock garden, with a backdrop of broom, while *Sedum spathulifolium* 'Purpureum' makes a subtle contribution in the foreground.

With boundless energy in July and August, *Sedum spurium* spreads its tangled mat of succulent foliage, interspersed with rich pink flowers.

After the July flowering the rosettes of *Sedum spathulifolium* 'Cape Blanco' can clearly be seen.

Sedum spathulifolium

STONECROP

Height 3in
Planting distance 1½ft
Best June-July

The thick, fleshy leaves of *Sedum spathulifolium* are spoon-shaped – hence the specific name. They form a tight mound of rosettes that are so pleasing in colour and form that the bright yellow haze of starry summer flowers is regarded as little more than a bonus.

Among the various forms there are two that are particularly striking when grown together – *S. s.* 'Cape Blanco', with foliage apparently cut from dove-grey felt; and *S. s.* 'Purpureum', whose leaves have a waxy sheen, and are richly suffused with burgundy.

S. spathulifolium adapts to a wide range of conditions and is equally at home among rock garden companions or planted in front of its giant relative, *Sedum* 'Autumn Joy'. It is also most attractive when contrasted with *Dianthus* 'La Bourboule' and *Zauschneria californica*.

CULTIVATION Plant any time in well-drained soil, in sun or part shade. Leave dead flower stems until spring, then snap them off. Propagate by transplanting rosettes in spring or summer.

Sedum spurium

STONECROP

Height 4in · *Planting distance* 2ft
Best August-September

Let this species ramble over banks, or spread its tangled mats of little, round, crimped leaves beneath shrubs and dwarf trees. Although originally from the Caucasus and Armenia, it is semi-naturalised in Britain and will grow almost anywhere in the garden. The fleshy, light green leaves remain all year round, and throughout July and August there are crops of starry flowers, available in various shades of white and pink to the stronger purple-red of the cultivar 'Splendens'.

Sedum spurium will enhance the colour and shape of dark dwarf conifers, keep weeds at bay, and do much to ensure moisture retention in the soil. The sedum's tangle of roots

Though a sun lover, *Sedum spurium* will settle in almost any situation, even under trees.

Among the many varieties of *Sempervivum tectorum* – houseleek – is the pretty and popular *S. t. calcareum*.

(*Sedum spurium* cont)
is so shallow, and takes so little from the soil, that the plant makes a useful filler around any established companion.

CULTIVATION Plant in autumn or spring in any soil, preferably in full sun. Propagate by division or cuttings after flowering and plant the pieces directly into the open ground.

Sempervivum tectorum

HOUSELEEK

Height 6-8in
Planting distance 1ft
Best June-July

Sempervivums used to be grown on rooftops as protection against lightning and witchcraft – which is at least an indication of the spartan conditions that the plants will tolerate. All produce rosettes of leaves like fleshy miniature

cabbages; these are often flushed with pink or purple, and vary in diameter from ½in to 8in, depending on the cultivar. Stout stems topped by small pinkish-purple, star-shaped flowers rise from the centres in July.

Of the many forms available, two of the most attractive are *Sempervivum tectorum calcareum*, whose thick red-tipped leaves have a pale blue sheen, and *S. t.* 'Triste', which has fresh green leaves suffused and tipped with reddish-brown.

A combined planting of sedums and sempervivums will make an intricate mosaic of colours and texture at ground level; the sunnier the spot, the more pronounced the foliage tones. Planted in cracks of walls, sempervivums will gradually form a living mortar.

CULTIVATION Plant in late spring or early summer in full sun and in light soil. Propagate by replanting rooted rosettes.

The traditional bed for houseleeks is on the rooftop, whence they are said to protect the household from lightning strike and witchcraft.

Affectionate colonisers of human habitation since time immemorial, the many varieties of houseleek grow nowhere with more enthusiasm than on a wall, where they insert themselves into the tiniest cracks and flourish on apparently no nourishment at all.

Thymus praecox arcticus

THYME

Height 2in
Planting distance 1ft
Best June-July

This is the tough little wild thyme of our chalk and limestone hills – and a rewarding plant in any garden. Minute, dark evergreen leaves make a dense, springy mat that releases a strong, tangy aroma on hot days, or when bruised. Early summer brings a froth of tiny, two-lipped flowers that are invariably humming with bees.

A most satisfactory situation for the carpet-forming *Thymus praecox arcticus* is the pavement garden, where it spreads across the stone to make a purple pool about the white pea flowers of *Dorycnium hirsutum*.

Viola labradorica 'Purpurea' will happily take over even in a shady site where the soil is poor.

Excellent for ground cover is *Waldsteinia ternata*, whose flowers resemble those of the dog rose.

Selected forms, mainly found in the wild, have greater clarity of colour than the basic species, ranging from the pure white of *Thymus praecox arcticus* 'Albus' to shell-pink and carmine.

Thymes are often planted to edge or creep over garden paths, so that their scent can be appreciated. They are also superb ground-cover plants to combine with the spring-flowering *Aubrieta* hybrids or *Arabis caucasica*. Cut these hard back after flowering, to provide contrasting foliage colour and a lengthy flowering succession that will go on from April to July.
CULTIVATION Plant during autumn or spring in a sunny part of the garden, such as a south-facing stony bank in any well-drained but moist soil. To ensure that cultivars run true, propagate by division in autumn or spring, or by cuttings in summer.

Viola labradorica
'Purpurea'

VIOLET

Height 4-5in
Planting distance 6in
Best May-June

As befits a native of Greenland and Labrador, *Viola labradorica* 'Purpurea', a sturdy, evergreen creature, gallantly carries its heart-shaped, purple-tinted leaves through the most severe of winters. The leaf tints are reflected in the flat-faced, rich mauve flowers that stand on strong stems above the crowded horizontal patchwork of leaves from late April onwards.

This is a plant for dotting about in shady nooks and crannies of the rock garden, especially if it is contrasted with the stiff, silver forms of *Saxifraga callosa* or *S. cochlearis*, planted a short distance away.
CULTIVATION Semi-shade is best in all but the most northerly gardens. Plant during early or mid-spring in any reasonable soil; in cool, moist conditions, the violet spreads rapidly by means of its self-catapulted seeds, but the seedlings are easily weeded out to keep them within bounds. The seed is usually plentiful and germinates well; it can be collected for controlled sowing in seed trays before planting out in spring.

Waldsteinia ternata

Height 4in
Planting distance 1-1½ft
Best May-June

Although rarely seen in rock gardens, *Waldsteinia ternata* with its rich evergreen leaves and sunny flowers, is a useful cover plant, charmingly tolerant of almost any soil. Its trifoliate leaves are rather like those of a strawberry plant and run freely to form a close-knit carpet. Late spring and early summer brings a profusion of bright yellow five-petalled flowers which may continue to brighten the garden until well into autumn.

Waldsteinia geoides is a larger species, about 9in in height, which holds its golden-yellow flowers in sprays above bright green kidney-shaped leaves. For earlier colour, plant clumps of blue *Iris histrioides* close by.
CULTIVATION Plant during early autumn, preferably in light shade or moisture-retaining soil. Propagate by division in autumn or spring.

A successful all-seasons garden depends largely on the imposition of a strong structure and definite style, coupled with a range of core plants that are attractive for most if not all of the year.

Many plants have one season of glory and then retire into relative passivity for the rest of the year, but there are others which never cease to catch the eye. Some may not even have to flower to achieve this distinction. *Acer griseum*, for instance, is a tree whose value rests entirely on its foliage and bark. A skeleton of mahogany-clad branches, glowing with

THE
All Seasons
GARDEN

every slanting ray of sunlight, enriches the winter scene. The contrast in spring and summer, between the bark peeling to reveal its soft brown and copper tones and the deep olive-green foliage, is quietly captivating, while a fiery climax is reached in autumn with the long-lasting display of jewel-brilliant, orange and vermilion leaves.

The shape and silhouette of a plant, the shadows it casts, and its general presence, all contribute to its through-season value. *Salix caprea* 'Kilmarnock', with its intensely weeping character, makes an impact in every season, but is most compelling in winter. The naked branches can be effectively highlighted against a dark evergreen background such as holly; and in a slightly elevated position, its profile against a low winter sky is dramatic.

The most obvious and constant feature of many gardens is the lawn. Even in winter a grassy sward can be green and restful to the eye – but only if it is well trimmed and its edges neat. Unless it is deliberate and controlled, as in a wild garden, untidiness is the enemy of beauty, and throughout the garden will fully reveal its destructive power in the colder seasons.

Lines outline spaces, and the demarcation between lawn and soil can be one of the most influential elements in the garden's design. It determines the overall style and shape of the garden and dictates how space is to be used. A combination of sweeping curves (which does not imply that a garden must be large) is likely to be satisfying to the eye all through the year. If one curve encloses a plant with a strong structure and all-seasons presence – the evergreen, spikily noble, winter-flowering *Mahonia japonica*, for example – the main elements of a garden for all seasons will be achieved in one stroke.

Spaces are outlined vertically as well as horizontally. If you haven't enough room for tall trees and shrubs, then a wall, fence, trellis, tripod or

Plants with interesting foliage and resistance to hard weather create a garden which is as attractive in the depths of a frost as it is in the full flood of June flowering. Bergenias and saxifrages, and low-growing shrubs like the small berberis, a hebe and helianthemums, are glorious in summer but also provide constancy through the seasons. The pond itself, the curve of the lawn, and the evergreen conifers integrate the planting.

The lines of a warm brick path draw the eye to the cottage, contributing as much to this garden's appeal through the seasons as the plants themselves. Against this charming background, one season melts into the next, the emphasis shifting from the flowering crab apple, hellebores and bluebells of late spring to the laburnum and arch of honeysuckle a month or so later.

simple pillar can support climbing and trailing plants and add an important new dimension to the garden. An ivy or the glossy dark evergreen *Clematis armandii* could, for instance, decorate a wall. A gently undulating carpet of heathers could lap about the orange trunk of *Arbutus* × *andrachnoides*, demonstrating brightly varied foliage and flowers for ten months of the year, and emphasising the steeply ascending branches of *Sorbus* 'Joseph Rock'.

Using your backbone plants to create illusions of space can add an intriguing new aspect to the garden's character, whatever the season. Parallel rows of as few as three or four small trees such as *Acer nikoense* and, in a less-than-severe climate, *Eucalyptus gunnii*, cut back to maintain size and young growths, can make a garden seem larger. If the intervals between the trees decrease, and the rows converge a little, the effect will be of a longer avenue, rather than two short rows.

The absence of a plant has as much potential for

Though it has its own season of flowering glory, a small rhododendron's evergreen foliage provides an enduring and effective foil to the dramatically changing moods of deciduous plants. An exochorda and a snowy mespilus are covered in a profusion of fresh blossom in late spring, and in autumn hold their own against the startling crimson of a Virginia creeper.

81

all-seasons appeal as its presence. If you plant large perennials with a view to what will be revealed when they disappear in winter, you will be utilising the space twice over. Imagine, for example, planting a colony of the shuttlecock fern *Matteuccia struthiopteris*, so that it framed a pond in summer; its absence in winter would open up a completely new vista – for example, a glaze of shimmering ice with the startling stems of *Salix alba* 'Britzensis' or a warm brick wall laced with ivy beyond.

Nothing is more likely to reduce the credibility of an all-seasons garden as much as great patches of bare soil. To solve the problem with 'ground cover' plants is to miss the point – which is that all soil provides opportunities for filling with plants of

year-round interest. Fill the gaps, certainly, but do it with plants that really earn their keep, that are chosen for their individual character and strengths, and not purely as quick and easy cover-ups.

Far from just hiding the embarrassingly bare soil, plants such as the hart's-tongue fern, *Asplenium scolopendrium*, can play a dominant role in a layered, season-to-season planting. The ferns are natural colonisers of ground among shrubs, and their glossy, evergreen fronds could lend support to the stems of small narcissi in spring, and keep the root runs of summer lilies cool.

Resist the temptation to plan a too-restricting planting scheme – a summer border, perhaps, based on a single colour, that will look glorious in

one season but be a total anticlimax for the rest of the year. Go instead for a succession of colour, incorporating a good mix of seasonal and backbone plants. Gold or silver variegated evergreens like *Ilex × altaclarensis* 'Golden King' or *Euonymus fortunei* 'Silver Queen', for example, could be the constant factors in a succession of yellow or cream narcissi, hostas and *Helleborus niger*.

When designing the all-seasons garden, plan the winter scene first and use this as a framework for the more abundant displays of the other seasons. Aim for a balance of evergreen and deciduous plants so that the winter profiles and changing moods – of deciduous trees and shrubs, for example – contrast with the constancy of the

evergreens. The basic design can then be fleshed out with plants of shorter-term value – perennials with follow-on flowering periods, annuals, and successions of bulbs throughout the year.

There is no need to immediately dispense with all your favourite plants or totally reorganise an established garden. As you recognise the seasonal strengths of the established plants, combine them with other plants with all-season appeal or whose glories precede or follow on. As you gradually learn to make the most of shape, structure and space as well, you will start to enjoy your garden in a full range of seasonal moods – the subtleties, shadows and silhouettes of winter as well as the pomp and circumstance of the summer border.

Getting the winter scene right is a good starting point for planning a successful all-seasons planting. Here, the golden leaves of an evergreen shrubby honeysuckle and the muted grey and blue tones of the evergreen rue and phlomis give the border substance in winter. They form a perfectly attractive skeleton planting that is fleshed out in other seasons – by the sunshine-yellow broom, pink aubrieta and phlox in late spring, and the mallow-like lavatera and a blood-red dahlia in late summer.

Spring

S PRING IS A SERIES of explosions that are dispatched to delight or betray at almost any time from the beginning of the year. Thus, a few short weeks after Christmas, a Cornish hedge or an English garden may produce a riot of flowers that would cause comment if it appeared on the shores of the Mediterranean at that season. April may lie prostrate in a heat wave, or breathe a bitter breath to strip the blossom from the apple trees.

These entertainments apart, there is also the true spring, the inexorable tide that stirs the dull roots in the ground and drags the year into wakefulness. In the garden, a green mist, too nebulous to be called foliage, graces the willows; crumpled leaves burst from sticky buds on the chestnut; and pale crocuses push impatiently through last year's debris. To the gardener, it is a stirring and optimistic time. His only real anxiety is the weather which, as Mark Twain said, 'gets through more business in spring than in any other season. In spring, I have counted 136 different kinds of weather in four-and-twenty hours'.

The sweet flamboyance of cherry blossom loudly proclaims the return of spring.

Spring *SHRUBS*

THEIR HABIT of branching at ground level makes shrubs ideal companions for crocuses, daffodils and other spring bulbs, whose colours will scintillate against the shrubs' new leaves. The spring shrubs create a constant parade of blossom throughout the season, providing a major thrust of flower colour in spring. They are generally plants of cool, temperate climates, and tolerate a wide range of conditions in the British garden.

Berberis darwinii

BARBERRY

Height 10ft · *Spread* 8ft
Best April-May

The first European, the first recorded one at least, to discover this dapper Chilean evergreen was Charles Darwin, during the voyage of HMS *Beagle* in the 1830s. No doubt he would have been struck by the shrub's veritable explosion of blossom. This is even more impressive in Britain, where it is one of the earliest-flowering barberries, cheering the darker end of spring with its clusters of yellowish-orange flower bells glowing against dark, polished, evergreen leaves that are spiny like miniature holly. Berries ripen to dark purple with a yeasty bloom in autumn, but seldom last long before the birds get them. The natural hybrid from the Argentine, *Berberis ×*

Some may find the orange-yellow riot of *Berberis darwinii* aggressive, but there is no doubt that it lights the garden in the early days of April.

lologensis has larger flowers of rich apricot hue, and would be quite a feature standing by itself in a medium-sized lawn.

B. darwinii is most effective at the back of a border, or used as a hedge. You could enjoy a continuous flowering shrub show from March to June with the lemon-yellow early spring flowers of *Stachyurus praecox* in front and the tiered, white, early summer flowers of

Viburnum plicatum tomentosum nearby. The fine heart-shaped leaves of *Brunnera macrophylla*, with spring flowers like forget-me-nots, would make jaunty cover at ground level.
CULTIVATION Plant during spring or autumn in any reasonable soil with adequate drainage and in full sun or partial shade. No pruning is necessary. Propagate by semi-hardwood cuttings in early autumn.

Berberis linearifolia offers the richest berberis blooms – occasionally in autumn too.

Berberis linearifolia

BARBERRY

Height 5ft · *Spread* 3-4ft
Best April-May

The back of a sunny border is an appropriate position for the upright, slightly asymmetrical character of *Berberis linearifolia*. Its most important contribution to the garden consists of rich apricot and reddish-orange bells massed around stiff stems and set against narrow, darkly shining, evergreen leaves. From late summer, berries ripen to black with a blue-white waxy bloom.

The gold flowers of *Euphorbia polychroma* will appear before the barberry blossom, and sustain a carpet of bright green leaves throughout the summer. To contrast with the

stiff-stemmed barberry, try *Kolkwitzia amabilis* whose pale pink blossom, thick on arching branches, would follow on into June. The pink theme could be continued with autumn-flowering *Colchicum* 'The Giant'.
CULTIVATION As for *B. darwinii*.

Berberis × stenophylla

Height 8ft · *Spread* 8ft
Best April-May

The mass of long, arching stems becomes transformed into a cascade of scented, lemon-yellow, bell-like flowers in spring. And for the rest of the year the barberry's graceful form clothed in narrow, dark evergreen leaves can make a rich backing in a border, an informal hedge, or can even stand alone as a special feature. The dwarf form, *Berberis × stenophylla* 'Irwinii', is suitable for the back of a rock garden.

As attention-getting as neon, *Berberis × stenophylla* arches its lemon-coated branches over a merry spring planting (right) that includes native forget-me-nots and the brownish-crimson of wallflowers. Beneath the berberis for autumn colour is the Japanese maple *Acer palmatum* 'Dissectum'.

The fragrant, tangerine-like flowers of *Buddleia globosa* make a good foil for a pastel planting.

Clematis alpina 'Frances Rivis' could be grown through the berberis and its lavender blooms would just overlap in most years. At their feet, why not grow a mixed planting of aquilegias and tall campanulas for summer-long colour? CULTIVATION As for *B. darwinii*.

Buddleia globosa

ORANGE BALL TREE

Height 10ft · *Spread* 8-10ft
Best May-June

The flower trusses are quite unlike those of any other buddleia – panicles of eight to ten scented, tangerine globes. The foliage, though, is fairly typical: big, wrinkled leaves that remain on the bush in mild winters.

This is a fine shrub whose great advantage is that it flowers when most spring shrubs are in decline, and summer perennials have not yet got going. Leaven the early spring foliage by

The shelter and reflected warmth of a south-facing wall will help *Ceanothus* 'Delight' to produce an abundance of blooms.

Tumbling *Ceanothus thyrsiflorus* 'Repens' makes an excellent edging for steps leading to a patio or terrace.

Like *Ceanothus* 'Delight', the cascading blooms and dense growth of *C. impressus* will flourish if sheltered by a wall or high fence.

(*Buddleia globosa* cont) trailing the earlier-flowering *Clematis alpina* through it, and try the sun-loving *Lespedeza thunbergii* in front for an early autumn show of purple, vetch-like flowers.
CULTIVATION Plant during spring or autumn in any reasonably well-drained soil with compost added. Occasionally cut back the oldest branches to about a foot from the ground. Propagate by semi-hardwood cuttings in late summer.

Ceanothus
'Delight'

CALIFORNIAN LILAC

Height 10ft · *Spread* 8ft
Best May

The intense blue of a tropical sky is captured in the clouds of spring blossom that clothe

Ceanothus 'Delight'. Glossy, neat-leaved foliage is almost concealed beneath the soft panicles of tightly packed tiny flowers. Despite its exotic appearance, this garden-bred ceanothus is hardy in all but the colder parts of the country, although it enjoys the warmth of a south or west-facing wall which it will swiftly ornament.

Use the ceanothus to provide a year-round backdrop for smaller shrubs such as *Daphne mezereum*, whose bare stems become spikes of scented pink blossom from February onwards. The vivid blue theme could be recalled in late summer, with *Agapanthus* Headbourne hybrids.
CULTIVATION Plant in autumn or spring in a reasonably sheltered, sunny position and in well-drained, not too rich soil. Prune back young shoots after flowering if necessary or, when

the shrub is grown against a wall, tie it back to encourage a flat, spreading habit. Propagate by taking semi-hardwood cuttings during late summer.

Ceanothus impressus

Height 8-12ft · *Spread* 6-10ft
Best April-May

In mid-spring, the young stems of this Californian native are crowded with an abundance of soft, clustered flowers of deepest azure. This ceanothus is dense and fairly low-growing in character as a free-standing specimen, and is best against a

warm south or west-facing wall or fence, where it will grow taller and even more dense. The dark evergreen leaves, polished above and downy beneath, are tiny and deeply furrowed.

Plant some earlier-flowering shrub such as *Daphne mezereum*, whose scented pink blossom on bare stems will show up well against the ceanothus foliage. Pink could return again in autumn, with a group of *Colchicum* 'Waterlily'; in between, the ceanothus colour would be recalled with the twisted blue summer flowers of *Osteospermum ecklonis* 'Whirligig'.
CULTIVATION Plant in autumn or spring in a sunny but sheltered

position, in well-drained but moisture-retentive, fertile soil. Propagate by semi-hardwood cuttings in autumn.

Ceanothus thyrsiflorus
'Repens'

Height 2-4ft · *Spread* 6-8ft
Best May-June

The edge of a paved terrace or a sunny bank is transformed into a haze of powder blue in late spring with this compact, slightly spreading ceanothus. The shrub eventually forms a compact, regular dome of tidy, bright green, glossy leaves

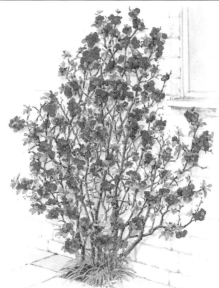

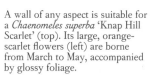

A dogwood sets off the yellow of *Corylopsis pauciflora* and *Erica carnea* 'Springwood White'.

providing a valuable all-season asset, but in its season of glory the foliage is overwhelmed by a profusion of flower clusters like soft puffs of cloud. A sprinkling of flowers can still be seen in the early days of autumn.

A foreground planting of *Pulsatilla vulgaris* (pasque flower) brings an early display of purple flowers, and continues interest into summer with lacy foliage and feathery seed heads. *Aconitum napellus* has rich green, deeply divided foliage to provide a strong contrast from spring through to autumn. In late summer, its deep blue, hooded flowers suggest a return to the colour range of the ceanothus, only accompanied by a change of mood.
CULTIVATION As for *Ceanothus* 'Delight' on page 88.

Chaenomeles superba
'Knap Hill Scarlet'

JAPANESE QUINCE, JAPONICA

Height 5-8ft *Spread* 5-8ft
Best March-May

A flash of brilliant red can be a welcome relief from the dominant blues and yellows of spring, and if you haven't the acid soil needed for rhododendrons, *Chaenomeles superba* is a less choosy alternative. It brings a spring-long display of plump buds and cup-shaped flowers, vibrantly coloured against bare branches where young leaves tinged with bronze unfurl as flowering continues. There will even be a scattering of blooms during winter if the weather is mild. In late summer, handsome yellow fruit ripens and can be used to make quince jelly. The shrub is compact and twiggy in character, with spined stems. Varieties with pink, white and orange flowers are available.

Lead up to the chaenomeles' flowering period with a show of *Crocus chrysanthus* cultivars such as 'Blue Pearl', 'Gipsy Girl' and 'Cream Beauty'. A companion shrub with a follow-on blossoming, like *Kolkwitzia amabilis,* would add colour between the japonica's flowers and its late summer fruit.
CULTIVATION Plant during spring or autumn in any reasonable well-drained soil and in a sunny position. If the shrub is trained against a wall, the new growth can be cut back after flowering. Propagate by taking softwood cuttings in midsummer, or by layering in spring or autumn.

Corylopsis pauciflora

Height 5-8ft · *Spread* 4-6ft
Best March

Fill a lightly shaded corner in spring with the tracery of wand-like stems and primrose-scented blossom of *Corylopsis pauciflora*. Two or three small, pale yellow cup-shaped flowers make up a short, drooping raceme, to give a catkin-like effect. The slender twigs are bare of leaves when the flowers are at their peak in March and April, but open later, pink at first then developing into bright green, pointed ovals.

Extend the delicate, yellow display with a group of *Narcissus cyclamineus,* and the May-flowering Virginian cowslip, *Mertensia virginica,* with its nodding flower heads that go well with the corylopsis blooms.
CULTIVATION Plant in autumn or spring in a well-drained neutral to acid soil with well-rotted compost or manure added. The site should be sheltered from cold winds, spring frosts and scorching sun. Best would be a west-facing wall, or a situation among other shrubs or beneath trees that will give protection. No pruning is necessary. Propagate by layering during spring and summer.

A wall of any aspect is suitable for a *Chaenomeles superba* 'Knap Hill Scarlet' (top). Its large, orange-scarlet flowers (left) are borne from March to May, accompanied by glossy foliage.

Born of French and Spanish parents at Kew Gardens a century ago, *Cytisus × kewensis* bears masses of cream and yellow flowers in May.

One of the many advantages of *Cytisus × praecox* is its compactness, desirable in the smaller garden. Another is its mass of flowers, thousands strong, that stirs a dollop of cream into the richness of spring.

Cytisus × kewensis

BROOM

Height 2ft · *Spread* 5ft
Best May

A mass of tiny, sweet-pea-like flowers swathe the broom in sheets of deepest cream. And even when the flowers are over, the shrub's graceful, spreading form, with the long slender stems closely covered in delicate leaves, remains an attractive choice for a patio or as cover over a low wall.

The Maytime flush follows such winter hints of spring as the brightly coloured *Iris reticulata* hybrids and the yellow-flowered *Crocus flavus*. For a summer display, the mauve-pink flowers and silvered leaves of *Cistus* 'Silver Pink' look very well in conjunction with the broom's matt green stems.
CULTIVATION Plant during spring or autumn in any well-drained soil, preferably not too chalky, with some coarse sand added, and in a sunny position. Propagate by semi-hardwood cuttings taken in summer and placed in a cold frame.

Cytisus × praecox

WARMINSTER BROOM

Height 4-6ft · *Spread* 3-5ft
Best April-May

Spray upon spray of arching wands, packed with small, acrid-smelling, sweet-pea-like flowers, form a spectacular cream cascade in late spring. You can also ring the changes with white and yellow-flowered cultivars – 'Albus', and the outstanding 'Allgold' with wide-spreading sprays of richly coloured, long-lasting flowers. When the display has finished, the green, whippy stems with hardly noticeable leaves maintain the shrub's graceful shape. Brooms are not long-lived and can become ungainly after a few years, though during their brief span they are excellent for ground cover, in large rock gardens and as wall shrubs.

To introduce early spring interest, and to get the ground cover scheme under way, try a group of the deep blue-flowered *Pulmonaria angustifolia* at the base of the broom. The bold foliage of *Hosta fortunei* would compensate for the broom's economy of leaf, and produce lilac flowers in late summer.
CULTIVATION Plant during spring or autumn in any well-drained soil and in a sunny position. No pruning is necessary. Propagate by taking semi-hardwood cuttings in July.

Daphne mezereum

MEZEREON

Height 2-4ft · *Spread* 2-3ft
Best February-March

Catching a waft of the daphne's exquisite scent is one of the great pleasures of early spring. Then, the stout, upright little bush suddenly erupts into

Daphne mezereum 'Alba' has white flowers and bright yellow berries.

Flowers like clusters of miniature bells emerge in spring to justify the name of *Enkianthus campanulatus*.

EVERY AUTUMN *Enkianthus campanulatus* puts on a fiery display of astonishing range, depth and clarity.

Given a warmish spring, the scented flowers of *Erica arborea* 'Alpina' will last for months.

colour, the tightly packed, purple-pink to reddish-violet, waxy flowers all but concealing the fleshy stems beneath. Soft green leaves develop towards the end of the flowering period, and then, in summer, the branches are covered with scarlet berries, highly poisonous to humans but apparently relished by birds. *Daphne mezereum* 'Alba' has white flowers and bright yellow berries. There is also the form 'Grandiflora', which has larger, bright purple flowers that may easily appear as early as autumn.

Plant the daphne near a frequently used path or doorway to make the most of the scent, and combine it with the Wedgwood-blue *Iris histrioides* 'Major' beneath. *Osmanthus delavayi* could be planted behind to continue a show of conspicuous white flower clusters in April and May.

CULTIVATION Plant during spring

The fragrant, early spring flowers of *Daphne mezereum* are followed by poisonous scarlet berries.

or autumn in deep, well-drained but moist soil in sun or light shade. No pruning is necessary. Propagate by cuttings of nonflowering shoots in summer or by seed when ripe.

Enkianthus campanulatus

Height 8-12ft · *Spread* 6-8ft
Best May

There are two sound reasons for growing this tall, upright shrub. The first is the delightful spring display of tiny flowers, like clutches of miniature bells, subtly shaded sulphur to rich bronze and veined with red. The second is the grand autumn finale, when the spear-shaped leaves, a dullish green in summer, turn to every conceivable shade between brilliant red and yellow, and shelter pendent seed cases. *Enkianthus cernuus rubens* has fringed, deep red flowers; those of the slowgrowing *E. perulatus* are white and shaped like tiny urns. All three species come from Japan, and are to be treasured. The flowers are admired, while the breathtaking quality of their foliage in autumn is surpassed by few shrubs of similar size.

Their companions must be chosen with care, but the earlier-flowering spring shrub *Corylopsis pauciflora* with its pale yellow, cowslip-scented flowers, or the evergreen *Viburnum × burkwoodii* could introduce a long season of continuous flowering. Later on, *Buddleia alternifolia* and a dense, rosy foreground carpet of the native heath *Erica tetralix* 'Alba Mollis', perhaps, could be used to link summer and autumn.

CULTIVATION Plant during spring or autumn in moist, acid soil and in sun or light shade. No pruning is necessary. Propagate by semi-hardwood cuttings in late summer or by layering pliable shoots in spring.

Erica arborea
'Alpina'

TREE HEATH

Height 10ft · *Spread* 6-8ft
Best March-May

Tree heaths grow throughout the Mediterranean lands, the honey scent of their myriad tiny bell flowers filling the air. The cultivar 'Alpina', from the mountains of Spain, is tougher, more erect and slightly shorter than the species, and hardy in all but the chilliest parts of Britain. It is at its best in spring when the fresh green, feathery foliage bears a froth of honey-scented white flowers. In a mild season

Erica erigena 'Brightness' is a useful plant for bridging the height gap between ground-hugging heathers and the tall tree heathers.

Erica australis is a mass of vibrant colour for many weeks from mid-spring; backed here by the sultry purple foliage and orange fruits of a berberis, it makes a tremendous impact on a shrub border.

(*Erica arborea* cont) they will continue for months.

Combine the tree heath with other acid-soil plants, using them to add height to a heather bed, or to contrast with evergreen azaleas like the later-flowering white *Rhododendron* 'Palestrina'. *Erica carnea* 'Pink Spangles' could start a complementary pink theme in the winter months, with the young leaves of *Pieris japonica* 'Flamingo' to follow on at the latter end of spring, and the Irish heath, *Daboecia cantabrica* for summer flowering.

CULTIVATION Plant during early spring in a sunny position and in well-drained, fertile, acid soil. When it is necessary, prune back leggy growths after flowering is over in spring. Propagate by taking semi-hardwood cuttings in summer.

Erica australis

SPANISH HEATH

Height 3-4ft · *Spread* 2-3ft
Best April-June

Darker-leaved and more contained in its spread than *Erica arborea*, *E. australis* is another tall heather with a satisfyingly long and abundant display of 2-3in long flower clusters from mid-spring. Although not quite as tough as *E. arborea* 'Alpina' in that it might suffer some damage in a severe winter, the Spanish heath should be fine in a sheltered position. If supported or tied against a wall it can grow 6-8ft high. The species has lovely, bright purplish-red, tubular flowers; 'Riverslea' is a fuchsia-purple form, and 'Mr Robert' is slightly hardier and pure white.

The twiggy stems with their needle-like, evergreen leaves benefit early in the year from an underplanting of the glowing red flowers of the fine cultivar *Erica carnea* 'Myretoun Ruby'. Summer colour would be provided by *Cistus* 'Silver Pink' and *Fuchsia magellanica* 'Versicolor'. *Hosta* 'Royal Standard' and, on a larger scale, *Stipa gigantea* would contribute contrasting foliage.

CULTIVATION Plant during spring in well-drained, neutral to acid soil with leaf mould or peat added. Clip the plants over after flowering to promote growth. Propagate by semi-hardwood cuttings in summer.

Erica erigena

(syn *E. mediterranea*)
'Brightness'

Height 2-4ft · *Spread* 2ft
Best March-May

Picture a bed or bank of different heathers, each with its particular season of glory. Dominating the entire display throughout the spring, in the midfield position between the tall tree heaths and the low, spreading heathers in the foreground, is *Erica erigena*. 'Brightness' is probably the hardiest cultivar, and slower growing than the species. Early in the season, tiny bronze-red buds open to deep pink, honey-scented, bell flowers, and for the rest of the year its compact, bushy, bronze-green foliage provides an attractive foil for later-flowering companions.

There are other cultivars in white and other shades of pink and red. Although a native of Ireland and France, *E. erigena* is not fully hardy in cold, exposed areas of Britain. It is lime-tolerant, but shallow, chalky soils would not be suitable.

The pink-purple, heavily scented flowers of *Daphne odora* 'Aureomarginata' would herald the erica's colour in late winter. Use something like *Festuca glauca* 'Blue Glow' to provide

The flowering season of *Exochorda × macrantha* is not particularly long, but its abundance of dazzling white blossom is eagerly awaited each year. It is accompanied here by euphorbias.

A splash of brilliant, canary-yellow from *Forsythia* 'Karl Sax' is nicely set off by the pink buds and emerging blue flowers of *Pulmonaria saccharata*.

complementary foliage or – in mild areas – *Euryops pectinatus*. In the foreground, plant *Gladiolus* Butterfly hybrids to brighten the summer scene.
CULTIVATION Plant during spring or autumn in well-drained, moisture-retentive, fertile soil and in a sunny, sheltered position. Propagate by semi-hardwood cuttings in summer.

Exochorda × macrantha

PEARL BUSH

Height 8-12ft · *Spread* 8-12ft
Best May

This shrub is the centre of attraction in May, bedecked with an opulence of virginal white blossom. Light lettuce-green, deciduous leaves appear before the flowers and provide a perfect foil for luxuriant racemes of single, 1¼ in diameter blooms. 'The Bride' has a sweeping train of branches, and flowers prolifically.

A dark evergreen such as *Sarcococca confusa* will make a handsome partner, with scented flowers at the turn of the year.

The pale leaves and shell-pink blossom of *Rosa rugosa* 'Fru Dagmar Hastrup' and *Lilium* Mid-Century hybrids would harmonise with the exochorda's summer foliage, the rose following on with hips in autumn.
CULTIVATION Plant in a sunny position during autumn or spring. Any fertile, well-drained soil is suitable, but shallow chalky or sandy soils should be enriched with a mulch. Propagate by detaching rooted suckers in autumn or spring.

Forsythia
'Karl Sax'

Height 8ft · *Spread* 8ft
Best March-April

The glorious sunshine effect of this forsythia's blossom, packed along stout bare stems, is intensified by the touch of orange at the throat of each flower. This cultivar is dense and twiggy in habit. Fresh green leaves, which appear after the flowers, occasionally have a purplish flush in autumn. 'Beatrix Farrand' is almost identical.

Later in the year, move into a cream theme with the weeping stems of *Cytisus × praecox* in late spring, then switch to white and let *Clematis* 'Henryi' show off its very large, snowy flowers in late summer. A lower-level planting of *Pulmonaria saccharata* 'Argentea' would give funnel-shaped flowers that are first pink, then sky-blue in March, and bold, silvery-leaved ground cover in summer.
CULTIVATION Plant in a sunny or partially shaded position in autumn or spring, and in ordinary soil. Prune old branches to encourage new growth after flowering. Propagate by hardwood cuttings in October.

The large flowers of *Forsythia suspensa* 'Nymans' are best when flattered by a dark background.

At spring's chilly opening, when few other flowers are in evidence, sprays of blossom of *Hamamelis japonica* 'Zuccariniana' soar up leafless stems to illuminate the garden like a celebratory firework display.

Forsythia suspensa

Height 8-10ft · *Spread* 8-10ft
Best March-April

This shrub's sweep of branches is laden with tufts of four-petalled bell flowers for many a spring week. Its pendulous character and slightly softer yellow blooms suggest a more elegant effect than the upright-growing forsythias. If left to its own devices it forms a mound-like bush, but if trained against a wall – even a north or east-facing one – it will provide a vertical sheet of cheering spring colour and fresh green summer foliage. The variety *Forsythia suspensa sieboldii* is a weeper of particularly pronounced habit; if you want short-term interest, try *F. s. atrocaulis* whose young stems are purple-black, highlighting the pale yellow flowers.

Train *Clematis alpina* through the weeping stems of a well-established forsythia to produce its blue cups in April and May, and partner it with the blue *C. macropetala*. For pink blossoms in February, plant *Daphne mezereum* in front, while an evergreen conifer touched with gold, such as the horizontally orientated *Juniperus × media* 'Gold Coast', would make a rich all-year foil for the forsythia.

CULTIVATION Plant during spring or autumn in a sunny position and in any fertile soil. Prune to remove old growth after flowering. Propagate by hardwood cuttings in October.

Hamamelis japonica
'Zuccariniana'

JAPANESE WITCH HAZEL

Height 8-10ft · *Spread* 8-10ft
Best February-March

The light fragrance of the witch-hazel blossom carries far on the chill air to marry with that of other early spring-flowering plants. The flowers, curiously twisted and crimped on the bare twigs, have a delicacy long appreciated by Japanese gardeners and even more by the flower painters of that nation. This witch hazel is very nearly as attractive in summer, and in autumn too, when its boldly veined, oval leaves turn to a clear, singing yellow before they fall.

A succession of low-growing bulbs will do much to emphasise the witch hazel's graceful, open habit. *Cyclamen coum, Eranthis hyemalis, Galanthus ikariae* and *Scilla mischtschenkoana* will flower at the same time or just before, and *Erythronium tuolumnense, Ipheion uniflorum* and *Convallaria majalis* 'Rosea' can follow later on in the season. Finally, train *Tropaeolum speciosum* through the witch hazel's branches, where its flame flowers will add a gaudy touch to the summer foliage.

The crimped, sulphur-yellow flowers of *Hamamelis japonica* have a curious scent that hovers between sweet and pungent.

CULTIVATION Plant during spring or autumn in sun or light shade and in well-drained neutral to acid soil. Prune after flowering to remove straggly older growth. Propagate by layering in spring or autumn.

A WARM RED brick wall is as necessary an adjunct to the traditional English garden as a woman in a broad sun hat carrying a trugful of long-stemmed roses. But such walls are rarer than calendar illustrations would have us believe, so if you are fortunate enough to possess one, it is more or less mandatory to dress it in as nostalgic a manner as possible. Here the main plant chosen for spring is *Kerria japonica*, a shrub immensely popular in Victorian gardens. Sturdy and well suited to a sunny wall, the kerria lends beginning-of-season colour to the surrounding foliage of roses that will not flower for some time yet. Balancing its warm, yellow, buttercup-like blooms are the purple flowers of *Pulmonaria officinalis*, 'called of Apothecaries Lungwurt, or the herbe for the lunges', for the simple reason that the white spots on its leaves were held to resemble those on diseased lungs. Therefore, it was believed that an infusion made from its leaves would cure ailments of the lung. Rounding off the spring display is a handsome little group of white *Tulipa* 'Purissima'. As summer advances, homage to Englishness is continued by the roses – the richly fragrant, pure yellow 'Graham Thomas' and the large, pink, long-lasting 'Mary Rose'. Ascending the wall behind is the climbing version of 'Iceberg', whose sprays of pure white flowers are set off by the shiny leaves and stems of the kerria. ❧

Tough, sunny and early flowering, *Kerria japonica* has long been assured of its welcome in the cottage garden. Here it is seen with other similarly honoured companions – the lungwort *Pulmonaria officinalis* and white *Tulipa* 'Purissima'.

Even when flowering is finished, *Kerria japonica* makes a fine framework for a collection of roses – yellow 'Graham Thomas', pink 'Mary Rose' and 'Iceberg', scrambling up the wall. Later, the kerria's green stems will help to add brightness to winter.

Kerria japonica 'Pleniflora' is a double-flowered form, sometimes known as bachelor's buttons.

In its single form, *Kerria japonica* has solitary flowers like single roses, 1½in across.

The pure white flowers of *Ledum groenlandicum* are borne in showy clusters at the branches' ends.

Pendent clusters of white flowers are neatly arranged to hang along the length of each gracefully arching stem of *Leucothoe fontanesiana*.

Kerria japonica

JEW'S MALLOW

Height 4-6ft · *Spread* 4-6ft
Best April-May

The pompon-flowered *Kerria japonica* 'Pleniflora' is by no means a rarity in British gardens, but the less familiar, true species is more compact and graceful in form. From mid to late spring, its arching stems carry a good show of single, buttercup-yellow flowers, and throughout summer the small, serrated leaves make a pleasing, fresh green foliage effect. When they have fallen, the green stems remain for an attractive winter profile. *K. j.* 'Variegata' combines single flowers with irregularly white-edged foliage.

The bare winter stems can be supplemented by the winter-flowering *Viburnum* × *bodnantense* 'Deben', and the flame-coloured flowers of the bushy perennial *Euphorbia griffithii* 'Fireglow' would add colour in early summer.
CULTIVATION Plant in spring or autumn in any ordinary, fertile soil, in any aspect. Propagate by division after flowering, or by semi-hardwood cuttings in late summer.

Ledum groenlandicum

LABRADOR TEA

Height 2-3ft · *Spread* 2-3ft
Best April-June

Small, sturdy and evergreen, this useful little shrub is a native of boggy moorland in Green-land and North America. For several weeks in spring, the dark, aromatic, narrow-leaved foliage forms a striking background for starfalls of small, long-stamened flowers. 'Compactum' is a smaller, neater form with broader leaves.

As plants of heath and moor-land, heathers are natural companions for the ledum; *Erica darleyensis* 'Arthur Johnson' would begin to show its flowers earlier in the year, while *E. ciliaris* 'Alba Mollis' would follow on into summer. Dwarf bulbs like *Scilla mischtschenkoana* and *Erythronium revolutum* can be planted at the ledum's feet for winter and spring colour.
CULTIVATION Plant during spring or autumn in acid organic soil which must be kept moist during dry periods. A site in full sun helps the shrub maintain its dwarf, bushy habit. No pruning is necessary. Propagate by layering in spring or by semi-ripe cuttings in late summer.

Leucothoe fontanesiana
(syn *L. catesbaei*)

Height 4ft · *Spread* 4ft
Best May

Even a small, shaded garden can benefit from the evergreen elegance of this shrub. In spring the leucothoe is at its finest, with dark, leathery pinnate groups of leaves, sheltering weighty spikes of tiny cream flowers shaped like miniature pitchers. But in every other season, too, there is much to offer. The long, arching stems and the willow-like leaves are dark, glossy green throughout the summer, but turn a wonderful shade of reddish-purple in winter. The shrub's spreading character and grace of form make it a valuable part of the garden's all-season framework.

Think of other shade-loving woodland plants for companions. *Helleborus foetidus*, with its unusual, green spring flowers, and *Hosta plantaginea* with lilac flowers in late summer would both contribute interesting foliage contrasts too. *Leucothoe fontanesiana* will also make

Framed by bare trees, a host of pale pink stars fills a corner of a garden just awakening from its winter slumbers. Beneath the *Magnolia stellata* 'Rosea', a sprinkling of dwarf daffodils and anemones completes a picture of springtime informality.

The profusely borne, large white flowers of *Magnolia stellata* have a delicate fragrance.

an interesting contrast with the bold shapes and foliage of rhododendrons, enjoying as it does the same acid conditions. CULTIVATION Plant during spring in moist, acid soil with plenty of humus, in a shady site. Propagate by division in autumn to late winter, by layering during spring or summer, or by cuttings taken in midsummer.

Magnolia stellata

STAR MAGNOLIA

Height 6-10ft · *Spread* 7-12ft
Best April

Ravishing star-like flowers and delicacy of form make this shrubby magnolia suitable for the smallest of gardens. Even when the plant is young, its silky buds open out into a profusion of white or pink blooms, 3-4in across, over several spring weeks before narrow, deep green leaves develop. 'Rubra' and 'Rosea' are pink cultivars, while 'Royal Star', a star indeed, has larger blooms with more petals.

Dwarf bulbs such as *Narcissus bulbocodium* and *Erythronium dens-canis* can be grown around the magnolia's base, with evergreen azaleas such as the rich red, low-growing *Rhododendron* 'Addy Wery' or 'Vuyk's Scarlet' to present flamboyant follow-on colour. Add the company of dwarf Japanese maples for foliage contrast and brilliant autumnal pyrotechnics.

CULTIVATION Plant during spring or autumn in moist but well-drained neutral to acid soil, although moderately alkaline soils will suffice as long as they are humus enriched. Though quite hardy, this magnolia does best in a sunny situation sheltered from frost. Support the plant with stakes for the first few years. Avoid disturbing the roots, and feed each year with a top-dressing of well-rotted organic matter. Pruning is rarely required.

Propagate by cuttings in early summer, or by layering in March or April, although it takes up to two years for the layers to root.

The small, neat leaves of *Osmanthus delavayi* and clusters of whiter than white flowers are perfectly proportioned to present a brave and dazzling display.

The magnificent *Paeonia lutea ludlowii* has larger flowers, some 2in across, and is more robust than most other peonies.

Osmanthus × burkwoodii bears lustrous leaves that make a handsome setting for its flowers.

Osmanthus × burkwoodii

(syn × *Osmarea burkwoodii*)

Height 7-10ft · *Spread* 5-8ft
Best April-May

The contrast between the polished, dark, evergreen leaves of *Osmanthus × burkwoodii* and its exquisitely shaped, pure white spring flowers is stunning. The flowers – axillary clusters of small, four-petalled bells – are deliciously perfumed, and even when they are over, the semi-glossy, compact foliage is pleasing throughout the year; it can even be used as an informal hedge or divider.

O. × burkwoodii is a moderately fast-growing shrub, and with its eventual height and spread needs to be situated towards the back of a mixed border. Create an exciting foliage combination with a nearby planting of *Euphorbia characias wulfenii*, which has grey leaves and golden flower heads in March, and clumps of the 4ft high, grey-green, ornamental grass *Stipa gigantea*.
CULTIVATION Plant during spring or autumn in sun or shade in ordinary garden soil enriched with humus. Pruning is generally unnecessary unless you are trimming the plants into shape for a hedge, which should be done after flowering. Propagate by taking semi-hardwood cuttings in late summer or by layering in September.

Osmanthus delavayi

Height 6-10ft · *Spread* 6-10ft
Best April-May

The small, gleaming, dark green leaves are reminiscent of holly. Set against them from mid to late spring are fragrant sprays of slender-tubed, pristine white flowers. Slow-growing, smaller and more compact than *Osmanthus × burkwoodii*, this species is a good choice for small gardens.

If you have the space, a companion shrub such as the beauty bush, *Kolkwitzia amabilis* would extend the flowering display into June, and provide contrasting, greyish-green leaves and silvery-brown winter stems. Contrasting grey could come, too, from the felted leaves of *Salix lanata,* or on a smaller scale from *Pulmonaria saccharata* which has blue, early spring flowers and mottled silver foliage.
CULTIVATION Plant during spring or autumn in any well-drained soil enriched with humus, and in sun or partial shade. No pruning is necessary. Propagate by taking semi-hardwood cuttings in late summer.

Paeonia lutea ludlowii

TREE PEONY

Height 6ft · *Spread* 6ft
Best May

Glorious golden bowls of single blooms, up to 4 or 5in across, make a relatively short but sensational appearance when this native of the Tibetan mountains takes the stage in late spring. With a crowd of golden stamens at the heart of the tissue-paper petals, the peony's spectacular display should not be contested by simultaneously flowering close companions. Rather let *Paeonia lutea ludlowii* stand alone, or in the company of later-flowering plants.

The foliage is equally dramatic, with 12in long, deeply divided, light green leaves held on reddish stems, and long seed pods filled with black seeds the size of peas.

Make the most of the foliage by underplanting with *Narcissus* 'Tete-a-Tete' and, if you have room, *Corylopsis willmottiae* nearby, both of which will give a hint of the peony display to

The opulent, 7in blooms of *Paeonia suffruticosa* 'Black Pirate' have won many prizes.

All peonies are exotic, and none more so than the lovely *Paeonia suffruticosa* 'Reine Elizabeth'. Grown against a wall, the weathered brickwork provides a sombre backing and helps to heighten the dramatic effect.

come in their yellow blooms. The white, scented sprays of *Clethra alnifolia* and *Lilium* Mid-Century hybrids would do justice to the peony's summer leaves, while a smoke tree, *Cotinus coggyria* 'Velvet Cloak', grown nearby would give strong foliage contrast from spring to autumn.

CULTIVATION Plant in a sunny position during spring or autumn in any soil that is well drained. No pruning is necessary. Propagate by detaching and transplanting suckers in spring, or by seed when ripe.

Paeonia suffruticosa
(syn *P. moutan*)

Height 4-6ft · *Spread* 4-6ft
Best May

These are the flowers whose grandeur and elegance inspired Chinese screen painters, and which make an astonishing and exotic impact on the ordinary British garden. The blooms are simple bowls of tissue-textured petals on a giant scale – up to 9in across. As they open, a dash of deeply contrasting colour at

the base of each petal and a forest of fine stamens is revealed. The leaves, deeply cut and often tinged with pink and grey, are large-scale too, and make a dramatic contribution to the garden scene in summer. Both single and double forms are available in a range of colours. 'King George V' (scarlet flecked with white), 'Duchess of Kent' (bright pink), 'Montrose' (pale mauve), and 'Rock's Variety' (white with crimson blotch) are cultivars to look out for.

Choose a few shade-loving

The peony 'Rock's Variety' is perhaps one of the most interesting of the species, with crimson blotches inside the petals.

companions which will flower at different times and not detract from the peony show. You could have *Primula vulgaris* or yellow shades of polyanthus for spring, with *Alchemilla mollis* or *Aquilegia* 'McKana' hybrids to follow in summer. The recipe for autumn should include the cool yellow shuttlecocks of *Kirengeshoma palmata* or pink

Physostegia virginiana. Yellow *Jasminum nudiflorum*, grown behind the peony, would be ideal for winter.

CULTIVATION Plant in autumn or late winter in a cool site where spring sun will not stimulate too early growth. The foot of a north wall or the north side of a large shrub is best. Propagate by layering in spring.

Pieris formosa forrestii 'Forest Flame' puts on a Maytime show of white flowers and scarlet leaves.

Pieris formosa forrestii 'Forest Flame'

Height 6-8ft · *Spread* 6-8ft
Best April-May

It is the fiery-tipped foliage of the pieris that makes the first spectacular contribution to the spring scene. Gleaming, narrowly elliptical leaves make this vigorous, hardy shrub a splendid foliage plant throughout the year, but the surprise comes with the young leaves that open an astonishing scarlet, then fade gradually to shrimp pink, then to white, and finally mature to dark green. The show is enhanced in May, when the sprays of tight, pinkish buds that have been lying in wait through the winter, burst into

In a summer-long cyclical display, the pieris foliage fades from youthful scarlet to interim pink and at last to mature green.

drooping bunches of flowers, white and jug-shaped, not unlike those of lily of the valley.

Grow the evergreen hart's-tongue fern, *Asplenium scolopendrium,* at its feet to create a year-long foliage combination, and the hardy, crimson and purple *Fuchsia magellanica* for follow-on colour from July

through summer into autumn.
CULTIVATION Plant during spring in acid soil that is well drained yet moisture retentive, with added peat or leaf mould. Shelter from cold winds is essential, though young growths killed by late frosts will be replaced by buds lower down. Propagate by taking semi-hardwood cuttings in late summer.

Rhododendron

DECIDUOUS AZALEAS

Height 6ft · *Spread* 5ft
Best May-June

The glorious flowers of the deciduous azaleas are all the more radiant for appearing

From modest 19th-century beginnings, deciduous hybrid azalea clones now number hundreds, each seemingly outdoing the other in floral display, in suavity or raucousness of colour, and in autumnal fireworks.

ahead of the foliage, though this too, rising in elegant tiers of light green throughout the summer, has a loveliness of its own. The leaves unfold with the last blooms, then in autumn flare into wondrous crimson and yellow.

The azaleas were originally placed in a genus of their own, but are now classified with the rhododendrons. Their story begins in the late 18th century, when the seeds of *Rhododendron luteum* were sent to Britain from the shores of the Black Sea. It became the parent of many splendid azalea hybrids, but is still itself valued for its simple beauty, its hardiness and ease of growing. Its funnel-like yellow flowers have a delicious scent.

In the mid-19th century, an azalea, *R. japonicum*, was introduced to Europe from Japan, and became the predominant parent of the Mollis group of azaleas. Their large trusses of trumpet-shaped blooms are unscented, but come in a dazzling range of colours, from the apricot-yellow, of 'Lemonora' to the rich orange-scarlet of 'Dr M. Oosthoek'. A decade or so later, *R. occidentale* from California was used to found the Knap Hill strain of hybrids. These have a similar colour range but slightly bigger flower trusses than the Mollis azaleas. Well-tested cultivars include 'Persil', white with an orange blotch; 'Satan' and 'Devon', pure blood red; 'Frome', frilled

A forebear of deciduous azalea hybrids is *Rhododendron luteum*, a native of the Black Sea area.

AS AUTUMN draws near, the deciduous azaleas make a breathtaking, yet at the same time wistful, acknowledgment of the year's end.

The cascade of flowers, each like a muted trumpet, produced by *Rhododendron* 'Palestrina' is considered outstanding even among azaleas. Here it has an audience of *R. luteum* and a red rhododendron cultivar.

and bright yellow; 'Homebush', semi-double rose-pink; and the beautifully scented 'Ghent' and 'Rustica' azaleas.

Plants with late winter colour like *Pulmonaria saccharata* and its varieties, or *Erica carnea* and *E. × darleyensis* cultivars can be set beneath the azaleas. Summer colour and a woodland effect would be provided by the hairy, cream-edged leaves and bright, gracefully nodding blue flowers of *Symphytum × uplandicum* 'Variegatum', together with candelabra primulas that rival azaleas for variety of colour.

CULTIVATION Plant during autumn or spring in acid soil – the sandier the better. Ensure that the azaleas are not planted any deeper than they were in their nursery containers, and add compost to the planting hole. Mulch annually with compost or peat. Lightly shaded woodland situations are ideal, but the shrubs will thrive in full sun as long as the soil is moist. No pruning is necessary. Propagate by layering lower branches in spring or autumn.

Rhododendron

EVERGREEN AND SEMI-EVERGREEN AZALEAS

Height 2-4ft · *Spread* 2-4ft
Best April-May

Smaller than their deciduous counterparts, the compactly leaved evergreen and semi-evergreen azaleas were originally brought to Europe from Japan and are perfect for adding a touch of the Orient where space is limited. Their exquisite blooms are small and widely flared, produced so freely as to smother the shrub in shades of white and light pink to red, lavender and blue, according to variety. They are at their best just before the deciduous azaleas. Recommended cultivars include the greeny-white 'Palestrina'; the clear pink 'Hinamayo', originally from the Emperor of Japan's garden; vermilion-red 'Addy Wery'; 'Vuyk's Scarlet'; pale pink 'Fedora' and 'Rosebud'. Provided the winters are not unduly severe, the leaves will usually remain on these azaleas throughout the year.

Tiarella cordifolia is a neat, low-spreading plant, whose froth of creamy flowers will last beyond the azalea display. If space is available, *Fuchsia magellanica* 'Versicolor' would provide a continuing show of colour through to autumn, when a drift of *Crocus goulimyi* could bloom at the azalea's base.

CULTIVATION Plant during spring in acid soil with well-decayed old leaf mould. No fertiliser

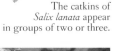

The catkins of *Salix lanata* appear in groups of two or three.

Leaves like silvered felt give the woolly willow its common name.

(*Rhododendron* cont) should be used at this stage, and the shrub should not be planted any deeper than it was in its nursery container. Mulch annually. The situation should be in dappled shade. No pruning is necessary. Propagate by semi-ripe cuttings in summer.

Salix lanata

WOOLLY WILLOW

Height 2-4ft · *Spread* 2-4ft
Best March-April

Salix lanata, unlike its willowy relations, is a squat, bushy, deciduous shrub, with short, thick stems, suited to a special place in a large rock garden, as a specimen shrub on a patio, or cutting a dash in a large pot on a terrace. In spring, fat buds burst open into a fine display of

The densely packed pink flowers of 'Hinomayo', one of the Kurume hybrids, spread a roseate apron at the feet of *Rhododendron* 'Pink Pearl' with its heavier, delicately shaded blooms.

catkins, silver at first, then gradually becoming dusted with yellow pollen. For the rest of the growing season, the dense covering of oval, silver-felted leaves is a great foliage asset to the garden.

Dwarf bulbs such as *Scilla sibirica* 'Spring Beauty', *Crocus chrysanthus*, and autumn crocus species could be cultivated around the lower branches. The large-scale ornamental grass *Stipa gigantea* and the blue-grey leaves and blue summer flower spikes of *Hosta sieboldiana* would provide some interesting foliage contrast. In a rock-garden situation, the vivid blue *Gentiana acaulis* contrasts wonderfully with the silver shrub in spring, light yellow

Like a fall of unseasonal snow, the white flowers of *Spiraea thunbergii* completely conceal the bare, arching branches in spring. Beneath, a creeping *Euonymus fortunei* provides a glossy, evergreen contrast.

As early as March, *Stachyurus praecox* will adorn a border with its translucent pendulous flowers.

The blossom of *Spiraea × arguta* has inspired the common names foam of May and bridal wreath.

Hypericum olympicum 'Citrinum' makes a different picture in summer, and *Polygonum vacciniifolium* with its pink flowers completes a fascinating autumn sequence.

CULTIVATION Plant in spring or autumn in a sunny position with any reasonably well-drained yet moisture-retentive soil. Propagate by taking hardwood cuttings in autumn.

Spiraea thunbergii

Height 4-5ft · *Spread* 4-6ft
Best March-April

Tiny white flowers with lemon-yellow centres give a sparkling display in early spring. They appear on the tangled arching stems and are later joined by the fresh young foliage in a splendid finale to the season.

Grow this spiraea as a flowering hedge, or in the middle of a mixed border with bright golden *Eranthis hyemalis* planted beneath for late winter colour. The upright, sword-like leaves and creamy summer flower spikes of *Sisyrinchium striatum* and the variegated gold foliage of *Symphytum grandiflorum* 'Variegatum' would go well with the spiraea's pretty leaves in summer.

Occupying a rather different niche in the garden is an offspring of *Spiraea thunbergii*, *S. × arguta*, which in May presents layer upon graceful layer of arching stems, topped by a foam of chalk-white flower clusters. The narrow, pale green leaves turn soft yellow before they fall. The weeping, slender stems would supply a suitable background for the winter-flowering *Sarcococca humilis*, while the feathery, bronze foliage of *Foeniculum vulgare* 'Purpureum' and the thistle-like flowers and leaves of *Eryngium planum* would make interesting contrasts with the spiraea's summer foliage.

CULTIVATION Plant during spring or autumn in fertile, well-drained soil in an open, sunny site. Propagate by semi-hardwood cuttings taken in summer, or by hardwood cuttings taken in autumn.

Stachyurus praecox

Height 6-8ft · *Spread* 6-8ft
Best February-April

Like miniature Chinese lanterns suspended on a slender rod, 4in long stems of up to 24 little rounded flowers hang from smooth, slim branches. The reddish-brown buds of winter open to flowers of the palest shade of lemon, making a striking contrast to the purple-brown bark of the branches. The summer leaves are big, pointed ovals, mid-green and strongly veined.

Enhance the subdued woodland colour scheme with the pale green flowers of *Helleborus foetidus* and the later-flowering Solomon's seal (*Polygonatum × hybridum*). Herbaceous plants like the golden-globed *Trollius × hybridus* and spiny *Morina longifolia* would bring summer interest, but die down as winter comes to leave the stage clear for the stachyurus.

CULTIVATION Plant during spring or autumn in sun or semi-shade, and in well-drained, fertile soil. No pruning is necessary. Propagate by semi-ripe cuttings in late summer, or by layering in spring or autumn.

Syringa × *josiflexa* 'Bellicent' bears panicles of rosy flowers.

Of the many *Syringa vulgaris* cultivars available, one of the most useful for background effect is the white-flowered 'Ellen Wilmott'.

Syringa vulgaris – common lilac – is the very essence of springtime.

For all-season value, and long-lasting flowers, it is hard to beat *Viburnum* × *burkwoodii*.

Syringa × josiflexa
'Bellicent'

Height 10ft · *Spread* 8ft
Best May-June

The work of Canadian horticulturist Isabella Preston in the l920s was a major breakthrough in lilac breeding. It led to the development of *Syringa* × *josiflexa,* a much more open, informal and graceful shrub than *S. vulgaris.* 'Bellicent', generally said to be the best clone of this superb hybrid, has large, loose plumes of rose-pink flowers, and big, deep green leaves on whippy, purple stems.

Flatter the lilac's lower stems in early spring with a group of *Anemone coronaria* 'De Caen', in manifold shades of blue and red, and during summer with *Campanula persicifolia* – tall, light blue spikes of smiling, saucer-shaped flowers. The fresh, light green foliage of *Rosa rugosa* 'Fru Dagmar Hastrup' would

perform a similar task, with the bonus of fragrant, pink blooms through summer and large crimson hips in autumn.
CULTIVATION Plant during spring or autumn in fertile, well-drained, but moisture-retentive soil in a sunny position. No pruning is necessary. Propagate by taking semi-hardwood cuttings in late summer, or by layering in spring.

Syringa vulgaris
COMMON LILAC

Height 10ft · *Spread* 10ft
Best May-June

When the lilac blooms – its big, conical flower trusses, with their heady fragrance, tossing among the fresh young leaves – it is a landmark in the gardening year. The common lilac, a native of the rocky hills of eastern Europe, develops into a large, upright shrub or small tree, equally attractive in either

guise. There are now many cultivars available, some of which have remained firm favourites since they were raised by the famous French nursery Lemoine at the turn of the century. Among them are: 'Blue Hyacinth' (mauve opening to lavender-blue); 'Congo' (dark red opening to deep pink); 'Maud Notcutt' (large white panicles); 'Mme Lemoine' (creamy-yellow, then opening to double white); 'Souvenir de Louis Spath' (wine red); and 'Primrose'.

Lilacs are plants for the back of a sunny border with, perhaps, *Spiraea thunbergii* in front to provide introductory blooming a little bit earlier, and the giant poppy *Papaver orientale* 'Mrs Perry' and *Penstemon* 'Garnet' in the foreground for additional colour.
CULTIVATION As for *Syringa* ×

The late-flowering *Syringa vulgaris* cultivar 'Charles Joly' is perennially popular.

josiflexa. Prune only to shorten ungainly main branches in April; they will regrow vigorously. Dead flower heads can be removed for tidiness sake.

Viburnum × burkwoodii

Height 6-8ft · *Spread* 6-8ft
Best February-May

There is hardly a time in the year when this large, open viburnum is not contributing

something to the garden, but its glory is in spring. Deliciously perfumed flower clusters, white with a hint of pink from unopened buds, are set against glossy, bottle-green leaves, brushed with bronze beneath. Heads of tiny rust-coloured buds form in autumn, and will open intermittently from late winter on. Many of the leaves remain on the bush well into winter, and even into spring in mild weather; in autumn, some of them turn bright crimson.

Place the viburnum towards the back of a sunny border, with boldly flowering summer perennials like *Echinacea purpurea* 'Robert Bloom' and *Cosmos atrosanguineus* in front. *Liriope muscari* could provide mid-autumn colour.
CULTIVATION Plant during spring or autumn in any well-drained, fertile soil and in a sunny, sheltered position. No pruning is necessary. Propagate by semi-hardwood cuttings in late summer.

Viburnum plicatum tomentosum 'Mariesii', in its spreading ball gown of white flowers, takes the lead in a parade that includes *Centranthus ruber* in bud, *Geranium sanguineum,Tellima grandiflora* and tall bearded irises.

In late spring, *Viburnum plicatum*, dressed overall in white mophead flowers, is supported by *Viola cornuta* and *Senecio* 'Sunshine'.

IN AUTUMN *Viburnum plicatum tomentosum* 'Pink Beauty' still shows the tattered remains of warm pink blossom among its rich red fruits.

Viburnum plicatum tomentosum

Height 8ft · *Spread* 8ft
Best May-June

A queen among shrubs, this viburnum is at its most regal in spring, when its stately form is outlined by double rows of white blossom along the layered branches. The rounded clusters of tiny fertile buds and infertile, five-petalled flowers are like miniature white mophead hydrangeas. In autumn, the viburnum has another period of glory when its matt-green leaves turn wine red; sometimes too it produces red-stalked bunches of scarlet berries that blacken with age.

There are a number of cultivars that are highly regarded. Their beauty lies not only in their magnificent show of spring flowers, but in the form of the shrubs. The shapely, crinoline-like skirt of *Viburnum plicatum tomentosum* 'Mariesii', for example, is draped in a veil of white blossom in spring. The branches sweep out in very pronounced horizontal layers and, as the shrub grows, new layers develop. The graceful fall of the tiered branches is emphasised by the long-lasting display of flat flower heads ranged along the upper surfaces of the branches, flanked by young, bright green leaves.

The form *V. p. t.* 'Pink Beauty' is slightly smaller, with blooms that slowly turn from white to soft pink as they age. The blossom is followed by red-stalked bunches of berries that turn, in early autumn, from bright red to black against a romantic background of wine-red leaves. 'Lanarth' resembles 'Mariesii', but is stronger-growing. Like

In full flower, *Viburnum plicatum* is a hydrangea look-alike, though its blooms are smaller.

(*Viburnum plicatum tomentosum* cont) 'Mariesii', it is unreliable in its production of berries; but the foliage of both turns to a handsome shade of burgundy in autumn.

Viburnums are not at their best in early spring, so introduce informal groups of *Narcissus* 'February Gold' or *N.* 'Suzy' and 'Ice Follies'. Later in the year, the dark summer foliage and autumn colours will be enhanced by the red flower spikes of *Polygonum amplexicaule*, and the white-flushed yellow and red-purple *Lilium regale* would make a stately and indeed regal, companion.

CULTIVATION Plant in spring or autumn in a part-shaded position and in any well-drained, fertile soil. Propagate by semi-hardwood cuttings in late summer, or by layering in autumn or spring.

Spring *TREES*

THE ARRIVAL of spring is evinced more in the blossoming of trees than in anything else. Certainly, bulbs and other low-growing spring flowers have considerable impact, and their quality of occurring with the rebirth of the year is endearing. But it is the joyful colouring of the landscape by spring-flowering trees that truly lifts the spirits – the pinks and whites of dogwood and malus, the glorious blossoms of magnolia and prunus that magically appear almost overnight. Together they proclaim that winter is finally over.

Cornus florida

FLOWERING DOGWOOD

Height 10-15ft · *Spread* 8-15ft
Best May and October

In spring, the maritime states of America are a spectacular sight when the small, multi-branched flowering dogwoods become swathed in clouds of variously coloured blossom. In favoured areas in this country, the show can be just as breathtaking, but even in districts where it is not, the autumn foliage alone is worth travelling a considerable distance to see, as the dark green leaves turn to brilliant orange and scarlet.

There are several named cultivars, each possessing delicate shades. They include pink *Cornus florida* 'Rubra'; the deep pink 'Cherokee Chief', paler

Cornus florida 'Rubra' in full blossom, a carpet of bluebells and a dark backdrop of rhododendron foliage compose a perfect springtime scene.

'Apple Blossom', and the rich creamy 'White Cloud'.

Richly scented and vividly coloured azaleas of the Ghent group such as *Rhododendron* 'Narcissiflora' and *R.* 'Nancy Waterer' break into flower as the dogwoods cease, and also colour well in autumn. For late summer to mid-autumn effect, try the bold, silver-green leaves and large, papery-white, yellow-centred flowers of the

tree poppy *Romneya coulteri* or the tall, pure white spires of *Cimicifuga foetida* 'White Pearl' that blooms in September.

CULTIVATION Plant in autumn, or spring in cold areas, in rich, moist, neutral to acid soil. The aspect should be open and bright, but sheltered from chilling winds and frosts. Pruning is generally unnecessary. Propagate by taking softwood cuttings in early summer.

IN AUTUMN the dark green leaves of the flowering dogwood burst into a kaleidoscope of bright colour.

The exotic flowers of *Magnolia denudata*, with just a hint of pink, measure up to 6in across.

Two of spring's finest performers combine to create a panoply of pink. The delicate chalices of *Magnolia × soulangiana* 'Pink Shell' are highlighted by the frothy backing of a flowering cherry.

IN AUTUMN the vivid orange-yellow dress of the yulan tree is just as distinctive as its display in spring.

Magnolia denudata

YULAN TREE

Height 10-15ft · *Spread* 8-12ft
Best April

Mature yulans can carry several hundred lemon-scented blooms like glistening white goblets. This is a slow-growing plant, eventually forming a well-branched, spreading, shrub-like small tree. The variety 'Purple Eye' tends to be more upright in habit and has somewhat larger flowers stained with purple.

Clematis macropetala or *C. alpina* 'Frances Rivis' can be trained into the magnolia, their wispy blue flowers beginning as those of the host tree fade. Bulbous plants such as *Anemone blanda* and *Erythronium revolutum* planted at the base give early season colour, and the yellow flowers of *Roscoea cautleoides* would provide summer interest. In a border, if space permits, the compact and slow-growing *Rhododendron williamsianum* and *R. w.* 'Pink Pebbles' would give an all-season deep green background and flowering link into late spring.

CULTIVATION Plant in spring in moist, acid soil in a sunny, sheltered site, protected as much as possible from late spring frosts.

Magnolia × soulangiana

Height 15-25ft · *Spread* 10-15ft
Best April-May

Gleaming, waxy, tulip-shaped blooms open out over a period of four to six weeks, while the branches remain bare of leaves. This is one of the most tolerant of magnolias and the most popular grown in this country.

There are many cultivars available, ranging in colour from white to dark wine purple, and varying a little in size. All are faintly scented, and many branch out at, or just above, ground level, often to become as broad as they are tall. 'Brozzonii' has white flowers, 10in in diameter and flushed purple at the base, appearing early to mid-May. It is a vigorous and comparatively upright form. 'Lennei' has thick-textured, 4in long blooms of rose-purple, white inside. It needs space to spread. 'Lennei Alba' produces splendid ivory-white blooms. Both flower from late April to early May and sometimes produce a secondary flush in early autumn. 'Rustica Rubra' is similar to 'Lennei' but has smaller flowers that are much more intensely coloured.

Autumn-flowering clematis can be successfully grown into soulangianas; the deep purple *Clematis viticella* 'Royal Velours'

The purple-stained flowers of *Magnolia* × *soulangiana* 'Lennei' stand erect at the end of each twig.

(*Magnolia* × *soulangiana* cont) offers a delicate tracery of flowers, while *C. orientalis* 'Burford Variety' or *C.* 'Bill Mackenzie' produce more abundant yellow flowers followed by fluffy seed heads. The spiky *Mahonia* × *media* 'Charity', or rhododendrons such as the brilliant 'Windlesham Scarlet', 'Vanessa Pastel' or 'Hydon Dawn' contribute dense evergreen backing and extend the spring flowering season.

CULTIVATION Plant in autumn in ordinary garden soil enriched with humus. Moderately lime tolerant; and though hardy, it should be set in a sunny situation sheltered from frost. Avoid disturbing the roots. Prune to keep within bounds immediately after flowering. Propagate by taking semi-ripe cuttings in summer.

Fluttering petals are the eye-catching feature of *Magnolia* 'Wada's Memory'.

Magnolia
'Wada's Memory'

Height 10-15ft · *Spread* 6-10ft
Best April-May

'Wada's Memory' set against a cloudless blue, late April sky is an electrifying sight; the entire tree forms a glistening white pyramid of blooms. Not long after opening, the petals expand rapidly and arch over to dance in the gentlest of breezes. The young leaves are mahogany-red, unfurling as the flowers finish, and when crushed, smell faintly of aniseed. Conical in shape and relatively compact and upright in habit, this magnolia is one of the best trees that can be suggested for inclusion in the smaller garden.

Plant spring bulbs such as

Erythronium tuolumnense and *Narcissus* 'February Gold' around the base of the tree. Then use shrubby evergreens like the spring-flowering *Camellia* × *williamsii* 'Donation', *C. japonica* 'Adolphe Audusson', or late summer-flowering *Eucryphia* × *nymansensis* 'Nymansay' to make a dramatic background.

CULTIVATION As for *M.* × *soulangiana*, but is even less lime tolerant. Propagate by semi-ripe cuttings taken in summer.

Malus baccata mandschurica

MANCHURIAN CRAB APPLE

Height 15-25ft · *Spread* 15-20ft
Best April-May

During late April or early May, billowing clouds of ivory-white, slightly fragrant flowers almost obliterate this crab apple's branches. The magnificent display, however, lasts only a couple of weeks at the most, and then the petals fall like confetti. But the tree still looks handsome in its summer

Though short-lived, the delicate blooms of the Manchurian crab apple are one of the most welcome and memorable sights of the season.

Clusters of deep-red, miniature crab apples provide the rich autumn display of *Malus baccata*.

leaf, and puts on another show in autumn with the appearance of small, deep-red fruits.

To follow on from the spring display, train *Clematis rehderiana* into the crown of the tree for a show of small greenish-yellow flowers during August and September, or *C.* 'Bill Mackenzie' that will give a display of yellow flowers in autumn. Brighten up the ground under the tree with variegated foliage such as *Hosta* 'Thomas Hogg', *H. fortunei* 'Albopicta'

or the tri-coloured *Tovara virginiana* 'Painter's Palette'.

CULTIVATION Plant between October and March in moisture-retentive but well-drained soil, in full sun but sheltered from strong winds though it is one of the hardiest of the genus.

Prunus dulcis
syn *P. amygdalus*

DOUBLE ALMOND

Height 15-20ft · *Spread* 10-15ft
Best February-April

The almond blossom is one of the first cheering signs of spring in the relatively mild environment of south-east England. In colder areas, however, it may not produce its froth of fine blossom until March or early April. A particularly lovely ornamental variety is 'Roseoplena', with its double pink flowers; 'Macrocarpa' produces edible nuts, but they are rarely of good quality in Britain.

The ornamental almond *Prunus dulcis* makes a dazzling show with its clear pink flower clusters clinging to the naked branches.

The almond needs sun-loving, summer and autumn-flowering companions to set against its light green foliage. The white flowers and aromatic foliage of *Cistus ladanifer*, the scented *Philadelphus microphyllus* and *P.* 'Sybille' would be suitable, with agapanthus, diascias and *Penstemon* 'Garnet' and 'King George' as border companions – but take care not to disturb the almond's roots when planting these.
CULTIVATION Plant in autumn in a sunny, well-drained site, preferably with alkaline soil. Propagate by budding in mid to late summer.

Prunus mume
'Beni-shidon'

JAPANESE APRICOT

Height 10-15ft · *Spread* 8-12ft
Best February-April

Prunus mume combines the delicacy of a Japanese water-colour with the bonus of a wonderfully sweet fragrance.

Dainty and deliciously fragrant are the rose-pink blossoms of *Prunus mume* 'Beni-shidon'.

Crimson buds, followed by carmine-pink, single flowers are studded along naked green stems, but the overall effect is a haze of colour. Pointed, dark green leaves develop later. The Japanese apricot grows into a neat, round-crowned tree, but can also be trained to fan a south or west-facing wall.

Encircle the base of this tree with autumn-flowering bulbs such as *Nerine bowdenii*, or in a mild spot, *Amaryllis belladonna*. Dwarf shrubs such as fuchsias that flower into autumn or *Ceratostigma willmottianum* will give weeks of colour up to the time that the Japanese apricot begins to lose its leaves.
CULTIVATION Plant in autumn in any reasonably good, well-drained but moisture-retentive soil in a sheltered site and in sun or dappled shade. Propagate by budding in mid to late summer.

Freshly emerged red-tinged leaves intermingle with the foaming, pale pink blossoms of the vigorous *Prunus sargentii*.

Prunus sargentii

SARGENT'S CHERRY

Height 25-35ft · *Spread* 20-30ft
Best April

Young copper-red leaves begin to open as the cherry blossom starts to fade, replacing the spectacular effect of the heavy clusters of blush-pink, single blooms. 'Accolade' is a smaller hybrid – about 20ft in height and spread – with graceful arching branches and pendulous, semi-double, soft pink flowers. These cherries are among the first trees to change colour, assuming spectacular scarlet tones in autumn.

To make the very most of the vibrant spring and autumn colours, make *Prunus sargentii* a solitary feature surrounded at its base by early flowering bulbs like *Narcissus* 'February Gold', 'St Keverne' and 'Thalia', or *Hyacinthoides hispanica*. An alternative planting scheme

The fiery *Prunus sargentii* is one of the first deciduous trees to change colour in autumn.

could incorporate grasses such as *Hakonechloa macra* 'Aureola', *Milium effusum* 'Aureum' and *Helictotrichon sempervirens* for an attractive combination of

Prunus serrulata 'Taoyama Zakura' puts on its full springtime dress of deliciously scented, semi-double flowers and emerging coppery leaves, prettily set off by *Forsythia × intermedia* and *Erica arborea*.

(*Prunus sargentii* cont)
foliage colour and flower. CULTIVATION Plant in autumn in a sunny, sheltered site in any ordinary, moist but well-drained soil. Prune in late summer, but only during the first five years of the tree's life.

Prunus serrulata
Cultivars

JAPANESE GARDEN CHERRIES

Height 10-30ft · *Spread* 10-25ft
Best April-May

This large group of oriental trees captures the very essence and elegance of Japanese gardens and art. Even young trees are heavily laden with blossom,

and most turn vibrant gold and scarlet in autumn. They vary in stature from low and wide-spreading to fairly tall – 30ft or so – and nearly as broad. The wide-spreading and weeping varieties look best in elevated situations, or trained so that their trunks reach about 7ft in height before branching out.

'Kiku-shidare Zakura', the lovely weeping chrysanthemum cherry, is a small tree with steeply arching branches covered in early April with large clusters of deep pink flowers. The leaves appear later, pale bronze at first, then turning light green in summer.

'Shirotae', often known as 'Mount Fuji', is a stunning white-flowering cultivar – the

individual, very slightly fragrant blooms can measure 2in across. The flowers, which usually appear in mid-April, are semi-double, but may be single in young trees. A low-growing, but wide-spreading tree, the branches lie horizontally in youth before arching.

'Shimidsu Zakura' is a small, May-flowering tree with a broad, flattened crown. Delicate pink buds open into long bunches of big, double white flowers set against unfolding bronze-green young leaves.

'Tai Haku', the great white cherry, was known only from an 18th-century painting until it turned up in a Sussex garden in 1923. It is vigorous, reaching 20-25ft in height and spread,

Prunus serrulata 'Amanogawa', tall and slim, makes an ideal attention-getter for the smaller garden.

and is one of the finest white cherries in cultivation. The single, bright white flowers coincide in mid-April with warm, rich, coppery-red young leaves. 'Ukon' bears a profusion of semi-double, pale yellowish-green flowers and bronze young leaves in April.

Encourage a carpet of dwarf bulbs, combined with *Primula vulgaris* or *P. denticulata*, to form beneath the smaller growing cherries, or create some denser ground-level interest with the (cont on page 112)

THERE ARE SOME plantings that so combine the colours and optimism of spring as to be akin to tapestry, or even music. This one, whose centrepiece is a truly splendid *Prunus* 'Tai Haku', with its blobs of dazzling white flowers enhanced by the first hint of coppery leaves, also has something of the delicacy of Japanese ceramics. Such a tree would be an eye-catcher on its own, but with the yellow blaze of *Kerria japonica* in the background and an underplanting of spring flowers gathered about the bare twigs of a *Rosa glauca*, it becomes the foundation of an image that will long linger in the mind.

The rose produces its single, red-purple flowers in June, but as a set piece, the group comes into its own again in about mid-October, when the coppery-red leaves of the cherry turn to yellow and tawny-orange that catch the sun, and even in shade illuminated from within. By way of contrast, the leaves of the rose, looking as though dipped in burgundy, are punctuated by round, red hips; the foliage of the nearby kerria is a delicate green. In a dry, sunny patch below the rose and the tree, there is now an underplanting of mauve and pale pink drifts of leafless *Cyclamen hederifolium* and of the autumn snowdrop *Galanthus nivalis reginae-olgae*. For good measure among the primula leaves left over from spring, there are bright lilac-blue *Crocus speciosus* and purple and lilac *C. medius*. ❧

Here is as sprightly a set-up for spring as may be imagined. *Prunus serrulata* 'Tai Haku' waves its snowy blossoms over a yellow fountain of *Kerria japonica* and a mixed planting of tulips, hyacinths and primroses. Skeletal twigs of *Rosa glauca* add focus and structure.

IN EARLY AUTUMN the group remains just as lively as in spring. The cherry's white blossom has been replaced by tawny-yellow autumnal leaves and the spring flowers by swathes of cyclamens and autumn snowdrops. The hips and leaves of the rose make a fine centrepiece.

The garden pear *Pyrus communis* 'Beech Hill' is also grown for the beauty of its spring blossom.

In this planting, the pure white spire of *Pyrus calleryana* 'Chanticleer' gives status and emphasis to a colourful carpet of spring bulbs.

Creating a secret garden within the embrace of its fountain of snow-white, delicately scented blossom is *Prunus × yedoensis* 'Perpendens'. At its foot is *Erythronium* 'Pagoda', which flowers in April.

(*Prunus serrulata* cultivars cont) late spring-flowering evergreen *Euphorbia polychroma*, perennial honesty (*Lunaria rediviva*), or the prettily tinted, evergreen leaves of an epimedium. Such hardy geraniums as *G. wallichianum* 'Buxton's Blue' and *G. endressii* could bring early summer colour, followed by the delicate star-like flowers of *Saxifraga fortunei* 'Wada's Variety' or the big-leaved *Bergenia purpurascens* for glamorous, all-seasons ground cover.
CULTIVATION As for *P. sargentii*.

Prunus × yedoensis

YOSHINO CHERRY

Height 20-30ft · *Spread* 15-25ft
Best March-April

The Yoshino cherry forms a graceful, rounded canopy that in early spring is cloaked with almond-scented blossom. Groups of single, pinkish-white flowers crowd every shoot to create an eye-catching display. Named forms include 'Ivensii', a smaller form with a horizontal network of branches that curve downwards at their tips, and the pink, weeping 'Moerheimii'.

Clematis 'Bill Mackenzie', with its yellow flowers followed by fluffy seed heads, or *C. flammula* with scented white flowers, could be trained into the canopy of the cherry to extend interest into summer and autumn. For all-season companions, ivies used as ground cover such as *Hedera canariensis* 'Ravensholst' and *H. helix* 'Glacier' would look effective. The kind of plants suggested as companions for *Prunus serrulata* varieties would also flatter the Yoshino cherry and carry the picture through the year.
CULTIVATION As for *P. sargentii*.

Pyrus calleryana
'Chanticleer'

CALLERY PEAR

Height 25-35ft · *Spread* 10-20ft
Best April

A handsome display of pure white flowers is shortly followed by silvery foliage which changes to a glossy grey-green as it matures. Autumn colour varies in Britain – the hotter the summer, the better it is.

Plant the callery pear as part of a border scheme or as a lawn specimen. Dwarf bulbs like *Crocus tommasinianus*, *Anemone blanda* and the bright yellow *Narcissus* 'Tete-a-Tete' or 'St Keverne' are good spring companions. A deciduous ornamental quince such as *Chaenomeles × superba* 'Knap Hill Scarlet', or the common pear cultivar 'Beech Hill', also grown for its dazzling white blossom, would make stunning garden companions in spring, while *Abelia × grandiflora* could provide follow-on pink and white colour from July to November.
CULTIVATION Plant in autumn in any ordinary garden soil that does not get waterlogged, and in a sunny site sheltered from strong winds. No pruning is

Spring
CLIMBERS

Beautiful *Xanthoceras sorbifolium* can easily become the talking point of the spring garden, particularly if grown against a south-facing wall.

CLIMBERS CAN LINK together the different elements in a garden – the trees, the shrubs, flower beds and buildings – as no other plants can, even if they take a few years to accomplish the tasks assigned to them. The quietness of tone of the spring climbers is perhaps their greatest asset, as they act as a gentle backdrop to some of the brighter colours, while expressing the ardour of the season in the sheer vigour of their growth.

Most in tune with the season, perhaps, are spring-flowering clematis which, by their habit of growing through other plants to add their own many-hued blooms, extend the display in both duration and power.

The rose-red flowers of *Clematis alpina* 'Ruby' are really seen at their best when the plant is encouraged to scramble over a wall or large rock.

necessary, apart from grooming the tree in winter to give it shape during its early years. Propagation is by budding in summer or by grafting in early spring – not a job for the amateur.

Xanthoceras sorbifolium

Height 10-15ft · *Spread* 5-8ft
Best May

The exotic and elegant xanthoceras is related to plants of tropical and subtropical regions, yet it is perfectly hardy. Plumes of white flowers, with coloured splashes at their hearts that turn from yellow to bright red, stand erect on long stems. The bright green leaves, com-

posed of many leaflets, are a further attraction all summer.

Train the xanthoceras against a south or west-facing wall, giving it a planting about its feet of autumn-flowering *Nerine bowdenii* or colchicums, followed by the winter-flowering *Iris unguicularis*. As a border plant, the scented *Philadelphus microphyllus* or the deep carmine flowers of *Deutzia* 'Rosealind' could follow in early summer with hardy fuchsia hybrids to round off in autumn.
CULTIVATION Plant in autumn in a well-drained, hot site against a south-facing wall, especially in the north. A slightly acid soil is preferable but not essential. No pruning is needed. Propagate in early spring by root cuttings.

Clematis alpina

Height 6-8ft
Best April-May

As befits a plant from the mountains of Central Europe and other alpine areas, this climber is one of the hardiest of clematis. It will grow and flower even in a draughty corner or against a north-facing wall. The violet-blue, bell-like flowers hang from long, slender stalks and are set in motion by the slightest breeze. After they have finished, the flowers are replaced by attractive silky seed heads. The plant looks at its best when grown over a low wall or allowed to scramble happily

over a small bush, a shed perhaps, or a tree stump.

Several sorts are available, including the pale blue 'Columbine', deeper blue 'Pamela Jackman', and the white-centred blue 'Frances Rivis'. White and dusky-pink forms include the double 'White Moth', reddish-pink 'Ruby', and 'Willy', whose pale pink sepals are deeper tinged at the base.

Blue cultivars would mingle delightfully with the last yellow flowers of *Forsythia suspensa*, the cooler branches of *Kerria japonica* 'Picta', and with the orange blooms of *Berberis darwinii*. Try the rich blaze of *Chaenomeles* × *superba* 'Knap Hill Scarlet' with the white sorts and, with the pink cultivars, an underplanting of the pale and dark blue stars of *Chionodoxa*

Low-growing *Clematis alpina* will mingle happily with a bushy shrub such as *Juniperus sabina*.

(*Clematis alpina* cont)
luciliae 'Rosea' and the dusky pink summer flowers of *Astrantia maxima*.

CULTIVATION Plant in autumn, in sun or shade, in enriched soil. Pruning, if needed, consists of removing flower-bearing stems immediately after the flowers fade. Propagate by cuttings taken in early summer, then spray them periodically as a precaution against fungus. Sow seed as soon as it ripens in late summer or early autumn.

Clematis armandii

Height 20ft
Best March-early May

Though slightly tender, this evergreen clematis will grow vigorously when trained on a warm and sunny, sheltered wall. Veined oblong leaves provide a

Clematis armandii 'Apple Blossom', with its flowers flushed with pink and long, slender leaves, is one of the few evergreen varieties.

dark glossy background for vivid sprays of vanilla-scented saucer-shaped, creamy-white flowers. The variety 'Snowdrift' has larger, pure white flowers, and 'Apple Blossom' has pink-tinged flowers and light bronze young foliage.

You can let *Clematis armandii* stems intertwine with wall shrubs such as *Ceanothus* ×

veitchianus, whose clusters of blue flowers would extend the display of colour. *Cistus ladanifer*, planted in front, and a climber needing a similarly sheltered site, such as *Passiflora caerulea* 'Constance Elliott', could continue a white-flowering theme into summer.

CULTIVATION Plant in spring, in humus-enriched soil, and take

care to protect against frost in very cold winters. Prune hard after flowering to keep the clematis tidy and within bounds. Propagation is not easy, either by cuttings or by seed, which may produce plants inferior to their parent.

Clematis montana

Height 30ft
Best April-June

In late spring, masses of vanilla-scented, white flowers grace this tall, vigorous climber from the Himalayas and China. The flattish blooms, each with a cluster of yellow anthers at the centre, contrast strongly with the dark green, three-pronged leaves. Several named forms, all vanilla-scented, are widely available. *Clematis montana rubens* has deep pink sepals, golden stamens and bronze-purple foliage; 'Elizabeth' is the softest of pinks; small-flowered 'Picton's Variety' a deeper pink; and 'Tetrarose' has deep rosy-mauve flowers and bronzed foliage. White-flowered varieties include the creamy-white 'Alexander', and the pure white 'Grandiflora'.

The white cultivars can highlight a tall, dark conifer or holly, and will transform a high, dark north wall. Plant *Helleborus orientalis* at the base for late winter and early spring colour,

The foliage of *Clematis montana* 'Tetrarose' is bronze-tinged.

and *Nicotiana sylvestris* for fragrant white summer trumpets. All forms will camouflage an unsightly shed or outhouse (but do not let the stems get under the roof tiles).

If you have a deciduous tree, such as a malus, grow a montana through it and add a climbing rose, such as 'Sander's White', to continue flower and

Wisteria floribunda 'Alba' creates a dazzling, frozen-fountain effect in a dark corner of a garden.

After its flowers have had their day, the luxuriant foliage of *Clematis montana* provides shady cover for a garden nook in summer.

For a heady cocktail, mix the fragrance of honeysuckle with that of pink icing-sugar *Clematis montana* 'Elizabeth'.

The tulip-shaped flowers of *Holboellia coriacea* hang in clusters of three on long stems. They are followed by purple fruits.

perfume through the summer.
CULTIVATION Plant in good soil in autumn or spring, or if container-grown, at any time when the weather is suitable.

Pink varieties need sun for good colour. Propagate by semi-hardwood cuttings in early summer; seed from named varieties produces inferior forms.

Holboellia coriacea

Height 15-20ft
Best April-May

A memorable feature of this twining evergreen climber from China is its strong, sweet fragrance that is carried from half-hidden clusters of purplish-white flowers in spring. After warm, sunny summers, long and thick purple pods may form. As a valuable extra, its trifoliate leaves provide a year-round display of polished green.

This holboellia can form luxuriant cover over a sunny wall, effectively masking eye-sores such as drainpipes, or can be grown through a tree with light, open habit.

Combine it with sun-loving climbers such as *Rosa banksiae* 'Lutea', whose double yellow flowers appear at much the same time, and *R.* 'Climbing Iceberg' for sprays of lightly perfumed white flowers in summer. Shrubs such as *Ceanothus* 'Autumnal Blue' or *Cytisus battandieri* would give follow-on colour, and *Cosmos atrosanguineus* with its flowers like cocoa-scented dahlias, would continue interest until the first frosts of autumn.
CULTIVATION Plant in spring in fertile, well-drained soil. This

climber does reasonably well in light shade but flowers more freely in a warm, sunny position. Keep well watered until established. Prune once the flowers have faded only if needed to keep in bounds. Propagate, if the season has been sufficiently warm, from fresh, ripe seed. Alternatively, take semi-hardwood cuttings or layer in late summer.

Wisteria floribunda

JAPANESE WISTERIA

Height 20-30ft
Best May-June

Like a spring waterfall in the clearest river under blue skies, the flowers of this climber fall in 1 to 2ft long tresses of fragrant violet-blue. Grow it on walls, pergolas and arches where its showy cascade makes a splendid late spring and early summer picture. The form *Wisteria floribunda* 'Multijuga' is even more spectacular, with

115

The lilac-blue streamers of *Wisteria floribunda* 'Macrobotrys' are one of the joys of the gardener's year. The 3ft long chains of fragrant flowers make a perfect frieze for an open conservatory or pergola.

(*Wisteria floribunda* cont)
fragrant chains of lilac-blue flowers growing up to 3ft long.

The Japanese wisteria can join other fragrant climbers which flower later. Try combining it with *Jasminum officinale*, with large-flowered clematis hybrids, or with semi-climbing roses such as 'New Dawn'.

At a lower level, sweet peas (*Lathyrus odoratus*) would add more summer fragrance. *Lavandula angustifolia* would provide a wealth of aromatic, grey-green foliage all year.
CULTIVATION Plant in full sun in ordinary garden soil. Enrich chalky soil with organic material. Provide a permanent support, preferably on a south or west-facing wall, and tie the

growths to it until the twining stems can gain a firm hold. Propagate by semi-hardwood cuttings in summer, or by layering supple stems in early autumn. Young plants can take up to ten years or more before they bloom. Prune in July, cutting back to within two or three buds of the base of the previous year's growth.

Wisteria sinensis

CHINESE WISTERIA

Height 40-60ft
Best May-June

If you want to make more of a tall tree or a high wall, this vigorous wisteria provides the

perfect answer. Its fragrant, deep lilac-mauve flowers decorate the bare stems before the leaves appear. It can be distinguished from the Japanese wisteria (*Wisteria floribunda*), by the fact that its stems twine in the opposite direction – that is, anticlockwise.

The cultivars of *W. sinensis* include 'Black Dragon', with double, dark purple blooms, and the white 'Alba'.

The Chinese wisteria is often grown to great effect on house walls, especially in town gardens. Try setting it around a south-facing front door with an early yellow rose such as *Rosa* 'Maigold', and aromatic *Rosmarinus officinalis* 'Miss Jessop's Upright' standing sentinel on

The best place to grow a *Wisteria sinensis* is on the wall of a house, and a large one at that, for it is an amazingly vigorous climber.

either side. Add *Hebe* 'Alicia Amherst' alongside with its deep violet-flowered spikes in summer and autumn. For an interesting contrast, plant the grey-leaved *Santolina chamaecyparissus* in the foreground, though it must be pruned in spring to make neat mounds.

CULTIVATION Plant containerised *W. sinensis* in ordinary garden soil at any time between autumn and spring when the soil is suitable. Provide supports in the same way as for *W. floribunda*. Propagate by taking semi-hardwood cuttings in summer, or by layering in early autumn.

Spring
ROSES

THOUGH THE ROSE is the flower that is held to characterise summer, those few that bloom in spring present us with a grand and welcome surprise. That they will grow in adverse conditions, either – like 'Maigold' – on a north wall, or as 'Frühlingsgold', in a poor soil in a hot, dry place, makes them even more valuable.

Rosa banksiae lutea

YELLOW BANKSIAN ROSE

Height 15-25ft
Best May

The Banksian rose is one of the first rambling roses of the year, its falling sprays of rich butter-yellow blooms anticipating the golden days of summer to come. First introduced to England from western China in 1824, it is one of the enduring classic roses. Although not recurrent, the wealth of small, cupped double blooms on almost thorn-less stems lasts from four to six weeks. *Rosa banksiae lutea* is more free-flowering, slightly less vigorous and slightly hardier than the other Banksian forms available, but only lightly scented.

To introduce late summer colour into the rose's pale green foliage, *Clematis* 'The President' could grow through it, with sun-loving summer perennials such as *Hemerocallis* 'Golden Chimes' or *Rudbeckia*

Ivy-like, climbing *Rosa banksiae lutea* can be trained to cover the entire south wall of a house.

The double, 1in diameter blooms of *Rosa banksiae lutea* are borne in clusters and are lightly scented.

fulgida 'Goldsturm' grown in the foreground.
CULTIVATION Plant in suitable weather and soil conditions between autumn and early spring in any reasonable, well-drained soil, enriched with organic material. *R. banksiae lutea* needs a south or west-facing wall to flourish. Prune in late winter or early spring only to remove very old or dead branches, and to thin out sur-plus shoots. Propagate by taking softwood cuttings in summer, or hardwood cuttings in autumn.

Rosa
'Canary Bird'

Height 5-7ft · *Spread* 5-7ft
Best May

Despite the informality of its name, 'Canary Bird' is in fact a species rose, a selection from

Magnificent *Rosa* 'Canary Bird' dominates a secluded corner of a cottage garden, with a demure escort of forget-me-nots providing a ribbon of light blue in the background.

the wild *Rosa xanthina spontanea* of north China and Korea. Being one of the first roses to flower, its month-long display is an exciting event in the garden year. It bursts upon the spring scene with a single but glorious profusion of canary-yellow blooms, similar in form to our native dog rose. The blooms are beautifully set against graceful, pale grey foliage. The abundance of its single, 2in diameter flowers, carried in generous sprays along chocolate-brown stems, is matched by the vigour of the shrub's growth. Upright shoots arch over at the top, and are not too prickly. Later, small maroon hips develop to embellish the autumnal scene.

'Canary Bird' can be grown as a standard or as a rose hedge, and in either case a bright annual climber such as the flame creeper, *Tropaeolum speciosum*, or morning glory (*Ipomoea purpurea*) would enhance its summer foliage.
CULTIVATION Plant in suitable weather and soil conditions between autumn and mid-spring in a sunny, uncrowded position. Any reasonably fertile, well-drained soil is suitable, with the addition of some organic material at planting time, especially in light soils. Prune two to three-year-old growths as necessary, to avoid the shrub becoming too twiggy, in late winter or early spring. Propagate by taking hardwood cuttings in autumn.

All the freshness and vivacity of spring is in this mingling of sweetly fragrant *Rosa* 'Frühlingsgold' with *Laburnum* × *watereri* 'Vossii'.

With its delicate combination of pink and gold, and red and yellow, the exquisite *Rosa* 'Frühlingsmorgen' is a decoration for the gates of dawn.

Rosa
'Frühlingsgold'

Height 6-8ft · *Spread* 6-8ft
Best May

Though the scented, clotted-cream blooms fade to pearly white in hot sun, the central crown of stamens remains bright gold. The great arching canes of this hearty shrub rose almost vanish beneath big, single to semi-double blooms, and the effect is spectacular. There is only one magnificent flush of flowers, but the display lasts for up to six weeks. 'Frühlingsgold' is one of the earliest roses and easy to grow, even in conditions that are poor by most rose standards.

A large-flowered rock rose such as *Cistus ladanifer* would make an excellent companion; its wide, papery flowers are not unlike those of 'Frühlingsgold', and would continue the theme of pale, open flowers well into summer. For a change of colour, try the crimson-pink flowering *C.* × *purpureus*.

CULTIVATION Prune gently in early stages of growth to establish symmetry, and remove some of the oldest growth completely in late winter. 'Frühlingsgold' flowers best on a poor, well-drained soil. Otherwise, cultivate in the same way as *R.* 'Canary Bird'.

The pale, ghostly flowers of *Rosa* 'Frühlingsgold' are warmed by the rich gleam of its golden stamens.

Rosa
'Frühlingsmorgen'

Height 5-6ft · *Spread* 5-6ft
Best May

The large, slightly cupped blooms have an exquisite perfection and symmetry of form and a light fragrance. Their colours are those of a clear spring dawn, varying according to sun strength from deep pink to pale rose, and fading to a cream centre with an elegant corona of dark red stamens.

Often, there will be a scattering of blooms throughout the summer, but the dark leaden-green foliage has an attraction of its own, especially if the pink stars of *Clematis* 'Duchess of Albany' can trail through it. *Geranium endressii* planted at the rose's base would follow through with sprays of pink flowers from midsummer until the first frosts, and bright, evergreen ground cover.

CULTIVATION Plant and propagate as for *R.* 'Canary Bird'.

Rosa
'Maigold'

Height 8-12ft · *Best* May

Cascades of burnished gold and glossy, rich green foliage that almost glows with health are the

Despite its soft flowers, *Rosa* 'Maigold' is one of the very best climbers for exposed situations.

most obvious rewards if you have the space for this vigorous climber. 'Maigold' is loose and open in habit, and very thorny, but richly clothed for four to six weeks with big, semi-double blooms, whose strong scent carries a considerable distance. There are no hips, but autumn will often bring a secondary flush of blooms. 'Maigold' is very tough, reliable and easy to grow, even in difficult or exposed conditions, and is one of the few roses that will flower on a north-facing wall.

Most at home rambling up a pillar, or trained against a fence or wall, 'Maigold' could be partnered with that fine winter climber *Clematis cirrhosa balearica*, or with the sweetly scented, shrubby honeysuckle *Lonicera fragrantissima*.
CULTIVATION 'Maigold' can be pruned into a self-supporting bush. Otherwise, cultivate as for *R.* 'Canary Bird'.

Spring PERENNIALS

JUST AS spring shrubs tend to be denizens of woodland in nature, so spring-flowering perennials show a preference for similar habitats. In the wild, they hasten to flower and set seed before summer's leafy canopy closes over them. In the garden, therefore, glade-like spaces between shrubs make ideal plots for perennials.

Anemone narcissiflora

Height 1½ft
Planting distance 1½ft
Best May-June

Anemone narcissiflora has sprays of cup-shaped flowers whose pure white interiors and petal backs are flushed with pale bluish-pink – reminiscent of apple blossom. The dark green foliage, with deeply cleft lobes, stays well below the flower spikes, which appear in late spring. The root system is fibrous but does not run, so plants are slow to increase.

The spring flowers replace those of the autumn-flowering *A.* × *hybrida*, although they are much smaller and more delicate. Placed among shrubs and set in the foreground, *A. narcissiflora* makes a lovely contrast with *Brunnera macrophylla*, whose bold heart-shaped foliage is a foil for the lobed anemone leaves. The subtle charms of the anemones would be smothered against showy, pale flowered shrubs such as philadelphus or

Columbine – *Aquilegia vulgaris* – has been a star of the cottage garden since time immemorial.

exochorda, but near pink or red camellias, or alongside dark bronze foliage, their effect is considerably enhanced.
CULTIVATION Plant at any time between autumn and spring in fertile, well-drained but moisture-retentive soil, in sun or partial shade. Propagate by offsets or by dividing and replanting rhizomes in summer.

Aquilegia vulgaris

COLUMBINE, GRANNY'S BONNET

Height 2-3ft
Planting distance 1½-2ft
Best May-June

Cottage-style perennials of great charm, columbines have spurred flowers like a cluster of doves. The species is blue, but garden forms come in a range of shades from white and pale pink through mauves and grubby violets to clear blue. The foliage

A few columbines will populate the garden. When this happens, bring in their traditional companions; forget-me-nots, honesty and pansies.

is grey-green, with attractively scalloped lobes.

A prolific natural hybridiser, the columbine has given rise to many hybrids, some strikingly beautiful, others peculiar. Gertrude Jekyll's white form, 'Munstead White', has exceptional foliage, particularly large white blooms and breeds true from seed. Among the oddities are 'Norah Barlow', whose double flowers are pink and white tufts.

No spring border can reach its full glory without columbines. Though less spectacular than summer perennials, if planted in large groups they play a role in linking isolated large-flowered plants. Combined with tulips, *Euphorbia epithymoides* and epimediums,

119

The many varieties of *Bellis perennis* – the common daisy – contribute cohesion to the border.

(*Aquilegia vulgaris* cont) they help to bring about the first floral climax of the year.

Columbines will often spread among shrubs where there is dappled shade or full light, and look natural in an informal woodland setting.

CULTIVATION Plant in autumn or spring in any fertile soil, and in sun or part shade. Aquilegias seed freely but, to ensure continuance of true colour, can also be propagated by division between autumn and spring.

Bellis perennis

DAISY

Height 4-6in
Planting distance 6-8in
Best April-June

It may seem eccentric to commend wild daisies to gardeners who already have a fine crop naturalised in the lawn. But there are numerous cultivated varieties which make a carpeting or edging display that will last from March to October. Try *Bellis perennis* 'Goliath', whose first flush of flowers may be as

BRIDGING THE SEASONS
WITH
Bellis perennis

M UCH TO BE desired is a massing of herbaceous and bulbous plants that will give a good balance of form and colour in a border through two whole seasons, and suffer scarcely a weed to live in the process. Linking the theme and the seasons are varieties of none other than the common daisy *Bellis perennis*, whose white, pink and scarlet pompons will front the border from March to October, long outlasting the lordly tulips – *Tulipa* 'Golden Oxford' and black-purple *T.* 'La Tulipe Noire', that make two distinctive and eye-catching clumps beside the stone-flagged path. Also in evidence in May, among the controlled jungle made up of the foliage of daffodils, geraniums, polyanthus, tall foxgloves and the distinctive wide leaves of hostas, are yellow-green florets of *Euphorbia characias*, the fading bells and top-knots of *Fritillaria imperialis*, a good, wide scattering of forget-me-nots (*Myosotis*) and the arched stems and flowers of Solomon's seal, *Polygonatum × hybridum*, to add its graceful drama to the border.

In early August the tide of daisies will have receded, and the place of the tulips largely usurped by the white bells of *Galtonia candicans* and a modern shrub rose 'Golden Wings' that produces single, pale gold flowers in profusion. In front of

This opulent planting, containing an encyclopedic collection of perennials and bulbs, swings into late spring with tulips and forget-me-nots, Solomon's seal and crown imperials, handsomely bound together by daisies.

the galtonia, *Hosta fortunei* is now showing its lilac-purple flowers, while to its right there is a tall clump of *Macleaya microcarpa*. Though credited with the invasive capabilities of Genghis Khan, there is no doubt that its buff-white plumes do ornament the front of a border. The euphorbia's florets are now a brighter green, but the Solomon's seal is done with flowering for the year; however, the leaves and black berries along the curving stems still

handsomely punctuate the run of foliage. The real eye-catchers now though are the geranium and the foxglove – *Geranium psilostemon* with its extraordinarily vivid, black-centred magenta flowers, and *Digitalis × mertonensis*, whose bells, the colour of crushed strawberries, crowd all around the tall stems. Altogether, this is a most successful planting, offering plenty of variety and, once established, requiring little attention from the gardener. ❦

SUMMER brings great changes to the border as the tulips give way to the golden flowers of the modern shrub rose 'Golden Wings', to hostas and geraniums, to euphorbias, and a clump of pink foxgloves.

Vivacious *Brunnera macrophylla* makes colourful ground cover for a dull or shady corner.

much as 4in across and appear in various colours. Contrast them with *B. p.* 'Pomponette', white and crimson, whose quilled petals are tightly packed into highly attractive pompons.
CULTIVATION Plant in any fertile soil, in sun or part shade. Propagate by seed in June.

Brunnera macrophylla

Height 2ft · *Planting distance* 3ft
Best April-July

In spring, brunneras produce a profusion of airy sprays of mid-blue flowers, rather like forget-me-nots, that last for many weeks. By high summer, the heart-shaped matt-green leaves have grown to become a

IN SUMMER the broad leaves of *Brunnera macrophylla* are heavily veined with a hide-like pattern.

THE SUMMER foliage of *Brunnera macrophylla* 'Variegata' has bright, elegantly patterned white margins.

The lacy foliage and nodding white flowers of *Corydalis ochroleuca* are a perfect foil for weathered, lichened stone in a rock garden.

Dicentra formosa, with its heart-shaped flowers on arching stems, is an excellent border plant.

(*Brunnera macrophylla* cont) valuable foliage background.

Several named forms include 'Langtrees', whose foliage is decorated with silver spots, and 'Variegata', which has white-margined foliage. The beautiful variety 'Hadspen Cream' has creamy leaf margins, and the leaves adorning the flower sprays are also cream. They contrast with the blue flowers to make this one of the loveliest spring perennials, but it is less vigorous than the other forms and is easily smothered.

As woodland plants, brunneras look well among most other spring perennials, especially primrose-coloured oxlips or white honesty. They associate perfectly with bulbs such as daffodils or yellow crown imperials, and make excellent companions for classic, spring-flowering shrubs; try contrasting their blue with the yellows of forsythia or the pinks and whites of a prunus.

CULTIVATION Plant between autumn and spring in a shady position and in soil which does not become too dry. Propagate by division in autumn.

Corydalis ochroleuca

Height 8-12in
Planting distance 1-1½ft
Best April-June

Grow *Corydalis ochroleuca* on an old wall, where it will anchor itself in damp crevices. Its curiously shaped flowers, each with a little snout, range from pale lemon-cream to greenish-white, and the fern-like foliage is vivid green with greyish overtones when young. There is a second flush of flowers when the weather begins to cool in autumn, and the foliage lasts for most of the year.

The plants do well alongside *C. lutea*, but are seen at their best if their creamy flowers are contrasted with strong blues, such as that of gentians. They also make fine companions for scillas or grape hyacinths – in gravel, for instance – if left to seed themselves at will.

CULTIVATION Plant in spring, where the plants will receive only short bursts of full sun – that is, facing north, north-east or north-west. They need a cool spot to multiply well, but dislike dense shade – it stops them flowering. In good conditions, plants will seed freely and colonies will develop of their own accord.

Dicentra formosa

Height 1-1½ft
Planting distance 1-1½ft
Best April-July

The mauve-pink flowers of this North American native hang like wild hyacinths above ferny leaves. The foliage forms dense mats on underground stems, and stays decorative until late summer. Of named varieties, 'Alba' is white with green leaves; 'Langtrees', near white with tiny pink tips; while

'Adrian Bloom' and 'Bountiful', both shades of plum-like red-pink, take the prize for vigour. The closely related *Dicentra eximia* 'Stuart Boothman' is also a superb spring plant. It has bluish or bronze foliage which is even more fernlike, and produces ruby flowers for several months in spring and early summer.

Dicentras make perfect companions for plants with bold foliage – notably the hostas, which enjoy similar growing conditions. The flowers go well with primroses or polyanthus, and with bold spring blooms such as the huge cream tulip 'White Emperor'. In mixed borders, their foliage makes a pleasing foreground to shrubs with gold or purple leaves. *D. e.* 'Stuart Boothman' looks superb when paired with the downy, silver foliage and woolly catkins of the willow *Salix lanata*.

CULTIVATION Plant and propagate as for *Dicentra spectabilis*.

BRIDGING THE SEASONS
WITH
Dicentra formosa

I T IS SURPRISING what can be done to ring the changes even in the most unpromising situation. This one is small – no more than 8ft by 8ft – a woody patch that is cool, dampish and shady. Yet with a little thought, great play can be made with it. The story begins in spring, as two ferns, *Polystichum setiferum* 'Divisilobum' and the lady fern *Athyrium filix-femina* begin to stretch their fronds, though their spread is nothing like what they will achieve later. Both enjoy cool, woody conditions, an appreciation that is shared by the plants that occupy the ground between them. The pure blue nodding heads of English bluebells, *Endymion non-scriptus*, are the first to catch the eye, but among them, and even more exquisite, are the delicate, heart-shaped flowers of *Dicentra formosa* 'Alba'. There too can be seen the leaves of *Digitalis grandiflora* that next year will produce tall foxglove flowers of soft creamy-yellow.

In autumn, the ferns will have reached their full spread – as much as 4ft in the case of *P. setiferum* – and the bluebells are no longer to be seen. *D. formosa* still shows a few flowers however, and contributes its own pale green, ferny leaves about the hump of the digitalis. But the main colour now is provided by glorious, multi-hued drifts of *Colchicum* hybrids – from the double, pinkish 'Waterlily', to the crimson-purple 'Atrorubens' and the gold-centred white of 'Album'. ❧

The flowers of *Dicentra formosa* 'Alba' are delicate and oddly shaped – rather like lockets designed for small girls. Their paleness here is emphasised by the vivacity of English bluebells.

IN AUTUMN two wide-spreading ferns almost overwhelm the dicentra's remaining flowers as they offer shelter to a vivid group of colchicum hybrids.

The flowers of *Dicentra spectabilis* hang from arching stems.

Wallflowers filling the spaces between *Doronicum orientale* make an informal gathering of lemon-sharp yellow and shades of red.

Dicentra spectabilis in full flower makes a distinctive backing for a show of scarlet *Tulipa* Greigii hybrids mingled with *Narcissus* 'Thalia'.

Dicentra spectabilis

BLEEDING HEART, LYRE
FLOWER, LADY IN BATH

Height 1½-2ft
Planting distance 3ft
Best May-June

One of the show stoppers of spring, bleeding heart first bears graceful, lobed foliage that emerges reddish flushed but turns green as the stems lengthen. The heart-shaped rose-red flowers open to allow the creamy-white, drop-shaped central petals to protrude.

Turned upside down, the flower resembles a figure sitting in a bath – hence 'lady in bath'.

Plants so distinctive are a feature in themselves. So despite their height, plant them near the front of a spring border; soon after summer's beginning, they will die away to make room for other perennials or annuals. In the meantime, the lobed foliage contrasts nicely with the solid leaf forms of such plants as hostas and bergenias. *Dicentra spectabilis* 'Alba' has pure white flowers with no trace of pink. Its foliage superbly complements large, glaucous-leaved hostas, and combines well too with dark shrubs. An excellent suggestion is the bronze fennel *Foeniculum vulgare* 'Purpureum', which would perfectly emphasise the flowers of *D. s.* 'Alba'.

CULTIVATION Plant in autumn or spring in any well-drained garden soil enriched with peat or compost, it does best when sheltered from frosts and strong winds. Propagate by carefully dividing and replanting the roots in early spring, or by root cuttings in late winter.

Doronicum orientale

LEOPARD'S BANE

Height 1½-2ft
Planting distance 1½ft
Best March-May

According to Turner's *Herball* of 1551, leopard's bane is not only a leopardicide; in addition, if 'layd to a scorpione (it) maketh hyr vtterly amased and Num'. As scorpions are not a problem in British gardens, the bright yellow daisies are chiefly valued for their contribution to spring, and for the way they help to bridge the gap when the daffodils have finally faded. Saw-toothed leaves, wavy-edged like scallop shells, grow into neat mounds of green foliage. The plants respond to the first warmth of the spring sun by pushing golden-yellow flowers well above the leaves; by April, if planted in proximity, the mounds will unite to create a carpet of gold.

Attractive cultivars include an old favourite, the hybrid cultivar 'Miss Mason', whose bright yellow flowers stand high above compact clumps of heart-shaped leaves. On the whole, this is a better plant to grow than the wild species, which is inclined to be invasive.

There is also a double-flowered sort, a charming, low-growing cultivar called 'Spring Beauty'.

Doronicums go well with tulips, especially those in the coppery-orange and red ranges, and you can link spring with summer by growing them with both kinds of honesty, the spring pea *Lathyrus vernus* and the blue varieties of lungwort. All these plants enjoy dappled woodland light, and can be used to cover the ground between rhododendrons and syringas, or among large shrub roses that will bring out their show later in the year.

CULTIVATION Plant between autumn and spring in sun or dappled shade, and in deep, ordinary soil. Dead-head regularly and cut stems down to the ground in autumn. The species may gently self-sow; propagate the cultivars 'Miss Mason' and 'Spring Beauty' by division during early autumn.

Epimedium pinnatum colchicum has a hearts-and-flowers display.

The young, veined and reddish foliage of *Epimedium × rubrum* shows up well against a ground cover of *Hedera helix* 'Buttercup'.

The *Euphorbia griffithii* cultivar 'Fireglow' lives up to its name when massed like glowing embers in front of dark green foliage.

Epimedium

BARRENWORT, BISHOP'S HAT

Height 10-12in
Planting distance 1-2ft
Best March-June

The various epimediums are valuable foliage plants for much of the year. In spring, the fresh green of the emerging leaves is often tinted copper, pink or red, though they turn a deeper green in summer. The early spring flowers vary from deep coral-red, through orange and yellow, to pure white. Though not in the top flight of floral beauties they have great charm, especially in dappled shade.

Epimedium × rubrum carries crimson flowers. *E. pinnatum colchicum*, with bright yellow flowers, has particularly long-lasting foliage and is especially colourful in autumn. *E. × cantabrigiense* has green foliage and

A mophead hydrangea stands out in sharp relief against the burnished purple and bronze autumn foliage of *Epimedium × rubrum*.

rusty-orange flowers, and the very much smaller *E. youngianum* 'Niveum' has shapely leaves and pure white flowers.

Their very nearly year-round greenery makes epimediums useful as ground-cover plants, for they will form weed-proof clumps without being invasive.

They make harmonious companions for spring woodlanders like *Uvularia grandiflora* or even perennial honesty. Or, set at the feet of such deciduous shrubs as corylopsis or hamamelis, they provide colour when the shrubs' flowers begin to fade.

CULTIVATION Plant in early spring, in a partially shaded position in moist, ordinary, well-drained soil. Propagate by carefully dividing and replanting during spring, before or immediately after flowering.

Euphorbia griffithii

SPURGE

Height 2-3ft
Planting distance 3ft
Best May-June

Rusty red predominates on this species' cultivars in spring, making them useful plants for warming up a mixed border. The young stems become suffused with shades of red at their tips, while the flowers that emerge in late spring are fiery orange. The frost-touched foliage also gives a good display in autumn. The improved cultivar 'Fireglow' is among the most widely grown, but 'Dixter'

is an excellent compact form.

The plants look well against yellows and golds, and provide highlights that relieve areas of dark foliage. They give an especially warm lift to the bronze foliage of berberis or *Prunus × cistena*. Suitable herbaceous companions include the doronicums, the yellow *Kniphofia* 'Early Buttercup', or yarrow, *Achillea* 'Moonshine'.

Euphorbia griffithii lends grace to a poolside, and will grow vigorously and half as high again in a bog garden. Try it with moisture-loving irises, or skunk cabbage (*Lysichiton americanus*) and golden marsh marigolds (*Caltha palustris*).

CULTIVATION Plant at any time between autumn and spring in moist, fertile soil. Propagate by division and replanting in early spring or late autumn, making sure that when the plants are lifted, there is a generous root system attached.

The vivid yellow of *Euphorbia polychroma* glows fluorescently alongside soft-hued bluebells and the palmate leaves of *Alchemilla mollis*, through which grow the budded stems of *Aquilegia vulgaris*.

Together, *Geranium macrorrhizum* 'Bevan's Variety' and 'Album' form a scarlet-white bouquet.

Euphorbia polychroma
(syn *E. epithymoides*)

SPURGE

Height 15in
Planting distance 2ft
Best March-May

One of the most vividly coloured of the spurges, and one of the finest early perennials for a golden theme. The stems begin to show golden-yellow flower buds in early spring, when they are no more than a few inches high. By April, they have grown to 1ft or more, and are topped by chrome-yellow bracts, whose colour fades in late spring.

The plant makes a brilliant splash of colour among other euphorbias, and is spectacular too, if mingled with clear blue companions, such as bluebells (*Endymion hispanica*) or forget-me-nots (*Myosotis*). Combining the euphorbia with bold reds is even more startling; try it with 'Red Riding Hood' or 'Texas Flame' tulips, and bright scarlet *Anemone × fulgens*. Such golden shrubs as *Physocarpus* 'Dart's Gold' or the rich purple foliage of *Berberis thunbergii* 'Atropurpurea' would provide a fine background.

Of clump-forming habit and therefore without creeping roots, *Euphorbia polychroma* is long-lived and trouble-free.
CULTIVATION Plant September-April in any well-drained soil, preferably in dappled shade. Propagate from cuttings of basal shoots in July, or by division in autumn.

Geranium macrorrhizum

Height 1ft · *Planting distance* 2ft
Best May-November

The rounded, downy, aromatic leaves of *Geranium macrorrhizum* make it one of the finest of ground-cover plants. Some of the leaves colour well in autumn and last until spring when new ones arise; thus the plant is almost evergreen. The exquisitely shaped soft magenta-pink flowers each have protruding stamens and a reddish calyx, the outer case of the bud. Garden forms include the exquisite 'Walter Ingwersen', of a deliciously soft pink, and 'Bevan's Variety', which has cerise blooms. There is also a lovely white form with contrasting pink stamens and calyx, and a variegated one with cream deformed-edged leaves.

Masses of soft pink flowers crowd the downy foliage of *Geranium macrorrhizum* 'Walter Ingwersen'.

This geranium will grow almost anywhere, and never looks out of place. Use it as weedstopping ground cover before a shrubbery, which it will enhance with drifts of flowers from May to July. Planted in a

In a well-stocked border a lighter shade of pale is created by the mid-green foliage and warm white flowers of *Geranium macrorrhizum* 'Album', flanked on either side by the large, dark tongues of *Symphytum × uplandicum*.

Cow parsley makes a suitably rustic companion for the woodland-dwelling *Geranium sylvaticum*.

Meconopsis cambrica 'Aurantiaca' is a cultivated, orange-flowered variety of the native Welsh poppy.

border to provide spring colour, it contrasts with columbine (*Aquilegia vulgaris*), or with later-flowering geraniums. The blue flowers of monkshood (*Aconitum*) – both summer-flowering varieties like 'Sparks' and the autumn species *Aconitum carmichaelii* with light blue hoods – look handsome standing above the russet tints of the geranium foliage.

CULTIVATION Plant between early autumn and mid-spring in any well-drained soil, and in any position from deep shade to full sun. The plant will spread naturally by growing new rhizomes and by self-seeding. Propagate by division between autumn and spring.

Geranium sylvaticum

WOOD CRANE'S-BILL

Height 1½-2½ft
Planting distance 2ft
Best May-June

Widely grown in cottage gardens, wood crane's-bill is a beautiful native plant with rounded, seven-lobed, mid to deep green foliage. It forms a pleasing mound of green before flowering begins in late spring.

The tall-stemmed flowers need no support, and like so many of the crane's-bills, their petals are coloured in fine pastel shades and patterned with veining. In the wild, the flowers of the wood crane's-bill are bluish-mauve with pale centres, but one of the finest garden forms, 'Mayflower', is rich violet-blue. There is also a superb white, 'Alba', and a purplish-pink, 'Wanneri'. The plant's natural habitat is open woodland rides, or hedgerows where there is direct sunlight for part of the day. Therefore, it makes a perfect companion for shrubs in open mixed borders. The white form looks well when backed by sombre foliage. Equally, it can take over from shrubs like winter-flowering *Mahonia japonica*, or serve as an overture to *Euonymus europaeus* which flowers later. A lazy gardener's dream, wood crane's-bill can be left to itself, and self-seeds plentifully, although clones do not always come true from seed.

CULTIVATION Plant between September and March in any soil that does not dry out too much in summer. Propagate by division between early autumn and mid-spring.

Meconopsis cambrica

WELSH POPPY

Height 3-5ft
Planting distance 3-5ft
Best May-October

The charms of the Welsh poppy are hard to resist, even when it colonises a shady area at the expense of its neighbours. Its fresh, green foliage develops into a thick mass from which slender stems topped with nodding green flower buds arise in May. When the crinkled petals open and expand, they are clear lemon-yellow. A bright orange form is available, which mixes well with the yellow, and there are double-flowered forms in both shades.

Grown with dwarf rhododendrons, the little Welsh poppy makes up for its smaller flower size by its superior numbers. Its soft citron hues also go well with the bright green fronds of *Asplenium scolopendrium* (the hart's-tongue fern), and the plants form a grand ensemble along with gold hostas, particularly 'Golden Prayers' or 'Gold Edger'.

Welsh poppies can be invasive and need careful siting, but they will sometimes thrive where very little else will grow – even in fairly dry shade by the sides of buildings.

CULTIVATION Plant in March or April in any soil or position. Hoe out any newcomers that appear in unwelcome places and control existing colonies by cutting plants to ground level before the seed capsules ripen. This will encourage a fresh flush of flowers later in the season. Propagate by seed sown when ripe or in spring.

Here beside a woody path is a sturdy, self-perpetuating community that, once established, goes through its yearly cycle with hardly any further help from the gardener. Pillars of the community are a dark, spiny holly, *Ilex aquifolium* 'Bacciflava', and a male fern *Dryopteris filix-mas* which, in May, is still stretching its fronds. About it are English bluebells, *Endymion nonscriptus*, of a wonderful innocent blue and, almost eclipsing them in brightness, the clear lemon and vivid orange flowers of the old Welsh poppy *Meconopsis cambrica*. Though fairly short-lived, it is a determined coloniser by seed and makes a brave show in late spring. Another important flower at this time is *Smilacina racemosa* with its sweetly scented, Solomon's seal-like, creamy plumes, while already apparent among the greenery are the mid-green ovate leaves of *Campanula latifolia* 'Brantwood'.

In July, the campanula puts out its towering spikes of tubular, purple-blue flowers, overbearingly regal among the few remaining poppies, whose ferny foliage nevertheless pleasantly complements the fronds of *D. filix-mas*, now at full stretch. But the leaves that really take the eye, and now triumphing over what is left of the bluebell foliage, are those of *Hosta fortunei*, a notable shade-lover. Cultivars 'Albopicta' and 'Aureomarginata' are both represented – the first, by this time, in two shades of soft green, while

Yellow Welsh poppies and vivid English bluebells together set the springtime trend for this crowded, jostling woodland community.

As summer advances, it is the spikes of *Campanula latifolia* that dominate in this self-regulating planting, aided by the distinctive foliage and lilac flowers of hostas and cool fronds of fern.

the leaves of the other are edged with gold. Standing tall over both are flowers of pale lilac.

It would be quite an idea to plant evergreen *Hypericum* 'Hidcote' and allow its bowl-shaped, golden flowers to carry the association through to autumn, but until the gardener gets round to it, the next period of interest is late winter, with pale blue *Iris reticulata* 'Cantab' pushing up through the snow near the hummock made by the male fern, and accompanied by a crowd of snowdrops, *Galanthus nivalis*. In the background, the 'Bacciflava' holly makes a splendid cone of yellow berries; these are of particular value, since birds, for some reason, are reluctant to eat them. ❧

Winter snow brings holly to the fore, that in other seasons provides a self-effacing background. Its sombre note is lightened by snowdrops and the arrival of *Iris reticulata* 'Cantab'.

Pink flower parasols precede the leafy umbrellas of *Peltiphyllum peltatum.*

autumn and spring in any well-drained but moist, fertile garden soil. Rake in bone meal after planting. Propagate by division in early autumn, or by seed as soon as they ripen.

Peltiphyllum peltatum

UMBRELLA PLANT

Height 3ft
Planting distance 3ft
Best March-September

In early spring this North American bog plant throws up a mass of naked stems, topped by starry clusters of pale pink flowers that are given emphasis by dark pink stamens. As the flowers begin to fade, huge rounded leaves emerge to create a magnificent mound of bold foliage. In maturity, the leaves open to reach 1ft or more in diameter, and in autumn turn bronze-pink. There is a dwarf form, 'Nana', which is slightly less exuberant.

Though far too big for a small pond, the plant is superb at the margin of a muddy stream, where the binding, sprawling

Paeonia mlokosewitschii

Height 1½-2ft
Planting distance 3ft
Best May-June

Do not be put off by the jaw-breaking name of the species, for this peony is stunning at all its stages. The deeply lobed, bronze foliage handsomely unfolds to become a wonderful unifier of spring bulbs, especially fritillarias and yellow and orange species tulips. Later, the leaves mature to grey-green, then brighten once more to yellow and orange in autumn. The glistening lemon-yellow petals of the goblet-shaped flowers, up to 5in across, are curled about a crowd of golden stamens. Later, three-pointed seed capsules, like jesters' caps, are produced and split open to display jewel-like blue and red seeds.

This peony deserves a place of honour, and looks at its best when backed by dark green or bronze foliage. Maples, *Cotinus* 'Grace', or *Berberis thunbergii*

The noble flowers of *Paeonia mlokosewitschii* are exactly right for this corner of a walled garden, with the foliage of foxgloves and the fronds of dryopteris ferns creating an old world charm.

'Atropurpurea' would all be perfect, with primroses at the foot of the peony to provide fresh early colour in the year.
CULTIVATION Plant between

The leaves of *Peltiphyllum peltatum* present a seasonably warm spectrum of colours in autumn.

(*Peltiphyllum peltatum* cont) network of roots helps to hold the banks together. Skunk cabbage (*Lysichiton americanus*) can hold its own with the umbrella plant, as can the more rampant rushes and water irises. The larger-than-life kingcup (*Caltha polypetala*) makes a good companion and flowers at about the same time.

CULTIVATION Plant in moist to wet ground, in sun or shade, in autumn. Propagate by lifting pieces of rhizome and re-planting in spring.

Polygonatum × hybridum

SOLOMON'S SEAL

Height 2-3ft
Planting distance 1½-2ft
Best May-June

The gracefully arching stems of *Polygonatum* × *hybridum* emerge from fleshy rhizomes in April and put out their waxy-white, green-tipped bells about

A slender framework of *Polygonatum × hybridum* arches over a border of forget-me-nots, a hosta and an edging of *Origanum vulgare* 'Aureum'.

a month later. The smooth, oval, boldly veined leaves turn yellow before falling in autumn. Good companions that enjoy similar conditions and flower at the same time are lily of the valley and the false spikenard (*Smilacina racemosa*). For later colour, plant lilies nearby.

Solomon's seal looks well among most rhododendrons and azaleas, and among small maples or daphnes, though they might overcrowd some of the dwarf varieties.

CULTIVATION Plant between autumn and spring in well-drained soil and in dappled shade. Propagate by division in autumn or early spring.

Primula

PRIMROSE, POLYANTHUS AND AURICULA PRIMULAS

They may be delicate and modest in form and flower, but the spring primulas are indomitable, and will bloom for week upon week, to return in increasing force for many a subsequent year. Some are plants suited to moist, boggy conditions, and others – the auricula primulas – favour drier alpine soils.

A PRIMULA CALLED 'WANDA'
Perhaps the most familiar primulas of them all, including our native common primrose (*Primula vulgaris*), come from the Vernales group. The Latin word *vernales* means literally 'of the spring', but is in fact used to cover the species and their hybrids that enjoy woodland conditions of light, shade and moist, leafy soil. From the plain *P. vulgaris*, itself a worthy contributor to a wide variety of garden schemes, have come many cultivars, including the fancy, double 'Miss Indigo', its petals frilled with silver. Some cultivars, like the tough little purple hybrid 'Wanda', derived from *P.* × *pruhoniciana*, are true primrose-style with delicate stems, each with its own bloom, rising from the base. Others, like the petite 'Lady Greer', are 'polyanthus-style' in form, with a number of flowers carried on each sturdy stem.

THE VERSATILE AURICULAS
Perfect *P. auricula* cultivars, with not a petal or colour out of place, are interbred for exhibition. But there are many

The common primrose is equally at home in a garden border or on a grassy woodland bank.

cultivars with the essential qualities of velvet-textured petals and precisely zoned colours that are quite suitable for the open garden. Those known as border auriculas are particularly reliable. With their smooth, fleshy leaves and many flowers carried proudly on sturdy stems, these primulas also make fine container or rock-garden plants. Combine them with dwarf tulips like *Tulipa tarda*, backed perhaps by *Rosmarinus officinalis* or a small *Lavandula angustifolia* cultivar.

The moisture-loving primulas can be used to create a woodland atmosphere in the

Spring would not be spring without bluebells, and there could be no better companions in a cottage garden than primulas and veronicas.

Primula vulgaris is a woodland flower, and here a delightful sylvan scene is created by an apron of mixed varieties spread around the base of a gnarled apple tree and flanked by the arching sprays of *Dicentra spectabilis*.

Closely related to *Primula vulgaris*, the polyanthus garden hybrids are sometimes listed as *Primula polyantha* or *P. vulgaris elatior*.

fragmented shade beneath shrubs and trees, with other small, shade-tolerant plants. The March-flowering *Narcissus* 'Jack Snipe', and April to June-flowering *Brunnera macrophylla* would extend the period of colour. The strap-shaped leaves and late spring flowers of bluebells make a luscious background, or for pretty mounds of leaves and a later haze of crimson, try *Heuchera sanguinea*. Another taller companion could be *Helleborus argutifolius*, which bears its fragrant, greenish-yellow flowers during winter, and retains its dark, serrated leaves all year.

Ferns like *Asplenium scolopendrium* make fine partners for *P. denticulata* and *P. rosea*, while the candelabra primula cultivars could follow on deep into summertime. *P. sieboldii* prefers neutral to acid soil and would complement rhododendrons or camellias.

CULTIVATION

Buy pot-grown plants just beginning to flower, so that you can be sure of the colours, and plant in spring. Auricula primulas like well-drained but not dry soil in full light or partial shade; but all the other primulas need soil that is reasonably moist, but

not waterlogged, in a lightly shaded position. Primulas may be divided every third year to increase, and every five years for healthy plants, by breaking each plant into individual rosettes immediately after flowering.

Pure white hyacinths (*Hyacinthus* 'L'Innocence') rise from a quilted patchwork bed of *Primula* 'Wanda'.

Primrose variations

Primulas are the modest stars of dappled shade
in the rock garden. Auriculas, with their velvet-textured
precision of flower, originate in the alpine regions of
Europe and like well-drained soil. The cultivated forms of
our native wild primroses and oxlips have a more gentle
beauty and prefer moist conditions and light shade. All the
primulas flower for many weeks, adding their charms
to the whole of spring.

Painted from plants supplied in late March by Craven's Hall Barn Gardens, Beaconsfield,
Buckinghamshire and Martin Nest Nurseries, Gainsborough, Lincolnshire.

Primula 'Cowichan'
An 'eyeless' strain
of polyanthus; leaves
burnished bronze-red.
Height 8-12in.
Spread 10-15in.
Best April-May.

Primula
'Garryarde Guinevere'
Leaves tinged purple-bronze;
polyanthus-style flowers. Height 6-10in.
Spread 8-12in. Best April-May.

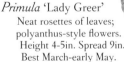

Primula vulgaris
'Miss Indigo'
Slightly scented double primrose.
Height 6in. Spread 10in.
Best March-April.

Primula denticulata
Available in various pink
and mauve shades,
and white; good in damp
soil; leaves develop
considerably after flowering.
Height 6-10in. Spread 10-15in.
Best March-early May.

Primula 'Lady Greer'
Neat rosettes of leaves;
polyanthus-style flowers.
Height 4-5in. Spread 9in.
Best March-early May.

Primula 'Gold Lace'
Tall-stemmed cultivar;
annual splitting essential.
Height 6-8in. Spread 9in. Best March-May.

Primula 'Wanda'
Free-flowering and tolerant of
a wide range of conditions. Height 3-4in.
Spread 9-12in. Best March-May.

Primula
'Dawn Ansell'
Lightly scented.
Each flower is set
in a ruff of leaves.
Height 6in. Spread 12in.
Best March-April.

Primula auricula
'Old Irish Blue'
Lightly scented,
tough border auricula.
Height 6-8in. Spread 6in.
Best May.

Primula sieboldii
'Snowflake'
Pink, mauve and
blue forms available.
Height 6-9in.
Spread 8-12in.
Best April-May.

Primula auricula
'Old Yellow Dusty Miller'
Vigorous, scented border auricula.
Height 6-8in. Spread 6in.
Best April-early May.

Primula rosea 'Grandiflora'
Needs moist spot. Height 4-8in.
Spread 6-9in. Best March-April.

The lovely white buttercup *Ranunculus aconitifolius*, whose double form 'Flore Pleno' (right) is claimed by both sides of the Channel as either Fair Maids of France or Fair Maids of Kent.

Smilacina racemosa has all the poise of its relation, Solomon's seal, with the bonus of fluffy flowers and blood-red berries. Here it makes a good backing for *Paeonia mlokosewitschii* and a *Helleborus orientalis* hybrid.

Ranunculus aconitifolius

Height 1½-2ft
Planting distance 1½ft
Best April-May

Explosions and showers of lovely white stars identify this not too far-removed cousin of the field buttercup. Like that pervasive but picturesque plant, it too produces armfuls of dark green, deep-lobed leaves that last all summer long. The flowers, however, arrive a month or so earlier to charm with their shining faces. Even more exquisite is the double form, *Ranunculus aconitifolius* 'Flore Pleno', known as Fair Maids of France. The name, if not the plant, is thought to have been imported by 16th-century homesick Huguenot refugees.

All the forms prefer dappled shade and are excellent for the spring border or as companions for flowering shrubs. The brightly shining petals enliven the quiet tones of shrub roses or hydrangeas in the time before they flower, and can also take over from the fading winter flowers of hellebores. In early summer they provide snap and sparkle before the phloxes, asters, lupins and lilies come into flower.

CULTIVATION Plant from autumn to spring in cool, moist soil and in light shade, though they will also thrive in full sun so long as their roots are protected. Propagate from division or fresh seed sown after flowering. In the particular case of *R. a.* 'Flore Pleno', propagate by division only in autumn.

Smilacina racemosa

FALSE SPIKENARD

Height 2-3ft
Planting distance 2-3ft
Best May-June

By late May, the arching stems of false spikenard are each topped with a fluffy spray of fragrant, creamy-white flowers among glossy lance-shaped leaves. In autumn, if conditions are good, the stems are bright with red berries, before they die away completely, leaving the way open for later plants.

False spikenard is a natural companion for its close relatives, Solomon's seal and lily of the valley. It brightens the shadows of woodland gardens with its elegant, creamy spring sprays, and provides fresh, vibrant greenery in summer. It relieves the darkness of holly foliage, and makes a lovely show with summer-flowering trees and shrubs before they are fully in bloom.

It looks particularly well near the dark-leaved, June-flowering *Cornus kousa* or among young camellias, as it flowers after they have finished and the white plumes are beautiful against the dark, glossy green. Add the July-flowering Turk's-cap lily, *Lilium martagon*, or *Liriope muscari*, which flowers in autumn, to the group to ensure

An attractive and efficient way to keep shade-loving weeds at bay is to put in a planting of *Symphytum grandiflorum* and give it its head.

A delightful plant for cool, dappled shade is *Trillium erectum* which, like all other members of this American genus, does everything in threes.

a long and colourful display. CULTIVATION Plant in early autumn or spring in lime-free soil rich in organic material. Propagate by division in autumn or early spring.

Symphytum grandiflorum

COMFREY

Height 9-12in
Planting distance 1½-2ft
Best March-July

Comfrey's vigorous, creeping rhizomes root as they go and soon form dense ground cover. The flower stems, held just clear of the mass of foliage, end in clusters of buds which produce tubular, red-hued flowers that change to pale blue or creamy-white as the flower opens. Flowers begin to show in late winter, have their main flush in spring, and turn up here and there during summer. The hairy, oval-shaped leaves are rough to the touch and can grow to 8in or more.

The invasive common form needs thoughtful positioning, but the cultivar 'Variegatum' is less intrusive and far more decorative, with its young foliage stippled and streaked with shades of gold and green.

Because it tolerates shade, creeping comfrey is fine as ground cover between shrubs. But even 'Variegatum' can be troublesome in a border, though it is not difficult to weed out. The plant's early spring blooms blend well with the pink, violet or blue flowers of pulmonarias, and enhance the effect of early flowering shrubs. Creeping comfrey is fine for planting among shrub roses, as it flowers before they begin to bloom, and looks well with emerging rose leaves.
CULTIVATION Plant in autumn or spring in any moisture-retentive soil. Propagate in autumn or spring by replanting short lengths of root.

For a good strong statement among more prostrate plants, try the spikes of *Thermopsis montana*.

Thermopsis montana

Height 2ft
Planting distance 1½ft
Best May-June

The mountains of the name are the Rockies, where, as in demure British gardens, the plant produces bright yellow flowers that open in May and stand in dense spikes that make them look rather like lupins. When they first emerge in April, the feathery three-lobed leaves are dark green; later they fade to grey-green.

The dark young foliage makes a good backing for early spring bulbs, especially tulips and narcissi. Later, the flowers blend well with the silvery foliage of lavender or artemisia, and the blooms of such shrubby potentillas as *Potentilla fruticosa* 'Elizabeth' and 'Tangerine', or with Jew's mallow, *Kerria japonica*. Since the foliage loses much of its appeal after the plant has flowered, back it up with later-flowering perennials such as *Potentilla recta*.

Other good shrubs to accompany the bold *Thermopsis montana* include purple-leaved acers, *Berberis thunbergii* 'Atropurpurea' or *Choisya ternata*. Clothe a wall or fence at the back of the plants with *Ceanothus veitchianus,* which has blue flowers and glossy dark foliage for a noble contrast, or with blue *Clematis macropetala*.
CULTIVATION Plant from autumn to spring in well-drained soil, and in full sun. Propagate by division in early spring, before the roots go too deep.

Trillium

Height 1-2ft
Planting distance 1-2ft
Best April-May

These joys of the North American woodland spring are distinguished by, and named from, the fact that everything about them is in threes. Each sturdy stalk bears three leaves, sometimes marbled white or purple, and a solitary flower with three petals and three pointed green sepals. The flowers of some species open flatly on the leaves while others stand erect; all would be exquisite in a woodland setting, even if their flowering is brief.

One of the loveliest is

Here triple-petalled *Trillium grandiflorum* makes a carpet on the floor of a glade, in which it has been provided with such agreeable companions as a rhododendron, *Smilacina racemosa* and a sprinkling of bluebells.

Trillium sessile is low growing, with tulip-like flowers making dramatic ground cover.

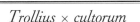

Creamy-gold *Trollius × cultorum* 'Alabaster' brings out the best in rusty-hued azaleas.

(*Trillium* cont)

Trillium erectum, whose dark maroon flowers mix well with such other North American shade lovers as false spikenard (*Smilacina racemosa*). Plant it among handsome shrubs, dwarf rhododendrons or purple-pink *Phyllodoce caerulea* to cheer the trillium leaves once flowering is over; other, larger spring-flowering shrubs in the neighbourhood could have the slender *Clematis viticella* growing through to brighten the scene from June to September.

Another delightful trillium is *T. grandiflorum*. It produces flowers of startling showiness – pure white, with gold stamens gleaming in the middle. Planted in groups in a leafy, shady place, dappled by light filtered through trees and shrubs, and accompanied by, say, pink andromedas and Asiatic primulas, it becomes one of the highlights of the spring garden. Then give extravagance to the scene with groups of fritillaries and the distinctive, pale Wedgwood-blue *Aquilegia alpina* 'Hensol Harebell'.

A very different trillium is *T. sessile*, which has low-growing, marbled leaves. The stemless flowers, rising straight up from the leaves, are somewhat tulip-like and emerge in dark shades of red and brown. These admirably complement the more usual hues of spring; those of jonquils, daffodils and white trilliums. To extend the season, plant *T. sessile* with that old-fashioned cottage garden favourite, *Helleborus foetidus*, which produces yellow-green flowers from March to May. A mountain laurel, *Kalmia latifolia* growing nearby, would carry a rich pink glow into spring.

CULTIVATION Plant from autumn to spring in any moist, humus-enriched soil, in partial shade. Propagate by dividing the rhizomes in late summer.

Trollius × cultorum

GLOBE FLOWER

Height 2-3ft
Planting distance 1½-2ft
Best May-June

A garden relative of the buttercup, the globe flower has bold, goblet-shaped blooms in luminous hues that range from pale lemon-yellow to rich glowing orange. The hybrid *Trollius × cultorum* embraces a wide range of cultivars, including 'Orange Princess', with flowers of warm, coppery-orange, and 'Alabaster', the colour of clotted cream. One parent, *T. europaeus*, is a handsome wild plant with cool lemon flowers that enjoys marshy ground. The other, *T. asiaticus*, which has yellow flowers of a more golden colour, will tolerate slightly drier conditions.

Some kinds of globe flower are earlier than others, so planting a selection gives a lengthy season. One magnificent cultivar that flowers bright and early is *T. ledebourii* 'Golden Queen', which needs rich, moist ground.

Trollius × cultorum 'Canary Bird' has gleaming, buttercup blooms.

Its glowing orange flowers are made conspicuous by their long, elegant, petal-like stamens.

Globe flowers, especially those with orange tones, are useful for 'hot' colour schemes alongside *Euphorbia griffithii* 'Fireglow', *Lathyrus vernus,* doronicums, or *Potentilla recta.* In marshy ground they team well with kingcups and yellow flags, especially *Iris pseudacorus* 'Variegata', whose leaves also have yellow stripes, at least in spring, though they turn green in summer. The hot theme can be cooled with deep blue *Iris sibirica* – 'Blue King' say – to bridge the gap between spring and high summer.

CULTIVATION Plant from autumn to spring in any moist soil. Globe flowers will thrive in alkaline soil, and will flower in either dappled shade or in full sun. Propagate plants by division in early autumn. They also seed themselves freely.

Spring
ALPINES

BECAUSE so many alpines flower in the spring, it is all too easy to occupy all the available space with nothing but early flowering plants. Once it is appreciated that there are many others flowering in different seasons, a balanced use of alpine plants will follow.

Nevertheless, in the context of the garden as a whole, spring is when alpines can be called upon to make a special impact in celebrating the onset of the gardening year. At this time, when their jewel-like qualities are yet unshadowed by larger plants, they are at their best.

Androsace primuloides

Height 3-4in
Planting distance 9in
Best May-June

In May, bright pink flowers, each with a prominent yellow eye, peer up from a mat of loosely packed leaf rosettes. These are partially evergreen and can provide splendid all-the-year-round ground cover. In autumn, clumps of small silvery-haired leaves form button-like rosettes, and the larger summer leaves die away. The plant advances from the parent by runners, each bearing a small replica of the rosettes.

Although *Androsace primuloides* will cover the ground in an almost perfect carpet, it will allow dwarf spring bulbs such as *Narcissus asturiensis* with its

Androsace primuloides chumbyi is one of the toughest forms of a species from the Himalayas.

tiny yellow trumpets and the hooped petticoats of *N. bulbocodium* to push through and give a show of yellow before it puts on its own display.

CULTIVATION Plant in spring in full sun in very gritty, well-drained soil top dressed with gravel. Propagate by detaching rooted rosettes in early autumn for immediate replanting.

Arabis caucasica
(syn *A. albida*)

Height 6-9in
Planting distance 1-1½ft
Best February-May

On a dry wall, *Arabis caucasica* will spread steadily, smothering it with its white flowers and grey-green leaves. Let it grow in contrast with the violet-purple of the aubrietia hybrid 'Dr Mules' and the pure gold of *Alyssum saxatile* and your

garden wall will excite the admiration of everyone.

For a rock garden there are less invasive cultivars, such as *A. c.* 'Variegata', also white-flowered but with compact cushions of white-edged leaves that will bring cheer to the garden all winter, as will the double white and likewise fairly restrained 'Flore Pleno'.

CULTIVATION Plant in autumn or spring in well-drained soil and full sun. Propagate by stem cuttings after flowering, or by division in autumn.

Too invasive for a rock garden, *Arabis caucasica* is better suited to growing on a bank or wall.

The pink cultivar *Arabis caucasica* 'Rosabella' is considerably less invasive than the parent species.

Purple cloaks of aubrietia draping a dry-stone wall is one of the loveliest spring sights, especially when embroidered with daffodils and muscaris.

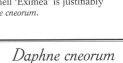

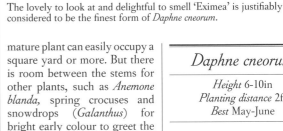

The flowers of *Daphne blagayana*, about ½in across, are borne in dense heads set amidst clusters of leaves at the ends of the branches.

The lovely to look at and delightful to smell 'Eximea' is justifiably considered to be the finest form of *Daphne cneorum*.

Aubrieta
Hybrids

Height 3-6in
Planting distance 1ft
Best April-May

Every year, more cultivars of aubrietia appear, each one, it is claimed, better than those that have gone before. The variations are usually in shades of red and purple, as are many of the old favourites which can still hold their own, such as 'Dr Mules' with its violet-purple flowers, the bright purple 'Godstone' and the long-lasting rose-purple 'Barker's Double'. All are evergreen, and form cushions of grey to green foliage smothered in bright flowers in the later weeks of spring.

Aubrietia hybrids are at their best growing in a wall or rock face, on a sloping bank or in containers. A striking plant to share the same conditions is lemon-flowered *Alyssum saxatile* 'Citrinum'.

CULTIVATION Plant in full sun on a wall, bank or slope in any soil between autumn and spring. Clip back the plants after flowering to ensure a good display the following year. To increase particular hybrids, take stem cuttings of growing shoots in June or July, including ½in of old wood, and root in moist sand; grow on until well established before planting out.

Daphne blagayana

Height 6-9in
Planting distance 2ft
Best March-April

In spring, the sight and smell of this dwarf shrub's dense creamy blooms is exquisite. Sparsely leaved stems splay out close to the ground to form a loose mat, and the tips produce clusters of leaves and heads of 20 or more flowers.

This daphne needs plenty of space to sprawl, as in time a mature plant can easily occupy a square yard or more. But there is room between the stems for other plants, such as *Anemone blanda*, spring crocuses and snowdrops (*Galanthus*) for bright early colour to greet the gardening year.

CULTIVATION Plant in autumn or spring in light soil with added leaf mould, coarse peat or good garden compost to help retain moisture. The daphne suffers if its roots dry out. A gritty slope or raised bed in light shade is a good planting site. *Daphne blagayana* has a natural tendency to layer itself, giving a constant supply of ready-rooted branchlets which need only to be severed and replanted in the autumn. Weight the branches with stones, or peg firmly to encourage rooting.

Daphne cneorum

Height 6-10in
Planting distance 2ft
Best May-June

Dense clusters of waxy, rose-pink flowers clad the *Daphne cneorum* in spring, and their heady fragrance is a delightful bonus. The shrub is low growing with small, neat, evergreen leaves on slim branches. The most widely cultivated form is *D. c.* 'Eximea', which is larger in stature and flower than the normal species. As a backdrop to the daphne is the softly green, new growth of *Pulsatilla vulgaris*, which has flowers resembling small mauve goblets. These are followed by silvery seed heads, to make an

Sprouting happily from the crevices of a dry-stone wall, *Erinus alpinus* is accompanied by the mat-forming foliage of *Pterocephalus perennis*, which later will bear pink-lavender flowers.

The deep-throated trumpets of *Gentiana acaulis* stand erect on stems little more than 3in high.

The intense blue of jewel-like *Gentiana verna* is accentuated by tufts of foliage.

admirable contrast. Nearby, the taller stems of *Hypericum olympicum* 'Citrinum' will provide a foliage contrast and bright yellow flowers in summer. CULTIVATION Plant in autumn or spring in a mixture of garden soil and peat, in a sunny site. Propagate by cutting semi-hardwood side shoots in late June or July, and rooting them in trays of sandy compost.

Erinus alpinus

FAIRY FOXGLOVE

Height 3-6in
Planting distance 6-10in
Best May-June

Though bearing no resemblance to the foxglove, the cheerful little *Erinus alpinus*

certainly has a fairy-like appearance with its hosts of starry, pink flowers and low tufts of leaves. It will grow almost anywhere, and is seen at its best when sprouting from the joints between paving or stone walls. Left to its own devices it will infiltrate the rock garden and path edges, yet seldom becomes a nuisance. Popular cultivars include *E. a.* 'Mrs Charles Boyle' with large, pink flowers, the clear, white 'Albus' and the carmine-flowered 'Dr Hanele'.

The glossy, evergreen *Globularia cordifolia*, with its tufted blue flowers, will have just the right quiet colour tones to blend with the soft pink of *E. alpinus*. To get the show under way, it would be hard to beat a random planting of tough, hardy *Crocus tommasinianus*, that seeds freely

to produce a solid mass of mauve, purple or lilac in late winter and early spring. CULTIVATION Plant in light, dry soil between autumn and spring. Propagate by seed in April, or by self-seeding.

Gentiana acaulis

TRUMPET GENTIAN

Height 4-6in
Planting distance 9-12in
Best April-July

Fanfares of deep blue trumpets thrust straight up from the squat clumps of evergreen leaves of *Gentiana acaulis*, and below the petals the flower tube is speckled with green. It is perhaps the most spectacular of the gentians and, though sometimes unpre-

dictable in flowering, is well worth a try for the hordes of lovely blooms it can produce.

Mass the trumpet gentians around drifts of dwarf narcissi and crocuses for a colourful start to spring, and follow with *Daphne cneorum* for a rose-pink contrast with the gentian's deep blue. On heavy, fertile soil that has good drainage, trumpet gentians can be vigorous enough to make an edging to a border that is almost heraldic in its richness of colour. CULTIVATION Plant in autumn in a warm, sunny position and in a good loamy soil. If flowering becomes unreliable, feed with a low-nitrogen content fertiliser. Division of mature clumps in July or August is the simplest and most reliable means of propagation.

Gentiana verna

SPRING GENTIAN

Height 3in
Planting distance 6-8in
Best April-May

Growing wild in the short turf of the mountains of Europe, these small gentians glow like jewels. For gardens, *Gentiana verna angulosa* is the best choice, with five-petalled flowers of the most intense and purest blue, emphasised by a snow-white, downy eye and tufts of pointed leaves.

This gentian looks and performs best in the controlled

Hepatica × media 'Ballardii' has soft, lavender-blue flowers which start to open in late winter.

The pale green leaves of Hepatica transsilvanica, with their delicately scalloped edges, compete for attraction with the blue-mauve flowers.

Pink, sugar-icing flowers of Lewisia cotyledon stand out against a grey stone wall, with Saxifraga moschata 'Cloth of Gold' as a companion.

(*Gentiana verna* cont) environment of a trough, a raised bed or part of the rock garden. It is a sociable plant and prospers in the company of other small mountain-dwellers such as thyme, *Pulsatilla vernalis,* with its pearl-white flowers, *Saxifraga oppositifolia,* or the soft blue *Cyananthus microphyllus.*

CULTIVATION Plant in spring or autumn in a mixture of equal parts loam, leaf mould and small limestone chippings. Propagate by fresh seed.

Hepatica transsilvanica

(syn *H. angulosa*)

Height 4-5in
Planting distance 1ft
Best February-April

The soft colours and character of this gentle plant from Romania are reminiscent of the little native anemone of British woodlands. A downy finish to the young leaves and stems lends a silvery sheen to the plant, and the blue-mauve flowers unfurl on slender stems from a bed of nearly evergreen leaves that are lobed at the edges.

The closely related *Hepatica nobilis* has flowers ranging from white to deep red and purple, and the hybrid *H.* × *media* 'Ballardii' bears blooms of an almost luminous mauve.

As woodland natives, hepaticas find a comfortable home in a small-scale setting in dappled shade. In such a position they can be used to follow autumn crocuses and such winter snowdrops as *Galanthus elwesii.*

CULTIVATION Plant in autumn in light soil with added peat or composted bark if the fibre content is low. Although hepaticas will tolerate a moderately sunny spot, they prefer light shade. Propagate by division in August or September, or sow seed immediately after it has been collected.

Lewisia cotyledon

Hybrids

Height 8-12in
Planting distance 12-15in
Best May-July

A touch of springtime in the Rockies comes to the British garden with *Lewisia cotyledon,* a glorious alpine from northern America where it grows on wind-swept rocky slopes. Its hybrids come in several colours, shapes and sizes, but all are formed of fleshy-leaved rosettes and sprays of striped, wide-open flowers. New varieties are offered from time to time, but three old varieties worth considering are: 'Sunset Strain' which ranges in colour from orange and yellow to apricot, pink and crimson; 'Phyllellia' which bears rose-coloured flowers throughout summer; and 'George Henley' with its heads of brick-red flowers.

A neat and compact plant, *L. cotyledon* is at its best planted in the crevices of a dry wall, combining with silver saxifrages and small campanulas.

CULTIVATION Plant on its side – it rots otherwise – in full sun. Propagate by taking side shoots in summer, and rooting in sand.

Phlox douglasii

Height 2-4in
Planting distance 1ft
Best May-June

With its profusion of blooms during spring, *Phlox douglasii* competes with aubrietias for flower power. The dense flower clusters sit close to the small, evergreen leaves and form mats of colour varying from white to rich violet. The white variety is

'Boothman's Variety' is a popular cultivar of *Phlox douglasii*.

Phlox subulata can be used to drench a rock garden in bold colour. Here the starry, lilac-blue flowers of 'Emerald Cushion Blue' make a wonderful contrast with the deep red of 'Scarlet Flame'.

With its compact form, *Primula frondosa* is an ideal plant for a tub display on a patio or terrace.

P. subulata 'Beauty of Ronsdorf' has a profusion of white blooms.

'Snow Queen', of medium height, and there is also a crimson form, 'Red Admiral'. 'Boothman's Variety' has clear, mauve blooms and the rich violet is found in 'Apollo'.

To create an interesting display, grow *P. douglasii* in a rock garden or dry wall, where it will combine well with the pink *Armeria juniperifolia* or white *Campanula cochleariifolia* 'Alba'.

CULTIVATION Plant between autumn and spring in a sunny position, in well-drained, fertile soil with a low lime content. Propagate as the last flowers fade by 1in long softwood cuttings rooted in a 50/50 peat-sand mixture. Pinch out the tips when growth is beginning, to encourage branching.

Phlox subulata

MOSS PHLOX

Height 4-6in
Planting distance 15-20in
Best May-June

For bold, billowing patches of spring colour, few plants can equal *Phlox subulata*. So dense are its blooms that the mats of spiky leaves are barely visible when the plant is in full flower.

There is an excellent range of varieties available, including 'G.F. Wilson' with clear blue flowers; 'Temiscaming' whose magenta flowers mass on low mats of foliage; the deep pink flowered 'Marjorie'; and lastly, 'Model', a neat plant with clear lilac blooms.

Before *P. subulata* bursts into life in late spring its rather flat, uninteresting foliage can be brightened by a planting of the yellow and red *Tulipa clusiana chrysantha* nearby. Then the rich blues and sparkling whites of *Campanula carpatica* can follow to illuminate the scene during the summer months.

CULTIVATION Plant in autumn or spring in a sunny position, close to large rocks and in fertile, well-drained soil. Propagate by taking 2-2½in cuttings from soft, new growth between June and September and insert the cuttings in equal parts of peat and sand in a cold frame.

Primula frondosa

Height 3-4in
Planting distance 6-8in
Best April-May

Easy to grow and delightful to behold, the perennial *Primula frondosa* is an early herald of spring, with clusters of 10-15 lilac-pink flowers appearing on each stem in April. Come rain, frost or snow its rosettes will continue to bloom, amid its powdered, grey-green leaves. As the first blooms fade, others take their place to maintain the glow of colour for several weeks.

Confirm the image of a mountainside meadow with *Scabiosa columbaria* 'Alpina Nana', which flowers in July, and one or two corms of *Cyclamen intaminatum* nearby, to greet the autumn with its exquisite white flowers.

CULTIVATION Plant between autumn and spring in a well-drained soil, in sun or partial shade. Lift clumps and divide after flowering in autumn every three years to maintain health and vigour. Look out for self-sown seedlings, which can be lifted and potted for setting out in their flowering positions at any time of spring or summer.

141

The velvety crimson petals and soft green leaves of *Primula × pubescens* 'Faldonside' bring a warm glow to the alpine garden.

Every leaf of *Primula marginata* has a silver lining, making it as valued for the sparkling effect of its foliage as for the charm of its flowers.

A harmonious blend of spring blues and mauves is created by the grape hyacinth, *Muscari armeniacum,* and *Pulsatilla vulgaris.*

Primula marginata

Height 4-6in
Planting distance 8-10in
Best April-May

In the French Maritime Alps *Primula marginata* threads its way along rocky crags, and in an English garden its mauve spring flowers will cloak a sheltered wall or vertical crevice in the rock garden. The leaves are just as attractive – powdered with a silvery dust and delicately outlined with a greater concentration of the silver at the margins. There are several cultivars, including 'Linda Pope' which has large, deep lavender-blue flowers.

The fine, white-plumed silver saxifrages *Saxifraga callosa* and *S. cochlearis* come from the same alpine environment as *P. marginata*, and so make excellent companions, especially as their blooms follow on from those of the primula.

CULTIVATION Plant in mid-autumn, in a spot sheltered from rain – by an overhanging rock, perhaps – to prevent the leaf powder being washed into smudges. Propagate by taking stem cuttings in early summer and root in moist sand.

Primula × pubescens

Height 4-6in
Planting distance 8-10in
Best April-May

There are almost 40 cultivars of this hybrid, covering a colour range of white, pink and purple to carmine-red and terracotta. Common to all is the crowded head of flowers at the top of a strong stem, standing proud of partially evergreen rosettes of slightly leathery leaves. The leaves vary a little in form, and some varieties are dusted with a waxy white powder of uncertain purpose called farina.

Among typical cultivars are 'Faldonside' – a neat plant with deep, dusky-pink, white-eyed flowers; 'Bewerley White' – a vigorous form with creamy-white flowers; and 'Rufus', which has pale green foliage and brick-red flowers.

Most of the flower colours tone well with the blue trumpets of *Gentiana acaulis*, and an adjacent planting of the golden-yellow *Ranunculus gramineus*, with its upright grassy leaves, will provide later colour and foliage contrast.

CULTIVATION As for *P. marginata*.

Pulsatilla vulgaris

PASQUE FLOWER

Height 10in
Planting distance 1ft
Best April-May

The common name is a reminder that this is the traditional flower of Easter – the

Set *Pulsatilla vulgaris* in an open position where the little mounds of goblet flowers amid finely dissected leaves can be seen to best effect.

IN SUMMER, *Pulsatilla vulgaris* bears glistening, globular seed heads.

word 'pasque' is derived from the Old French *pascal,* meaning 'of Easter'. A rich green dye obtained from the petals was once used to stain Easter eggs. On England's southern chalk downland the Pasque flower is now a rare wild treasure, but it is fortunately widely available in its cultivated forms.

The whole plant is covered with silken hairs that give a blurred softness to its outlines. The young leaves are pale green and heavily silvered, later darkening and expanding to form a spreading, feathery mound. The shallow goblets of gold-centred flowers appear in a number of colours including rust, purple, pink and white. Their charm persists even as summer approaches, and the dying blooms are transformed into glistening, globular seed heads.

When these have gone, the pulsatilla looks drab and requires plants with fresh green foliage and light-coloured blooms nearby, such as the evergreen, summer-flowering *Veronica teucrium*.

CULTIVATION Plant in autumn in any fertile, well-drained, but moisture-retentive soil in an open, sunny position. The pulsatilla has deep roots and does not transplant easily. To propagate, sow seed immediately after collection.

The modest flowers of *Viola odorata* 'Vaughan Fleming' contrast with the handsome leaves.

Viola biflora brings freshness of flower and leaf colour to the spring scene.

Viola biflora

Height 4-6in
Planting distance 8-10in
Best April-May

Vivid yellow flowers make *Viola biflora* a welcome spring arrival. The leafy stems are smooth and have a succulent appearance, while the handsome, heart-shaped leaves have slightly serrated edges.

The double-flowered snowdrop, *Galanthus nivalis* 'Flore Pleno', enjoys similar conditions and will be in bloom for several weeks before the viola. The crocus *Colchicum agrippinum* would give autumn colour.

CULTIVATION Plant in autumn in a porous soil rich in humus, lightly shaded against the sun and drying winds. Propagate by dividing clumps in autumn or after flowering.

Viola odorata

SWEET VIOLET

Height 4-6in
Planting distance 1ft
Best March-April

The fragrant and dainty sweet violet has been a symbol of love for thousands of years. It was the flower of Aphrodite, goddess of love, a connection not lost upon London's Piccadilly

Circus flower sellers who sold bunches beneath the statue of Eros, son of the goddess. As a garden plant it has been rather eclipsed by the larger, showy bedding pansies, but *Viola odorata* plays a valuable part as a charming ground-cover plant in softly shaded places. Tufts of heart-shaped evergreen leaves eventually form a small carpet by means of rooting runners.

In woodland fringes and hedgerows *V. odorata* can be found in the company of the wild wood anemone (*Anemone nemorosa*), and the combination looks well in the garden, too. For later interest, try placing a drift of autumn snowflakes (*Leucojum autumnale*) nearby for their delicate white and pink bells in September.

CULTIVATION Plant in autumn or spring, in any moisture-retentive soil. Add leaf mould or composted bark to sandy or heavy soils. Detach and replant self-rooting runners in July; if kept moist, they will be established by autumn.

Spring *BULBS*

THERE IS a distinction to be made, just as there is with trees and shrubs, between those bulbs which flower in spring and those which flower later. In general, spring-flowering bulbs come from cooler climates and do not need the summer baking that later bulbs do. This means that bulbs such as scillas, narcissi, erythroniums, anemones and fritillaries can be grown as they might in the wild, permanently planted in drifts or naturalised in patches among the grass of the lawn. Alternatively, use them with other plants, to create spring highlights, or to provide continuity of colour through the season.

Anemone blanda

Height 6in
Planting distance 6in
Best March

Small groups of *Anemone blanda*, with its blue, daisy-like flowers, make a delightful subject for the rock garden or mixed border. Or the plant can be naturalised in cropped grass beneath trees where it will spread to form an enchanting floral carpet. In its native Greece, *A. blanda* colours the hillsides in February; in Britain it will flower just as early.

Several forms of *A. blanda* are generally available from nurseries. Named varieties include 'White Splendour', the pink 'Charmer', magenta 'Radar'

Anemone blanda varieties 'Melange Deal' and 'White Splendour' make an attractive partnership.

and dark blue 'Atrocaerulea'.

The plant looks well with fancy forms of dwarf, hardy, evergreen ferns. For example, hart's-tongue fern (*Asplenium scolopendrium* 'Cristatum' or 'Undulatum') or feathery *Polypodium vulgare* 'Pulcherrimum'. In the mixed border, *A. blanda* can be used to provide flower colour beneath almost any deciduous shrub from February to April. If planting beneath a tree, choose one which has attractive young foliage, such as a birch or witch hazel.

CULTIVATION Buy dry tubers in autumn and plant immediately. Plant tubers 3in deep in any moist, well-drained soil in full sun or partial shade. They reproduce freely, form sizable clumps within a few years, and are easily propagated by division once the leaves wither.

BRIDGING THE SEASONS
WITH
Anemone blanda

RATHER IN THE manner of a painter composing a picture, so the gardener here has used forms and colour to compose an underplanting for a birch tree. The gardener's advantage is that his picture, unlike the artist's, will change with the seasons. The show opens in spring, as the silver birch begins to trail its young green leaves before the ever-present, evergreen, spotted leaves of *Aucuba japonica*. To its right is the spectacular, narrow, blue-grey column of *Juniperus virginiana* 'Skyrocket', while in front of the aucuba are young *Fritillaria imperialis* and *Tulipa* 'Keizerskroon', whose yellow and red flowers open flat in the sun.

The ground planting consists of starry *Anemone blanda*, intermingled with *Erica carnea*; the snowdrops among them have ceased to flower, but their slender, strap-like leaves still play a part.

In July, the picture changes considerably. The dark background remains the same, but all that is left of the anemones and the erica is their foliage. The place of the erica has been usurped by *Calluna vulgaris* 'Caerketton White', but the real attention-getter for summer is the swathe of *Lilium martagon*, the Turk's-cap lily, whose swept-back, rose-purple flowers have been so positioned as to conceal the fading foliage of the tulips and the crown imperials (*Fritillaria*).

The winter facet too has been planned for. Then, a thin covering of snow helps to highlight the aucuba's annual dramatic gesture – the bright scarlet berries that with luck will last through to spring. Beside them are the gaping seed pods of the martagon lilies and the foliage and dried-out blossoms of the calluna. Once again the erica is in flower, among which can be seen anemone leaves, just unfurling. True representatives of the season, though, are the generous clumps of snowdrops – *Galanthus nivalis* – rising above the heather. ❧

A carefully composed planting of bulbs, heathers and evergreens about a silver birch makes a colourful feature of a previously neglected corner.

IN SUMMER the planting is dominated by *Calluna vulgaris* and the rich exotic blooms of martagon lilies.

WINTER's offering is scarlet aucuba berries supported by *Erica carnea* and a drift of snowdrops.

The various shades of *Anemone coronaria* De Caen blend to make a brilliant impact in early spring.

Anemone coronaria
De Caen group

Height 8in
Planting distance 6in
Best March-April

These brightly coloured, poppy-like flowers are widely grown for cutting and are well known in florists' shops. They are native to the Mediterranean, and are available in vivid reds and purples as well as white. Named varieties include the scarlet 'Hollandia', blue-purple 'Mr Fokker', and 'The Bride', which is white.

The plants look best in isolation, massed together in tubs, outdoor containers and window boxes. They also make startling splashes of colour if scattered among the bold green columns

In a good year, *Anemone coronaria* De Caen may produce 20 or more flowers in a season.

Anemone nemorosa 'Robinsoniana' is one of the best anemones for open woodland planting.

(*Anemone coronaria* cont)
of well-established conifers. CULTIVATION Plant the raisin-like tubers during autumn immediately after buying. Set tubers 2-3in deep in any well-drained soil, and in a sheltered, sunny situation. The flowering period can be varied by planting at different seasons – in spring to provide summer flowers and in summer to ensure an autumn display. Propagate by dividing and replanting tuber clumps when they become crowded.

Anemone nemorosa

WOOD ANEMONE

Height 6-8in
Planting distance 6in
Best March-April

A charming, elegant, native anemone with white, starry, yellow-centred flowers on slender stems above fern-like foliage, tiny *Anemone nemorosa* revels in a shady, woodland setting. It is most useful for providing much of the early colour – blues, purples and pinks – in shady places.

In an ideal world, plant wood anemones in sizable colonies among established trees – not in grass, but where they will be seen in drifts pushing up through the vestiges of last year's fallen leaves.

In smaller gardens, use wood anemones to provide carpets of spring colour beneath shrubs. They will blend in with the colour displays of early flowering shrubs such as forsythia. If planting them in a flower bed or rock garden, use 'Royal Blue' or 'Vestal', which is white. The species itself is a little too invasive for such situations.

CULTIVATION Plant the root-stocks in autumn, in soil that includes plenty of well-rotted organic material. Choose a cool shaded place among established trees and shrubs. Propagate by dividing dormant rootstocks.

BRIDGING THE SEASONS
WITH
Anemone nemorosa

LIKE A STRING of pearls, this native woodland jewel will mix with and enhance almost anything. It is easy to grow, an eager coloniser, and its pinkish-tinged white flowers look particularly well with the spring foliage of such wood and shrubbery dwellers as hostas, Solomon's seal and ferns.

A classic role for anemones is for them to enhance the juvenile stage of another plant – in this case *Polygonatum × hybridum*, Solomon's seal. It is a particularly happy association, for the contrasting foliage shapes of the two plants perfectly complement one another and will continue to do so when the anemone flowers have gone and the leaves serve as a carpet below the rising polygonatums. Surely one of the loveliest of garden plants for a shady site, Solomon's seal produces its delightful little greeny-white bells in June, borne on graceful stalks clasped by sweetly curving leaves. It has always been considered a valuable plant. John Gerard, in his *Herball* of 1597, says 'The roots . . . taketh away any bruise gotten by fals or women's wilfulnesse, in stumbling upon their hasty husband's fistes . . .'

Stars of *Anemone nemorosa* light the leaves of *Polygonatum × hybridum*.

IN SUMMER, Solomon's seal flowers above a carpet of anemone foliage.

It is a curious fact, but the farther west you go in England and thence into Wales and Ireland, the greater is the chance of seeing the odd anemone in shades of blue, rather than their accustomed blushful white. Generally, in south-east England, only a hint of pink touches these flowers as they push through the woodland floor, or in this case, through the shining spears of *Hosta lancifolia*. As with all hostas, the leaves give long-lasting ground cover in shady spots that other plants have difficulty in colonising. But the flowers too have charm. *H. lancifolia* has deep lilac trumpets borne on slender stems; they are produced in September, when the anemones are only a memory.

Anemone nemorosa can also be used to lend importance to *Hosta lancifolia*.

IN AUTUMN, hosta flowers rear above anemones gone to ground.

For a perfect expression of the promise of spring, it would be hard to beat this picture of *Anemone nemorosa* lightening the muted colours of last year's fern fronds. Again, the anemones have been used to enhance associated woodland plants before they reach their best, but as it happens, these particular ferns, *Polystichum setiferum* and *Polypodium vulgare*, can be grown to fill almost any moderately shady corner of the garden. In early summer, when the anemone flowers have faded, the ferns begin to put out new fronds among the old. The contrast in greens and textures is striking, particularly in *Polystichum setiferum*, whose young, unfurling fronds are of an exquisitely soft hue. ❧

Bright *Anemone nemorosa* pays a spring compliment to last year's ferns.

IN SUMMER, unfurling fronds mingle with the anemones' foliage.

Light and dainty *Chionodoxa luciliae* hugs the rough contours of a cypress trunk, and is neatly confined by a lawn in a perfect partnership.

In a moist and shady spot, lily of the valley, *Convallaria majalis,* is a modest but harmonious companion for the bold *Hosta plantaginea.*

Chionodoxa luciliae

GLORY OF THE SNOW

Height 6in
Planting distance 2-4in
Best March, early April

Vigorous and reliable, *Chiono-doxa luciliae* spreads quickly to form a shimmering spring carpet among all kinds of shrubs. Its spikes of star-shaped blue flowers have conspicuous white centres, and its leaves are narrow and grass-like. There are also white and pink-flowered cultivars.

Because it likes moist condi-tions, *C. luciliae* makes a good companion for shrub willows like *Salix hastata* 'Wehrhahnii', which bears large, attractive catkins in spring. Its tolerance of a wide range of conditions also makes the chionodoxa useful for growing in narrow borders – as between fence and drive – that are unsuitable for most plants for much of the year. Its rapid spread and scanty foliage also make it suitable for colonising rock gardens, where it goes well with yellow alyssum (*Alyssum saxatile*), which follows on flowering from April to June.

Where space is particularly limited, try *C. sardensis*, whose

Chionodoxa sardensis is later flowering and spreads less rapidly than *C. luciliae.*

flowers are of a richer blue than those of *C. luciliae*, which is equally good for naturalising. It also grows well in containers, and looks good in a pocket of the alpine garden – particularly against a grey-white back-ground of limestone. It is toler-ant of alkaline conditions.

CULTIVATION Plant dry bulbs in the autumn as soon as possible after purchase. Put them in 2-3in deep in large groups in any well-drained soil, even where it is full of shrub roots – competition rarely presents a problem. Propagate by division after flowering, if you wish to start a new colony elsewhere.

Convallaria majalis

LILY OF THE VALLEY

Height 5-8in
Planting distance 6in
Best April-May

Arching stems of the sweet-scented, snow-white bell-like flowers of this popular plant grow out from pairs of broad, lance-shaped green leaves. They are occasionally followed by rounded orange or red fruits. The plant can spread rapidly by slender rhizomes, eventually forming sizable colonies, and is excellent for carpeting the soil beneath deciduous shrubs. By autumn the foliage has died away. There are several culti-vars, including 'Plena' (double-flowered), 'Variegata' (with gold-striped leaves), 'Rosea' (pink), and the large white 'Fortin's Giant', which flowers 10-14 days after the species.

Traditionally, lily of the valley is grown alone in a narrow border, and for many gardeners this is still the most effective way to grow it. It also looks good beneath the flowering currant (*Ribes san-guineum*). But to bring colour to the area from late summer to early autumn, *Crocosmia* hybrids

For best effect, naturalise *Crocus vernus* cultivars as in this mixture of dark 'Purpureus Grandiflorus', 'Striped Beauty' and white 'Jeanne d'Arc'.

Beneath dark-leaved rhododendrons, the Spanish bluebell, *Endymion hispanicus*, runs wild with *Hosta fortunei* 'Albopicta'. Later, the hosta darkens and spreads over the fading bluebells, and produces summer flowers.

could push through the convallaria foliage to display their arching stems of flowers.

CULTIVATION Plant short pieces of rhizome (pips) in autumn. Choose an open site in moist but well-drained soil containing plenty of well-rotted organic matter. Put each pip just below the soil surface, with its pointed end uppermost. Propagate by separating pips in autumn.

Gleaming goblets of *Crocus vernus* 'Purpureus Grandiflorus' look splendid clustered in pots or tubs.

Crocus vernus
Varieties

Height 4-5in
Planting distance 3in
Best March

Crocus vernus, star of the alpine meadows, was the forerunner of all the many named large Dutch cultivars. Affectionately known by gardeners as the 'big boys', they provide bright drifts of colour every spring. Their handsome, cup-shaped, upright flowers vary in colour from white to lilac and deep purple, and are often strikingly veined with dark purple.

The bold goblet blooms of the 'big boys' are best seen against soft, green grass – perhaps mixed with groups of the bright yellow narcissus 'February Gold'. They also look good on their own in containers, and even better if planted around the bases of trees or among deciduous shrubs.

CULTIVATION Plant crocus corms in early autumn, as soon as they are available. Plant them 3in deep (up to 6in in light soils) in any moist, free-draining situation, ideally in an open, grassy spot. Crocuses multiply naturally, but can be propagated by removing young corms from established plants. Lift the plants when the leaves turn yellow and replant the corms.

Endymion hispanicus
SPANISH BLUEBELL

Height 12-15in
Planting distance 6in
Best April-May

This is the best garden bluebell. It is bigger than the native bluebell, easier to grow, and soon forms large majestic clumps. Cultivars include the snowy 'White Triumphator', deep pink 'Queen of the Pinks', the clear blue 'Myosotis' and deep blue 'Excelsior'.

Bluebells do best beneath the shade of trees and shrubs. They suit a wild garden admirably, where they will happily thrive untended for many years, especially when grown with the red campion (*Silene dioica*). In a mixed border, bluebells make a wonderful impression with groups of polyanthus.

CULTIVATION Plant bulbs as soon as they are available in early autumn. Put them 3in deep in any fertile soil that is moderately moist. The plant prospers in most situations, but prefers a little shade. Propagate from young bulbs, which are produced quite freely. Lift and divide congested clumps when flower quality diminishes.

Erythronium revolutum 'Pink Beauty' has yellow-centred flowers and mottled leaves.

With its delicate yellow flowers reminiscent of the roofs of oriental temples, the hybrid *Erythronium* 'Pagoda' is well named.

Erythronium revolutum

AMERICAN TROUT LILY

Height 1ft
Planting distance 4-6in
Best April-May

The American trout lily, from western North America, is named for its handsome green leaves, which have trout-like brown and white mottling. They are surmounted by spikes of pale to deep pink blossoms with attractively reflexed petals. This is an ideal plant for a shady mixed border, and it will also prosper in damp, free-draining soil by a stream or pool.

Although the plant looks good on its own, it is most effective when scattered among low-growing plants of the woodland floor like the clear, bright *Geranium endressii* 'Wargrave Pink', or the golden variegated coral berry (*Symphoricarpos orbiculatus* 'Variegatus'). Or try it among a group of giant Himalayan cowslips (*Primula florindae*), which burst into growth as the erythronium blossoms fade.

Another attractive species is *Erythronium tuolumnense*, that hails from the banks of California's Tuolumne River. It bears glossy green leaves and upright flower spikes with as many as ten pendent, backward-curving, bright yellow blossoms on each. This erythronium is quite often grown among deciduous shrubs such as small-leaved rhododendrons, where it brightens low-level gaps in spring. The flowers have a distinctly Eastern flavour, and so will fit in well with an oriental planting theme. Fo. example, they could be grouped to advantage beneath some of the attractive varieties of the Japanes maple (*Acer palmatum*) or the Chinese *Acer griseum*. Alternatively they will look well in an oriental urn placed beside a pond or stream.

CULTIVATION Plant in early autumn, 3-4in deep in moist, well-drained soil rich in organic matter, and in partial shade. Propagate by periodically lifting and dividing tubers from well-established clumps.

Fritillaria imperialis

CROWN IMPERIAL

Height 2-3ft
Planting distance 1-1½ft
Best April

The showy, stately crown imperial is distinguished by a topknot of green, leafy bracts above its cluster of handsome bell flowers. Cultivars include orange-red 'Aurora', bronze-red 'Rubra', and lemon 'Lutea'.

Few modern cottage gardens are without a treasured group of crown imperials, which provide excellent early colour. Their bright colours, tall stature and rapid growth make them difficult to mix with other flowers, but a mass of low-growing spring flowers such as *Viola labradorica* at their feet accentuates their dramatic beauty. They also look well against such dark evergreens as *Osmanthus delavayi* and *Ilex aquifolium*.

CULTIVATION Plant the potato-like bulbs in early autumn, as soon as they are available. Put them 8in deep on their sides in well-drained but moisture-retentive soil, and in an open site. Propagate by offsets taken in autumn, or by separating clumps as soon as the foliage dies down and then replanting immediately.

Like a gathering of noble lords, a group of tall *Fritillaria imperialis* 'Aurora' thrust their crowned heads above a mixed border.

Purple *Fritillaria meleagris* are here mixed with the white-flowered variety 'Aphrodite'.

The spiky blue heads of grape hyacinths punctuate the pale blue of *Ipheion uniflorum*.

Carefully selected mixed colour groups of Dutch hyacinths share a border edge with red and yellow-flushed *Tulipa kaufmanniana*.

Fritillaria meleagris

SNAKE'S-HEAD FRITILLARY

Height 8-12in
Planting distance 4-6in
Best April

The species gets its common name from the chequered patterning that looks like scales and from the cup-shaped flowers that are said to resemble a *fritillus* – a Roman dice box. Purple or lilac, they nod gracefully on slender stems above narrow, grey-green leaves. Varieties include white-flowered 'Aphrodite' and 'Alba' (veined green) and violet-red 'Saturnus'.

A native of water meadows, the fritillary will flourish in a damp pocket on a rock garden, but is most at home in a grassy setting. Grown alongside a group of the hooped-petticoat narcissus (*N. bulbocodium conspicuus*), it can bring a touch of an alpine meadow to the smallest suburban garden. It is happy in quite damp conditions, and looks well with its pendent blossoms reflected in a pool CULTIVATION Plant bulbs as soon as they are available in early autumn. Put them 4in deep in any moist soil, and in any situation, though they do best in sun. The fritillary can be propagated from offsets which are produced freely, but established clumps are best left undisturbed. Better to buy fresh bulbs for new plantings.

Hyacinthus orientalis
Cultivars

DUTCH HYACINTH

Height 8-12in
Planting distance 9-12in
Best April

The wild hyacinth (*Hyacinthus orientalis*) is now rare. Most of those in gardens are its large-flowered progeny, with dense spikes of brightly coloured, highly fragrant blossoms and stiff, strap-like green foliage. Among the most popular of these are the soft yellow 'City of Haarlem', the pure white 'L'Innocence', as well as 'Pink Pearl' and 'Delft Blue'.

Because of their stately, stylish appearance, hyacinths look best in a formal setting. Grow them in tubs, window boxes or sunny beds, or in groups of a single colour among tulips or pansies. The modern multi-flowered types, which have one or more stems, can be naturalised in grass.
CULTIVATION Plant 4-6in deep in autumn, in any light, well-drained but moisture-retentive soil, and in a sunny situation. Propagation is by offsets, but it is a lengthy business and it is really better to buy fresh bulbs each year. However, hyacinths grown in the garden are generally longer-lived than those that have spent their brief existences in pots.

Ipheion uniflorum

Height 5-8in
Planting distance 3-4in
Best April-May

Face-up, soft blue, starry flowers and grassy foliage make this South American plant one of the nicest small bulbs for massing in a sunny rock garden or dryish border. The bulbs and pale green leaves have a garlic-like smell, but the 1½-2in wide flowers are sweetly scented. Cultivars include 'Wisley Blue', 'Violaceum', 'Froyle Mill' and 'Caeruleum'.

Ipheions do well beside a south or west-facing wall – you might try them below wall-trained fruit trees or shrubs to provide colour – or in front of a border of mixed shrubs. As the plants tend to look scruffy after flowering, grow them with taller, later companions such as *Primula auricula* or *Pulsatilla vulgaris* which have good summer leaves, or with dwarf annuals like ageratum.
CULTIVATION Plant bulbs in early autumn as soon as they are available. Put them 2in deep in free-draining, gritty soil in an open, sunny but sheltered position. Propagate by lifting and dividing established clumps, or remove offsets during the dormant period.

With flowers larger than those of the snowdrop, *Leucojum vernum* does best in moist soil.

Leucojum vernum

SPRING SNOWFLAKE

Height 6-10in
Planting distance 6in
Best March

The spring snowflake is more robust than its name suggests, and looks like a tall snowdrop. Its white bowl-shape blossoms hang bell-like above erect, fresh green, strap-like leaves. *Leocojum vernum carpathicum* has white petals which are tipped with greenish-yellow.

A lovely plant for growing beside a stream or pool, the spring snowflake enjoys damp conditions. It tolerates both sun and shade, so use it to brighten moist, dappled corners where ferns hold sway. Or grow it among groups of later-flowering, moisture-loving perennials such as giant cowslips

The grape hyacinth *Muscari armeniacum* grows and spreads rapidly, and will soon provide clumps of vivid blue among other spring flowers.

(*Primula florindae*), filipendulas and ligularias.

CULTIVATION Plant bulbs as soon as they are available in autumn, 3-4in deep in any soil that is moist in spring, in sun or shade, and in a site that will not be disturbed for a number of years. Propagate by lifting and dividing clumps when they become overcrowded and flowers diminish in quantity and quality.

Muscari armeniacum

GRAPE HYACINTH

Height 8-10in
Planting distance 3-4in
Best April

Grape hyacinths have a host of white-rimmed blue flowers closely packed on a single, spike-like stem. Named varieties of this grape hyacinth from Turkey include 'Cantab' (pale

blue) and 'Heavenly Blue'.

Plant these hyacinths extensively in less formal areas, most especially among well-established shrubs; they tolerate root-filled soil and are capable of colonising under difficult circumstances. Use them to carpet the ground beneath bright spring-flowering shrubs such as *Forsythia × intermedia* 'Spectabilis', *F.* 'Beatrix Farrand' or *F. × intermedia* 'Lynwood', so that they rise in golden mounds from blue seas of grape hyacinths. Supplement them with a white foam of *Ornithogalum nutans*.

CULTIVATION Plant bulbs in autumn, 3in deep, in any ordinary garden soil in sun or partial shade. Do not remove fading foliage until it has turned yellow. Colonies rapidly establish themselves. Propagate by dividing clumps that have become overcrowded.

Narcissus

The trumpeted golden daffodils are the stalwarts of the spring scene in town and country. But there is a host of hybrids that has extended the colour range to include combinations of cream, yellow, orange, and even salmon-pink. Some cultivars are big and bold, others are small enough to make an important in-scale contribution to window box and rock garden displays.

INFORMALITY THE KEY

Most bulbs take readily to naturalising in grass, and are reliable, adaptable and easy to grow. The bulbs may be left undisturbed in the soil for at least three years, and will produce an increase of flowers each year. A planting of different narcissus cultivars whose flowering periods overlap will bring fresh, bright colour to the garden for a good three months of the year.

The opportunities for stunning planting associations are legion, but informality is the key to the most effective use of daffodils and narcissi. Plant irregular groups of each cultivar in settings that reflect the woodland origins of their wild ancestors. Robust cultivars like 'Dutch Master' can push through a light carpet of ivy, such as *Hedera helix* 'Glacier'.

PICKING PARTNERSHIPS

Heathers, too, will make good ground-level companions; *Erica carnea* and *E. erigena* in winter and spring, perhaps, with *Calluna vulgaris* to follow in late summer. Pick out the colours

that predominate in the foliage and bark of particular shrubs and trees, and plant complementary narcissi beneath. Yellow daffodils could be set against *Hedera colchica* 'Goldheart', for example, or cream cultivars like 'Thalia' and 'Ice Follies' beneath the unfurling soft greys and whites of *Pyrus salicifolia* 'Pendula'. In a mild season, the gold-toned foliage of *Spiraea japonica* 'Goldflame'

Cream and yellow *Narcissus* 'Jack Snipe' decorates a stone seat when the weather is yet too chilly for sitting out in the garden.

Groups of *Narcissus* 'Dutch Master' help to dress a rather plain gate while proclaiming spring's arrival to the garden as a whole.

could coincide with an orange and gold narcissus such as 'Suzy'. The darkness and density of many an evergreen shrub can be lightened, and its personality changed, by a pool of narcissi at its base – 'Tete-a-Tete' or 'Minnow' among dwarf conifers, for example, or big yellow daffodils with *Mahonia × media* hybrids. The winter-flowering evergreen, *Viburnum tinus*, will be producing its white, pink-budded blooms when the first narcissi appear, to form a lasting partnership throughout the spring.

CULTIVATION

Plant narcissi from September onwards and no later than the end of October. Dappled shade is ideal, but full sun is tolerated as long as the soil is rich and reasonably moist. Simply scatter the bulbs and plant them where they fall. Allow the plants to grow on for at least six weeks after flowering before cutting the leaves back. Propagate by dividing clumps of bulbs after the leaves have died and replant in autumn.

In an old-fashioned garden, complete with mini-pagoda, nothing could be more fitting than old-fashioned narcissus cultivars around a liquidambar, with a carpet of anemones and eranthis.

Defining and illuminating a path's edge is a mingling of *Narcissus* 'Actaea' with *Primula vulgaris*.

A random mixture of narcissi encompasses the late winter bareness of the deciduous shrub *Rubus biflorus*, with its blue-white stems.

Like a bevy of ladies in a flying hurry, a group of *Narcissus* 'Beryl' appears to be rushing past the shrub *Pieris japonica* 'Blush'.

'Ice Follies'
Height 16in.
Best late March.

'Golden Ducat'
Height 20in.
Best late March.

'Dutch Master'
Height 18in. Best late March.

'Actaea'
Height 16in.
Best mid-April.

'Minnow'
Height 7in.
Best April.

'Barrett
Browning'
Height 16in.
Best early April.

'Tete-a-Tete'
Height 9in. Best April.

'Jenny' Height 9in.
Best March-early April.

'February Gold'
Height 14in.
Best March.

154

Reflections of spring sunshine

Let informal groups of the cheerful daffodils and narcissi
introduce all the optimism of spring to your garden. Create pools of
brightness among shrubs, bring drifts of sunshine colours to the dappled shade
beneath trees, or use the delicate grace and symmetry of the smaller forms
as highlights in rock gardens and window boxes.

Photographed in March at Springfield Gardens, Spalding, Lincolnshire.

'St Keverne'
Height 18in.
Best mid-March.

'Passionale'
Height 16in. Best mid-April.

'Suzy'
Height 18in.
Best late April.

'Cheerfulness'
Cream and
yellow forms;
scented.
Height 14in.
Best mid-April.

'Thalia'
Height 12in.
Best mid-April.

'Jack Snipe'
Height 9in.
Best March.

'Professor
Einstein'
Height 12in.
Best early April.

A native of the tougher regions of western Asia, *Puschkinia scilloides* will fit in almost anywhere.

Puschkinia scilloides

STRIPED SQUILL

Height 4-6in
Planting distance 3in
Best March-April

Pale blue petals with a conspicuous darker blue central stripe nobly distinguish the star-shaped flowers of the striped squill. Up to six blooms are clustered on one stem rising from strap-shaped leaves, rather like those of a hyacinth.

The striped squill is a good rock-garden plant, especially when allowed to colonise, and looks particularly attractive in the grey-white of a limestone rock garden. In a border, the plant blends well with any of the purple varieties of *Aubrieta deltoidea* or the pasque flower, *Pulsatilla vulgaris*, all of which will link late spring to early summer. Plant the striped squill

The early waking, china-blue forerunner of spring, *Scilla bifolia* here makes a lively and congenial companion for *Aubrieta* 'J.S. Barker'.

too with the low-growing deciduous shrub *Potentilla fruticosa*, whose leaves can become the point of attraction as the squill fades.

CULTIVATION Plant bulbs 3in deep in autumn in any well-drained soil, preferably in full sun, though partial shade will do. Leave the foliage to die down naturally. Propagate by periodically lifting and re-distributing the bulbs to ensure a goodly population.

Scilla bifolia

ALPINE SQUILL

Height 4-6in
Planting distance 3in
Best March

This hardy squill has at least ten small, starry, blue flowers set on a wiry stem above strap-shaped leaves. Cultivars of other colours are 'Alba' (white) and 'Rosea' (pink). The alpine squill

Scilla sibirica 'Atrocerulea' is of a blue so electrifying that it will illuminate the entire border.

is charming on its own, particularly in a pocket top-dressed with fine grit in a rock garden. Alternatively, grow it through ground-cover plants, such as acaena or moss phlox (*Phlox subulata*).

Its relation, the Siberian squill, *Scilla sibirica*, has brilliant blue bells that make a startling splash of colour in the garden in early spring. It makes an effective carpet in a shrub border, beside *Daphne mezereum* for example, and looks well in grass that later on will be shaded by the foliage of deciduous shrubs. Try it too with hellebores, or among old-fashioned shrub roses.

CULTIVATION Plant bulbs 2-3in deep in autumn, in any free-draining soil, and in sun or part shade. Do not remove foliage until it turns yellow. Propagate by dividing established clumps of bulbs after the leaves die down.

The feminine grace of *Tulipa clusiana* has justly earned it the popular title of lady tulip.

Tulipa clusiana

LADY TULIP

Height 9-12in
Planting distance 3in
Best April

The elegant lady tulip has grey-green leaves edged with exquisite red and white flowers flushed and striped with pink. When the pointed petals are open, each bloom is star shaped. There is also a slightly shorter, red-flushed yellow form, *Tulipa clusiana chrysantha*.

The best place for this tulip is in a bed with other plants that have greyish leaves, such as purple sage (*Salvia officinalis* 'Purpurascens'). It also makes a splendid group in a container.

CULTIVATION Plant bulbs in

Despite appearances, Greigii hybrids, such as 'Cape Cod', can withstand spring winds.

autumn, 3-4in deep in free-draining, gritty soil and in full sun. Leave foliage until faded. Propagate by dividing natural-ised clumps, but in formal beds replace bulbs yearly.

Tulipa
Greigii hybrids

Height 9-12in
Planting distance 6in
Best April

The vivid colours of these hybrid cultivars range from bright orange-scarlet, through mixtures of apricot, yellow and pink. The blossoms are cup-shaped, rising on strong stems from broad grey-green leaves mottled with red and purple. Among the best cultivars to grow are orange-scarlet 'Red Riding Hood', carmine and yellow 'Oriental Beauty', primrose-yellow 'Zampa', and

'Red Riding Hood' is another favourite Greigii hybrid.

yellow-margined red 'Plaisir'.

Sturdy Greigii tulips are well suited to exposed gardens and windy places, whether natural-ised or in formal beds. Use different cultivars in single groups of colour. Good com-panion plants to intermingle with the tulips are grape hya-cinths and yellow alyssum.
CULTIVATION As for *Tulipa clu-siana*. Greigii hybrids are gen-erally long-lasting, except in the heavier clay soils.

The shape of the flowers of *Tulipa kaufmanniana* has earned it the name of water-lily tulip. A popular hybrid is 'Heart's Delight'.

Tulipa kaufmanniana
WATER-LILY TULIP

Height 6-10in
Planting distance 6in
Best March

With its short stems, handsome grey-green leaves and cream and pink cup-like blossoms, often with vivid orange centres, this tulip from Turkestan indeed looks very like a water lily. It is

one of the earliest tulips to flower. The hybrids derived from it are superb, displaying its compact growth and early flowering blooms of almost every colour imaginable. Popular cultivars are 'Cesar Franck', red edged with yellow, lemony 'Chopin', 'Johann Strauss', striped white and red, and the pink and yellow 'Heart's Delight'. Then there are the 'royals', graceful and clear-hued; creamy 'White Emperor', shining

Starry *Tulipa kaufmanniana* contrasts well with the lowered heads of *Narcissus asturiensis*.

'Orange Emperor' and 'Red Emperor', pure glowing scarlet.

The brilliant colours of the water-lily tulips are fine for most beds and borders, and they are also very welcome as patio container fillers. They can be left to naturalise in close-mown grass, and give a cheerful air to a rock garden if planted in groups among spring-flowering peren-nials like spring cinquefoil, *Potentilla tabernaemontani*, with its bright yellow flowers.
CULTIVATION As for *Tulipa clu-siana*. Do not clear foliage away until it has withered.

Tulipa tarda

Height 4-6in
Planting distance 3in
Best April

One of the smallest tulips, *Tulipa tarda* has four or five flowers clustered together on a

157

The dwarf *Tulipa tarda* with its flower clusters and glossy foliage makes an exuberant display in a garden urn or tub.

(*Tulipa tarda* cont)
stem. They are yellow with white-tipped petals that shine out from glossy green leaves.

These lovely dwarf tulips look marvellous in tubs or other outdoor containers, and are ideal for rock gardens or sunny borders. The purple pasque flower (*Pulsatilla vulgaris*) makes a good companion. Or plant them round dwarf evergreens like *Ilex crenata* or low-growing berberis such as *Berberis thunbergii* 'Atropurpurea' and *B.* × *rubrostilla*.

CULTIVATION As for *Tulipa clusiana*. The plant often dies out in wet soils, but is usually long-lived elsewhere.

Tulipa

A Persian legend tells of a youth who, on hearing that his love had died, hurled himself over a cliff; red tulips grew where his blood spilt. And so red tulips became a symbol of perfect love, just as yellow tulips came to represent hopeless love, and purple tulips, undying love in the language of flowers.

In nature, tulips extend from the eastern Mediterranean to Japan. They were introduced to Europe when the Ottoman Turks planted them in the gardens of Constantinople in the 16th century. Since then, selection and hybridisation has led to an overwhelming range of named varieties. The garden hybrids have a symmetry and simplicity of form that has made tulips popular subjects in the decorative arts. They can add the same formal decorative touch to borders – or to the house as cut flowers.

ELEGANT AND EXOTIC
Most weather resistant of all are the early flowering hybrids, which tend to be short-stemmed and sturdy, with single or double blooms. In the mid and late seasons come the classic, tall-stemmed cultivars, categorised according to flower shape and colours – from the erect satin-petalled goblets of the

Just about all the cottage-garden favourites are here in this charming and deceptively casual setting, with tulips planted seemingly at random near a wall draped with daphne (on the left), and a pale pink *Aethionema grandiflorum* (right).

Darwin and Triumph hybrids to the elegant lily-flowered and exotically fringed Parrot groups.

PLANTING WITH PERENNIALS

Tulips can be treated like annuals – lifted and replanted or replaced annually, or they can be left undisturbed in the ground for several years. If they stay in the ground, the foliage must be left to draw nourishment for the following year's growth, after the flowers have died, so plant them in the first place among sun-loving perennials which will take over in summer. *Pyrethrum roseum* cultivars, with their vibrantly coloured daisy flowers, and *Polemonium caeruleum* or *P. foliosissimum*, all have the bonus of attractive foliage which will disguise but not overwhelm the tulip leaves. *Cheiranthus cheiri* and pelargonium cultivars would continue strong colours into the summer months.

CULTIVATION

Plant bulbs in autumn so that the plants have time to build up a strong root system before cold weather sets in. Plant bulbs that are to remain in the ground undisturbed for a number of years at three to four times the depth of the bulb. This allows overplanting with summer annuals and leads to longer-lasting colonies and more substantial blossoms. The site should be open and sunny, in any free-draining soil. Deadhead blooms as the first petals fall, and top dress the soil with coarse bone meal in autumn. To propagate, divide established groups of bulbs.

Tulipa 'Gold Medal' and the rich red 'Greuze' dominate a border busy with forget-me-nots.

The variegated foliage of hostas makes a pleasing foil for the lily-flowered *Tulipa* 'Aladdin'.

Nothing could brighten a shady corner more than a tubful of *Tulipa* 'Apricot Beauty'.

Trooping the tulip colour

Hybrid tulips can be rallied into smart parades in bed or border,
their symmetrical flowers providing painter's-palette blobs of colour.
Together, the different cultivars span a flowering season from March until May.
But the attraction of these hybrids lies not only in the satin-petalled goblets
of the blooms at their peak. Buds, lined with a hint of colour to come,
stand sentinel-like on pencil stems, and later become the mature blooms
that are the open stars of the lily tulips, the luxuriance
of the doubles, or the startling hearts of the singles.

Photographed in April at Springfield Gardens, Spalding, Lincolnshire.

'Amulet'
Triumph.
Best mid-April
Height 22in.

'Apricot Beauty'
Triumph.
Best mid-April.
Height 16in.

'Charles'
Single early.
Best mid-April.
Height 15in.

'Dutch Princess'
Triumph.
Best late April.
Height 22in.

'Monte Carlo'
Double early.
Best mid-April.
Height 16in.

'Esperanto'
Viridiflora.
Best late April.
Height 9in.

'Snow Queen'
Double early.
Best mid-April.
Height 11in.

'Keizerskroon'
Single early.
Best mid-April.
Height 12in.

'Golden Artist'
Viridiflora.
Best mid-May.
Height 10in.

'Queen of
the Night'
Single late.
Best mid-May.
Height 24in.

'Red Parrot'
Parrot.
Best mid-May.
Height 22in.

'Flaming Parrot'
Parrot.
Best mid-May.
Height 26in.

'Marilyn'
Lily-flowered.
Best early May.
Height 22in.

'Gudoshnik'
Darwin hybrid.
Best late April.
Height 26in.

'Prominence'
Triumph.
Best mid-April.
Height 18in.

'Hermione'
Double late.
Best late April.
Height 20in.

'Pax'
Darwin hybrid.
Best late April.
Height 22in.

'Estella Rijnveld'
Parrot.
Best mid-May.
Height 24in.

'Aladdin'
Lily-flowered.
Best early May.
Height 20in.

161

Spring
BIENNIALS

◆

ANNUALS AND biennials have a limited time in which to germinate, grow, flower, set seed and die. Even for a good display in summer, gardeners need to start their annuals into growth as early as possible. Spring-flowering annuals are few, simply because of the shortness of time that exists for them to make any headway after sowing. The part that the summer annuals will later play is carried out by spring-flowering bulbs such as crocuses and narcissi. Just one or two biennials, however, with their two year life cycle, can add that extra element to the bulb-dominated spring scene.

An edging of the daisy *Bellis perennis* echoes the tulip colour, while a creamy-yellow wallflower binds the display together.

Cheiranthus 'Golden Bedder' with golden-eyed polyanthus.

Cheiranthus cheiri

WALLFLOWER

Height 9-18in
Planting distance 9-12in
Best April-May

A crowd of wallflowers with their velvet-soft flowers and rich, old-fashioned scent evokes cottage gardens and the first balmy days of late spring. Although strictly a hardy, shrubby perennial, especially when growing on walls, wallflowers are short-lived and give of their best if they are grown as biennials.

The species has given rise to a host of free-flowering cultivars that vary in height and cover an extensive range of colour. The taller cultivars, 1½ft high or

In this traditional combination of wallflowers and tulips, the profusion of *Cheiranthus cheiri* flowers softens the starkness of the tall tulip stems.

more, include 'Blood Red', 'Carmine King', the red-purple 'Purple Queen', very deep crimson 'Vulcan' and rich scarlet 'Fire King'; also 'Golden Monarch', 'Cloth of Gold', 'Primrose Monarch' and 'Ivory White'. 'Persian Carpet' is a fine mix of subtle shades. Smaller cultivars, 6-12in high, include 'Orange Bedder', 'Golden Bedder', 'Primrose Bedder' and 'Scarlet Bedder'.

Plant wallflowers in the gaps between shrubs and perennials with a nostalgic ring to them – for instance, a rambling rose like 'Mme Alfred Carriere', *Paeonia lactiflora, Papaver orientale* 'Mrs Perry' or 'Perry's White'. A bank of Michaelmas daisies nearby could continue the country-garden theme through to autumn.

CULTIVATION Sow seed outdoors in shallow drills between late May and July; when the seedlings are large enough to handle, transplant them 6in apart in nursery rows, and bed out young plants to their final positions in autumn for flowering the following spring. The ideal soil is light, well drained and alkaline in a sunny position. If you have a rich soil, it is advisable to sow the seed as late as possible, otherwise oversized plants may develop which have weak root systems that are vulnerable to frost. When the plants are 6-9in high, pinch out the tips to encourage branching growth.

Myosotis

FORGET-ME-NOT

Height 1ft
Planting distance 9in
Best April-May

A myriad tiny flowers, each one brightened by a white or yellow eye, make a haze of lightly scented blue. *Myosotis alpestris* is a wild plant of the highlands of Britain and Europe. Small, tough and bushy, it is a short-

Biennials *Myosotis sylvestris* and *Cheiranthus cheiri* lay a bright band of colour through the spring garden.

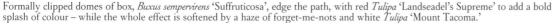

Formally clipped domes of box, *Buxus sempervirens* 'Suffruticosa', edge the path, with red *Tulipa* 'Landseadel's Supreme' to add a bold splash of colour – while the whole effect is softened by a haze of forget-me-nots and white *Tulipa* 'Mount Tacoma.'

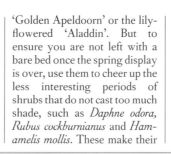

Myosotis 'Blue Ball' will still be a mist of blue when the first *Dianthus* 'Doris' blooms appear.

lived hardy perennial, though best grown as a biennial. The biennial wood forget-me-not *M. sylvatica* is a larger, more showy species. Most of the cultivated forget-me-nots are derived from these two species. Recommended varieties include 'Bluc Cloud', the compact, 6-8in high 'Blue Ball', and the rich pink, 8in high 'Carmine King'. Forget-me-nots are good for cutting for indoor arrangements, where the dainty precision of the flowers can be fully appreciated.

Forget-me-nots are classic covering and edging plants for spring borders packed with later-flowering tulips such as 'Golden Apeldoorn' or the lily-flowered 'Aladdin'. But to ensure you are not left with a bare bed once the spring display is over, use them to cheer up the less interesting periods of shrubs that do not cast too much shade, such as *Daphne odora*, *Rubus cockburnianus* and *Hamamelis mollis*. These make their major contribution to the garden in winter and early springtime. The forget-me-nots could be set among old-favourite perennials such as *Geranium endressii* or *Dianthus* 'Doris' to carry on the blue and pink into summer.

CULTIVATION Sow seed outside between June and July in a cool, shady and moist site. When the seedlings are large enough to handle, transplant them 6in apart in nursery rows and keep well watered. Set plants into their permanent positions in a sunny or lightly shaded spot in autumn, for flowering the following spring. Any ordinary garden soil is suitable.

The alpine garden need not be an expanse of stony outcrops. Raised beds, cracks in stone walls and paving, sinks and troughs, and drilled tufa blocks can all be hosts to a range of dwarf plants, and simulate in miniature the mountain landscapes from which many of the true alpines come.

The impact of each small rock plant on the garden as a whole is minimal, but the combined effect of a number grouped together with an eye to what each contributes in flower and foliage colour through the year will be a telling part of the all-season garden framework.

Given a mainly sunny aspect with a prepared mixture of equal proportions of ordinary garden soil, leaf mould, composted bark or a peat substitute, and coarse grit or fine gravel, you will be surprised at how easy it is to fill just a few square yards with year-round interest in flower, foliage and shape. Blanket the whole soil surface with a ½in layer of stone chippings, as rock-garden plants will benefit from a well-drained, quick-drying surface, and weeds will be kept to a minimum. Make sure, too, that every part of the alpine bed is accessible from a path or stepping stones – and you will find that your rock garden becomes one of the least demanding parts of the garden to maintain.

CREATING THE FRAMEWORK

While spring is the peak time for alpine plants, with careful planning and planting the follow-on will not be an anticlimax. Plan the rock garden as you would the garden as a whole, but in miniature. The rocky structure is the backbone on which dwarf shrubs and trees can provide accent, height, and diversity of shape and texture. Even a raised bed or trough can support one or two miniature conifers, or an evergreen like *Daphne retusa* or the tiny *D. arbuscula*. In a full-sized rock garden, small shrubs like *Berberis thunbergii* 'Atropurpurea Nana', compact forms of the shrubby potentillas and naturally dwarfed rhododendrons such as *Rhododendron calostrotum*, *R. kiusianum* and *R. sargentianum* can establish individual points of

THE *Alpine* GARDEN

Juniperus communis 'Compressa', with thyme, dianthus and sempervivums at its feet, dominates a small alpine display that turns a retaining wall into a colourful garden feature.

permanent interest. A shallow-rooting dwarf conifer (see pages 42-45), such as a slender column of *Chamaecyparis lawsoniana* 'Pygmaea Argentea' or a squat *Abies balsamea* 'Nana', could punctuate the lower levels, while ground-hugging *Juniperus squamata* 'Blue Star' spreads its tiered foliage over higher ground.

Against such a framework, the alpine plants are set. Ring the changes between carpeting plants and hummock-forming species, and keep in mind what each plant will look like once its main display is over. Even if you stick to the alpine staples – saxifrages, gentians, primulas and campanulas – you will have a succession of flower from January to November. Add the maroon-tipped leaves of *Sempervivum tectorum* with a flattering background of the grey-white foliage of *Sedum spathulifolium* 'Cape Blanco', and perhaps some vertical lines from the blade-like leaves of *Sisyrinchium angustifolium*, for strong year-round contrasts in foliage pattern and tone. Dwarf bulbs and small herbaceous perennials can inject extra variety and colour in particular seasons.

THE ALPINE YEAR

Spring comes very early to the rock garden. By early February, some plants are already in bloom. The Kabschia, or cushion saxifrages, with their hummocks of mossy or silver-encrusted leaves, are first to show their colours, different cultivars producing a run of short-stemmed, pink, white or yellow flowers through to April. They contrast handsomely in form and colour with bright-eyed *Anemone blanda* and the dainty *Iris reticulata*. Small groups of *Tulipa tarda* could push through the trailing evergreen foliage of *Dryas × suendermannii* which will flower later, in early summer. The glorious blue of the spring-flowering European gentians (*Gentiana verna* and *G. acaulis*) will catch the eye later in the season, to coincide with *Pulsatilla vulgaris*. At a respectable distance so as not to be smothered by the pulsatilla leaves, could be the clear pink thrift, *Armeria juniperifolia*, whose neat grassy cushions of leaves never lose their attraction. The primulas of the European mountains enjoy gritty, nutritious soils in pockets of the rockwork and are at their best in mid-spring. The softer-toned Himalayan species flower around the same time, but need light shade and moist leafy soil. Following on into June are the New World primulas such as *Primula rusbyi* and *P. parryi*.

Continuity between spring and summer is provided by the mossy saxifrages in May and June, when they overlap with the silver-leaved species, whose snowy plumes of flowers last until July. But there is plenty else happening. The flowers of *Pulsatilla vulgaris* are replaced by fluffy white seed heads, and the white flowers of the mountain avens, *Dryas × suendermannii* appear. Small crane's-bills, like *Geranium cinereum ×* 'Ballerina', flower all the way from late spring to autumn, and pockets of the mat-forming *Dianthus alpinus* will not be far behind, with flowers until August.

HIGH SUMMER TO AUTUMN

High summer is the season for the alpine campanulas, which are reluctant to bloom until their demands of sun and warm earth are met.

The foliage of *Silene schafta* is attractive in its own right, but its pink flowers provide a bridge of colour from July to October. If *Potentilla tabernaemontani* is planted nearby, fresh green prostrate leaves and golden flowers that often appear intermittently until autumn will tone in perfectly. The leaves of the mossy saxifrage are now often tinged with bronze and yellow. The glories of the autumn rock-garden scene, however, are the Asiatic gentians, which raise trumpets of many different blues for weeks on end.

THE WINTER SCENE

The miniature landscape in winter is a tapestry of all-season foliage colours and textures. But flower colour can be provided by little groups of *Galanthus caucasicus* or *G. nivalis,* growing through light ground cover, or *Iris histrioides* pushing through a creeping carpet of thyme. As a general rule, avoid planting any bulbs beneath vigorous carpeting plants with strong, hungry root systems or densely interwoven surface stems. *Iris danfordiae* likes to stand alone, and other highlights can be provided by a group of *Narcissus asturiensis,* carmine *Cyclamen coum* and winter crocus cultivars suitable for a dry, open position (see pages 360-363).

As the individual rock plants merge, this level scree area becomes a floral carpet of colour in spring and summer and a sea of green and grey foliage in winter, and always enhances the strong all-seasons background.

Summer

H ORACE WALPOLE, the 18th-century writer and wit, was of the opinion that the only way to ensure summer in England is to have it framed and glazed in a comfortable room. Such a degree of pessimism is not shared by most of his countrymen, who have placed their most important tribal rites within that climatically uncertain season. Wimbledon, the British Open and Henley are doggedly held in summer, whether in typhoon, hail or blistering heat. Most optimistic is the gardener, who each year envisages that summer will reward twelve months of effort with a glorious bouquet. Alas, if the roses are at their most rampant, so too are the weeds, while hedges and grass grow almost visibly.

But though summer in the garden is a time of war, it is also one of great beauty, when even the rain falls softly and with sparkle. June offers evenings of hushed expectancy leading to dawns of awesome fulfilment, while August is a cornucopia of opulent fruitfulness. Whatever its drawbacks, we never see summer depart without a pang; 'its lease hath all too short a date'.

Lilies, roses and delphiniums capture the overbrimming luxuriance of summer.

Summer *SHRUBS*

The dense arching stems of *Abelia schumannii* are covered with flowers all summer long.

MANY OF our shrubs that flower in summer come from warmer climates, and their young leaves and shoots may be sensitive to late spring frosts. This is no obstacle to their use, however, provided that they are planted in well-drained soil which is never waterlogged during winter. Using summer shrubs means that the flowering season of shrubs in general can be extended from the familiar displays of the hardier spring cultivars right through the summer months.

Abelia schumannii

Height 6-8ft · *Spread* 6-7ft
Best June-September

Introduced from China at the beginning of the century, this is a small abelia which will earn its keep in a sunny spot throughout the summer months. The flowers are like rose-pink elfin caps lined with white and a touch of yellow. They have a quiet charm but appear in profusion from midsummer to early autumn. The abelia is a dense, bushy, deciduous shrub, its leaves turning from bronze when young to glossy green. If a hard winter does knock the plant back, it will usually push up new growth from the roots.

A glorious scented background of *Philadelphus* 'Beauclerk' would complement the abelia in summer, and brilliant effects in autumn could be introduced by the intense blue flowers and scarlet foliage of *Ceratostigma willmottianum*.

CULTIVATION Plant during spring or autumn in any well-drained fertile soil in a sunny, sheltered position – as a severe winter could cause some damage. Propagate by semi-hardwood cuttings in late summer.

Buddleia alternifolia

Height 12ft · *Spread* 12ft
Best June

With its cascading form and delicate, narrow leaves, this graceful species is more reminiscent of a weeping willow than of other buddleias. In early summer, the previous year's growths are covered with fragrant, 1in wide clusters of tiny flowers, alternately placed along the ends of whippy young stems to produce a fall of soft lavender. *Buddleia alternifolia*

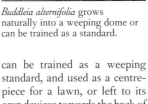

Buddleia alternifolia grows naturally into a weeping dome or can be trained as a standard.

can be trained as a weeping standard, and used as a centrepiece for a lawn, or left to its own devices towards the back of a mixed border. The silvery-grey-leaved cultivar 'Argentea' is even more decorative.

The evergreen fern *Polystichum setiferum*, interplanted with *Narcissus* 'Thalia' and *Campanula persicifolia* would make fine ground-level companions from early spring to the summer's end. Alternatively, *Hebe* 'Midsummer Beauty' and *Anemone × hybrida* could be planted alongside the buddleia in the mixed border for an extended display until autumn.

CULTIVATION Plant in spring or autumn in a sunny position in any fertile, well-drained soil. Pruning is done immediately after flowering, but is only necessary if the shrub is trained as a standard, or to keep growth within bounds. Propagate by taking semi-hardwood cuttings in late summer.

Buddleia davidii

COMMON BUDDLEIA

Height 6-8ft · *Spread* 6-8ft
Best July-August

Considering that this buddleia was only introduced to Britain at the turn of the century, its ubiquitous presence in garden

Buddleia davidii is sometimes known as the butterfly bush because the insects are so attracted by its rich, scented trusses of tiny flowers.

and wasteland is quite an achievement. Nevertheless, the cultivated forms like the red-purple 'Royal Red' or brilliant 'Empire Blue', which carry luscious, vibrantly coloured cones of tiny fragrant flowers, are highly regarded garden plants, and are equally popular with butterflies.

The common buddleia is seen at its best in the company of other shrubs, like *Lavatera thuringiaca* 'Rosea', which bears pink flowers throughout the summer. The autumn and winter blossom of *Viburnum × bodnantense* 'Deben' would detract attention from the buddleia's rather ungainly habit when it is not in flower.

CULTIVATION Plant during spring or autumn in any well-drained

Calluna vulgaris 'Spring Torch' flowers in late summer, but its name is inspired by the foliage which is delightfully tipped with pink and red in spring.

Clematis florida 'Alba Plena' leavens the density of *Ceanothus* × *burkwoodii* and doubles the value of the midsummer display.

Calluna vulgaris

COMMON HEATHER, LING

Height 1½ft · *Spread* 1½ft
Best July-October

From the common ling of heaths and moors has sprung an extraordinarily wide range of cultivars, each with quite distinct leaf and flower colours. The habit common to all is a small, erect bush, covered with tiny evergreen leaves and, from late summer onwards, tall soil, preferably in a sunny position. Prune the stems back to 1-2ft in early spring to encourage large flower spikes. To propagate, take hardwood cuttings during autumn.

spikes of miniature flowers. They are excellent for dried flower arrangements.

Among the first calluna cultivars to flower in summer is 'County Wicklow', a low, compact but spreading form with double pink flowers. 'Spring Torch' is mauve flowered, with mid-green foliage tipped with pink and red in spring. 'Orange Queen' has pink flowers and leaves that turn from spring gold to orange late in the year. 'Gold Haze' is a taller form with massed white flowers and yellow foliage.

Best planted in groups, the heather could be put near the gold-leaved grass *Hakonechloa macra* 'Aureola' for striking foliage contrast, or combined with other heaths and heathers.

Calluna 'Gold Haze' is worth growing for its foliage alone; the summer flowers are a bonus.

CULTIVATION Plant at any time in an acid, peaty soil. Trim spent flower spikes in winter or spring to keep the plants compact. Propagate by taking 1in cuttings in summer.

Ceanothus × burkwoodii

Height 6-10ft · *Spread* 6-8ft
Best July-October

Most evergreen ceanothus flower in the spring, but this one bursts into life in midsummer with large clusters of rich blue flowers that last until autumn. And when the blooms have gone, the arching, glossy grey-green foliage will still give the garden a fresh look throughout the winter months.

Ceanothus × *burkwoodii* is an ideal plant for the middle of a mixed border. In front, put in *Arum italicum* 'Pictum' for a spring display of white-veined leaves, and behind, *Callicarpa bodinieri giraldii* would provide lilac-purple autumn berries.

CULTIVATION Plant in full sun, preferably against a south or west-facing wall, especially in cold districts, during autumn or spring. The soil should be well-drained. To propagate, take softwood cuttings in early summer, or semi-hardwood cuttings in early autumn.

Ceanothus 'Gloire de Versailles' carries its soft blue blossom until autumn.

Ceanothus
Deciduous cultivars

Height 6-8ft · *Spread* 5ft
Best July-September

'Perle Rose', 'Marie Simon' and 'Gloire de Versailles' are deciduous ceanothus cultivars, with long spikes of pink, pale pink and pale blue flowers respectively. They strongly resemble lilac, but their blooms appear later in the year, and continue into autumn.

As they do not have the evergreen advantage of *Ceanothus × burkwoodii,* these forms are better partnered with evergreen shrubs like *Pernettya mucronata*, with its rosy berries in winter, or grown against a

Hedera colchica 'Dentata Variegata' looks magnificent all year, but in summer it sets off the blooms of *Cistus ladanifer* to perfection.

wall with *Choisya ternata,* which has white blossom in spring.
CULTIVATION Plant in spring or autumn in a sunny, preferably south or west-facing position with well-drained soil. Prune hard annually in spring. Propagate by taking softwood cuttings during early summer or semi-hardwood cuttings in early autumn.

Cistus ladanifer
GUM CISTUS

Height 6ft · *Spread* 5ft
Best June-July

This cistus is a shrub of the dry hillsides of southern Europe and North Africa and, in a sunny, sheltered spot, will bring a

Cistus 'Peggy Sammons' evokes the mood of Mediterranean hillsides with its felted evergreen leaves and rose-like flowers.

touch of the Mediterranean to the British garden. The common name, gum cistus, comes from the sticky, leathery, evergreen leaves and stems. These provide a striking background for the paper-white, 4in diameter blooms which have a dash of maroon-crimson at the base of each petal. The variety 'Albiflorus' has pristine white flowers with no blotch.

This species is upright and open in character. When it has reached its full height and girth, it is well suited to the middle or back of a mixed border.

The long, whippy stems of *Cytisus × praecox* would provide foliage contrast in summer, and its late spring, creamy flowers would herald those of the cistus. Follow on with the red and purple flowers of *Fuchsia* 'Riccartonii' to the first autumn frosts, and use *Helleborus viridis,* with its deeply cut evergreen leaves, for year-round ground cover.
CULTIVATION Plant during late spring in a warm, sunny and

sheltered position in any well-drained soil. Prune only to shorten leggy young growth in March or after flowering. Propagate by taking semi-hardwood cuttings in summer.

Cistus
'Peggy Sammons'

Height 4-6ft · *Spread* 3-4ft
Best June-July

Hardier than some other cistuses, this little shrub could display its southern charms at the back of a rock garden or the edge of a path or patio. The leaves are silver-brushed evergreen, with clusters of round buds among them, that over a period of weeks, open to reveal delicate pink flowers.

The cistus could be backed by *Rosa virginiana* for its brilliant autumn leaf colour and hips. The low, spreading broom, *Cytisus × kewensis,* would bring a flush of creamy-yellow in May. At the

A warm, sunny wall of grey-white stone and well-drained soil beneath provide a perfect setting for the glory of a satin-flowered sun rose, *Cistus × purpureus* emphasised by a wandering tendril of purple-blue periwinkle.

Clethra alnifolia is open in habit, and can support a clematis hybrid as long as it is not too vigorous.

old and leggy, or in case it is damaged by frost.

This is a middle-sized cistus which develops into a bushy shrub with matt, greyish, evergreen leaves. Combine it with other sun-loving plants like *Rosa* 'Frühlingsgold', whose own, light gold flowers are not unlike those of the cistus and finish as the first cistus flowers commence. *Potentilla fruticosa* 'Manchu', with summer-long, buttercup-like, white flowers, or the yellow 'Goldfinger' would also go well.

CULTIVATION As for *Cistus ladanifer*.

Clethra alnifolia

SWEET PEPPER BUSH

Height 7ft · *Spread* 7ft
Best August

When it was introduced from North America in the 18th century, the sweet pepper bush became one of the most sought-after plants in a vogue for 'American gardens'. With its late summer spires of white, scented flowers and its acid soil requirement, it is an ideal, quieter second act to follow the camellias and rhododendrons of spring. *Clethra alnifolia* 'Paniculata' carries a mass of long, white flower panicles, while the buds and blooms of 'Rosea' are flushed pink. The handsome leaves turn crimson in autumn before falling.

Winter to spring-flowering *Erica carnea* cultivars would make valuable ground-level companions, and the pale blue of *Clematis alpina* blooms could trail through the clethra in mid to late spring. Hardy chrysanthemums, particularly the Korean hybrids, would enhance

base of all, *Crocus tommasinianus* could make a lavender carpet in early spring.

CULTIVATION Plant in late spring in a warm, sheltered, sunny position with well-drained soil. Prune only to cut back leggy young growth in early spring or after flowering. Propagate by taking semi-hardwood cuttings in summer.

Cistus × purpureus

SUN ROSE

Height 3-4ft · *Spread* 3-4ft
Best June-July

The satin-textured, crimson-pink blooms open with the morning sun and shed their petals at noon. But the following morning, a fresh crop takes over, and so the delightful process continues for week after week. Although this is one of the least hardy cistus, given a warm, sunny and sheltered position, the rewards are great. But carefully nurture new plants taken from cuttings, so that you have new stock ready to replace the parent shrub as it becomes

Each blossom of the lovely flowering dogwood *Cornus* 'Ormonde' is set among leaf bracts which clothe the shrub like layers of cream lace.

IN SUMMER the dogwood is heavy with blossom, flushed pink where it catches most light. A cool blue drift of campanulas, tradescantias, and spires of delphiniums and ligularias bring pools of colour to the shade beneath.

(*Clethra alnifolia* cont)
the clethra's autumn foliage.
CULTIVATION Plant in spring in a sunny position with moist, lime-free soil. Propagate by taking semi-hardwood cuttings in late summer.

Cornus kousa chinensis

FLOWERING DOGWOOD

Height 10-15ft · *Spread* 8-12ft
Best June

At the height of its summer flowering, the wide, spreading branches of *Cornus kousa chinensis* are evocative of a flared, layered petticoat. Though the flowers themselves are insignificant, they are surrounded by petal-like leaf bracts that turn from lime green in spring to white, and then pink-tinged cream. In their profusion, they almost obliterate the glossy, pointed ovals of leaves beneath. In warm summers the flowers may be followed by pinkish-red, strawberry-like fruits. The pageant continues into autumn, as the dogwood's foliage turns through purple to glowing red and bronze before falling.

The dignified shape of the cornus deserves a position uncluttered by other tall shrubs, except perhaps another dogwood, the equally handsome 'Ormonde', much valued for its broad, overlapping bracts. To extend the flowering season, add an underplanting of *Lilium* 'African Queen' and the vibrant *Cosmos bipinnatus*.
CULTIVATION Plant during spring or autumn in deep, fertile, well-drained soil in full sun or very light shade. No pruning is necessary. Propagate by layering in June or July.

BRIDGING THE SEASONS
IN A
Woodland setting

AT THE HEART of this woodland-style scheme are the tiered branches and seasonal displays of *Cornus kousa chinensis*. In a fairly open position with a reasonable depth of soil, it provides the framework for a year-round variety of perennials and bulbs.

In midsummer, the cornus is in full bloom, some of its petal-like bracts flushed with pink, a colour that is echoed in a haze of *Astilbe* 'Europa' beneath. A peal of blue *Campanula latifolia* bells rings the changes among shades of foliage.

Throughout summer, there's a flow of activity, with *Ligularia* 'The Rocket' providing yellow highlights until August, while the spires of *Delphinium* Belladonna hybrids and the three-petalled blooms of *Tradescantia* 'Blue Stone' spill their colours well into autumn. In a mild year, the cornus may be hung with baubles of strawberry-like fruits. Early autumn is the time to trim any remaining flower spikes from the ligularia to gain full effect from its

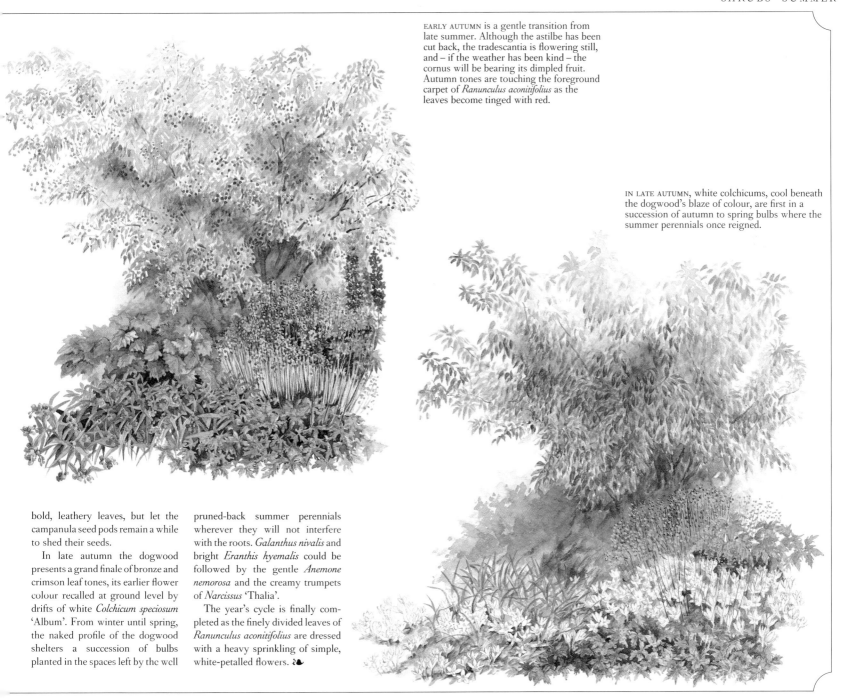

EARLY AUTUMN is a gentle transition from late summer. Although the astilbe has been cut back, the tradescantia is flowering still, and – if the weather has been kind – the cornus will be bearing its dimpled fruit. Autumn tones are touching the foreground carpet of *Ranunculus aconitifolius* as the leaves become tinged with red.

IN LATE AUTUMN, white colchicums, cool beneath the dogwood's blaze of colour, are first in a succession of autumn to spring bulbs where the summer perennials once reigned.

bold, leathery leaves, but let the campanula seed pods remain a while to shed their seeds.

In late autumn the dogwood presents a grand finale of bronze and crimson leaf tones, its earlier flower colour recalled at ground level by drifts of white *Colchicum speciosum* 'Album'. From winter until spring, the naked profile of the dogwood shelters a succession of bulbs planted in the spaces left by the well

pruned-back summer perennials wherever they will not interfere with the roots. *Galanthus nivalis* and bright *Eranthis hyemalis* could be followed by the gentle *Anemone nemorosa* and the creamy trumpets of *Narcissus* 'Thalia'.

The year's cycle is finally completed as the finely divided leaves of *Ranunculus aconitifolius* are dressed with a heavy sprinkling of simple, white-petalled flowers. ❧

Even when it is young, *Crinodendron hookerianum* gives a fine summer display of waxy lantern flowers.

Despite its southern origins, the Moroccan broom *Cytisus battandieri* is quite tough and a fine plant for a high wall, whence its pineapple scent will permeate the garden.

The flowers of *Cytisus battandieri* are borne in soft racemes that resemble bright yellow pine cones.

Crinodendron hookerianum

LANTERN TREE

Height 8-12ft · *Spread* 6-10ft
Best May-June

Soft, glowing red lanterns are suspended among slim, dark evergreen leaves like out-of-season Christmas decorations. The build-up to the festive summer display begins in autumn, when tiny flower buds are formed on long, pendulous stalks. The buds gradually swell through winter and spring. This is a big, upright shrub from the forests of southern Chile, and is easy enough to grow provided it has the mild, moist conditions it needs.

As an acid soil plant, it could partner *Erica arborea* 'Alpina' for a contrast in foliage and early spring flowers. *Hydrangea villosa* enjoys a similar, lightly shaded yet sheltered aspect and would continue the display into autumn. *Lilium regale* planted underneath the shrubs would further illuminate the scene in the summer months.
CULTIVATION Plant during spring in moist but well-drained acid soil in a sheltered position with sun or light shade. The mild, moist areas of the west coast of Britain are favoured locations. No pruning is necessary. Propagate by taking hardwood cuttings during autumn.

Cytisus battandieri

MOROCCAN BROOM

Height 10ft · *Spread* 8-10ft
Best July

An excellent wall shrub, Moroccan broom is quite unlike European brooms in habit, leaf and flower. Its young shoots and leaves are covered with silky white hairs, giving the whole plant a silvery appearance, and its golden-yellow flowers, borne in midsummer, are pineapple scented.

A south or west-facing wall is the best place for *Cytisus battandieri*, where it could enjoy the company of other sun-loving plants. The cool, powder-blue flowers of *Ceanothus thyrsiflorus* 'Repens' would blend with the silvery foliage in May and June, followed by the spikes of white, bell-like flowers of *Galtonia candicans* in summer. The silvered leaves would also look most effective with the rosy pea-like flowers of the bush clover, *Lespedeza thunbergii*, which will bloom in autumn.
CULTIVATION Plant during spring in any well-drained, reasonably fertile soil in full sun. Propagate by sowing seed in a greenhouse or propagator in spring.

Deutzia
Hybrids

Height 5ft · *Spread* 5ft
Best June

A long, bitter winter suits these hardy shrubs, for a warm spell in early spring or too sheltered a position will prompt the leaves and young shoots to develop early and so be vulnerable to late frosts. The hybrids are generally easy to grow, however, especially in chillier parts of the country, and when in full bloom the branches are weighed down with clusters of star-

Deep cherry-pink *Erica ciliaris* 'Corfe Castle' is a low, spreading heath whose flowers carry memories of midsummer deep into autumn.

shaped flowers for nearly a month. *Deutzia × hybrida* is a collective name for a number of cultivars which vary in colour from light to rich mauve-pink. A more compact hybrid, *D. × rosea*, has arching branches and pink, bell-shaped flowers.

The hybrids' bushy, twiggy growth and matt-green leaves need enlivening before and after the flowering period. Try the ferny foliage and earlier pink flowers of *Dicentra spectabilis*, and the later pink mallow flowers of *Lavatera thuringiaca* 'Rosea' or 'Barnsley' through summer into autumn.

CULTIVATION Plant during spring or autumn, in any fertile, well-drained soil in full sun or light shade. Remove old, straggly flowering shoots immediately after flowering to encourage new growth. Propagate by hardwood cuttings in autumn.

Soft clouds of *Deutzia × rosea* blossom contrast with the bright foliage of *Weigela* 'Looymansii Aurea' behind, and recall its earlier pink flowers.

Erica ciliaris

DORSET HEATH

Height 1ft · *Spread* 1½ft
Best July-October

Erica ciliaris is said to survive from a period when the British climate was warmer than it is today. Now it grows wild only in the heathlands of the south-west of Britain. The spikes of tiny flowers persist throughout summer and autumn, and spill over well into winter. The cultivar 'David McClintock' bears white flowers tipped with pink, and light grey-green foliage that turns bronze in winter; 'Aurea' has golden foliage and pink flowers.

As well as mixing this erica with other heaths and heathers with widely different flowering periods, try introducing some height with a small shrub like *Salix lanata*. Drifts of *Scilla sibirica* 'Spring Beauty', and *Erythronium revolutum* could be grown through and around

A mass of *Erica cinerea* 'E.C. Best' provides a vivid carpet against sombre conifers; later its pink flowers will fade to form russet bells.

(*Erica ciliaris* cont)
the heather in spring, with *Cyclamen hederifolium* in the foreground for autumn colour.
CULTIVATION Plant any time in autumn or spring in a sunny position and in moist, acid soil. Shear off the dead flower heads immediately after flowering. Propagate from 1in semi-hardwood cuttings in summer.

Erica cinerea 'Alba Minor' is easy to grow, small and compact, reaching to about 6in in height.

Erica cinerea

BELL HEATHER

Height 6-12in · *Spread* 1ft
Best June-September

Erica cinerea is the earliest summer heather to flower, and tolerates drier conditions than other hardy summer-flowering heathers. It is a small, wiry-stemmed shrub with spikes covered in little bell-shaped flowers that fade in autumn and winter to russet-brown. The many cultivars available span a range of flower colours, though the foliage is usually mid-green. 'Alba Minor' is compact and white-flowered, 'C.D. Eason' has glowing dark pink flowers, and 'Eden Valley' has distinctly bicoloured blooms of lavender and white.

Compatible moorland-style companions would be the blue grass *Festuca glauca* and the silver-leaved willow *Salix lanata*. For combining with other heaths, see page 376.
CULTIVATION Plant at any time of the year in well-drained acid soil. Clip after flowering to keep compact. Propagate by taking 1in cuttings during the summer and placing them in peat and sand in a propagator.

Erica tetralix
'Alba Mollis'

CROSS-LEAVED HEATH

Height 6-12in · *Spread* 9-15in
Best Late June-August

Although the cross-leaved heath's natural habitat is wild boggy moorland in Britain, the cultivated forms are rewarding garden plants given a reasonably moist soil. The particular attraction of 'Alba Mollis' is the combination of the small, white, urn-shaped flowers that crown the stems, and the soft silver-grey foliage that is a year-round bonus. Other varieties include

Chamaecyparis lawsoniana cultivars make a fine backing for *Erica tetralix* 'Alba Mollis'.

'Con Underwood', with crimson flowers, and the apricot-pink 'L.E. Underwood'.

Plant 'Alba Mollis' with a range of other heaths and heathers for a through-season flower and foliage display among dwarf conifers or silver birch (*Betula* species).
CULTIVATION Plant any time in autumn or spring in acid soil that is moist all year. A thick dressing of peat or leaf mould will help to retain moisture. Propagate by taking semi-hardwood cuttings in summer.

Named *Erica vagans* cultivars like 'Mrs D.F. Maxwell' are much more striking in appearance than the species itself.

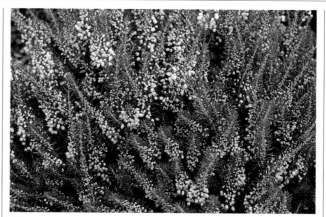

Erica vagans is our most vigorous native heath, and 'Grandiflora' is a particularly strong-growing cultivar, with long flowering stems.

Like all the Cornish heaths, *Erica vagans* 'St Keverne' makes a good cut flower for indoor decoration.

The cultivar 'Slieve Donard' is one of the hardiest of escallonias and excellent for hedging.

Erica vagans

CORNISH HEATH

Height 1-1½ft · *Spread* 1½-2ft
Best August-November

In mainland Britain, the last wild outpost of *Erica vagans* is the Lizard Peninsula, where it creates a haze of vivid pink-purple in late summer. In the context of the garden, the heath's dense, rounded hummocks, spiked with crowded sprays of bright bell flowers, provide a glowing link between late summer and autumn, and give year-round foliage too. Cultivars range from the white-flowered 'Lyonesse' which has bright green leaves, and 'Valerie Proudley', with white flowers against golden foliage, to the salmon-pink 'St Keverne' and cerise 'Mrs D.F. Maxwell'.

Grouping a number of Cornish heath plants together looks more effective than isolated specimens. Evergreen azaleas such as splendid *Rhododendron* 'Blue Danube', 'Palestrina' and 'Rosebud' would anticipate the heath's vibrant colours with their spring displays, and add their gleaming foliage to the all-season framework.

CULTIVATION Plant in a sunny position at any time of the year in acid, peaty soil. If necessary, clip over immediately after flowering to keep the shrubs compact. Propagate by taking 1in cuttings in summer.

Escallonia

Donard cultivars

Height 5-7ft · *Spread* 5-7ft
Best July-August

As South American natives, escallonias can be tender in this country, but with the raising of the Donard cultivars, the area in which they can be confidently grown has enlarged considerably. A good thing, too, for these bushy shrubs can certainly earn their keep in the all-seasons garden, with gleaming dark evergreen or semi-evergreen leaves, and a splendid, long-flowering season from midsummer well into autumn. 'Donard Brilliance' has rose-red flowers on graceful, arching stems; 'Donard Seedling' is a vigorous, whip-stemmed cultivar with pale pink and white flowers; 'Donard Radiance' is compact with rose-red flowers.

Escallonias can serve as dense hedging or windbreaks, and are particularly useful in seaside areas as they do not mind salt-laden air. For companions, look for a contrast in leaf shape with the North American, summer-flowering *Echinacea purpurea* and, for bright autumn flowers, use something like *Ceratostigma willmottianum*. Then carpet the ground beneath with the fresh green of *Waldsteinia ternata*.

CULTIVATION Plant any time in autumn or spring in any well-drained, fertile soil and in full sun. Little pruning is necessary, but if trained as a hedge, prune immediately after flowering. Propagate by semi-hardwood cuttings in summer, or by hardwood cuttings in autumn.

Fremontodendron californicum, with its sensational and long-lasting waxy blooms, does equally well on both chalky and acid soils, providing it is given a well-drained sunny spot against a south or west-facing wall.

Fremontodendron californicum

Height 15-25ft · *Spread* 8-15ft
Best May-October

The rich, butter-yellow flowers of this bold shrub are 2-3in across, and in a mild year will still be brightening the garden as late as October. *Fremontodendron californicum* is a sun-loving native of California and is an excellent shrub for a warm wall. The best form to grow is 'California Glory', which has even larger flowers than the species and is more hardy.

For an early display of bright blue flowers, plant *Ceanothus thyrsiflorus* 'Repens' at the foot of the shrub. *Rhamnus alaternus* 'Argenteovariegata', if planted nearby, will provide a subtle foil with its cream-edged leaves.
CULTIVATION Plant in spring in well-drained soil, in a sunny position. Propagate by softwood cuttings in summer.

Fuchsia

Hardy fuchsias, unlike the highly bred cultivars of show and greenhouse, can become rewarding outdoor plants, especially in mild, maritime areas. Natives of Central and South America and New Zealand, fuchsias are named after Leonard Fuchs, a 16th-century German botanist. The hardier cultivars range in size from low, spreading shrublets valuable for filling spaces at the front of a border, to large shrubs suitable for the middle or back of a mixed border. The ultimate height of an individual plant varies according to how sheltered the aspect. The degree of hardiness varies too; fuchsias may be cut down to ground level by winter frost, but often set up fresh growth in spring. In the midlands and north, they are generally treated as half-hardy plants and lifted in winter.

PENDENT BELLS
The hardy fuchsia's flowering period bridges summer and autumn, and is useful for when the main flush of spring and summer colour is spent. Some cultivars, however, can begin to flower as early as June. The beautifully fashioned, bell-like flowers, in rich shades of pink, red and purple, hang from slender stems that grow from the leaf axils. The sepals of some cultivars curve back to reveal the skirt of petals and long stamens beneath. In some cultivars, like the cerise and lilac 'Abbé Farges', or rose-pink and white 'Alice Hoffman', the flowers are small but profuse

Fuchsias can make a valuable contribution to container displays, but must then be treated as tender.

and clothe the foliage in a haze of contrasting colour. Others, such as 'Mission Bells' and 'Santa Cruz', carry big, striking blooms, and are particularly arresting when viewed from below. They look splendid growing from a higher level, from hanging baskets or as weeping standards in a large container. In containers, however, all fuchsias must be treated as tender and overwintered in a greenhouse or conservatory.

COMPANION PLANTS
Hardy fuchsias can be used towards the front of a mixed border, or against sunny walls, to supplement the blue flowers of *Caryopteris* × *clandonensis* 'Kew Blue', or *Ceratostigma willmottianum*. *Ceanothus impressus* and *Cytisus* × *kewensis* are sun-loving shrubs that could provide spring colour nearby. *Hosta crispula* could add substance and form to the foliage of

In a classic blend of architecture and horticulture, warm-toned brick links the already turning late summer colours of Virginia creeper and the rich crimson and green of *Fuchsia magellanica* 'Riccartonii'.

Lonicera periclymenum mingles with a luxuriant show of fuchsia cultivars, *Lilium regale*, tuberous begonias and *Lobelia erinus*.

the larger cultivars at ground level throughout the summer, and a semicircle of *Iris reticulata* hybrids could furnish the late winter and early spring scene.

CULTIVATION
Plant in late spring in any fertile, well-drained, though moisture-retentive, soil. The situation should be sheltered and in full sun or partial shade. Protect from severe weather by covering the roots with sand, bark chips or ashes. Prune back to ground level in spring. To propagate, take semi-hardwood cuttings in summer or spring, and place them in a closed frame or propagator until rooted.

Fuchsia 'Lady Thumb' is neat enough in habit to join sedums in a trough.

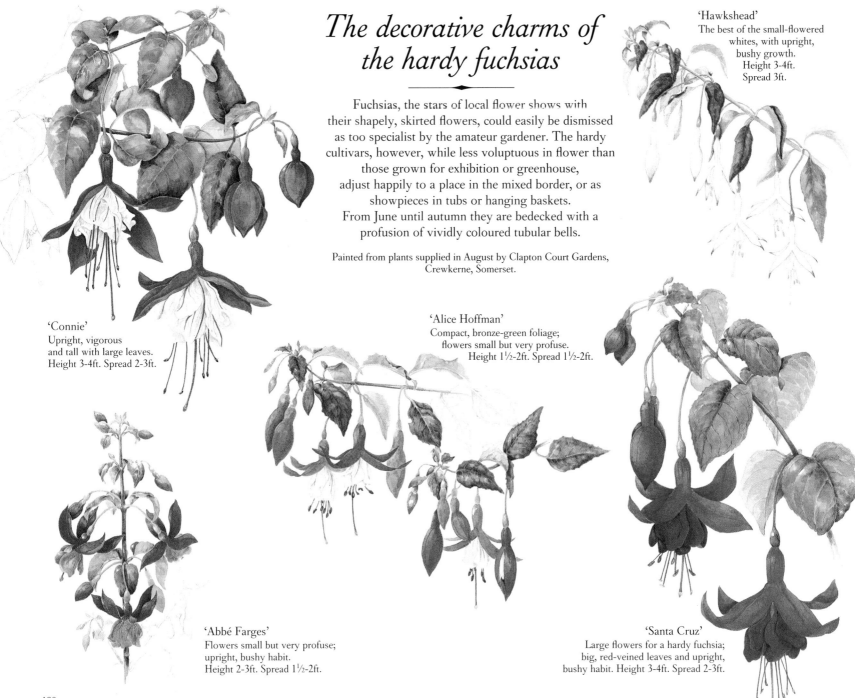

The decorative charms of the hardy fuchsias

Fuchsias, the stars of local flower shows with
their shapely, skirted flowers, could easily be dismissed
as too specialist by the amateur gardener. The hardy
cultivars, however, while less voluptuous in flower than
those grown for exhibition or greenhouse,
adjust happily to a place in the mixed border, or as
showpieces in tubs or hanging baskets.
From June until autumn they are bedecked with a
profusion of vividly coloured tubular bells.

Painted from plants supplied in August by Clapton Court Gardens,
Crewkerne, Somerset.

'Hawkshead'
The best of the small-flowered
whites, with upright,
bushy growth.
Height 3-4ft.
Spread 3ft.

'Connie'
Upright, vigorous
and tall with large leaves.
Height 3-4ft. Spread 2-3ft.

'Alice Hoffman'
Compact, bronze-green foliage;
flowers small but very profuse.
Height 1½-2ft. Spread 1½-2ft.

'Abbé Farges'
Flowers small but very profuse;
upright, bushy habit.
Height 2-3ft. Spread 1½-2ft.

'Santa Cruz'
Large flowers for a hardy fuchsia;
big, red-veined leaves and upright,
bushy habit. Height 3-4ft. Spread 2-3ft.

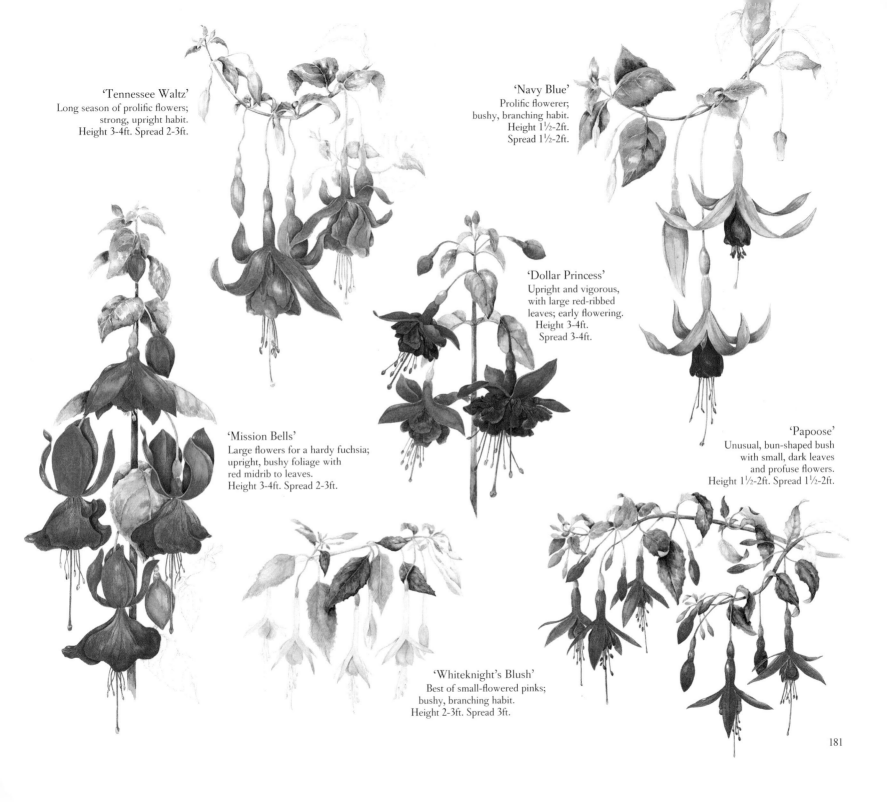

'Tennessee Waltz'
Long season of prolific flowers;
strong, upright habit.
Height 3-4ft. Spread 2-3ft.

'Navy Blue'
Prolific flowerer;
bushy, branching habit.
Height 1½-2ft.
Spread 1½-2ft.

'Dollar Princess'
Upright and vigorous,
with large red-ribbed
leaves; early flowering.
Height 3-4ft.
Spread 3-4ft.

'Mission Bells'
Large flowers for a hardy fuchsia;
upright, bushy foliage with
red midrib to leaves.
Height 3-4ft. Spread 2-3ft.

'Papoose'
Unusual, bun-shaped bush
with small, dark leaves
and profuse flowers.
Height 1½-2ft. Spread 1½-2ft.

'Whiteknight's Blush'
Best of small-flowered pinks;
bushy, branching habit.
Height 2-3ft. Spread 3ft.

181

Here is a duo for a garden not too far from a branch of the Gulf Stream. Though *Fuchsia magellanica gracilis* 'Versicolor' and *Zantedeschia aethiopica* are not unhardy, they do best in a balmy clime.

Much prized among the rich abundance of hebes available is long-lasting 'Midsummer Beauty'.

Not to be outdone, *Hebe* 'Simon Delaux' presents spikes of brightest crimson.

Fuchsia magellanica gracilis
'Versicolor'

Height 4ft · *Spread* 3ft
Best July-October

The species, *Fuchsia magellanica*, is a tough creature that can be left in the garden throughout the year; in the West Country and in Ireland it is even grown in hedgerows. Though not so muscular as this, some of its offspring are still pretty hardy as fuchsias go, and are even more attractive. The cultivar *F. m. gracilis* 'Versicolor', for example, is a small, spreading shrub that produces slender, long-stalked flowers from midsummer onwards. Its particular beauty, however, lies in its splendid foliage. The slim stems carry leaves that are pink-tinted when they first unfold, then become grey-green with a striking red midrib; later still, they are variegated with creamy-white. Only the most severe frosts will cut this cultivar to ground level, and even then it will bounce back to reach 2-3ft by summer's beginning.

If you live in a mild, moist westerly area with a hint of sea air, *F. magellanica* cultivars may not need to be cut back each year, and could instead support *Clematis alpina*. This would advance the annual flowering display by a month or so. Spring bulbs like *Tulipa* 'Hermione' or the lily-flowered, cream and strawberry-stippled 'Marilyn' would do a similar job at the fuchsia's feet. Contrasting form would then be provided by striking all-seasons foliage plants such as *Phormium tenax* 'Purpureum', or the winter-flowering *Bergenia cordifolia*.

CULTIVATION Plant in late spring in any fertile, well-drained soil in a sheltered, sunny position. Prune back to ground level in spring – if large plants are required, remove dead stems only. Propagate from semi-hardwood cuttings in summer.

Hebe speciosa
Hybrids

SHRUBBY VERONICA

Height 4-5ft · *Spread* 4ft
Best July-August

These reasonably hardy shrubs from New Zealand will thrive in relatively frost-free coastal areas, or in sheltered districts inland. All are evergreen, with handsome leathery leaves.

Hebe 'Simon Delaux' has large spikes of crimson flowers. 'Alicia Amherst' is magnificent with long spikes of rich, purple flowers, and handsome 'Midsummer Beauty', the hardiest of the three, makes a spectacular show throughout summer with long, lavender flower racemes

If the *Hebe speciosa* hybrids are too large for your garden scheme try the dwarf *H. albicans*. This will make a dense, rounded clump to fill out a small, sunlit corner.

Eye-catching form is scarce in the late summer garden. One excellent remedy is the greenish-white, fragrant cascade of *Itea ilicifolia*.

Even among the opulence of early summer, the graceful, soft pink and yellow drapery of *Kolkwitzia amabilis* is quite outstanding.

set against light green foliage.

Good companions for these shrubs are *Hypericum* 'Hidcote' which, with 'Alicia Amherst', will give a summer display of purple and gold. The rosy-white flowers of *Viburnum bodnantense* 'Dawn' will provide fragrance and colour behind 'Midsummer Beauty' from late autumn, and *Cimicifuga simplex* 'White Pearl', with its graceful white plumes, will contrast with the dark green foliage of 'Simon Delaux'. All three hybrids would benefit from a nearby spring showing of yellow, such as *Euphorbia characias wulfenii*.

CULTIVATION Plant in spring, in any well-drained soil in a sunny position. Propagate by semi-hardwood cuttings in autumn.

Itea ilicifolia

Height 8-12ft · *Spread* 6-10ft
Best August-September

Long tassels of greenish-white flowers hang catkin-like from this tall and graceful evergreen in late summer, adding to the quiet charm of its glossy, holly-like leaves.

Itea ilicifolia is best grown on a sheltered west-facing wall, where *Daphne mezereum* 'Alba' with its sweet scent and white flowers could light up the scene in spring, and a carpet of *Osteospermum ecklonis* beneath will give a succession of large daisy-like flowers, deep blue, white and purple, throughout the summer. It is also the perfect host for that joyful companion of springtime, *Clematis alpina* 'Frances Rivis', whose large blue flowers are dramatically enhanced by bright, contrasting sheaves of white stamens.

CULTIVATION Plant in spring in any well-drained, fertile soil in a sunny but sheltered position. Propagate by semi-hardwood cuttings in late summer.

Kolkwitzia amabilis

BEAUTY BUSH

Height 7-10ft · *Spread* 6-8ft
Best May-June

In May and June the spreading branches of *Kolkwitzia amabilis* are covered in glorious, soft pink, yellow-throated flowers, like breezy fanfares of miniature trumpets, fully justifying the shrub's common name. The cultivar *K. a.* 'Pink Cloud' has an abundance of flowers of a richer, deeper pink. Although it is deciduous, the shrub maintains its attractiveness in winter with a display of peeling, silvery-brown bark.

Plant this tall bush at the back of a mixed border with *Magnolia stellata* for a spring display of white, starry, fragrant flowers. A generous ground cover of *Geranium endressii* 'Wargrave Pink', which enjoys light shade, will ensure a continuing pink floral display into the autumn.

CULTIVATION Plant in spring or autumn in well-drained soil in full sun. Increase by semi-hardwood cuttings in summer.

Lavatera thuringiaca 'Rosea' has flowers that fit in perfectly with perennials in a mixed border.

Lavatera thuringiaca
'Rosea'
(syn *L. olbia* 'Rosea')

SHRUBBY MALLOW

Height 6-8ft · *Spread* 5-7ft
Best July-September

Come rain or shine, *Lavatera thuringiaca* 'Rosea' is a fine spectacle in late summer, and lasts until the first frosts. 'Barnsley' is more compact, with white, pink-centred flowers.

The shrubby mallow suits a mixed border situation with the evergreen *Ceanothus thyrsiflorus* 'Repens'. Add *Anchusa* 'Loddon Royalist' and *Agapanthus* Headbourne hybrids for contrasting blue flowers.

CULTIVATION Plant in spring in any well-drained, but moisture-retentive soil, not too rich, and in a sheltered, sunny position. Propagate by semi-hardwood cuttings in late summer.

IN SUMMER, the flamboyant display of pink from *Lavatera thuringiaca* 'Rosea' and *L. t.* 'Barnsley' is such a show-stopper, it is almost impossible to imagine the stunted, bare stems of only a couple of months before They are ably supported by rosy penstemons and the spiky lilac flowers of hostas.

BRIDGING THE SEASONS
WITH *Lavatera thuringiaca*

THE GLORY and abundance of the shrubby, richly hued mallows throughout the summer months make them well worth growing. But what happens in winter, when they are cut back? In fact, the space they leave can open up a completely different vista in the garden, and ground space which can be used to good advantage.

In July, the dark pink of *Lavatera thuringiaca* 'Rosea' and the pink and white *L. t.* 'Barnsley' are echoed until autumn in the deep rose-red of *Penstemon* 'Garnet' and the lilac-pink flower spikes of hostas in the foreground. A splash of campanulas rival the penstemons in stature, and flower until August, their colour reflected for a time by purple-blue sage (*Salvia officinalis*) flowers set among the hostas.

Trees play second fiddle to the vigorous lavateras, but add welcome contrast to the riot of pink in the summer months, and give constancy of structure throughout the year. The dark purple foliage of *Prunus cerasifera* is picked up again in the round leaves of the smoke tree *Cotinus coggygria*.

In autumn the cotinus comes into its own with a flash of bright crimson foliage, extending the colour after the mallow flowers have gone. The sculptural hostas, their flower heads removed, are focal points until October, and the faded campanula seed heads remain until they shed their seeds.

Magnolia grandiflora is joined here by another all-seasons faithful, *Ruta graveolens* 'Jackman's Blue'.

Magnolia grandiflora

Height 15-25ft
Spread 10-15ft
Best July-October

Magnolia grandiflora is a magnificent large shrub with glossy, evergreen leaves and huge, cup-shaped flowers. It excels when grown against the south or west-facing wall of a house or outbuilding. Two good forms of *M. grandiflora* are 'Goliath' with its huge blooms, and the fragrant 'Exmouth', both of which flower when quite young.

Underplant with the white, spring-flowering *Choisya ternata*, and for an autumn follow-on, try *Lespedeza thunbergii* with its pink, pea-like flowers.
CULTIVATION Plant in spring in any well-drained fertile soil. Propagate by layering the previous season's growth in spring or the current season's growth in late summer.

There is a dramatic change of scene in late autumn, when the lavateras' main stems are cut back to 2ft, and the penstemons and campanulas are cut back too. A wall is revealed, draped with the variegated ivy *Hedera colchica* 'Variegata'. Married to the neatly domed *Sarcococca confusa* and the variegated *Euonymus fortunei* 'Silver Queen', both shade-lovers, it forms a backdrop for a procession of bulbs through winter and into spring.

Winter trees are etched against the sky, while at a lower level are the graceful bare branches of the cotinus. The evergreen shrubs add solidity and the scent of the sarcococca's winter flowers carries for yards. But the show-stoppers are the flowering bulbs. Winter crocus or small early daffodils like *Narcissus* 'Ice Follies' can build up to a crescendo of spring colour provided by the cultivar 'Barrett Browning'. *Prunus cerasifera* 'Pissardii' explodes into a shock of white blossom with just a hint of unfurling purple leaves. The hosta leaves cut through the earth, and the nodding maroon and green bells of *Allium siculum* swell. Later the light violet flowers of *Allium rosenbachianum* take centre stage among the perennials and the lavateras poised once more for their summer performance.

IN SPRING, *Narcissus* 'Ice Follies' and *N.* 'Barrett Browning' are the climax of a succession of bulbs that have rung the changes against a late autumn and winter backdrop of bare-branched trees, evergreen shrubs and the year-round, soft green of *Salvia officinalis*.

The luxuriant golden-green foliage of *Philadelphus coronarius* 'Aureus' provides the background to fragrant early summer blossom.

The flowers of *Philadelphus* 'Belle Etoile' have a red-purple blotch at the base of each petal, a colour that is effectively picked out in the surrounding hardy geraniums, heucheras and foxgloves.

Philadelphus coronarius
'Aureus'

Height 6-10ft · *Spread* 5-8ft
Best June-July

Fountains of white flowers, which are deliciously fragrant, have given philadelphus the nickname of 'mock orange'. *Philadelphus coronarius* 'Aureus' has the added attraction of leaves that open bright yellow, and soften to greeny-gold. It is a strong-growing, medium-sized shrub with dense, bushy foliage, and is particularly well suited to dry soils.

Plant in a mixed border, with herbaceous plants sited in front of the shrub's lower stems. *Euphorbia griffithii* 'Fireglow' is a good choice for a spring display of brick-red flowers, and pink-ribbed foliage in autumn. An underplanting of *Geranium wallichianum* 'Buxton's Blue' will give a long succession of blue flowers from late summer until late autumn.
CULTIVATION Plant in autumn or spring in any well-drained soil. Philadelphus need plenty of light, but too much direct sun may cause leaves to bleach. Prune after flowering to keep within bounds. Propagate by taking semi-hardwood cuttings in late summer or hardwood cuttings in autumn, and place them directly outside.

Philadelphus
Hybrids

Height 3-6ft · *Spread* 4-6ft
Best June-July

A wide choice of philadelphus hybrids is available, many of them raised in France at the turn of the century. All have the distinctive 'mock orange' scent of the philadelphus genus. Particularly suitable for smaller gardens is 'Sybille', with its arching stems of single, purple-stained flowers. 'Avalanche' has loose-growing, arching stems bearing small but profuse, richly scented flowers. At the medium

Scents mingle sweetly when *Rosa* 'Old Blush' is planted next to *Philadelphus* 'Beauclerk'.

to large end of the scale are 'Beauclerk', whose large, single blooms are flushed pale cerise around the stamens, and 'Etoile Rose' with petals splashed deep purple-pink.

Like *Philadelphus coronarius* 'Aureus', the hybrids are best suited to a mixed border, with herbaceous plants such as low-growing asters in front of the shrub's stems to continue a colourful display into autumn.
CULTIVATION Plant in autumn or spring in a sunny, well-drained position. Prune after flowering to keep within bounds. Propagate by semi-hardwood cuttings in late summer or hardwood cuttings in autumn, and place directly outside.

The soft apricot blooms of *Rosa* 'Buff Beauty' and the creamy flowers of *Potentilla* 'Vilmoriniana' recur throughout summer. The rose's glossy, deep green foliage contrasts beautifully with the potentilla's silvered leaves.

Potentilla 'Princess' forms the background for *Paeonia officinalis* 'Rosea Superba Plena'.

Potentilla
Shrubby cultivars

Height 1-4ft · *Spread* 2-4ft
Best May-September

Shrubby potentillas are wonderfully versatile. They are very hardy, they will flourish in any soil, and they are equally at home in a mixed border or as individual specimens on a terrace or patio. Their 1in wide, saucer-shaped flowers are like little dog roses, and they appear over many months. Colours range from pure white and yellow to flaming orange-red, and the leaves vary from silver to mid-green. Some cultivars, such as the bright 'Tangerine' and 'Sunset', show better colour when planted in light shade, but most shrubby potentillas are at their best in full sun.

There's a potentilla for every garden, as size and habit vary.

The pendulous, softly coloured flower heads of *Robinia hispida* are rather like those of a wisteria.

Reliability, compactness of habit and rewardingly long flowering won *Potentilla* 'Elizabeth' a Royal Horticultural Society award.

(*Potentilla* cont)
'Mandschurica', with pure white flowers, and 'Longacre' with bright sulphur-yellow flowers, are dwarf and mat-forming. 'Tangerine' grows into a dense, wide-spreading mound that becomes covered with pale coppery-yellow blooms, and 'Sunset' is a small shrub with flaming orange-red flowers. Upright 'Vilmoriniana' bears a profusion of cream flowers against silver leaves. 'Elizabeth' is a big, dome-shaped shrub with canary-yellow flowers set against silvery-green leaves.

In a border, plant roses in complementary colours behind potentillas. *Waldsteinia ternata* will spread a carpet of green starred with bright yellow flowers through the summer, while *Mahonia* 'Charity' will provide glossy, dark evergreen foliage throughout the year and yellow flower spikes in autumn and winter. Potentillas also associate well with heathers.
CULTIVATION Plant in spring or autumn in any well-drained soil. Prune weak or old stems at ground level as necessary to keep the plants bushy. Propagate by taking semi-hardwood cuttings in late summer.

Robinia hispida

ROSE ACACIA

Height 6-10ft · *Spread* 6-8ft
Best May-June

Robinia hispida is fast-growing, tolerant of pollution, and useful for dry, sunny situations. Plump racemes of pea-like flowers, are set among slender branches of dainty leaflets and are a delight in early summer.

Train a robinia against a sunny wall with *Wisteria sinensis* for a sensational display of pendulous pink and lavender flowers in spring and early summer. Nearby, a haze of china blue from *Ceanothus* 'Gloire de Versailles' could follow in late summer, and *Daphne mezereum* could provide a late winter show of rose-pink.
CULTIVATION Plant during spring or autumn in a sunny, well-drained position protected from strong wind. To propagate, remove suckers in early spring.

Weigela florida

Height 5-7ft · *Spread* 4-6ft
Best June

The arching branches of *Weigela florida* are laden with closely packed, foxglove-like flowers in early summer. Sometimes there's the bonus of a secondary display in late summer or early autumn. The shrub is easy to grow and, as it is resistant to pollution, is a good candidate for town gardens.

W. f. 'Variegata' has a two-fold beauty, with fresh pink blossom set against creamy-white-margined leaves. 'Bristol Ruby' has rich ruby-red flowers and mid-green leaves that are prominently veined.

The weigelas are useful for a mixed border, where *Centranthus ruber* could continue the red theme through the summer after 'Bristol Ruby' blossom has faded. The white-variegated leaves of *Cornus alba* 'Elegantissima' will offset the flowers of 'Bristol Ruby' in early summer, and offer naked red stems in

Weigela florida 'Variegata' combines creamy-margined leaves with an abundance of flowers that crowd along the previous year's new stems.

Summer *TREES*

WHILE THE trees of spring have a joyous prettiness about them, in summer there's more emphasis on glamour and exotic dignity. The flowers tend to be individually spectacular or collectively dramatic, and the colours are often more dashing than the spring equivalents. This is not to say that summer-flowering trees are in any way vulgar – merely that they clothe themselves in the appropriate summer fashion.

Catalpa bignonioides
'Aurea'

INDIAN BEAN TREE

Height 15-25ft
Spread 15-25ft
Best July-August

Ravishing in both appearance and fragrance, this catalpa is at its most beautiful when clad in its summer dress of sweet-scented, golden-throated, white flowers. These, however, only appear on mature trees between 15 and 20 years old, and they fade comparatively quickly. They leave behind long brown seed pods like narrow beans which remain long after leaf-fall. The soft, broad, heart-shaped leaves, however, are magnificent throughout the summer, and release a pungent smell when touched. *Catalpa bignonioides* is a broad, spreading tree best suited for a medium-sized or large garden, perhaps as a lawn specimen. But

Although slender of trunk, this fine specimen of *Catalpa bignonioides* 'Aurea' is mature enough to bear a good head of blossom.

C. b. 'Aurea', with its beautiful golden-yellow leaves, is slower growing than the species, and appropriate for a smaller garden. *C. b.* 'Koehnei' is a variegated form.

Herbaceous plants with bold foliage combine well beneath the catalpa's broad canopy. Bergenias and *Helleborus argutifolius* will make a display of purple and yellow-white in springtime, before the catalpa foliage begins to develop. *Euphorbia polychroma* will give a bright display of yellow flowers to herald the golden-yellow foliage of 'Aurea'.

CULTIVATION Plant at any time between mid-autumn and early spring in fertile, well-drained but moist soil, in a sunny site sheltered from winds that could damage the leaves.

winter. Both weigela cultivars would benefit from a group of *Pulsatilla vulgaris* at their feet, for the purple spring flowers and tousled seed heads to follow. The feathery spires of *Cimicifuga simplex* 'White Pearl' and chocolate-red flowers of *Cosmos atrosanguineus* would be fine autumn companions.

CULTIVATION Plant during spring or autumn in fertile, well-drained soil in full sun. Prune old flowering shoots when flowering has finished. Propagate by taking semi-hardwood cuttings in late summer.

In early summer, *Weigela* 'Bristol Ruby' gives a luxuriant display of intense, eye-catching crimson.

Variously suggesting ghosts, doves and handkerchiefs, the dancing white bracts of *Davidia involucrata* are a special ornament of early summer.

The graceful *Davidia involucrata* was discovered by the missionary Père David in China in 1869.

Cornus controversa
'Variegata'

Height 8-15ft · *Spread* 6-10ft
Best May-October

Cornus controversa 'Variegata' is an aristocrat of the garden. Its silver-frosted foliage is borne on slender branches that spread in layers like the iced tiers of a wedding cake, and the effect is enhanced on mature trees in summer when diminutive, decorative clusters of creamily-white flowers are added. In October the foliage turns to a variegated purple.

The tree's charm can best be appreciated in a lawn, with a carpet of spring bulbs around it,

Outstanding among any plant companions is a mature specimen of *Cornus controversa* 'Variegata', rising tier upon tier like a giant Victorian cake stand.

such as the purplish *Anemone blanda*. Among other suitable companions are the perennials *Brunnera macrophylla*, with its blue flowers, and the lilac-mauve to maroon *Geranium phaeum*. The changing hues of *Epimedium* × *rubrum* leaves would make a low-growing feature, and *Iris foetidissima* could provide evergreen leaves and orange seeds when the cornus display fades in autumn.
CULTIVATION Plant in autumn in any good soil, in a sheltered, sunny position.

Davidia involucrata

POCKET-HANDKERCHIEF TREE

Height 20-30ft · *Spread* 10-15ft
Best May-June

The creamy-white leaf-shaped bracts, up to 8in long, have given this tree its best-known

common name. They hang in unevenly sized pairs beneath the branches and dance in the slightest breeze, suggesting a fluttering of doves or an agitation of spectres – hence the tree's other names of dove tree and ghost tree.

Small shrubs make the best companions for *Davidia involucrata*. Try the splendid spring-flowering Japanese azaleas, the Kurume hybrids, among the best of which is the richly pink 'Hinomayo'. For a continuation of colour it would be hard to beat hydrangeas, especially the smaller cultivars, like 'Ami Pasquier', 'Pia' or 'Grayswood'. The golden-yellow flowers of *Hypericum* 'Hidcote' would also provide glorious company until late summer.
CULTIVATION Plant between autumn and spring in a rich, moisture-retentive soil, in a sunny, sheltered site.

Eucryphia × nymansensis
'Nymansay'

Height 15-20ft · *Spread* 6-10ft
Best August-September

Eucryphia × nymansensis
'Nymansay' has gleaming bowls
of blooms against dark foliage.

Late summer is made glorious by this magnificent evergreen, when white flowers, up to 2½in in diameter, cover the entire tree. Even when not in flower 'Nymansay' is still a handsome specimen, with lustrous, dark green leaves.

This tree is splendid enough to stand on its own, but a nice contrast with its pristine snowy whiteness would be the blue of *Hydrangea macrophylla* 'Blue Wave' or 'Blue Bonnet', or the pink of *H. m.* 'Mariesii'. To provide spring and early summer colour there is a useful range of evergreen azaleas, the Japanese Kurume hybrids. Some good examples are 'Kureno-Yuki' (white), 'Hinomayo' (pink) and 'Hinode-giri' (crimson). However, since it is essential to plant eucryphias with their heads in the sun but their roots in cool shade, you could plant heathers right up to their low-growing branches. In soils that are not acid enough, use *Erica carnea* instead and go for foliage colours.

CULTIVATION Plant in autumn in a sunny, sheltered site with moist, acid or neutral soil. Keep the roots shaded. Propagate by taking semi-hardwood cuttings during late summer.

Gleditsia triacanthos
'Sunburst'

GOLDEN HONEY LOCUST

Height 15-25ft · *Spread* 10-15ft
Best May-June

Gleditsia triacanthos 'Sunburst' is well named, as can be seen in late spring when its golden-yellow foliage erupts like the sun bursting through overcast skies. During summer and through to autumn, the foliage retains its golden-green hue,

Despite its aristocratic appearance, *Gleditsia triacanthos* 'Sunburst' is indifferent to industrial pollution, and can therefore bring its feathery golden foliage to brighten city gardens deep into autumn.

unless the weather is very hot; then the leaves darken, leaving the paler shade only as a delicate edging at the tips.

With its elegance of branch, the golden honey locust is excellent for a small garden, especially if it can be featured in a lawn. To complement it, plant perennials with contrasting foliage for ground cover, such as the grey-green leaves of *Hosta sieboldiana* 'Elegans'. Alternatively, try *H. fortunei* 'Albopicta' or 'Aureomarginata', both with dark green foliage and clotted cream-coloured centres or margins. For the benefits of both spring blooms and foliage contrast, plant bergenias, favourites of that great gardener Gertrude Jekyll, choosing the white-flowered *Bergenia* 'Silberlicht' or *B. purpurascens* with crimson flowers and red winter leaves.

CULTIVATION Plant at any time between mid-autumn and early spring in full sun, in any fertile, moisture-retentive garden soil.

As it flowers best in warm, dry conditions, *Koelreuteria paniculata* is a good choice for sunny, sheltered town gardens.

IN AUTUMN – if the summer has been long and hot – *Koelreuteria paniculata* may show pretty seed capsules, which remain until November.

The glorious, paper-white, scented blooms of *Magnolia sieboldii* appear intermittently from late spring to late summer.

Koelreuteria paniculata

GOLDEN RAIN TREE

Height 25-35ft · *Spread* 10-15ft
Best July-August

The golden rain tree really lives up to its name in a hot, dry summer, when it flowers most prolifically. Large clusters of fragile yellow flowers, like golden raindrops, speckle the foliage. These may be followed by inflated, bladder-like seed capsules of the palest green flushed with red, that last until late autumn. The foliage, too, changes with the seasons, the handsomely divided leaves unfurling shrimp-red in spring, maturing to pale greenish-yellow and turning bright yellow in autumn. *Koelreuteria paniculata* is also sometimes called 'Pride of India', though since it hails from northern China, it is difficult to see why. But it will be the pride of any English garden, on its own in a lawn, or among sombre evergreens in a herbaceous border.

The stately blue *Agapanthus* Headbourne hybrids and the erect, soft orange *Kniphofia* 'Underway' can be combined effectively beneath the tree's delicate colours. Alternatively, consider a scattering of autumn-flowering bulbs beneath, such as *Colchicum speciosum* and *C. autumnale*, whose purple-pink display could be followed by the yellow of *Sternbergia lutea*.

CULTIVATION Plant between autumn and spring in a sunny, sheltered position with any free-draining soil. This tree is not suitable for colder parts of the country. Propagate by taking root cuttings in winter and placing in a cold frame.

Magnolia

Height 7-9ft · *Spread* 5-7ft
Best May-June

Taken all in all, magnolias are the most exotic and lovely flowering trees that can be persuaded to grow outdoors in these northerly climes. Persuasion, in fact, is unnecessary, for with their tolerance of deep clay and city fumes, they are eager to bring glamour to the most unlikely situations. *Magnolia wilsonii*, for example, is a broad, spreading tree with gracefully arching branches, which in May and June, bear pendent, white satin flowers with crimson stamens. The rather similar *M. sinensis* gives a wonderful display at the same time of year, of slightly larger and more strongly lemon-scented blooms of the purest white with bright red centres. Both species flower when the oval, glossy leaves have opened. Another excellent, and longer-flowering, magnolia is *M. sieboldii*, whose nodding, oval buds open into silky, sweetly scented, snow-white flowers with claret stamens. From late spring to late summer, these appear intermittently, and are followed by clusters of dark pink seed capsules which open in mid-autumn to reveal orange seeds.

The tree magnolias make excellent lawn specimens that require little back-up when in flower. But beneath their branches, and to get the show on the road in spring, polyanthus, or drifts of chionodoxas and scillas could be planted. For a lasting sensation in the shrub border, set the tree magnolias among early flowering shrubs such as *Rhododendron* 'Praecox' or the later *R.* 'Pink Pebble'. In autumn, a flare of orange-yellow from *Fothergilla major*, or the red-purple *Disanthus cercidifolius* could take over.

CULTIVATION Plant in spring in well-drained, moist soil, in a shady, sheltered site. The magnolias do not like chalk soils, and *M. sieboldii* is particularly intolerant of lime. Propagate by cuttings in summer or by layering in spring.

The dainty, drooping flowers of the Japanese snowbell, *Styrax japonica*, are carried along the undersides of the fanning branches, so if possible, plant the tree where they can be seen from below.

Sorbus thibetica 'John Mitchell' has the light-catching qualities of all the whitebeams, but is a particularly splendid, large-leaved form.

Sorbus thibetica
'John Mitchell'
(syn *S.* 'Mitchellii')

Height 20-30ft · *Spread* 10-20ft
Best May-October

When a summer breeze catches this whitebeam its leaves dance and twist to reveal their silvery undersides, and the whole tree shimmers in the light, taking on the silver-grey look of beaten pewter. In autumn there's a new colour scheme as the leaves take on shades of russet and yellow.

'John Mitchell' is more robust than the common whitebeam, *Sorbus aria*, with broad leaves up to 8in long. It looks splendid standing alone on a lawn, where its pyramidal shape and handsome foliage can be best admired. The lower branches arch gracefully to the ground, but it is unlikely that they will obscure a spring display of the small, bluebell-like *Scilla sibirica* and dwarf narcissus. For summer colour, train a large-flowering, non-strangling clematis, such as *Clematis* 'Ernest Markham', to clamber among the whitebeam's branches.

CULTIVATION Plant between autumn and spring in any well-drained soil. The sorbus will withstand an exposed situation but is at its best in an open, sunny position.

Styrax japonica
JAPANESE SNOWBELL

Height 10-15ft · *Spread* 8-10ft
Best June

Styrax japonica bears outstretched, fan-like branches that spread out horizontally and droop at their slender tips. In June, the flowers line up along all the undersides to hang like snowdrops and bring a touch of the orient to occidental gardens. If there is room, you might also grow its relation, *S. hemsleyana*, for contrast. Its June flowers, too, are white, with yellow anthers, but have elongated, lax racemes. In autumn, the leaves of both species are delicately shaded with orange and russet.

Herbaceous plants with attractive foliage as well as a good flower display go well with *S. japonica*, like *Rodgersia pinnata*, while *Kirengeshoma palmata* will bring yellow flowers in autumn. If you wish to plant shrubs with the snowbell, choose *Hydrangea serrata* 'Grayswood' or 'Preziosa' for late colour, and *Hypericum* 'Rowallane' for large yellow flowers that will bloom from

IN AUTUMN, *Styrax japonica* glows with russet and orange tones.

midsummer until the autumn.
CULTIVATION Plant between mid-autumn and mid-spring in a slightly acid, moisture-retentive soil. Propagate by taking cuttings in midsummer, or by layering in spring.

Summer
CLIMBERS

S OME OF the headiest scents of summer are provided by exotic climbers which, allowed to roam free in trees and shrubs, give the garden an air little short of intoxicating. While many other kinds of scented plants keep their olfactory charms to themselves, climbers, by their very nature, distribute their perfumes at just the level at which they can be most appreciated. A warm evening, spent among the fragrances of jasmine and honeysuckle, amid a visual feast of clematis, will linger on in the mind long after summer's other joys have gone.

Campsis × tagliabuana
'Madame Galen'

TRUMPET VINE

Height 20ft
Best July-September

The *Campsis* genus consists of only two species, *C. grandiflora* and *C. radicans*. This, their offspring, is the most suitable trumpet vine for British gardens, since it will flower well even though the hot sun of a continental climate is lacking. The plant is deciduous, the foliage rather like that of an ash, the stems are more or less self-clinging, though requiring some support, and the flowers are wide, flared trumpets of bright salmon-rose. Clambering up a wall or fence, it is quite an awesome sight.

Match it in summer with

For a sound, showy wall covering, it would be hard to beat *Campsis × tagliabuana* 'Madame Galen'.

other sun-lovers, such as the splendid blue or white globes of agapanthus, the stately yellow or bicoloured kniphofias, or the tubular flowers of a phygelius. Even before the campsis flowers, its luxuriant foliage will make a fine backdrop for blue *Ceanothus* 'Delight', while in winter the evergreen, fragrant *Daphne odora* 'Aureomarginata' will distract the eye from the bare stems.

CULTIVATION Plant in spring in any well-drained soil, in full sun and preferably against a south-facing wall. Tie young plants to a support. Prune as little as possible, as this encourages leafy growth at the expense of flowers. Propagate by semi-hardwood cuttings in summer.

Clematis
Large-flowered hybrids

The large-flowered clematis hybrids are spectacular, long-lasting in bloom, and suited to many garden situations. The various cultivars produce their magnificent flowers, 3-6in or more across, in great profusion all summer long. Some present their first flush in late spring or midsummer, then a second show in autumn. Others have one major explosion of colour, then bloom intermittently for several weeks afterwards. Even the individual blooms have impressive staying power, for they are made up, not of fragile petals, but of tough, brightly coloured sepals.

Clematis cling by their leaves; each one is made up of small leaflets, whose stems entwine about any suitable support, and may need tying in as they grow.

A popular plant partnership is to marry clematis hybrids with climbing or shrub roses. Each plant bears blooms so opulent that any shortcomings in the rose's shape is overlooked. But hybrid clematis flowers can fill any shrub whose season of glory is past or yet to come, or add to the host's display so that each plant gains from the contrast.

CULTIVATION

Clematis are greedy feeders, and need plenty of humus and a well-drained soil if they are to thrive. Plant them during autumn or spring, a little deeper than they were set in their containers, in a sunny or lightly

The lovely and vigorous *Clematis* 'Comtesse de Bouchaud' contributes its rose-pink, yellow-stamened flowers from June to August.

shaded position. Some of the striped cultivars look their best in light shade as they tend to fade in full sun. The roots must be shaded – for example, by the foliage of low-growing shrubs or perennials planted about 2ft away from the clematis stem. Prune early flowering hybrids in February or March. Cut out all dead growths and shorten the remaining stems to the topmost pair of strong buds. Prune late-flowering hybrids by cutting all growths hard back to 1-3ft in February or March.

Propagate by taking semi-hardwood stem cuttings in midsummer. Dip the cuttings in rooting powder incorporating a fungicide, and insert in a mixture of peat and sand. Cover with plastic to maintain humidity until roots have formed.

To lend an opulent touch to the garden, partner the long-flowering *Clematis* 'Marie Boisselot' with the climbing rose 'New Dawn'.

Clematis go well in tandem with other plants, for example in such partnerships as *Clematis* 'Mrs N. Thompson' with a berberis (above) and *C.* 'Lasurstern' with *Rosa* 'All Gold' (right).

195

'Mrs George Jackman'
First flush of semi-double flowers;
later flowers are single. Height 10ft.
Best May-June, and August.

'Horn of Plenty'
Produces the largest flowers
of all when well grown.
Likes sunny aspect.
Height 10ft. Best May-June.

'Richard Pennell'
Any aspect. Height 12ft.
Best June-September.

'Marie Boisselot'
(syn 'Madame le Coultre')
Very free-flowering. Height 10ft.
Best June-September.

'Vyvyan Pennell'
First flowers double; later flowers
single. Needs sunny position.
Height 10ft. Best May-June,
and August.

'Lincoln Star
Plant in shade
to avoid fading.
Height 10ft.
Best May-June,
and September.

'Bee's Jubilee'
Plant in shade to prevent
fading. Height 10ft.
Best May-June,
and August.

'Mrs N. Thompson'
Very free-flowering.
Height 12ft.
Best June-August.

Spinning
a web of clematis

Every wall, fence or pergola, every decent-sized tree or shrub,
is a potential support for these flamboyant beauties. With flowering periods
that together span nearly six months, the large-flowered hybrids provide
a continuous, graceful link between late spring and autumn. At the
cost of very little ground space, a number of different
cultivars can trail their great starry blooms
through the upper levels of the garden.

*Photographed in May at Treasures,
Tenbury Wells, Worcestershire.*

'Elsa Spath'
(syn 'Xerxes')
Almost constantly in flower;
flourishes in any aspect.
Height 10ft. Best May-June,
and August-September.

'Duchess of Edinburgh'
Early blooms double; later
blooms single. Height 8ft.
Best June-August.

'Dawn'
Flourishes in sunny position.
Height 8ft. Best May-June,
and August.

'Niobe'
Glossy leaves; thrives
in any aspect. Height 10ft.
Best June-July.

'Royalty'
First blooms double; second flush
single. Needs sunny position.
Height 8ft. Best August.

197

With its dense mass of stems, the vigorous *Clematis flammula* is the ideal plant to clothe a high unsightly wall or to enliven a dull hedge.

Clematis flammula

FRAGRANT CLEMATIS

Height 10-15ft
Best August-October

In late summer and early autumn this vigorous clematis metamorphoses into a cloud of small, starry white flowers redolent of almonds and hawthorn; as they fade, they are replaced by silky 'old man's beard' seed heads. Since this species makes a tangle of stems, it is best grown through a tall hedge or trained up a high wall and allowed to cascade down from the top. There, its froth of blossom would contrast well with the changing colours of mophead hydrangeas; both the deep pink 'Altona' and 'Ami Pasquier', for instance, turn coppery-crimson as autumn advances. Enliven the autumnal picture still further by planting pink colchicums at the foot of the hydrangeas, together with a carpet of forget-me-nots or bluebells (*Endymion hispanicus*) for spring. Deep blue columbines, *Aquilegia* 'Hensol Harebell', could carry the group through to early summer.

CULTIVATION Plant in spring or autumn in fertile soil, preferably with its roots in shade and its head in the sun. Prune hard back in spring if it has to be kept in bounds, or lightly to remove dead wood. Propagate by semi-hardwood cuttings in summer.

A native of southern Europe, *Clematis viticella* has been grown in Britain since the 16th century. Among the cultivars to emerge since then is the lovely crimson 'Kermesina', perfect for training up an old brick wall.

Clematis viticella

Height 12ft
Best July-September

Clematis viticella flowers nod demurely like open bells from their long stems. In the wild – in southern Europe – the blooms are purple, but there are many cultivated forms, mostly in the blue to reddish-violet range. 'Alba Luxurians', however, has white flowers tinged with green. If you set it against a dark background of yew or holly, you could add spring-flowering *Helleborus corsicus* and white daffodils, ferns, white variegated *Hosta crispula* and white hydrangeas for a cool green and white scheme to last all year.

Clematis viticella cultivars 'Abundance' and the similar 'Kermesina', both claret-red and tall growing, would look well

One of the most subtly hued hybrids of *Clematis viticella* is the green-tinged 'Alba Luxurians'.

Jasminum officinale, common white jasmine, has been scenting cottage gardens since the mid-16th century. Plant it where its fragrance can be best appreciated and perhaps support it, as here, by a white 'Iceberg' rose.

Another traditional favourite valued for its sweet scent is the honeysuckle *Lonicera caprifolium*.

growing through a large *Juniperus* 'Pfitzeriana', or with white agapanthus at their feet. Deepest hued of all viticellas is 'Royal Velours', of a dark wine velvety purple. It would be superb against grey foliage, with a planting of crimson nicotianas added for good measure.

CULTIVATION Plant in spring or autumn in fertile soil and in sun, but with shade for the roots. Prune hard back in spring. Propagate by layering in spring.

Jasminum officinale

SUMMER JASMINE

Height 20-30ft
Best June-September

Vigorous, twining summer jasmine makes a tangle of deliciously scented white flowers that can be trained over a wall or allowed to make their way through a tree. Despite its vigour, one of the nicest ways to grow it is around a window that is left open on warm summer evenings. There, it might be accompanied by other scented flowers, especially those that emit their fragrance at night, such as white *Nicotiana alata*, or night-scented stocks. Just as fragrant is *Osmanthus delavayi*, which produces flowers in spring, while its dark, evergreen foliage would look well in winter when the jasmine is bare. *Rosmarinus officinalis* 'Benenden Blue' could offer its bright blue, early spring flowers set against aromatic foliage.

CULTIVATION Plant in autumn or spring in any well-drained soil, in full sun or partial shade. Choose a sheltered spot in chilly areas. Plants may be thinned out in early spring. Propagate by taking semi-hardwood cuttings in mid to late summer.

Lonicera caprifolium

EARLY CREAM HONEYSUCKLE

Height 15-20ft
Best June-July

As its common name implies, this is one of the first honeysuckles to flower; its profuse creamy blooms are sometimes faintly tinged with pink, and are always very fragrant. Like the common honeysuckle *Lonicera periclymenum*, it is a creature of cottage gardens where it is often seen clambering over rustic porches. More imaginatively, it could be used on an arch or between two old and adjoining trees to make a scented bower, with *Lilium regale*, night-scented stocks and tobacco plants added for later summer fragrance. Despite its name, *Hebe* 'Midsummer Beauty' will carry its lilac flower spikes through to the first frosts of autumn, while male skimmias such as 'Rubella' would add sweetness to spring.

CULTIVATION Plant in autumn or spring in any fertile garden soil. Train the stems over or through their supports. Propagate by cuttings in summer or autumn.

'Florida' is one of several cultivars of *Lonicera periclymenum*; its superb flush of pink in summer is followed by bright red berries in autumn.

Lonicera periclymenum

WOODBINE

Height 20ft
Best June-September

As befits a plant of full summer, *Lonicera periclymenum*, the common honeysuckle of Britain's countryside, is more vigorous than *L. caprifolium*, and its sweet fragrance is particularly noticeable at dawn and dusk. The cultivar 'Serotina', known as late Dutch honeysuckle, is brighter and later flowering (July to October) than the species, its creamy flowers flushed rich red-purple on the outside.

Beware of the vigour of this species, for it can strangle a weaker host tree or shrub. Try growing it on a stout stake in the middle of a border. The scheme could be extended by the shrub rose 'Mutabilis', whose single flowers change from buff to crimson. Clove-scented ruby and cream wallflowers could precede this show in spring, and chrysanthemums of similar hues round off the year. Winter pansies will bridge the brief gap in this cottage-style planting. Shrewd honeysuckle fanciers can extend the season of their favourite climbers by planting 'Serotina' with *L. caprifolium*, which flowers a little later.

CULTIVATION Plant and train as for *Lonicera caprifolium*.

Lonicera periclymenum cultivar, 'Graham Thomas', makes a pastel pattern with *Rosa* 'Albertine'.

Lonicera sempervirens

TRUMPET HONEYSUCKLE

Height 20ft
Best July-September

It seems eccentric to grow a scentless honeysuckle, but what this species lacks in fragrance is compensated for by exuberant, 3in long orange-scarlet trumpets and rich, semi-evergreen foliage.

For such boldly coloured flowers, companions must be chosen with caution; kindest are soft yellow, white and pure blue, with some silvery foliage thrown in. *Ceanothus* × *burkwoodii*, and a white large-flowered clematis hybrid such as 'Henryi' or 'Marie Boisselot' would contribute towards a long summer of flower. For colour earlier in the year, plant the winter-flowering *Iris histrioides* 'Major', followed by a

With its head in the sun, and *Santolina chamaecyparissus* to shade its feet, *Lonicera sempervirens* is an exuberant companion for *Rosa* 'Albertine'.

spring programme of *Tulipa* 'Purissima' with primrose wallflowers. *Iris pallida dalmatica* bridges the flower gap in late spring and adds good glaucous sword-leaves for the summer.

CULTIVATION Plant in autumn or spring in any fertile garden soil, with its roots shaded and its head in the sun. It grows

The intricate blooms of *Passiflora caerulea* are said to represent features of Christ's Passion.

The cultivar *Solanum crispum* 'Glasnevin' has a longer flowering season than the species.

IN AUTUMN, if you are lucky and the summer has been long and hot, *Passiflora caerulea* may reward you with its soft apricot-orange passion fruits, although they seldom ripen and are barely edible if they do.

particularly well against a wall. Spray at the first sign of aphid infestation. Propagate by taking and planting semi-hardwood cuttings in late summer.

Passiflora caerulea

BLUE PASSION FLOWER

Height 20ft
Best July-October

Despite its exotic appearance, the blue passion flower is one of the hardiest of its genus. In mild areas it retains its fingered leaves all winter, and even when it is cut down by frost it will usually grow again from the roots. The flowers are zoned in blue, white and purple, and their intricate structures were said by Spanish missionaries in South America to represent certain features of Christ's Passion. The five sepals and petals are the apostles, less Peter and Judas; the three stigmas are the three nails, the five stamens the five wounds, the corona the crown of thorns, and the fine tendrils the scourges. In the same mould, but with exquisite, ivory-white flowers, is the slightly less hardy form 'Constance Elliott'.

During its long summer blooming, the passion flower's colours are echoed by blue ageratum, the mallow *Lavatera* 'Mont Blanc' and purple heliotrope, while form is added by the sword leaves of a yucca. There are the bright mauve spikes of *Liriope muscari* for autumn, and for spring, *Ipheion uniflorum* could make a wide carpet of lilac-blue stars. Those who prefer a scheme of greater contrast should nevertheless keep the colours soft. The delicate pink of *Cistus* 'Peggy Sammons' would be a good idea, or the primrose-yellow of *Phygelius* 'Moonraker'.

CULTIVATION Plant in spring against a warm wall or sheltered fence, and in well-drained soil enriched by a general fertiliser. In cold winters, protect the roots with a layer of peat or grit. Cut out frost-killed stems and growths that are too vigorous in spring. Propagate by semi-hardwood cuttings in summer.

Solanum crispum
'Glasnevin'

(syn *S. c. autumnale*)

Height 10-15ft
Best June-October

This semi-evergreen plant is a native of Chile. It is particularly effective when trained up a wall where its long succession of rich violet flowers, lit by cones of bright yellow stamens, will be seen to best advantage.

The solanum's colours would go well with the yellow climbing rose, 'Golden Showers', or

The flowers of *Solanum crispum* bear a strong resemblance to those of the potato plant.

(*Solanum crispum* cont)
with the soft, shell-pink 'New Dawn', both of which match its long flowering season. The red and purple *Fuchsia* 'Corallina' can be trained up a wall to mingle with the solanum; or, if you prefer a paler contrast, *Lavatera thuringiaca* 'Barnsley', with pink and white, mallow-like flowers, could be planted nearby. All these plants flower on and on until the frosts.
CULTIVATION Plant in spring in full sun, and in any well-drained soil; solanums flourish on chalk. Propagate by taking cuttings in late summer.

Tropaeolum speciosum

FLAME FLOWER

Height 8-12ft
Best July-October

One of these slender, herbaceous climbers is something of a star at the National Trust garden at Hidcote, where its

Give *Tropaeolum speciosum* a cool, moist spot and let its profusion of jewel-brilliant flowers trail through a dark host plant.

vivid, scarlet flowers, like open nasturtiums, are allowed to scramble over a clipped yew hedge. This is a combination that could hardly be improved upon, though a dark green conifer would also be effective. The foliage would show up both the flowers and the bright blue fruits that follow, and remain after the tropaeolum died down in autumn.
CULTIVATION Plant from containers in autumn, in peaty, moist soil on the shady side of the host shrub or hedge. Propagate by division of the rootstock, or by taking hardwood cuttings in late spring.

The autumn fruits of *Tropaeolum speciosum* are well set off by *Chamaecyparis* 'Boulevard'.

Summer ROSES

SUMMER AND roses are inextricably interwoven. By choosing from the vast range that is available, roses can be made to complement every aspect of the garden. Whether it is the formality of the bush rose, the scrambling informality of climbers and ramblers, or the solidity which shrub roses bring to the mixed border, every garden can benefit from some aspect of the rose's versatility.

Rosa

BUSH ROSES

For sheer brilliance and abundance of bloom – from midsummer until autumn – nothing can match the bush roses. They include the famous hybrid tea and floribunda groups – now known respectively as large-flowered and cluster-flowered roses.

The large-flowered roses were developed in the late 19th century, specifically for display in specimen rose beds and for the splendour of the individual blooms. They married the hardiness, vigour and fragrance of hybrid perpetual roses with the thick petals and pointed buds of tea roses. A completely new flower was born, as arresting in its perfectly conical buds as in the symmetrical beauty of its mature blooms. Many rich colours, hitherto unknown among roses, came too, some of which bordered on the gaudy; recently, there has

The clustered blooms of *Rosa* 'Memento' have little or no scent, but are aflame with colour.

been, on the whole, a welcome trend to return to softer shades.

The cluster-flowered roses bear sprays of many blooms. They evolved from crossing hybrid teas with the polyantha roses, and are tough and very free-flowering. The individual flowers are smaller and less reliably scented than hybrid teas, but this is compensated for by the luxuriance of their massed effect.

THE RIGHT SETTING

With their upright stature and richness of bloom, bush roses are often grown in solitary splendour, in beds set aside exclusively for roses, or in groups of single cultivars. There is no reason why they should not form a part of a more informal, mixed border, softened by 'ever-grey' foliage plants such as *Stachys byzantina* 'Silver Carpet' or perhaps *Ruta graveolens*. Plant them among shrubs that can provide colour

Rosa 'Just Joey', with its scented, coppery-apricot blooms and long, elegant buds, rises boldly above a subtly shaded sea of *Alchemilla mollis*.

A good, vigorous bedding rose, *Rosa* 'Matangi' (above) has vermilion petals with a silvery sheen on the outside.

Helleborus foetidus and *Sedum spectabile* (left) add substance to the galaxy of bush roses 'Pristine', 'Harry Edland', 'Silver Jubilee' and 'Margaret Merril'.

and scent in winter like *Daphne odora*, with low-growing perennials such as hostas and *Helleborus orientalis* placed in the foreground.

CULTIVATION

Plant bare-rooted roses in mid to late autumn or in mid-spring, in well-drained soil enriched with well-rotted organic material and bone meal. Prune the large-flowered roses to the first three or four buds on each stem in mid-spring. Prune cluster-flowered roses to about five to seven buds from the base. Remove old and diseased wood.

The enduring glory of the bush roses

To grow the large-flowered and cluster-flowered bush roses in exclusive specimen beds limits their versatility, for they can look splendid as part of a mixed border, planted in groups of two or three for best effect. They are all outstanding garden plants, flowering long and vigorously into the autumn and even beyond in favourable weather.

Photographed in July at the Royal National Rose Society Gardens, St Albans, Hertfordshire.

'Fragrant Delight'
Wonderfully scented.
Medium height.

'News'
Slight scent.
Vigorous and bushy;
medium height.

'Just Joey'
Very large, moderately
scented blooms. Spreading;
medium height.

'Paul Shirville'
Large-flowered, but several
blooms to a stem; good scent.
Bushy; medium height.

'Pristine'
Very large, well-scented
blooms. Upright; medium height.

'Memento'
Slight scent. Bushy;
medium height.

'The Times'
Very long flowering period
compensates for lack of scent.
Upright; medium height.

'Matangi'
Lightly scented.
Bushy; medium height.

'Amber Queen'
Award-winning,
sweet-scented, pretty buds.
Height medium to short.

'Peaudouce'
Very full, moderately
scented blooms. Bushy,
upright growth; medium height.

'Margaret Merrill'
Deliciously fragrant.
Vigorous and bushy;
medium height.

'Champagne Cocktail'
Moderate scent.
Bushy, upright growth;
medium height.

'Invincible'
Light scent.
Upright growth; tall.

'Silver Jubilee'
Magnificent buds open to large,
lightly scented blooms.
Medium height.

'Harry Edland'
Sturdy growth
and good scent.
Height medium to short.

Rosa

CLIMBING AND RAMBLING ROSES

Nothing can rival the repeat-blooming climbing roses for their combination of fragrance, beauty and remarkable length of flowering. From late spring to autumn, and sometimes beyond, they flower prolifically. Most are fragrant, and some carry autumn hips.

Their cousins, the rambling roses, can be coaxed into cascading from trees or to transform unsightly buildings into a profusion of foliage and flower. Each year, several new stems come from the base of the plant, resulting in long, loose, arching growth. But the beauty of most ramblers is transitory; they flower only briefly, and so are hardly suited to the garden for all seasons. 'Albéric Barbier', however, is a notable exception for its toughness of spirit, handsome, almost evergreen foliage, and the possibility of a sprinkling of later flowers after the midsummer flush.

CLIMBING STYLES

Generally speaking, the climbing roses have larger, more formal flowers than the ramblers, which are held on strong, upright stems. Unlike the ramblers, too, a climber throws out new shoots from anywhere on the plant, and can be trained effectively over a pillar, wall or fence, and responds well to formal fan-shaped pruning. Alternatively, leave a climber free to wander over a pergola and trellis, or to introduce summer blossom into

Rosa 'Golden Showers' dramatically lights up a backcloth of *Hedera helix* 'Atropurpurea'.

a large spring-flowering tree.

Clematis, apart from the more vigorous of the species, can trail in harmony with climbing roses for the most wonderful combinations of colour and flower, but give the rose a two or three-year start before establishing the partnership. The winter and early spring flowering *Clematis alpina* would add substance and violet flowers to the rose's winter profile. For more companions, see *The Climbing Garden* on page 334.

CULTIVATION

Plant during mid to late autumn or in mid-spring, in fertile, well-drained soil with extra organic material added. Prune at planting time, and otherwise in spring or after flowering to encourage fresh growth.

Rosa 'New Dawn' (above) is assertive enough to be partnered with the flamboyant *Clematis* 'Hagley Hybrid' for a symphony of soft pink and mauve blooms in summer and autumn.

The essence of an English country garden (right) is captured by a profusion of rose blooms and the mingling of their scents.

The arching stems of the fragrant, repeat-flowering rambler *Rosa* 'Phyllis Bide' rise from evergreen mounds of *Hebe albicans*.

'Climbing Ena Harkness'
Very rich fragrance; needs training
horizontally on south or west-facing wall.
Best late May–November.

'Sympathie'
Widespreading, thick,
dark foliage; fair scent.
Needs careful training.
Best June–September.

'Dortmund'
Widespreading;
slight scent.
Best June–October.

'Mme Alfred Carrière'
Well-scented; bushy,
nearly thornless.
Any aspect.
Best May–December.

'Albéric Barbier'
Very hardy, semi-evergreen;
green-apple fragrance.
Best June–July, and October.

'Climbing Arthur Bell'
Well-scented and upright;
almost thornless.
Best June–September.

'Climbing Iceberg'
Widespreading; light foliage;
good scent. Best June–September.

'Golden Showers'
Bushy and almost thornless;
sweet lemon fragrance. Any aspect.
Best June–November.

A tracery of climbing roses

The climbing roses, with their fragrance and profusion
of flower, are redolent of the atmosphere of old-fashioned country
gardens and long summer days. Supported by fences,
walls, trellises or trees, in gardens traditional or modern, they will
soften harsh outlines. And from one small patch of ground,
they can fill the garden's higher levels with blooms
that simply carry on appearing from late May to autumn,
and sometimes beyond.

Photographed in early July at the Royal National Rose Society Garden,
St Albans, Hertfordshire.

'Compassion'
Upright-growing;
award-winning scent.
Best June-September.

'New Dawn'
Sweetly scented; widespreading.
Best June-October.

'Zéphirine Drouhin'
Bushy, thornless, sweet-scented
Bourbon. Needs open site.
Best June-September.

'Handel'
Upright-growing;
light fragrance;
almost thornless.
Best June-September.

'Summer Wine'
Strongly perfumed;
upright-growing.
Best June-September.

'Pink Perpétue'
Widespreading;
free-flowering
fruity fragrance.
Any aspect.
Best June-November.

209

Rosa

SHRUB ROSES

Because shrub roses are pruned only lightly, to encourage plenty of blooms, they are more relaxed in habit than bush roses. They were bred for use as shrubs rather than as specimen plants, and their deluge of summer blossom merges easily into the profusion of the border. When necessary, they can be carefully pruned – to keep them orderly and contained, or to coax low-growing cultivars to spread in the right direction, or to guide taller, arching types against a wall. Some, like the tough 'Robusta' or 'Fountain' can even be encouraged to form luxuriant hedges.

The shrub roses as a whole embrace hybrids of the tough rugosa roses, delicate, scented hybrid musks, modern shrub and prostrate roses, and draw on a wealth of captivating flower shapes. The elusive scents of the species are often reproduced too. The modern shrub roses, in particular, combine the sweet fragrance of old-fashioned roses with persistence of flower and reliability.

SEASONAL HIGHLIGHTS

Some shrub roses, in the context of the all-season garden, are worth growing for their display in other seasons, so that their early blossom (see page 117), autumn hips or late flowers (page 304) can really be appreciated. The choice for summer is based predominantly on cultivars with flowering displays that start in June and often continue until autumn. The

Rosa 'Charles Austin',
Lilium regale and *Phormium tenax*
'Variegatum' harmonise cool creams and greens.

exception is 'Pink Bells' which, like its red and white forms, is covered by a mass of pompon, fully double blooms from late June to August. It has dark, glossy, small-leaved foliage, very dense and spreading, which makes excellent ground cover, or a fine backdrop.

Spring-flowering shrubs like *Exochorda* 'The Bride', *Paeonia lutea ludlowii* and *Spiraea × arguta* 'Bridal Wreath' will have passed their principal season of glory, but still have attractive summer foliage to enhance the rose in bloom. Old time cottage garden favourites like *Lavandula angustifolia* would coincide in flower, and also provide all-season support.

CULTIVATION

Plant potted roses at any time between autumn and mid-spring when soil and weather conditions are favourable. If possible, prepare a 2-3ft diameter hole for each rose a month in advance, adding bonemeal and well-rotted compost. The situation should be sunny and well-drained. Deadhead faded flowers; prune, if necessary, in late autumn. Shorten long growths and remove old or dead wood. Propagate by hardwood cuttings in autumn.

The informal character of shrub roses lets them merge easily into a busy border, where they provide constancy of colour into autumn.

Modern hybrid pinks and *Rosa* 'Felicia' retain all the charm of their ancestors but are in flower for a longer period.

Some shrubby roses, particularly the species, have only one flush of blooms, but compensate by their fine displays of hips in winter.

The gentle beauty of shrub roses

The casual quality of shrub roses, often combined
with a flowering season that can rival that of the bush roses in length,
allows them to blend easily into the mixed border. They can provide an atmospheric
background, or introduce flushes of blossom among the summer foliage
of spring-flowering shrubs. They are, for the most part, larger and more spreading
than bush roses, but careful pruning will keep them in check.

Photographed in late June at the Royal National Rose Society Garden,
St Albans, Hertfordshire.

'Aloha'
Scented, strong-growing,
fairly upright; also effective
as a climber. Height 6ft.

'Angelina'
Fragrant modern shrub;
medium height,
bushy habit. Height 5ft.

'Felicia'
Vigorous, sprawling
hybrid musk; strong,
aromatic scent; suitable
for hedging. Height 5ft.

'Robusta'
Dense, wide-growing
hybrid rugosa suitable for
hedging; lemony scent.
Height 5ft.

'Graham Thomas'
Scented English modern shrub;
vigorous, healthy, sprawling. Height 5ft.

**'White Bells', 'Red Bells'
and 'Pink Bells'**
Shorter flowering season,
but attractive glossy foliage;
suitable for ground cover;
light scent. Height 2½ft.

'Fountain'
Growth upright and wide;
suitable for hedging;
slight scent. Height 5ft.

'Bonica'
Spreading and bushy;
particularly disease-resistant.
Height 3ft.

'Marjorie Fair'
Bushy, widespreading
modern shrub; polyantha-like
sprays and delicate foliage.
Height 3ft.

'Charles Austin'
Well-scented English
modern shrub; sprawling
habit. Height 4-6ft.

'Mary Rose'
Well-scented English
modern shrub; robust,
bushy, widespreading.
Height 5ft.

'Golden Wings'
Scented modern shrub;
bushy and widespreading. Height 6ft.

213

Summer
PERENNIALS

Summer is high season for perennials. There is almost no restriction to the uses and colour combinations that are possible. Some gardeners have a preference for quieter-hued perennial plants following a bright pageant of colour in spring. Others feel that rich, emphatic colour themes should be flaunted in the strong light of summer. In fact, judicious planting, using the softer hues at a distance and the bolder tones near at hand, allows the best of both worlds.

The sculptural grace of *Acanthus spinosus* recalls motifs of classical architecture; hardly surprising, since the leaf shapes appealed to both Greeks and Georgians as the ideal decoration for pediments and capitals.

The versatility of *Achillea* is revealed by two hybrids, 'The Beacon' and 'Great Expectations'.

Acanthus spinosus

BEAR'S BREECHES

Height 3-4ft
Planting distance 3-4ft
Best July-September

A handsome plant with spine-tipped, divided foliage and sculptured flower spikes that are also spiny. The leaf shapes were echoed in the carved column tops of ancient Greece and widely used in classical design. The flower spikes, which rise majestically above the dark green foliage, begin to appear from midsummer and have strangely shaped flowers in which green, white and mauve-pink are blended to create a cool colour effect.

The larger hostas give fine leaf contrast all through the growing season and, where space permits, the broad purple-red foliage of *Rheum palmatum*

'Rubrum', with its creamy-pink flowers in June, makes a handsome companion for the acanthus. The foliage lasts well into winter, making a foil for autumn perennials, such as Michaelmas daisies. Alternatively, clumps of acanthus grown between shrubs along with daffodils for spring and colchicums for autumn, can be particularly effective, since the acanthus flowers when few shrubs are looking their best.
CULTIVATION Plant autumn or spring in any well-drained soil, in sun or light shade. Protect

young plants with a mulch in their first winter. Propagate by root cuttings in winter or by division in spring.

Achillea
Galaxy hybrids

YARROW

Height 2-3ft
Planting distance 2ft
Best June-August

Only recently introduced, these brightly coloured hybrids are simply descendants of yarrow,

the well-known roadside weed. However, their solid, close heads of tiny daisy-like flowers are most attractive, and are enhanced still further by a lacy background of ferny foliage.

The hybrids presently available include the pale pink 'Apple Blossom'; sandstone-yellow 'Great Expectations'; 'The Beacon', brick-red; and 'Salmon Beauty', pale salmon-pink. The darker pink *Achillea millefolium* 'Cerise Queen' has a stronger, brighter colour that is quite distinctive.

As border plants, the Galaxy

hybrids are better grown as patches of individual colours rather than in mixed groups. The yellow or brick-red shades would fit well into a 'hot' scheme with *Euphorbia griffithii* and *Lathyrus aureus* (syn *L. luteus aureus*), as they follow late spring bulbs, and with kniphofias or crocosmias to take over in late summer and autumn. Any suggestions for shrubs to precede or continue the yellow display should certainly include *Forsythia* 'Beatrix Farrand' or *Kerria japonica* for spring colour, and varieties of *Cotinus coggygria* for the late show. *C.* × 'Grace' is a relatively new cultivar with sumptuous foliage that in October turns rich mahogany-red.
CULTIVATION Plant autumn or spring in any, even impoverished, well-drained soil, in full sun. Propagate by cuttings in spring, or by division in spring or autumn.

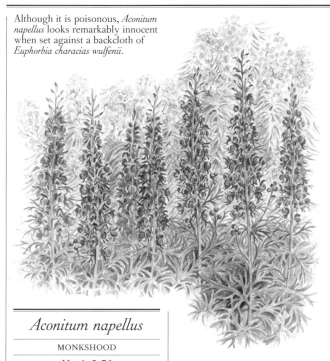

Although it is poisonous, *Aconitum napellus* looks remarkably innocent when set against a backcloth of *Euphorbia characias wulfenii*.

The sun-loving *Agapanthus* Headbourne hybrids were developed in a garden at Headbourne Worthy, near Winchester, in the 1960s.

The close-bunched flower heads of *Anaphalis cinnamomea* are perfect for dried flower arrangements.

Aconitum napellus

MONKSHOOD

Height 3-5ft
Planting distance 2-3ft
Best June-August

Recommended for their useful height, sturdy indifference to support and extended flowering period, monkshoods are characterised by spikes of hooded flowers. The dark green foliage is finely divided, and emerges in early spring. Unlike its look-alike, *Aconitum anglicum*, which produces single flower spikes in spring, *A. napellus* and its hybrids delay flowering until after the longest day. Once the main spike has faded, numerous side shoots continue flowering into late summer. The flowers are in shades of blue: 'Sparks', the deepest, at one end of the scale, and 'Bicolor', blue and white, at the other.

The related *A. septentrionale* 'Ivorine' is altogether different, growing to more than 4ft, and bearing dense spikes of pale cream, elongated flowers that open a month after the others.

Monkshoods make superb border plants, providing rich violet-blues and a strong silhouette for many weeks. Their fresh young foliage forms a soft, ferny background for spring-flowering perennials and bulbs. The duskiness of some of the blues makes a particularly good setting for yellow achilleas or the light mauvy-pink of *Campanula lactiflora* 'Loddon Anna'. CULTIVATION Plant during spring or autumn in any fertile soil and in sun or partial shade. Propagate by dividing crowded clumps in autumn or spring.

Agapanthus
Headbourne hybrids

Height 2-3ft
Planting distance 2ft
Best August

Agapanthus species are native to South Africa, but these handsome hybrids originated in the Hon. Lewis Palmer's garden at Headbourne Worthy, Hampshire, and are therefore more tolerant of northern climes than the species. However, in late summer a hint of the exotic still appears as stems topped with rounded flowers, ranging from deep blue to near white, rise clear of the strap-like foliage. They give delight for weeks and the seed heads are attractive too.

The soft blues are perfect for blending with yellow or lemon. Potentillas, either the shrubby 'Elizabeth' or the herbaceous *Potentilla recta*, are suitable companions and extend the season. In the pink to mauve range, perennial phloxes blend well, as long as they are chosen to avoid clashing, and a white phlox, such as 'White Admiral', would provide perfect contrast. Roses, especially in shades of apricot, white or yellow, like 'Buff Beauty', 'Iceberg' or 'Golden Showers', for example, also go well with agapanthus. CULTIVATION Plant during spring or autumn in any fertile, well-drained soil, and in a sunny, sheltered position. Propagate by dividing crowded clumps during the spring.

Anaphalis cinnamomea

PEARL EVERLASTING

Height 2-2½ft
Planting distance 3ft
Best August-September

The thickly felted silvery stems and leaves of this plant are decorative from the moment they emerge in spring until they die down in late autumn. In late summer, they produce sprays of small, white flowers that rustle when touched. Fresh or dried, they make perfect contributions to indoor arrangements.

Useful when an alternative to a green background colour is needed, the white-felted young shoots contrast well with the dark stems of peonies or with the emerging foliage of cotinus. Later, red penstemons, especially 'Firebird' or 'Garnet' – but not the two together – will make a handsome, long-lived

Vivid *Anchusa azurea* 'Loddon Royalist' needs hot-coloured partners for best effect.

Vigorous, bicoloured 'McKana' hybrids are among the best of the long-spurred aquilegia strains.

Few plants contribute a merrier range of colours than *Aquilegia* long-spurred hybrids, descendants of several North American columbines. Shapes and shades mingle well with the furry, silver foliage of *Stachys byzantina*.

(*Anaphalis cinnamomea* cont) contrast. Red shrub roses or a dark-flowered buddleia, such as 'Black Knight', form a good midsummer background, and for autumn, asters or chrysanthemums can take over.

CULTIVATION Plant between autumn and spring in a sunny position and in ordinary fertile soil. Propagate by division during spring or autumn.

Anchusa azurea

Height 3-5ft
Planting distance 1½-2ft
Best June-August

The flowers of this anchusa resemble largish forget-me-nots – except that they are of a much stronger blue. Though short-lived as individuals, the branched sprays that develop above the hairy foliage last for many weeks and provide a colour quality that other plants are hard put to equal. The cultivar with the richest blue flowers is 'Loddon Royalist', and there is also a fine paler form, 'Opal', and a charming dwarf form, 'Little John'.

These astonishing blues make a striking picture with the hot colours of red oriental poppies, or with lemon and yellow flowers such as *Achillea* 'Great Expectations' or the early flowering *Kniphofia* 'Buttercup'.

The blues too are exquisite with silver foliage, and might be given support by cornflowers (*Centaurea*), *Campanula lactiflora* and *Iris sibirica* to create a cool effect. A fine companion shrub would be the orange-flowering *Buddleia globosa*.

CULTIVATION Plant between autumn and spring in fertile, very well-drained soil and in full sun. The stems may snap in windy weather and need support. Cut back stems as soon as the flowers fade, to promote new shoots. Propagate by taking root cuttings in late winter or early spring.

Aquilegia
Long-spurred hybrids

Height 2-3ft
Planting distance 1-1½ft
Best May-June

Flowers possessed of longer spurs and warmer colours distinguish North American columbines from their European relative, *Aquilegia vulgaris*. The long-spurred hybrids have been evolved from a number of gaily-hued transatlantic species, resulting in a wide range of colour and flower size. Among several hybrid strains, bold 'McKana' remains the most popular with its 2in wide bicoloured blooms of red, pink, orange, blue, cream or yellow borne throughout the summer months. 'Crimson Star' is also outstanding, shorter but with large flowers that alternate rose-crimson with white.

While the more delicate columbines are ideal for planting in drifts among shrubs, the American strains really need a border in which to show off. They could be preceded by bright tulips, and followed by day lilies or dahlias and border chrysanthemums. In shrub plantings, bronze or silvery foliage, perhaps contributed by *Berberis thunbergii* 'Atropurpurea' or *Pyrus salicifolia*, would help to promote the cheerful picture.

CULTIVATION Plant between autumn and spring in well-drained soil in sun or part shade. Cut stems to ground level after flowering. Propagate by division between autumn and spring, or by seed.

The form and colours of *Astilbe × arendsii* are particularly well-suited to an old-fashioned border.

Astilbe × arendsii

Height 2-4ft
Planting distance 1½-2ft
Best June-August

The slender, graceful astilbes find a welcome in many gardens, delighting their audience from the moment their ferny foliage emerges. At first deeply bronzed, the leaves later turn green and remain so until late autumn. The plumed flowers last for many weeks and come in a rich variety of shades that eventually fade to russet and soft brown as autumn comes to an end. Numerous named cultivars are available, including pale pink 'Europa' and deep pink 'Bressingham Beauty'; the dark red 'Fanal' and 'Red Sentinel'; and lilac to magenta 'Purple Lance' and 'Amethyst'.

Astilbes can be found a niche in many summer plantings. Their colours, delicate or strong, are always positive without being garish. Pink and white cultivars go especially well with wetland plantings of irises, hostas and pink Asiatic primulas. Purple forms make elegant companions for day lilies and ligularias. The deep red 'Fanal' is outstanding when backed by the broad, crinkled, bronze-tinted leaves of rodgersias, accompanied by ferns or grasses. Even during winter, the warm mahogany of the dead flower stems and the reddish-brown seed heads contribute to a winter scene that could also include groups of hellebores and winter bulbs.

CULTIVATION Plant between autumn and spring in light shade. Boggy conditions are ideal; ordinary soil should be mulched each year and kept moist. Propagate by division between autumn and spring.

The greenish Elizabethan ruffs of *Astrantia major* 'Shaggy' are nicely offset by the darker hues of the leaves and the various shades of green provided by *Helleborus argutifolius* (top left) and a skimmia (top).

Astrantia major

Height 2-3ft
Planting distance 1½ft
Best June-November

The flowers of this lovely Caucasian wild plant are in themselves insignificant, but they nestle in ruff-like white collars streaked or fringed with green, and are set among divided foliage. The wild species is pretty enough to hold its own anywhere, but there are also several superb garden forms including 'Rubra' with wine-red ruffs, as well as a number of variants tinted with shades of pink. 'Rubra', which flowers over several months, will produce seedlings with just such a range. The vigorous *Astrantia major* 'Shaggy' (syn 'Margery Fish'), which comes fairly true from seed, has ruffs that are much larger than the type, and ragged with greenish extensions so that the collar edges look like rays. The leaves of 'Sunningdale Variegated' are splashed with gold in spring although they may turn wholly green by August.

An easy plant to associate and one which colonises freely – a little too freely sometimes – by self-seeding. Following on where columbines and other semi-shade-loving spring perennials leave off, *A. major* ensures a continuation of interest through to the first frost. It is particularly useful for a cottage-garden effect, interwoven with old-fashioned border pinks and the tiny, bell-shaped flowers of heucheras.

CULTIVATION Plant between autumn and spring in any soil, wet or dry, and in partial shade. Propagate by division from autumn to spring.

A bold plot, where *Campanula lactiflora* 'Pouffe' complements *Rosa* 'Graham Thomas'.

Campanula lactiflora

Height 5ft · *Planting distance* 2ft
Best June-August

This bold, upright-growing perennial would make a glorious background in any well-planned herbaceous border. With its soft green, pointed leaves and luxuriant sprays of lilac-blue, bell-shaped flowers, it is eye-catching for much of the summer. 'Loddon Anna' is slightly shorter – 4ft – than the species, with light pink flowers. Since self-sown plants display considerable variation, it is better to rely on nursery-grown cultivars, such as 'Prichard's Variety', which is dense in flower and strong in colour.

Campanula lactiflora and its cultivars are particularly useful in mixed and shrub borders, where, as foreground subjects, they can take over the display from such spring-flowering shrubs as the porcelain-pink *Kolkwitzia amabilis*. They could assume supporting roles too in front of repeat-flowering climbing roses such as 'Pink Perpétue' or 'New Dawn'. In the herbaceous border, the cultivars associate particularly well with modern hybrid pinks, or carnations, whose blooms will carry on the display into early autumn when the campanulas have finished flowering.

For gardens where space is limited, the dwarf *C. lactiflora* 'Pouffe' is the ideal choice. At only 1½ft tall, its dense mass of foliage is almost smothered in pale blue flowers, making it a fine companion for old-fashioned or modern shrub roses of almost any colour.

CULTIVATION Plant during spring or autumn in moist but well-drained soil, in full sun or light shade. Cut back stems with faded flower heads by half to encourage a second flush. Propagate by dividing crowded clumps in autumn, or by taking basal cuttings in spring.

Here is a grand opera of a planting, in which *Campanula persicifolia* takes centre stage, with a chorus of stately delphiniums in the background and hardy geraniums in the wings. A warmer note comes from pink sweet williams – *Dianthus barbatus* hybrids.

Campanula persicifolia

PEACH-LEAVED BELLFLOWER

Height 2-3ft
Planting distance 1½-2ft
Best June-August

Sturdy of stature, these are useful campanulas for the middle or front of the border where the flowers can be enjoyed at close range. Glossy leaf rosettes maintain an ever-green ground cover. During June, firm stems are topped by nodding bells which appear sporadically for the rest of the summer. The flowers are cup-shaped but open out flatter than most campanulas and come in deliciously cool colours. There is a stunning double, 'Fleur de Neige', and a semi-double blue, 'Pride of Exmouth'.

The subspecies *Campanula persicifolia sessiliflora*, sometimes listed as *C. latiloba* or *C. grandis*, is similar, but the large bell flowers are almost stalkless and face stiffly outwards. The cultivar 'Percy Piper' has flowers like little blue saucers, pale at the centre bosses and darkening

Centranthus ruber – valerian – is a welcome decorator of old walls and rubble patches; a frequently grown form is *C. r.* 'Coccineus'.

Pretty and wholesome as a daisy, *Chrysanthemum maximum* smiles upon all summer's days.

Sturdy, and as good for indoor arrangements as it is for outdoor display, *Chrysanthemum maximum* 'Phyllis Smith' is excellent for town gardens.

towards the rims. There is also a dazzling white form, 'Alba', and a soft lilac-mauve called 'Hidcote Amethyst'. All varieties are excellent for cutting and for inclusion in long-stemmed flower arrangements.

Such cool colours harmonise perfectly with soft yellows, lemons, beiges and some pinks. *Viola cornuta* makes a fine long-season ground cover at the front, with a background of softly variegated or golden foliage, such as *Symphytum* × *uplandicum* 'Variegatum'. Like *C. lactiflora*, the peach-leaved campanulas are excellent companions for roses of all shades and look equally at home among rhododendrons, providing fresh colour when these have finished flowering. The winter rosettes take well to the company of hellebores and spring bulbs.

CULTIVATION As for *Campanula lactiflora*. This species tolerates even poor soils. Propagate by division in spring or autumn.

Centranthus ruber

RED VALERIAN

Height 2-3ft
Planting distance 1½ft
Best June-November

One of the easiest perennials to grow – so much so, that it can be a problem to keep it within bounds. On the other hand, it thrives on practically nothing and cheerfully fills odd cracks and unpromising corners where little else would survive. The foliage is luxurious and makes a charming foil for the myriads of tiny florets which make up the floral plumes from June onwards. Generally a subdued pink, they crowd walls in the south and west of Britain, occasionally interrupted by the form 'Atrococcineus', which is the shade of old Tudor bricks.

This goes well with most hardy geraniums and also makes a fine association with the creamy-yellow *Centaurea*

ruthenica. On a wall, a blue clematis, such as *Clematis* × *jackmanii*, tumbling through red valerians, makes a wonderful combination that lasts for much of the summer. In gravel or paving, valerian teams handsomely with *Alchemilla mollis* and with the dark foliage of *Viola labradorica*.

CULTIVATION Plant in spring, in any, even the poorest, well-drained soil and in full sun. Propagate by cuttings in late spring or late summer.

Chrysanthemum maximum

SHASTA DAISY

Height 2-3ft
Planting distance 2ft
Best June-September

The victims of recent botanical reclassification, these vigorous, Pyrenean relatives of our wild ox-eye daisies should now be called *Leucanthemum*. Set aside

the confusion over names, and the shasta daisy remains an old favourite, valued for its total indifference to wind and poor weather. Bottle-green foliage emerges in spring, and from the thick basal mat rise many stems topped with large, yellow-centred, white daisy flowers. Among old and popular cultivars 'Wirral Supreme' is a fine double, and 'Phyllis Smith' has fringed petals reminiscent of shredded coconut. 'Snowcap' is an outstanding recent introduction, little more than 1ft high.

Single and double-flowered

forms are striking in orange, gold or yellow colour schemes, especially if gold foliage as well as gold flowers is included in the planting. *Philadelphus coronarius* 'Aureus', golden-leaved hostas and *Oenothera tetragona* 'Fireworks' would make a dazzling mix that could be toned down with nepetas or blue-leaved grasses, such as the hardy *Helictotrichon sempervirens*.

CULTIVATION Plant in spring, in well-drained but moisture-retentive soil. Propagate by dividing crowded clumps in autumn or spring.

Graceful bell-shaped flowers hang from the curving stems of the herbaceous *Clematis integrifolia*.

In massed array, the flowers of *Cynoglossum nervosum* harmonise with the deep green foliage.

Stately wands of *Cimicifuga racemosa* climb sky-high among a bed of blue-flowered hostas.

Cimicifuga racemosa

Height 4-5ft
Planting distance 2-3ft
Best July-August

Huge, multi-branched wands, clothed with hundreds of tiny white flowers which give a bottle-brush effect, rise from clumps of *Cimicifuga racemosa* in July and August. The divided, fresh green foliage is handsome all summer and makes an impressive show before the flowering period.

This tall perennial creates a grand effect among other large herbaceous plants, and can take over from earlier flowering *Aconitum* 'Ivorine' or creamy lilies. Among shrubs, it can relieve monotony at dull times, and it also makes a handsome pond-side plant, with its spire-like stems reflected in the water. CULTIVATION Plant during late autumn or spring. Marsh is the natural habitat, so enrich the soil in the border with organic matter. Propagate by dividing roots in autumn or spring.

Clematis integrifolia

Height 2-3ft
Planting distance 2ft
Best June-August

The herbaceous clematis is marvellous for scrambling through herbaceous and mixed borders and for flowing down low walls and steps. The species is usually a deep, dusky violet-blue, and there are also pink forms as well as a white. The most popular cultivar is the deep blue 'Hendersonii' whose large flowers are elegantly recurved.

Clematis integrifolia does best supported on twiggy pea sticks in the mixed or perennial border. It is too stiff and short to train over a shrub, but there is a very fine hybrid, *Clematis × durandii*, which grows up to 8ft and has large royal blue flowers with a satiny texture. It is at its most attractive when allowed to flop over shrubs that have flowered rather earlier in the year – dwarf rhododendrons for instance – or left to lounge among small conifers.
CULTIVATION Plant between autumn and spring in any good, moist soil, in sun or part shade. Propagate by division or basal cuttings in spring.

Cynoglossum nervosum

HIMALAYAN HOUND'S TONGUE

Height 2ft
Planting distance 1½-2ft
Best June-July

Vivid blue flowers, like large forget-me-nots, grow in showy clusters at the tips of the hound's tongue's stems, which uncurl as the flowers open. The narrow tongue-shaped leaves are rough and hairy.

Such an intense blue contrasts well with gold or yellow companions such as yarrow (*Achillea* 'Great Expectations') or lemon-coloured red-hot poker (*Kniphofia uvaria* 'Buttercup') – or gold-leaved shrubs or golden grasses. For a yellow succession behind the hound's tongue, try crown imperial (*Fritillaria imperialis*) or doronicums for spring, yellow day lilies (*Hemerocallis*) for summer, and rudbeckias or golden rods (*Solidago*) for late summer.

Silver foliage also combines well with the hound's tongue's blue, so *Anaphalis cinnamomea*, with its felty young shoots, makes a fine companion, following on with white flowers.
CULTIVATION Plant between autumn and spring in full sun in any well-drained, reasonably fertile soil. Support plants in exposed sites. Propagate by seed sown in early spring, or by division in autumn or spring.

BRIDGING THE SEASONS IN A *Herbaceous Border*

IT MIGHT BE CONSIDERED that a herbaceous border is a notion too fleeting for the all-season garden, since by definition it is composed of plants that year by year die back to their roots. Yet with cunning, the gardener can also introduce an air of permanence to the border, without diminishing the summer show by one jot. In this instance, when the display is at its June climax, the bed is filled with stately columns of large-flowered delphinium hybrids, massed hardy geraniums and serried ranks of campanulas. It is hard to imagine the scene without them, but with other plants in the wings there will be plenty to please throughout the year. The feathery leaves of *Foeniculum vulgare* add a piquant touch and the plant contributes its bright yellow flowers in August. Though the spring flowers of *Euphorbia robbiae* are modest, the foliage is evergreen, as are the broad, shining leaves of *Bergenia* 'Ballawley'.

The creamy flowers of *Pyracantha* 'Mohave' are coming to an end, but later on it dresses in scarlet berries that last through winter. The conifers, too, have greater significance then, and the bergenia leaves are crimsoned by frost. The mid border is filled with bulbs of pale blue *Scilla mischtschenkoana* and creamy *Narcissus cyclamineus*, to carry a touch of summer into spring. With them, the bergenia's crimson flowers hail the next perennial takeover. ❧

Tall delphinium hybrids form the centrepiece of a classic summer border display that includes geraniums, fennel, bergenia and the creamy foam flowers of *Pyracantha* 'Mohave'.

IN LATE WINTER attention is focused on the reds of pyracantha berries and bergenia leaves that help to highlight the early flowering *Narcissus cyclamineus* and *Scilla mischtschenkoana*.

The all-white border is a theme for the enthusiast, but those who attempt it should certainly include – as here – white *Delphinium* 'Moonbeam'.

Delphiniums
Large-flowered hybrids

Height 4-7ft
Planting distance 2½-3ft
Best July-August

The typical large-flowered delphinium has a tall, stately spire of blue flowers – each one sporting a distinctive eye – above handsomely, lobed foliage. The hybrids are descendants of *Delphinium elatum* crossed with various other species. There is a vast range of large, vigorous cultivars, mostly blue but with some white, mauve, pink and red forms. They include the Pacific hybrids from California, such as the giants 'Black Knight' (dark blue), 'Blue Jay' (mid blue with a white eye) and 'Galahad' (pure white). Dwarf cultivars include 'Blue Fountains' and 'Blue Heaven', both under 3ft.

Make use of the delphiniums' height to punctuate a large border – where they will hold their own among standard shrub roses and hollyhocks. For a diversion, plant hostas in the foreground and dicentras, with their fern-like leaves and pendulous flowers.

CULTIVATION Plant from autumn to spring in moist but well-drained, preferably alkaline, fertile soil, in a sunny, sheltered spot. Support tall plants. Propagate by basal cuttings in spring.

Dianthus
GARDEN PINKS

The flowers of the modern garden pinks come in a delicious assortment of colours and scents. However, neatness of flower and spiky, cool, grey-green foliage are common to all. The modern hybrids have contributed tints of salmon and purple to the more traditional range of pinks and whites; some are flecked, others banded, with contrasting tones. All certainly earn their place in the all-season garden, not only by virtue of their evergreen foliage, but because they flower repeatedly through the summer, peaking between June and July. And, of course, they are some of the most rewarding flowers of all for indoor arrangements.

POOR MAN'S CLOVES

Though sweetly scented laced and old-fashioned pinks, traditional favourites of the summer border, flower profusely, they do so only for two or three weeks in midsummer. Their place in the all-season garden is therefore limited except in a supporting role, to link the flowering border plants of spring and late summer. Among the most rewarding of old-fashioned pinks are: 'Sops in Wine', whose heavily scented flowers are said to have been used by the Elizabethans as a poor man's substitute for cloves in mulled wine; 'Laced Monarch', a free-flowering, petunia pink cultivar; the perennial favourite 'Mrs Sinkins' and the 17th-century 'Bridal Veil', both white and heavily fragrant.

Another border theme is one that centres upon *Dianthus* – in this case, 'Doris', supported by *Dicentra eximea* 'Alba' and *Begonia semperflorens*.

Expertly chosen ingredients for an old-fashioned planting would certainly include *Dianthus* 'Laced Monarch' and *Salvia officinalis atropurpurea*.

With a height and spread of around 1ft, pinks are natural front-liners for any well-drained, sunny border and can be incorporated into all kinds of planting schemes. To evoke a cottage garden atmosphere, combine them with a background of roses, or with annuals like *Nigella* 'Miss Jekyll', *Lupinus hartwegii* and sweet peas. For a flow of colour through the year, and to convey a hint of an Elizabethan garden, back an array of pinks with evergreen herbs like rosemary and sage, and use soft-toned wallflowers (*Cheiranthus cheiri*) to precede the pinks in spring.

CULTIVATION

Plant at any time from spring to autumn in a sunny position with well-drained, preferably neutral to alkaline soil. The plants are not long-lived and should be replaced every few years. Propagate by cuttings in July.

Accompanied here by the sombre foliage of *Astrantia major* 'Rubra' is the highly scented, old English favourite *Dianthus* 'Sops in Wine'.

Dianthus 'Haytor' makes a busy picture with pansies, euonymus and *Senecio maritimus*.

Here is the best possible use of *Dianthus* – as the foremost, low tier at the front of a classic, mixed border. Rising behind its cool flowers and foliage are roses, gladioli, *Penstemon heterophyllum* (bottom right) and, at the top, the blue spikes of false indigo, *Baptisia australis*.

The very pinks of perfection

The delicacy of old-fashioned pinks and the durability of border carnations were captured and encapsulated in the lasting perfection of modern hybrid pinks. Fine of foliage and neat of flower, the modern pinks bring sweet-scented, feminine grace to sunny borders, in a succession of flowers from early summer to early autumn.

Painted from plants supplied by Three Counties Nurseries, Bridport, Dorset.

'Letitia Wyatt'
Superb fragrance.

'Diane'
Unscented but
particularly free-flowering.

'Haytor'
Strong, upright habit
and sweet scent.

'Doris'
Heavily perfumed;
excellent cut flower.

'Becka Falls'
Low growing, unscented,
but eyecatching.

224

'Joy'
Free-flowering
and strongly scented.

'Houndspool Ruby'
Scented and
very free-flowering.

'Valda Wyatt'
Compact and well-scented.

'Cranmere Pool'
Heavily scented
and low-growing.

'Monica Wyatt'
Very free-flowering
and clove-scented.

'Bovey Belle'
Strongly clove-scented;
particularly good cut flower.

225

The abundant spherical blooms of *Echinops ritro* can be dried and enjoyed in winter arrangements.

Echinops ritro

GLOBE THISTLE

Height 3-4ft
Planting distance 2-3ft
Best July-August

Not only does the globe thistle have large, rounded bright blue flowers that attract bees and butterflies, but it has handsome foliage that makes a pleasant display on its own. The jagged, deeply lobed leaves, borne on thick, rigid stems, are green on top and felty white on the undersides. The flowers last for many weeks, and in autumn the seed heads keep their outline for some time.

Although it is robust enough to survive in grassland, the globe thistle is never invasive. Use it to add body to the centre or back of a border – it can take over from earlier-flowering irises and oriental poppies. The rugged outline and blue flowers

Give *Eryngium variifolium* a dry, sunny spot, and the reward will be a year-round display of attractive foliage, and thistle-like summer flowers.

of the thistle will contrast well with a softer mass of phloxes in shades of purple, mauve, pink and white, or with pink and white shrub roses. *Chrysanthemum maximum* 'Snowcap' would make an attractive addition in the foreground.

Globe thistles fit in well with a cottage-garden-style planting in company with lavenders, pot herbs and summer annuals.
CULTIVATION Plant between autumn and spring, in full sun. *Echinops ritro* does best in a fertilé, well-drained soil, but will tolerate poor soil and flowers fairly freely even if neglected. It does not need staking. Propagate by division in autumn, root cuttings taken in late autumn, or seed sown in mid-spring.

Eryngium variifolium

MOROCCAN SEA HOLLY

Height 1½ft
Planting distance 1ft
Best July-September

This lovely North African sea holly has decorative evergreen foliage and a fine show of flowers in summer. The leaves, veined with silver, form rosettes from which rise short, branched, sharp-spiked flower stems with clusters of small blue blooms.

The sea holly's leaf markings contrast well with broad, smooth-leaved plants such as bergenias. These evergreens take the stage with their spring flowers, and make a fine backing for the sea holly in summer.

The blue of the sea holly's flowers is so discreet that it blends with most other colours, and looks wonderful in company with purple or variegated sage. In a mixed border, natural companions are shrubs that relish hot, dry conditions, such as lavender, rock roses and cotton lavender (*Santolina*).
CULTIVATION Plant between autumn and spring in a sunny position, in well-drained soil. It does best in hot, dry conditions, and flowers well even in thin soils. Propagate by dividing mature plants in early spring, or by root cuttings in February.

Foeniculum vulgare

FENNEL

Height 5-6ft
Planting distance 3ft
Best April-October

Fennel's hair-thin, fern-like foliage emerges in spring to form a waving, feathery mist of green. Heads of tiny greenish-yellow flowers, rather like cow-parsley in outline, appear in July and August. Not only is *Foeniculum vulgare* decorative, it is also a culinary herb with a fragrant scent reminiscent of

The scarlet flowers of *Papaver orientale* punctuate an early summer border dominated by the fern-like leaves of bronze fennel, *Foeniculum vulgare* 'Purpureum'.

Glossy rhododendron foliage provides a strong background for the long flower display of *Geranium endressii*.

Cool flowers clothe *Geranium* 'Johnson's Blue', lightening the dense blooms of *Paeonia officinalis* 'Rubra Plena' and *Rosa* 'Charles de Mills'.

aniseed. The cultivar 'Purpureum' has rich purple-bronze foliage throughout the summer although the colour is most intense on the emerging leaves.

Green-leaved fennel is a good, filmy background for plants of any colour. Bronze-leaved fennel looks striking against yellow, gold or peach flowers, such as roses, late tulips, summer marigolds and yellow-flowered shrubs. For a more subtle contrast, plant it near silver foliage or the lime-green leaves of *Philadelphus coronarius* 'Aureus'.

CULTIVATION Plant in spring or autumn in any well-drained soil, in full sun. Deadhead before seed ripens to prevent prolific self-seeding. Propagate from seeds taken just as they ripen in mid-autumn. Sow in early spring under glass, or outdoors in mid to late spring.

Geranium endressii

CRANE'S-BILL

Height 1-1½ft
Planting distance 1½-2ft
Best July-October

This good-natured geranium from the Pyrenees produces bright pink flowers in more or less continuous sprays from midsummer until the frosts. Its bright green, rounded, deeply lobed leaves have rough upper surfaces and toothed edges. One of the finest of the garden varieties is 'Wargrave Pink', a larger, more robust plant with brilliant salmon-pink, faintly veined flowers. Others include 'A.T. Johnson' (silver-pink) and 'Rose Pink'.

In a summer border, this geranium looks good with the blues of pansies (*Viola cornuta*) and bugle (*Ajuga reptans* 'Purpurea'). It will form vigorous colonies between shrubs, as long as the shade does not get too dense, brightening the ground when the shrubs are not in flower. The geranium foliage makes a bright contrast with rhododendrons and other dark-leaved evergreens.

CULTIVATION Plant between autumn and spring in any soil, in a sunny position with occasional shade. Plants can be cut back in late summer to ensure better autumn flowering. Propagate by dividing clumps in autumn or spring.

Geranium
'Johnson's Blue'

CRANE'S-BILL

Height 1ft
Planting distance 1½ft
Best June-July

'Johnson's Blue' has large rich lavender-blue flowers with clearly marked veins, and is a cross between our native meadow crane's-bill (*Geranium pratense*) and *G. grandiflorum* (syn *G. himalayense*). Masses of deeply lobed, rounded leaves begin to appear in spring before the main flush of blooms. Occasional flowers appear in late summer, and in autumn some of the leaves turn rust red.

This is a fine geranium to plant under roses, especially

227

The spreading stems of *Geranium wallichianum* 'Buxton's Blue' bear exquisite flowers into autumn.

In midsummer, an old brick wall provides a mellow backdrop for the bright double flowers of *Geum chiloense* 'Mrs Bradshaw'.

A gauzy pillow of *Gypsophila paniculata* veils *Chrysanthemum maximum* and *Alstroemeria aurantiaca*, with *Erigeron speciosus* in the foreground.

(*Geranium* 'Johnson's Blue' cont) those in the primrose-apricot colour range, such as the climbers 'Golden Showers' and 'Mermaid', and the shrub roses 'Buff Beauty' and 'Graham Thomas'. Pink roses are also good companions, especially old cultivars such as 'Old Blush China' or 'Zéphirine Drouhin'. For a really old-fashioned effect add lavender and rosemary.
CULTIVATION As for *Geranium endressii* on previous page.

Geranium wallichianum
'Buxton's Blue'

CRANE'S-BILL

Height 6-12in
Planting distance 2ft
Best August-October

Geranium wallichianum originates in the Himalayas. 'Buxton's Blue' is covered with a succession of beautiful sky-blue, white-centred flowers

carried on radiating, ground-hugging stems from late summer to the end of autumn. Its three-lobed leaves are finely marbled and elegantly toothed.

This geranium is at home on a bank under spring-flowering shrubs or at the border front. Among *Erica* and *Calluna* cultivars, its foliage and flowers stand out delightfully against the needle-like leaves and tiny flowers of the heaths. The geranium is still in flower when autumn gentians and colchicums are blooming, and it looks particularly good near the white *Colchicum speciosum* 'Album'.
CULTIVATION Plant at any time between autumn and spring in cool, moist conditions, in fertile, well-drained soil. Mulch with leaf mould or well-rotted manure to ensure the soil does not dry out. Propagate by division in spring.

Geum chiloense

AVENS

Height 1½-2ft
Planting distance 1½-2ft
Best June-July

Two gaily coloured *Geum chiloense* cultivars, 'Mrs Bradshaw' (bright red) and 'Lady Stratheden' (bright golden-yellow) have been dependable border plants for most of this century. There is also a useful dwarf yellow sort, 'Georgenberg'. All have rosettes of bright green, slightly hairy, toothed foliage.

At dusk, the elegant sprays of flowers appear stemless, hovering above the foliage. The red of 'Mrs Bradshaw' can shout at similar colour shades, so needs planting where it will contrast. It looks lovely against the bronze foliage of the smoke tree

(*Cotinus coggygria*), or against purple fennel. The yellow of 'Lady Stratheden' can share a similar background, and the two planted near each other make a striking contrast.

The related water avens (*Geum rivale*), has two outstanding garden hybrids, 'Leonard's Variety' (coppery-pink) and 'Lionel Cox' (primrose). Their softer colours blend with blues or mauves such as those of columbines (*Aquilegia*), especially 'Hensol Harebell', and Jacob's ladder (*Polemonium*), which enjoy similar conditions.
CULTIVATION Plant any time from autumn to spring in moist, well-drained soil, in full sun or partial shade. Mulch to keep the soil moist. As soon as the early flowers begin to fade, remove them to encourage following blooms. Propagate by dividing plants every two or three years.

Gypsophila paniculata

Height 2-3ft
Planting distance 2ft
Best July-September

Myriads of tiny flowers on stems as thin as fuse wire give the impression of a soft mist. There is very little foliage, only a tracery of grey-green, multi-branched sprays. 'Bristol Fairy' is a fine cultivar, producing sprays of dazzling white, tiny double flowers for months. 'Flamingo' is pale pink, similar in habit and also double, but fractionally less vigorous.

This species gives softness and light to strong reds and bronzes in a summer border and blends well with silver foliage plants. It can follow tulips or daffodils to bloom alongside *Penstemon* 'Garnet', dark blue

'Stafford' is one of many sparkling hemerocallis hybrids, bringing colour to a sunny border.

delphiniums or dahlias such as 'Bishop of Llandaff'. *Cotinus coggygria* would add a strong background and carry interest beyond late summer.

CULTIVATION This species does not last for many years, and is tender in the coldest counties. Plant in mid-spring in a sheltered position in full sun. It thrives in the poorest of limy soils, but dies quickly if waterlogged. In rich soils it grows well at first but is short-lived. Propagation is not easy; buy grafted plants from a nursery.

Hemerocallis
Garden hybrids

DAY LILY

Height 1½-4ft
Planting distance 2-3ft
Best July-September

Fresh sprays of exotic lily flowers are produced in succession throughout late summer,

Fragrant *Hemerocallis citrina* is particularly free-flowering. In this mixed border the wide-mouthed blooms are massed in front of spires of Russell lupins, and a scattering of *Papaver orientale* and *Anchusa azurea*.

although each bloom lasts only for a day. There is a huge range of cultivars, some scented, which, while mostly yellow to orange in hue, include shades of pink and blood-red. All rise above generous shocks of long, strap-shaped leaves. *Hemerocallis flava* is a fragrant yellow species, *H. minor* is a compact form, and *H. citrina* has lemon-yellow flowers. Outstanding cultivars include the dwarf form, 'Corky', with much-branched sprays of sharp yellow blooms; 'Stafford' (red with yellow throat); the flesh-pink 'Penelope Vestey'; the deep

mahogany-red of 'Missenden'; and the remarkably fine, rich yellow 'Gold Chimes'.

Yellow and orange cultivars contrast well with sombre evergreen shrubs. Their flowering could follow on – in neutral to acid soil – from rhododendrons such as 'Golden Torch' or 'Logan Damaris', or the cream, yellow-tinted *Camellia* 'Jury's Yellow'. Some slightly earlier-flowering summer companions could include *Aconitum* 'Ivorine' or *Cimicifuga racemosa*.

CULTIVATION Plant between autumn and spring, in any fertile soil, in sun or light shade.

Feed annually with a general fertiliser to encourage free flowering. To propagate, divide clumps in autumn.

Heuchera

CORAL FLOWER

Height 1½ft
Planting distance 1½-2ft
Best May-July

Edging a pathway or border, the tiny bell flowers on their long, graceful stems, will produce a haze of colour. And even when this display is over, the crowds

Evergreen *Heuchera* 'Red Spangles' provides all-seasons ground cover and sprays of summer flowers.

of heart-shaped leaves, often marbled beneath, remain decorative throughout the year. The hybrids of *Heuchera sanguinea* and *H. americana* are invariably better than the original species, and while similar in form and use, vary in leaf and flower colour. *H. americana* itself has glossy foliage, suffused and veined coppery-brown when young. *H.* 'Red Spangles' has scarlet flowers above marbled foliage; *H.* 'Palace Purple' carries creamy flowers set against its deeply bronzed leaves.

Clump-forming heucheras make excellent ground cover in a woodland setting or between shrubs. They combine well with the foliage of winter-flowering hellebores, and with large grasses like *Miscanthus sinensis* or *Helictotrichon sempervirens*.

CULTIVATION Plant from autumn to spring in moist soil, in sun or light shade. Propagate by division in spring or autumn.

229

Hosta 'Thomas Hogg', with its cream-edged leaves and mauve flowers, makes elegant dressing for *Rosa multiflora* and an old brick wall.

Hosta crispula

Height 2-2½ft
Planting distance 2-3ft
Best May-August

This elegant, variegated hosta has large, regular, tapering leaves, each with a narrow but conspicuous streak of white round its margin. One of its great uses in a garden is to add brightness to a border, where its white-edged green goes well with bronze, gold and grey-green foliage, and with flowers of almost any colour. Japanese maples enjoy similar conditions and so make good companions, as do the spring-flowering *Smilacina racemosa* and Solomon's seal (*Polygonatum*). The deep green, cream-margined leaves of *Hosta* 'Thomas Hogg' would also be welcome in such a spot. It is one of the best hostas for planting under trees, for it will tolerate shade without losing its variegation, while its tall spires of lilac flower trumpets look well with such pure white, graceful blooms as *Polemonium caeruleum* 'Album'.

For a further variation on the theme, you might try *H. undulata*, whose curved and twisted leaves – hence the name – have broad, creamy splashes at their centres; its lilac-mauve flowers are produced in early summer. Use it to brighten up shrubs that flower but briefly – magnolias, camellias, azaleas – which lack bright colour for so much of the year.

CULTIVATION Plant between autumn and spring in a fertile, well-drained but moisture-retentive soil, in a sheltered spot in sun or light shade. Propagate by division in spring.

BRIDGING THE SEASONS
WITH
Greens and whites

ROSE BEDS NEED not be exclusively for roses, nor lie fallow between the peak flowering and fruiting times. In a reasonably well-nourished soil, a variety of plants can be added at ground level for a quietly attractive planting theme through the seasons. The sculptured leaves of *Hosta crispula* reflect, in their creamy margins, a cool white rugosa rose such as *Rosa* 'Schneezwerg', and add body to its lower stems. The peaceful colour focus gradually shifts from the recurrent flushes of blue, mauve and white of *Viola cornuta* varieties, to the fragrant cream flower heads of *Filipendula ulmaria* and, in late summer, back to the hosta's stems of lilac flowers.

Autumn is a harmony of foliage tones, uplifted by the glorious salmon-pink of *Schizostylis coccinea* 'Sunrise'. The hosta's flowering stems are cut back to concentrate once again on the leaves, contrasting with the carpet of viola foliage, the golden filipendula and dark *Viburnum* × *burkwoodii* in the background. The first sharp autumn frosts bring yellow and orange tones to the rose leaves before they fall, and signal the hosta's retreat to

This thoughtful planting would be equally valid for a large or small garden. In summer (left), the centrepiece is the white-margined foliage of *Hosta crispula* backed by *Viburnum* × *burkwoodii* and the repeat-flowering *Rosa* 'Schneez-werg'. The groundwork is made up of multicoloured *Viola cornuta* varieties and *Filipendula ulmaria*.

a bare root crown, and the time to cut back the violas. The hosta crown must be left undisturbed, but it can be encircled by alternate clumps of the common snowdrop of our woodlands, *Galanthus nivalis*, and the later flowering Grecian snow-drop, *G. ikariae*. These will continue the green and white theme until early spring. A staggered planting (to allow for its two-year flowering cycle) of fragrant *Iris danfordiae*

adds cheering golden-yellow to the early spring scene.

As the weather warms up, spears of new hosta leaves pierce the ground, and the golden-green tufts of filipendula foliage begin to emerge. The viburnum now plays its part, heralding the white summer rose display as its tight pink buds open into sweetly scented clusters of waxy white flowers that last until late spring. ❧

IN LATE WINTER the viburnum still retains its leaves and, though the roses have gone, a few defiant hips remain. The main display is now at ground level, where two snowdrop species emerge and *Iris danfordiae* pushes up through the viola leaves.

IN AUTUMN the rose puts out hips at the same time as its last flowers; shortly the leaves will turn orange-yellow. The hosta's flowers have come and gone, and the main floral colour now is provided by *Schizostylis coccinea* 'Sunrise', climbing through the contrasting greens of viola and filipendula foliage.

In this bouquet of greenery, the dominant factor is the white-edged leaves of *Hosta fortunei* 'Albomarginata', with *H. sieboldiana* below.

Making a bold match are *Hosta lancifolia* and *Polygonum amplexicaule* 'Atrosanguineum'.

A favourite American cultivar, *Hosta sieboldiana* 'Frances Williams', dominates a group of irises and smaller hostas in a waterside setting.

Hosta fortunei

Height 2-3ft
Planting distance 2-3ft
Best May-July

Unusually for this genus, *Hosta fortunei* is valued more for its flowers than its foliage. Its leaves are attractive enough – a soft grey-green – but its tall, midsummer flowers of lilac-mauve are quite spectacular. However, several of its cultivars have superb foliage. 'Albopicta' (syn 'Picta') has leaves that are at first yellow, edged with light green. Later, the yellow fades and the green becomes darker, so that by late summer the leaves are two-tone green, with the lighter shade in the middle.

These hostas make wonderful companions for the sky-blue Himalayan poppies *Meconopsis betonicifolia* that flower in June. Another hosta grown mainly for its flowers is *H. lancifolia*, whose deep lilac trumpets are borne in mid to late summer. Its neat mounds of small, polished leaves make excellent ground cover, and the flowers create a striking picture with the red *Polygonum amplexicaule* 'Atrosanguineum', which has an even longer flowering period. In winter and spring, encircle the bare hosta crowns with crocuses or snowdrops.

CULTIVATION As for *H. crispula*.

Hosta sieboldiana

Height 2ft
Planting distance 3-4ft
Best May-September

This, the king of hostas, has broad – 1ft across – blue-green leaves that are boldly marked with deep, seam-like veins. They make a most impressive display in any garden situation. It is a touch let down by the pale lilac flowers which, though dense, only just rise above the leaves. This is also the case with *Hosta sieboldiana* 'Elegans', whose leaves are crinkled and even more sumptuous. 'Frances Williams' has similar leaves which are margined with a bright yellow that gradually deepens in shade, bestowing a glow upon its surroundings.

Broad, cool, luxuriant foliage puts these hostas among the most sought after plants for mixed borders. Placed between shrubs, their simplicity offsets the complexity of spring and summer foliage, and looks well too when contrasted with the swordlike leaves and purple flowers of *Iris sibirica* and the vivid colours of Candelabra primulas. *H. s.* 'Elegans' is particularly valued for the blue effect it imparts to the border.

CULTIVATION As for *H. crispula*.

The American *Hosta* 'August Moon' is grown for its leaf colour, which it maintains all summer.

One of the loveliest and richest of its genus for colour and fragrance is *Iris pallida dalmatica*.

In this small town garden, the scene is commanded by the huge leaves of *Hosta sieboldiana* 'Elegans'. Among its companions are *Geranium platypetalum* and, suitably for the situation, *Saxifraga urbium* – London pride.

Hosta
Hybrid cultivars

Best May-September

The obliging and adaptable nature of hostas – they thrive in shade, and don't in the least mind damp – has led to their being used in a constantly widening range of garden situations. In recent years, this in turn gave rise to the development, particularly in the United States, of numerous cultivars, each intended for a particular purpose and ranging in height from 2in to 5ft. Among the best is 'Royal Standard' which grows to 3ft and more, and has large, boldly veined, lightly waved leaves and fragrant white flowers. It looks well with other large foliage plants, especially ferns, where its oval leaves provide a perfect foil for the more delicate, lacy fern leaves. The flowers are produced in late summer, and are excellent for cutting.

'Gold Edger', as the name suggests, is a fine edging plant for a border or path. Growing to only 6in, its yellow-green leaves mature in full sun to a vibrant gold. Pale lilac flowers stand well clear of the foliage.

A similar hybrid, 'Golden Prayers', grows about 3in taller and colours to a deeper gold. The golden hybrids are seen at their best surrounding a bed of mixed hostas, which should certainly include the dark, leathery *Hosta tardiflora*, that

Most attractively, *Hosta* 'Golden Prayers' has been planted in a pot, where it will demand frequent feeding and daily watering. The *Liriope muscari* alongside will flower in October when the hosta is past its best.

flowers in October. Other good North American hostas include 'August Moon', gold of leaf and pale mauve of flower; 'Zounds', that makes a 2ft mound of puckered golden foliage; and 'Francee', which has heart-shaped, white-edged leaves and lavender flowers.

CULTIVATION As for *H. crispula*.

Iris pallida dalmatica

Height 3ft · *Planting distance* 2ft
Best June-August

This iris from the Adriatic has perfumed lavender-blue flowers with golden beards. Its broad, sword-like leaves are blue-grey, and retain their colour from spring to autumn. There are also two forms with variegated leaves – *Iris pallida* 'Argentea Variegata', which has white stripes, and *I. p.* 'Aureo Variegata', which has gold stripes.

The grey leaves make a good background for flowers in blue or pink shades. They would soothe the gaudiness of red or salmon oriental poppies. The poppies flower at the same time as the irises, and the reds and blues go well together. Crane's-bills, such as *Geranium* 'Johnson's Blue', also go well, with rounded, deeply lobed leaves to contrast with those of the iris, and a succession of blue flowers that lasts until September.

The white-striped leaf form

Iris pallida 'Argentea Variegata' and *Brunnera macrophylla* make a good border combination.

(*Iris pallida dalmatica* cont) is a perfect candidate for a blue and white theme. It will look superb planted with creamy-white *Smilacina racemosa* and the blue *Brunnera macrophylla* 'Hadspen Cream', combined with lavender-blue *Campanula lactiflora* behind. The gold-striped leaf form goes well with yellows and oranges, or with the golden foliage of *Philadelphus coronarius* 'Aureus', for example, with golden-leaved hostas in the foreground.

CULTIVATION Plant in either early autumn or midsummer, in neutral soil in full sun. Propagate by division after flowering.

A large garden needs tall-growing border plants, and here a solitary group of *Iris sibirica* among the brilliantly coloured spires of Russell lupins provides a fine show against a dark background of shrubs.

Iris sibirica

SIBERIAN IRIS

Height 3-4ft
Planting distance 2ft
Best June

Siberian irises are beardless, and have clusters of richly coloured flowers carried well above their generous mid-green foliage. In autumn the seed capsules turn a rich tan, contrasting with the beige-brown of the dying foliage. Good garden varieties include 'Emperor' (rich purple-blue), 'White Swirl' (pure white) and pale blue 'Papillon'.

Its dense, upright foliage and vigorous growth makes *Iris sibirica* a useful mid-border plant for filling space quickly, or for colonising between shrubs such as mahonia and berberis, which together can provide a succession of flowers for much of the year. The flowers harmonise well with peonies or oriental poppies early in the summer, and in autumn the dying foliage and tan seed capsules are a foil for such emphatically blue flowers as asters or monkshoods.

CULTIVATION Plant in spring or late autumn in moist, fertile soil in sun or very gentle shade. Apply a mulch of well-rotted compost in late spring, especially to those plants that have been grown in dry borders.

Propagate by division in autumn, or grow from seed sown in autumn. Young plants should flower within two years of sowing. If you have room, let all seedlings flower and select the best colours.

Kniphofia
Hybrids

RED-HOT POKER

Height 1½-4ft
Planting distance 1½-3ft
Best July-September

A number of kniphofia species, mainly South African, have been crossed to produce a large and richly coloured range of garden varieties. Among the best are the dwarf 'Yellow Hammer' and 'Gold Else' in different shades of yellow; and 'Little Maid' – light yellow and ivory. Taller cultivars include

The aptly named *Kniphofia* 'Royal Standard' is a noble plant both in its colour and commanding height.

the early flowering 'Buttercup' whose custard flowers are enhanced by extra strong green foliage, and 'Royal Standard' in red and gold.

Although neater in habit than *Kniphofia uvaria*, all pokers except *K. caulescens* have rather scruffy foliage and need something in front to disguise this defect. The short hybrids go well with broad-leaved plants not far away – *Bergenia cordifolia*, perhaps, or low-growing, sun-loving hostas like 'Golden Prayers'. Taller hybrids can be set farther back and will not be lost among asters or lavenders with which the flowers will make an attractive contrast. As long as they are in full light, the larger red-hot pokers will relieve the monotony of spring-flowering shrub foliage when the shrubs are at their dullest.

CULTIVATION Plant in autumn or spring, in any well-drained soil and in full sun. They will not survive extremes of drought or sogginess. Protect young plants

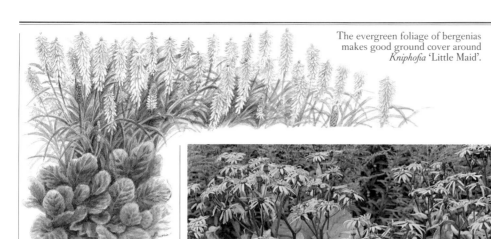

The evergreen foliage of bergenias makes good ground cover around *Kniphofia* 'Little Maid'.

with straw during their first winter after planting. Propagate by division in spring only.

The huge and heavily veined leaves of *Ligularia dentata* 'Desdemona' are as eye-catching as the daisy-like flowers on their purple stems.

Ligularia dentata
'Desdemona'

Height 3-4ft
Planting distance 3-4ft
Best August

The large sprays of vivid yellow-orange daisy flowers of *Ligularia dentata* grow above a mass of heart-shaped leaves that are green on top and deep purple beneath. The leaves emerge in spring and the flowers in late summer. Other notable cultivars are 'Othello', even darker orange, and the related *Ligularia* hybrid 'Gregynog Gold' with flowers that are slightly paler orange.

Such a large, robust plant needs plenty of room. Good companions are flag irises (*Iris pseudacorus*) which flower in late spring, rodgersias of all kinds, which flower in mid-summer, and cimicifugas, which flower during August and September. Big *Aruncus dioicus*, with its feathery foliage and cream flowers, enjoys similar conditions, and both look well with red, purple or cream astilbes in the foreground. If you have enough space, vigorous grasses such as miscanthus or *Glyceria maxima* contrast well. CULTIVATION Plant any time between autumn and spring in damp, fertile soil, in sun or in light shade. They make fine bog plants, but wilt quickly during dry sunny spells. Protect plants from slugs, which will eat the flower stems. Cut down to ground level in winter. Propagate by dividing the plants in spring or autumn.

Lupinus × regalis
Russell strain

LUPIN

Height 3ft
Planting distance 2-3ft
Best June

This familiar perennial has spires of close-packed, pea-like flowers rising above emerald-green leaves radiating from the stalk like the spokes of a wheel. The flowers appear in May, and their spicy scent confirms the arrival of summer. Hybridisation has led to the improvement of stock, and newer cultivars with extra long spikes include the blue and white 'Barnsdale', delicious cream 'Deborah Woodfield', pristine

In a mixed border, blue columbines and purple honesty pods make a subtle contrast to a salmon-pink variety of Russell lupins.

white 'Pope John Paul' and scarlet 'Chelsea Pensioner'.

Lupins are traditional plants for the summer border, and are useful because, when over, they can be cut back to make room for later perennials. They make a good early summer show in company with perennials such as crane's-bills (*Geranium*), geums, columbines (*Aquilegia*) and dicentras. For continued colour, plant *Monarda didyma*, *Echinacea purpurea* and *Anaphalis cinnamomea* nearby. Chrysanthemums and asters could continue the display in autumn. CULTIVATION Plant any time between autumn and spring in sun or partial shade in good soil. Lupins respond to plenty of potash and phosphorus. Feed in spring, then mulch lightly with well-rotted compost.

Meconopsis grandis makes a noble companion for the delicate blooms of *Rhododendron occidentale*.

A stately plume of *Miscanthus sinensis* arches gracefully over a froth of sugar-candy pink and magenta *Phlox paniculata* cultivars.

The fiery heads of *Monarda didyma* 'Cambridge Scarlet', some 2½-3in across, make a dramatic impression in a large border.

Meconopsis
Species

Height 2-3ft
Planting distance 2-3ft
Best May-July

Among the most breathtaking of the early perennials, the poppies from the Himalayan regions have large, sky-blue petals with a mass of bright gold stamens at their centres. The colour fades to lavender-blue if the soil tends towards the dry and alkaline. The leaves are oblong, and the young basal foliage is covered with russet-coloured hairs.

Meconopsis betonicifolia has sky-blue to purple flowers in May and June, while the rich blue flowers of *M. grandis* may appear a little earlier. The hybrid *M. × sheldonii* 'Branklyn'

has blooms 6-8in wide. 'Slieve Donard' is slightly taller, but its flowers are less sensational.

Blue poppies are perfect companions for yellow Asiatic primulas such as *Primula sikkimensis* and the giant cowslip (*P. florindae*). They also look good with ferns – the soft shield fern (*Polystichum setiferum*), for example, or the dramatic shuttlecock or ostrich feather fern, *Matteuccia struthiopteris*. Hostas make good companions too, especially *Hosta sieboldiana* and *H.* 'Thomas Hogg'.

CULTIVATION Plant early to midspring in partial shade. For the best flower colour, the soil should be neutral to acid, well-drained but moist. Propagate from seed sown in late summer, or by dividing plants in early spring. The seeds of *M. × sheldonii* are sterile, so propagate by division.

Miscanthus sinensis

Height 5-8ft
Planting distance 3ft
Best June-November

This tall, elegant grass has several striking garden varieties. They include: 'Zebrinus', which has yellow bands across its green leaves and may bear feathery panicles of pinkish flowers in autumn; 'Variegatus', with a silver stripe along each leaf; 'Silver Feather', with plain green leaves but which usually bears enormous sprays of pinky-brown, silky flowers in autumn; and handsome 'Purpureus', which has a purplish tinge to its young stems.

Although the grass is very tall, it need not be placed at the back of the border – when it is tucked behind other perennials,

some of its striking beauty is lost. It does, however, make a superb backing for mid and late-summer perennials such as asters, phloxes, globe thistles (*Echinops*) and *Campanula lactiflora*. Or try a border devoted exclusively to grasses, using a variety of miscanthus cultivars as a background for shorter, colourful *Holcus mollis* and *Hakonechloa macra* 'Aureola'.

CULTIVATION Plant in March or April in any moist soil. A sunny position is best, as the variegations of 'Zebrinus' and 'Variegatus' are more pronounced in sun than in shade. The grass will generally flower only in warm areas. Propagate by division of clumps in spring.

Monarda
Hybrids

Height 2-3ft
Planting distance 2ft
Best July-September

Perfect for a semi-wild setting in a large garden, these aromatic plants are a delight throughout their development. The first shoots, with pungent, nettle-like leaves, emerge in spring and grow steadily into substantial plants that seldom need staking. The hybrids are derived from *Monarda didyma* and *M. fistulosa* (wild bergamot). Monardas with flowers on the red side descend from *M. didyma*,

In a wild garden the indefatigable catmint's billowing clouds of lavender-blue flowers crowd around shrub roses to provide a colourful contrast with the red, pink and cream blooms throughout the summer.

There is no need to wait for Guy Fawkes' Night for the *Oenothera tetragona* 'Fireworks' display.

while the purple-inclined take after *M. fistulosa*. 'Cambridge Scarlet' has dark stems with scarlet flowers, while 'Prairie Night' has rich purple flowers. 'Snow Maiden' is a white form.

The deep scarlet flowers, enhanced by the dark stems, make 'Cambridge Scarlet' a superb subject for a border featuring warm colours. Evening primroses, kniphofias, red oriental poppies and *Euphorbia griffithii* all display similar warm tones that would harmonise well. For colour contrast, you could introduce shades of blue with catmint, crane's-bill and veronica. 'Prairie Night' will make a dramatic companion for the golden bamboo *Arundinaria viridistriata*.

CULTIVATION Plant in autumn, in sun or light shade. Red-toned hybrids require a moist soil; those with purple tones prefer a drier position. Propagate by division in autumn or spring.

Nepeta × *faassenii*

CATMINT

Height 1-2ft
Planting distance 1½ft
Best June-September

Few plants can rival the faithful performance of the common catmint. Its hazy clouds of lavender-blue are a constant source of delight to gardeners and swarms of bees alike. It repays a little judicious trimming with an endless succession of bloom, from early summer until autumn frosts. 'Six Hills Giant' is a large form of *Nepeta* × *faassenii* – nearly double the size of the species in height, flower and foliage.

The small grey-green leaves are almost hidden by sprays of nectar-rich tubular flowers, and the soft blue colouring makes catmint the perfect companion for roses of all colours. As an edging plant it can replace or be teamed with lavender, used to enhance the cooling effect of silver-foliaged plants or planted in a happy, traditional association with pink carnations.

CULTIVATION Plant between autumn and spring in well-drained soil, in sun or light shade. Propagate by division in spring or by cuttings in summer.

Oenothera tetragona

EVENING PRIMROSE

Height 1-2ft
Planting distance 1-1½ft
Best June-September

The funnel-shaped blooms of this oenothera open almost flat to reflect the evening sun from their rich yellow petals, and to release their faint scent on the still air. Compact in habit, the plants have short, stiff stems topped with clusters of flowers that decorate the garden for month after month. Named forms include 'Fireworks', with petals streaked with orange-red on the outside, and 'Yellow River' which is similar but grows slightly taller. The cultivar 'Glaber' more closely resembles the species, but bears warm, golden-yellow flowers above glossy, deeply bronzed foliage.

Such bright yellows are valuable for teaming up with other shades, from cool lemon to bright orange, and as a contrast to blue. Planted among *Euphorbia griffithii*, marigolds and rudbeckias, a yellow scheme could extend from early summer until autumn, with the contrasting richness of blue lupins or delphiniums and *Iris sibirica*.

CULTIVATION Plant autumn to spring in any well-drained soil. Propagate by dividing clumps in autumn or early spring.

The weathered brickwork of a garden wall makes an excellent backing for *Paeonia lactiflora* 'White Wings', with red and cream shrub roses, a pink clematis, and in the foreground *Geranium endressii* in shades of pink.

Paeonia lactiflora

PEONY

Height 2-3ft
Planting distance 2-3ft
Best May July

The stunning centres of peony 'Bowl of Beauty' blooms are semi-petals derived from stamens.

Although the flowering season of our garden peonies is short – just one splendid burst in early summer – they give pleasure for much longer, from the moment the fat, pale green and bronze shoots emerge from the ground. And then, in autumn, the handsome foliage takes on autumn tints that delight any flower arranger. The large cup or bowl-shaped flowers are made up of single or double layers of satiny petals.

The Doubles include 'Sarah Bernhardt', apple-blossom pink and scented; 'Festiva Maxima', white; and 'Knighthood', deep crimson. The smaller Singles group, in which the flowers have a centre of golden stamens, includes 'Hyperion', a reddish-purple; 'White Wings'; and the light pink 'Dayspring'. The Imperial group blooms have bosses of narrow petal-like stamens, and include 'Crimson Glory'; 'Bowl of Beauty', rose-pink with cream boss; 'Barry-more', white with cream centre; and 'Emperor of India', red with gold-brushed boss.

Lactiflora peonies are long-term perennials, at home in shrub, mixed or herbaceous borders. They create spectacular displays in summer when spring trees and shrubs have finished, and contribute to a continued show near camellias or other evergreens. Their large flowers and warm but soft colours blend well with plants of more hazy outline, such as anchusas, aquilegias, astrantias,

The blood-red double flowers of the handsome *Paeonia officinalis* 'Adolphe Rousseau' are borne erect on single stems.

This gloriously mixed border has the soft pink *Papaver orientale* 'Mrs Perry' at its centre, alongside towering delphiniums, while the pink theme is taken up by the spikes of *Polygonum bistorta* 'Superbum'.

crane's-bills and many grasses. CULTIVATION Plant in autumn, in moist but well-drained fertile soil. These peonies do best in full sun, but light shade is acceptable. Once planted they should be left undisturbed.

Paeonia officinalis

PEONY

Height 2ft
Planting distance 2-3ft
Best May-June

Medieval monks are thought to have introduced this peony for medicinal purposes – the plant name is said to be derived from Paeon, physician to the Greek gods. The vigorous, lobed foliage is set on thick stems, each of which carries a large, single, crimson-petalled flower with a centre of golden stamens.

The species itself is rarely seen, but several fine double forms, all sweetly scented, are readily available including the crimson 'Rubra Plena', and 'Alba Plena', a near white flushed with pink in the bud.

These are large and space-hogging plants, but their foliage looks superb with spring perennials like *Lunaria rediviva* and with blue columbines, especially *Aquilegia* 'Hensol Harebell'. CULTIVATION As for *P. lactiflora*.

Papaver orientale

ORIENTAL POPPY

Height 2-3ft
Planting distance 2ft
Best June-July

No garden should be without a clump of this kind of poppy, whose flowers, carried on tall hairy stems, are available in both the fiercest of reds and in ice-cool pastel shades.

Papaver orientale and *P. bracteatum* are the main sources of some magnificent garden forms. *P. bracteatum* has a ruff of leaves at the base of each flower and is glowing vermilion. The form 'Goliath' is the reddest and tallest of any garden poppy. *P. orientale* has dark green, hairy and deeply cut leaves and spectacular cup-shaped flowers, with petals like crinkled tissue paper, with a black blotch at the base. The species itself is orange-scarlet, and other red forms include the striking red-orange double, 'May Queen'.

The soft-coloured cultivars include old favourites such as 'Mrs Perry', ice-cream pink, and 'Perry's White', white flushed dull pink. Newer forms include 'Black and White', and 'Blue Moon', with huge lilac flowers. 'Picotee' is white with reddish flushing along the edges of the frilled petals.

The oriental poppies can make up the bulk of June colour in traditional herbaceous borders. The reds need careful placing but the fiery-red 'Goliath' looks marvellous near the pure blue *Anchusa* 'Loddon Royalist', or yellow *Thermopsis montana*. Pink and lavender shades blend into white or blue schemes; obliging 'Mrs Perry', for instance, goes splendidly with the crane's-bill, *Geranium* 'Johnson's Blue'. 'Black and White' is a pleasing companion for any colour; the black petal blotches stand out particularly well in white planting schemes. CULTIVATION Plant in autumn or spring, in good, well-drained soil and in full sun. Staking may be necessary. Propagate by division in autumn or spring or by root cuttings in late winter.

For long-flowering cheerfulness in the summer border it is hard to beat penstemons. One of the most optimistic in hue is *Penstemon* 'Firebird'.

The clear, singing pink of *Phlox paniculata* 'Eva Cullum' is given point and emphasis by a planting of annual phloxes and yellow hemerocallis.

Of well-tried pedigree, the lovely *Polemonium caeruleum* was grown in the gardens of ancient Rome.

Penstemon
hybrids

Height 2ft
Planting distance 1-2ft
Best July-October

Penstemons give colour in the border from midsummer until the autumn frosts; week after week they present their elegant stems clothed with long, tubular flowers. Their only disadvantages are that they are short-lived and are not fully hardy. The hybrids are raised from various North American species including *Penstemon campanulatus* and *P.* × *gloxinioides*.

A rule among penstemons seems to be, the narrower the leaf, the hardier the plant, and the narrowest leaves belong to the light pink 'Evelyn' and 'Pink Endurance' – a plummy pink. Almost as hardy, and broader in the leaf are 'Apple Blossom', pink and white; 'Garnet', rosy-red; 'Firebird', red; and 'Sour

To name such an obviously happy plant as this *Penstemon* 'Sour Grapes' seems a little unkind.

Grapes', greenish-blue.

Penstemons make handsome companions for almost everything. Their discreet foliage merges into the background and the flowers provide bright focal points when grouped according to colour. Pink forms go well with lavender, and reds are strikingly handsome in white arrangements. Blue and purple-blue forms contrast splendidly with orange and yellow flowers.

CULTIVATION Plant in spring, in sun and shelter, and in well-drained but moisture-retentive soil. Propagate by taking semi-hardwood cuttings in summer.

Phlox paniculata

Height 2-4ft
Planting distance 1½-2ft
Best July-September

As indispensable and traditional in the border as a rose, but much more easy-going, this phlox demands little apart from the odd mulch, and in return can furnish both the garden and house with colourful clusters of flowers. The species, lilac-purple in colour, is rarely seen, but it has provided a range of hybrids, some with *Phlox maculata* in their ancestry.

The stems, clothed with willowy foliage, are topped in summer with sprays of brightly coloured flowers, which range from white to pink, purple, mauve and crimson. Whites include the late, long-flowering 'Fujiyama'. It grows taller than most and has cylindrical flower spikes. 'Eva Cullum' is a clear pink with a red eye; 'Franz Schubert' is lilac; 'Sandringham', soft pink; and 'Harlequin' a startling purple. Darkest of the near reds is 'Starfire'.

Phloxes look their very best grouped in harmonious shades, but because of the sheer mass of colour they can clash with other plants unless carefully placed. The flowering season coincides with that of russet and gold-coloured plants – golden rods, rudbeckias and heleniums; the best companions for these are white and lilac phloxes, while the red and pink hues would be better off near the blues of Michaelmas daisies.

CULTIVATION Plant in autumn or spring, in fertile, moisture-retentive soil, in full sun or partial shade. Propagate by division in autumn.

Polemonium caeruleum

JACOB'S LADDER

Height 2-3ft
Planting distance 1½-2ft
Best April-July

With a fair bit of imagination, it can be seen that the common name of this perennial is derived from the structure of the foliage: the narrow leaflets, set at right angles to the leaf stalks, do vaguely resemble the rungs of a ladder. But it is the flowers that catch the eye – borne in tight clusters at the tips of the stems, startlingly sky blue in colour, and each with a central tuft of

It would be a tough weed that could fight its way through the handsome, sturdy leaves and bottle-brush flowers of *Polygonum bistorta* 'Superbum'.

Few things better express the richness of high summer than tumbling masses of potentillas. However, hues like that of *Potentilla* 'Gibson's Scarlet' are not to be trifled with, and companions must be chosen with care.

golden stamens. There is also a pretty white form, 'Alba'.

Polemonium caeruleum can provide drifts of colour in herbaceous or shrub borders. When naturalised in grass, it joins the bridge between early daffodils and crocuses, and the advent of autumn colchicums.
CULTIVATION Plant between autumn and spring, in any moisture-retentive soil, and in full sun or the dappled shade of overhead shrubs. Propagate by dividing the fibrous root mass during the dormant season. It seeds freely, so deadhead to prevent it spreading.

Polygonum amplexicaule

Height 4ft
Planting distance 3-4ft
Best July-October

Scarlet spikes of tiny bell flowers grow in profusion on this robust Himalayan plant.

From July to the first frosts, the flowers stand erect above a bush of deep green, heart-shaped leaves. The cultivar 'Firetail' is bright crimson.

A large plant that needs plenty of space to develop, it is decorative all the way down to the ground, and is impressive standing on its own. The flowers blend well with blues and oranges, so asters such as the blue-flowered *Aster × frikartii*, make fine companions.

If you want a smaller polygonum, try *Polygonum bistorta* 'Superbum'. It carries soft pink flower spikes sporadically all summer, and the dock-like leaves form an impenetrable and extremely attractive ground cover. It harmonises well with cottage-style perennials, such as *Astrantia maxima* and the white-spotted leaves of pulmonarias. The pink blooms also show up well against dark evergreens like rhododendrons.
CULTIVATION Plant between autumn and spring in moist,

fertile soil, in sun or partial shade. Propagate by dividing clumps in spring or autumn.

Potentilla
hybrids

CINQUEFOIL

Height 1½ft
Planting distance 1-1½ft
Best June-August

Sprays of small, brightly coloured cinquefoil flowers will lend sprightliness to a sunny border throughout the summer. Many of the hybrids are descended from two herbaceous species, *Potentilla atrosanguinea* and *P. argryophylla*. They have strawberry-like leaves of green and silver and include the bright 'Gibson's Scarlet', the slightly taller, intense red 'Flamenco', and 'Helen Jane' which is rose-pink with a deeper pink centre. Their flowers show up well against silver-leaved plants such as *Anaphalis cinnamomea*, or the feathers of bronze fennel.

Another group, descended from *P. nepalensis*, form neat mounds of deep green leaves. The best garden forms include the coppery-orange 'Roxana' and cherry-pink 'Miss Wilmott'. The pink form blends with rosy-tinged astrantias and some of the reddish penstemons. Try 'Roxana' with shrubs that have golden foliage for a particularly striking combination.
CULTIVATION Plant between autumn and spring in moist, well-drained soil in full sun. Propagate hybrids by division in early spring.

The dignified *Primula japonica* 'Postford White' can bring summer elegance to the margins of a pool, or a moist, partially shaded spot.

Primula
Waterside species

Height 1½-3ft
Planting distance 1½-2ft
Best June-July

Most of these moisture-loving plants belong to the Candelabra group. They have flowers arranged in whorls up their tall, elegant stems. *Primula bulleyana* is an example, with light orange flowers that first appear in May and rise from large rosettes of dark green, oval leaves. Two particularly attractive Candelabra primulas are *P. pulverulenta* and *P. japonica*. The flowers of *P. pulverulenta* are a striking crimson-red with deep, purple-red eyes. A magnificent garden form is 'Bartley', with flowers of sugar-pink with a carmine eye. *P. japonica* cultivars include 'Miller's Crimson', 'Postford White', as well as 'Buttermilk' and 'Tresco Purple'. The fine

The trumpet flowers of *Primula helodoxa* are arranged like cartwheels along its tall stems.

yellow flowers of *P. helodoxa* are held gracefully above leaves that remain light green and shiny throughout the winter.

P. florindae, the giant cowslip, takes a different form from the Candelabras, its yellow, sweetly scented flowers hanging umbrella-like from tall stems. Similar, but smaller and more delicate, is *P. sikkimensis*, the Himalayan cowslip, with tiny yellow flowers and spoon-shaped, light green leaves.

All the waterside primulas go well together in groups. The yellow varieties also associate well with blue or purple flowers, such as *Campanula lactiflora* and Siberian irises.

CULTIVATION Plant between autumn and spring in moist, fertile soil that will not dry out – either in sun or shade. Propagate by division in autumn or early spring, or by sowing freshly collected seed in pans in a cold frame.

Rheum palmatum
ORNAMENTAL RHUBARB

Height 5-6ft
Planting distance 4ft
Best June-August

Massive flower spikes of red, pink or cream appear in mid-summer, but these are a bonus. It is the huge deeply lobed leaves, which in good conditions grow to 2ft across, that are the rheum's most dramatic feature. They are dark green and conspicuously veined on top and crimson or bronze underneath. Garden forms include 'Atrosanguineum' and 'Bowles Variety', with wine-red flowers and deeply tinted leaves.

Such plants can stand on their own, and need little around them to enhance their magnificence. Candelabra primulas create a cool effect against the fresh new foliage, and the bronze-leaved fennel, *Foeniculum vulgare* 'Purpureum', contrasts superbly with the rheum foliage. If there's a drier, sunny spot nearby, bold perennials like *Acanthus spinosus* and *Veratrum nigrum* would add to the overall tropical effect.

CULTIVATION Plant between late autumn and early spring in a bog garden, or in moisture-retentive, fertile soil, in sun or

The great umbrella leaves of the ornamental rhubarb, *Rheum palmatum*, the grace of a *Primula bulleyana* hybrid, and rodgersias come together in a dramatic, moist soil partnership.

partial shade. Propagate by division in spring or autumn. The rootstock can be huge but is split easily with a spade.

Rodgersia pinnata

Height 3-4ft
Planting distance 3ft
Best June-September

As with other rodgersias, the striking foliage makes this bold plant rewarding even when not

Rodgersia pinnata 'Superba' goes well with rhododendrons and moisture-loving woodland plants.

in flower. The young bronze leaves change to rich emerald green as they mature, and finally become like burnished copper. In July, generous sprays of bright pink and white starry flowers rise above the leaves. There is a white form, 'Alba', and a pink-flowered variety, 'Superba', whose brave foliage remains bronze.

The plant is fine for a bog garden or a damp border with plenty of space for its clumps to expand, with perhaps the blue-green foliage of *Hosta sieboldiana* nearby. The bronze leaves go well with the cream plumes of *Aruncus dioicus*, which also contrast well with the pink rodgersia flowers.

CULTIVATION Plant in spring in moist soil, preferably rich in humus, and in sun or light shade. Plants will survive in shade that is fairly dense, but flowering will be sparse. Propagate by division in spring.

Romneya coulteri

TREE POPPY

Height 4-6ft
Planting distance 3ft
Best July-October

Romneyas are large-scale herbaceous perennials with woody bases. They can be temperamental, and are hardy only in warm sheltered areas. Once established, however, they can get out of hand, the vigorous rootstock spreading far and wide. Their redeeming virtue, quite apart from the handsome, deeply divided and blue-green leaves, are the poppy-like flowers. Huge, snowy-white blooms, crinkled like silk skirts that have been crammed into suitcases, grow in seemingly endless succession. The petals spread flat to reveal a centre of golden-yellow stamens.

Position romneyas where

Both *Romneya coulteri* and the large-flowered clematis hybrid above bloom continuously from midsummer until autumn.

they will not encroach on other plants, perhaps with silvery artemisias at the front for an ice-cool composition, or backed by dark-leaved plants to accentuate the snowy flowers – for example, the evergreen *Ceanothus* 'Autumnal Blue'.

CULTIVATION Plant in late spring, in any light, even poor, sharply drained soil and in full sun, ideally in the shelter of a south or west-facing wall. They resent being moved. Cut stems to near ground level in autumn and cover the crowns with a protective winter mulch. Propagate by replanting suckers in late spring, or by root cuttings in late winter.

The single-flowered yellow-gold *Rudbeckia nitida* 'Herbstsonne' is also known as 'Autumn Sun'.

Rudbeckia laciniata

CONEFLOWER, LAZY SUSAN

Height 5-7ft
Planting distance 2-3ft
Best August-September

In late August the showy, vivid golden-yellow flowers of *Rudbeckia laciniata* appear above jagged, bright green foliage. The flowers are daisy-like with a green cone at the centre. Garden varieties of this species and the very similar *R. nitida* include 'Goldquelle', which has double blooms of bright yellow, and the brassy, golden-flowered, single 'Herbstsonne'.

Excellent plants for a late-summer border of yellow and orange, the coneflowers bridge the gap between high-summer blooms such as blanket flowers (*Gaillardia*) or day lilies (*Hemerocallis*) and late-summer flowers such as chrysanthemums and perennial asters. Grouped with heleniums, with crocosmias and red-hot pokers (*Kniphofia*) in the foreground, the rudbeckias can contribute to a superb and long-lasting display of glowing oranges, yellows and russets. Acers or berberis also make good companions, providing a backing of foliage in shades of crimson, scarlet, gold and bronze.
CULTIVATION Plant in autumn or spring in any moist, fertile, well-drained soil. The rudbeckias do best in full sun, but will tolerate partial shade. Propagate by division in autumn.

The *Sedum* hybrid 'Ruby Glow' is a magnificent plant for the front of a border, with its dazzling display of crimson flower clusters some 3-4in in diameter.

Sedum spectabile

Height 1-1½ft
Planting distance 1½ft
Best July-October

A native of China, *Sedum spectabile* has waxy, fleshy foliage and large fluffy heads of clustered tiny flowers which are very attractive to butterflies. The flowers vary in colour from creamy-pink to deep, dusky purple. Cultivars, some of hybrid origin, include 'Ruby Glow' (which does not attract butterflies as it is sterile), 'Sunset Cloud' (purple leaves, claret flowers), and 'Bertram Anderson' (dark foliage, wine-purple flowers).

Sedums are ideal for the border front interplanted perhaps with border pinks, whose fine blue-grey foliage contrasts delightfully, and whose flowers reach their peak a little earlier in the season. Or try the smaller crane's-bills such as *Geranium wallichianum* 'Buxton's Blue', and silver-foliaged plants, particularly artemisias. Plant some autumn and spring-flowering crocuses nearby to ensure a long succession of flower.
CULTIVATION Plant between autumn and spring in dry, well-drained soil in full sun. Propagate by division in spring.

Sidalcea malviflora

Height 3-4ft
Planting distance 2ft
Best July-August

A relative of the mallow from western USA, this sidalcea has shapely pink mallow flowers that are borne on spikes from

Tall stems of deep shell-pink flowers are borne by *Sidalcea malviflora* 'Loveliness'.

July onwards. Its glossy, rich green rounded leaves form thick, weed-smothering clumps in spring. Garden varieties include 'Oberon' (rose-pink), 'Loveliness' (compact and shell pink) and 'Mrs T. Anderson' (taller, dark pink).

These superb border plants contrast well with blue crane's-bills, such as 'Johnson's Blue', and with the later-flowering bell flowers, particularly *Campanula persicifolia* and the cultivar 'Percy Piper'. Shrubs such as *Weigela florida* 'Foliis Purpureis' and *Ceanothus* × 'Gloire de Versailles' go well with the sidalcea in a mixed border.
CULTIVATION Plant any time

One of the most showy but shorter and non-invasive *Solidago* hybrids is 'Goldenmosa'. Its golden-yellow flowers, borne in late summer on arching plumes 6-9in long, are reminiscent of mimosa.

The wide, flat-headed flowers of the *Sedum* hybrid 'Autumn Joy' provide a contrast for the silvery spikes and leaves of *Stachys byzantina*.

between autumn and spring in fertile, well-drained but moist soil in full sun or light shade. Taller cultivars may need staking. Propagate by division in autumn or spring. Divide the plants at least every third year to maintain vigorous growth and promote free flowering.

Solidago
Hybrids
GOLDEN ROD

Height 3-6ft
Planting distance 1½-2ft
Best August-October

Vigorous golden rod, with its long plumes of bright yellow flowers, can bring a fine show of colour to, and even take over, the late summer border. The tall North American *Solidago canadensis* and its hybrid cultivar 'Golden Wings' grow to around 6ft high. Less invasive, and more suitable for all but the smallest gardens, are hybrids of *S. canadensis* and shorter species such as the European *S. virgaurea*. They include 'Goldenmosa', about 3ft high, whose bunched golden flowers resemble mimosa, and 'Lemore' with soft, primrose-yellow flowers.

In a bank or corner, golden rod contributes a splendid drift of autumn brightness if used as a space filler between vigorous, spring-flowering shrubs such as flowering currant (*Ribes sanguineum*), lilac (*Syringa*) and forsythia. 'Goldenmosa' looks good in a border – in an all-gold theme with, for example, golden privet (*Ligustrum ovalifolium* 'Aureomarginatum'), rudbeckias and heleniums, or contrasted with the blue of asters such as *Aster* × *frikartii* or *A. amellus*.

CULTIVATION Plant between autumn and spring in any soil, in full sun or light shade. Some cultivars may suffer from powdery mildew; mulching to keep the soil moist will discourage this. Propagate by dividing clumps and replanting them between autumn and spring.

Stachys byzantina
LAMB'S EARS

Height 1-1½ft
Planting distance 1½ft
Best April-October

A silver-foliaged ground-cover plant, lamb's ears has felty leaves that form thick silver mats in spring and go on producing new leaves for many months. The flower spikes, like the leaves, are fleeced with silvery hairs, and spikes of small magenta flowers peep through in June and July. The plant is sometimes listed in catalogues as *Stachys lanata* or *S. olympica*.

The garden cultivars include 'Silver Carpet', a non-flowering variety; the silvery-flowered 'Sheila Macqueen', and yellow-leaved 'Primrose Heron'. Any of these are natural low-level

The dock-like *Tovara virginiana* is grown for its distinctively marked and compact foliage.

The non-flowering *Stachys byzantina* 'Silver Carpet' provides good and unusual ground cover.

Tall clusters of soft-hued, powder-puff flowers of *Thalictrum aquilegifolium* make a charming display in a mixed border, and its lacy foliage provides a delicate contrast with the broad and deeply veined blue-green leaves of *Hosta sieboldiana*.

(*Stachys byzantina* cont) companions for roses, especially the old-fashioned pink sorts. It makes a superb plant for the border front, and can be encouraged to line paths or edge terraces and walls. Modern hybrid pinks (*Dianthus*) go well with 'Silver Carpet', as do the light blue flowers of *Geranium* 'Johnson's Blue', or the delicate filigree blue-green foliage of *Ruta graveolens* 'Jackman's Blue'. Lamb's ears can also be grown in containers with busy lizzies or ivy-leaved geraniums.
CULTIVATION Plant any time between autumn and spring in any well-drained soil in full sun. It thrives in poor soil and tolerates warm, dry weather without showing signs of stress. Propagate by dividing root clumps in autumn or spring.

Thalictrum aquilegifolium

MEADOW RUE

Height 2-3ft
Planting distance 1½-2ft
Best May-July

The lilac flowers of *Thalictrum aquilegifolium* appear in late May or early June above elegant, bluish-grey foliage that looks strikingly fresh in spring. A good form is 'Album', with similar foliage and with fluffy white flowers.

It is worth planting meadow rue among evergreen shrubs for the lightening effect of the lacy foliage alone, but such gently coloured flowers are an added attraction. In a mixed border, the young leaves make a fine background to late bulbs, including tulips. The lilac-mauve flowers harmonise well with lavender and pink, or with pale lemons and creams, so roses make good companions, as do crane's-bills such as pale pink *Geranium endressii*, or any of the filipendulas.

The flower sprays of the taller *T. delavayi* are more open and stand well above the lobed foliage; golden-yellow stamens contrast with lilac flowers. This plant thrives in a sheltered site in partial shade, and may need support, which could be provided by shrubs that have finished flowering, such as rhododendrons and camellias.
CULTIVATION Plant in early spring in moist but well-drained, fertile soil. Full sun is ideal, but the plants tolerate partial shade. Propagate by division in spring or by seed sown in spring in a cold frame.

Tovara virginiana

Height 2-2½ft
Planting distance 1½-2ft
Best May-October

A relative of the dock, this compact, mound-forming plant is grown for its foliage. It has oval leaves each marked with a conspicuous half-moon across the centre. The best varieties are 'Variegata' (cream markings) and the decorative, cream and pink marked 'Painter's Palette'.

Its fine colours and tidy appearance make *Tovara virginiana* ideal for a restricted border where every plant must contribute fully. It goes well near plain green hostas, which thrive in similar conditions. Include winter-flowering hellebores for earlier colour, and perhaps the Japanese toad lily (*Tricyrtis hirta*) for a later show. Its white-spotted, purple blooms are at their best in late summer. Yellow or white flowers look fine with the tovara's foliage, so dark-leaved *Cimicifuga ramosa* 'Atropurpurea' would help to create a good colour combination. The tovara also makes a fine container plant, grown in a low-sided trough with, perhaps, the variegated grass *Hakonechloa macra* 'Aureola'.
CULTIVATION Plant from autumn to spring in moisture-retentive soil in full sun or partial shade. Choose a sheltered site, as late frost and chilly winds can damage young growths, even though the plants are completely hardy. Propagate by dividing crowded clumps in early spring or by taking stem cuttings during the summer.

The yellow-tinged foliage and pale blue flowers of *Veronica austriaca teucrium* 'Trehane' stand out well in a border backed by grey stone.

Veronica austriaca teucrium

Height 1-2ft
Planting distance 1-1½ft
Best July

The small, sky-blue flowers cluster like foxes' tails at the stem ends above neat, slow-spreading mats of lance-shaped leaves. Cultivars include 'Crater Lake Blue' (Oxford blue) and 'Royal Blue'. 'Trehane' (pale blue with gold-flushed leaves) is a cultivar of the lower growing *Veronica prostrata*.

Veronicas provide sound, clean, deep blue flowers for the border front, and make a useful contrast with the yellow of *Oenothera missouriensis* or *O.* 'Fireworks'. They also look beautiful with pinks or with greenish-white or pink-tinted *Astrantia major*, and are good companions for penstemons, and particularly the pink of the cultivars 'Evelyn' and 'Apple Blossom', which will continue flowering into autumn.

CULTIVATION Plant any time between autumn and spring in any fertile soil in sun or part shade. The plants tolerate a range of conditions. Propagate by division in autumn or spring.

Viola cornuta

HORNED VIOLET

Height 6in · *Planting distance* 1ft
Best May-November

These are among the most valuable plants in the garden. They form leafy, persistent clumps and bloom throughout the summer and beyond. The flowers are fragrant, and each

Pushing up through a bush rose, *Viola cornuta* 'Lilacina' and the white form 'Alba' blend happily with their host. The sharp pink of dianthus below balances the pink of the rose.

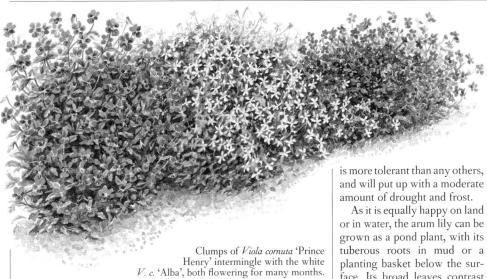

Clumps of *Viola cornuta* 'Prince Henry' intermingle with the white *V. c.* 'Alba', both flowering for many months.

(*Viola cornuta* cont)
one bears a slender spur, or horn. There are several fine cultivars, including the white 'Alba', royal purple 'Prince Henry', 'Lilacina' in a subtle lavender-blue, and *Viola cornuta minor*, a half-sized version in blue and white.

All the cultivars work well as ground cover at the feet of shrubs, where they will self-propagate. They often grow up to flower among the shrub's lower branches. These violets are perfect below shrub roses because their colours harmonise well and their flowering period overlaps that of the roses at both ends of the season. In cottage borders horned violets might mingle well with orange marigolds or pinks, or can be mixed with other violas to produce a constant supply of colour and interest.
CULTIVATION Plant in autumn or spring in any moist, well-drained soil. They tolerate all but the driest or darkest of spots. Propagate either by dividing mature plants in spring or autumn, or by taking cuttings during spring or late summer.

Zantedeschia aethiopica

ARUM LILY

Height 3ft · *Planting distance* 2ft
Best June-July

The curled, snow-white 'petal' of the arum lily that encircles a central yellow spike is in fact a modified leaf (spathe). As the spathe opens, it flattens around the erect spike. The leaves are large and soft, pointed at one end and borne on fleshy stalks. In its native South Africa, the lily is a weed that clogs water-courses. The plant is not hardy enough to be a reliable perennial except in warm areas. One hardy cultivar, 'Crowborough', is more tolerant than any others, and will put up with a moderate amount of drought and frost.

As it is equally happy on land or in water, the arum lily can be grown as a pond plant, with its tuberous roots in mud or a planting basket below the surface. Its broad leaves contrast splendidly with the reediness of water irises or sedges.

An ideal spot would be the banks of a stream or pond, interplanted with ferns such as the sensitive fern, *Onoclea sensibilis*. In a warm border, as long as the soil is moist, it cohabits happily with other warmth-loving perennials such as red-hot pokers (kniphofias), which flower at the same time, or crocosmias, which flower in July and August. It would also look good with true lilies such as the orange-red panther lily (*Lilium pardalinum*) or white *L. speciosum*.
CULTIVATION Plant in spring in moist, fertile soil. In winter protect the roots with a thick mulch, and put a cloche over them during the coldest months. As water plants, so long as the tubers are below the level at which the water freezes, they should survive in all but the coldest years. Propagate by division in spring.

In the dappled shade of this border, the eye is drawn to the striking white *Zantedeschia aethiopica*, planted beside *Hosta sieboldiana*.

Summer
ALPINES

As with any other group of plants, the effectiveness of alpines depends to a large extent on their foliage. After the spring flush, the alpine garden need not be by any means flowerless over the summer months. Indeed, with planning, it will be almost as colourful in summer as in spring. But if proper attention is paid to the creative use of alpine foliage, the overall effect will be greatly enhanced.

Campanula cochleariifolia

Height 3-4in
Planting distance 9in
Best June-August

One of the loveliest of the campanulas, this species has thimble-shaped bell flowers on the thinnest of stems, hanging just an inch or two above the tiny, spoon-shaped leaves. In summer, the crowded bells almost hide the foliage. There are various shades available including several blues as well as a delightful pure white.

A wanderer by nature, *Campanula cochleariifolia* flourishes in one spot for a year or two, then spreads out on its underground runners to establish itself a few inches away. Self-sown seedlings may also spring up in the same locality. Planning companionship and continuity for a wanderer is difficult, for although small, it is vigorous enough to overgrow those of its

Easily grown without being rampant, *Campanula cochleariifolia* softens the edge of a gravel path with its great multitude of flowers throughout the summer months. In its native Alps it grows on rock and scree.

neighbours of similar size. One solution is to let it spread around a small, prostrate willow such as *Salix myrsinites*, where it will fill the spaces between branches without detriment to the willow. It also looks good bordering gravel paths or edging a driveway or terrace where its wanderlust need not be restrained. Always include the white form in a planting, as it enhances the blue varieties.

CULTIVATION Plant in early spring in moist but well-drained soil in a sunny spot. It is one of the easiest campanulas to grow, and is less troubled by slugs than most of its kin. Propagate

from self-sown seedlings, or dig up a few of the creeping stems with roots attached and replant or pot them in autumn or spring.

Campanula garganica

Height 3-4in
Planting distance 1ft
Best July-August

A leafy member of the bellflower family, *Campanula garganica* forms crowded little evergreen clumps of heart-shaped leaves. The rock-hugging stems bear sprays of lavender-blue flowers. They

open, at the height of summer, into five-pointed stars and last for many weeks. The variety 'W. H. Paine' has blue flowers with white centres, and 'Hirsuta' has grey hairy leaves.

A plant best suited to a sunny crevice or scree, it needs companions of similar inclination. The silvery leaved *Achillea tomentosa* is one – its foliage makes a good contrast, and its dense yellow flower heads begin to appear several weeks before those of the campanula. For an unconventional display, plant blue and white forms of the campanula in a strawberry tub together with earlier flowers

Campanula garganica 'Hirsuta' quickly fills a corner, the open flowers masking its grey leaves.

like aubrieta. Fill the tub with garden soil mixed with equal quantities of peat, limestone chippings and coarse sand.

CULTIVATION Plant in early spring in light, well-drained soil in a sunny position. This is an easy-to-please plant that repays moderate attention with steady growth and abundant flowers. Do, however, keep slugs at bay. Propagate by dividing plants in autumn or spring, or by taking cuttings from young shoots during spring.

Campanula × haylodgensis becomes a mound of lilac-blue flowers.

A neat, 2in high hummock of *Dianthus alpinus*, with its glossy leaves and pale-pink flowers, is set in a carpet of *Raoulia australis*.

There are many dianthus hybrids available to suit every rock garden colour scheme; this eye-catching cultivar is 'Kesteven Kirkstead'.

Campanula × haylodgensis

Height 6in
Planting distance 1ft
Best July-August

One of the very few double campanulas, this plant has multi-petalled flowers of lilac-blue. It is a hybrid of *Campanula cochleariifolia* and the larger-flowered *C. carpatica*, and is closer to the first-named in size and shape. The influence of its larger parent has been to curb the wandering habit, so this bell flower can be planted in a crevice or pocket of soil to form a slowly developing tuffet.

The campanula can be mixed with the early blooming mossy saxifrages, its neat green leaves making a good foil for the saxifrages' smooth cushions of foliage and earlier flowers. As a wall plant campanula goes well with silver saxifrages, semper-vivums and the smaller sedums.

A quite different use for this hybrid campanula is as the permanent central feature for a ring of traditional annuals, such as trailing lobelia and alyssum, in a tub, urn or chimney pot.
CULTIVATION Plant during mid-spring in a sunny site – although the plant will tolerate some shade. Light, well-drained fertile soils are best. Be sure to protect the plants from slugs. Propagate by division in mid-spring, or by softwood cuttings in late spring.

Dianthus alpinus

ALPINE PINK

Height 2in
Planting distance 9in
Best June-August

Although the plants are sometimes rather short-lived, they are spectacular. *Dianthus alpinus* forms a mat of glossy, deep green foliage and large flowers. The broad, toothed petals overlap slightly to form a disc 1-1½in across. They range in colour from pale pink to deep rose, and always have a zone of speckled crimson at the centre. There are white forms, but see them in flower before buying, as they vary in quality. The variety 'Joan's Blood' is noted for its deep rich colour.

The dianthus is well suited for interplanting with kabschia saxifrages (which also like limy soil), and comes into bloom a few weeks after the saxifrage flowers are spent. The dark, long and narrow leaves of the dianthus make an interesting contrast with the grey-green foliage of the saxifrages all through the year.
CULTIVATION Plant in mid-spring in light, preferably limy soil. Choose a fairly sunny location, and keep the soil moist during dry spells. Propagate from softwood cuttings taken in mid to late summer and rooted in sand or equal parts peat and coarse sand. Alternatively, sow seed in a cold frame in spring. The dianthus grows well for several seasons, but may then decline rapidly, so keep new stock in the pipeline for replacements.

Dianthus

Hybrids

Height 3-4in
Planting distance 9-12in
Best June-July

Dozens of these little evergreen dianthus hybrids are available, many of which are fragrant. *Dianthus* × 'Little Jock' and *D.* × 'La Bourboule' (syn 'La Bourbrille'), share a well-deserved popularity and are particularly suitable for the rock garden.

The double-flowered 'Little Jock' forms a solid mat of small sword-like leaves that spread to occupy about a square foot of ground. In June, apple-blossom pink flowers appear singly on 2in long stems and, if the weather is kind, stay fresh and colourful for two or three weeks. 'La Bourboule' forms a neat, squat cushion of grey-green foliage that is smothered with a host of small pink flowers as June begins, and flowering often continues well into July.

Both hybrids have attractive evergreen foliage, but further

Dianthus 'La Bourboule' blooms follow on from those of *Androsace sarmentosa.*

Unlike many of the hardy geraniums, or crane's-bills, *Geranium cinereum* 'Ballerina' is a dainty cultivar, that is contained enough in habit and vigour for all but the smallest of rock gardens.

plants are needed to provide interest in spring and autumn. *Androsace sarmentosa* has rose flowers from April to June and attractive leaf rosettes all year. *Acaena microphylla* could be planted nearby for its colourful autumn fruits and bronze-green foliage, but not too close. Keep it in check with a little snipping now and again.

CULTIVATION Plant in autumn or spring, and cultivate as for *Dianthus alpinus.*

Dianthus pavonius
(syn *D. neglectus*)

Height 3-4in
Planting distance 6in
Best June-July

A blue-green central eye, and petals that are buff-coloured on the underside, distinguish this dianthus. Otherwise the colours

Dianthus pavonius flowers rise on short stems above dense, grey-green tufts of grass-like leaves.

are very variable – from pale pink to rich rose. The flowers are borne singly on stems 2-3in high. Outside the flowering season the evergreen foliage, like a small hummock of fine grass, is attractive all year.

More temperamental than many other dwarf dianthus, the plant may be fickle in one garden and amiable in another. It does seem to respond better if

grown in a trough rather than the open garden. A perfect companion, especially in a trough, and which blooms earlier, is the spring gentian, *Gentiana verna.* For an autumn display, plant the dianthus with clumps of the petite *Cyclamen intaminatum*, which bears white flowers all through October.

CULTIVATION Plant in spring, preferably in a trough or specially prepared raised bed. The plant will tolerate limy soil, although reputed not to. Spray regularly to destroy aphids, otherwise plants may be seriously crippled or infected by aphid-borne disease. Propagate from cuttings taken in mid to late summer.

Geranium cinereum
'Ballerina'

Height 6-8in
Planting distance 12-15in
Best June-September

Most geraniums are too big and vigorous for the rock garden, but 'Ballerina' is sufficiently restrained for use in alpine plantings, except for small beds and most troughs. The broad-petalled flowers, slightly dished in form, are light purplish-pink and strikingly marked with a purplish-red eye. They flower in steady succession throughout summer. The maple-like leaves are greyish-green and form a

low mound of foliage which may develop autumn tints if the plant is in a sunny position.

The white-flowered early snowflake, *Leucojum vernum*, will fill the bare ground around the geranium's crown in March. By the time the geranium is fully active, the snowflake will have faded and will not resent being overgrown.

CULTIVATION Plant in autumn or spring in any well-drained soil. It is content in either full sun or partial shade. To propagate, lift the plant in early autumn or spring and divide the crown, or take off one or two well-rooted offsets from the edge. Replant the divisions immediately, or pot them for later planting.

Vivid blooms embellish the deeply cleft foliage of *Geranium riversleaianum* 'Russell Prichard', the longest-lasting of all crane's-bill cultivars.

A sunny position brings out the best in rock roses, and *Helianthemum* 'Beech Park Red' makes a colourful and vigorous contribution to the rock garden. Each short-lived bloom is immediately replaced by others.

Geranium × riversleaianum
'Russell Prichard'

CRANE'S-BILL

Height 9-12in
Planting distance 1-1½ft
Best June-September

'Russell Prichard' is the longest-lasting of all the hardy geraniums, and neat enough in habit for a reasonable sized rock garden. Its brilliant pink flowers are nearly an inch across, and are subtly veined with darker pink which fades with age. The flowers grow on trailing stems above grey-green, toothed, lobed foliage that forms attractive clumps from spring until the colder days of late autumn.

The rich blues of *Gentiana verna* would make a strong precedent in spring to the geranium's magenta-pink, and brilliant *Gentiana sino-ornata* could follow in autumn. Alternatively, saxifrages could carpet the ground in front of the geranium to provide noble year-round foliage. *Saxifraga cochlearis* brings white flowers in summer, but its mounds of silvery rosettes would come to the fore when the geranium leaves die back to the rootstock in winter. It could be combined with *S. apiculata*, for contrasting leaves and white or yellow spring flowers. Whites and creams make subtle same-season companions – you could try *Helianthemum nummularium* 'Wee Bride', as a foil to the geranium's hot pink.

CULTIVATION Plant any time between autumn and spring in fertile, well-drained soil, in full sun or dappled shade. Propagate by division in spring, when new growth is evident but not advanced. Roots that are not divided every few years will grow woody and lose vigour.

Helianthemum 'Wisley Primrose' makes a colourful ground cover for border foregrounds.

Helianthemum nummularium

ROCK ROSE

Height 4-8in
Planting distance 1½-2ft
Best June-August

Centuries ago wild yellow rock roses were cultivated to front the borders of cottage gardens. Since then, many colour varieties of hybrid origin have been produced, including orange, pink, red and white, as well as different colours and textures of the oval leaves. Just a few varieties from the dozens on the market are: 'Ben Afflick', whose muted orange flowers have a terracotta eye (6in); 'Ben Heckla' which is coppery gold (6in); crimson-scarlet 'Beech Park Red' (8in); white 'Wee Bride' (4in); the double-flowered, pale yellow 'Jubilee' (6in); large-flowered 'Wisley Pink' (6in), and primrose yellow 'Wisley Primrose' (6in).

Rock roses grow vigorously, and need a foot or so all round them for the new flowering stems to spread. Although each flower lasts only a day or two, successive new ones maintain the display for many weeks.

By carefully selecting plants with differing foliage, and setting the grey, woolly-leaved forms against others of varying green, evergreen rock roses can look attractive well beyond their summer flowering time.

Helianthemum 'Wisley Pink' quickly forms a hummock of grey foliage, with larger than average flowers.

A golden dome of the flax *Linum* 'Gemmel's Hybrid' enhances the sunniest part of the garden.

From midsummer into autumn, a carpet of *Lithodora diffusa* blooms among bright fronds of the hart's-tongue fern, *Asplenium scolopendrium*.

With such a choice of colours to offer, the plants mix well with a host of garden favourites. A nearby planting of the prolific *Ornithogalum umbellatum* (Star of Bethlehem) will give a display of white, star-shaped flowers in May before the rock roses appear. For colour after they have finished flowering, try growing evergreen, mat-forming *Acaena* 'Blue Haze' between the rock roses. In late summer and early autumn it bears distinctive burr-like seed heads with russet spines.

CULTIVATION Plant any time between autumn and spring in any well-drained but not too rich soil where there is plenty of sun. In early autumn, cut back to within a few inches of the soil to keep plants compact and pre-vent them invading their neigh-bours. Propagate by cuttings of non-flowering shoots in mid or late summer. Plants do not come true from seed.

Linum
'Gemmel's Hybrid'

Height 6-9in
Planting distance 1ft
Best June-July

One of the finest of the dwarf forms of flax, *Linum* 'Gemmel's Hybrid' bears a dazzling mass of large golden flowers with a distinctive sheen. Although it is something of a prima donna, this hybrid is well worth a bit of extra attention. The bluish-green leaves form a mound from which many short, upright flower stems produce succes-sive blooms for several weeks.

For early colour, set *Iris reticulata* 'Cantab' round the flax to bear its Cambridge-blue flowers in February and early March, and ripen its next year's bulbs in the summer-warmed soil. Plant *Crocus pulchellus* to take the place of the irises in

October. The veined, pale lavender flowers rise naked from the ground, and then, when the blooms are past, narrow leaves develop.

CULTIVATION Plant in spring in fertile, well-drained soil in the sunniest corner of the garden. This hybrid can be short-lived, and should be regularly propa-gated to ensure a stock of replacements. Take cuttings of semi-hardwood non-flowering shoots in midsummer.

Lithodora diffusa

Height 4in
Planting distance 2-2½ft
Best June-October

The lovely trumpet flowers, each with five petals of intense azure blue, cling tightly to a spreading mat of small, ever-green leaves. In time, this native of southern Europe, which is

also sold as *Lithospermum diffusum*, will spread for several feet and scramble happily over and among low shrubs. Richest of all in colour, and with the greatest wealth of flowers, is the variety *Lithodora diffusa* 'Heavenly Blue'. 'Grace Ward' bears slightly larger and paler flowers which are less abun-dant, but it is a more robust cultivar and easier to grow.

Stunning effects can be achieved by garlanding the lithodora's blue-spangled stems round gold-leaved plants such as the heathers *Erica ciliaris* 'Aurea' and *Calluna vulgaris*

'Golden Haze'. Or it could be trained around a dwarf conifer, such as the very slow-growing *Chamaecyparis obtusa* 'Nana Lutea'. This forms a bright yellow conical bush which retains its colour through the winter months.

CULTIVATION Plant in mid or late autumn in lime-free soil in a sunny, open position. Make sure that the soil never dries out at the roots. Propagate *L. diffusa* by taking semi-hardwood cut-tings in mid or late summer. Apply a hormone rooting powder and insert in equal parts of peat and coarse sand.

For a sunshine glow at the front of the border, it would be hard to better *Oenothera missouriensis*.

The grassy foliage and buttercup flowers of *Ranunculus gramineus* make a fine foil for the denser foliage of *Picea glauca albertiana* 'Conica'.

The wild relations of *Scabiosa columbaria* 'Alpina Nana' are found on chalk downland.

Oenothera missouriensis

EVENING PRIMROSE

Height 9in
Planting distance 1½ft
Best July-September

The purity of colour in this evening primrose – denying its name by flowering during the day as well – is rarely if ever matched by any other yellow. Its low and spreading, rather untidy, habit is instantly forgiven as soon as the first canary-yellow flower opens above the narrow, glossy green foliage. From midsummer until early autumn, at regular intervals, an enchanting succession of large (3-4in), satiny blooms studs each plant.

Let the evening primrose spread along the edge of a raised bed or atop a rocky outcrop. Add substance behind with a dwarf conifer such as *Chamaecyparis lawsoniana* 'Pygmea Argentea', whose gilded foliage will echo the yellow of the primrose blooms. Nearby, or in front, *Aubrieta deltoidea* 'Aurea' could spread its mat of gold-edged, evergreen leaves and contribute a mass of purple flowers to the spring scene.
CULTIVATION Plant between autumn and spring, in ordinary garden soil and in full sun. Good drainage is essential. Propagate by basal cuttings in spring.

Ranunculus gramineus

Height 12-15in
Planting distance 9in
Best May-June

Gardeners are understandably wary about growing a member of the invasive buttercup genus. But this species is well behaved. It provides no threat to other plants, and it keeps up a late spring to early summer display of shiny yellow flowers, shaped like flat bowls, in sprays of five. Before and after flowering, the foliage looks like a small, upright clump of grey-green, broad-bladed grass.

A good companion for *Ranunculus gramineus* is *Pulsatilla vulgaris*, whose purple flowers will mingle with the buttercup's in May. In a lightly shaded place, surround the buttercup with a mat of *Primula* 'Wanda'. This hardy little plant bears a profusion of rich ruby blooms lying close against its huddled leaves, often from late winter until the beginning of June.
CULTIVATION Plant in autumn or spring in well-drained but not dry soil, in sun or light shade. The plant needs very little attention. Propagate by division in early or mid-autumn.

Scabiosa columbaria
'Alpina Nana'

Height 5-8in
Planting distance 9in
Best July-October

Typically of the scabious genus, this dwarf, evergreen form is a sun-lover whose natural habitat is dry, stony mountainsides. It is presented by nurseries and garden centres under a number of pseudonyms including *Scabiosa columbaria* 'Dwarf Form', *S. alpina* and *S. c. alpina*; so to be sure of correct identification, check that mature plants are of the right height. The lilac-blue flower heads are about 1in across and rise from clusters of grey-green leaves.

To get the best from 'Alpina Nana', plant it in groups of at least five, with other small, earlier-flowering plants such as *Dianthus gratianopolitanus*.
CULTIVATION Plant during spring in well-drained soil and in a sunny position. Propagate by dividing clumps in spring.

Summer
BULBS, CORMS AND TUBERS

UNLIKE SPRING BULBS, which tend to come from temperate climes, many summer bulbs hail from such warmer quarters of the globe as South Africa, tropical Asia and South America. Their origins are reflected in the shapes and colours that look so exotic in our homely native gardens. Apart from lilies, which prefer cool soil, most summer bulbs are used to heat and ill-adjusted to frost. However, in well-drained soils and sunny sites, they will usually survive happily.

Allium christophii

Height 1-1½ft
Planting distance 1ft
Best June

The flower heads of this ornamental member of the onion family are a dark rosy-purple borne on tall, stiff stems. The big spidery balls of fragile, slightly metallic-looking starry blooms can make an important focal point in the summer garden. They can be dried in their coloured state, or be left to form skeletal seed heads that open to reveal shiny black seeds. Either way, they can be employed to give dramatic effect to flower arrangements.

The arching strap-shaped leaves and unusual flowers of *Allium christophii* (also listed as *A. albopilosum*) make attractive eyecatchers among the stones of

In this gorgeous planting, the lacy heads of *Allium christophii* are mingled with the hybrid musk rose 'Ballerina', *Silene dioica* 'Rosea Plena' and a few indigo bells of the herbaceous *Clematis integrifolia*.

Though the leaves release a strong garlicky odour when crushed, there is no doubt that *Allium moly* will bring sunshine into sombre corners.

a patio or terrace. Alliums need to be set in groups in the middle of a mixed border, with later-flowering plants such as the low-growing perennial asters or a dwarf solidago hybrid in the foreground to disguise the alliums' dying foliage.

CULTIVATION Plant as soon as the bulbs become available during autumn in sun or partial shade in any well-drained soil. Propagate by separating new bulbs from established clumps in the autumn, or sow seed in trays of compost under a cold frame and grow on for a year before planting out.

Before a backdrop of Japanese anemones, the spectacularly decorative globe-like seed heads of *Allium christophii* open to reveal coal-black seeds.

Allium moly

Height 6-10in
Planting distance 4-6in
Best June

This allium is tough and vigorous, and most useful for placing in dry, difficult areas, such as the base of a wall, where few other plants would thrive. It quickly builds up large clumps of broad, strap-shaped leaves, lit in midsummer by many loose clusters of golden-yellow stars. There is a powerful garlic odour, but no problem with lingering foliage, as the leaves die back rapidly after flowering.

The evergreen shrub *Ceanothus* 'Cascade' that produces rich blue flowers in May, would make an attractive companion, and provide interest in the plot throughout the year.

CULTIVATION Plant during early or mid-autumn in a sunny or partially shaded position in any free-draining soil. Remove faded flower heads to prevent seeding, and top dress plants with bone meal in autumn. Propagate by lifting and dividing clumps in autumn or spring when they become congested.

Alstroemeria aurantiaca

PERUVIAN LILY

Height 2-3ft
Planting distance 1-1½ft
Best June-July

The delicate appearance of the flame-orange blooms, flecked with maroon and ornamented with long elegant stamens, belies the Peruvian lily's hardy nature. It is a strong-growing and immensely rewarding plant for the summer border, and the firm stems, clothed in small,

Sprightly *Alstroemeria* Ligtu hybrids bring the fresh colours of spring into summer. *Geranium magnificum* and *Papaver somniferum* give support.

Crinum × powellii contributes a touch of real ostentation to the summer bedding plan.

Though South African in origin, *Crocosmia × crocosmiiflora* is now widely seen in British gardens. The cultivar 'Solfatare' is more unusual.

(*Alstroemeria aurantiaca* cont) lance-shaped leaves, make it an excellent flower for cutting. Also highly desirable among alstroemerias are the justly famed Ligtu hybrids, which on their tall stems produce sprays of up to 20 trumpet flowers, each as delicately shaped as orchids, and in a colour range of sunset pink, gold and apricot, all freckled with deep red. Though they are slightly shorter than *Alstroemeria aurantiaca*, their stems are just as straight and strong, and carry attractive grey-green foliage.

Draw inspiration from the dark flecked petals, and plant the tubers near the maroon-leaved smoke tree *Cotinus coggygria* 'Royal Purple', which has splendid autumn colours; back them up with the flowering spires of *Cimicifuga simplex* 'White Pearl'. The many-hued Ligtu hybrids make a glorious and lasting mid-border display, and are perfect for cutting. Plant them behind the all-season, aromatic foliage of *Santolina chamaecyparissus* or the dense silver filigree leaves of *Artemesia* 'Powis Castle'.

CULTIVATION Plant the tubers as soon as they become available in autumn, in an open, sunny position, and in any free-draining soil. Deadhead regularly and cut to ground level in autumn. Propagate by dividing crowded clumps in early spring.

Crinum × powellii

Height 2-3ft
Planting distance 2-3ft
Best August-September

South African in origin, and a member of the amaryllis family, this charming plant introduces a touch of tropical elegance into the garden. Each sturdy stem can carry up to ten glorious trumpet blooms, set against a shock of long, narrow leaves. In nurseries, the pale pink original hybrid is often known as 'Roseum', to distinguish it from the white form, 'Album'. The foliage is killed off by frost in most winters.

The magnificent display of the crinum entitles it to stand alone, basking in the reflected warmth of a wall uncluttered by close companions. However, the strong, shapely forms of *Phormium tenax* or of *Yucca filamentosa* nearby would add a further hint of the exotic, and a succession of crocuses could be scattered in the foreground for autumn to spring colour.

CULTIVATION Plant during spring in a warm, sunny position, preferably against a south or west-facing wall, with rich, well-drained soil. Leave the necks of the bulbs just above the ground. Protect the emerging shoots against late frosts with straw or bracken. Propagate by division in spring.

Crocosmia × crocosmiiflora

MONTBRETIA

Height 1½-2ft
Planting distance 1ft
Best August-September

Flares of orange montbretia flowers that arch from stiff blades of leaves for several weeks of summer are a familiar sight in many gardens, and not unfamiliar either in the luxuriant and unsprayed hedgerows of Wales and Cornwall. There are now variously coloured hybrids available, including the spectacular deep orange 'Emily McKenzie', soft lemon-yellow 'Citronella' and perhaps the

One of summer's peaks is the flowering of *Crocosmia* 'Lucifer'.

Long-lasting, sweetly fragrant and tough, *Cyclamen purpurascens* is a good choice for odd corners – in this case, beneath a caryopteris.

The cool, white elegance of *Galtonia candicans* is outstanding even among a summer collection that includes monardas, alliums and dahlias.

loveliest of them all 'Solfatare', whose warm apricot flowers are balanced by pale bronze foliage. Apart from *Crocosmia × crocosmiiflora*, there is quite another range of hybrids raised not so long ago at Bressingham Gardens, Norfolk. They are the offspring of *C. masonorum* and *Curtonus paniculatus* and combine the most majestic features of each species. Both are worth growing in their own right – *Crocosmia masonorum* for its pleated leaves and startling orange flowers, and *Curtonus paniculatus* for its 4ft stature and sprays of scarlet blooms. The

hybrids include 'Lucifer', a triumphant, shining red; the fiery orange 'Spitfire', and burnt orange 'Emberglow'.

Not surprisingly, crocosmias were great favourites in the more opulent Victorian gardens, and generous groups of the plants still mesh very smoothly indeed with traditional border perennials. *Helenium autumnale* and perennial asters, for example, backed by the orange-red hips of *Rosa moyesii* 'Geranium', would nicely extend the display well into autumn.

CULTIVATION Plant corms during spring in an open, sunny position or light shade, in any well-drained soil. Top dress with general fertiliser in spring as the new spears are just emerging. Propagate by lifting and dividing overcrowded clumps just after flowering or during early spring.

Cyclamen purpurascens

Height 4in
Planting distance 8-10in
Best July-September

Although modest in appearance – its leaves are less strikingly marked than those of many cyclamens – this species has a delicious fragrance and virtually evergreen foliage. The flowers, rich in tone, range from lilac to purple-red, and include a gorgeous carmine.

Coming as it does from the mountains of Eastern Europe, it is a hardy plant and will grow quite happily in the less sunny quarters of the rock garden. Plant it with equal confidence beneath small-leaved deciduous trees or among shrubs, such as white-flowered eucryphias or *Caryopteris × clandonensis*.

CULTIVATION Plant young, pot-grown plants in spring in well-drained soil, and in a site with some shade. Apply bone meal in spring. Propagate early in the autumn from freshly gathered seed sown immediately in seed compost in a cold frame.

Galtonia candicans

SUMMER HYACINTH

Height 2-3ft
Planting distance 9-12in
Best August

With its waxy, white flowers hanging like ornamental bells above a mass of narrow, grey-green leaves, the cool grace of *Galtonia candicans* can soothe the hot colours of late summer in a south or west-facing border. As the foliage dies down in autumn, divert attention from it with a clump of the later-

flowering *Amaryllis belladonna*.

If the soil is acid, galtonias can also be used to highlight a mixed shrub border in front of camellias and rhododendrons. Another good summer notion is to plant them in a large tub or urn, either by themselves, or mixed with *Agapanthus campanulatus* for follow-on colour.

CULTIVATION Plant during spring in an open, warm and sunny situation with any free-draining soil. Apply general fertiliser in spring, and do not cut back the leaves in autumn until they have turned yellow. Propagate by seed sown in early spring.

Gladiolus byzantinus, sometimes known as the sword lily, has a wonderful intensity of colour.

Gladiolus byzantinus

Height 2-3ft
Planting distance 6-9in
Best June

Hardy, vigorous, and elegant too, this species comes from the Mediterranean, and is easier to grow and more adaptable to British gardens than the large-flowering hybrids from South Africa. Slightly arching stems carry unpretentious flowers of vibrant purple-red set against narrow blades of leaves that are handsome throughout summer.

Other plants of Mediterranean origin make good companions, such as the evergreen *Rosmarinus officinalis* 'Benenden Blue', or *Cistus × purpureus*, or the fleecy, silver leaves of *Stachys olympica*. This gladiolus can also be naturalised in grass – as long as the grass is not too vigorous.

CULTIVATION Plant corms as soon as available in autumn or spring, in any reasonably fertile, free-draining soil. An open, sunny position is ideal, but partial shade is tolerated. Top dress with bone meal in spring. No staking is necessary and the corms can be left in the ground over winter. Propagate by dividing established clumps.

Iris xiphioides

ENGLISH IRIS

Height 1½-2ft
Planting distance 6in
Best June-July

The slender elegance of *Iris xiphioides* is useful for enhancing a waterside planting scheme

The royal purple of *Iris xiphioides* finds its match in the vivid cerise *Centaurea dealbata* 'Steenbergii' behind, and the softer mauve *Viola cornuta* cultivars; dwarf irises in the foreground will star in another season.

in the difficult dryish margins often bordering artificial pools. It will grace an uncluttered part of an informal border too, the fresh green of its firm, fluted leaf blades contributing pleasant vertical lines to the summer garden scene. There are forms available in blue, violet, purple-red and white, all with a blaze of yellow on the lower petals. Reliable cultivars include 'Mont Blanc' and 'La Nuit'.

The Spanish iris, *I. xiphium*, is more refined in character than *I. xiphioides*, and as it flowers earlier, could bring forward the iris flowering display. It has classic, clear-cut blooms in blue, white or yellow. The slender blades of grey-green leaves are attractive after the flowers have

faded. Particularly reliable cultivars include the blue 'Wedgwood', yellow 'Lusitanica', and white 'Queen Wilhelmina'.

Sedum spectabile planted in front of the irises would conceal the dying leaves and reach its own peak in autumn. Or the iris theme could be continued in winter with *I. reticulata* planted among a carpet of *Thymus praecox arcticus*.

CULTIVATION Plant in autumn in an open, sunny or partially shaded position in any free-draining soil. Apply general fertiliser in late winter. Cut back foliage in late winter when it has turned brown and papery. Propagate by dividing overcrowded clumps as soon as the plants are dormant.

Lilium

GARDEN LILIES

From when they first break the topsoil in spring, lilies command attention. The stems, with their spirals of fresh, clean-cut, narrow leaves, lengthen at an almost visible rate, and are soon topped by fecund buds that hint of the exotic blooms to come.

The splendour of the Asiatic species and the hybrids that have been developed from them makes up for a lack of scent. Luscious and prolific, the flowers open into wide, waxen-petalled stars, several crowning each slender, fine-leaved stem. Most members of the Asiatic group flower during early to midsummer and grow to around 3ft in height. There are pendent-flowered forms, such as *Lilium tigrinum* 'Splendens', and the tough Turk's-cap lily, *L. martagon*, whose flowers tend to be more delicate in character. The blooms are staggered at the heads of slender stems, and the petals are curved back upon themselves to show off eye-catching stamens.

TRUMPETS AND ORIENTALS

Trumpet-flowered hybrids are generally taller and later-flowering than the Asiatic lilies, and have a heady scent.

The Oriental hybrids were raised from Japanese species. Their mid to late summer blooms open into elegant stars, and the whorled leaves are broader than those of the other hybrids. They will grow vigorously if they are planted in dappled sunlight, with soil on the acid side of neutral.

Lilium tigrinum is bold enough in colour to partner another high summer special, agapanthus.

Plant lilies in groups of at least three, set in triangular formation. Let them reign autocratically, uncluttered by bright plants nearby. Instead, try a dramatic background of rich evergreens or purple-leaved shrubs like *Berberis thunbergii* 'Atropurpurea' and *Cotinus coggygria*. Rhododendron blooms could blaze a fittingly exotic trail in spring, or for a softer effect, the foaming blossom of *Spiraea × arguta*. In lightly shaded situations, hardy ferns like *Dryopteris filix-mas* and hostas would enhance the summer lily display and later deflect attention from the dying leaves.

CULTIVATION

Select fresh, plump bulbs and plant between late autumn and spring in any well-drained soil enriched with organic matter. The Oriental hybrids do best in lime-free soils. A lightly shaded, south-facing position sheltered from strong winds is ideal, but

A subdued setting of cool ferns is appropriate for the exquisite Turk's-cap lily, *Lilium martagon*.

most hybrids tolerate full sun as long as they are shaded and cool around the roots. Stake tall, heavy-headed cultivars at the time of planting. Propagate from undamaged bulb scales at the end of the growing season. All plants should be divided every three to five years.

Creamy-yellow *Sisyrinchium striatum* and purple *Tradescantia andersoniana* shelter the root runs of *Lilium regale*, their colours echoed in the lily's subtle shades.

259

A fair prospect of lilies

Lilies create different moods according to their colour and to where they are placed in the garden. They can reign serenely in peaceful corners of dappled shade, be imposing in their tropical beauty if planted in tubs on a patio or terrace, or be extrovert and exotic in the summer border.

Photographed from plants supplied by J. Walkers Bulbs, Spalding, Lincolnshire.

Lilium tigrinum
'Splendens'
Pendent-flowered
Asiatic. Height 4ft.
Best August-September.

Lilium
'Mont Blanc'
Asiatic. Height 2-3ft.
Best June-July.

Lilium regale
Trumpet-flowered,
scented.
Height 4ft.
Best July.

Lilium 'Golden
Splendour'
Trumpet-flowered,
strongly scented.
Height 4-5ft.
Best July.

Lilium
'Journey's End'
Oriental, scented.
Height 3ft. Best August.

Lilium
'Marilyn Monroe'
Asiatic. Height 3½-4ft.
Best July.

260

Lilium
'African Queen'
Trumpet-flowered,
scented. Height 4-5ft.
Best July-August.

Lilium
'Enchantment'
Asiatic. Height 3ft.
Best July.

Lilium
'Pink Perfection'
Trumpet-flowered,
lightly scented.
Height 5ft. Best July.

Lilium
'Festival'
Trumpet-flowered,
scented. Height 4ft.
Best July.

Lilium
'Sterling Star'
Asiatic.
Height 3ft.
Best July.

Lilium
'Stargazer'
Oriental, scented.
Height 3-4ft.
Best July-August.

Summer
ANNUALS
& BIENNIALS

T HE PLANTS classified as annuals are those that last for one season only; once their flowering season is over, they die. Yet these transitory creatures have a part to play even in gardens that depend on long-life plants for through-season appeal. In these, the secret is to use their range of colour and form as stylish accessories to the whole. The public park treatment of annuals, using them en masse in a series of replacement plantings to inject instant colour, lacks subtlety in the domestic garden, and is labour-intensive and expensive. Instead, within the all-season context, it is better to let the annuals earn their keep by using them to bridge seasonal gaps. They can fill the spaces left by early bulbs, cover up for developing perennials, or give importance to young shrubs that have not yet realised their full height and spread. Use them to add colour to terraces or hanging baskets, or to fill tubs that later will be planted with bulbs.

How you grow and use annuals and biennials depends on whether they are half hardy or fully hardy. Among the hardy annuals and biennials are such old-fashioned favourites as love-in-a-mist (*Nigella*), fox-gloves (*Digitalis purpurea*), and

In this delightful planting, petunias, pansies and nemesias demonstrate how a shrewd use of annuals can bring invaluable colour to a mixed border.

larkspur (*Delphinium ajacis*). Refined versions of the wild flowers of Europe, they are well inured to northerly climes. Hardy annuals and biennials are cheaper to buy and easier to grow than half-hardy plants. They can be sown into their flowering positions as early as March, and while the flowering season of some cultivars is short, staggered sowings will ensure a continuing display. Left to their own devices, they will self-seed year after year, but generally it is better to dig up faded plants and replace them with fresh stock. Often more subtle in hue and more graceful than the half-hardy plants of tropical regions, hardy annuals and biennials are suited to planting in individual groups to create summer colour in a harmonious blend of cottage-garden flowers.

CULTIVATION Sow seed into open ground in spring, following packet instructions for aspect and planting distance. Otherwise, buy young plants for setting out in mid or late spring. Propagate by seed.

Antirrhinum
The new snapdragon cultivars combine the charm of the old ones with a greater colour range, and flower from June to September. Dwarf forms, such as 'Tom Thumb Mixed', are longer-flowering.

Campanula medium
Let the soft-hued spires of June-flowering Canterbury bells join other old-fashioned biennials before a sunny wall or fence. The species has large single bells in white, blue or pink. Doubles may be taller.

Bartonia aurea
A cheerful annual that is quick to bloom and flowers from June to September. A sun-loving plant from California, it grows to about 1½ft, and looks well with plants such as yucca or the Chusan palm.

Chrysanthemum parthenium 'Aureum'
This cultivated form of feverfew makes a neat edging plant over the summer months. The golden tints of the soft-textured, aromatic foliage are intensified in full sun.

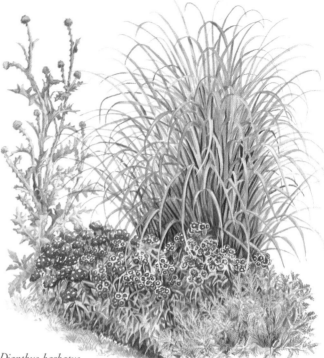

Dianthus barbatus
Well known as sweet william, this June-flowering biennial has velvety, flat-topped flower heads in colours ranging from white and pink to scarlet and crimson. Most cultivars are about 2ft in height, but the dwarf *Dianthus barbatus* 'Wee Willie' grows to only 6in. In the group above, the tall grass *Miscanthus sinensis* towers over the dianthus, with grey-leaved *Santolina chamaecyparissus* and *Onopordum acanthium* (Scotch thistle) on either side.

Agrostemma githago 'Milas'
A cultivated form of the wild corn cockle, this agrostemma fits in with other country annuals. The five-petalled flowers are short-lived but appear in a succession that lasts from June to September.

Brassica oleracea
The Japanese have long appreciated the decorative qualities of the ornamental cabbages with their rosettes of variegated, fringed or waved leaves. The pink types intensify to crimson in late summer.

Clarkia
Clarkia cultivars produce a water-colour wash of white, rose and lilac in summer. The elegant, 1½-2ft high flower spikes may need some support, although dwarf forms are available.

Coreopsis
Build a golden flame that lasts from July to October with cultivars of coreopsis. Though heights vary from 1¼ to 2ft, the vivid golds and reds of the daisy flowers and erect bushy habit are common to all.

Digitalis purpurea
The garden forms of foxglove, grown as biennials, bring wonderful pastel colours to partly shaded situations in June. The flowers of 'Excelsior' lie almost horizontally, showing their flecked interiors.

Eschscholzia californica
Sun-loving Californian poppies appear in July and August. Grow them at the front of a border, to show their feathery foliage and satin-finish petals of orange, pink, cream, crimson and mauve.

Lavatera trimestris
Within three months, this Mediterranean mallow grows into a bushy, 2-2½ft plant, able to hold its own among shrubs and perennials. The flowers are pink or white, and appear in July and August.

Matthiola bicornis
The flowers of night-scented stock are modest, but the scent released on summer evenings is delicious. Straggly in habit, the plant is best grown in small groups with other annuals of similar size.

Phacelia campanularia
A small plant suitable for edging a border or setting among paving stones, this Californian bluebell will flower profusely from early to late summer on poor soil, provided it has a sunny position.

Reseda odorata
The flowers of mignonette are unremarkable, but from June to August their scent will fill the air. It is easily grown in sun or light shade, and will add depth and support to displays of more showy annuals.

Godetia
With silky, azalea-like flowers that almost conceal the pointed leaves beneath, the July and August-flowering godetia makes a fine container plant. Taller cultivars, up to 2ft high, mix well with mallows.

Layia platyglossa
Given a sunny position and soil that is not too rich, the 1-1½ft high *Layia platyglossa* will produce its bright yellow, white-tipped daisy flowers in a rich profusion that lasts from July until September.

Nigella damascena
The common name of love-in-a-mist is well suited to the soft-toned flowers that appear in a haze of feathery foliage from June to September. The seed pods look well in dried flower arrangements.

Ionopsidium acaule
The diminutive violet cress can be sown in a lightly shaded spot and left to look after itself. It forms low tufts covered with a myriad tiny flowers from June to August; it is a useful rock garden gap filler.

Lupinus 'Pixie Delight'
If you haven't the space for perennial lupins, this 1ft high annual is an effective alternative. Given a sunny position, it will display its pink, blue or bicoloured flowers from July until September.

Papaver nudicaule
The delicacy of Iceland poppy is at odds with its Arctic origins. Best grown as a biennial, it flowers from early to late summer. Colours range from cream and yellow to orange and scarlet. Plant in full sun.

Tropaeolum majus
A sunny position and poorish soil are essential ingredients in obtaining a good show of nasturtiums. There are trailing and non-trailing cultivars, some with variegated or dark bronze foliage, and with flowers that may be anywhere in the yellow, orange and deep crimson ranges. The dwarf Tom Thumb strains are more compact, with single flowers in many colours, and grow to only 10in – the standard trailers can spread for 6ft or more.

Half-hardy annuals

Introduce half-hardy annuals to the garden with care, for many are plants from warmer lands, and their vibrant colours can easily eclipse the softer tones of plants from temperate regions. Some are, in truth, not annuals at all, but tender perennials that cannot survive cold winters, and must be replaced each year with fresh stock. They demand more initial attention than the hardy annuals, and must not be planted out until all risk of frost has passed. But once happily established, their impact is immediate, and their flowering long and brilliant.

CULTIVATION Sow seed in compost, and in a temperature of about 18°C (64°F) under glass from early March. Prick out seedlings into trays or pots as soon as they are big enough to handle, and set young plants outdoors from late April to late May. Propagate tender perennials by cuttings in late summer. Overwinter young plants in frost-free conditions.

Amaranthus caudatus
Love-lies-bleeding takes its name from long tassels of tiny blood-red flowers that appear from July to October. These, and its 3-4ft height, make this amaranthus a special feature for the border.

Begonia semperflorens
The specific name, meaning forever-flowering, is particularly apt, as these vigorous small plants perform from early summer to autumn, in light shade or sun. The leaves are bright green or bronze.

Cosmos bipinnatus
The sizzling colours of the flowers, set against feathery foliage, make this Mexican plant an eye-catcher in late summer, when it thrives in sun or part shade. There are short and long-stemmed strains, in single and semi-double forms; all are gorgeous in flower arrangements. Equally impressive is the plant's performance as backup in a mixed border. Here it presides over a summer gathering that includes buddleia, lavender, zinnias and valerian.

Dianthus chinensis
Whether you use the dwarf or taller cultivars for use in border-front groupings, annual carnations will reward you with freely produced summer-long flowers in shades of white, pink and rosy-red.

Gazania
Gazanias are lowish, mat-forming plants good for raised beds and containers. The flowers, in bright shades of yellow, red and orange, open with the sun, and appear from June until the first frosts.

Ageratum houstonianum
Masses of tiny powder-puff flowers that appear from June to September on 6-12in stalks, make this a superb edging plant. Colours are mainly in the lavender to reddish-blue range. Taller cultivars (1½-2ft) exist.

Callistephus chinensis
The intense colours of China asters are best massed rather than mixed with less extrovert flowers in the late summer border. The long-stemmed cultivars make excellent cut flowers.

Cosmos sulphureus
The flaming yellow, orange and scarlet flowers appear on slender 2-3ft flower stems in late summer. They may need some light twiggy support, but there are shorter, sturdier strains such as 'Sunny Bell'.

Dahlia
The bedding dahlias come in a similar range of colours and forms as border dahlias, but are smaller in stature, and are grown annually from seed. They flower prolifically from July to September.

Helichrysum petiolare
Helichrysum, a tender sub-shrub, is kept going each year by cuttings rather than by seed. It is grown for its creeping, silver-felted foliage which blends well with taller, pastel-shaded annuals.

Heliotrope
The fragrance emitted by the long-lasting, tiny flowers has given this plant its name of cherry pie. It reaches about 1½ft or more in height, and while happiest in sun, also tolerates light shade.

Lobelia erinus
A bright edging of lobelia, whether trailing or clump-forming, will add substance to your displays of annuals from June to September. Colours range from light blue to rich azure and deep red.

Impatiens walleriana
Indomitably cheerful busy lizzie brightens window boxes, hanging baskets, tubs and border edges from June to September. Its numerous hybrids are available in a wide range of startling colours.

Mimulus
Some musks are reliably hardy but others are less so and best treated as half-hardy annuals. These flower from June to September in colours ranging from white to deep red, pink and orange.

Nicotiana
Evening brings out the tobacco plant's delicious scent. The simplicity of the flowers, in wonderful colours from an unusual, creamy lime-green to bold pink, red and purple, create a rewarding show from July to September. Up to 2ft in height, nicotiana thrives in semi-shade, which makes it a good plant, as here, for the front of a tallish border. Its companions include *Dahlia* 'Bishop of Llandaff', Michaelmas daisies in bud, pinky-red *Penstemon gloxinioides*, yellow hemerocallis, achillea, and *Lilium speciosum album*, also in bud. Altogether, they make a classic planting, as evocative of an English summer as Devon cream teas and village cricket.

Lathyrus odoratus
Modern sweet peas include the wavy-petalled Spencer cultivars; old-fashioned cultivars are the sweetest scented and carry smaller blooms. Remove seed pods to encourage further flowering.

Moluccella laevis
The green calyces, sheltering small white flowers, crowd at the top of 3ft stems. Its interesting shape and subdued tones make it useful backing for gaudier annuals. Dry the stems for indoor displays.

Ocimum basilicum 'Dark Opal'
It is the purple-black, aromatic foliage that earns this cultivar of the culinary herb sweet basil its place in the summer garden. It combines well with nicotiana and golden-leaved bedding plants.

Petunia
Velvet trumpets in dazzling colours that appear from June to September make the petunia an annual favourite for both containers and summer borders. But it needs full sun to show at its best.

Verbena
Seed strains produce tightly-clustered flowers in pink, red, mauve and white, from early summer until September. The finely divided leaves are a further attraction. Best in full sun and well-drained soil.

Pelargonium

Pelargoniums are perennials, and most of them are evergreen, but they succumb to cold winters and are treated as half-hardy annuals when grown outside. They can contribute a vivid show of colour to border, terrace or patio throughout summer and into autumn.

The common name – geranium – that is often applied to zonal and ivy-leaved pelargoniums, should apply to the hardy crane's-bills of the genus *Geranium*. Unlike them, the pelargoniums are shrubby and tender, most of them originating in South Africa. They vary considerably in habit, foliage and flower, and can be tiny and delicate, or tall and robust. Colours range from white to every shade of pink, through to black-purple and scarlet.

DIFFERENT GROUPS

Zonal pelargoniums, which vary in height from 6in to 6ft or more, are the most shrub-like of all, with rounded, pale to mid-green or golden leaves that are often strikingly 'zoned' with horseshoe-shaped markings. They have rounded flower heads, densely packed with single, semi-double or double blooms ½-1½in across. These are the most common border 'geraniums', best used as fillers for spaces among plants that have finished flowering.

Regal pelargoniums have exotic, open flowers, often veined or blotched with contrasting shades. The flower heads are grouped on shorter stems than the zonals. The

This model of pelargonium planting is a movable feast; it has to be, for the plants are tender and must be removed before the first frosts. Both zonal and ivy-leaved pelargoniums are on display, with such traditional companions as *Lobelia erinus, Impatiens walleriana* and fuchsias.

plants are shrubby, erect and branching, and mostly 1-3ft in height. Their matt, mid-green leaves are firm-textured, with edges that are slightly toothed.

The scented-leaved species and their hybrids emit fragrances such as peppermint, lemon or balsam at the slightest touch.

Ivy-leaved pelargoniums are trailers, and are used almost exclusively to tumble from hanging baskets. Their stems reach 3ft or more in length; the leaves are polished and fleshy, and the heads carry up to seven blooms.

Pelargoniums are often most striking when grown on their own to create a bank of colour, but a silver foliage plant such as *Stachys byzantina* 'Silver Carpet' would make an attractive, if rather exuberant, partner. When flowering is over, lift the pelargoniums from their containers and replace with bulbs for a bright display in spring.

CULTIVATION

Plant in late May, in well-drained soil in full sun. Lift plants before autumn frosts, cut back by half, pot up and over-winter, providing only minimal watering, in a cool, frost-free place. Propagate by cuttings in late summer.

267

Pelargonium
'Blandfordianum'
Pungent-scented leaves.
Height 1½ft. Spread 2ft.

A riot of carnival colour

Geraniums – or more correctly, pelargoniums – trailing from baskets,
spilling over tubs and borders are the nearest you're likely to get to evoking the
vivid profusion of flowers found in whitewashed Mediterranean villages. These tender
perennials revel in full sun and dry heat, and so are grown as half-hardy annuals
in this country, putting on a reliable show of flamboyant
colour for four to five months.

Photographed in July at Clapton Court Gardens, Crewkerne, Somerset.

Pelargonium
× *hortorum*
'Bridesmaid'
Dwarf, fancy-
leaved zonal.
Height 9in.
Spread 9in.

Pelargonium × *hortorum*
'Rio' Compact,
self-branching zonal.
Height 10in. Spread 10in.

Pelargonium × *hortorum*
'Double Skies of Italy'
Fancy-leaved zonal.
Height 1½ft. Spread 1ft.

Pelargonium peltatum
'Mini-cascades'
Compact, ivy-leaved;
flowers red, pink or lilac.
Trails to 1½ft.

Pelargonium × *hortorum*
'Alba'
Compact, semi-double zonal.
Height 1ft.
Spread 1ft.

Pelargonium crispum
'Variegatum'
Very compact, with
lemon-scented leaves.
Height 1½ft. Spread 10in.

Pelargonium × *hortorum*
'Golden Ears'
Compact,
miniature zonal.
Height 8in.
Spread 8in.

Pelargonium × *domesticum*
'Miss Australia' Tall, upright regal.
Height 2½ft.
Spread 2½ft.

Pelargonium peltatum
'Duke of Edinburgh'
Variegated ivy-leaved cultivar.
Trails to 2ft or more.

Pelargonium × *hortorum*
'Alcyone'
Free-flowering, miniature zonal.
Height 8in. Spread 8in.

Pelargonium × *domesticum*
'South American Bronze'
Compact regal.
Height 2ft. Spread 2ft.

269

Water brings year-round tranquillity to the garden, reflecting light and mirroring the sky and the surroundings. It will introduce a welcome change of pace and become a haven for wildlife. Even a tiny plot can accommodate a water-lily tub, and a pool 1½-2ft deep is adequate for fish and all but the most vigorous water lilies. A pool with a surface area of 10ft × 5ft would accommodate one or two water lilies, three floating aquatic plants, about twenty oxygenating plants, and six marginal plants. If the borders of the pond are allowed to merge into a marshy margin you will also be able to grow a range of plants that flourish in shallow water and moist soil. Preformed pools have built-in shelves for this purpose.

Some plants are functional as well as decorative, and help keep the pool clean. To prevent the growth of algae, for example, about a third of the surface area should be covered with deep-water floating aquatic plants, such as water lilies or *Aponogeton distachyos*. These provide shade and hiding places, too, for fish and frogs which help keep the midge population down. Other aquatics,

A simple combination of a hosta and a water lily among boulders makes a striking water garden on a small scale.

THE
Water
GARDEN

known as 'oxygenators', also help to keep algae at bay. These plants include *Elodea canadensis* and *Myriophyllum spicatum*. However, these rampant growers will need thinning out from time to time.

SUMMER REFRESHMENT

In high summer the pool comes into its own. Stars of the show are exotic water lilies that bloom until the first autumn frosts. They grow in a range of colours, both soft and brilliant. Cup-shaped flowers, sometimes up to 8in across, open to reveal layers of pointed petals around a yellow-orange boss of stamens. Many named hybrids are available, varying in vigour and required water depth. The miniature *Nymphaea* × *pygmaea*, including the canary-yellow 'Helvola' and the pure white 'Alba', or the dainty water-lily-like *Nymphoides peltata*,

When dry land meets water, new planting opportunities arise – like this grouping of *Primula japonica*, *Pernettya mucronata*, ferns and irises.

with bright yellow blooms above tiny leaf pads, are suitable for small pools and water tubs. Laydekeri hybrids like 'Fulgens', 'Lilacea' and 'Purpurea', and the tea-scented white 'Alba', need a water depth of 1-1½ft. The more vigorous types, like the red, peony-flowered 'James Brydon', the white double 'Gonnère' or the flouncy, primrose-yellow 'Sunrise', flourish in 2½-3ft of water.

Introduce vertical lines with the water soldier, *Stratiotes aloides*, which lives a submerged existence for much of the time, but in summer pokes its white flowers and sword-shaped leaves above water.

Tall, upright marginal plants can be used to frame the pool mirror – the sweet flag, *Acorus calamus*, has 2ft tall, iris-like leaves, edged creamy-white in 'Variegatus', and its flowers are sweetly aromatic. It makes a fine companion for lilac-blue water mint (*Mentha aquatica*) and the elegant water musk (*Mimulus ringens*), whose 1½ft tall stems are studded with pale lavender blooms. The smaller monkey musk (*M. luteus*) bears a profusion of golden-yellow, red-spotted flowers throughout summer. As the days shorten, the emphasis shifts to long-flowering marginal plants like the purple loosestrife, *Lythrum salicaria*. Although its flowering display begins in early summer, its 4ft stems topped with pale pink to vivid magenta flower spikes take centre stage in autumn.

AUTUMN TINTS

Grassy foliage plants such as the green and silvery zebra rush, *Scirpus tabernaemontani* 'Zebrinus', grown around the pool fill out the scene strikingly when the summer flush of colour has past. The arching stems of the royal fern, *Osmunda regalis*, turn russet, and there are autumnal tints in the water too, where the surface-floating, pale green fronds of *Azolla caroliniana* become red-tinted. Also at its best in autumn, with small, three-petalled flowers above floating, bright green kidney-shaped leaf pads, is the frogbit, *Hydrocharis morsus-ranae*. Keep these floaters under control by removing excessive growth.

WINTER FROSTS

With the arrival of frosts, most aquatics die down to overwinter on the pool bottom, though the evergreen acorus stands a lonely sentinel through winter. Colour focus can be shifted to the pond surrounds, where shrubs with vividly coloured winter stems can be grown. The bright and showy crimson-stemmed dogwood, *Cornus alba* 'Sibirica', or yellow-green *C. stolonifera* 'Flaviramea', the orange-scarlet willow, *Salix alba* 'Chermesina', or the violet *S. daphnoides* all enjoy a moist position.

RENEWED LIFE IN SPRING

Spring is the time for overhauling the pool, setting out new plants and lifting and dividing others. For a while algae may cloud the water but will diminish with the developing cover of foliage pads.

At the waterside, the giant golden buttercups of *Caltha palustris* appear, and join the little water buttercup, *Ranunculus aquatilis*, whose white flowers float above foliage submerged in the pool itself. Hooded spathes of the pure white bog arum, *Calla palustris*, and the butter-yellow skunk cabbage, *Lysichiton americanum*, whose dramatic leaves later reach 3-4ft, break through the shallow water. In shallow water too, at the end of spring, the lovely blue, pink, white and purple flowers of *Iris laevigata* appear, and *I. pseudacorus* cultivars grow in water about 1½ft deep. Plants like the arrowhead, *Sagittaria sagittifolia*, link spring and summer, the fleshy, spear-shaped foliage rising majestically from the water to be later crowned with small white flower clusters. At the water's edge, *Eriophorum angustifolium* presents its cotton-wool tufts in late spring, and the flowering rush, *Butomus umbellatus*, is topped with rose-pink flower heads in early summer. At lower levels, in the pool itself, the submerged water violet, *Hottonia palustris*, lifts stems of pale lilac blooms. These make perfect companions for the waxy, white water hawthorn, *Aponogeton distachyos*, whose sweet-scented flowers appear from late spring until autumn. Water forget-me-not (*Myosotis palustris*) scrambles at the margins, and in up to 1ft of water, the golden club, *Orontium aquaticum*, radiates metallic grey-green leaves and white-stemmed, gold-tipped flower spikes over the pool's surface.

The verdant growth of aquatic and water-margin plants blends gloriously with azaleas in late spring; later, summer-flowering water lilies, hostas, ligularias and mimulus will be radiant against a green backdrop.

Autumn

IT IS A SEASON of nostalgia, and it would be a stolid soul who could watch the swallows eagerly discussing their holiday plans without a wistful glance at the travel posters. Fortunately, nature has undertaken to divert us from this moment of weakness with one of its most generous displays. Lustrous golden mists at morning and rinsed afternoon skies send spirits soaring to match the near-audible hues of foliage exquisitely dying. For a brief while, the mildest-mannered garden throws decorum to the winds and puts on a performance more usually associated with the frost-painted falls of New England. Foliage commands the scene, but it is by no means the sole contributor of colour in the autumn garden. There is the startling brightness of hips, haws and cotoneaster berries; the warmth of chrysanthemums, the pinks and mauves of asters and the delicate, luminous carpets of autumn bulbs; crocuses, colchicums and cyclamens. The show flares and fades at last . . .'No fruits, no flowers, no leaves, no birds; November', as the poet Thomas Hood pithily, but not too accurately, put it.

The ripening year culminates in a cornucopia of burnished leaves and glowing fruits.

Autumn
SHRUBS

SHRUBS HAVE A variety of roles to play in autumn. There are many that flower at this time of the year, including some of the most beautiful of all shrubs. Others bear colourful, long-lasting fruits. But it is for their foliage colours that most autumn shrubs are prized, with a glowing range of tones that become dominant focal points in the autumn garden.

Abelia × grandiflora

Height 5ft · *Spread* 5ft
Best July–September

A vision remarkably spring-like for so late in the year, is the arching branches of *Abelia × grandiflora*, laden with an abundance of pink and white, gently fragrant flowers. The blossom first appears at midsummer, and not infrequently delays its exit until the first frosts.

The shrub's soft colouring and handsome, semi-evergreen leaves make it a most useful bridge between summer and autumn, especially in a mixed border where it can be a companion to a whole range of plants. For autumn, try matching it with such other late flowerers as *Anemone × hybrida* and the lovely deep red kaffir lily, *Schizostylis coccinea* 'Major'. Somewhere nearby – if you have the space for its 9ft spread – you might well grow *Viburnum × bodnantense* for its dark, plum-red autumn leaf

The branches of *Abelia × grandiflora* are tipped with numerous, fragrant, long-lasting flowers.

colour and the sweetly scented pink flower clusters that grow on the bare wood in winter.
CULTIVATION Plant abelia during autumn or spring in any well-drained soil in a sheltered, sunny spot. Propagate by taking semi-hardwood cuttings in summer.

Aesculus parviflora

SHRUBBY CHESTNUT

Height 8–10ft · *Spread* 10–15ft
Best July, August and October

Striking yellow-orange autumn foliage covers this deciduous, horse-chestnut-like shrub, a native of the southern USA. Its bushy, upright habit and strong outlines would look fine in a

Aesculus parviflora, a shrubby member of the chestnut family, needs plenty of space to be seen at its best.

IN SUMMER, *Aesculus parviflora* carries stately flowers.

lawn as an all-season architectural feature. Upstanding, 1ft long panicles of white, pink-stamened flowers are a welcome sight in late summer when few other shrubs are in bloom.

Helleborus foetidus planted under the shrub would carry fond memories of summer into winter – the hellebore leaves are similar to those of the chestnut, but are darker and evergreen. *Narcissus* 'Golden Harvest' or 'February Gold' would strike a sprightly note to take the grouping into spring.
CULTIVATION Plant in autumn in a sunny, open site in any reasonably fertile soil which is well drained but stays moist. Propagate by removing and replanting the suckers which form at the base.

Aronia arbutifolia

RED CHOKEBERRY

Height 6–8ft · *Spread* 4–6ft
Best October

The glory of this shrub lies in its combining brilliant autumn foliage with startlingly bright red berries, in a display which can last through to December. In late spring, it produces clusters of hawthorn-like white flowers and, in summer, dark green leaves that make a good backdrop for perennials.

Aronia melanocarpa 'Brilliant'

is a black chokeberry, smaller in stature and noted for the exceptionally fine colour of its autumn leaves, which coincide with berries of lustrous purple-black. The splendour of both red or black chokeberries can be matched with the red flowers and rich golden leaves of *Fuchsia magellanica* 'Aurea', with autumn-flowering *Crocus speciosus* and winter and spring-flowering crocuses for a continuing display beneath.
CULTIVATION Plant any time between autumn and spring in a sunny or partially shaded position, where the soil is neutral to

The flaming foliage of *Aronia arbutifolia* brings the vibrant colours of the North American fall to British autumnal gardens.

acid and moisture retentive. Propagate by semi-hardwood cuttings in summer.

Berberis × rubrostilla

Height 4-5ft · *Spread* 4-5ft
Best October

Since birds do not seem too keen on the coral-red, pear-shaped berries, this is one berberis whose fruits are more or less guaranteed to be long-lasting. Set amidst autumnal foliage of ruby and orange, the ensemble is a showy display that illuminates the garden for yards around.

Its companions must be equally emphatic. Try the blue-purple varieties of aster or some of the brilliant, long-lasting Korean hybrid chrysanthemums. And plant shade-tolerant *Liriope muscari* right under the arching berberis branches, allowing its blue spires to reach up towards the berries, and its leaves to provide evergreen ground cover. Use *Geranium*

The showy autumn fruits of *Berberis × rubrostilla* are among the largest of all berberis berries.

macrorrhizum to fill the early summer slot. Its pale, magenta-pink flowers could be preceded by *Ipheion uniflorum* bulbs, of which there are several cultivars in colours ranging from white through to violet-blue.

CULTIVATION Plant between autumn and spring in any good, well-drained, though moisture-retentive, soil, and in full sun. Propagate by heel cuttings in late summer or early autumn.

Berberis thunbergii
'Atropurpurea'

PURPLE-LEAVED BARBERRY

Height 4-6ft · *Spread* 5ft
Best May-October

Dense, dark purple summer foliage turns flaming red in late autumn, when it is brilliantly highlighted by a host of luminous scarlet berries. The colour contrasts are equally dramatic in spring, when red buds, opening into dainty, golden-yellow flowers, are set against the new season's plum-purple leaves. Even after the leaves' departure in autumn, a sprinkling of berries often remains dotted along the bare

The berries of *Berberis thunbergii* 'Atropurpurea' contrast startlingly with the rich damson of the shrub's early autumn foliage colours.

branches into the depths of winter. 'Atropurpurea Nana' is a dwarf form, about 1½-2ft high, and suitable as an edging or rock garden plant.

'Atropurpurea' is a compact, purple barberry making a useful back of the border plant. But take care to avoid colour clashes with companion plants. Soft pinks and greys work well: a foreground of pink phlox, a nearby shrub rose such as the warm pink 'Fantin Latour' or 'Penelope', a late summer-flowering mallow, *Lavatera thuringiaca* 'Rosea' or *L. t.* 'Barnsley', or an underplanting of spring-flowering cyclamen or tulips are all attractive combinations. But for a truly stunning partnership, try the glowing red *Dahlia* 'Bishop of Llandaff', which has unusual bronzed foliage, and perhaps

Berberis thunbergii 'Atropurpurea Nana' in late autumn colour.

add some grey-leaved companion, such as *Senecio bicolor*.

CULTIVATION Plant any time between mid-autumn and mid-spring in full sun or partial shade in any fertile soil. Propagate as for *B.* × *rubrostilla*.

The opulent autumn berries of *Callicarpa bodinieri giraldii* decorate its leafless stems.

Callicarpa bodinieri giraldii

Height 6ft · *Spread* 5ft
Best October

Widely tipped as a champion among shrubs for its handsome fruits is this callicarpa, with its autumn abundance of lilac-purple berries. Carried in heavy bunches on upright, twiggy stems, their effect is further enhanced as the lance-shaped, dark green summer leaves turn deep rose-purple in October. The leaves drop to reveal bare stems festooned with glistening swags of fruit. Pretty lilac flowers appear in summer.

Plant the shrub in the middle or back of the border, though it is quite attractive enough to stand as an individual in a lawn. Grow the white *Colchicum autumnale* 'Album' and mixed

An agreeable companion for *Calluna vulgaris* 'Darkness' is the autumn-flowering *Crocus kotschyanus*.

plantings of autumn, winter and spring crocuses beneath the callicarpa.

CULTIVATION Plant in a sunny, sheltered site with rich soil any time between October and March. Propagate by heel cuttings in June or July. Prune the previous year's growth back to young wood in February.

Calluna vulgaris
'H.E. Beale'

HEATHER, LING

Height 2ft · *Spread* 15-18in
Best September-November

True heather, or ling, contributes much to the character of the mountains and moors of the

Let heathers show themselves at their best – as a massed band. Way out in front in this parade is the double pink *Calluna vulgaris* 'H.E. Beale'.

west and north, and is the main covering, too, of the sandy heaths of southern England. It has produced many sports, of which 'H.E. Beale' is one of the best of the late flowerers. Spikes of tiny flowers like pink icing sugar rise above long shoots of scale-like leaves in September and remain until late November.

Heathers look best when planted in groups. A carefully planned planting of a number of heath and heather cultivars with different flowering periods can give a quite astonishing continuance of colour. Try for example, planting St Dabeoc's heath, *Daboecia cantabrica*, whose rose-purple flowers last from spring to autumn, and mixing it with *Erica carnea*

'Springwood White' and 'Myretoun Ruby'. The two ericas will provide snow-white and deep red flowers from November to May.

CULTIVATION Plant in full sun in autumn or spring in acid soil, with added peat. Lightly clip to keep in trim when the flowers have faded. Propagate by cuttings in late summer.

Caryopteris × clandonensis

Height 2-3ft · *Spread* 2-3ft
Best September-October

In early autumn, a froth of feathery blue flowers erupts from the strong, upright stems

For a small, exuberant, early autumn display, it would be hard to beat *Caryopteris* 'Kew Blue'.

and aromatic, grey-green leaves of this small deciduous shrub. Caryopteris does well almost anywhere, but thrives particularly on chalk. Exuberant and showy, it makes a delightful foliage plant for near the front of the border throughout summer. It can be used as a wide, spreading feature, or cut back to form an attractive, compact dome. There are two excellent cultivars available – the bright blue 'Arthur Simmonds', and the deeper, richer 'Kew Blue'.

For flowering company, plant the deep red Kaffir lily, *Schizostylis coccinea* 'Major', and some autumn crocuses nearby. Such a combination will help to divert attention from fading summer perennials, and can be followed by a succession of winter and spring bulbs.

CULTIVATION Plant in autumn or spring in full sun, and in soil that is well drained but not too rich. Prune back the previous season's stems to two pairs of buds in winter or spring. Propagate by cuttings in summer.

Ceanothus 'Autumnal Blue' is gaily illuminated by a background of *Hamamelis japonica*.

BRIDGING THE SEASONS
WITH
Caryopteris

Blue and gold for autumn is the decree of this planting. The first colour is provided by *Caryopteris × clandonensis* 'Kew Blue', a deciduous, aromatic shrub that puts out its bright blue tubular flowers in September. Compact in form, this shrub is excellent in gardens where limestone or chalk predominate. Its gilded, graceful companion is the pampas grass *Cortaderia selloana* 'Gold Band' which, just as the caryopteris flowers begin to fade in October, raises tall, silky plumes to wave enticingly in the lightest, wandering breeze.

March is the time to cut the shrub's leafless twigs back to some 6-8in high. However, with a light trim for tidiness sake, the pampas grass's leaves remain to complement the clumps of *Narcissus* 'Tete-a-Tete'.

In summer, the caryopteris forms a grey-green cushion. Beside it and the pampas grass, a large pot is sunk into the soil. It contains the easily grown *Lilium regale* 'Aureum', a sun-loving lily that grows to 5ft high and more. In July the flowers are produced, trumpet-shaped and fragrant, and of a soft gold marked with rose-purple. Though happy in ordinary soil this lily does better in its own environment. Hence the pot, which also allows greater latitude within the association.

AUTUMN *Caryopteris* 'Kew Blue' is admirably set off by *Cortaderia* 'Gold Band'. This is compact as pampas grasses go, but still attains 4-6ft.

SPRING Twiggy branches of caryopteris are partly hidden by a graceful group of *Narcissus* 'Tete-a-Tete'.

SUMMER A tangle of caryopteris foliage is given distinction and height by a pot of *Lilium regale* in the back of the bed.

Ceanothus
'Autumnal Blue'

Height 6ft · *Spread* 6ft or more
Best July-October

As the glories of the herbaceous border begin to fade, *Ceanothus* 'Autumnal Blue' brings welcome clouds of fluffy blue flowers from midsummer to well into autumn. It is one of the hardiest of ceanothus hybrids, and evergreen too, with a dense, bushy growth that gives constant value as a background shrub in almost any garden, great or small.

Add a bright touch in late spring by growing *Clematis*

Neatly arranged leaves and a well-ordered appearance make *Ceratostigma willmottianum* suitable for a forward position in the border.

(*Ceanothus* 'Autumnal Blue' cont) *alpina* 'White Moth' over the dark ceanothus foliage. For companionship in summertime, plant *Buddleia alternifolia* or one of the *B. davidii* varieties behind, and a *Fuchsia magellanica* 'Versicolor', with its rose-tinted leaves, in front.

CULTIVATION Plant in early autumn or spring in a light soil, and in a sunny, sheltered site. Propagate by cuttings of new growth in late summer.

Ceratostigma willmottianum

CHINESE PLUMBAGO

Height 3ft · *Spread* 3ft
Best August-October

Clusters of rich blue flowers appear at the ends of the wiry stems in summer; they last well into autumn, when some of the leaves flush red.

The plumbago's extra-long flowering period makes it a useful companion to a whole succession of plants. In July and August, for example, it might accompany *Agapanthus praecox* 'Bressingham White' and the lilac-pink Cape marigold *Osteospermum ecklonis* 'Whirligig'. Then, in September and October, you might try adding bright scarlet kaffir lilies, *Schizostylis coccinea*, and the vivid blue of *Caryopteris* × *clandonensis*. Lastly, a foreground planting of the Lenten rose, *Helleborus orientalis*, would bring some interest to the site in winter.

CULTIVATION Plant in spring in well-drained but moisture-retentive soil and in a sheltered, sunny position. Propagate by taking summer cuttings of the current year's growth.

The autumn fruits of *Clerodendrum trichotomum fargesii* are produced in great profusion, and their colours have an almost fluorescent quality.

SUMMER In August, *Clerodendrum trichotomum fargesii* bears delicate, 6in-wide sprays of scented flowers.

Clerodendrum trichotomum fargesii

Height 8-10ft · *Spread* 9ft
Best August-October

An unusual and eye-catching display of colour is created from late summer onwards. First come sprays of star-like white flowers, each one set in a crimson casing which remains after the flowers drop. In autumn, these develop into red stars, each holding an astonishing turquoise berry. The attractive leaves smell unpleasantly when crushed.

If the suckers are regularly removed, this clerodendrum grows like a small tree, with a central stem topped by an umbrella of branches. This can provide a haven for ferns and species geraniums, or perhaps a spring-flowering azalea. It would also make a welcoming spot for the dwarf holly, *Ilex aquifolium* 'Ferox Argentea', or a flowering currant, such as the deep rose-red *Ribes sanguineum*.

CULTIVATION Plant in autumn or early spring in well-drained soil, and in a sunny, sheltered position. Propagate by detaching and replanting suckers in early spring.

The magical autumn foliage colours of *Cotinus coggygria* 'Royal Purple' and *Acer palmatum* glow like an alchemist's furnace.

Cotinus coggygria 'Notcutt's Variety'

SMOKE TREE

Height 8ft · *Spread* 8ft
Best May-October

The smooth, round, deep wine-purple leaves make a real eye-catcher from when they first unfold in spring, right through until autumn. Just before leaf-fall they turn a rich plum-red. This spectacular array is joined in midsummer by feathery panicles of flowers, which resemble plumes of smoke from a distance, and gradually fade in

Berries like jewels clothe *Cotoneaster franchetii* after the small, pinkish-white flowers of midsummer.

A native of the peaty moorlands of Ireland, *Daboecia cantabrica* fits companionably into a heather garden.

SUMMER The deep purple leaves of *Cotinus coggygria* 'Notcutt's Variety' contrast strikingly with the soft grey leaves of a cistus.

colour as autumn approaches. A similar cultivar is 'Royal Purple'; the species itself has green leaves.

Sited west of the house, the shrub will warm to a rich, red translucent glow when the setting sun shines through the leaves. Choose pink and white flowers to set off the purple foliage – phlox, for example, with, say, *Lavatera thuringiaca* 'Barnsley' – and continue the colour theme with autumn crocus and *Helleborus orientalis*.

CULTIVATION Plant between autumn and spring in a sunny position, and in any well-drained soil. Propagate by semi-hardwood cuttings in late summer, or layering in spring.

Cotoneaster franchetii

Height 5ft · *Spread* 5ft
Best October-March

It is fortunate that the berries of this species are not particularly palatable to birds, for they are among the biggest and brightest of all cotoneaster fruits. Many of the older leaves on this compact shrub take on autumnal tones in autumn, but the real spectacle is the splendid display of bright scarlet berries. If ignored by birds, the fruits may last throughout winter.

Groups of colchicum bulbs planted beneath the shrub will flower in succession from late August to late October. Their flowers – lilac-pink to purple or white – will combine well with the cotoneaster's scarlet berries and neat, polished leaves. This association could be expanded by planting a group of autumn-flowering *Anemone × hybrida* varieties among the colchicums – try for example, the pink 'Queen Charlotte' or white 'Honorine Jobert'.

CULTIVATION Plant between autumn and spring in any type of well-drained but moisture-retentive soil, in a sunny position. Prune only if necessary to keep in trim, in April. Propagate by taking cuttings in autumn.

Daboecia cantabrica

ST DABEOC'S HEATH

Height 15-24in · *Spread* 15-24in
Best June-November

For five months – nearly a flowering record – clusters of this noble shrub's rosy-purple, pitcher-shaped flowers contrast vividly with dark, glossy, silver-backed leaves. The flowers are larger than those of most heathers, and are available in a range of colours including white and rich purple.

Winter and spring-flowering varieties of *Erica carnea* could be planted nearby to follow on in winter, and a background of dwarf evergreen azaleas such as *Rhododendron* 'Rosebud' and 'Palestrina' could take the display into early summer.

CULTIVATION Plant between autumn and spring in acid, peaty soil, in full sun. Propagate by cuttings taken in late summer. Shear off the dead flower heads in spring.

One of the joys of autumn is the slow warming of *Disanthus cercidifolius* to a rich wine red.

Disanthus cercidifolius

Height 8-10ft · *Spread* 6-8ft
Best October

Give this tree-like shrub the sheltered, dappled shade it likes, and it will reward you with a flaming autumn show of claret-red foliage highlighted with orange. Tiny, dark red flowers also appear in autumn, but they have little significance against the spectacular leaf display.

In summer, the heart-shaped leaves can offer a cool bluish-green backdrop to small shrubs, such as the Knaphill azalea *Rhododendron* 'Homebush' and the calico bush, *Kalmia latifolia*. Plant evergreen *Liriope muscari* around the base of *Disanthus cercidifolius* for the blue of its autumn flower spikes.

CULTIVATION Plant in acid, moisture-retentive soil, adding plenty of well-rotted leaf mould or composted bark as a late spring mulch. Propagate by cuttings in early autumn.

The glowing reds and yellows of *Fothergilla gardenii* recall shafts of autumn sunlight on the shrub's native North American hillsides.

The branches of *Euonymus europaeus* bow beneath the weight of the deep rosy-coloured fruits that punctuate the hedgerows of the South Country.

Euonymus alatus

WINGED SPINDLE

Height 6ft · *Spread* 8ft
Best October

The downward-arching, tapering leaves of this slow-growing shrub turn extraordinary shades of shrimp-pink and crimson in autumn, coinciding with small purple fruits. Even after the autumn show is over, winged spindle still pays its way with a most unusual winter profile of corky wings along the stems.

Euonymus alatus, in near-audible scarlet dress, presides over a terrific collection of shrubs shrewdly chosen for autumnal contrast. Its chief supporters are the pale grey *Helichrysum splendidum*, dark, empurpling *Mahonia nervosa* and the turning leaves of *Spiraea* 'Bumalda'.

Euonymus europaeus
'Red Cascade'

SPINDLE

Height 10ft · *Spread* 8ft
Best October–December

The fluorescent effect of the wild spindle's bright orange seeds in their red-pink casings can be a startling sight in the

The bright leaf colours make the spindle an uneasy partner for other shrubs and trees whose leaves turn. Try planting it as a specimen flanked by evergreens, such as *Osmanthus delavayi* or *Euonymus japonicus*. *O. delavayi* produces fragrant white flowers in mid-spring, while its partner *E. japonicus* bears green-white flowers in early summer.

CULTIVATION Plant in full sun in autumn in well-drained neutral to acid soil. Propagate by taking semi-hardwood cuttings in late summer or early autumn.

hedgerows of Britain's chalk and limestone country. 'Red Cascade', a cultivated, free-fruiting form, offers the added reward of dense, green summer foliage that softens to rose-pink in autumn. The berries are poisonous.

Since mature spindles carry most of their foliage on the upper branches, they are best planted at the back of the border with spring-flowering shrubs like the evergreen *Osmanthus delavayi*, which produces fragrant white flowers in April. A willow, such as *Salix* 'Melanostachys', with its unusually dark catkins in late winter and spring would also be effective.

CULTIVATION Plant in any well-drained soil, including chalky, between autumn and spring. Propagate by layering in spring or by cuttings in autumn.

Fothergilla gardenii

Height 3ft · *Spread* 3ft
Best April, May and October

The 2–3in long oval leaves turn brilliant shades of red, orange and yellow in autumn. It is quite a sight in spring, too, when it is covered with fragrant white flower clusters.

This small, twiggy bush would enhance a planting of heathers and some evergreen azaleas – which like similar growing conditions – to give a variety of year-round colour effects. Ferns would make another delightful combination.

CULTIVATION Plant in autumn or spring in well-drained but moist, neutral to acid soil, and in sun or dappled shade. Propagate by cuttings in late summer.

Fothergilla major opens its autumn show with a fine display of old gold and orange foliage.

Fothergilla major

Height 6-8ft · *Spread* 5-6ft
Best April, May and October

In the midst of the fairly restrained British autumn, this shrub puts on a tempestuous show of deep orange and yellow, more reminiscent of the North American fall. The reason is not far to seek, since the shrub's ancestral habitat is the Allegheny Mountains where it plays its part in the orchestra of the first frosts. Its springtime contribution is sweet-smelling, brush-like white flowers.

It would be unkind to conceal such a paragon, and the best place for it would probably be at the edge of a lawn, its fiery autumnal dress providing a

The autumn leaves of *Fothergilla major* gradually deepen in colour.

highlight, perhaps, against a backdrop of dark evergreen azaleas or rhododendrons. Such a combination would also provide a shift in colour tones in other seasons. Any Japanese maple (*Acer palmatum*) would make a fine autumn companion.
CULTIVATION Plant between autumn and spring in well-

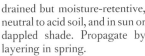

drained but moisture-retentive, neutral to acid soil, and in sun or dappled shade. Propagate by layering in spring.

Gaultheria procumbens

PARTRIDGE BERRY, CREEPING WINTERGREEN

Height 4-6in · *Spread* 2-3ft
Best September-October

In autumn, cheerful red berries stand out brightly against shiny dark green leaves, and look good enough to eat – and, indeed, they are edible. They are preceded in late spring or early summer by delicate, pale pink, bell-shaped flowers.

A low, creeping evergreen shrub, introduced from North America in the mid-18th century, it can be used as an

all-season front of the border plant, or allowed to form a glossy carpet beneath open deciduous shrubs or trees.
CULTIVATION Plant at any time of the year in neutral to acid soil, with added peat. Propagate by carefully separating the underground rooted stems in spring.

Hebe
'Autumn Glory'

SHRUBBY VERONICA

Height 2ft · *Spread* 2ft
Best August-September

Luxuriant violet-blue flower spikes form this plant's special offering from late summer onwards, when many shrubs and herbaceous plants are beginning to look a bit jaded. It thrives in mild coastal areas,

The brilliant autumnal fruits of *Gaultheria procumbens* are rendered all the more outstanding by the dark, shiny foliage.

IN SPRING the handsome foliage of *Gaultheria procumbens* makes a satisfying backdrop for a planting of *Narcissus cyclamineus*.

even in windswept places where few other shrubs will survive, making it invaluable for seaside plantings. Farther inland, it may be cut back by hard winters, but replacements may easily be grown anew from cuttings and kept in reserve.

The dark evergreen foliage of *Hebe* 'Autumn Glory' makes it a valued, year-round resident of the mixed or shrub border when emphasising such foreground plants as creamy-flowered *Cytisus* × *praecox* and the rich canary-yellow *Potentilla fruticosa* 'Elizabeth' for spring and summer colour. It looks well too with a pink-flowered shrub such as *Weigela florida* 'Variegata', which has broad, cream-white leaf margins.
CULTIVATION Plant in autumn or spring or from containers at any time of the year, in well-

One of the hardiest and latest-flowering of the hebes, 'Autumn Glory' carries its intense violet spikes almost until the first frosts.

drained, fertile soil in full sun. Propagate by semi-hardwood cuttings during autumn.

Hebe
'Marjorie'

Height 2-3ft · *Spread* 3-4ft
Best July-September

Hebes in general owe their fondness for sea breezes and dislike of frost to their New Zealand ancestry. Less explicable is their ability to thrive in an urban atmosphere, but they do. And since this one is hardier than average, the chances are it would do well in most British situations, excepting only the chilliest. The reward for taking it on is a mass of clear, mauve-blue flowers that fade to white in summer, and a wealth of fleshy, spearhead-shaped, mid to yellowish-green leaves for the rest of the year.

A fine companion would be the semi-evergreen *Cotoneaster franchetii*, a shrub from 10,000ft up in the mountains of China. With its graceful, curving branches, it complements this shrubby veronica very well, producing autumnal foliage and a crop of brilliant orange-scarlet berries when the hebe's flowers have faded. The cotoneaster's attractive show of small pink and white flowers in June, precedes the hebe's display.

CULTIVATION Plant in autumn or spring in any well-drained soil and in full sun. Propagate by softwood cuttings in summer. Prune leggy shrubs in April.

The paler flower spikes of *Hebe* 'Marjorie' help to cheer even the smokiest of industrial areas.

The attractive 'Woodbridge' variety of *Hibiscus syriacus*.

Hibiscus syriacus

Height 6-8ft · *Spread* 4-6ft
Best August-October

Hope for a warm, dry summer to enjoy to the full this hibiscus's sumptuous, deep blue-mauve blooms with their dramatic cones of stamens. A good year will produce a succession of large, single flowers from July to October. This hibiscus is one of the best in terms of clear colour and good flower size. From early summer, its fresh green leaves earn their place in the middle of a mixed border as a backdrop to early-flowering herbaceous plants such as *Hemerocallis* 'Stella d'Oro' and the hardy *Geranium* 'Johnson's Blue'. A nearby *Hydrangea* 'Preziosa' would provide warm complementary autumn shades of red and pink. CULTIVATION Plant in a sunny, sheltered position in any good soil between mid-autumn and early spring. Propagate by heel cuttings of semi-hardwood, non-flowering shoots taken in late summer.

BRIDGING THE SEASONS WITH *Potted plants*

POTS ARE A MEANS of stealing a march on the seasons. Terracotta pots like those shown here are not exactly cheap, but only half a dozen are needed; the flowers they contain are grown elsewhere in plastic pots that are slid into the ornamental ones when you want to ring the changes.

They are used here in association with *Hibiscus syriacus* 'Blue Bird', through which a clematis has been grown – *Clematis alpina* 'Frances Rivis'; both grow to around 6ft tall. From July until October the hibiscus puts forth its large, mid-blue, red-centred flowers that emerge rather charmingly from the contrasting leaf shapes. The pots at this time contain petunias, single colour F$_1$ varieties of *Petunia × hybrida*. There are plenty of choices, all of whose flowering spans match that of the hibiscus.

From May there is an entirely different scenario. The hibiscus flowers have been replaced by those of the clematis – large, and of a blue as deep as a tropical sky. The terracotta pots are now filled with Japanese azaleas (Kurume hybrids) which are evergreen and come in a spectacular range of colours. They are represented here by two each of the following: 'Hinode-giri', three-quarters of whose visible surface is covered with crimson flowers; 'Hino-mayo', a clear, rich pink; and 'Kure-no-Yuki' – a near-solid mass of white, each bloom holding another flower within. ❧

This charming association can be created in quite a small space. The centrepiece in autumn is *Hibiscus syriacus* 'Blue Bird' which has been ringed with *Petunia × hybrida* in pots. The leaves of a clematis grown through the hibiscus can also be seen.

SPRINGTIME reveals a different show. *Clematis alpina* 'Frances Rivis' is in flower and the terracotta pots are now filled with bright blossoms of *Rhododendron* Kurume hybrids – neat Japanese azaleas.

Hydrangea

Hydrangeas are worthy choices for the all-season garden; their great flower heads flamboyantly bridge summer and autumn, many fading into dusky, metallic colours which continue into winter after the leaves have fallen. From the original wild hydrangea species, two cultivated forms with distinctly different flower styles have emerged – the lacecaps and the mopheads. The delicate effect of the lacecaps is due to a combination of tiny, fertile florets at the heart of each flattened flower head, surrounded by four, or sometimes five-petalled, sterile flowers. The more ostentatious mopheads consist almost entirely of sterile flowers.

Hydrangea colours vary according to soil conditions and climate. The milder the climate, the purer the blues and pinks. Otherwise, the colour depends on the amount of aluminium the plants can draw from the soil. Growing in acid soils that release traces of aluminium, blue hydrangeas are blue, pinks are pink, and the white forms have blue centres. Neutral and alkaline soils release little or no aluminium, and while hydrangeas survive on all but very chalky soils, lack of the aluminium element has a very odd effect on their flower colours. White lacecaps will have pink rather than blue centres; the pinks may darken; and though the blues – depending on variety – may become perfectly acceptable pinks and reds, they may also turn muddy purple, as

in the case of 'Ayesha'. If you are lucky, a hydrangea such as 'Blue Wave' will reward you with a delightful blend of blues and pinks. Should you still be determined to cultivate blue hydrangeas on a neutral or slightly alkaline soil, water in a blueing powder every fortnight during the growing season.

As medium-sized shrubs that are happy in sun or light shade, hydrangeas are ideal for a patio or lining a path or border.

CULTIVATION Plant in autumn or spring in fertile soil that will not dry out; mulch in spring. Light shade is ideal – too much direct sun can scorch the leaves – and the site must be sheltered from cold winds. Prune only to remove old, diseased, or weak wood from the base of the shrub in early spring. Propagate by taking 3in softwood cuttings in late summer or early autumn.

In a Kentish garden, hydrangeas are massed under a canopy of climbers (right).

IN SPRING the bright green foliage of the hydrangea makes a lively association in a border (below).

The fading beauty of mopheads and lacecaps

The clear, crisp colours of hydrangeas can overshadow any neighbouring plants of more subtle character in late summer and early autumn. But the bold, clustered flower heads add brightness to dappled shade or a north or west-facing wall for many weeks. Some cultivars continue their display even longer, the flower heads taking on more muted tones to provide a welcome bridge of colour through to winter. Blue hydrangeas fade to the palest of turquoise and green, and the pinks deepen to ruddy reds and purples.

Painted in early October from plants at Abbotsbury Subtropical Gardens, Dorset.

Hydrangea paniculata
'Grandiflora'
Plumes of white flowers
gradually turn soft pink.
Flower heads up to 1½ft long.
Height 8ft. Spread 8ft.

Hydrangea macrophylla
'Générale Vicomtesse de Vibraye'
Bright rose-pink or sky-blue mophead
flowering from midsummer.
Striking after-colour. Flower heads 6½in.
Height 4ft. Spread 5ft.

Hydrangea macrophylla
'Lanarth White'
Compact-growing lacecap.
White flowers, with pink or blue
centres. Flower heads 8-9in.
Height 6ft. Spread 5ft.

Hydrangea macrophylla 'Pia'
Small mophead with red flower heads
deepening to purple-red after-colour.
Flower heads 4in. Height 2ft.
Spread 2ft.

Hydrangea macrophylla 'Mariesii'
A lacecap with flat flower heads of rose-pink
and good after-colour. Flower heads 7½in.
Height 6ft. Spread 6ft.

Hydrangea macrophylla
'Madame Émile Mouillière'
Mophead with white florets,
centred pink or blue, and green
after-colour. Flower heads 9in.
Height 4½ft. Spread 5ft.

Hydrangea macrophylla
'Blue Wave'
Ranges from gentian-blue to clear pink,
or combines both. A lacecap with after-colour.
Flower heads 8in. Height 6ft. Spread 8ft.

Hydrangea macrophylla 'Ayesha'
Clear blue mophead that turns muddy pink
or purple in alkaline soil. Flower heads 8in.
Height 6ft. Spread 6ft.

Hydrangea macrophylla
'Quadricolor'
A lacecap with variegated leaves
and pale pink blooms fading to white.
Flower heads 6in. Height 5½ft. Spread 5ft.

Hydrangea serrata
'Preziosa'
A mophead with rose-red florets
that deepen to burgundy.
Flower heads 6in. Height 5ft.
Spread 5ft.

287

The bright berries of *Hypericum × inodorum* 'Elstead' look splendid in the garden and on cut stems for indoor display.

Hypericum 'Hidcote' towers over the lower-growing *H. androsaemum* and the grey and yellow of *Santolina chamaecyparissus*.

Hypericum 'Hidcote'

Height 4ft · *Spread* 4ft
Best August-September

With its glowing mound of saucer-like golden flowers, this – the largest of any of the hardy hypericums – provides a link from late summer until October. It is a superb shrub for the all-season garden. The semi-evergreen leaves may fall in a very hard winter, but the plant recovers to give just as fine a show the following year.

Create a cream and gold theme with *Carex elata* 'Aurea' and a drift of the spring-flowering comfrey, *Symphytum grandiflorum* 'Variegatum'.

CULTIVATION Plant in autumn in any well-drained soil in sun or light shade. Shorten previous year's shoots to within a few buds of the old wood in early spring. Propagate by planting suckers, or by semi-hardwood cuttings in late summer.

Hypericum × inodorum 'Elstead'

Height 4-5ft · *Spread* 3-4ft
Best October

Rich golden clusters of small flowers, like pools of sunshine against cool green leaves, appear from late summer into autumn. They are the heralds of the brilliant orange-red handfuls of upright, oval fruits that arrive as the leaves assume a crimson-copper tinge.

This is a compact and upright shrub that links summer and autumn, and would mix well with the scarlet kaffir lily, *Schizostylis coccinea* 'Major'. Or try an evergreen shrub of similar size, like the black-berried *Sarcococca confusa*.

CULTIVATION Plant during early autumn, in any moisture-retentive but well-drained, humus-enriched soil in sun or partial shade. Propagate by planting semi-hardwood cuttings in late summer, or by very carefully dividing established, mature plants in early spring.

Lespedeza thunbergii

BUSH CLOVER

Height 6ft · *Spread* 5-6ft
Best September-October

Clover-like leaves covered in a film of grey hairs form a soft background for large panicles of rosy-purple, pea-like flowers. To ensure a good display, bush clover should be cut back in spring and left to grow up again with renewed vigour through the summer.

The long arching stems of the lespedeza look effective on a

Arching stems of *Lespedeza thunbergii* are heavy with flowers.

bank. Plant evergreen perennials, such as hellebores, *Primula vulgaris*, polyanthus or bergenias to fill the dormant winter period. In a mild area, *Fuchsia magellanica* 'Versicolor' would complete a very pretty grouping.

CULTIVATION Plant during early spring in a sunny position and in well-drained but moisture-retentive soil. Propagate by division in spring.

Rhus typhina

STAG'S-HORN SUMACH

Height 8-10ft · *Spread* 8-10ft
Best October

At the first touch of frost, the sumachs shout their fall colours to the blue skies of eastern North America – and even in the British garden, some of this

The flaming foliage and torch-like fruits of *Rhus typhina* 'Laciniata' combine in one of the most vividly coloured ensembles of autumn.

The polished fruits of *Sambucus racemosa* hang like swags of scarlet gems.

Symphoricarpos × doorenbosii 'Mother of Pearl' is laden with berries which remain, untouched by birds, until winter.

magic can be captured. Fern-like ranks of leaflets turn fiery red, orange and yellow, contrasting with torches of furry, dark crimson fruit. 'Laciniata' is a particularly fine cultivar.

The sumach is a large, angular, suckering shrub with a widespreading crown, lending itself to underplanting with glossy evergreens such as *Sarcococca confusa* or *S. humilis.* Another plan could figure the winter-flowering heath, *Erica carnea*, and the pink-flowering shrub *Kolkwitzia amabilis* for early summer flowers.

CULTIVATION Plant between autumn and spring in any well-drained soil, preferably in full sun. Propagate by replanting suckers in early spring.

Sambucus racemosa

RED-BERRIED ELDER

Height 10ft · *Spread* 10ft
Best May-October

Sambucus racemosa has long been valued as game cover in parts of Scotland and northern England – and has been cultivated here since the 16th century. Clusters of scarlet berries ripen in late summer and, if not devastated by birds, last through autumn. They are preceded by conical, creamy-yellow spring flowers. The cultivar 'Plumosa Aurea' is slow growing with handsome, finely cut leaves that mature to bright yellow. The shrub grows well even on exposed sites and in heavy, wet soils.

The rose 'Climbing Iceberg' grown through the shrub would add white, lightly scented blooms throughout summer and autumn. A group of *Euphorbia griffithii* 'Fireglow' beneath would give pastel autumn colours and bracts of rich terracotta in early summer.

CULTIVATION Plant in any aspect or soil between mid-autumn and early spring. Cut back in winter if the shrub becomes too large. Propagate by hardwood cuttings in mid-autumn, grown on for a year in a nursery bed.

Symphoricarpos × doorenbosii
'Mother of Pearl'

Height 4-6ft · *Spread* 4-6ft
Best September-October

Masses of full, round berries weigh down wiry, erect to spreading stems and add a quiet charm to the autumn garden. The deciduous leaves turn pale yellow in autumn. 'Mother of Pearl' is a small, dense cultivar, carrying white berries with a rosy blush; 'Magic Berry' is a compact and spreading shrub with rose-lilac fruits.

Plant the shrub near a spring-flowering cherry, like one of the *Prunus serrulata* cultivars, for a fine pink and white colour scheme. In autumn, *Cyclamen hederifolium* and purple *Crocus medius* could be planted beneath, with *C. tommasinianus* and *C. chrysanthus* varieties to follow. Evergreen *Erica carnea* cultivars could provide winter and spring flowers.

CULTIVATION Plant between October and March in any well-drained garden soil in partial shade. Propagate by replanting suckers or taking hardwood cuttings in autumn.

The berries of *S. paniculata* give it its common name, sapphire berry.

IN SPRING, white flower clusters drape *Symplocos paniculata*.

Symplocos paniculata

SAPPHIRE BERRY

Height 7-10ft · *Spread* 6-8ft
Best October

Warm summers and plenty of room are required if this elegant shrub is to give of its best, but if these conditions are provided, then the proud owner's autumn reward will be crops of brilliant blue berries like ultramarine jewels. The reason why *Symplocos paniculata* requires space is that at least another one must be grown close by to ensure pollination and successful fruiting, but they offer charm and dignity in return, as well as an elegant, open profile for the back of the border. There, when not fruiting, they will provide deciduous, tapered leaves and fragrant, starry white flowers in May and June.

The shrimp-pink to red foliage and purple fruits of the spindle *Euonymus alatus* would make it a striking autumn companion, and in the foreground, *Gaultheria procumbens* could display its red autumn and winter berries. In spring, the area immediately around and beneath will be enhanced by a few Japanese azaleas, especially the white cultivars such as *Rhododendron* 'Kure-no-yuki'.

CULTIVATION Plant in a sheltered position in sun or light shade, and in well-drained, lime-free soil between autumn and spring. No pruning is needed. Propagate from heeled, semi-hardwood cuttings in autumn.

Autumn TREES

I
T IS in their autumn foliage that trees and shrubs join forces most effectively. Spectacular though the colours are, they fall into tonal ranges in which clashes are impossible. So for this short, entrancing season, there is a harmony which only nature could possibly manage effectively. Counterpoint is provided by the abundance of fruits of all sizes, from tiny clustered berries to crab apples.

Acer

MAPLE

No other major group of trees can boast as many species with such a glorious range of autumn colour shades as the maples. Among the ornamental species and varieties, every possible shade of yellow, orange and deep crimson is represented.

Maples are usually associated with spectacular autumn displays in the northern USA and Canada, or with tranquil Japanese gardens. There is a wide range of forms to suit gardens both great and small.

Although their great season of glory is autumn, many species and varieties contribute attractive flowers, seeds and noble leaves in other seasons. Common to all species are the winged seeds that hang like bunches of keys against the summer foliage. In spring, the unfurling leaves often have their own distinctive livery, from the bright yellow of *Acer cappadocicum* to the brilliant red of *A. capillipes*. The flowers vary from the slender drooping racemes of *A. pensylvanicum* to the small, erect flower heads of *A. palmatum* varieties, or the small red sprays of *A. rubrum* which appear before the leaves develop. The summer foliage of the maples is often so sumptuous that it almost totally conceals the branches.

WINTER ATTRACTIONS

Even in winter, acers earn their keep in the all-season garden with their graceful profiles, particularly the snake-bark maples, among which are *A. davidii* and *A. grosseri hersii*. *A. griseum* has flaking bark of burnished copper, and the branches of *A. palmatum* 'Senkaki' are bright coral.

The Japanese maples, especially *A. palmatum* 'Dissectum', are small and delicate enough in form for a large tub or raised bed, a patio or small lawn. The larger varieties can make splendid features where space allows.

Plant a succession of bulbs that will flower from autumn to spring – such as the autumn and winter crocus, *Chionodoxa luciliae*, or the winter aconite, *Eranthis hyemalis* – beneath a maple to add colour during and after leaf-fall. If you have the space, the winter-flowering witch hazel *Hamamelis mollis* 'Pallida' could be planted nearby. As a late summer curtain-raiser to the fiery

The fiery red of *Acer palmatum* 'Osakazuki' and rich gold of *A. p.* 'Heptalobum Lutescens' blend beautifully with the pale orange tints of a flowering cherry.

IN SUMMER, *Acer palmatum* 'Dissectum Atropurpureum' adds the colour of mulled wine to the garden scene.

In autumn the bark of *Acer griseum* peels away to show a gleaming orange-brown surface beneath.

One beauty of *Acer davidii* is its white-streaked bark, which provides winter interest.

autumn show, *Hosta fortunei* 'Albopicta', *Ceratostigma plumbaginoides* and a massed band of mophead hydrangeas would provide a colourful link.

CULTIVATION

Plant the young trees between October and March, in reasonably fertile, well-drained soil. *A. rubrum* does best in lime-free soil, but most of the other species are tolerant of some lime. However, extremes of alkalinity and thin, chalky soils should be avoided. The ornamental acers need a sheltered, lightly shaded position – a site catching the sun at either end of the day would be ideal. Add plenty of organic material when planting, and give an annual dressing. To propagate, sow seed in a cold frame in autumn.

Acer palmatum
Broad canopied and hardy; rich
green in summer, crimson to gold in
autumn. Height 15ft. Spread 8-10ft.

Acer capillipes
Bright red young leaves and
greenish-white spring flowers;
whitish stripes on bark.
Height 15-20ft. Spread 10ft.

Acer japonicum
'Aconitifolium'
Upright and compact
habit. Height 8-10ft.
Spread 6-8ft.

Acer palmatum
'Dissectum'
Rounded, shrubby
habit with
cascading branches.
Height 4-6ft.
Spread 5-8ft.

Acer japonicum
'Vitifolium'
Centre often remains
green, while outer leaves
take on autumn tones.
Height 15-25ft. Spread 8-10ft.

Acer palmatum
'Senkaki' (syn 'Sango Kaku')
Bright coral young stems;
light green spring leaves
are tinged red.
Height 15ft. Spread 8-10ft.

Acer pensylvanicum
Young leaves brushed with red.
Young bark green then red-brown
with jagged white lines.
Height 15-20ft. Spread 10ft.

Going out in a blaze of glory

The ornamental maples bring a last great blaze of colour to the garden, glowing like fire even in the dullest weather or as dusk falls. As the year declines, the leaves change dramatically to royal burgundy and vivid scarlet, sunset orange and butter yellow – sometimes all on one tree! When the branches are at last bare of leaves, a graceful profile is left to enhance the winter scene.

Photographed in October at The Forestry Commission, Westonbirt Arboretum, Tetbury, Gloucestershire.

Acer rubrum
'Schlesingeri'
Best on neutral to acid soil. Red spring flowers followed by dark red keys.
Height 25ft.
Spread 10-15ft.

Acer grosseri hersii
Grey-green bark, striped white. Pendulous early summer flowers.
Height 10-15ft.
Spread 8-12ft.

Acer palmatum 'Osakazuki'
Neat and sturdy habit. Rich green summer foliage.
Height 10-15ft.
Spread 8-10ft.

Acer ginnala
Hardy, small and multistemmed. Fragrant early summer flowers.
Height 10-15ft. Spread 8-10ft.

Acer cappadocicum
'Aureum'
Spring leaves yellow; small, erect yellow flower heads. Height 30-40ft.
Spread 15-25ft.

The burnished foliage tones of *Cercidiphyllum japonicum* are startlingly effective against a dark, evergreen background.

The heart-shaped leaves of the katsura are tinted with delicate shades in autumn.

As the leaves of *Crataegus prunifolia* fall, bright red berries take the stage for a winter display.

Cercidiphyllum japonicum

KATSURA TREE

Height 40-60ft · *Spread* 15-20ft
Best October and April

When the katsura tree is wearing its autumn shades of gold, amber, pink, orange and red, it will bring new life to the garden when all else is beginning to fade. The shades vary from tree to tree, and from year to year. In late spring the tree almost glows as the coral-red young foliage unfurls before turning sea-green. When the flowers are opening, before the leaves appear, a pleasant aroma like roasting coffee beans fills the air around the tree.

If space permits, grow the tree in a lawn against a backcloth of dark evergreens or the bamboo *Pleioblastus viridistriatus* to ensure the prominence of the beautiful autumn colours. An incense cedar (*Libocedrus decurrens*) as a companion would provide aromatic year-round foliage.

CULTIVATION Plant in autumn or spring in moisture-retentive soil, acid or alkaline, in a sunny, sheltered position. Propagate from seed sown in early spring.

Crataegus prunifolia

PLUM-LEAF THORN

Height 12-20ft · *Spread* 10-18ft
Best October-November, May-June

The glossy, dark green leaves of this ornamental thorn turn to brilliant shades of orange and scarlet in autumn, and then gradually darken to crimson-purple. Bunches of bright red berries last through the winter, if the birds don't get them. In addition, clusters of white blossom cover the tree in early summer. A closely related ornamental thorn, *Crataegus × lavallei*, is larger and more spreading, and turns an even deeper red in autumn.

Plum-leaf thorn looks attractive on a lawn because of its low, spreading shape. Plant early flowering spring bulbs around it to offset the bareness of the dense twiggy crown. Large-cupped varieties of narcissi, such as 'Fortune', 'St Keverne', and 'Salome', are particularly suitable. Tough, low-growing dwarf shrubs *Sarcococca humilis* and *S. hookeriana digyna* of the box family will thrive in the shade of the tree, and produce a mass of tiny white, very fragrant, flowers in winter.

CULTIVATION Plant from autumn to late winter in any fertile soil, preferably in a sunny position. Propagate by seed sown as soon as it is ripe; germination may take a year.

Liquidambar styraciflua

SWEET GUM

Height 30-60ft · *Spread* 15-30ft
Best October-November

Two months of blazing autumn colour is the reward if you have the space for this magnificent foliage tree from North America. The maple-like leaves gradually change from glossy green to deep purple, and then progress through shades of red, orange and yellow. Shape may vary considerably – some trees are broad-spreading, while others, such as 'Lane Roberts' and 'Worplesdon', have upright branches. In winter, the heavily fissured, corky bark on some older trees is an attractive feature.

To provide a contrast in both shape and colour, try an ornamental grass nearby. For example, the white plumes of *Cortaderia selloana* 'Sunningdale Silver' look stunning set against the dark splendour of the sweet-gum foliage in autumn. For an equally effective combination, try *Aralia elata*, whose billowing white flower heads and bold foliage appear in late summer. In autumn, plant large-cupped narcissi beneath the tree to add spring sparkle to the scene.

CULTIVATION Plant between mid-autumn and early spring in rich, moisture-retentive soil in full sun. Propagate by layering.

In a mixed border (right), the scarlet and crimson of *Liquidambar styraciflua* set off lemon-yellow African marigolds and rose-pink *Cosmos bipinnatus*, while black-eyed Susan around the birdbath completes a charming picture.

The compact shape of the crab apple *Malus tschonoskii* makes it perfect for a lawn.

The foliage of *Nyssa sylvatica* glows with an almost incredible brilliance in the autumn sun.

Malus tschonoskii

Height 15-25ft · *Spread* 5-10ft
Best October

Because of its upright habit, this ornamental crab apple is suitable for places with limited space, such as courtyards or small front gardens. It is noted for its succession of brilliant autumn colours, the leaves turning yellow at first and then passing through a range of oranges to crimson, culminating in a flaming pyramid of colour. In summer, the thick leathery leaves are dark green with a hint of grey beneath.

Plant a spreading, not-too-vigorous conifer for greenery around the base of the malus – for example, the dwarf *Juniperus communis* 'Depressa Aurea', or *J.* × *media* 'Gold Coast'. To add colour, train a clematis to climb through the crab apple crown. *Clematis macropetala* and *C.* 'Bill Mackenzie' will provide colour in late spring and late summer.

CULTIVATION Plant between autumn and spring in any well-drained soil, preferably in a sunny position. Propagate by seed sown as soon as it is ripe.

Nyssa sylvatica

TUPELO

Height 15-25ft · *Spread* 10-15ft
Best October

Each autumn, the glossy green leaves of the American tupelo quickly turn to a brilliant, fiery red, revealing, in a mature tree, an elegant pyramidal network of branches. Insignificant June flowers are followed by clusters of small, fleshy, blue-black seeds. The named variety, 'Sheffield Park', has an upright habit. The quite closely related Chinese tupelo, *Nyssa sinensis*, has similar autumn colouring,

The massed scarlet berries of *Sorbus commixta* ripen in August, but are still around when the foliage takes on its fiery autumn colours.

(*Nyssa sylvatica* cont)
but is generally not as tall and has a broader, spreading habit.

As a feature in a lawn, the tupelo could be underplanted with spring bulbs such as crocus and narcissi. Alternatively, grow the tall ornamental grasses *Cortaderia selloana* or *Miscanthus sinensis* close by. For winter interest, the brightly coloured stems of *Salix alba* 'Britzensis' or the dogwood *Cornus alba* 'Sibirica' would make good companions.

CULTIVATION Plant at any time between mid-autumn and early spring in rich, moist, acid soil in a sunny, sheltered position. Propagate by seed when ripe, or by layering in spring.

Sorbus commixta

SCARLET ROWAN

Height 25-35ft · *Spread* 8-15ft
Best October

The glossy leaves of this elegant and upright-growing rowan from Japan turn purple in autumn, and in October erupt into the flaming scarlet that gives the tree its common name. Its large clusters of bright red berries persist several weeks after leaf-fall. The related *Sorbus* 'Embley' has equally rich autumn colour, which starts later, and is less column-like in stature.

Low-growing heathers look

As the season advances, *Sorbus vilmorinii* marks its passage with berries that fade from rose-red to pink to a blushing white.

well with this tree, especially the summer-flowering *Calluna vulgaris* 'Kinlochruel' (white), 'H.E. Beale' (pink) or 'Peter Sparkes' (deep pink). The ornamental dogwood, *Cornus alba* 'Spaethii', with golden variegated leaves, or the acid-loving evergreen *Pernettya mucronata*, with urn-shaped June flowers and pink, white or purple berries in autumn and winter, would provide striking foliage and colour contrast.

CULTIVATION Plant between mid-autumn and early spring in any well-drained soil, in sun or shade. Propagate from seed sown in autumn.

Sorbus vilmorinii

Height 7-15ft · *Spread* 5-10ft
Best August-November

The fern-like, dark green leaves of this small, spreading tree from China turn rich orange-red in autumn. Clusters of pea-sized berries mature in August or September, changing from deep pink to rose-flushed white. They seem to be unpalatable to birds, and hang on the bare branches through the winter.

Winter-flowering heathers make effective companions for *Sorbus vilmorinii*. Plant selections of *Erica carnea*, such as 'Springwood White', 'Myretoun Ruby', or 'Westwood Yellow' with its golden foliage, or use the slightly taller, white-flowered *Erica* × *darleyensis* 'Silberschmelze'. *Mahonia aquifolium*, a dark evergreen shrub with leathery leaves that often turn red or purple in winter, would contrast well, and has the added attraction of yellow flowers in spring.

CULTIVATION Plant between autumn and spring in well-drained soil in a cool, moist position. Propagate by seed sown in mid-autumn.

Autumn
CLIMBERS

THE GRAND parade of clematis is by no means over when autumn arrives. Some of the most luxuriant are at their best, and many which flowered in early summer give a repeat performance. But foliage colour is dominant too, and the true Virginia creeper and vines find support from garden features and house walls, clothing them in scarlet and crimson to join the splendid autumn show.

Celastrus orbiculatus

STAFF VINE,
CLIMBING BITTERSWEET

Height 40ft
Best September-November

The bright autumnal fruits of this robust, twining climber are as handsome for indoor arrangements as they are in the garden. Fleshy, scarlet-coated seeds, lying within a glossy, yellow-lined, gaping capsule, last well into winter. The rounded leaves turn clear yellow in autumn before falling. Make sure to get the self-pollinating form which bears fruit without the need for an extra plant as a pollinator.

Because of its vigour, the staff vine needs a fair-sized host tree, such as a 20ft pine, larch, alder or lime. A well-grown birch (*Betula*) or *Acer cappadocicum* 'Aureum' of at least 10ft in height might also cope with the climber's rampant growth. On a smaller scale – though likely to be overwhelmed in time –

Celastrus orbiculatus climbs with great vigour, its thick coat of leaves creating a mantle of bright golden-yellow in autumn.

Celastrus orbiculatus fruits; brown husks split to reveal gold linings and gems of scarlet within.

Cotoneaster lacteus is a possibility. *Prunus sargentii* or *Amelanchier lamarckii* could be neighbours for their splendid autumn colour, and also for their displays in spring when the celastrus has nothing to offer. At their feet *Hypericum × inodorum* 'Elstead' would add clear yellow flowers in summer followed by bright salmon-red fruits later in the year.

CULTIVATION Plant in any soil during autumn or winter in full sun or half shade. The staff vine will grow on north or east-facing walls. Prune, if required, in late winter. Propagate by semi-hardwood cuttings in midsummer or by transplanting suckers in autumn or spring.

Clematis
'Ernest Markham'

Height 10ft
Best June-September

Many gardeners regard this plant as the best 'red' clematis because of its reliability and the deep petunia-red and rich velvety sheen of its blooms. But 'Ernest Markham' has more to offer, for if pruned annually it flowers continuously for nearly four months, providing a valuable bridge of colour between summer and autumn.

Let the clematis climb through shrubs whose autumn berries or winter flowers will remain to give a splendid display after the climber has died back. For instance, a wall-trained evergreen *Pyracantha* 'Mohave', with orange-red berries from late summer through to midwinter, or *Viburnum × bodnantense* 'Deben', with clusters of fragrant, pink-tinted white flowers from October until about February, would both be suitable. With a ground-level planting of autumn and winter-flowering bulbs such as large mauve *Colchicum* 'Waterlily' and *Crocus tommasinianus* 'Ruby Giant', you will achieve a long-lasting colour scheme of pink, purple and plum.

CULTIVATION Plant in suitable weather conditions any time from autumn to spring in soil enriched with general fertiliser

The rich, velvet blooms of *Clematis* 'Ernest Markham' will bring late summer and autumn life to a host shrub or tree which has had an earlier season of glory.

Subdued rosemary can be given a long-term uplift by the brilliant trumpets of *Clematis* 'Gravetye Beauty' which gradually change to crimson stars, illuminating their surroundings.

Pink and chocolate *Clematis* 'Hagley Hybrid' would not be out of place on the set of a Hollywood musical; in a British garden, it can be soothed with cool colours and soft leaves.

(*Clematis* 'Ernest Markham' cont) and humus. Make sure that the roots are in shade, but the top growth is in the sun. Prune hard in late winter or early spring. Propagate by leaf-bud cuttings or layering in midsummer.

Clematis
'Gravetye Beauty'

Height 6-8ft
Best July-September

'Gravetye Beauty' is a hybrid of a species from Texas, and is quite unlike the large-flowered or lantern-flowered clematis. The blooms, which provide a spectacular display for many weeks, are like tulips at first – narrow, nodding trumpets that open out as they mature to form wide, cherry-crimson stars. The effect is quite breathtaking, and the selection of companions is a task to be undertaken with caution.

The slender, crimson and white *Tulipa clusiana*, spearing through the young purple-tinted foliage of *Sedum* 'Vera Jameson' in spring, could be the harbinger of the clematis flowers, with pink peonies and hybrid pinks for later company. Trail a few strands of 'Gravetye Beauty' through the soft greys of a group of *Salvia officinalis* or the bright, steely foliage of *Ruta graveolens* 'Jackman's Blue' for contrasting back-up colour and all-season interest.

CULTIVATION As for *C.* 'Ernest Markham', page 297.

Clematis
'Hagley Hybrid'

Height 8ft
Best July-September

This glamorous clematis, with its 3-4in wide, star-shaped blooms of mauve-pink with chocolate-coloured anthers, is exceptionally free-flowering. Its height may be limited, but it is not hard to grow, and would not overwhelm a shrub rose such as 'Magenta' with harmonising mauve blooms, or *Rosa glauca*, with its plum-flushed leaves. Plant *Salvia officinalis* 'Purpurascens', with soft grey-purple foliage, to provide through-season interest.

Pink Japanese anemones, *Anemone × hybrida*, or perhaps *Chrysanthemum rubellum* 'Clara Curtis', would intensify the autumn effect. In summer *Campanula* 'Loddon Anna' would repeat the pale mauve-pink tones and heliotrope would add a deep note of colour combined with an almond perfume.

CULTIVATION As for *C.* 'Ernest Markham', page 297.

Clematis × jackmanii

Height 10-12ft
Best July-October

Not for nothing is this the best known of the large-flowered clematis. It is both showy and easy to grow, with violet-purple blooms up to 5in across, which are borne in long succession deep into autumn. Their velvety darkness can be heightened if the clematis twines through a pale backcloth – the weeping silvery foliage of *Pyrus salicifolia* 'Pendula', for example.

To create a lasting theme of lilac, purple, mauve and pink, plant early summer-flowering thalictrums and *Allium christophii* beneath the clematis. The violet, star-like flowers of the allium eventually produce superb seed heads like skeletal footballs. Use pink *Geranium endressii* to bridge spring and summer, and clear lilac-blue *Aster × frikartii* 'Mönch' to echo the clematis colour and match its flowering season.

CULTIVATION As for *C.* 'Ernest Markham', page 297.

A climber of distinction, *Clematis × jackmanii* scrambles up a Cotswold wall (right), cheered on by red roses and pink hydrangeas in a show both colourful and fragrant.

Purple *Clematis* 'Mme Baron-Veillard' brings an aristocratic air to the autumnal garden.

The cheerful yellow bells of *Clematis rehderiana* take walls in their stride, and turn sheds into pagodas.

The densely growing bells of *Clematis tangutica* are ideal for decorating low fences and trellises.

Tousled silky seed heads accompany the later flowers of *Clematis tangutica obtusiuscula*.

Clematis
'Madame Baron-Veillard'

Height 15ft
Best August-October

A late-flowering clematis is a real boon in a garden that is just beginning to resign itself to the coming winter; this one has the added advantage of uplifting the slightly shop-soiled last days of summer as well. A vigorous climber, it flowers from the end of August to the end of October, when its wide, rose-lilac stars – up to 6in across – consort very well with Japanese anemones. The crimson buds of the fine old *Chrysanthemum* 'Emperor of China' would contribute much to the scene and its soft rose-coloured flowers even outlast those of the clematis.

Earlier occupants of the stage could include *Clematis* 'Gypsy Queen', which shows velvety-purple flowers from July to September. For spring, plant purple crocuses, and add the wine-red *Gladiolus byzantinus*

for a rich display in summer.
CULTIVATION Plant a container-grown clematis in autumn or spring, in soil enriched with plenty of humus, and preferably against a warm, sunny wall. Prune hard in spring and tie in new growths as required. Propagate by layering or leaf-bud cuttings in late summer.

Clematis rehderiana

Height 25ft
Best August-October

Dainty, pale primrose-yellow flowers appear in late summer and carry on well into autumn. They hang in loose clusters

from stiff stems among softly hairy, serrated leaves. Despite its delicate appearance, this clematis can soon cover a shed or fill a medium-sized tree, creating a breathtaking sight out of a mediocre feature.

The gentle colouring calls for quiet companions, such as *Nicotiana alata* 'Lime Green' and *Phygelius aequalis* 'Yellow Trumpet' or *P.* × *rectus* 'Moonraker', both with flowers that link summer and autumn. A backdrop of dramatic, variegated ivy such as *Hedera colchica* 'Dentata Variegata' or 'Sulphur Heart' would pick up the clematis colours and detract attention from its bare winter stems.
CULTIVATION Plant at any time

between autumn and early spring in any ordinary moist, well-drained garden soil. Prune after flowering, retaining a framework of 6-8ft of growth. Cut back hard in early spring if growth becomes excessive. Propagate by taking leaf-bud cuttings in midsummer or by seed when ripe in spring.

Clematis tangutica

Height 25-30ft
Best August-October

Yellow flowers like hanging lanterns and leaves elegantly dissected into small leaflets make *Clematis tangutica* a wel-

come midsummer friend, and as the flowers fade in October they form globes of silky, feathery-tipped seed heads. A named cultivar of *C. tangutica*, 'Bill Mackenzie' has larger, longer lanterns. *C. t. obtusiuscula* has broad saucer-shaped flowers and leaves that are less distinctively dissected than the species. It is very similar to the 'Orange Peel' and 'Lemon Peel' clematis, *C. tibetana vernayi*, so called because of its very thick, petal-like sepals.

Although *C. tangutica* is ideal for training up a wall trellis, it will also grow through the crown of a good-sized tree (say, 15-20ft high). Alternatively, it can be trained to grow along a fence or rough hedge, or even encouraged to cascade down a

Tumbling over a wall, *Clematis tangutica*, with its lantern flowers and fluffy seed heads, makes a splendid background (right) for an informal autumnal bed of Michaelmas daisies and the yellow flowers of *Rudbeckia fulgida*.

Carmine and gold *Clematis* 'Ville de Lyon' is of a richness and stature well suited to the style of its turn-of-the century origins.

bank. Try linking it between large neighbouring shrubs, such as bold, bright-berried, ever-green pyracantha and *Cornus alba* 'Spaethii', with *Bergenia* 'Sunningdale' beneath. The ber-genia's leaves turn crimson-mahogany in autumn if planted in full sun, and pink flowers are borne in spring.

CULTIVATION Plant any time between autumn and late winter in ordinary fertile soil that does not dry out. Prune back to a framework of 6-8ft in early spring, although this clematis can be cut hard back if growth is excessive. Propagate by leaf-bud cuttings in midsummer.

Clematis
'Ville de Lyon'

Height 10ft
Best June-October

The carmine-red flowers, deeper-coloured at the margins and enhanced with creamy stamens, place *Clematis* 'Ville de Lyon' among the most striking of the large-flowered clematis. As they mature, the centres fade slightly to mauve. With good cultivation and pruned hard in spring *C.* 'Ville de Lyon' pro-duces a tremendous late crop of blooms; on the other hand, a light pruning will encourage a first flowering as early as May.

The blue-silver foliage of *Eucalyptus gunnii* would pro-vide a splendid through the season backcloth. The clematis could ramble on a trellis or pergola in dramatic partnership with a white climbing rose such as 'Mme Alfred Carrière', which has flowers faintly blushed with soft pink. *Colchicum speciosum* 'Album' and *Dicentra spectabilis* 'Alba' could add ground-level colour in autumn and spring.

CULTIVATION Plant at same time between autumn and spring in humus-enriched soil, with the addition of a general fertiliser. Propagate by taking leaf-bud cuttings or by layering in July.

Parthenocissus quinquefolia

VIRGINIA CREEPER

Height 60ft or more
Best September-October

In autumn the leaves of this vigorous vine flare into brilliant scarlet, orange and crimson. The stems cling to their supports by means of adhesive pads at the end of the stem tendrils.

The most suitable position for the climber is against a tall wall or scrambling into a large tree. It combines well with those vigorous, creamy-yellow and green Persian ivies *Hedera colchica* 'Dentata Variegata' or 'Sulphur Heart', which mask the creeper's bare stems in winter and enhance its autumn tints.

CULTIVATION Plant in mild weather between late autumn and spring in any fertile soil and in almost any situation except heavy shade. Support the young plant against a wall or tree trunk with a cane at first. Cut back hard in summer to keep within bounds. Propagate by cuttings in late summer.

A well-established Virginia creeper will provide a spectrum of autumn colours, making the closing months of the year a season well worth waiting for.

Pileostegia viburnoides is one of the few evergreen flowering climbers that is hardy in Britain.

Pileostegia viburnoides

Height 10-15ft
Best August-October

Though rather slow growing, this climbing relative of the hydrangeas eventually makes a dense cover of leathery, mid to deep green leaves. The wide flower heads, foaming with tiny creamy florets, appear in late summer and autumn. *Pileostegia viburnoides* is a fine plant for a north wall, and as an evergreen has great all-season value. At its feet could go variegated hostas, white *Anemone × hybrida* or wand-like *Cimicifuga simplex* 'White Pearl' for a cool blend of cream, white and green. *Corydalis lutea*, which enjoys similar cool conditions, would introduce sprays of soft yellow flowers from spring to late autumn, over fern-like foliage.

CULTIVATION Plant between autumn and spring in fertile soil in either shade or sun. Ensure roots are cool. Propagate by layering or by semi-hardwood cuttings in late summer.

BRIDGING
THE SEASONS
WITH
Vitis coignetiae

Perceived by a contemplative cat is one of those autumn days when the year is held in perfect balance. The sun is bright, but the shadows are not so sharp as at midsummer. Mornings and evenings have an edge to them, there is a hint of bonfires in the air, and foliage hangs languidly, awaiting the colours that frost imposes.

About to show the way are the broad, already-turning leaves of *Vitis coignetiae*, the Japanese crimson glory vine, that in its full autumnal dress of yellow, orange-red and purple will illuminate the white-edged, evergreen leaves of *Euonymus fortunei* 'Silver Queen', which forms both ground cover and wall decoration behind the stone seat. In the shadows above the cat's head are the glowing, deep red spikes of *Polygonum millettii* that flowers well into autumn. A few pink flowers of *Saponaria officinalis* – the lather-producing soap-wort – are still in evidence and some silver pods of honesty. Much of the remainder of the scene is green – the fingered leaves of stinking hellebore (*Helleborus foetidus*) under the seat, and the dark, shiny foliage of *Daphne odora*.

As autumn goes into winter, the vitis loses its glorious leaves and shows only bare twigs until late spring. In May, it produces green flowers in 3in long clusters that are followed by purple-black fruits; however, unlike those of the related grape vine, they are inedible.

Well satisfied with a gleaming backdrop of *Euonymus fortunei* 'Silver Queen', given point and substance by the broad autumn-flushed leaves of *Vitis coignetiae*, a contented cat basks in the approval of the late sun.

Through winter and into spring, attention is drawn to the scene by the pale purple flower heads of the daphne and the crowded yellow-green blooms of the hellebore, against the background of the euonymus's handsome foliage.

With the return of summer, the main interest in the little corner is provided by foliage. The leaves of the vitis are mid-green and shapely, and those of the luxuriant euonymus almost silvery from a distance. The honesty (*Lunaria annua*) provides young pods, but the polygonum is once more in flower, and the saponaria is about to be. *Felis domesticus* 'Ginger Tom', it will be noticed, has abandoned the seat, at least for the time being. ❧

IN SUMMER the stone stage is empty, but the now green leaves of vitis, punctuated by *Polygonum millettii*, still make a stately backcloth.

Bold veining emphasises the leaf colours of *Vitis coignetiae*.

Vitis coignetiae

ORNAMENTAL VINE

Height 50ft or more
Best September-November

The huge, rounded leaves, up to 1ft across, of this lusty vine form bold, decorative patterns all through spring and summer. In autumn, this effect is enhanced by the blood-red and burnished copper of the leaves.

A plant of such strong character is most effective for adding a distinctive touch to a terrace or patio wall. It can also be encouraged to climb through a large tree. *Clematis tangutica* would make a stunning climbing partner. The striking evergreen foliage of *Helleborus foetidus* would provide interest when the vine is leafless. Plant it at the foot of the vine with clumps of spring bulbs.

CULTIVATION Plant at some time between autumn and early spring in any well-nourished soil. Propagate by layering or by single bud cuttings taken in late winter or early spring.

Autumn
ROSES

THE GARDEN for all seasons can be well served by roses, which continue flowering well into autumn. But it is not only flowers with which roses grace the garden. Their fruits, particularly those of the species roses and their near hybrids, are decorative, brightly coloured, fascinatingly shaped, and unexpectedly varied. Foliage, too, should not be forgotten. The crinkled leaves of the rugosa roses and the burgundy-dipped foliage of *Rosa glauca* are of longer value than any flowers.

Rosa
'Ballerina'

Height 3-4ft · *Spread* 3-4ft
Best July-October

Swathed in clusters of blooms like apple blossom, this dainty hybrid musk rose is a sight to treasure in autumn. The small, single flowers are soft pink with a white eye, and almost overwhelm the low-growing, light green bush beneath. 'Ballerina' is sufficiently vigorous and spreading to be used as a hedge.

The evergreen, pink winter-flowering *Sarcococca hookeriana digyna*, with a foreground planting of snowdrops (*Galanthus*) or *Crocus chrysanthus* 'Snow Bunting', is worth considering if you feel the need for foliage and colour when the rose bush is finally bare.

CULTIVATION Plant between late autumn and early spring in any

Rosa chinensis 'Old Blush' retains all the charm of old-fashioned roses in its relaxed, fragrant blooms.

soil in sun or light shade. Remove faded flower clusters to encourage another flush. Prune in late winter to maintain shape. Propagate by taking hardwood cuttings in late autumn.

Rosa chinensis
'Old Blush'

Height 4ft · *Spread* 4ft
Best June-December

Also known as the 'last rose of summer' and 'Parson's Pink China', this traditional rose is often still showing the odd spray of small, semi-double blooms at Christmas. The fine combination of a scent reminiscent of old-fashioned sweet peas, 'perpetual' flowering and quality of colour (pale pink,

The wonderfully reliable, recurrent flowers of *Rosa* 'Ballerina' dance with simple grace against the soft grey of a stone wall.

The flowers of *Lavatera thuringiaca* 'Barnsley' complement *Rosa glauca* in its autumn livery, the hips recalling the rose's earlier blooms; in the foreground, the silver-grey foliage of *Santolina chamaecyparissus* echoes the smoky tones of the rose's leaves.

IN SUMMER, the modest, clear pink blooms of *Rosa glauca* add exquisite highlights to its tinted leaves.

that deepens with age), was to revolutionise European rose-growing when 'Old Blush' was introduced in the late 18th century. Its fusion with other old roses led to the creation of many new hybrids.

Evergreen *Daphne odora* 'Aureomarginata' as a planting companion could bring all-season elegance and scented flowers from winter to early spring, and a stately group of *Digitalis purpurea* 'Excelsior' nearby would bring pastel shades in summer.

CULTIVATION Plant bare-rooted specimens between late autumn and early spring in any well-drained soil in a sunny position. No pruning is necessary, except to remove old wood and weak growth. Propagate by taking hardwood cuttings in autumn.

Rosa glauca
(syn *R. rubrifolia*)

Height 6-8ft · *Spread* 4-6ft
Best September-October

Of all roses, this is one of the finest for foliage. The leaves of *Rosa glauca* are purplish-grey in sun or greyish-green in light shade, and dusted with a smoky bloom. The stems are smooth, almost thornless, and coloured a bluish-red. In autumn, the branches arch under the weight of cheerful bunches of scarlet hips, and in June the bush is studded with fragile, clear pink roses with white eyes.

Emphasise the greeny-grey foliage, and provide year-round continuity after leaf-fall, with the white-flowering *Lavandula* *spica* 'Nana Alba' and early spring-flowering *Narcissus bulbocodium* 'Nylon'. If you have the space, a taller companion to give a magnificent spring show of porcelain-pink blossom is *Kolkwitzia amabilis*. A shrewd collection of annuals in the blue and pink colour ranges, like *Nigella* 'Miss Jekyll', *Lupinus hartwegii* or *Clarkia elegans*, would bridge the gap between the rose's summer flowers and autumn hips.

CULTIVATION Plant in full sun or light shade between late autumn and early spring in any well-drained but water-retentive soil. Little pruning is needed, but remove dead wood and straggly growth in winter or after flowering. Propagate by taking cuttings in early autumn.

IN EARLY SUMMER, soft, fragrant blooms cover *Rosa* 'Mme Grégoire Staechelin', justifying the rose's popular name of 'Spanish Beauty'.

'Mme Grégoire Staechelin' presents a magnificent autumn display of luscious, flask-shaped hips.

Rosa
'Mme Grégoire Staechelin'

Height 20ft or more
Best October, and May-June

Few roses can beat the autumn display of this voluptuous climber – enormous, apricot-coloured hips hanging in abundance from its stems. Also known as 'Spanish Beauty', it is one of the earliest roses to flower if grown against a warm wall, and in early summer there is a billowing display of slender buds that open into richly scented, loose, double blooms. On a north-facing wall, blossom and fruit will be delayed by a month or so, but will be just as prolific.

When the rose is finally bare, the winter-flowering, partially evergreen scented honeysuckle *Lonicera fragrantissima* could take centre stage at a lower level, and *Clematis alpina* 'Ruby' as a climbing companion would flower just before the rose.

CULTIVATION Plant bare-rooted specimens in good, well-drained soil enriched with well-rotted manure or bone meal between late autumn and early spring, in sun or light shade. Secure stems to supports as they develop. Prune to keep within

A cascade of glowing hips from *Rosa moyesii* pours over *Vinca major* 'Variegata' beneath, and the turning leaves of *Mahonia japonica*.

THE SUMMER flowers of *Rosa moyesii* have a simple grace, and though unscented are popular with bees.

bounds by cutting back lateral flowering shoots to two or three buds in spring. Propagate by hardwood cuttings in autumn.

Rosa moyesii
'Geranium'

Height 8-10ft · *Spread* 6-8ft
Best September, June-July

The first *Rosa moyesii* to arrive in Britain was discovered growing at 9000ft in China near the Tibetan frontier. *R. moyesii* 'Geranium', a fine cultivar developed at the Royal Horticultural Gardens at Wisley, is smaller and bushier than the species, with luscious, flagon-shaped hips in autumn. Although intense crimson-red single flowers make a vivid display in summer, it is the fruit, hanging in sealing-wax red clusters from long, upright canes, that is the outstanding feature of this shrub.

Try planting a bluish evergreen shrub such as *Ruta*

Even in poor, sandy soils, *Rosa rugosa* will present a glorious display of enormous hips, each an inch or more across.

graveolens 'Jackman's Blue' in front to disguise the rose's rather gaunt base, or grow it before a wall covered in winter-flowering *Jasminum nudiflorum*.
CULTIVATION Plant in fertile, well-drained soil in sun or light shade between late autumn and early spring. Remove any weak or dead stems in winter. Propagate by taking cuttings of strong, non-flowering lateral shoots in early autumn and place in a cold frame.

SUMMER *Rosa rugosa* blooms recur over many weeks, the later ones often coinciding with the first hips.

Rosa rugosa

Height 4-5ft · *Spread* 4-5ft
Best July-October

Particularly healthy and hardy, with displays of foliage, flowers and fruit to link spring, summer and autumn, the Rugosa cultivars are among the front

runners in the garden competition for seasonal continuity. Fruity hips, as big and bright as cherry tomatoes, are set against a mass of wrinkled, apple-green leaves that take on autumn tints of gold, while the stems are thick with fine prickles. The

flowers are happily recurrent throughout summer, and the last autumnal blooms often coincide with the first hips.

'Fru Dagmar Hastrup' is a spreading yet compact cultivar that is suitable for hedging. It bears large, dark red hips and fragrant, clear pink single blooms with cream stamens. The tomato-red hips of 'Scabrosa' are the largest fruits of all the Rugosas. 'Scabrosa' is extra vigorous, with sweetly fragrant, magenta-pink flowers.

For a low-level companion, × *Fatshedera lizei* – a hybrid of ivy and *Fatsia japonica* – would look well in the foreground.
CULTIVATION Plant bare-rooted specimens between late autumn and early spring in full sun in any soil other than heavy clay or chalk. *R. rugosa* does well in poor and sandy soils not suited to other roses. To encourage compact growth, prune hard in winter; otherwise simply cut out old and weak wood in early spring or autumn. Propagate by suckers or by hardwood cuttings in autumn.

Lighting the garden, *Rosa virginiana* hips are set against fiery autumn foliage.

Rosa virginiana

Height 3-5ft · *Spread* 5-7ft
Best September-November, and July-August

The autumn foliage of this rose is enough to make it remarkable: the outer leaves turn purple, then orange-red and crimson, and the inner leaves turn yellow, the whole effect highlighted by scarlet hips. But there is an equally vivid show in summer, when cerise-pink flowers are set against glossy, bronze-tinted leaves.

This low, suckering, spreading shrub has a distinctive appearance for a rose. It makes a splendid specimen for the corner of a border, or isolated in a lawn. Flank it with *Alchemilla mollis* and spring bulbs.
CULTIVATION Plant in moist, fertile, well-drained soil in an open, sunny site in late autumn or early spring. Prune only to keep within bounds in March. Propagate from suckers in autumn or early spring.

Autumn
PERENNIALS

Seasons are an invention of mankind, not nature. Late summer and autumn merge slowly together, and it is often difficult to categorise perennials that flower at this time of the year as belonging to one season or to the other. To a large extent, the autumn perennials form a bridge between the two seasons.

Aconitum carmichaelii
'Arendsii'

MONKSHOOD

Height 4ft · *Planting distance* 2ft
Best September-October

The common name results from the curious cowl-shaped or helmet-like upper petal on each bloom. Tall spires of deeply cut foliage provide body and background all summer until, in late September, blue delphinium-like flower spikes begin to open. These last for many weeks and are perfect for cutting for indoor arrangement.

In dry weather, the leaves start to turn yellow before the flowers fade, and create an attractive colour contrast.

Of the half-dozen cultivars available, 'Arendsii' is the clearest mid-blue; for darker, violet-blue, try the cultivar *Aconitum* 'Kelmscott'.

Plant aconitums between shrubs, or at the back of the border where they can tower above shorter summer and autumn perennials. The cool

Tall spires of dark blue *Aconitum carmichaelii* contrast boldly with strong red *Sedum* 'Autumn Joy'.

'Honorine Jobert' is a pure white form of Japanese anemone.

The prolific *Clematis* 'Perle D'Azur' makes a stunning backdrop for Japanese anemones, with added sparkle from *Nicotiana sylvestris* and *Chrysanthemum maximum*.

blue flowers blend equally well with strong reds and russets of autumn foliage on shrubs such as *Euonymus europaeus* 'Red Cascade' or among variegated evergreens like *Elaeagnus × ebbingei* 'Limelight'. They also make perfect companions for ripening rose hips.

CULTIVATION Plant in autumn or spring in cool, water-retentive soil; avoid thin sandy soils which dry out. Monkshood is lime-tolerant. Propagate by division of the tuber-like roots in autumn or late winter, when

new leaves appear above the ground. Caution – all parts of the plant are poisonous.

Anemone × hybrida

JAPANESE ANEMONE

Height 2½-3½ft
Planting distance 2-3ft
Best August-October

As summer fades, the tall branched flower stems that rise from a solid cover of foliage become crowded with gold-

centred blooms up to 3in across. The usual colour is pink but one of the finest varieties, 'Honorine Jobert', is pure shining white. Good pink forms include 'Queen Charlotte' and the near double 'Lady Gilmour' whose flowers tend to hang under their own weight. 'Luise Uhink', raised in Germany at the beginning of the century, has semi-double, white blooms.

Japanese anemones look best planted in drifts rather than in isolated clumps. They are perfect for the mixed border,

where the foliage can form a cover between shrubs and other perennials during summer. In autumn, if shrubs are becoming dull, the flowers can be star performers. Spring shrubs such as azaleas, cytisus or *Viburnum plicatum* are good companions.

CULTIVATION Plant during autumn or spring in sun or partial shade, allowing plenty of room for the roots to spread. Propagate by division in autumn or by root cuttings in winter. Once established, they can be difficult to eradicate.

Aster

MICHAELMAS DAISY

There is a much greater range of Michaelmas daisies than the traditional pale mauve species would suggest. A host of different forms embraces plants short and tall, compact and spreading, and a surprising range of flower colour and size. From the shocking-pink *Aster novae-angliae* 'Alma Pötschke' to the rich blue rays of *A. amellus* 'King George', there is a perennial aster to suit every garden. Some forms, like the lavender-blue *A.* × *frikartii* 'Mönch', begin to flower as early as July and there are plenty of hybrids which carry colour into November.

Hybrids of *A. novi-belgii* can be prone to mildew and, though they offer some of the best colours, need careful siting and regular spraying. The mildew-resistant *A. novae-angliae* has an interesting colour range including 'Herbstschnee', a fine white cultivar growing to 4ft, and 'Harrington's Pink' which has flowers of the clearest shell-pink. Among dwarf forms, ideal for border fronts, is neat, deep pink *A. dumosus* 'Rosenwichtel'.

COLOUR AND HEIGHT

Asters can be grouped to create a bank of rich, blended colour, increasing in height from dwarf forms at the front to tall hybrids at the back. *A. ericoides* 'Ringdove' or 'Pink Cloud' can be planted in front of the taller hybrids, for example.

Place earlier-flowering plants near the asters for a continuous display of colour while the foliage is developing. For spring, *Lathyrus vernus* will provide red-purple flashes. By adding wallflowers you can enrich the planting with colour and scent, especially if backed up by tulips and geums.

CULTIVATION

For best results, plant in fertile soil in a sunny position which drains well but which does not bake too hard in summer. Tall cultivars need support from pea sticks, canes and string, or interlocking metal stakes. Cut back the dead stems in March. Propagate by lifting, dividing and replanting the rootstock in autumn or spring. Do this every three years or sooner to maintain vigour and to ensure free flowering.

Massed asters (right) can create a billow of luxuriant colour for many weeks if you combine cultivars of varying heights. Plant low-growing evergreens in front to take over when the aster display is over.

Brilliant *Aster* × *frikartii* holds its vibrant colours until October.

Aster dumosus
'Chatterbox'
Erect, bushy and almost
top-heavy with powder-puff
blooms. Height 1½ft.

Aster dumosus 'Rosenwichtel'
Forms a neat mound with surprisingly
large flowers and tiny, dark green leaves.
Height 10in.

Aster amellus 'Violet Queen'
Fine mid-border plant;
bold, single flowers above
compact foliage.
Height 1½-2ft.

Aster × *frikartii* 'Mönch'
Mildew-resistant; masses of large,
single flowers from July to October.
Height 3ft.

Aster novi-belgii
'Royal Ruby'
Small and sturdy;
big flowers for its size.
Height 1½ft.

Aster ericoides
'Ringdove'
Drifts of tiny
flowers cover sprays of
heath-like leaves.
Height 3ft.

Aster novi-belgii
'Chequers'
Chequerboard contrast
between petals and bright
gold centres; firm, fine-
leaved foliage. Height 20in.

Aster novae-angliae
'Alma Pötschke'
Very compact, large variety;
mildew-resistant.
Height 3ft.

Aster lateriflorus
'Horizontalis'
Spreading bush with small
dark leaves, and wealth of
tiny flowers. Height 2ft.

Aster ericoides 'Pink Cloud'
Clouds of delicate flowers almost obscure feathery foliage. Height 2¾ft.

A tapestry of Michaelmas daisies

Picture a tapestry of blues, mauves and pink,
alive with butterflies and bees and gilded by autumn sunshine.
You can fill a section of border from front to back with the vibrant colours of
Michaelmas daisies, for the varieties embrace a surprising range of form – from low
mounds, densely packed with tiny leaves, to tall, back of the border types.

Photographed on Michaelmas Day, September 29,
at The Royal Horticultural Society's Garden, Wisley, Surrey.

Aster novae-angliae 'Harrington's Pink'
Mildew-resistant. Height 4ft.

Aster novae-angliae 'Herbstschnee'
Splendid for the back of the border, with luxuriant show of blooms. Height 4ft.

Aster cordifolius 'Golden Spray'
Tight, white buds open into white, gold-centred flowers ageing deep pink; tiny, close-packed leaves. Height 2½ft.

Aster turbinellus
Open, grey-green foliage and a succession of small, rayed flowers. Height 4ft.

Aster novi-belgii 'Fellowship'
Shapely sprays of flowers with slightly ragged petals. Height 3¼ft.

Aster novae-angliae 'Lye End Beauty'
A tall form with flowers of striking lavender. Height 4½ft.

311

Cerise-pink *Centaurea hypoleuca* 'John Coutts' harmonises happily under the rose-pink flowers of tall *Syringa × josiflexa* 'Bellicent'.

'Mei-Kyo', a pompon chrysanthemum, needs little attention and will flower until mid-November.

The flowers of *Centaurea hypoleuca* 'John Coutts' first appear in June.

The luscious red hybrid Korean chrysanthemum 'Mabel' is one of a wide range providing strong colours for the autumn garden. Eminently suitable for cutting, their sprays of flowers will equally enliven a room.

Centaurea hypoleuca
'John Coutts'

PERENNIAL CORNFLOWER

Height 2ft · *Planting distance* 1½ft
Best June-November

Flowers, held well above the foliage, are produced in a rush in midsummer and then appear sporadically until early autumn when a second flush usually appears. Each flower has a hard, scaly base above which rests a large ruff of cerise-pink florets. After several weeks, these give way to handsome seed heads, silvery in colour, papery in texture, with a lustrous sheen.

Fresh green, deeply lobed leaves, each with a silvery underside, create a decorative effect even before the plant commences flowering.

'John Coutts' makes a fine subject for the mixed border, filling spaces between shrubs and yielding a nearly continuous run of rich, sumptuous colour over many months.

CULTIVATION Plant during spring in well-drained soil in full sun.

Chrysanthemum
indicum
Pompon hybrids

Height 2-3ft
Planting distance 3ft
Best October-November

For a spectacular flourish at the end of the season, it is worth having a bed devoted entirely to these bright, showy plants. Such is the range of colour available they can be planted to produce a graduation of tones from bronze through yellow to primrose and white, and then through pinks and mauves to red. Button-shaped flowers are produced in generous, many-branched sprays that last for weeks in autumn. Cultivars

Deadhead to extend flowering, but for a winter show of seed heads, leave the later blooms. Propagate by division.

include: 'Anastasia', with pale pink flowers, 'Bronze Fairie', 'Salmon Fairie', the orange 'Peterkin' and hardy 'Mei-Kyo'.

To provide colour while the chrysanthemums are out of season, underplant them with tulips for a spring display, and dot a few bedding plants among them for a summer show.

CULTIVATION As for Korean hybrids (see below).

Chrysanthemum
Korean hybrids

Height 3-4ft
Planting distance 2ft
Best October-November

Korean chrysanthemums have generous sprays of small, double, semi-double, or single flowers, and were originally raised in the United States. They need little attention, and can provide strong colour to

The Korean chrysanthemum 'Wedding Day', like others in the group, is fine for cutting.

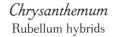

Spectacular *Chrysanthemum* 'Clara Curtis', a Rubellum hybrid, dazzles autumn with its brilliance.

The feathery flowers of *Cimicifuga simplex* 'Elstead' float above its fern-like foliage.

The bright yellow flowers of *Corydalis lutea* shine for almost all the year. Here they combine with the evergreen fern *Polystichum setiferum*.

enliven the autumnal border.

In colours ranging from the dark red 'Apollo' (one of the original hybrids) to the pink 'Venus' and the white 'Wedding Day', Korean chrysanthemums are easy to fit into a planting scheme. The bronzes and yellows blend well with the colours of autumn foliage, and the whites and pinks make good companions for perennial asters, often continuing to flower as the asters die down. A foreground of yellow chrysanthemums will brighten up sombre evergreens – rosemary, say, and other herbs.

CULTIVATION Plant in late spring, in any fertile but well-drained moisture-retentive soil in sun.

Chrysanthemum
Rubellum hybrids

Height 1½-2½ft
Planting distance 1½ft
Best September-October

Single, daisy-like blooms bring old-world charm to the garden. This group of plants was developed from a Welsh fore-bear of the 1920s. Perhaps the oldest variety in cultivation is 'Clara Curtis', with slightly irregular pink flowers; 'Duchess of Edinburgh' is rusty-red and has yellow centres; and 'Apricot' has orange petals that blend with its yellow centre; 'Mary Stoker' is pale yellow.

These chrysanthemums go

well with other late perennials, such as asters, sedums and mauve-lilac *Liriope muscari*. Randomly mixed with dianthus, astrantia, lupins, poppies and Jacob's ladder, which all flower earlier, the hybrids would be the mainstay of a late-season show.
CULTIVATION As for Korean hybrids, on this page. In rich, moist soil, plants may need supporting with canes or pea sticks, but in light soil should be self-supporting.

Cimicifuga simplex
'Elstead'

BUGBANE

Height 5ft · *Planting distance* 2ft
Best September-October

Among the cultivated bug-banes, 'Elstead' is a reliable performer. For a sharper and purer white, try 'White Pearl'. The branched, feathery spires of

tiny flowers are like bottle-brushes, and rise above the foliage. Side shoots continue to flower for weeks after the main display has faded. The small, divided leaves provide a useful low-key show throughout the summer. The cimicifuga display could follow on from astilbes, or plant it with other moisture-lovers such as *Ligularia dentata* 'Desdemona' or any of the rodgersias. The white cimici-fuga flowers are valuable also for relieving the darkness of off-season rhododendrons.
CULTIVATION Plant during autumn in light shade and in moist, leafy soil. Stems may need support in exposed posi-tions. Propagate by division in autumn or late winter, or by seed sown in gritty compost,

and set in a shaded corner or open cold frame where frost action can assist germination.

Corydalis lutea

YELLOW CORYDALIS

Height 8-12in
Planting distance Random
Best May-October

Seldom out of flower except in the depths of winter, *Corydalis lutea* produces tiny bright yellow snapdragon-like flowers which glow above the mounds of cool grey-green filigree foliage. Few plants are so useful for filling crevices or dull cor-ners, brightening old walls, softening harsh building lines or colonising paths and drives.

Delphinium Belladonna hybrids have a country-garden charm about them and their long flowering period bridges summer and autumn.

A soft mist of *Gypsophila* 'Bristol Fairy' provides a perfect setting for the rich, burnt reds of *Helenium autumnale* 'Moerheim Beauty'.

(*Corydalis lutea* cont)

C. lutea makes a good companion for almost any yellow, gold or blue flowers. Try it with tough early spring bulbs such as *Chionodoxa luciliae*. Alternatively, for an evergreen association, plant *C. lutea* alongside ferns or evergreen shrubs.

CULTIVATION Plant this corydalis almost anywhere – it thrives in the poorest soils and flowers most freely in sun. Cut straggly plants to ground level in summer. Propagate by scattering seed; once established the plants multiply unaided.

Delphinium
Belladonna hybrids

Height 5ft · *Planting distance* 2ft
Best June-October

The gracious spires of these hybrids provide the perfect alternatives, where spread and height are limited, to the tall, back of the border delphiniums.

Although their character is more open and branched than the dense, vertical spikes of the big delphiniums, they are just as elegant. And as they flower at a medium height, they do not need staking. Colours range from light to deep blue: 'Blue Bees' flowers are pale blue with a conspicuous white eye; those of 'Lamartine' are rich royal blue with a dash of purple.

Belladonna delphiniums can be used to provide contrast in a rose bed or in a mixed herbaceous border among shrubs. They would blend beautifully with cottage-garden annuals in blue or mauve shades, such as *Nigella*. Or combine them with the pale lemon *Potentilla recta* 'Citrina' in June, and later with the deeper yellow *Helenium autumnale* 'Butterpat'.

CULTIVATION Delphiniums are lime-tolerant, but respond well if planted in any humus-rich soil. Deadhead regularly to encourage further flowering. Keep the plants well fed, and

Helenium autumnale 'Butterpat' brings bold splashes of golden autumn sunshine to the border.

water copiously in dry spells to discourage mildew. Propagate by division or by taking basal cuttings in early spring.

Helenium autumnale

Height 2-4ft
Planting distance 2ft
Best September-October

The helenium's distinctively shaped flowers, with their prominent central cones surrounded by rays of slightly swept-back petals and available in colours ranging from rich mahogany through russet to gold, are like giant bumblebees. They are held in generous sprays on long stems, and make good cut flowers. The foliage reaches stately dimensions, sometimes exceeding 5ft in rich soil, but has no particular off-season attraction. 'Butterpat' is one of the finest hybrids, with clean yellow petals and matching cones. 'Wyndley' is a mixture of yellow and copper with contrasting dark cones. 'Moerheim Beauty' has darkly glowing, deep red to mahogany petals and dark brown cones.

Heleniums are favourites for the herbaceous border and make good companions for shrubs and trees. Place pale foliage plants such as *Stachys byzantina* 'Silver Carpet' in front, and add cream or white-flowered subjects to bring out the strong colours. Heleniums would also look well near variegated shrubs such as *Cornus alba* 'Elegantissima'.

CULTIVATION Plant at some time in autumn or spring in rich soil

Hosta plantaginea 'Royal Standard' contributes to the garden scene from May, but in autumn, graceful flowers enhance the sculptured foliage.

Iris foetidissima is native to woods and thickets, but its strong leaves and arresting seed pods fit just as well into a garden context.

Given a deep, moist soil, the handsome leaves and delicate hooded flowers of *Kirengeshoma palmata* will flourish.

which is regularly mulched or dressed with manure, in full light. All but the shortest cultivars need supporting with stakes or large pea sticks. Propagate by dividing as soon as the flowers have faded in late autumn, or in cold areas on heavy soil, in spring.

Hosta plantaginea

PLANTAIN LILY

Height 2ft · *Planting distance* 3ft
Best May-November

Tall stems bearing pure white and faintly fragrant trumpet flowers emerge in late summer or early autumn, depending on seasonal warmth. The leaves are green and lustrous, and on mature plants arch gracefully to give a fine show throughout summer. At the end of the season, however, the foliage turns yellow and then quickly dies down.

Careful siting in front of evergreen shrubs such as *Pieris* 'Forest Flame' will divert attention from the hosta crown in winter, and the pieris will display its young red leaves in spring. Winter bulbs around the perimeter can serve the same purpose – try planting either *Narcissus* 'February Gold' or perhaps *N*. 'Thalia'.

CULTIVATION Plant in spring in a sunny or partially shaded spot. As long as the ground is well mulched, hostas will tolerate almost any soil. Keep well watered during dry spells. The young foliage is prone to slug damage, and may need to be protected. Propagate by division in early spring.

Iris foetidissima

STINKING IRIS

Height 1½ft
Planting distance 1½ft
Best June, November-March

Do not be put off by this plant's name – there is only a mildly unpleasant smell when the leaves are crushed. *Iris foetidissima* earns its place in the garden with a fiery show of autumn berries. Long green seed pods split open to expose rows of brilliant orange beads, which will last for weeks if not eaten by birds. Small flowers appear in early summer in the subtle shades of lilac with greenish veining. The variety 'Citrina' has larger, yellow flowers. Upright blades of leaves – dark green in the species, and with a white stripe in the form 'Variegata' – are evergreen and a useful vertical feature through the year.

For a well-balanced woodland group, plant the iris beneath a light canopy of deciduous trees with summer-flowering *Geranium endressii* and spring-flowering *Brunnera macrophylla*. Alternatively, in a border situation, combine a group of the iris with a bold-leaved perennial such as *Bergenia cordifolia*.

CULTIVATION Plant in autumn in any free-draining soil that does not dry out, in sun or light shade. Propagate by dividing and replanting the clumps of rhizomes in autumn.

Kirengeshoma palmata

Height 4ft · *Planting distance* 2½ft
Best September

The keeled flowers, with thick petals and bell-shaped calyx, have a unique texture which looks waxy but is soft to the touch. Dark stems contrast with bright vine-like leaves, which retain their fresh green all summer. The sprays of flowers continue for several weeks during autumn.

The creamy-yellow blooms show up beautifully against the dark leaves of evergreen azaleas or rhododendrons. Hostas or

The orange-red flowers of *Kniphofia caulescens* gradually turn to pale yellow in late autumn.

Delicate, drooping flower tubes with long stamens identify *Kniphofia galpinii* from *K. caulescens*.

(*Kirengeshoma palmata* cont) rodgersias would also contribute to an extended season of harmonious flower and foliage. CULTIVATION Plant during spring or autumn in neutral to acid soil enriched with plenty of organic material, and keep well watered during dry spells. The plant is not lime-tolerant.

The young shoots are susceptible to late spring frosts, so protect with cloches. Propagate from seed or by division of rooted clumps in spring.

Kniphofia caulescens

RED-HOT POKER, TORCH LILY

Height 3-5ft
Planting distance 3-4ft
Best September-October

Tall, straight stems with torchlike flower heads of massed, flame-coloured flowers give this plant its common names. A near-hardy species from South Africa, *Kniphofia caulescens* has a trunk-like base, from which emerge strap-like leaves.

As this tall poker tends to produce untidy leaves from summer onwards, grow perennials in front to hide them – the large-leaved evergreen *Bergenia* 'Silberlicht', for example, which has white bell-flowers in April and heart-shaped leaves that sometimes turn bronze in autumn. In July, the clear blue flowers of *Ceratostigma willmottianum* make a cooling contrast to the pokers, and can be grown right up against them. The purple flowers of the butterfly bush, *Buddleia davidii*, or of *B. fallowiana*, which last until autumn, contrast pleasantly with the poker flowers.

CULTIVATION Plant in autumn or spring in any well-drained soil, in full sun. Do not cut back the foliage until spring, as frost can damage the crowns and halt flowering for a year. Propagate by division in late spring, or sow seed in spring in a greenhouse or cold frame.

Kniphofia galpinii

RED-HOT POKER, TORCH LILY

Height 2ft
Planting distance 1-1½ft
Best September-October

A neater plant than *Kniphofia caulescens*, this red-hot poker bears flowers of a colour midway between orange and apricot in late autumn. It also has tidier leaves than its relative. One of the forms of *K. galpinii*, named 'Underway', grows much taller and more vigorously than its parent and has the attraction of long, conspicuous stamens protruding from its narrow, tubular flowers. For a cooler effect, the hybrid (cont on page 318)

ANYONE FORTUNATE enough to own a mellow brick wall with a strategically placed arch should certainly dress it as richly as this. The rest of us who don't might still make a creditable attempt upon a tall fence and a pergola. Either way, it is a worthwhile planting that carries summer deep into the shortening days of autumn and provides a focal point in the garden during most of the rest of the year.

Central to the theme are two vigorous climbing 'Pink Perpétue' roses, scrambling up on either side of the arch and still putting forth their two-tone pink double flowers in early October. Growing through and uniting the two roses is the spring-flowering *Clematis montana* 'Tetrarose', whose dark green leaves emphasise the strikingly brilliant orange-yellow spikes of *Kniphofia galpinii* and the golden-eyed, mauve Michaelmas daisies *Aster novae-angliae* 'Barr's Pink'.

Also attuned to the imperial note are the purple leaves of *Ajuga reptans* 'Atropurpurea', those of the purple sage, *Salvia officinalis* 'Purpurascens', and the purplish-pink flowers of *Origanum laevigatum*. In

IN SPRING the flowers of *Clematis montana* burst through the climbing *Rosa* 'Pink Perpétue' to overhang the border flowers and foliage.

the wings awaiting their season are *Geranium macrorrhizum* with its lobed, aromatic leaves – from which is derived oil of geranium – a fading iris or two and the Old-fashioned pink 'Inchmery'.

An opulence of hue is carried over into spring. There are still plenty of purple leaves, now leaned over by the lilac-pink flowers of the clematis. The geranium responds with a blaze of magenta that carries through from May to July, and the purple flag, *Iris germanica*, justifies its name with a display of rich blue-purple and white. Plants yet to flower provide interesting leaf shapes and textures; the bright green, grass-like leaves of the kniphofia, for instance, and the neat,

faintly scented origanum foliage.

In early summer, the obliging 'Pink Perpétue' roses have their first flowering, richly glowing rose-pink among the slowly fading blossoms and handsome bronze foliage of the clematis. The pink, *Dianthus* 'Inchmery', provides a paler ground echo of the rose next to the small, violet flowers of the salvia and the deeper blue whorls of the ajuga. The geranium continues to knit the scheme together with its attractive leaves and a few flowers. 🌿

The last display of the year still includes a few roses, but the main blaze of colour is provided by the spikes of *Kniphofia galpinii* and the rosy-mauve of *Aster novae-angliae* 'Barr's Pink'.

IN SUMMER, 'Pink Perpétue' takes command over a flowering collection that includes origanum, ajuga, salvia and a tall group of *Iris germanica*.

Flower spikes of *Liriope muscari* enhance the glossy green foliage of a euphorbia, intermingled with a purple-leaved berberis.

Planted in a group of two dozen or so, the tall spikes of *Lobelia fulgens* will create a blaze of red at the back of a border.

The papery orange lanterns of *Physalis alkekengi franchetii* can be dried for indoor decoration.

(*Kniphofia galpinii* cont)
'Maid of Orleans' is about the same height as the species, and carries tall creamy-white spikes from July to September.

A good companion for *K. galpinii* is the stonecrop, *Sedum spectabile*, which has white-green leaves and flat, 3-5in wide, heads of tiny pink flowers with a mauve tinge borne in September and October. As a bridge from summer, you could plant lady's mantle (*Alchemilla mollis*) around the kniphofia. CULTIVATION As for *Kniphofia caulescens*, page 316.

Liriope muscari

LILY TURF

Height 1½ft
Planting distance 1-1½ft
Best September-November

The slow-growing clumps of grassy foliage look unspectacular all year until the conspicuous flower spikes, like outsize grape hyacinths, turn bright amethyst in autumn.

Mix with pink, blue or white flowers in autumn, possibly to liven up the evergreen foliage of *Sarcococca confusa* or *Viburnum tinus*. Or plant in drifts around shrubs like *Viburnum plicatum* 'Mariesii' that have flowered earlier in the year. The foliage of this liriope can be effective in January as a background for winter bulbs such as *Cyclamen coum*, or flanked by hellebores. CULTIVATION Plant in groups during spring in any well-drained soil in sun or partial shade. Propagate by division of overcrowded clumps in spring; plants may not flower well until the second year after splitting.

Lobelia fulgens

Height 2-3ft
Planting distance 1-1½ft
Best July-October

Although tender in the coldest parts of Britain, this is such a magnificent plant for moist soil situations that it is well worth a little extra care. Glossy, deep-bronze foliage begins to appear in late spring, and by mid-summer stately flower spikes have arisen from among the leaves. Long-lasting and start-lingly red, the flowers are highly dramatic against the dark background. Colour variations among the cultivars include the blood-red 'Dark Crusader' or the brighter 'Cherry Ripe'.

If associated with bog plants in full sun, the flowers of these tall lobelias will stand out as if illuminated. Alternatively, plant them in the shadow of larger bronze-leaved plants such as handsome *Acer palmatum* 'Dissectum Atropurpureum' or the big, bold, summer-flowering ornamental rhubarb *Rheum palmatum* 'Atrosanguineum'. CULTIVATION Plant in late spring in a permanently humus-rich moisture-retentive soil. Protect the roots with straw or bracken in cold areas. Lift the plants in late autumn and overwinter in a well-ventilated cold frame, giving extra protection during severe weather. Propagate by dividing clumps in spring, as growth starts.

Physalis alkekengi franchetii

CHINESE LANTERN

Height 2ft · *Planting distance* 2ft
Best September-November

The orange lanterns that give this plant its common name are papery seed pods, each containing a bright red berry. For the rest of the year, both foliage and off-white summer flowers are undistinguished.

This plant, with its erect stems hung with bright spotlights of orange, looks marvellous among rhododendrons or other dark evergreen shrubs. CULTIVATION Plant during spring

Physostegia virginiana 'Vivid' offers an appropriately bright display of neatly arranged pink blossoms.

Masses of rose-pink flowers swamp the heather-like foliage of *Polygonum vacciniifolium* in autumn.

IN WINTER, the polygonum becomes a mat of russet leaves.

The pinks, mauves and purples of asters are splendid companions for the bright yellow of *Rudbeckia fulgida*. Together they create a delightfully informal effect against the weathered brickwork of a wall.

in any well-drained soil, allowing plenty of space for the roots to run – but take care, the plant can become invasive. Propagate by division in spring, when the new shoots are emerging.

Physostegia virginiana

OBEDIENT PLANT

Height 1½-2½ft
Planting distance 1½ft
Best August-September

Bend a flower of this North American plant sideways, and it will stay in its new position – which is how the plant earned its reputation for obedience. Its flowering habits are equally obliging; the slender, pink, snapdragon-like blooms neatly arranged along the stem, flower for weeks in full sun. The best garden variety for the front of a traditional border is the compact, rich pink 'Vivid'; there are also white forms, like 'Alba'. This is a classic plant for the

traditional perennial border, but it can easily become swamped by more vigorous neighbours. Early asters, such as *Aster × frikartii* 'Mönch', nepetas or white-flowered phloxes would provide a pleasing backdrop.
CULTIVATION Plant in autumn or spring in any soil in full sun. It does not thrive on highly alkaline soils, especially those which dry out in summer.

Propagate by taking basal cuttings in spring, or by division in spring. Keep newly planted divisions well watered until the root systems are established.

Polygonum vacciniifolium

Height 3-6in
Planting distance 1½-2ft
Best August-October

It is hard to believe that so comely a plant is related to the coarse wild dock. Its thick,

contour-hugging mats of small, diamond-shaped leaves gradually turn from cool green to shades of rusty-red, and its beads of tiny shell-pink flowers crowd stiff upright stems from August to November.

On limy soils, *Polygonum vacciniifolium* is a good substitute for summer heathers. It makes a fine ground-cover plant for sunny banks or for the shady sides of stone walls. It can also be used for edging borders.
CULTIVATION Plant during autumn or spring in ordinary soil, in sun or partial shade. In

shade, flowering will be less prolific, and autumn leaf colour less pronounced. Propagate by division in early spring.

Rudbeckia fulgida

BLACK-EYED SUSAN

Height 2-3ft
Planting distance 1½ft
Best September-October

With her forceful personality, black-eyed Susan can become the centre of attraction in the autumn border. Bold, daisy-like

Dazzling white flowers like sparklers adorn the tall, mahogany-red stems of *Saxifraga fortunei* 'Wada'.

With its months-long display of soft flowers and fine-cut leaves, *Scabiosa caucasica* brings a touch of summer's pastel hues to cool the fires of autumn.

Schizostylis coccinea 'Major' has larger flowers and stronger stems than the less ebullient species.

Autumnal *Saxifraga fortunei* bears luminous red-tinged foliage.

(*Rudbeckia fulgida* cont) flowers, with narrow golden petals radiating from prominent central knobs of darkest brown-black, bloom for many weeks. They appear in such profusion that the rough-textured, dark green foliage beneath is almost concealed. 'Goldsturm' bears exceptionally large flowers.

Rudbeckia fulgida provides a bridge of colour between summer and autumn. Bright, fiery-berried shrubs such as *Pyracantha* 'Orange Glow' or bold *Cotoneaster lacteus* planted nearby will continue a strong display of colour into winter.

CULTIVATION Set young plants in reasonably fertile, moist soil in full sun or light shade in autumn or spring. Propagate by division or by seed in spring. Divide at least every second year to ensure strong, sturdy plants.

Saxifraga fortunei

SAXIFRAGE

Height 15in
Planting distance 1ft
Best October-November

Like sparklers in a firework display, the saxifrage's starfalls of glistening, pure white flowers, elegant on slim stems, introduce light into shady spots on darkening October days. The handsome leaves are an attraction between spring and autumn – rosettes of glossy green, or bronze in the case of the variety 'Wada' – becoming red-tinged in autumn.

A native of China and Japan, and almost a woodlander in its natural habitat, *Saxifraga fortunei* will combine effectively with small plants such as primulas, *Polygonum vacciniifolium* or spring gentians.

CULTIVATION Plant during mid-spring in moist but free-draining, lime-free soil with plenty of humus and in a cool, semi-shaded position. Propagate in spring just as growth starts by carefully dividing the plants. Plant in situ or pot up individual rosettes in humus-enriched, lime-free compost. Plant out in mid-autumn when the roots are established.

Scabiosa caucasica

Height 2-3ft
Planting distance 1½ft
Best June-November

The cultivars of this garden scabious are larger-flowered but just as delicate in colour and texture as their wild relatives of chalk and limestone grassland. They are easy to grow and flower nonstop for months.

The finest blue form is 'Clive Greaves', a glorious lavender-blue. There are several other cultivars including the magnificent white 'Mount Cook', introduced from New Zealand.

The long-stemmed flowers with their divided foliage would look well under shrub roses such as 'Golden Wings' or 'Buff Beauty'. In a mixed border, the filigree foliage of *Achillea* 'Moonshine' would blend well with the scabious, as would campanulas and aquilegias. It will also make a good successor to something like *Hemerocallis* 'Golden Chimes', and to earlier, shorter perennials such as *Geranium* × *magnificum*.

CULTIVATION Set young plants in any reasonably moist, fertile soil during spring. Although this scabious prefers a limy soil, it will flower without it. Propagate by dividing established clumps or from seed in spring.

Schizostylis coccinea

KAFFIR LILY

Height 2-3ft
Planting distance 1½-2ft
Best September-October

As its common name suggests, the elegant kaffir lily comes originally from South Africa. Its

A hint of winter to come is inherent in the frost-dusted, coppery-red flower heads of the clump-forming *Sedum spectabile* hybrid 'Autumn Joy'.

Vivid pink *Sedum* 'Autumn Joy' fronts a rich backdrop of dahlias and white *Cosmos bipinnatus*.

1½in cochineal-red, crocus-like flowers are carried on firm stems. Both blooms and sword-like leaves last well in indoor flower arrangements.

In a border, place schizostylis in front of a shrub of open habit that will provide vivid winter colour, such as the bright red-stemmed *Cornus alba* 'Sibirica'. A low-level foreground planting of some summer-flowering evergreen such as *Saxifraga × urbium* could be added. The more muted colours of some of the schizostylis cultivars, like 'Mrs Hegarty' (bright rose), 'Viscountess Byng' (pale pink), or 'Sunrise' (peach-pink), can also make ideal companions for tall, paler Michaelmas daisies.

CULTIVATION Plant in early spring in full sun and in well-drained, moisture-retentive soil with plenty of humus added. Mulch with compost or well-rotted manure in spring. Propagate by division – clumps should be divided at least every three years to prevent over-crowding and promote growth.

Sedum
'Autumn Joy'

STONECROP

Height 1-1½ft
Planting distance 1½ft
Best September-December

Flowers like huge pink broccoli heads in the autumn sunshine are a magnet for butterflies, especially small tortoiseshells. Fleshy, grey-green leaves make an attractive show from mid-spring, and even in winter this sedum provides interest when its dead flower heads are dusted with a sparkle of early frost.

Tradescantia 'Caerulea Plena' can make a sparkling filler between perennials that have faded.

(*Sedum* 'Autumn Joy' cont)
The drought-resistant foliage makes a good summer foil for shrubs and early perennials, but at flowering time it hogs the limelight while less dominant neighbours go into decline.
CULTIVATION Plant at some time during autumn or spring in any well-drained soil in full sun or partial shade. To increase stock, divide and replant in spring.

Tradescantia × andersoniana

SPIDERWORT

Height 2ft · *Planting distance* 1½ft
Best June-October

Small, three-petalled flowers set in a mass of rush-like leaves glow like gemstones and carry on blooming for months. Cultivars of merit include 'Osprey', white with a central dash of blue; sapphire-like 'Isis'; light blue 'Caerulea Plena'; and the

Glossy, deep green leaves accentuate the unusual blooms of *Tricyrtis formosana* – each one winged like an insect in flight atop the slim stems.

amethyst 'Purewell Giant'.
The foliage is inclined to be unruly, so place the plant between shrubs that have winter and spring interest like *Kalmia latifolia* (in lime-free soil) or *Mahonia japonica*.
CULTIVATION Plant during autumn or spring in moist, fertile soil in a sunny site or partial shade. Propagate by division in autumn or spring.

Tricyrtis formosana

TOAD LILY

Height 2-3ft
Planting distance 3ft
Best September-October

Even though this is quite a tall plant, it is all the better for being placed near the front of the bed so that the intriguing flowers

can be examined at close range. They open in sprays on firm, erect stems, their outcurved petals revealing splashes of lilac on white, and dark stamens.
As a late-flowering plant *Tricyrtis formosana* is best used in the border where other plants have finished – for example hemerocallis or monarda, among many. Plant with gold-leaved shrubs like *Philadelphus coronarius* 'Aureus', so that the subtle beauty of the lily will not be lost and interest is carried through to winter and spring.
CULTIVATION Plant during spring in full sun – or in partial shade in drier areas – in ordinary garden soil that stays moist. Annual mulching and feeding in spring will ensure clumps can be left for years without deteriorating. Propagate by division as the new growth starts in spring.

Autumn *ALPINES*

WHILE LARGER plants, such as trees and shrubs, are cooperating in producing a harmonious composition of colour they are joined on a miniature scale by equally spectacular changes in deciduous alpine foliage. At the same time, some of the most sumptuous of all alpine flowers, the Asiatic gentians, make their presence dramatically felt in a startlingly strong statement of blues.

Gentiana farreri

Height 4-5in
Planting distance 9in
Best September

A coolly elegant flower, this gentian bears the name of the English plant collector and gardener Reginald Farrer, who brought it back from the mountains of China in the early 1900s. The petals are the blue of a clear morning sky and curve out from a white throat. Each slender stem – up to 50 can rise from the plant's central tuft of foliage – carries a single bloom.
To emphasise such colour and delicacy, choose background plants with dark, rich tones such as *Oenothera glaber* with its deep bronze leaves and golden, late summer flowers.
CULTIVATION Plant from March to April in sun or dappled shade with humus-rich, free-draining soil low in lime. Propagate by cuttings in May and June, using the current season's growth.

Each deep, upturned flower of *Gentiana farreri* is striped with green and creamy white.

The display of royal-blue trumpets by *Gentiana sino-ornata* lasts well into October.

Gentiana sino-ornata

Height 6in
Planting distance 9-12in
Best September-October

On the mountains of Tibet, this gentian reaches its full glory when most other flowers have gone to seed. And thus too it does in the gardens of Britain. During September, crowds of royal-blue trumpets, over 2in long and their throats (cont page 324)

BRIDGING THE SEASONS
IN AN
Acid soil

HERE IS A WAY to use autumn's palette to its uttermost in a garden from which lime is absent. The leaves – madder, scarlet, hectic red – are those of the lovely deciduous Mollis azalea *Rhododendron* 'Lemonora'. Before it, mirroring the lustre of the autumnal skies, is a sweep of *Gentiana sino-ornata*, whose brilliant blue flowers are marked with stripes of a deeper blue and of greenish-yellow. Generally considered the best of autumn species, this Chinese gentian flowers from September to November; though it thrives only on moistish, acid soils, in that situation it is very easy to grow. Massed, it has a strength of colour that is quite remarkable to see.

By late winter, all that remain of the gentians are withered stems and leaves about the twiggy azalea. Their place has been taken by clumps of snowdrops, *Galanthus nivalis* 'Viridapicis', a delightful variety with green spots on the inner and outer petals.

The group greets the returning sun in a singularly apt manner. In early May, the azalea puts on its show of compact, funnel-shaped flowers in apricot-yellow flushed with pink. Beside them, among the fresh green of new gentian leaves, is a good broad scattering of *Erythronium revolutum*, more widely known as the American trout lily from its mottled leaves and petals. This variety is 'White Beauty', whose nodding, gold-centred flowers have six petals, pointed and turned back so that each resembles a Turk's cap. Leave them undisturbed in moistish soil and they will reappear year after year to make a joyous and jaunty array with the warm colouring of the azalea. ❧

Rhododendron 'Lemonora' and fathomless blue *Gentiana sino-ornata* glow like antique stained glass.

IN SUMMER the pink-tinged apricot hue of 'Lemonora' is flattered by the ivory and gold of *Erythronium revolutum*.

EVEN IN WINTER the reaching branches of 'Lemonora' make a strong background for a gathering of *Galanthus nivalis* 'Viridapicis'.

The flowers of *Sisyrinchium californicum* reward the gardener with colour from June to October.

The showy *Zauschneria californica* 'Glasnevin' has rich leaves and flowers of a deeper scarlet than the species.

Even after the floral energy of *Silene schafta* has flagged, its spreading tuft of green foliage retains its colour until well into winter.

(*Gentiana sino-ornata* cont) striped with green, stand on mats of fine, grassy foliage. In reasonable weather the blooms can last for more than two weeks. And even as they fade, a second generation of flowers, fewer in number perhaps, but equal to the first in beauty, appears and extends the display well into October.

Out of flower the plants are not unattractive, but some winter-flowering crocuses planted among them will give some colour as the leaves and stems die away to resting buds. CULTIVATION Plant from March to April in moist but well-drained, lime-free soil, laced with leaf mould. Select an open place with midday shade if possible. Propagate by division in early spring.

Silene schafta

CAMPION

Height 6in
Planting distance 1ft
Best July-October

A tuft of hairy, spear-shaped leaves throws up sprays of rose to magenta-pink flowers like those of its cousins, the wild campions. For colourful weeks, as summer passes and autumn sets in, the display never falters. Spent blooms are replaced with a vigour more usually found in a bedding annual.

Equally at home in the rock garden or border, the long-lasting cheer of colour can be intensified by setting the plant against an all-season silver foliage plant, such as *Euryops*

acraeus which has golden daisy flowers in late spring.
CULTIVATION Plant in autumn or spring in any reasonably fertile soil and situation, including shade, but avoid moist patches. It grows easily from self-produced seed, which is best sown in spring.

Sisyrinchium californicum
(syn *S. brachypus*)

Height 6in
Planting distance 6-8in
Best August-October

Though the bright yellow, six-petalled flowers are never profuse there are always some present – over a rewardingly long autumn period. The plant is a little sturdier than *Sisyrinchium angustifolium*, and although its flowering period is later (and longer), there is a time when the rich blue of the one and the gold

Sisyrinchium angustifolium bears a succession of delicate, starlike blooms from June to September.

of the other can coincide in a striking partnership.

For another bold colour scheme in autumn, grow this cultivar through the purple-leaved *Ajuga reptans* – which will go on to provide all-season foliage and spring flowers.
CULTIVATION Plant in autumn or spring in any soil in sun or light shade. Propagate from seed or by root division in early spring.

Zauschneria californica

Height 1ft
Planting distance 1½-2ft
Best September-October

Like many plants from America's Golden State, this native Californian is only fully satisfied in a warm, dry position, with little risk of hard frosts. It is a spreading, bushy plant with grey-green foliage and stems that set off to perfection the orange-scarlet autumn flowers.

Plant dwarf narcissi around it, such as *Narcissus* 'Tete-a-Tete' or *N.* 'Liberty Bells' to fill the space during spring.
CULTIVATION Plant during April-May in ordinary soil in full sun – against a south-facing wall would be ideal. Protect from hard frosts and waterlogging, if necessary during winter, by covering with glass. Take cuttings from small basal shoots in early June.

Autumn
BULBS, CORMS AND TUBERS

BULBS ARE almost universally thought of as being heralds of spring. This is to restrict their use, because some of the most fascinating flower in autumn. The true autumn crocuses, for example, are poorly represented in our gardens, as are the strikingly iridescent nerines. Bulbs present us with countless opportunities for blurring the floral boundaries between the seasons, and cyclamen and crocuses, well chosen, can eliminate them altogether.

Long before the leaves appear, the pink trumpets of *Amaryllis belladonna* sound their fanfare.

Like swan's-down floating on a dark lake, *Colchicum speciosum* 'Album', that pale jewel of autumn, lights up a shady, half-forgotten dell.

Amaryllis belladonna

CAPE BELLADONNA LILY

Height 2-2½ft
Planting distance 1½-2ft
Best September-October

The Cape belladonna lily adds an exotic highlight to any garden. Purple-tinted, rod-like stems rise naked from the bare soil, crowned with up to six or more magnificent trumpet blooms. Long, bright green, strap-shaped leaves develop after the flowers have faded, and last until the following summer.

Soften the starkness of the flowering stems by a foreground planting of low, shrubby plants, such as the winter-flowering *Erica carnea*, which will also contrast well with the bulbs' later foliage.

CULTIVATION Plant during spring in free-draining soil in full sun, preferably against a south or west-facing wall or fence. Propagate by lifting and redistributing the bulbs when they become crowded. Apply an occasional liquid feed in spring. Cover with a cloche or with straw in severe winter weather.

Colchicum agrippinum

Flower height 4-6in
Planting distance 6in
Best September-October

There are few chequered colchicums as fine as this, with its neat, chalice-like flowers tinted a delicate rosy-pink and patterned with deep lilac-purple. It is one of the smaller-flowered species, with blooms on the ends of sturdy, leafless white stems. Pointed, semi-prostrate leaves appear later in the year.

Spread colchicum bulbs beneath low-growing, carpeting plants such as *Primula* 'Wanda' or *Viola odorata*. They

A delicate purple-pink chequered pattern graces the chalice-like blooms of *Colchicum agrippinum*.

will give a nice background to the flowers and provide winter interest, while their flowers will complement the colchicum's shiny leaves in spring.

CULTIVATION Plant in late summer in any well-drained soil in sun or partial shade. No propagation is necessary as the bulbs rapidly increase naturally, but lift and divide them when they become crowded.

Colchicum speciosum

Height 9in
Planting distance 8-12in
Best September-October

A generous planting of colchicums will create a gem-like effect among the fallen leaves of early autumn, and will sparkle in shady areas beneath dark evergreen shrubs. *Colchicum speciosum* is particularly robust, and ranges in colour from rosy-lilac to deep reddish-purple. There is also a striking white form called 'Album'.

You can create a dazzling

IN SUMMER, the bright *Colchicum speciosum* leaves thrust through the soft rose-pink flowers of *Geranium macrorrhizum* 'Ingwersen's Variety'.

patchwork of colour by combining *C. speciosum* with a mixed variety of hybrid colchicums such as 'Autumn Queen' (rose-lilac); 'Waterlily' (large, double, rose-lilac flowers); 'The Giant' (deep rose-lilac goblets with gleaming white centres); 'Rosy

Colchicum speciosum 'Waterlily' gained its name from the majestic dimensions of its flowers.

'The Giant' is one of the many *Colchicum speciosum* hybrids.

(*Colchicum speciosum* cont)
Dawn' (bold rose-pink); or 'Conquest' (chequered purple-pink). Plant them near rhododendrons or evergreen azaleas, or let them push through evergreen periwinkles, *Vinca major* and *V. minor*, whose flowers will relieve the bulkiness of the colchicums' springtime leaves, which appear after the flowers are finished.

CULTIVATION Plant in late summer in well-drained soil in sun or partial shade. The bulbs increase naturally but should be lifted and divided when they become crowded.

Crocus kotschyanus
(syn *C. zonatus*)

Height 3-4in
Planting distance 2-3in
Best September-October

The goblet-shaped flowers are at their best set in fairly short grass – a last mowing in mid-August will avoid damage to the blooms. This is one of the earliest autumn crocuses to flower,

Crocus kotschyanus from Lebanon can be pot grown to bring colour to the patio in autumn.

The wide-spreading branches of *Prunus subhirtella* 'Autumnalis' (autumn cherry) will provide a display of white blossoms in winter, linking the colourful drifts of colchicums and autumn crocuses around its base with spring.

usually in September but sometimes in late August. It is also one of the easiest to naturalise, forming spreading colonies of neat, pale rosy-lilac blooms with gold throats.

Groups of *Crocus kotschyanus* can look effective in containers or in bare earth among shrubs, although they can collapse in heavy rain or wind. Mix plantings with later-flowering crocuses and colchicums for continuity until spring.

CULTIVATION Plant in late summer in an open position in ordinary soil. Natural propagation is by cormlets and seed. If flowering is poor, redistribute corms after flowering.

Crocus medius

Height 4-5in
Planting distance 2-3in
Best October-November

Inject cheerful spotlights of colour in the late autumn garden by planting the large-flowered *Crocus medius* in small, bold groups. Its deep lilac flowers, with veins of deep purple towards the base, are shaped like goblets and appear long before the leaves. A pale lavender species for similar conditions is *C. goulimyi*.

Small colonies of *C. medius* should stand alone for best

The flowers of the alpine *Crocus medius* are lightly scented.

effect, with a nearby planting of the robust snowdrop *Galanthus elwesii* to follow on in winter. *C. goulimyi* can grow through an evergreen carpeting plant such

Distinctively marked foliage makes *Cyclamen cilicium* attractive even after the flowers have faded.

Cyclamen hederifolium is long-lived, and regularly produces flowers from old tubers.

Cyclamen cilicium

Height 3-4in
Planting distance 6in
Best October-November

Small and deliciously fragrant, this cyclamen comes originally from the hill forests of southern Turkey, but in cultivation it tolerates full sun and is very much at home in a rock or scree garden. However, it may be too tender for some northern or eastern parts of Britain. Grow it on its own, surrounded perhaps by clean rock chippings so that its delicate pale pink flowers on their short, wiry stems and the handsome, heart-shaped leaves which follow can be fully appreciated to best advantage.
CULTIVATION Plant pot-grown young plants during spring in well-drained soil in a sunny sheltered position. Apply bone meal for a spring tonic. Propagate from freshly gathered seed sown immediately in seed compost in a cold frame.

Cyclamen hederifolium
(syn *C. neapolitanum*)

Height 4-6in
Planting distance 8-10in
Best September-October

Cyclamen hederifolium is a wonderfully versatile plant. Its rose-pink flowers, tipped with a carmine 'nose', appear in profusion for many weeks from late August to late October, and its dark green, marbled leaves, with silver markings above and red below, provide attractive ground cover for at least three seasons of the year. It is also one of the hardiest cyclamen species and one of the most commonly available. It has a pure white form, 'Album'.

Plant the cyclamen beneath small-leaved deciduous trees and shrubs whose leaf-fall will not obliterate the autumnal flowers. Alternatively, use it as a rock-garden plant and set it against grey-white limestone.
CULTIVATION As for *C. cilicium*.

---

as *Acaena microphylla*, with its bright red burrs in summer.
CULTIVATION Plant in well-drained soil in late summer, in full sun beneath a wall or in a rock garden. Apply bone meal in early spring. The crocus reproduces freely. Redistribute overcrowded corms.

Crocus speciosus

Height 5-7in
Planting distance 3in
Best September-October

The most frequently grown autumn crocus colonises readily to provide drifts of slender blooms, bare of leaves. Mix a number of varieties together to produce almost continuous carpets of lavender, blue, purple and white or better, to clothe bare earth beneath established shrubs. Add the later-flowering, but similar, *Crocus pulchellus* to extend the show until late October or early November.

The vivid leaf-fall of shrubs such as *Rhus typhina* 'Laciniata' or *Fothergilla major* will cover the fading crocus blooms with a tapestry of colour. A ribbon of crocuses can brighten the base of an evergreen hedge of *Ligustrum ovalifolium* or *Prunus laurocerasus*.
CULTIVATION Plant during late

Crocus speciosus is one of the easiest of autumn crocuses to grow.

summer in well-drained soil. The crocus reproduces freely from both cormlets and seed. Redistribute corms every three or four years if overcrowded.

BRIDGING THE SEASONS
WITH
Cyclamen

WHETHER YOUR 'woodland glade' is a few yards of ground in front of two or three trees, or a true glade, by summer's end it could be starting to look a little weary. But this may easily be forestalled by providing a Mediterranean uplift of *Cyclamen hederifolium* – sprightly pale pink to mauve, mingled with the brilliant white form 'Album'. In this case, from late August on, they illuminate a fading surround of *Senecio* 'Sunshine' (syn *S. greyi*) with its downy-topped leaves, and the broad, veined foliage of *Lunaria annua* – honesty. The link is a wandering, pale green branch of *Catalpa bignonioides*, the Indian bean tree, whose leaves pungently reek when crushed.

By midwinter, the senecio has only leaves to offer, but these are always attractive, grey-green above and white felt beneath. Next on the scene is the cyclamen, *C. coum*, whose pink, carmine and white flowers, like tiny ship's propellers, enliven the dark season through to early spring. They are perfectly set off by the silver-patterned leaves and by the mature, darker green foliage of *C. hederifolium*.

A few weeks' pause, to mid-spring, and the twisted, richly scented pink petals of *C. repandum* begin to appear among its silver and red leaves, highlighting the emerging young growth of the catalpa and the rest. But the real crescendo of this succession is saved for high summer, for July, when the strongly scented carmine flowers of *C. purpurascens* (syn *C. europaeum*) come forth to joyously compete with the young green pods of the honesty and the grey leaves of the senecio. The latter's buds have been sheared in early summer to maintain a pink and grey colour scheme. ❦

Trooping through the woodland's undergrowth is the brightly caparisoned, autumn-flowering *Cyclamen hederifolium*, resplendent in mauve and pink, while the form 'Album' wears sparkling white.

IN WINTER the genus is represented by *Cyclamen coum*, with its colourful propellers and silver-marked leaves. Suitable back-up is provided by the darker foliage of *C. hederifolium*.

IN SUMMER the silver and grey leaves of *Senecio* 'Sunshine' and the foxglove blooms of an Indian bean tree frame the fragrant, carmine flowers of *Cyclamen purpurascens*.

Dahlia

One of the chief delights of the vast range of dahlia cultivars is the dazzling choice they have to offer in the way of flower shape, size and colour. There are the tightly packed, perfectly formed petals of ball and pompon dahlias; the multi-spiked flower heads of the small, medium and giant cactus cultivars; the simple single-flowered forms; or the collerette dahlias with their inner ring of contrasting petals, which have a delightful neatness and grace. Other cultivars have blooms shaped like anemones, water lilies and peonies. Whatever their particular form, the dahlias' boldness of bloom and long season of flowering extend the summer season deep into autumn.

EXHIBITING AND CUTTING

Sturdy, mid to dark green foliage adds depth and body to planting schemes, and the flowers themselves can make dominant focal points in gardens big or small. Dahlias are easy to grow; even the giant flower heads grown for exhibition are no more than a matter of regular disbudding and feeding, while no effort at all is required to achieve a rewarding border display. Dahlias make excellent cut flowers – and have earned their 'cut and come again' reputation because of the obliging readiness and vigour with which new blooms appear.

Dahlias need careful placing in the mixed border, as their flamboyant presence can easily overwhelm more modest neighbours. They are at their best grouped together, and interspersed between shrubs that will take centre stage in winter and spring when the dahlia patch is bare. *Chimonanthus praecox* would benefit from the dahlia colour in autumn, and produce sweet-smelling flowers in winter; *Cornus alba* 'Variegata' has attractive cream and green leaves in summer, and eyecatching bare red winter stems. The berries of *Cotoneaster lacteus* or, against a wall, *Pyracantha* 'Fireglow' would continue a vibrant display into winter. In the foreground you could plant an evergreen edging of box (*Buxus*) enlivened by a succession of early spring snowdrops (*Galanthus nivalis*).

CULTIVATION

Plant tubers in mid-spring, covering them with 3-4in of soil, and a layer of straw to protect against frost. Tubers that have already sprouted should be planted in late spring when all danger of frost has passed. The situation should be open and sunny, in any well-drained soil enriched with moisture-retaining peat or well-rotted compost. Add general fertiliser or bone meal. Insert stakes at planting time, and secure the stems to them as the plants grow. Keep the dahlias well watered, especially in light soil, and deadhead regularly.

After the first significant frost, lift the tubers carefully and allow them to dry naturally, then lightly brush off the soil and store over winter in a cool, frost-free, dry place. Dust any raw, exposed surface with flowers of sulphur to guard against disease. Propagate by

The ruby-red dahlias seen above are anemone-flowered 'Comet'. The purple-black foliage of *Ricinus communis* 'Cambodgensis' provides dramatically dark contrast, while contributing uplift behind it is lordly *Kniphofia* 'Royal Standard'.

In a mixed border, 'Comet' breaks up a pink theme consisting of antirrhinums and *Lavatera trimestris* 'Loveliness' in front, and 'Chasamay' dahlias behind.

carefully dividing the tubers – ensuring that each has an eye – and replanting, or by cuttings of 3-4in shoots in spring. Pot them and place them in a greenhouse. After hardening off, plant out when fear of severe night frost has passed, usually in May or early June.

'Salmon Keene'
Large semi-cactus equally
good for garden display,
cutting and exhibition.
Height 4½ft.

'Alva's Doris'
Particularly free-flowering
small cactus; some disbudding
needed to encourage long stems.
Height 4ft.

'Mariner's Light'
Prolific small semi-cactus
of luminous colouring.
Height 4ft.

'David Howard'
Compact, bushy miniature
decorative with bronzed foliage.
Height 3½ft.

'Daddy's Choice'
Small semi-cactus with
ragged-tipped petals.
Height 4ft.

Bright splashes of autumn colour

Popularly known as 'cut-and-come-again' flowers, dahlias bloom profusely, adding depth and strong paintbox colours to the late summer and autumn garden. These varieties are chosen for their value as garden plants rather than for exhibition. All are free-flowering, easy to manage and excellent as cut flowers.

Photographed at the Royal Horticultural Society's Gardens, Wisley, Surrey, in September.

'Biddenham Fairy'
Very free-flowering miniature decorative; needs some disbudding. Height 3½ft.

'Mistill Delight'
Miniature decorative with flowers that stand well above the foliage. Height 4½ft.

'Bishop of Llandaff'
Deep bronze, dissected foliage is attractive in its own right. Height 3½ft.

'Lady Kerkrade'
Very free-flowering small cactus. Height 3½ft.

'Red Alert'
Miniature ball with continuous display of long-stemmed blooms. Height 3½ft.

'Pearl of Heemstede'
Water-lily blooms rise high above the foliage. Height 3½ft.

'Clair de Lune'
Graceful, free-flowering collerette that likes shade from early morning sun. Height 3½ft.

Pendent, trumpet-like flowers bend the delicate wands, slender as grass, of *Dierama pulcherrimum*.

A group of autumn snowdrops beside a garden wall glistens against a background of fallen leaves and a *Cotoneaster microphyllus*.

Looking a little like exotic birds in flight, the delicate flowers of *Gladiolus callianthus* stand tall in a sunny border.

A mat of *Silene schafta* makes an unobtrusive companion for the lordly *Leucojum autumnale*.

Dierama pulcherrimum

ANGEL'S FISHING ROD

Height 4-6ft
Planting distance 1½-2ft
Best September

The common name angel's fishing rod beautifully describes the graceful South African dierama. If possible, grow it beside a pond where its slender leaves and tall arching stems, hung with bell-shaped flowers, will be reflected in the water. Named varieties offer a colour range from white through to deep wine-red and purple.

Although the leaves die back in winter, dieramas contribute bold forms to the garden from early summer to late autumn, and grown in groups can make a strong focal point. The effect is muted if it is mixed with other plants of similar size. *Primula pulverulenta* would introduce welcome spring colour when the dierama has little to show.

CULTIVATION Plant pot-grown specimens in spring or summer in rich, moist, free-draining soil in a sunny site. Water well until established. Add bone meal in spring and cut to ground level in autumn when the leaves have faded. Leave the plants undisturbed, as the corms dislike being moved. Propagate from seed sown in spring under glass.

Galanthus nivalis reginae-olgae

AUTUMN SNOWDROP

Height 4-6in
Planting distance 3-4in
Best October-November

The pristine beauty of this snowdrop from the lands around the Adriatic Sea adds an unusual and welcome touch to the autumn garden. It looks almost the same as its cousin, *Galanthus nivalis*, that appears in late winter, with its drooping flowers as white as the snow that gives it its common name. But *G. n. reginae-olgae* blooms before the slender leaves develop, lending the flowers a solitary elegance and emphasis.

Set the autumn snowdrop in small groups in a rock garden, at the base of a wall or pushing through small-leaved creeping plants such as the common wild thyme *Thymus serpyllum*.

CULTIVATION Plant bulbs in full leaf in early spring in very free-draining soil in a warm, open situation. Propagate by dividing overcrowded clumps of bulbs when dormant in summer. Keep the bulbs from drying out and replant at the same depth as before.

Gladiolus callianthus

(syn *Acidanthera bicolor murielae*)

Height 3ft
Planting distance 9in
Best September-October

The open, white blooms with their deep maroon throats bring a touch of fragile simplicity to the garden. Tall stems carry ten or more flowers, set among narrow blade-like leaves. This gladiolus needs special care in the British climate, but the refreshing autumn display is well worth the trouble.

Plant the corms in groups of up to ten for the best effect, towards the back of a sunny border, with a low-growing evergreen such as summer-flowering rock rose, *Helianthemum nummularium*, or candytuft, *Iberis sempervirens*, in front.

CULTIVATION Plant corms in soil-based potting compost in a cold frame. In spring, plant in a sunny position. Lift corms before autumn frosts and store in a dry, frost-free place until replanting in early May.

Leucojum autumnale

AUTUMN SNOWFLAKE

Height 6-8in
Planting distance 3in
Best September

Because of its delicate form, the autumn snowflake needs to be savoured alone, planted in small groups to create pools of light. Its flowers, which hang like

The butter-yellow flowers
of *Sternbergia lutea* nestle on
a cushion of tightly packed leaves.

A bright yellow eye and the palest of pale cream
petals give the flowers of *Zephyranthes candida* a
starry quality in a firmament of grassy leaves.

Autumn comes to life when the flowers of *Nerine bowdenii* explode like
cascading rockets in a border of mixed evergreens.

miniature lampshades, are reminiscent of the snowdrop, but the white petals are slightly flushed with pink at the base.

Plant leucojums in groups in small pockets in the rock garden. Close companions might easily overwhelm this fragile plant, but a nearby group of *Iris unguicularis* could take centre stage in winter.

CULTIVATION Plant bulbs in late summer in a warm, sunny position with free-draining soil.

Dress with bone meal each spring. Propagate by dividing crowded clumps and replanting.

Nerine bowdenii

Height 1½ft
Planting distance 8-10in
Best October

A crowd of iridescent pink nerines will introduce a flamboyant, tropical flavour to the

autumn garden. Up to eight lily-like flowers, their crimped and waved petals curving back to expose long stamens, appear at the top of bare stalks before a mass of strap-shaped leaves develops at the base. 'Fenwick's Variety' is larger and more vigorous, and has flowers of a deeper pink than the species.

The nerine's exotic character and colour can clash with many temperate plants, but summer annuals such as Virginian stock (*Malcolmia maritima*) would disguise the nerine's rather untidy leaves. Nerines can make striking container plants too, but may need to be moved to a cool but frost-free and dry place in severe winters.

CULTIVATION Plant bulbs 6in deep in free-draining soil at the base of a south or west-facing fence or wall in spring. Nerines flower best when well established, and the bulbs should only be lifted, divided and redistributed if flower quality starts to decline, which generally happens about every four to five years.

Sternbergia lutea

Height 4-6in
Planting distance 4-6in
Best September-October

In full sunshine, the waxy yellow flowers of *Sternbergia lutea* open out like brilliant stars. Set against a profusion of narrow, deep green leaves, the effect is quite startling.

In the wild, sternbergia is a plant of dry Mediterranean scrubland, and a companion planting of aromatic shrubs from the same region, such as lavender (*Lavendula*) and rosemary (*Rosmarinus*), would provide a sympathetic backdrop and year-round interest.

CULTIVATION Plant during mid to late summer in free-draining soil in an open, sunny position. Apply a generous dressing of bone meal each spring. To propagate, divide overcrowded bulbs and replant immediately.

Zephyranthes candida

Height 6-8in
Planting distance 4-6in
Best September-October

The Latin name – *Zephyranthes* – of this slender, crocus-like plant from Argentina and Uruguay means 'from the west wind'. This species is the only zephyranthes hardy enough for British gardens in milder areas, where it will flourish in full sun.

Combine it with other sunloving bulbs such as *Nerine bowdenii* or the delicate autumn crocus, *Colchicum speciosum*, whose lavender-blue flowers will blend well with the pale cream of the zephyranthes. Plant winter-flowering bulbs such as *Iris histrioides* to follow on.

CULTIVATION Plant in spring in a warm and sunny position with free-draining soil, preferably at the base of a south or west-facing wall. Apply an occasional liquid feed during spring and autumn. Propagate by lifting and dividing clumps in spring.

THE *Climbing* GARDEN

At the cost of very little ground space, climbing plants introduce a large vertical dimension to the garden. They can mask ugly outbuildings, bring colour to trees or shrubs whose own seasons of glory are past, or transform and soften garden boundaries.

There are climbers for all aspects. On north and east-facing walls, or on solid fences that are not too densely shaded, some roses, including 'Golden Showers', 'New Dawn', 'Summer Wine' and 'Phyllis Bide', will perform well. Most honeysuckles (*Lonicera*) and many clematis – particularly *Clematis montana* – are also fairly hardy subjects. Between them, these three plant groups – roses, honeysuckles and clematis – will produce flowers from spring to autumn. In addition, ivies (*Hedera*) – the best climbers for camouflage – thrive in shady, cool areas with poor soil, and offer year-round mantles of rich foliage with a surprising variety of leaf designs. The hydrangea relative, *Pileostegia viburnoides*, with clouds of starry flowers that link summer and autumn, appreciates a certain amount of shade. The evergreen foliage is handsome throughout the year.

Reserve south and west-facing walls for tender species that need plenty of sun and for those which look better in sunlight. Although in many ways ideal for east and north walls, the fiery colours of Virginia creeper (*Parthenocissus quinquefolia*) are brighter in full sun. And in a sheltered position, attention could be diverted from its bare winter remains by the ferny, bronzed evergreen leaves and creamy, freckled bells of *Clematis cirrhosa*. The tropical charm of *Passiflora caerulea*, and later-flowering trumpet vines *Campsis radicans* or *C. × tagliabuana* 'Madame Galen', will bring spring and summer rewards to sheltered spots.

FOLLOW-ON FRAGRANCE

By a patio or frequently used doorway, plan a succession of fragrance as well as colour, rather than be overwhelmed by a jumble of scents all in one season. Roses such as 'Pink Perpétue', which will adapt to any aspect or, on a south or

Clematis 'Hagley Hybrid' scrambles through *Potentilla fruticosa* – a partnership of lasting value that will give colour from early summer to early autumn.

west-facing site 'Climbing Crimson Glory' could still be blooming in late autumn. When it's warm enough to venture outside in spring, you could be greeted by the vanilla scent of *Clematis armandii* or, a little later, the glossy-leaved, half-hardy *Holboellia coriacea*. *Lonicera caprifolium*, a June to July-flowering honeysuckle, could pave the way for any one of the later jasmines and roses. And a shock of old-fashioned sweet peas (*Lathyrus odoratus*) could be bedded at their feet for a grand finale in summer.

Fences can be much more than boundaries, and make useful supports for climbing plants. Solid fences can shelter tender climbers, although to a lesser extent than a warm brick wall. The flamboyant nasturtium, *Tropaeolum majus*, will do a rapid cover-up job over the ugliest of chain-link fences while you are waiting for more permanent climbers to get established. Combined with vigorous climbers such as *Celastrus orbiculatus* or *Parthenocissus quinquefolia*, the fence will become a 'fedge' with the appearance and function of a hedge but using up far less space.

SUPPORTING FEATURES

The seasonal succession of fragrance and colour can be applied to climbers on pergolas, trellises and arches. You may need to use a strong-growing plant such as *Wisteria floribunda* to clothe the horizontal parts of a structure, where the late spring flower tresses will droop elegantly from above. Shorter, large-flowered clematis hybrids, roses and sweet peas can be planted to cover the uprights. You don't need a great deal of space for such features – a simple arch could support a honeysuckle, rose and jasmine to give a flow of colour and scent from spring to autumn.

In a border where a tall shrub would be too space-consuming, climbers can be trained up a tripod or even a single stout pole. A pillar of dark, glossy ivy could introduce year-round contrast to more frivolous companions; a tripod of honeysuckles such as *Lonicera periclymenum* 'Belgica' and *L. caprifolium* would fill a bed with scent from April to July; a tree severed by gales could become a host for spring-flowering *Clematis alpina*, the later large-flowered clematis hybrids or *Hydrangea anomala petiolaris*, or in a sheltered spot, *Campsis × tagliabuana* 'Madame Galen'.

Particularly robust climbers such as rambler roses, *Clematis flammula* and *C. montana*, or the autumn-fruiting *Celastrus orbiculatus* can be encouraged to climb up one side of a wall and to cascade freely down the other side, their lower stems concealed by complementary shrubs.

One of the most effective all-season uses of climbers is to let them ramble through a host plant – a tree, a hedge, or to link two or three shrubs. Choose a plant that will flower simultaneously with the host for added impact in a particular season. Or extend the season by selecting one whose blossoming will precede or follow on from that of the host. Classic combinations include a large-flowered clematis hybrid running through a summer shrub rose; the rambling *Rosa* 'Alberic Barbier' or 'Phyllis Bide' could follow a fruit tree's spring blossom or brighten a dark holly (*Ilex*). Small-flowered *Clematis viticella* could make a trail through winter-flowering forsythia cultivars, or *Clematis* × *jackmanii* could combine with the handsome shrubby chestnut, *Aesculus parviflora*.

Wall shrubs like *Pyracantha* 'Fireglow' and *Cotoneaster horizontalis*, while not strictly climbers, play an important role in the all-season vertical garden – but take care that the colours do not clash. Trailing plants, such as *Lobelia erinus*, ivy-leaved pelargoniums, or the ever-ready *Corydalis lutea* are useful for filling in seasonal gaps, especially in walls and containers.

LINKING PLANTS

Ensure that any climbing plants you grow do not stand in isolation. Link them firmly with the rest of the garden by base plantings of shrubs and perennials such as all-season *Lavandula angustifolia*, santolina, *Caryopteris* × *clandonensis* or sage (*Salvia officinalis*) in sunny positions. Use large-leaved hostas, ferns such as *Asplenium scolopendrium*, or *Dryopteris* species, and spring-flowering skimmias in shade. Many climbers will, in any event, need to be covered at ground level by the foliage of neighbouring plants, or a low wall, for example, to prevent their roots becoming overheated, while their upper parts need sun for healthy flowers, fruits and foliage.

Be sure to match the vigour of the host tree or shrub with a suitable climbing partner. Often a post or tripod set near the host will share the weight and guide the climber in the right direction.

HOW DOES YOUR CLIMBER GROW?

❧ Climbers that twine take hold by curling stems, leaf stalks or tendrils around the host. They need wires, trellis, twigs or branches slender enough to catch hold of.

❧ Rambling plants have no clinging facility and trail long, slack stems. They need tying to any support and to be trained in the right direction.

❧ Most climbers that self-cling – like *Hydrangea anomala petiolaris* and ivies, for example, may initially need support or wiring, but from then on cling by tiny roots that embed themselves in the host. Virginia creeper, with its adhesive tendrils, is a very determined and robust self-clinger.

❧ Some very vigorous self-clingers can cause damage to buildings. If left untamed, they can force their way beneath roof tiles and prise them apart, their weight can bring down guttering, or their roots or tendrils weaken old brickwork. However, if brickwork is in good condition to start with, it will not suffer, and may even gain from the protection a climber can give.

❧ If a wall is likely to need maintenance work or painting at any time, train the climber against a wall-fixed trellis, which can be moved with the plant left intact.

A profusion of *Eccremocarpus scaber*, *Solanum jasminoides* and clematis, with delicate alstroemerias and pinks, transforms a small modern house for most of the year.

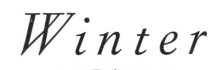

Winter

T HOUGH IT IS not necessary to take Lord Byron too literally when he speaks of 'the English winter, ending in July to recommence in August', there is no doubt that it has an identity problem. Sometimes, with a watery smile, it pretends to be spring and pushes up flowers weeks before their time. In others, howling like a wolf of the tundra, it sends blizzards to lay the garden flat. Then, just when escape is becoming mandatory, it produces a frosty day that sparkles like champagne.

Such lack of decision deters the average gardener. This is a pity, for there are many joys to find in the winter garden. There are gallant snowdrops and tough aconites; jasmine, witch hazel with its spidery blossoms, cyclamens, daphnes and a host of other winter-flowering plants. But really, this is a season that properly belongs to the shapes of twigs and branches, cleared of foliage and given substance by evergreens. Now bark can be appreciated – ghostly birches, brilliant dogwood, the extraordinary colour range of willows. Altogether, there is quite enough to see us through until spring.

The frozen assets of the winter garden – ivy leaves are crystallised into a fragile tracery.

Winter
SHRUBS

EVERGREEN shrubs provide much of the winter garden's vitality; it is their variety of greens, and the accents made by gold-leaved or variegated shrubs, that bring a sparkle to the darkest days of the year. Deciduous shrubs too make a valuable contribution at this time, for it is then that the strong and graceful shapes of their branches can be appreciated, unobscured by foliage. Upright and weeping shrubs provide contrast of line and structure and some offer even more – the bonus of brilliantly coloured stems. Most desirable of winter shrubs, however, must be those that produce blooms during this unlikely season, such as cornus and chimonanthus, hamamelis, sarcococca and jasmine.

Abeliophyllum distichum etches its delicate flowers and stems upon a pale winter sky.

Waxy blooms of *Chimonanthus praecox* sweetly perfume the crisp air of winter.

Cornus mas produces a golden sunburst in February; in this case it illuminates the evergreen foliage of *Elaeagnus pungens* 'Maculata'.

Abeliophyllum distichum

Height 4-6ft · *Spread* 4-6ft
Best January-February

The starry flowers that crowd along the stems have led to a popular description of this plant as 'white forsythia'. But the branches are more slender than those of true forsythia, the flowers are more delicate and, unlike forsythia, they have a sweet fragrance.

The sprays of purplish young winter stems, carrying their mass of white, pink-tinged blooms, stand out beautifully against bold backgrounds. The shrub would look equally distinguished before a brick wall, or against the dark green of a rhododendron or camellia. For lower-level springtime colour, add a group of pink and white lily-flowered tulips.
CULTIVATION Plant from late autumn to late winter in any well-drained soil and in a sunny, sheltered position. It does best trained up wires on a west or south-facing wall, a position which will encourage early flowering and counter any frost damage. Prune hard back after flowering. Propagate by semi-hardwood cuttings in summer.

Chimonanthus praecox

WINTERSWEET

Height 8-10ft · *Spread* 8-10ft
Best December

For centuries, *Chimonanthus praecox* has brought spicy fragrance and colour to the winter gardens of China and Japan. The straw-hued flowers, about an inch across, have waxy petals that curve claw-like over dark purple centres. They may appear on the young shoots at any time from November to March, but December is firm favourite for the best display.

It is a hard act to follow, and the plants chosen to do so should make a strong statement. Try daffodils for follow-on spring colour, then relieve the wintersweet's not altogether prepossessing summer dress of large, pointed leaves with the softer foliage and yellow flowers of *Clematis* 'Royalty'.
CULTIVATION Plant in spring or autumn in well-drained soil and in a warm, sheltered position. Trim back the longest shoots after flowering, and remove weak or overcrowded shoots. Propagate by layering.

Cornus mas

CORNELIAN CHERRY

Height 15ft · *Spread* 10ft
Best February-March

In late winter, the bushy, twiggy stems of the cornelian cherry are illuminated by clusters of golden-yellow flowers that appear on the leafless stems of the previous year's growth. The flowers are often followed by large, edible red berries. These look particularly well against the white-margined, ovate leaves of *Cornus mas*

Impervious even to sharp frost, the leathery leaves and red berries of *Cotoneaster lacteus* create a suitably festive picture in the garden from autumn until well into the other side of Christmas and the New Year.

A true winter partnership has been created here by combining *Daphne laureola* with the pale green, maroon-edged bells of *Helleborus foetidus* and the cream, pink-tinged flowers of *H. orientalis*.

'Variegata'; other forms are the golden-leaved 'Aurea' and 'Elegantissima', whose yellow-bordered foliage is sometimes tinged with pink.

This sturdy shrub may be given an additional role as support for a summer-flowering climber amongst its dark green leaves. You might, for instance, marry 'Variegata' to the clematis 'Perle d'Azur' or even more spectacularly to the flame-coloured creeper, *Tropaeolum speciosum*. A carpet of *Colchicum* 'Autumn Queen' would carry the display on until September, when the cornelian cherry's leaves turn to a spectacular reddish-purple before falling. CULTIVATION Plant in spring or autumn in any good garden soil, and in a sunny spot. Propagate by layering in late summer.

Cotoneaster lacteus

Height 10ft · *Spread* 10-12ft
Best November-March

The winter appeal of *Cotoneaster lacteus* lies in the bold contrast of the dark upper surfaces of the leaves and their silver-brushed undersides. It is a true bridging plant in that the bunches of red berries it produces in autumn last all the way through to winter – provided they are spared by birds.

In midsummer, too, it has much to offer in the clusters of creamy-white flowers. The rich purple *Clematis viticella* 'Royal Velours' could be trained through the cotoneaster as a link between summer and autumn; otherwise it provides its own seasonal continuity. The shrub is ideal for hedging. CULTIVATION Plant in sun or partial shade during spring or autumn in any fertile soil. Propagate by semi-hardwood cuttings in late summer or early autumn. Prune only when necessary to keep the shrub within bounds.

Daphne laureola

SPURGE LAUREL

Height 4ft · *Spread* 3-4ft
Best February-March

The little flower clusters are indeed like those of spurge and the dark green, shiny leaves like those of laurel. A native of British woodlands, it makes a useful and decorative shrub for a shady corner, for its handsome evergreen foliage puts on a perpetually cheerful show. This is further enhanced in spring by clusters of tubular, yellowish-green flowers. Though modest of hue, form and size, they release a sweet fragrance to the garden in the evenings. A compact, dwarf form, *Daphne laureola philippi*, grows to a height and spread of about 15in.

Grown beneath trees, spurge laurel becomes the heart of a strong plant combination. For its companions, try the evergreen Lenten rose, *Helleborus orientalis*, which bears flowers of various hues in spring, with the stately *Veratrum nigrum* beside it to make a show for summer. CULTIVATION Plant in spring or autumn in a shady, fairly moist spot. Full sun bleaches the leaves. Cut back any straggly growth; otherwise, no pruning is necessary. Propagate by taking semi-hardwood cuttings in late summer.

Daphne odora 'Aureomarginata' is tough enough to cope with quite severe but not prolonged frosts.

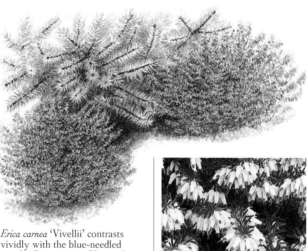

Erica carnea 'Vivellii' contrasts vividly with the blue-needled conifer *Picea pungens* 'Hoopsii'.

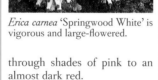

Erica carnea 'Springwood White' is vigorous and large-flowered.

Euonymus fortunei 'Emerald 'n' Gold' and a gold-leaved heather merge with pink and white *Erica carnea* for a glowing winter display.

Daphne odora
'Aureomarginata'

Height 3-5ft · *Spread* 3-5ft
Best February-April

The wonderful effect of the red-purple flowers against gold-rimmed, evergreen leaves makes this plant a handsome asset to any garden. The cut flowers are long lasting, and will fill the entire room with their fragrance. For the same reason it is a good idea to plant the daphne by a much-used path or door, where its perfume will cheer an even larger audience.

The long branches of older plants tend to sprawl, and a carpet of spring flowers such as the dapper evergreen violet, *Viola labradorica*, and starry *Tulipa kaufmanniana* hybrids could make a colourful halo about the shrub's low-growing foliage. In acid soils, the unusual pink-orange, bell-like

flowers of *Rhododendron* 'Fabia' behind the daphne would create a bridge of colour into summer. CULTIVATION Plant in spring in any well-drained soil in sun or in partial shade, with some shelter from strong, cold winds. Prune only to remove untidy branches. Propagate in summer by semi-hardwood cuttings.

Erica carnea

WINTER-FLOWERING HEATH

Height 6-12in · *Spread* 1-1½ft
Best November-April

One of the beauties of this heath is that, by a careful selection from the many cultivars with different flowering periods, you can have colour from November right through to April. 'Winter Beauty', which flowers in December, could be followed by the mid-season 'Vivellii' and the late-flowering 'Ruby Glow'. Colours range from white

through shades of pink to an almost dark red.

The leaves are usually dark green, but those of some cultivars are as rewarding as the flower display. 'Foxhollow', for instance, is bronze in winter, pink and red tinged in spring, and a lovely soft yellow-green in summer. The *Erica carnea* cultivars are, unlike many heaths, tolerant of lime.

Heaths look best when they are grown in groups. Try the bold combination of *E. c.* 'Foxhollow' and *E. c.* 'Springwood White' planting them around the silvery-blue dwarf conifer, *Picea pungens* 'Glauca Globosa'. For a warmer winter combination, you could add the deep

pink *E. c.* 'Myretoun Ruby' and the golden *Juniperus × media* 'Gold Coast' or 'Old Gold' instead. Either way, an underplanting of the purple and lilac *Crocus tommasinianus* will give a fine contrast in early spring. CULTIVATION Plant in spring or autumn in a sunny, open position, and in soil with added compost. Propagate by semi-hardwood cuttings in summer.

Erica × darleyensis

Height 1½ft · *Spread* 2ft
Best December-April

The hardiness of heaths is a gardening legend, and there can be few more uplifting sights in winter than the spectacle of this heath cheerfully flowering in the midst of ice and snow. A

The scented flowers of *Erica* × *darleyensis* 'Silberschmelze' provide a graceful backdrop for snowdrops.

hybrid between *Erica carnea* and *E. erigena*, it nicely combines the characteristics of its parents, and stays in bloom for months on end. It is also lime-tolerant, although it will not do well on shallow, chalky soils. There are a number of pink and white varieties of *E.* × *darleyensis*, and also a yellow-leaved form.

Make this heath a feature of the heather garden. Plant it with purple and pink callunas, which are at their best in late summer and autumn, and *E. carnea* to follow on. *E.* × *darleyensis* is too tall to permit bulbs to rise up and flower through its foliage, but such winter-flowering bulbs as snowdrops, aconites and *Iris reticulata* hybrids could be planted in artfully casual groups around the heath.

CULTIVATION Plant in spring or autumn in a sunny, open position, and in soil with added peat or compost. Propagate by taking semi-hardwood cuttings in late summer.

Frozen catkins of *Garrya elliptica* hang like icicles. Its frosted partner (left) is *Pseudotsuga menziesii*.

Garrya elliptica

SILK TASSEL BUSH

Height 12ft · *Spread* 12ft
Best January–February

The silvery-green tassels that drape the male *Garrya elliptica* in midwinter are remarkable for their length and grace – particularly on the variety 'James Roof', which has the longest catkins of all. Female forms produce shorter catkins followed by silky-haired fruits.

G. elliptica is a large shrub, with leathery, evergreen leaves, making it an excellent host for either *Clematis* × *jackmanii* or *C. viticella*. These are pruned back in early winter and so will not spoil the garrya's display with a tangle of leafless stems.

CULTIVATION Plant in a well-drained soil and in a site sheltered from searing east and north winds that may scorch the leaves and damage the catkins.

Shrub of surprises, *Hamamelis × intermedia* bears spidery flowers in winter (above) and fiery foliage hues in autumn (below).

A bonny fighter, *Hamamelis × intermedia* can withstand the worst that winter can throw at it. Here, a fine specimen produces its deceptively delicate blossoms along branches heavily draped with wind-driven snow.

Hamamelis mollis is valued for its sweetly scented winter flowers and golden autumn foliage.

(*Garrya elliptica* cont)
To keep the shrub to size, thin new growth in spring. Propagate by taking semi-hardwood cuttings in late summer.

Hamamelis × intermedia
'Jelena'

WITCH HAZEL

Height 8-10ft · *Spread* 8-10ft
Best December-March

'Jelena' is a hybrid of the two most popular species of witch hazel, *Hamamelis mollis* and *H. japonica* – and its coppery-yellow blooms would mix well in a companion planting with either or both of its parents. The hybrid has a particular oriental charm, with its long, ragged, twisted petals, like witch's fingers, emerging from the bare young winter stems. They have the austere delicacy of a Japanese flower painting, yet they are able to withstand the worst of the winter weather without flinching. In other seasons, too, this is a shrub that gives good value – especially when its large summer leaves flare into bronze and red in the autumn.

This witch hazel would show up well against the purple, white-dusted winter stems of *Salix irrorata*, while its spreading canopy would offer shelter to the shade-loving Lenten rose, *Helleborus orientalis*.

CULTIVATION Plant in spring or autumn, preferably in sun or light shade with acid soil, adding peat or leaf mould. Shallow, chalky soils are not suitable. To propagate, layer stems in early spring or late summer, though rooting may take up to two years.

Hamamelis mollis
'Pallida'

CHINESE WITCH HAZEL

Height 8-10ft · *Spread* 7-10ft
Best December-March

The darkest days of the year are lightened by this pretty witch hazel – one of the first of the winter-flowering shrubs to show its colours. The golden autumn leaves fall to reveal young branches covered with furry buds; eventually, these open into spidery, bright lemon flowers with a sweet fragrance. By early summer the new leaves, which are large and fresh green, much like those of the common hazel, are beginning to make their own rich contribution to the year-round garden.

The wide, open canopy of the witch hazel invites complementary planting beneath. *Scilla sibirica* 'Spring Beauty' and groups of *Helleborus orientalis* would provide a link with spring, and a low bushy evergreen such as *Sarcococca hookeriana digyna* provide contrast throughout the year.

CULTIVATION Plant in autumn or spring in well-drained, preferably slightly acid soil enriched with peat or leaf mould; shallow chalky soils are not suitable. No pruning is necessary. Propagate by layering in early spring or late summer.

O F ALL THE WINTER-FLOWERING shrubs, one of the most rewarding is the Chinese witch hazel, *Hamamelis mollis*. From bare twigs on the darkest days, it puts forth its spiky-petalled flowers, which seem impervious to frost and as happy in a smoky town as in a country garden. In either place, they will serenely persist from December to March. Moreover, the flower-laden twigs last well indoors, filling the room with fragrance and cheering it with their yellow glow.

In the garden, the witch hazel's upward-thrusting branches make it particularly suited to underplanting, in this case with the heather *Erica carnea* 'Springwood White', whose massed flowers emerge shortly after the witch hazel's. The best of the white cultivars of *E. carnea*, its branches are packed with urn-shaped flowers, and the fine-leaved foliage makes attractive and labour-saving ground cover throughout the year. The snowy carpet continues well into spring, when the witch hazel's soft green, felted foliage appears.

Spring is the time to plant some annual sweet peas (*Lathyrus odoratus*) beneath the witch hazel. Choose cultivars that will make their presence felt, like the deep scarlet, weather-resistant 'Red Arrow' or the sweetly scented, pristine 'White Leamington'. Even better, try one of the old-fashioned mixtures like 'Painted Lady', 'Butterfly Hybrids' and 'Antique Fantasy

A guarantee of returning spring is inherent in the spiky yellow winter flowers of *Hamamelis mollis* 'Pallida' above a carpet of white heather.

Mixed'. All appear in a wide colour range, are headily fragrant and good for cutting. If the soil is well manured, the sweet peas will grow to 7ft or more, and as summer advances, they will climb right up through the branches of the witch hazel and cascade down its sides. Remember to deadhead the faded sweet pea blooms regularly to

ensure a continuing display, and as soon as flowering is over, take out the plants, whose bare stems will be an unsightly tangle.

Autumn reveals that the witch hazel has one last shot left in its locker. Before the leaves fall they turn a rich gold. And the heather is already in bud, as a token of the display to come. ❧

IN SUMMER, the old-fashioned sweet pea 'Painted Lady' climbs right up through the witch hazel's branches.

THE AUTUMN colour of *H. mollis* rivals that of its winter flowering.

With a sparkle of yellow to enliven the dullest day, *Jasminum nudiflorum* commences flowering in November. Here it enhances a wall, and is supported by *Cotoneaster horizontalis* and *Bergenia* 'Ballawley'. For summer colour (above), a *Clematis × jackmanii* is encouraged to scramble through the jasmine's foliage.

Jasminum nudiflorum

WINTER-FLOWERING JASMINE

Height 8-10ft · *Spread* 6-8ft
Best November-March

Few winter shrubs can match this one for the sheer exuberance of its display, or for its hardiness, for though it flowers best on a sunny wall, it will also thrive very creditably against a bleak, north-facing one.

Apart from being trained

Lonicera × purpusii combines a heady fragrance with long-lived, creamy-white flowers and bark with ornamental interest.

against a wall, winter-flowering jasmine can be allowed to cascade down banks or old tree stumps, where it is often partnered with a rich, glossy, evergreen ivy such as *Hedera colchica* 'Sulphur Heart'.

CULTIVATION Plant at any time of year in almost any site or soil. Prune back old or dead wood immediately after flowering. Propagate by hardwood cuttings in mid-autumn.

Lonicera × purpusii

SHRUBBY HONEYSUCKLE

Height 5-7ft · *Spread* 5-8ft
Best January-March

Born of a union between *Lonicera standishii* and *L. fragrantissima*, this bush honeysuckle combines the best qualities of both parents. It forms a sturdy, twiggy bush with oval, bristly margined leaves and shreddy bark. The creamy-white sweetly scented flowers, sturdily emerging at the chilliest time of year, are good for cutting. They are followed by not very significant red berries in May.

Beside this paragon among honeysuckles, a swathe of *Narcissus cyclamineus* will carry a cream and yellow theme into spring. Later come the perennial plants, such as the 3ft high sweet bergamot, *Monarda didyma* – Oswego tea – to ring the changes with a scarlet, pink or purple display for summer.

CULTIVATION Plant from autumn to late winter in any well-drained soil and in sun or partial shade. Prune to remove old wood. Propagate by hardwood cuttings in mid-autumn.

Rubus biflorus

WHITEWASHED BRAMBLE

Height 6-8ft · *Spread* 6-8ft
Best October-April

An eye-catching garden feature can be created with the help of the bleached, skeletal frame of this bramble. The main show is in winter, when the arching young stems are covered by a gleaming white bloom; but they are attractive during the rest of the year as well, when they present blackberry-like leaves with a flash of white felt

Ornamental bark helps to highlight the shrubbery in winter. Here the dark, feathery, fan-like foliage of *Chamaecyparis lawsoniana* is given emphasis by being glimpsed through a veil of *Salix irrorata*.

The ghostly, skeletal stems of *Rubus biflorus* are brownish, but covered with a livid white, waxy bloom that is quite startling in the winter.

The contrasting spring catkins of *Salix irrorata* (left) and *S. gracilistyla* 'Melanostachys' (right).

beneath. White flowers appear in early summer, followed by yellow fruits somewhat reminiscent of raspberries. Immediately after the fruits have been eaten by birds or humans, cut the stems out at the base to encourage the growth of white shoots for the winter display.

For a really striking autumn picture, plant a deep red kaffir lily *Schizostylis coccinea* 'Major' at the foot of the rubus, and allow rich pink *Cyclamen coum* to carry the association through from December to March. A planting of *Iris sibirica* will contribute blade-like leaves and a splash of blue in front of the bramble in early June.

CULTIVATION Plant in sun or semi-shade in any soil in spring or autumn. To propagate, transplant suckers in autumn.

Salix irrorata

WHITE-STEMMED WILLOW

Height 8ft · *Spread* 8ft
Best October-April

In youth, the long shoots of this large, shrubby willow are a fresh and delicate green. As they mature, they turn a rich purple, powdered with white bloom that is particularly striking after leaves fall. Before the foliage returns in spring, the twigs are festooned with an array of dancing yellow male catkins, about an inch long.

From late spring to early autumn, the narrow, graceful leaves, glossy green above, greeny-grey below, will make an elegant backdrop for boldly coloured annuals. For structural effect and colour contrast, add a number of acanthuses that put up dark green, spiny leaves to a height of 2ft or more, and produce dramatic 1½ft white and purple flower spikes above them in July and August.

CULTIVATION Plant in autumn or winter in any soil, preferably in full sun. Prune old growth occasionally to encourage new stems. Propagate by hardwood cuttings taken between autumn and spring.

Salix gracilistyla
'Melanostachys'

Height 6-8ft · *Spread* 6ft
Best Late February-April

This medium-sized shrub has a strong personality, which it expresses in deep green, shining leaves produced on thick young shoots. Its most dramatic feature is the very dark, almost black, catkins that appear in late winter; the anthers are a brick red and ultimately turn yellow as they open and shed pollen.

Accompany the catkins with *Hepatica nobilis*, which provides a haze of blue flowers from February to April. If the willow is at the back of the border, follow on with bleeding heart *Dicentra spectabilis* and the densely packed, scented flower sprays of *Smilacina racemosa* – false spikenard – to make a pink and cream combination for a gorgeous late spring display.

CULTIVATION Plant in spring or autumn in almost any soil; it will flower best in full sun, but is tolerant of shade. No pruning is necessary, but to limit growth cut back hard after flowering. Propagate by hardwood cuttings in autumn.

Though small, the flowers of *Sarcococca confusa*, lying in clusters along the stems, bear a strong fragrance that carries far in mild weather.

The slender leaves of *Sarcococca hookeriana digyna* set off its delicate blooms, which consist of stamens only.

When the leaves of *Viburnum × bodnantense* 'Dawn' have fallen, tight clusters of pink flowers decorate the tall, naked stems.

Sarcococca confusa

SWEET BOX

Height 3ft · *Spread* 2ft
Best January-February

Not every plant would choose to flower in winter, nor do best in a damp, shady corner; but this shrub does, making it particularly welcome in the garden during the darker days of the year. The glossy, evergreen leaves grow into a dense mass that few weeds can penetrate, and in the depth of winter the fragrance of its tiny white flowers carries for yards on a mild, moist day. They are followed by black berries in early spring. Other sarcococcas include the smaller *Sarcococca humilis* with pinkish flowers and *S. hookeriana digyna* with white, pink-tinged blossom.

All would go well in an association of shade-lovers. If planted by a wall, a honeysuckle (*Lonicera*) can be trained up beside it with, say, evergreen *Helleborus foetidus* in attendance. This prince of the shady side carries green flowers edged with purple from late winter into spring, while *Vinca major*, also evergreen, can be used to take the display through into early summer with its intense purple-blue flowers.

CULTIVATION Plant in autumn or spring in any ordinary soil. Propagate by stem cuttings in late summer.

Viburnum × bodnantense 'Dawn'

Height 8-10ft · *Spread* 6-8ft
Best October-March

Plant this viburnum by the path to the front door – or similar well-trodden route – to obtain maximum enjoyment from its sweetly scented flower clusters that last from October to March. For despite its being one of the longest-flowering of all winter shrubs and moderately frost-tolerant, the blooms do drop quickly after cutting. Visually, too, it is a handsome creature, vigorous and upright-growing in habit. The dark green, ribbed leaves are tinted bronze when young, and plum-coloured in autumn, in which guise they coincide with the first rosy-white flowers before falling.

If the viburnum is used as a solitary feature for winter, an underplanting of the autumn-flowering *Colchicum* 'Waterlily' together with spring crocuses will give a long succession of low-level colour to the plot.

CULTIVATION Plant between autumn and spring in any reasonable, well-drained soil (a chalky soil is particularly suitable), and in full sun. Thin some of the old wood in spring. Propagate by semi-hardwood cuttings in late summer under glass, or by layering in autumn or winter.

Flower pompons of fragrant pink clothe the stems of *Viburnum farreri* throughout the winter.

Viburnum farreri

Height 8-10ft · *Spread* 7-10ft
Best November-March

Given a mild winter, the fragrant, rose-pink to white flowers will be produced continuously from late autumn to early spring. They do not, however, last long when cut. The leaves that replace the flowers in spring are tinged with bronze when young, but dull as the year advances. The main stems stand arrow straight and upright, but develop many twiggy side shoots that gradually combine to form a dense, dome-shaped bush.

The viburnum is sufficiently imposing for it to be made the background of a border containing such large perennials as lupins and Pacific hybrid delphiniums. When these die down in autumn, add a group of winter pansies to act as colourful harbingers of spring.
CULTIVATION Plant in spring or

From November to May the shoots of the bushy *Viburnum tinus* bear a profusion of fist-size flowers, from the lowest to highest branches.

autumn in a sunny position and in any well-drained soil. Thin out occasionally to invigorate growth. Propagate by layering from autumn to spring.

Viburnum tinus

Height 6-10ft · *Spread* 6-8ft
Best October-March

The pink buds open to become clusters of white flowers. Set against the shrub's dark, evergreen foliage, they insinuate their joyful glow into the darkest time of the year. In sunshine or shade, exposed to salt air, or in the poorest of chalky soils, the shrub looks cheerful in every season.

With its very low-sweeping branches, *Viburnum tinus* is especially effective in summer when it could make a dramatic

Viburnum tinus 'Eve Price' is a neat little cultivar with carmine buds opening to pink-tinged flowers.

background for the huge white, sulphur-yellow and red-purple trumpets of *Lilium regale*.
CULTIVATION Plant in spring or autumn in any well-drained soil, preferably in full sun. No pruning is necessary. Propagate by semi-hardwood cuttings, or by layering during late summer or early autumn.

Winter
TREES

A BALANCE BETWEEN evergreen and deciduous trees is particularly important in winter. If tilted too much towards an evergreen character, the garden can assume a sameness throughout the year; without evergreens, in winter it can lack depth and form. Bared of their leaves, deciduous trees reveal limbs that are hidden by foliage in other seasons. Their often bold, usually graceful, and sometimes richly coloured branches give the eye a different kind of experience as they hold centre stage uninhibited by competitors. A garden at dawn, after a clear, chill night can be captivating. A tracery of twigs and branches with hoar frost picked out by the sun is as stunning as any luxuriance of summer.

Alnus incana
'Aurea'

GOLDEN-GREY ALDER

Height 15-30ft · *Spread* 10-15ft
Best November-March

Glowing orange shoots tip the branches of this slender tree in winter, and cone-shaped fruits hang like baubles on a Christmas tree. In late winter, red-tinted catkins appear. Later the leaves are yellow at first, but then turn to a refreshing lime-green in early summer.

Perennials such as the bright yellow *Euphorbia polychroma* or the flaming reds of *E. griffithii*

As winter fades, the red-tinted catkins of *Alnus incana* 'Aurea' set the bare branches aglow.

'Fireglow' will echo the golden-grey alder's display in spring and early summer, and interest can be continued through the summer season with *Geranium* 'Buxton's Blue' and the dense, silver-filigree foliage of *Artemesia* 'Powis Castle'.

To fill the space between the herbaceous plants and the lower branches of the alder, try perennial grasses such as *Miscanthus sinensis* 'Silver Feather', 'Zebrinus' and 'Gracillimus', mixed with the dainty, mauve, double-flowered *Thalictrum delavayi* 'Hewitt's Double'.
CULTIVATION Plant at any time between autumn and spring, in any moisture-retentive soil that is reasonably fertile. Propagate from softwood cuttings under glass in late spring.

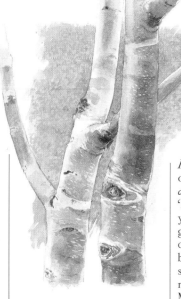

Betula albo-sinensis septentrionalis

CHINESE RED-BARK BIRCH

Height 18-30ft · *Spread* 8-15ft
Best October-April

The reddish-pink glow of the trunk and branches, highlighted by a waxy white bloom and peeling attractively in papery flakes, makes this one of the most elegant of birches, and the autumn colour is good too.

The vivid, greenish-yellow stems of *Cornus stolonifera* 'Flaviramea' will make a striking contrast, though this noble tree needs no embellishments in winter. The summer cloak of mid-green leaves can be augmented with a range of herbaceous plants and low-growing shrubs. Try *Euphorbia robbiae*,

Delicate, pinkish-orange shades make subtle patterns on the branches of Betula albo-sinensis septentrionalis.

Hemerocallis 'Golden Chimes' or 'Stella d'Oro', *Potentilla arbuscula* 'Beesii' or *Hypericum* 'Hidcote' to provide a host of yellow flowers, with hints of green and orange.

CULTIVATION Plant at any time between autumn and spring in a sunny position, preferably in a moisture-retentive, acid soil. Most soils are tolerated, however, except for chalky ones which dry out rapidly. Lichen can discolour the bark – scrub gently to remove.

Betula utilis jacquemontii

KASHMIR BIRCH

Height 30-40ft · *Spread* 15-20ft
Best October-April

The dazzling white bark of the Kashmir birch comes into its own in winter, when its naked profile has a ghost-like appearance. The varieties 'Inverleith'

With no concealing leaves, the shining white bark on the branches and trunk of a *Betula utilis jacquemontii* stands out with startling luminosity against a stretch of lawn and the fading beauty of autumn borders.

Superb yellow catkins drape the corkscrew hazel in spring. A planting of *Erythronium revolutum* beneath the tree (left) will eventually provide a carpet around the tree's base and roots.

Even the thread-like twigs of *Corylus avellana* 'Contorta' are twisted, looped and curled like a mass of tangled hair, creating a bizarre visual drama in an otherwise bleak winter landscape.

and 'Grayswood Ghost' have the whitest bark, while 'Jermyns' softens its eerie charm with a spring display of 6in long catkins. *Betula utilis jacquemontii* also makes a contribution to the autumn scene, when its leaves turn to golden-yellow.

The upright, shapely tree can be best admired gracing a lawn, with a few dwarf bulbs, such as the hoop petticoat daffodil, *Narcissus bulbocodium*, at its feet in spring and a through-season carpet of heather. The winter heathers *Erica carnea*, 'King George', 'December Red' or 'Myretoun Ruby', mixed with *Calluna vulgaris* 'Beoley Gold', 'Sunset' or 'Wickwar Flame' will provide a changing display of pinks, reds and golds.

CULTIVATION Plant between autumn and spring in any fertile, moisture-retentive soil, but allow plenty of space and add extra nutrients if placed near shrubs. Lichen can discolour the bark in winter – scrub gently with soap and water to remove.

Corylus avellana 'Contorta'

CORKSCREW HAZEL

Height 8-10ft · *Spread* 6-8ft
Best October-April

When the corkscrew hazel's branches are bare it is easy to see how it got its name. The branches twist, curve and spiral in delightful contortions, and have earned it the nickname 'Harry Lauder's Walking Stick', after the famous music hall artist's familiar prop. Late winter brings a mass of long, yellow catkins, and nuts may form among the crinkled leaves in summer and ripen in October. At this time also, the leaves gradually turn to yellow.

The fragrant honeysuckle *Lonicera standishii* and the subtly scented evergreen shrub *Sarcococca confusa* will add to the display and perfume the air on a still winter's day. In summer, the hazel's dark green foliage would be well complemented by a show of yellow flowers such as *Rudbeckia fulgida* 'Goldsturm'.

CULTIVATION Plant between autumn and spring in any fertile soil, in sun or in partial shade. Cut back the older stems periodically to promote multi-stemmed growth. Propagate by layering one to two-year-old stems at any time between autumn and spring.

Cupressus macrocarpa 'Goldcrest' is a fine specimen tree, seen here alongside evergreen *Fatsia japonica*.

Cupressus macrocarpa
'Goldcrest'

GOLDEN MONTEREY CYPRESS

Height 25-35ft
Spread 8-15ft
Best October-April

Winter brings out the best in the golden form of the Monterey cypress, when its yellowish-green, cone-shaped foliage turns to a feathery rich yellow.

Round-shaped, deciduous shrubs such as *Euonymus alatus* and *Fothergilla major* will complement the cypress's shape and, when they transform into brilliant shades of red and orange in autumn, will make a spectacular display alongside their golden neighbour.

Broad colonies of the blue-flowered *Chionodoxa luciliae* or *Scilla sibirica*, naturalised in the grass around the cypress, will get spring off to a good start. Combine these with a carpet of

The fruits of *Malus* 'Red Sentinel' sometimes remain on the bough through to March. It is the tallest of the varieties and may grow to 20ft.

Polygonum bistorta 'Superbum', whose clear pink summer flowers turn to crimson as autumn approaches.

CULTIVATION Plant at any time during autumn or spring in any soil, though the growth rate will be faster in a rich, moisture-retentive soil. Shelter the tree from severe frosts, which may 'scorch' the foliage, and do not plant it as a hedging plant as it does not respond to clipping. Propagation by rooting semi-hardwood cuttings is possible, but not easy.

Malus

ORNAMENTAL CRAB APPLE

Height 12-20ft · *Spread* 8-15ft
Best October-December

In autumn the miniature apples of the ornamental crabs take on their glowing colours of red, orange-red or golden-yellow, depending on the variety, and adorn the bare branches long after the leaves have fallen. In spring the trees blossom with clusters of delicate and slightly

Malus 'Golden Hornet' produces clusters of golden-yellow apples, which may last until December.

fragrant flowers. If space allows, it is worth growing more than one variety, to widen the fruit and flowering periods. 'Almey' (height 12-18ft, spread 8-10ft) has small, round, orange-red fruits from October to December. In late spring its large, pink flowers, paling to white in the centre, open at about the same time as the neat, reddish-bronze leaves. 'Golden Hornet' (height 10-20ft, spread 15ft) produces its yellow apples as early as September. 'Red Sentinel' (height 10-20ft, spread 10-12ft) is the slenderest of the varieties.

Low-growing evergreens such as *Pernettya mucronata* 'Mulberry Wine', 'Crimsonia' or 'Alba', as well as *Skimmia japonica reevesiana* will tolerate the light shade beneath a malus and produce red or white fruits of their own. They can be combined with the golden vari-egated leaves of *Hedera colchica* 'Sulphur Heart', or *H. helix*

SPRING The fragrant blossom of *Malus* 'Red Sentinel' is impressive.

The smooth, glossy bark of the Manchurian cherry glows like old polished leather in a wintry sun.

Fragrant white blossom decorates *Prunus maackii* in spring, and its dark green leaves turn yellow in autumn.

'Goldheart' as ground cover. CULTIVATION Plant in any moisture-retentive but well-drained soil in an open site between autumn and spring.

Prunus maackii

MANCHURIAN CHERRY

Height 18-25ft · *Spread* 10-15ft
Best November-April

The smooth, honey-brown bark of the Manchurian cherry makes the tree an appealing sight in the winter garden. It has the added attraction of small, sweetly scented spikes of white flowers in late spring, and dark green summer foliage that turns yellow in autumn. The aptly named 'Amber Beauty' is particularly handsome.

The Manchurian cherry looks good planted in a lawn, especially if surrounded at its base with spring-flowering *Narcissus* 'Tete-a-Tete' or *N.* 'February Gold'. Planted in a border, clumps of the tawny-orange *Hemerocallis fulva* and blue *Agapanthus* 'Headbourne Hybrids', or the starry gold flowers of *Hypericum* 'Hidcote', would flatter the bark in summer.
CULTIVATION Plant during early autumn in any fertile, reasonably moisture-retentive soil, in a sheltered site in sun or partial shade. Maintain the bark's gloss by wiping off algae with water each year.

Prunus serrula

TIBETAN CHERRY

Height 12-18ft · *Spread* 12-18ft
Best November-April

The glorious, polished mahogany bark of the Tibetan cherry comes into its own in winter when the foliage has gone, and is as pleasing to the touch as it is to the eye. Its small white flowers in spring are insignificant and mostly hidden by the willow-like foliage, but the grafted 'Sheraton' cherries combine the attractive bark with the spring display of a Japanese flowering cherry.

Polishing the bark of the Tibetan cherry with a soft cloth helps preserve its lovely sheen, so plant it in an accessible position, such as in the centre of a lawn, with a spring display of *Narcissus* 'Golden Harvest' or 'February Gold' at its base. Alternatively, place it near the front of a border, with *Rubus biflorus* and *Helleborus orientalis* or *H. corsicus* as white, pink and yellow-green companions in the planting.
CULTIVATION As for *P. maackii*, but will stand drier conditions and thrives on chalky soils.

Like a sculpture in polished bronze, *Prunus serrula* dominates a lawn. In the background stands a handsome partner, *Malus* 'Golden Hornet', with its golden apples still clinging to the boughs.

Prunus subhirtella 'Autumnalis' defies cherry convention by producing its pale pink flowers in winter.

Stems of *Salix alba* 'Britzensis' shoot up from coppiced bases to show their brilliant winter colour.

Prunus subhirtella
'Autumnalis'

AUTUMN CHERRY

Height 10-15ft · *Spread* 8-10ft
Best November-April

The chief delight of this cherry is the show of pink buds that open to semi-double, almost pure white flowers between November and April. If budded twigs are cut for indoor display, they will quickly flower at room temperature. An equally attractive rose-pink variety, 'Autumnalis Rosea', is also available.

For additional winter colour nearby, plant the spreading varieties of witch hazel, *Hamamelis mollis* 'Coombe Wood' and 'Gold Crest', with their scented golden flowers. Then, around the base of the autumn cherry, plant *Cyclamen hederi-*

folium and *C. coum* to provide bright splashes of white and pink in autumn and spring, and a glorious marbled carpet of leaves for the rest of the year.
CULTIVATION Plant in any sunny site that is protected from frost, and in soil that is fertile and moisture-retentive.

Salix alba
'Britzensis'

CORAL-BARK WILLOW

Height 8-10ft · *Spread* 6-10ft
Best November-March

Young willow stems will brighten any garden in winter. Two of the best for this purpose are *Salix alba* 'Britzensis', which has coral-red stems, and the related *S. a.* 'Vitellina', whose

bark is of an acid-yellow hue. It is important to stress that it is only the young shoots that possess these vivid colours, and in order to maintain a succession from winter to winter it is necessary to coppice or pollard the trees each spring or every other one. Also, without this pruning the trees could easily grow to 35ft in a decade.

Both can be combined with other plants that have vividly coloured stems, like the bright green *Cornus stolonifera* 'Flaviramea', the white *Rubus biflorus* or the dark purple *Cornus alba* 'Kesselringii'. For ground cover, use variegated ivy, such as *Hedera colchica* 'Sulphur Heart', interspersed with dark flowered forms of *Helleborus orientalis* hybrids.
CULTIVATION Plant in autumn

SPRING AND AUTUMN 'Loveliest of trees, the cherry now . . . ' The picture (top) shows *Prunus subhirtella* 'Autumnalis' in spring, at the very end of its flowering season. It flowers in bursts throughout winter, coinciding with mild spells. The lower picture shows the tree bedecked in its splendid autumnal livery.

SPRING. In March, long before the leaves appear, *Salix daphnoides* 'Aglaia', a male clone, puts out large, lemony catkins on its bare purple stems.

or spring in a sunny position with any moisture-retentive, though well-drained, soil. Propagate by taking hardwood cuttings during autumn.

Salix daphnoides acutifolia
(syn *S. acutifolia*)

VIOLET WILLOW

Height 10ft · *Spread* 6ft
Best November-March

The purple-violet, two-year-old shoots of *Salix daphnoides* are silvered with a whitish bloom in winter, and in latish

'A willow grows aslant the brook . . .' In fact, several of them grow there, against a background of snow-draped conifers. In the foreground there are the purple stems of *Salix daphnoides*, vying for attention with the red shoots of *S. alba* 'Britzensis'. Twisting over all are the corkscrew branches of *S. matsudana* 'Tortuosa'.

February this attractive display is augmented by the appearance of yellow catkins. Control the tree's height by cutting out half the shoots every other spring; this will also ensure a strong framework of stems.

The willow's upright lines will be emphasised by the blade-like leaves of *Iris sibirica*, which has bright blue flowers in late spring and early summer. To follow, try the strongly variegated foliage of *Miscanthus sinensis* 'Variegatus'.

Another excellent willow for winter colour is *Salix × rubra* 'Eugenei', whose stems turn from yellow-green to olive-grey as the season progresses; it also produces an abundance of grey-pink catkins. The low-growing, evergreen shrub *Euonymus fortunei* 'Emerald 'n' Gold', with green, gold and pink leaves, would make admirable ground cover under the tree.

CULTIVATION As for *S. alba*.

IN SUMMER cloak of green, the corkscrew willow's twisted branches are barely noticeable.

Salix matsudana
'Tortuosa'

CORKSCREW WILLOW

Height 15-25ft · *Spread* 10-15ft
Best December-April

When bare of leaves the twisted and contorted young branches of this Chinese willow make an interesting winter feature in the garden and provide it with another name – the dragon's-claw willow. The narrow, bright green leaves, too, have an appealing twist and curl when they appear in spring. Green-yellow catkins, about 1in long, arrive in April. As the branches mature and thicken they gradually become straighter. The young shoots are olive-green or, in its hybrid *Salix × erythro-flexuosa*, a bright orange.

Reinforce the tree's oriental look by planting it next to an ornamental pond if possible, or

The bare, contorted *Salix matsudana* 'Tortuosa' has a bizarre appearance, yet has an appealing charm when silhouetted against a wintry sky.

lay rock and gravel around its base. Clumps of *Hosta sieboldiana* or *H.* 'Halcyon', with their grey-green leaves and off-white flowers, will add to the effect. Otherwise, train *Clematis* 'Bill Mackenzie' into the crown of the tree for yellow flowers in summer and autumn and fluffy seed heads in winter.
CULTIVATION Plant between autumn and early spring in a sunny, warm position, in any moisture-retentive soil. Avoid light, sandy soil unless the roots have adequate moisture, such as beside a pool. Propagate by hardwood cuttings taken in autumn or winter.

Thuja occidentalis
'Rheingold'

Height 3½-5ft · *Spread* 2½-4ft
Best November-April

The yellow-green foliage of this slow-growing conifer turns to luminous old gold in winter. *Thuja occidentalis* 'Aurea' has the same conical shape, but grows more vigorously than 'Rheingold'. Both make handsome specimen trees for small gardens, and are also suitable for rock gardens.

Heathers go well with conifers; *Erica carnea* 'Springwood

Groups of *Adonis amurensis* 'Fukujukai' complement the gold of *Thuja occidentalis* 'Rheingold'.

White', 'Myretoun Ruby' and 'Pirbright Rose' flower from December to early April, while *E. erigena* 'Superba' and 'Irish Dusk' have pink flowers that last until May.

Dwarf brooms such as *Genista lydia*, *Cytisus × beanii* and *C. × kewensis* will complement the golden-yellow foliage display during spring and follow through until early summer.
CULTIVATION Plant in good weather between late autumn and spring, in any soil that does not dry out too rapidly. A sunny, sheltered site will bring out the best foliage colour. Keep the ground well watered and clear of weeds. Propagate by taking semi-hardwood cuttings in early autumn.

BRIDGING THE SEASONS
WITH
Thuja

IT IS NOT OFTEN that plants are valued chiefly for their appearance in the dormant season, but so it is with some willows, whose young, leafless shoots can contribute a quite startling flash of colour to the winter garden. The willow in this case is *Salix alba* 'Britzensis', whose young shoots are a brilliant orange; they are employed to emphasise the radiant old gold of *Thuja occidentalis* 'Rheingold', which grows rather slowly to a height of 5ft, and whose bright foliage looks its best in winter sunshine. Further riches are added by the bronze winter dress of *T. orientalis*, the bold, vivid, winter-flowering heather *Erica darleyensis* 'Springwood White' and the ivy *Hedera colchica* 'Variegata', whose leaves are marked with cream, yellow and pale green.

Winter is not the group's only season of glory. In spring, the willow adopts a greeny haze of new leaves, lending freshness to the thujas. The heather is still in flower, while growing up through the ivy are tall *Narcissus poeticus* 'Actaea', which have pure white petals and yellow, red-rimmed cups.

Summer creates a symphony of foliage. The willow's grey-green leaves show bright green as they toss in the breeze beside the green-gold *T. o.* 'Rheingold' and the now dark green *T. orientalis*. Completing the picture is the variegated ivy and, in the foreground, the pale green leaves of the heather. ❧

IN SPRINGTIME uniforms of green-gold and dark green, the thujas are supported by the misty young willow foliage, and the stately heads of *Narcissus poeticus* 'Actaea'.

THE SUMMER theme of the association is the contrasting foliage of thujas, willow, ivy and heather.

Perfectly in tune with the winter sunshine are the old gold of *Thuja occidentalis* 'Rheingold', the bronze of *T. orientalis* and an orange willow, set among white heather and variegated ivy.

Winter
CLIMBERS

GREENNESS AND FLOWERS are at a premium in winter, especially where links between the layers of interest are concerned. Evergreen climbers, including the many different kinds of ivy, lead the eye upwards from foliage at ground level to the winter density of evergreen trees. It is always a welcome moment when a winter-flowering species clematis is suddenly seen to have braved the cold and festoons an old tree or building with its fresh, delicate blooms.

Clematis cirrhosa balearica

FERN-LEAVED CLEMATIS

Height 10-15ft
Best December-March

One glance reveals the origin of this elegant, evergreen climber's common name. The leaves are handsomely divided into several segments, giving them indeed a fern-like appearance. The foliage takes on a bronze-green tinge in winter, prettily complementing the flowers – nodding cream-white bells, speckled with red-purple inside – which also emerge at the same time. On sunny winter days the flowers put forth a faint, attractive fragrance, suggestive of lemon.

Grow *Clematis cirrhosa balearica* firmly anchored to a sheltered wall, shaded from early morning sun. Some of

The bell-like flowers of *Clematis cirrhosa balearica* and its delicate leaves make a delightful display against dark supporting trelliswork.

its slender stems can be encouraged to thread through the dark green and white, aromatic leaves of *Rosmarinus officinalis* 'Benenden Blue'. The rosemary's blue flowers appear in spring, and can be followed in late summer by the greenish-white tassels of *Itea ilicifolia*. The three plants create a year-round pattern of contrasting foliage, ideal as a backdrop for bulbs. Try the elegant *Narcissus* 'Thalia' and *Tulipa* 'Artist' for spring, the white *Galtonia candicans* in summer, and the mauve and lemon *Gladiolus papilio* for autumn.

Alternatively, grow the clematis through a deciduous tree, such as a crab apple, or an old fruit tree perhaps, to decorate the bare branches in winter.
CULTIVATION Plant in late spring in soil enriched with humus and

The bronze-tinted winter leaves of *Clematis cirrhosa balearica* contrast well with its cream flowers.

general fertiliser. The ideal situation is a sheltered, sunny spot, but with shade for the roots. Propagate by stem cuttings in early summer.

Hedera

IVY

Don't be put off by the toughness and tenacity of ivy, for on a host tree or house wall it will be neither parasitic nor destructive. Indeed, it is one of the most versatile evergreen plants, not only for winter display but throughout the year. Ivies will adapt to virtually any soil, to sun or dense shade, and are even tolerant of most industrial pollution.

Many ivies have beautifully patterned leaves; some are delicately veined, and others are variegated with cream, gold or acid yellow, or tinged with pink, red and grey. They vary greatly in character, from the modest all-gold *Hedera helix* 'Buttercup' or the frilled, dark green 'Ivalace', to *H. colchica* 'Dentata' and its variegated forms with large leaves sometimes known as 'elephants' ears'.

TWO STAGES OF GROWTH

Ivy has two stages of growth: in the earlier, juvenile stage the climbing is done, followed by the mature stage when the flowers and fruit are formed. If left unchecked, ivies become tree-like as they reach the end of their support, the upper stems branching out to form a bushy canopy. The leaves of some ivies, such a *H. helix* 'Angularis Aurea', change in colour as they age and reach more light. The early growth characteristics – when the leaves are often more distinctively shaped and the plant is better suited to climbing and trailing – can be maintained by regular trimming.

Ivies can be grown up a tree trunk or a stout pole in a border, and are perfect for clothing sheds or walls. They spread by sending out long stems with aerial rootlets that attach themselves to any surface. But the degree of hold varies. Some species are good self-clingers, their rootlets strong enough to support the plant even if it is climbing upwards. Others have weaker rootlets in relation to the weight of foliage, and while they trail easily over the ground, making a most attractive blanket, they need artificial support to climb efficiently.

HARMLESS CLIMBER

As long as a host tree is healthy, the most vigorous, self-clinging ivy will remain a secondary plant. However, an ailing host with poor leaf production could be deprived of light and overwhelmed by the healthier ivy, especially when the main stems grow large and woody and twine about the host. Similarly, ivy will not damage a sound wall – it may even help to preserve it and have an insulating effect on a house. A weak or crumbling wall, however, could be pulled down by the weight of a vigorous ivy. Only if the mortar is soft will the roots penetrate sufficiently to cause further damage.

PARTNERSHIPS

The evergreen foliage of ivy could make a splendid partner for a deciduous climber. The vibrant crimson of Virginia creeper (*Parthenocissus quinquefolia*), for example, could be set off against the glossy greens and yellows of the magnificent

Hedera colchica 'Dentata Variegata' spills over an urn with *Origanum* 'Aureum' grouped around its base (above). On the left, *H. helix* 'Goldheart' drenches a high wall, above a cascade of *H. h.* 'Buttercup'.

Bluebells and Siberian wallflowers bring their springtime colour to a column of the ivy 'Goldheart'.

H. colchica 'Sulphur Heart'.

As ground cover, the smaller ivies look well with snowdrops and other winter and spring bulbs piercing through their dark leaves. An especially effective combination is the bronze-purple winter leaves of *H. helix* 'Atropurpurea' with *Galanthus* 'Sam Arnott'. Vigorous ivies can reach out to carpet difficult areas where other plants would perish.

CULTIVATION
Most ivies are very hardy and remarkably resistant to pests and diseases. *H. canariensis* and its cultivars may suffer in a severe winter, but usually recover. Check the situation requirements of each cultivar – leaf colour and degree of variegation can be affected by the amount of light to which the ivy is exposed.

Propagation is simple as the stems are constantly forming aerial roots in the climbing stage, and cuttings root very easily. Pruning consists of cutting back as required.

The evergreen all-rounder

Ivies really come into their own in winter
when deciduous trees and shrubs are stripped of foliage,
and flowering plants are but occasional treasures. Festoons of
glossy green or delicate traceries of trailing stems and shapely
leaves give depth, character and colour to the garden.
Different varieties vary greatly in vigour, leaf size and form,
providing a range of moods and effects. They can be trained
to climb up, cascade down or carpet the ground.

Photographed in December at Whitehouse Ivies, Maldon, Essex.

Hedera colchica
'Sulphur Heart'
Variegation best in full
light. Needs initial
support as a climber.

Hedera helix 'Goldheart'
Tough, and tight-clinging after initial support.
Not suitable for ground cover
as gold hearts are lost.

Hedera helix 'Atropurpurea'
Tight-clinging. Leaves turn
bronze-purple in winter,
especially in exposed sites.
Any soil or aspect.

Hedera helix
'Königer's Auslese'
Strong, self-clinging climber.
Any aspect and soil.

Hedera helix
'Deltoidea'
Strong-clinging climber,
and good ground cover.
Can be over-vigorous
in full light.

358

Hedera helix 'Palmata'
Tolerates any site, but leaves
more distinctively shaped
in poor soil. Good self-clinger.

Hedera colchica
'Dentata'
Very tough; tolerates
any soil or aspect.
Needs initial support as climber.
Leaves fragrant when crushed.

Hedera colchica
'Dentata Variegata'
Thrives in any soil or aspect
but full light shows off variegation
to best effect. Needs some support.

Hedera helix 'Glacier'
Fast-growing, hardy and tight-clinging trailer,
climber or ground cover. Any soil or aspect.
May lose variegation in full sun.

Hedera helix
'Buttercup'
Strong-clinging.
Leaves yellow in sun,
light green in shade.
Likes poor soil.

Hedera canariensis
'Gloire de Marengo'.
Strong-clinging. May suffer
leaf loss in a severe winter
but often recovers. Loses some
variegation in full light.

Hedera helix 'Ivalace'
Small, neat habit as climber,
trailer or ground cover.
Likes good soil.

Winter
ALPINES

IN THE MOUNTAINOUS regions of the world, alpines are never so happy in winter as when shrouded in a blanket of snow. Under their protective, insulating blanket, small hummocks of plants hibernate. Many have beautifully sculptured foliage to add to the winter scene when they emerge, and others, notably the lime-encrusted hillocks of Kabschia saxifrages, are tough enough to flower at the year's beginning.

Adonis amurensis

Height 10-12in
Planting distance 15in
Best February

The first sign of growth is the dark bronze-green shoots in January. Later, globular flower buds nest in a ruff of finely cut awakening leaves. Glossy petals unfurl to form a broad, shallow golden cup, while the leaves develop just a little to take on the appearance of young conifer shoots. The plant at this stage is little more than 3in high. Its crisp, bright look can be marred by soil splash in winter storms; avoid it by surrounding the plant with chippings or gravel. After flowering, the finely divided foliage continues to grow, doubling or trebling its height before dying down towards the end of summer.

The white and blue forms of *Anemone blanda* would make delightful winter companions.

Like a corsage on a white gown, a group of *Adonis amurensis* pushes through a layer of glistening snow.

Plant one or two *Cyclamen hederifolium* nearby. These would produce autumn flowers when the adonis foliage dies.
CULTIVATION Plant during late summer or early autumn in a well-drained soil with added leaf mould. The site must not be exposed to the hottest sun. Propagate by seed and division.

Arabis ferdinandi-coburgii
'Variegata'

Height 6-9in
Planting distance 9-12in
Best All year

Its ground-hugging masses of tightly overlapping rosettes ensure that *Arabis ferdinandi-coburgii* 'Variegata' puts on a fine display throughout the year. The narrow-based leaves are rich green with creamy-white edges, which in severe weather become flushed with purple. Although its clusters of ½in wide white flowers, which appear in spring, are not spectacular, they do contribute to the beauty of the foliage.

A. f-c. 'Variegata' is a versatile, fast-growing plant that may spread to cover a foot or more in one season. It will liven up many parts of the garden, such as a rock garden where its mats will tumble over rocks and boulders and fill crevices. Or it can be used to fill troughs and sinks, garnish the base of a wall, or carpet a gravel garden. If planted in front of a group of ferns, it will brighten an otherwise dull winter display.

Arabis ferdinandi-coburgii 'Variegata' cascades its tight packed tresses over a low wall.

IN SPRING, the arabis flowers highlight the two-tone leaves.

CULTIVATION Plant in September, October or March in well-drained soil and partial shade. Propagate by division in early autumn, or by cuttings in late summer. Thin out, divide and replant congested mats.

Winter
BULBS, CORMS AND TUBERS

A GREAT RANGE of bulb species from cool, rather than tropical climates, flower between autumn leaf-fall and the opening of buds in spring, when there is no leafy canopy to shade them. In the wild, the exact time of flowering within this period is geared to local conditions of weather and moisture levels in the soil. For the gardener it means that there is a wide choice of cultivated bulbs that will flower, when conditions are right, in a long succession between autumn and spring. In the inhospitable conditions of a hard British winter the flow is undiminished, and winter-flowering bulbs provide welcome vitality and splashes of colour near to the ground.

Crocus

Winter-flowering crocuses, if planted en masse to produce bright pools of colour, will generate a carnival-like atmosphere in the garden at a time when it is often at its most drab. Some varieties, like the November to late January-flowering *Crocus laevigatus, C. angustifolius, C. sieberi* 'Bowles' White' and *C. imperati*, can be outstanding when planted in small groups in a rock garden which catches the best of the winter sun. The more vigorous varieties such as *C. tommasinianus* are more suitable for enlivening a winter lawn or a border.

The cultivar 'Cream Beauty', one of the loveliest of the winter-flowering crocuses, will survive and flower in the most severe conditions.

The exact flowering period of the winter crocuses depends on weather and aspect, but the different species flower in a consistent order. For a succession of blooms over six months or more, plan an autumn display of colchicums and autumn crocuses in grass or borders. The soft lilac *C. tournefortii* will perform an intermezzo before the winter crocus show, and *C. vernus* cultivars extend the display into March.

In borders, winter crocuses can be planted in drifts between later-flowering shrubs, or near perennial plants with undemanding root systems which will not inhibit the crocuses' growth. Perennials like *Gypsophila paniculata* 'Bristol Fairy' or *Dicentra spectabilis* will conceal the dying crocus leaves in late spring and early summer. Small shrubs such as *Berberis thunbergii* 'Atropurpurea Nana' or the long-flowering Irish heath, *Daboecia cantabrica*, would give summer and autumn interest to the planting combination.

CULTIVATION

Plant in early autumn in any reasonably fertile, well-drained soil, preferably in an open position to encourage the bulbs to reproduce well. To plant in grass, lift a section of turf, break up the soil beneath, and plant the bulbs randomly, taking the thickness of the turf into account in the planting depth.

Crocus tommasinianus, snowdrops and winter aconites, and the dark foliage of cyclamen provide a happy kaleidoscope of colour on a terraced rock garden.

The winter crocus connection

It's possible to have a succession of crocus blooms all the way through from autumn to spring. But it is the winter-flowering species that are most welcome. Their shapely goblet blooms can provide bold dabs of colour beneath dark evergreens or naked deciduous shrubs in the border, or revitalise a tired winter lawn. In smaller groups, they can highlight rock-garden pockets or fill window boxes and pots to be enjoyed from indoors.

Painted in January and February from plants supplied by Broadleigh Gardens, Taunton, Somerset.

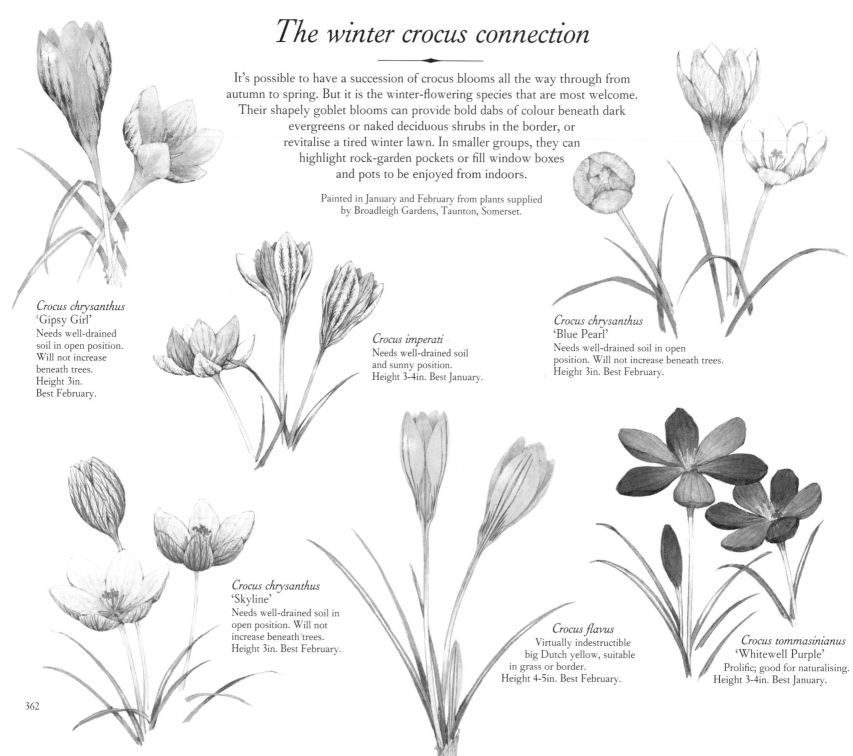

Crocus chrysanthus 'Gipsy Girl' Needs well-drained soil in open position. Will not increase beneath trees. Height 3in. Best February.

Crocus imperati Needs well-drained soil and sunny position. Height 3-4in. Best January.

Crocus chrysanthus 'Blue Pearl' Needs well-drained soil in open position. Will not increase beneath trees. Height 3in. Best February.

Crocus chrysanthus 'Skyline' Needs well-drained soil in open position. Will not increase beneath trees. Height 3in. Best February.

Crocus flavus Virtually indestructible big Dutch yellow, suitable in grass or border. Height 4-5in. Best February.

Crocus tommasinianus 'Whitewell Purple' Prolific; good for naturalising. Height 3-4in. Best January.

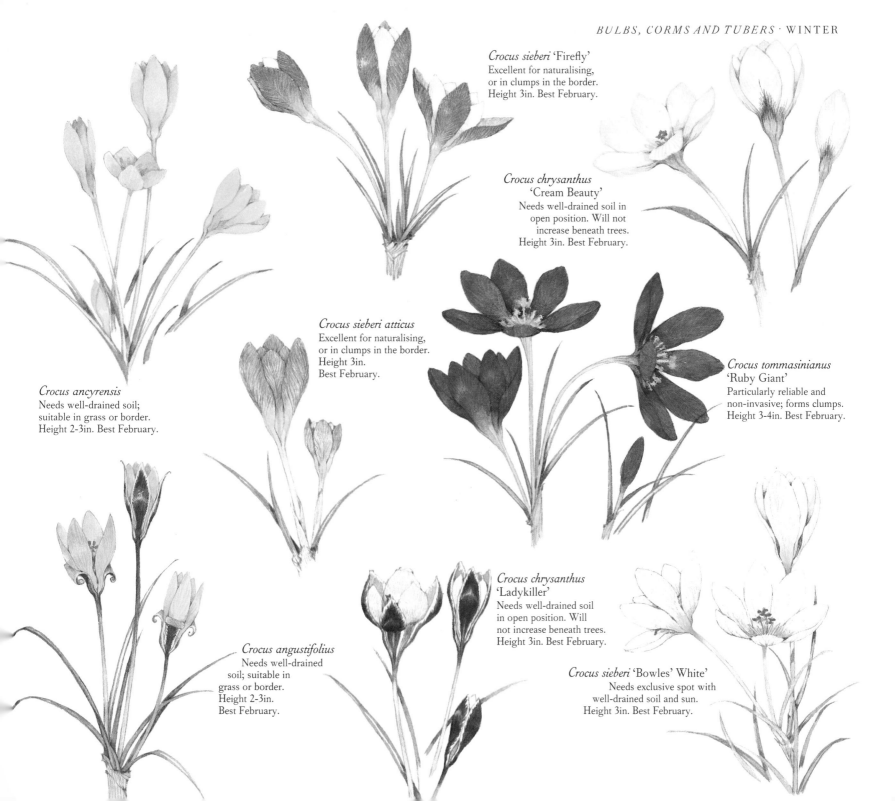

Crocus sieberi 'Firefly'
Excellent for naturalising,
or in clumps in the border.
Height 3in. Best February.

Crocus chrysanthus
'Cream Beauty'
Needs well-drained soil in
open position. Will not
increase beneath trees.
Height 3in. Best February.

Crocus sieberi atticus
Excellent for naturalising,
or in clumps in the border.
Height 3in.
Best February.

Crocus tommasinianus
'Ruby Giant'
Particularly reliable and
non-invasive; forms clumps.
Height 3-4in. Best February.

Crocus ancyrensis
Needs well-drained soil;
suitable in grass or border.
Height 2-3in. Best February.

Crocus chrysanthus
'Ladykiller'
Needs well-drained soil
in open position. Will
not increase beneath trees.
Height 3in. Best February.

Crocus angustifolius
Needs well-drained
soil; suitable in
grass or border.
Height 2-3in.
Best February.

Crocus sieberi 'Bowles' White'
Needs exclusive spot with
well-drained soil and sun.
Height 3in. Best February.

Nothing prunes back winter more effectively than the bright carmine splashes of *Cyclamen coum*. It is grown here as a companion of crocuses, as a herald of daffodils to come and as a source of handsome foliage.

Cyclamen coum

Height 3in
Planting distance 6in
Best December-February

In the depths of winter, when bright colours are scarce, this dainty cyclamen brings vivid splashes of carmine-pink to the garden. And when the flowers have finished, horizontal, heart-shaped leaves, marbled with silver, continue an attractive display as late as midsummer. Available varieties range from white to deep carmine.

Cyclamen coum is not sufficiently vigorous to compete with neighbours planted close by, but it is strong enough to form a sizable colony alone. Therefore, it is best suited to a pocket in the rock garden, or planted in groups, as highlights, in front of dwarf conifers such as *Picea glauca albertiana* 'Conica' or *Abies balsamea* 'Nana'; alternatively, try planting a group by a bed of heathers.

CULTIVATION Set young plants in humus-rich, free-draining soil in a sheltered site, ideally in partial shade. Shun the dormant tubers often sold by nurseries which may be slow to establish; buy young plants instead. Established plants multiply naturally; propagate by sowing seed when ripe in early summer, or in spring.

In the winter garden, *Cyclamen coum* 'Album' becomes a veritable snow princess with its pale flowers and silvery-marbled leaves.

Clumps of *Eranthis hyemalis* glow in the late winter garden like flecks of golden sunshine.

Eranthis hyemalis

WINTER ACONITE

Height 4in
Planting distance 3-4in
Best January-February

Let this cheerful little woodland aconite seed itself underneath deciduous trees and shrubs to form a glowing carpet of green and yellow. Brilliant buttercup-like flowers, surrounded by a smart green ruff, open with the sun, and when they are over the glossy leaves remain to provide an attractive ground cover through the spring.

Plant scattered groups of winter aconites beneath trees and shrubs whose canopies almost block the light. Use them to emphasise a white-trunked *Betula utilis jacquemontii*, or mahogany-barked *Prunus serrula*. The narrow, boldly white-veined leaves of *Arum italicum* 'Pictum', planted nearby, would coincide with the glossy aconite foliage. (continued on page 366)

BRIDGING THE SEASONS
IN A
Shady corner

EBRUARY 'fill-dyke' is not generally a month that gardeners look forward to. The ground is mica-hard or soggy, the air sepulchrally damp or razor-edged. But it may also be mild and, if so, it is a marvellous month for hellebores, and an association based upon these cheery plants will not only entice strollers down wintry paths, but bring colour and sparkle to a hitherto neglected corner of the garden through much of the year. The hellebore chosen here is the Lenten rose, *Helleborus orientalis*, which can be any kind of colour from cream to crimson to purple, though in this instance it is pink. Its companions through winter's darkest days are snowdrops, *Galanthus nivalis*, and winter aconites, *Eranthis hyemalis*, both often found naturalised in British woodlands. Offering the promise of balmier days ahead are the bare twigs of the hardy *Fuchsia* 'Madame Cornelissen', the glossy leaves of *Arum italicum* and the distinctive, white-veined foliage of *A. i.* 'Pictum'.

Towards the end of spring, in early May, the focus of attention is upon the arums, which have produced their extraordinary, palest yellow spathes, as much as 1ft long, and each half-curved about a spike of tiny, petalless flowers. They go well with the hellebores, most of whose flowers have faded to green, though there remains here and there a hint of rose. The aconites and snowdrops are still present as

Mild winters only would bring out the best in this romantic planting of snowdrops, aconites and a hellebore, but it is well worth trying.

IN SPRING the corner becomes a composition of gentle pastel hues – yellow arum spathes, the hellebore's green and rose, and the leaf shades of flowers past and those still to come.

IN SUMMER the formerly neglected corner turns into an English posy of fuchsias, crimson 'Stargazer' lilies, pansies and ageratums – with the jaunty scarlet spikes of arum berries.

clumps of leaves, and there is young foliage on the fuchsia twigs, which have been firmly cut back to promote good bushy growth later in the year. Also anticipating summer is a gathering of annuals – pansies and ageratums – set into the ground directly from their containers.

Come summer, and the pansies – *Viola* × *wittrockiana* – and the soft, blue powder-puffs of *Ageratum houstonianum* have opened and are in full fig. They are backed by a stand of crimson lilies, *Lilium* 'Stargazer', the waxy, cerise and white bells of the fuchsia, and what were the hellebore's flowers, now metamorphosed into seed pods. Another change has taken place among the arums, which have erected spikes topped by bright red berries.

Autumn need not ring the knell of the little colony. The 'Stargazer' foliage is still there, and the fuchsia will continue to flower until the first frosts. Encourage it by providing a succession of pansies and ageratums grown elsewhere in pots and kept in the wings to enliven the scene now. You could try *Viola* 'Roggli Giants', broad-faced pansies that flower deep into the autumn days, and team them with blue, mauve or pink ageratums with heart-shaped leaves and neat heads like shaving brushes, that last well into winter, so creating a cheering reminder that spring is not too far away. ❧

The elegant, drooping flowers of *Galanthus elwesii* are marked with deep green inside.

The bright green leaves of *Galanthus ikariae* appear in late winter, followed by butterfly-like flowers in early spring.

To make the best of *Galanthus caucasicus*, intersperse it with winter-flowering crocuses to create a colourful, thick-pile carpet of blooms.

(*Eranthis hyemalis* cont)
CULTIVATION Plant after flowering in moist, free-draining soil containing well-rotted organic matter, in a partially shaded site. Propagate by division or by sowing seed.

Galanthus caucasicus

CAUCASIAN SNOWDROP

Height 6in
Planting distance 4-6in
Best January-February

This charming, broad-leaved snowdrop is a close ally of *Galanthus elwesii*, though distinguished from it by the absence of the green spot at the base of the flower. But the chief joy of *G. caucasicus* lies not so much in the species, as in some of its subspecies – for example, in *G. c. hiemalis*, which often flowers in late November, and certainly in December. Since the species comes out in January and February, the two can be mingled together for a really long-lasting flowering succession.

G. caucasicus and its various offspring will make a splendid carpet beneath deciduous trees and shrubs; you could also try them in smaller groups, placed before dwarf evergreens like *Euonymus microphyllus*. They look well, too, growing through the kind of sprawling evergreen ground cover that the spring-flowering periwinkles *Vinca major* and *V. minor* make.
CULTIVATION Set young plants in any good soil, in an open or partially shaded position, in spring. Propagate by dividing the crowded clumps just after flowering; transplanted bulbs should be well watered until they are established.

Galanthus elwesii

GIANT SNOWDROP

Height 6-10in
Planting distance 4-6in
Best January-February

Originally from western Turkey, *Galanthus elwesii* has broad, blue-green leaves and bold green markings inside the large – up to 1¼in – flowers. It is not so free-flowering as some of the other snowdrops, and the 'floral carpet' treatment really does not suit it; rather it is a creature of individual beauty that demands a special location to be seen at its best.

Place it therefore in a rock garden, among low-growing plants such as *Phlox stolonifera* or *Arenaria caespitosa* 'Aurea' which bloom as the snowdrop leaves die back. Alternatively, mingle it in well-defined groups among evergreen shrubs with spring flowers that follow the snowdrops – Japanese azaleas or *Choisya ternata*, which has flowers sweetly scented, like orange blossom.
CULTIVATION Set young plants in spring in any good soil, avoiding heavy shade. Propagate by lifting and dividing crowded bulbs just after they have flowered.

Galanthus ikariae

Height 6-8in
Planting distance 4-6in
Best March

In its native Caucasus, this charming snowdrop comes out near the snow line in May and June; in balmier Britain, it throws discretion to the winds and emerges in March and April, carrying the genus *Galanthus* into spring. But before flowering, its buds and glossy, bright green leaves have been around for some weeks, mingling with, and enhancing, more intrepid snowdrops.

A minor problem is that once flowering is over, the dying-back leaves tend to linger. They can be camouflaged by accompanying *G. ikariae* with the periwinkles *Vinca minor* and

The miniature lampshades of *Galanthus nivalis* glow brightly to illuminate late winter.

Even the dazzling crystals of melting snow cannot compete with the brilliance of *Galanthus nivalis* 'Flore Pleno' with its double flowers.

Planted at random beneath deciduous trees, groups of *Galanthus nivalis* and *Cyclamen coum* speckle a coppery canvas of fallen leaves.

V. major. The periwinkles with variegated foliage would be particularly suitable as an evergreen ground cover, and as an attractive disguise for the dying snowdrop leaves.

CULTIVATION Set young plants in spring, in any moist, free-draining soil enriched with well-rotted organic matter. The bulbs self-propagate naturally, forming sizable clumps, and should be divided every few years to maintain flower size and quality. Keep from drying out during this process.

Galanthus nivalis

COMMON SNOWDROP

Height 4-6in
Planting distance 3-4in
Best January-February

The gallant wild snowdrop of British woodlands is the traditional herald of life returning after bleak winter. In the garden it can be planted in drifts beneath trees and shrubs, or among evergreen ground-hugging plants such as the

Galanthus nivalis 'Lutescens' is known by its yellow markings.

periwinkles, *Vinca major* and *V. minor*, or in smaller groups by small shrubs like *Euonymus fortunei radicans*.

There is a double-flowered variety, *Galanthus nivalis* 'Flore Pleno', and a host of hybrids derived from the species which vary considerably in stature, behaviour and also flowering

period. Each form has its own special characteristics and so deserves to be grown individually or with contrasting companions. The robust *G. n.* 'Sam Arnott' is a perfect companion to set off the exuberant, pink-flowered *Erica carnea* 'Springwood Pink' or 'Pink Spangles'. The vigorous *G. n.* 'Atkinsii' is useful for growing through evergreen ground cover such as *Vinca minor* cultivars. The less boisterous *G. n.* 'Viridapicis', which has a distinctive green spot on the outer as well as on the inner petals, can also be grown among light ground cover. *G. n.*'Scharlockii' is similar, but with two upright, leaf-like spathes above each flower which have earned it the nickname of 'Donkey-eared snowdrop'. *G. n.* 'Lutescens' is an unusual yellow and white form.

CULTIVATION Plant bulbs in

A green spot on the tips of the petals identifies *G. n.* 'Viridapicis'.

autumn in moisture-retentive, fertile soil. The hybrids can be bought as bulbs in full leaf – 'in the green' – and set in spring in soil refreshed with plenty of organic matter. Propagate by transplanting self-sown seedlings, or lift and divide crowded bulbs immediately after they have flowered.

BRIDGING THE SEASONS
IN A
Woody dell

Towards the end of February, days are some two hours longer than they were at the beginning of the month. Perhaps that is why our native snowdrop, *Galanthus nivalis*, seems at its best then, whether poking up through snow, grass or fallen leaves. The snowdrops are particularly suited to a situation like this – shady, sheltered and with plenty of humus. And if you don't happen to have a full-scale woody dell in your garden, it doesn't matter, for this simple but effective planting scheme can create a pool of colour little more than 4ft across beneath any suitable shrub or tree.

The snowdrops mingle with the lemon-yellow flowers of winter aconites (*Eranthis hyemalis*), set in their ruffs of glossy green, which emerge at about the same time. Like them, they can take quite a lot of shade, and in any case do their growing up before the trees put on their leaves and while the dell is still fairly well lit.

Certain small narcissus hybrids would also be happy in this little patch of woodland, and are much better suited to it than the large garden cultivars with their broad leaves and big, self-important trumpets. They have their place, but it is not here in this fragment of wilderness. The advancing spring brings forth the fragrant, creamy *Narcissus* 'Minnow', 7in high, and the slightly taller 'Jenny', white with a yellow trumpet, in good time to

mix with the pink-flushed stars of the native windflower, *Anemone nemorosa*, another plant that easily naturalises in woodland. A different effect could be achieved by substituting or adding the large-flowered, soft lilac-blue *A. n.* 'Robinsoniana', or the darker 'Royal Blue'. Both cultivars are just as vigorous as the species itself, and will happily reappear season after season.

Summer's contribution to the dell can also be left undisturbed for years. The attention-getters are the nicely compact hostas 'Thomas Hogg' (2ft high, 20in across), which has cream-edged leaves and mauve flowers, and 'Golden Prayers' (18in height and spread), with bright gold foliage and paler blooms. Apart from being one of the earliest hostas to flower, 'Thomas Hogg' is particularly well suited to this situation, since the smooth, shiny upper surfaces of the leaves shed water and remain free of the sediment that drips from the trees. The hosta leaves will linger into autumn, when they will make good company for a planting of the autumn crocus *Crocus speciosus*, with its delightfully slim mauve and grey-blue goblets, and lilac-blue *C. kotschyanus*. ❧

To give a woody corner the authentic air of a forest glade, plant it for winter with our native snowdrops and winter aconites. The aconites especially enjoy this setting, where they do not have to compete with grass.

IN SPRING the wild look is given encouragement by a swathe of jaunty narcissus hybrids and the delightful pink-washed stars of the windflower, *Anemone nemorosa*.

IN SUMMER, a certain formality is given to the glade by the presence of two brilliant hostas – 'Thomas Hogg' with its shiny, creamy-edged, water-resistant leaves, and the brightly gilded 'Golden Prayers' shining below the tree.

AUTUMN reveals that though the hostas' flowering is at an end, their bright foliage is still very much in evidence. It makes a cheerful shelter for a small army of *Crocus kotschyanus* and *C. speciosus* beginning to emerge in the foreground.

Iris danfordiae, with its distinctive, vivid yellow blooms, top-heavy on their short stems, came originally from eastern Turkey.

Iris histrioides 'Major' can flower as early as Christmas; it is remarkably tough, surviving all weather conditions, including snow.

Iris danfordiae

Height 3-4in
Planting distance 3-4in
Best February-March

In the first year after planting, a group of this dwarf bulbous iris forms a picture of golden light. The honey-scented blooms, 2½-3in across, are slightly top-heavy above short, narrow leaves. After flowering, the bulbs divide naturally into many smaller bulbils that take several years to bloom again. By planting newly purchased bulbs for three or more years in succession, a regular parade of flowers can be anticipated as each spring approaches.

Iris danfordiae does not grow well through ground-hugging plants, and needs to be set among fine stone chippings in an isolated position in a rock garden, or in a small bed that can be seen from the house. In spring, when the leaves die down, sprinkle seeds of an easy-going summer annual such as violet cress, *Ionopsidium acaule*, to fill the space left by the irises, yet not to interfere with the bulbs beneath.

CULTIVATION Plant bulbs during autumn in free-draining soil, in a sunny position, with 4in of soil above them. Once established, colonies are best left alone, and new plantings should come from fresh bulbs.

Iris histrioides
'Major'

Height 3-4in
Planting distance 3-4in
Best January-February

A most reliable and rewarding early flowering iris, this cultivar produces splendidly audacious blooms – bright blue and boldly marked with white and gold – which appear well before the leaves develop.

Iris histrioides prospers in the well-drained, sunny setting of a rock garden, in a patio bed or

The lordly air of hybrid *Iris reticulata* 'J.S. Dijt' is enhanced by the ermine markings on the petals.

Standing on delicate stems, the trumpets of *Narcissus asturiensis* are about an inch long.

Like ladies-in-waiting, prim snowdrops intermingled with variegated ivy, escort a flamboyant parade of *Iris reticulata* 'Joyce' in a winter border, backed by a periwinkle and the blue-grey foliage of rue.

(*Iris histrioides* cont) balcony container, or pushing up through a dense grey-green carpet of creeping *Thymus praecox arcticus*. This will flower in summer when the iris leaves have died back.

For an unusual colour display, try the hybrid 'Katharine Hodgkin'. Basically, it is a pale yellow washed over with purple. When the flowers open, it is yellow that predominates; later, purple comes to the fore. CULTIVATION Plant the dormant bulbs during autumn in any free-draining soil in a sunny position. Dress with bone meal

after flowering. To propagate, wait until the bulbs become overcrowded, then lift and divide them after flowering.

Iris reticulata
Hybrids

Height 4-6in
Planting distance 3-4in
Best February-March

A handful of *Iris reticulata* glowing blue-purple in a rock garden or in a border will do much to lift the garden from its post-Christmas doldrums; add

some of its hybrids and you have a real festival of colour. There are plenty to choose from – the debonair sky-blue 'Joyce', deep plum 'J.S. Dijt', the cream and azure 'Clairette', white-blue 'Natasha', pale blue 'Cantab', the violet-pink 'Pauline', and more.

If you plant the dwarf irises in a rock garden, emphasise their colours with a layer of limestone chips spread beneath them. They can also be planted under deciduous shrubs and trees such as the dwarf willow *Salix lanata* and the witch hazel, *Hamamelis mollis* 'Pallida', or

Pastel-shaded petals with creamy aprons are the joy of the hybrid *Iris reticulata* 'Clairette'.

Chimonanthus praecox. The witch hazel 'Pallida' will be in flower in January or earlier, while the chimonanthus will lead the association from December onward. The willow will follow the irises with a fine display of yellow catkins above grey-white felt leaves.
CULTIVATION Plant bulbs 3-4in

deep in autumn, in a sunny position and free-draining soil. Propagate by dividing bulbs.

Narcissus asturiensis
(syn *N. minimus*)

Height 3in
Planting distance 2-3in
Best February

The natural home of this sparkling, golden miniature daffodil – it is the smallest of all species narcissus – is the mountains of Spain, where it grows in clumps in the short alpine turf and on rocky slopes near the snow line. In cultivation in Britain, *Narcissus asturiensis* is unlikely to flourish in grass and does best established in pockets of well-drained soil in a rock garden. It is also a good plant for sink gardens, troughs, window boxes and urns.

Plant *N. asturiensis* between established clumps of saxifrages, such as the grey-leaved

The lemon-yellow flowers give *Narcissus bulbocodium citrinus* its name. It is one of the cultivars suitable for naturalising in a grassy setting.

A host of golden daffodils, in this case of *Narcissus cyclamineus*, that would gladden the poetic heart of William Wordsworth, form a brilliant carpet beneath a rose-purple bank of *Rhododendron* 'Praecox'.

Narcissus bulbocodium has a distinctive cup-shaped trumpet and slim, rush-like foliage.

Saxifraga grisebachii. There, the delicate 1in long trumpets will provide bright splashes of gold among the smaller alpines waiting to flower in the days ahead.
CULTIVATION Plant bulbs 2-3in deep in autumn, in any well-drained soil and in a sunny position. Propagate by dividing the bulbs in autumn.

Narcissus bulbocodium

HOOP-PETTICOAT DAFFODIL

Height 3-6in
Planting distance 3-4in
Best February-March

The large, cup-shaped trumpet, widening at the end like a hooped petticoat, distinguishes *Narcissus bulbocodium* from all other daffodils. There are a number of different forms and cultivars. *N. b.* 'Nylon' grows a little taller than its cousins, and has milky-white, scented blooms; *N. b.* 'Tenuifolius' has almost prostrate foliage.

A number of varieties and cultivars of *Narcissus* are ideal for naturalising and look their best when associated with other plants in a meadow-like setting. For example, a scattered mixture of crocuses – say *Crocus kotschyanus, C. medius* and *C. imperati* – could lead on from autumn through to late winter. Then, taking over from the daffodils and crocuses, you could have *Gentiana acaulis* and *G. verna* that would flower from late spring to early summer.
CULTIVATION Plant bulbs under turf in autumn, or about 4in deep in good soil. These daffodils naturalise in moistish sites, or can be propagated by replanting dormant bulb offsets.

Narcissus cyclamineus

Height 6-10in
Planting distance 4in
Best February-March

As the species name implies, these rich gold flowers, with their long cups and swept-back petals, do somewhat resemble cyclamen; the less botanically minded might also spot a more than faint likeness to miniature Christmas crackers.

With its smallish stature, *Narcissus cyclamineus* is best naturalised in clumps of a dozen or so about the base of a tree or shrub. They can be preceded in autumn by real cyclamen, such as *Cyclamen cilicium*, which produces pale pink flowers in October and November, and by the longer-flowering, lilac-rose coloured *Colchicum speciosum*. To carry the association into spring, plant groups of *Anemone nemorosa* or another dainty narcissus with a later flowering period than *N. cyclamineus*, such as 'Tete-a-Tete'.

There is no mistaking the swept-back look of *Narcissus cyclamineus*.

CULTIVATION Plant in the open or in partial shade in early autumn. The bulbs multiply naturally in moist soil; when overcrowded, lift and divide in autumn.

Scilla mischtschenkoana will carpet the ground beneath most deciduous shrubs when they are bare of leaves.

Scilla mischtschenkoana
(syn *S. tubergeniana*)

Height 3-6in
Planting distance 3-4in
Best February-March

When little else is in bloom this lovely scilla brings a hint of spring to winter. Each bulb produces up to five stems, each with four or five starry, bell-shaped, pale blue-white flowers with dark blue stripes.

Create a delightful winter picture by planting *Scilla mischtschenkoana* bulbs among and around the stark crimson stems of *Cornus alba* 'Sibirica'. The bulbs will be safely dormant by the time the shrub's foliage develops. Alternatively, plant *S. mischtschenkoana* in masses around medium-sized, columnar conifers, which in winter will look like tall ships on a sea of blue scilla blooms.

CULTIVATION Plant bulbs in autumn in any well-drained soil, with a generous scattering of bone meal over the site; repeat the dose each autumn. The bulbs multiply rapidly. Divide and replant them when they become overcrowded.

Winter ANNUALS

GENERALLY, annuals do not flower in winter because of the absence of insect pollinators. However, the flowering season of one or two groups of plants has been so reliably extended that winter annuals cannot be entirely dismissed. Some of them, too, after flowering, retain other attractions such as seed pods, which can contribute variety and charm to the winter scene.

Lunaria annua
HONESTY

Height 2-3ft
Planting distance 1ft
Best October-January,
April-June

Just let honesty run to seed and it will be with you always, to illuminate a dark corner in winter with its tissue-thin, silvery moons – the remains of its seed vessels. In late spring come masses of fragrant, reddish-purple to pink flowers; the variety *Lunaria annua* 'Alba' has white flower clusters, while *L. a.* 'Variegata' has crimson flowers and creamy-edged leaves. The flowers are replaced in summer by round, flat, green seed vessels which, as the year advances, dry and shed their

The translucent, mother-of-pearl discs of *Lunaria annua* catch the pale winter light, and with a drift of snowdrops (*Galanthus nivalis*) bring a touch of fairytale magic to a shady corner of the garden.

THE SUMMER flowers of *Lunaria annua* will self-seed and be even more prolific in following years.

outer casings to reveal the translucent discs that are often used in flower arrangements.

With its seed pods, winter-green leaves and spring flowers, honesty provides its own continuity of interest. However, it would be helped out in summer by a foreground planting of the button-shaped crimson daisy *Bellis perennis* 'Pomponette'. If the honesty itself is intended as an accompaniment, it would look very well beneath the showy, pink-flowering beauty bush, *Kolkwitzia amabilis*.

CULTIVATION Sow seed in late spring on the site where the plants are to grow; choose a shady spot in any light, well-drained soil. Despite its specific name, this lunaria is a biennial, but sometimes lasts for more than two years.

Viola × wittrockiana

PANSY

The round-the-year pansy has completely changed the face of many of our gardens in winter. The plant's natural preference for cool, moist growing conditions has led to the successful creation of varieties that cheerfully withstand northern climes and winter weather. By planting varieties with different flowering times, it is possible to have these bright, velvety flowers decorating the edge of the border, window boxes or containers throughout the year.

Plant the pansies in groups or packed along the edge of a border, so that despite their size they can make a colourful impact on the winter garden. Place groups of white, gold or blue pansies in front of evergreens – the variegated *Ilex × altaclarensis* 'Golden King',

Elaeagnus pungens 'Maculata', or dark dwarf conifers. *Skimmia japonica* or *S. j. reevesiana* would complement any of the pansy varieties and provide early spring flowers and winter berries. Summer annuals like mimulus and impatiens would continue a bright display after the pansies have been lifted.

CULTIVATION

Sow seed in June and July, directly outdoors in any reasonably fertile, moist soil in a cool, lightly shaded position, or in a shaded cold frame. If you use a cold frame, prick out seedlings 6in apart when they are large enough to handle and transfer to their final positions in autumn. Alternatively buy young plants as soon as they are available in early autumn and plant directly outside. Keep the ground free of weeds and deadhead regularly. Propagate by seed or by cuttings of basal shoots in July.

This could be a summer patio scene, but it isn't; there are many tough varieties of *Viola × wittrockiana* that flower over the winter months.

Winter pansies bring glorious colour to a border, in front of *Skimmia japonica* 'Rubella' and *Ceanothus thyrsiflorus*, whose flowering seasons are yet to come.

Summer colour in the depths of winter

Winter pansies free the garden from the monochrome tones
of winter, and stand out like refugees from the summer border.
Their vibrant colours and velvety texture can brighten the garden scene
from November to May in all but the very coldest of weather. Let them
be seen from the house, crowding in a hanging basket, a window box
or a patio container. Alternatively, they can be used to revitalise dark
winter evergreens with a dash of brilliant foreground colour.

Photographed in February at The Royal Horticultural Society's Garden,
Wisley, Surrey.

'Universal Purple'

'Universal White'

'Joker Light Blue'

'Imperial Pink Shades'

'Universal Red'

'Clear Crystal Mixed'

'Universal Yellow'

'Crystal Azure Blue'

'Majestic Giants Mixed'

'Supremo Early'

'Imperial Silver Princess'

THE *Heather* GARDEN

The colour focus in a bed of heathers shifts subtly from one part to another through the seasons, creating an ever changing tapestry of foliage and flowers. Most species are in bloom for many weeks, if not months, and by mixing different cultivars it is possible to have a heath or heather in flower at almost any time in the year. Strictly speaking the term heath applies to ericas, heather to callunas. In practice, heather is used for both genera. The evergreen foliage is an additional asset, the tiny, tough, densely packed leaves of dark green, silver-grey, gold, orange or fiery red providing a year-round foil for any plants nearby. It is not necessary to have a bed exclusively for heathers; neat hummock-forming species can be incorporated into an alpine bed or patio border to spill over rocks or paving slabs, and there are many varieties which are suitable for hedging. To grow a wide enough range of heathers for all-season interest, a neutral or acid soil free of lime is preferable. However, the winter-flowering *Erica carnea, E. × darleyensis* and *E. erigena* all tolerate lime and chalk soils. Otherwise, heathers are remarkably resilient and easy to grow. They spring back into place if trodden underfoot, are resistant to pests and diseases, and many are completely frost-hardy. Once they are well established, the plants need very little attention, and by covering the ground with their thick foliage almost eliminate any need for weeding.

Bulbs like the large Dutch *Crocus vernus* will push through *Erica carnea* for a coinciding display of flowers in early spring.

WINTER INTO SPRING

Only the most severe snowfall and frost affects flower development in the winter heathers; they invariably produce a display that lasts for months at the darkest time of the year when colour is most needed. *Erica × darleyensis* hybrids are the longest flowering of all: the white 'Silberschmelze' and the countless, strong rose-pink flowers of 'Furzey' can appear as early as late November and continue until May. By January, they are joined by the first of the *Erica carnea* varieties, such as 'Myretoun Ruby' – compact with glowing red flowers – or the more vigorous 'Pink Spangles'. The buds of 'Springwood White', a very strong-growing form, graduate from apple green to yellow over winter, before opening to glistening white in February. The warm brown, dead flower heads of *Erica vagans* cultivars will also add tone to the winter scene. And falling temperatures intensify the glorious golden foliage colours of *Erica carnea* 'Foxhollow', *E. × darleyensis* 'Jack H. Brummage', *E. vagans* 'Valerie Proudley' and the fiery *Calluna vulgaris* 'Orange Queen' and 'Robert Chapman'. By April, when the winter heaths are at last fading, the tree heathers – such as the charming rose-pink *Erica australis* and white *E. arborea* 'Alpina' – are in flower. The mid to late spring flowers of *E. erigena*, which is tolerant of salt spray if not of chill east-coast winds, vary in colour from white to a warm and cheerful rose-red, and take centre stage all the way through until May.

Although strictly speaking in a genus of its own, the Irish heath, *Daboecia cantabrica*, is a natural plant for the heather garden. Its flowers are larger than those of the true heaths (*Erica*), and its May to October flowering period probably longer than that of any other shrub. Unlike most of the heathers, it also tolerates light shade. 'Alba' and 'Alba Globosa' are superb white forms; 'Praegerae' is rose-red, and 'Atropurpurea' a splendid purple. *D. × scotica* 'William Buchanan' is another fine purple, with smaller, more freely produced flowers than the species.

THE SUMMER MONTHS

The delicate bell flowers of *Erica cinerea* not only bloom through the summer months from June to August, but may continue until October; varieties include the white 'Alba Minor' and 'Alba Major', the

IN AUTUMN, different *Calluna vulgaris* cultivars, with a succession of flowering periods, carpet the ground beneath the silvery *Picea pungens* 'Glauca' and *Acer palmatum*.

washed-mauve 'Eden Valley', rose-red 'C.D. Eason', the more compact, brighter red 'Atro-rubens', and vibrant purple 'P.S. Patrick'.

The late summer choice is enormous. From heathlands near Wareham in Dorset comes the Dorset heath, *Erica ciliaris*. Although slightly vulnerable to pollution and severe weather, it is worth growing for its spikes of larger-than-average flowers in shades of pink – or the white 'Sto-borough' – during July and August.

SUMMER INTO AUTUMN

Another county 'speciality' is the Cornish heath, *Erica vagans*, found in the wild only on the Lizard Peninsula in the extreme south-west of England. The flowers, closely set along elegant spikes, appear from August to October, and include 'Lyonesse' (white with distinctive brown anthers), the pale pink 'St Keverne' and the red 'Mrs D.F. Maxwell'. It is wide-spreading and grows well in heavy soils as long as peat is added.

The silvery-grey foliage of the cross-leaved heath, *Erica tetralix*, is attractive in its own right, and the flowers of the rose-red 'Con Underwood' or white 'Alba Mollis' bloom from July to October. Last to flower is the common heather or ling, *Calluna vulgaris*, a tough inhabitant of our heaths and moorlands. 'Tib' is a particularly free-flowering, red-purple form and one of the first to bloom in August. 'County Wicklow' is compact, with double mauve-pink blooms; 'H.E. Beale', a taller, deeper mauve cultivar, flowers from September to early November; double white 'Alba Plena' is September and October flowering; and double carmine 'Schurig's Sensation', which flowers from August to November.

PLANNING A HEATHER GARDEN

Heathers are at their best in open, sunny positions in an informal planting scheme.

• Plant in groups of odd, rather than even numbers, with at least three of any one variety.

• Ensure that the area devoted to heathers is in keeping with the size of your garden. If there isn't

A startling February scene is created as the winter and spring-flowering *Erica carnea*, smaller clumps of *E. erigena* and *Helleborus foetidus* bloom amid conifers and the brilliant naked stems of *Cornus alba* and *C. stolonifera* cultivars.

room for a full-size heather garden, plant a small group of winter, summer and foliage cultivars among complementary shrubs.

• Aim for a ratio of 45 per cent summer and autumn heaths, 30 per cent winter, and 25 per cent foliage varieties.

• Avoid planting in straight lines or regular patterns.

• Take height, spread and habit into account, so that the level of the heather bed graduates from the pincushion-like shrublets and ground-hugging forms to the heartier upright varieties, with the tree heathers in the centre or at the back of a bed.

• For companion plants, take a lead from the wild. Silver birch (*Betula*) could form a centrepiece; dwarf conifers (see pages 42-45), with their complementary foliage, can provide lower-level vertical interest – and form a windbreak if necessary. The acid-soil-loving rhododendrons could provide depth of background, but go for the smaller, compact varieties such as *Rhododendron* 'Pink Pebble', or 'Golden Torch'. Any dwarf broom (*Cytisus* and *Genista*), potentillas and smaller forms of spiraea would make good late spring and summer neighbours, with pernettya, cotoneaster or berberis to follow on into autumn.

Looking after your garden

SEASONAL JOBS IN YOUR GARDEN

A GUIDE TO GARDENING TECHNIQUES

TROUBLESHOOTING

SEASONAL JOBS IN YOUR GARDEN

A QUICK, READY REFERENCE and reminder to help you handle the year's workload. See pages 12-13 for a guide to seasonal variations according to locality. For soil preparation, planting and cultivation techniques, see page 388.

· EARLY SPRING ·

THE MOMENTUM OF WORK increases as the season advances. Much depends on the weather, for if the ground is saturated the tilth required for sowing seeds cannot be obtained, and the soil will be too cold for germination.

TREES AND SHRUBS
- Complete planting of bare-rooted trees.
- Layer shoots of chimonanthus, cotinus, *Magnolia grandiflora* and other shrubs that do not root easily from cuttings, as spring growth starts.
- Cut out flowering shoots of winter-flowering shrubs such as *Jasminum nudiflorum*.
- Cut back last year's stems of salix and cornus grown for winter colour almost to ground level.

CLIMBERS
- Layer *Vitis coignetiae, Pileostegia viburnoides* and other climbers.
- Complete pruning of large-flowered clematis.

ROSES
- Complete planting of bare-rooted roses when ground is neither frozen nor waterlogged.
- Prune repeat-flowering climbers, shrub, bush and miniature roses.

HERBACEOUS PERENNIALS
- Dress all plants with base fertiliser and rake in.
- Plant perennials when soil conditions are favourable.
- Divide clump-forming plants left over from autumn, including less hardy types such as peonies, as soon as new growth begins.

ALPINES
- Divide summer-flowering alpines such as *Campanula garganica, Ranunculus gramineus* and *Geranium* 'Ballerina'.
- Plant nursery-raised plants for spring and summer flowering.

WATER AND BOG PLANTS
- Remove dead and dying tops of marginal plants left on for winter protection.
- Put in all types of water plants for bog garden.

BULBS, CORMS AND TUBERS
- Lift, divide and replant snowdrops and aconites once flowers have faded.
- Plant *Anemone coronaria* cultivars for flowering in summer.
- Remove fading flowers from daffodils, narcissi and other late winter-flowering plants, but leave the foliage until it has died down.
- Continue feeding bulbs with general fertiliser as soon as the leaves start to appear.

ANNUALS AND BIENNIALS
- Sow half-hardy annual seeds under glass. In mild districts, sow hardy annual seeds outdoors.

- Harden off earlier-sown half-hardy annual seedlings in a cold frame. Protect frame against frost with, for example, an old piece of carpet.
- Plant out sweet pea seedlings sown the previous autumn.

LAWNS
- Rake over and reseed worn or bare patches.
- Apply a spring/summer general fertiliser.
- In a mild season, mow the grass as its growth rate dictates, with blades set about 1in high.

GENERAL MAINTENANCE
- Complete all digging as soon as possible, removing and burning perennial weeds.
- Clear weeds from paths and drives.
- Scrub stone paths and drives with a garden brush dipped in a dilute solution of potassium permanganate to kill algae.

· MID-SPRING ·

SEED SOWING MUST go on, because a late start can spoil the display in the flower garden. Cut back straggly, evergreen shrubs to encourage new growth from the base. If cold winds persist, shield newly planted shrubs with screens.

TREES AND SHRUBS
- Prune hardy fuchsias, buddleias and other shrubs which flower on current season's growth to two or three buds from base.

- Prune hydrangeas whose flower heads were retained for winter display.

- Plant bare-rooted evergreens as long as the ground is moist, but only plant deciduous trees and shrubs if they are containerised.

- Continue the layering of shrubs begun in early spring, and layer camellias, rhododendrons and other acid-loving evergreens.

- Prune early flowering shrubs, such as for-sythia, as the flowers fade.

CLIMBERS

- Tie in young shoots of large-flowered clematis hybrids to prevent them breaking in windy weather. Handle them carefully – they break easily.

ROSES

- Complete all pruning by mid-season and lightly rake a rose fertiliser into the surface soil.

- Mulch with well-rotted farmyard manure or garden compost when the ground is moist.

- Plant roses only if they are containerised, and conditions are frost-free.

- Tie in new growth on climbing and rambling roses.

HERBACEOUS PERENNIALS

- Finish dividing and replanting clumps of late summer to autumn perennials such as asters, rudbeckia, monarda and *Schizostylis coccinea*.

- Stake tall-growing plants such as delphiniums and Michaelmas daisies at an early stage of growth.

ALPINES

- Plant any alpine plants now and they will quickly establish themselves.

WATER AND BOG PLANTS

- If it is a reasonably mild season, plant aquatic plants, such as water lilies; otherwise postpone this job until late spring.

BULBS, CORMS AND TUBERS

- Deadhead spring bulbs but leave foliage for a minimum of six weeks or until foliage yellows.

- Plant *Nerine bowdenii* for autumn flowering.

ANNUALS AND BIENNIALS

- Plant out and stake spring-sown sweet peas.

- Complete indoor sowings of half-hardy annual seeds.

- Continue sowing hardy annual seeds in open garden when soil conditions permit.

LAWNS

- Apply selective weedkillers if necessary.

- Mow at least once a week, gradually lowering the blades to about ½in.

GENERAL MAINTENANCE

- Hoe to remove all weeds to prevent them seeding and taking nutrients from other plants.

· LATE SPRING ·

Though this is the first really rewarding time of the year, routine work – hoeing, sowing, thinning and planting – must continue. With the first grass cuttings available, this is a good time to start a compost heap. Now, too, is the time to apply selective weedkillers.

TREES AND SHRUBS

- Deadhead rhododendrons and azaleas to encourage the formation of next year's blooms.

- Plant out shrubs that are tender when young, such as choisya, hydrangea and fuchsia.

- Keep newly planted trees and shrubs moist at the roots during dry periods. Spray foliage with water from time to time.

- When the soil is moist, spread a mulch of pulverised bark, compost or well-rotted manure.

- Lightly dress all trees and shrubs with a high nitrogen general fertiliser.

ROSES

- Deal with any sign of aphid infestation or disease immediately; if you are using a systemic insecticide or fungicide, spray in the early morning or late evening.

HERBACEOUS PERENNIALS

- Remove growing tips of tall perennials such as asters and solidago, and thin out weak shoots from the centre of overcrowded plants to promote sturdy growth and better flowers.

- Mulch all plants with well-rotted manure or garden compost.

ALPINES

- Trim back spreading plants, such as aubrietia and arabis, 2-3in from the base when they have finished flowering.

WATER AND BOG PLANTS

- Divide and replant any marginal plants – such as *Primula japonica* – that have spread beyond their allotted spaces.

- Thin overgrown clumps of water lilies and remove some of the larger leaves.

- If necessary, water the bog garden to keep it moist during dry spells.

BULBS, CORMS AND TUBERS

- Plant half-hardy bulbs such as crinum in sheltered positions.

> Plant dahlia tubers in well-prepared ground that has been enriched beforehand with well-rotted manure or garden compost.

> Plant *Amaryllis belladonna* as soon as the bulbs become available.

> If you are going to lift bulbous plants to make way for summer bedding, heel them into a spare piece of ground until the foliage has died back. The bulbs can then be lifted, dried and stored in a cool, dry place.

ANNUALS AND BIENNIALS

> Complete sowing hardy annuals outside as soon as possible.

> Sow biennials in a seedbed outdoors, ready for next spring.

> Plant out half-hardy annuals when fear of frost has passed. In the south of Britain, this is usually around mid-May.

> Liquid feed any young plants still in boxes before planting out in the garden.

LAWNS

> Apply weedkiller – which is more effective when weeds are growing strongly – or cut out weeds with a knife.

> Mow the grass regularly. Trim the edges of the lawn after every cut.

GENERAL MAINTENANCE

> Remove suckers – shoots rising from ground level, directly from the roots – from roses, lilacs and other shrubs.

> Water plants copiously – at least 1 gallon per square yard at each watering – during dry spells over this critical growth period.

> Protect plants from slugs, especially when weather is warm and humid.

> Hoe frequently to remove weeds while they are still young.

· EARLY SUMMER ·

THIS, THE LOVELIEST HOUR of the gardening year, is also the time to keep a weather eye open for insect pests, diseases and weeds. Feeding plants with fertilisers or liquid feeds is also important at this season. Sow perennials in nursery beds for next year's display.

TREES AND SHRUBS

> Cut out any branches of variegated cultivars that are losing their variegation.

> Take softwood cuttings of hardy fuchsias and place them in a propagating frame to root. Shade during sunny periods.

> Plant out tender fuchsias when they have been well hardened off.

> Thin out the weak flowering shoots from deciduous shrubs which have finished flowering, such as deutzia, spiraea and *Hamamelis japonica*.

CLIMBERS

> Take leaf-bud cuttings of all clematis.

> Water wall-trained shrubs during dry spells, and mulch immediately afterwards to help retain the moisture.

ROSES

> Remove any suckers.

> Continue to guard against aphids.

HERBACEOUS PERENNIALS

> Cut back early flowering perennials such as aquilegia and doronicum – that need to be kept in

trim and discouraged from self-seeding – to about 4in, once the flowers have died.

> Lift and divide primroses and polyanthus after flowering and replant in a shady corner for the summer, in moisture-retentive soil containing plenty of humus.

> Lift and divide bearded iris after flowering.

> Finish sowing seeds of hardy perennials outdoors or in a cold frame for flowering next year.

ALPINES

> Keep rock gardens and patios free of weeds.

> Remove spent flower heads unless required for the seeds, and clip back any plants that are becoming straggly.

WATER AND BOG PLANTS

> If aphids attack water lilies, spray leaves with a powerful water jet.

> Keep water clear of algae before large masses form.

BULBS, CORMS AND TUBERS

> In mild districts, plant *Anemone coronaria* cultivars for autumn and winter flowering.

> Plant out young dahlia plants raised from cuttings or seeds.

> Continue to remove spring bulb foliage not less than six weeks after flowering has finished.

> Gather seed capsules of crocuses when they start to ripen, and sow.

ANNUALS AND BIENNIALS

> Plant out pelargoniums for summer bedding.

> Sow biennial seeds in a nursery bed for flowering next year.

> Deadhead annuals regularly to promote a longer flowering period.

> Hoe frequently to keep weeds in check.

🙿 Pick sweet peas each week to promote continued flowering. Do not let them form pods.

LAWNS

🙿 Mow regularly. Raise the blades slightly during dry, hot spells.

GENERAL MAINTENANCE

🙿 Watch out for greenfly and other aphids. Spray at first sign of attack.

🙿 If not already done, mulch beds after rain.

· MIDSUMMER ·

A REWARDING TIME for the gardener whose earlier work is now paying dividends, but guard against drought by watering well and providing mulches of well-rotted leaves or old compost. Keep a careful lookout for greenfly attack on any young, soft shoots, and prepare new and worn lawn areas for autumn sowing.

TREES AND SHRUBS

🙿 Continue thinning out shrubs that have finished flowering, including philadelphus and weigela, cutting old stems down to base.

🙿 Take semi-hardwood cuttings of shrubs whose new stems are starting to get woody, such as cistus and deutzia.

CLIMBERS

🙿 Prune the current year's growth of wisteria to the first five leaves to keep in trim and promote more vigorous flowering.

ROSES

🙿 Deadhead as soon as blooms fade to encourage new growth.

🙿 Feed with a proprietary fertiliser while the plants are in full bloom.

🙿 Take action against pests and diseases only if there are still signs of attack.

HERBACEOUS PERENNIALS

🙿 Deadhead and remove any yellowing foliage.

ALPINES

🙿 Sow freshly gathered seeds of *Pulsatilla vulgaris* and *Gentiana verna* for spring flowering.

🙿 Take healthy, non-flowering cuttings of spring-flowering alpines, including thyme, phlox, aubrietia, helianthemum and arabis.

WATER AND BOG PLANTS

🙿 Rake algae from ponds.

BULBS, CORMS AND TUBERS

🙿 Plant *Sternbergia lutea,* autumn-flowering crocuses and colchicums as soon as the bulbs become available.

🙿 Lift tulip bulbs when the foliage has started to die down. Dry and store.

🙿 Stake tall-growing plants such as dahlias.

🙿 Deadhead lilies.

ANNUALS AND BIENNIALS

🙿 Keep annuals flowering continuously by deadheading regularly.

LAWNS

🙿 Water regularly and copiously in dry weather and do not cut too close.

GENERAL MAINTENANCE

🙿 Hoe beds and borders regularly to keep them free from weeds.

· LATE SUMMER ·

M AKE A NOTE NOW of possible improvements that could be made to the herbaceous border when replanting in autumn. Cut suitable flowers, such as helichrysum and poppy seed heads, and hang them head downwards to dry for indoor displays in winter. Continue watering if drought threatens.

TREES AND SHRUBS

🙿 Take semi-hardwood cuttings of shrubs including hydrangea, cytisus, escallonia, euonymus, hypericum, ceanothus, philadelphus and shrubby spiraea.

🙿 Layer rhododendrons if not done in spring.

🙿 Take leaf-bud or semi-hardwood cuttings of camellias.

🙿 In dry weather, water newly planted trees well around their trunks – they can take several gallons a week.

CLIMBERS

🙿 Take semi-hardwood cuttings of *Solanum crispum* and other woody climbers.

ROSES

🙿 Order now for delivery of bare-rooted plants in late autumn.

🙿 Feed with fertiliser to give last blooms a boost.

🙿 When the last flowers of rambling roses have faded, remove those stems which bore flowers earlier in the year; new young shoots will have time to mature before winter arrives.

HERBACEOUS PERENNIALS

&. If asters show signs of mildew, spray with a systemic fungicidal solution before flowering.

&. Sow newly harvested meconopsis seeds for next year's flowering.

&. Take cuttings of violas, choosing young, healthy, non-flowering basal shoots.

&. Deadhead faded flowers, cut off tall weak stems from plants that have finished flowering, but leave foliage.

&. Plant autumn crocuses and colchicums.

ALPINES

&. Complete taking cuttings of healthy, non-flowering lateral shoots of helianthemum and arabis.

WATER AND BOG PLANTS

&. Thin out oxygenating plants such as water milfoil and water thyme to keep within bounds.

BULBS, CORMS AND TUBERS

&. Feed dahlias and support tall cultivars.

&. Propagate lilies using stem bulbils.

ANNUALS AND BIENNIALS

&. Continue deadheading to prolong the flowering period. Leave those which form decorative seed heads or from which you will gather seed.

&. Sow pansy and violet seeds for winter and spring flowering.

&. Take cuttings from non-flowering shoots of pelargoniums.

LAWNS

&. Prepare ground if seeding next year.

&. Apply summer dressing of lawn fertiliser.

GENERAL MAINTENANCE

&. Check all supports and ties on plants and replace any that are broken or missing.

· EARLY AUTUMN ·

THIS IS THE PERIOD for tidying up, for putting things to rights and preparing for the coming winter. The gardener would also be wise to devote some consideration to the requirements of the coming spring and, towards the end of the period, clear the ground of summer bedding plants, and fork it over.

TREES AND SHRUBS

&. Feed half-hardy shrubs with sulphate of potash to help ripen the wood and make the plants less susceptible to disease and frost damage.

&. Plant conifers and other evergreens while ground is moist and still warm.

&. Take hardwood cuttings of conifers.

&. Layer pliable stems of any deciduous shrubs.

CLIMBERS

&. Gather ripe seeds from clematis species for sowing in a cold frame over the next few weeks.

ROSES

&. Deadhead repeat-flowering shrub, bush and climbing roses.

&. Apply feed of sulphate of potash in the next few weeks to help ripen the wood and make the plants less susceptible to disease and frost damage.

HERBACEOUS PERENNIALS

&. Continue deadheading and cutting back; tidy borders, and mark the healthiest plants for later propagation by division.

ALPINES

&. Do any redesigning of the rock garden, or any necessary replanting and repositioning of plants.

WATER AND BOG PLANTS

&. Divide marginal and bog plants to prevent overcrowding around the pond.

BULBS, CORMS AND TUBERS

&. Plant bulbs during dry spells, starting with narcissi.

&. Plant bulbous irises for late winter and early spring flowering, and lily bulbs for next summer, as soon as they become available.

&. Check supports on dahlias; remove small buds below terminal bud if you want to encourage long-stemmed and larger blooms.

ANNUALS AND BIENNIALS

&. At the end of the month, lift any tender perennials that are treated as annuals because of their vulnerability to frost, such as *Helichrysum petiolare*, *Impatiens walleriana*, gazanias and heliotropes. Store in a frost-free place.

&. In warmer parts of the country, or in sheltered, sunny corners, sow hardy annuals outdoors for early flowers next year.

&. Fill gaps in borders with winter-flowering pansy plants as soon as they become available.

&. Start removing fading annuals to make way for spring bedding plants.

LAWNS

&. Sow seed on sites prepared earlier. Sow when ground is moist, but on a dry day.

&. Lay turf from mid-month onwards.

GENERAL MAINTENANCE

&. Tidy up beds – cut back dead stems and dead flower heads of perennials, and remove annuals that have finished flowering.

· MID-AUTUMN ·

Now TREES AND SHRUBS flare into autumn colour, the last of the border flowers are picked and only a few chrysanthemums and dahlias are left to defy the frosts. This is a good time to apply slow-acting fertilisers, such as bone meal.

TREES AND SHRUBS
🍃 Plant new trees and shrubs, including heaths and heathers, and stake standard specimens likely to be vulnerable to strong winds.

🍃 Take hardwood cuttings of deciduous shrubs, including forsythia, philadelphus and weigela.

CLIMBERS
🍃 Plant clematis and secure to supports.

ROSES
🍃 Cut back rose bushes by about one-third to help them withstand winter winds. Use the prunings as hardwood cuttings.

HERBACEOUS PERENNIALS
🍃 Divide and replant overcrowded clumps of tough-rooted perennials such as hostas and hardy geraniums.

🍃 Begin planting for flowering next summer.

WATER AND BOG PLANTS
🍃 Place netting over ponds to catch leaves.

BULBS, CORMS AND TUBERS
🍃 Continue to plant bulbs, such as *Iris xiphioides* and tulips, for early summer flowering.

🍃 Lift dahlias as soon as the foliage starts to yellow, or after the first frost, and store tubers.

🍃 At the end of the month, protect neck of tender bulbs such as *Crinum powellii* with a layer of straw.

ANNUALS AND BIENNIALS
🍃 Sow sweet peas in a sunny, sheltered site for early flowering.

🍃 Thin out and transplant hardy annuals sown last month.

🍃 Plant out wallflowers, *Campanula medium*, forget-me-nots and bellis daisy plants for spring.

LAWNS
🍃 Apply turf dressing and start to lay new turf.

GENERAL MAINTENANCE
🍃 Plan new planting schemes for next year, dig any beds needing an overhaul, and keep all parts of garden clear of fallen leaves.

· LATE AUTUMN ·

THIS IS THE SEASON for bonfires, and for gathering up leaves to add to the summer's lawn mowings to make compost. Plant bare-rooted trees and shrubs while the weather permits, and protect hellebores from mud splashes. They will reward you with their waxen blooms in the depths of winter.

TREES AND SHRUBS
🍃 Continue to plant deciduous trees and shrubs.

🍃 Protect tender specimens and exposed conifers which are prone to windburn by surrounding them with a windbreak material such as plastic sheeting.

🍃 Cover winter and spring-flowering shrubs with netting to deter bullfinches from eating the immature flower buds.

🍃 Bring container-grown fuchsias and hydrangeas into cold greenhouse or shed to overwinter.

CLIMBERS
🍃 Check all supports and make sure that ties are well secured, making any necessary replacements.

ROSES
🍃 Plant bare-rooted roses as soon as possible. Prune back any damaged roots to sound wood, and prune stems as necessary before planting.

HERBACEOUS PERENNIALS
🍃 Plant primulas and polyanthus.

ALPINES
🍃 Protect grey-leaved plants, and any tender specimens, with sheets of glass (secured against wind damage) or open-ended cloches.

🍃 Mulch hardier plants with a layer of fine gravel under the foliage, to prevent them coming into contact with wet soil.

WATER AND BOG PLANTS
🍃 Overhaul pool pumps, fountains and filters.

BULBS, CORMS AND TUBERS
🍃 Complete planting of tulips.

🍃 Continue planting lilies.

ANNUALS AND BIENNIALS
🍃 Remove growing points on sweet peas sown a few weeks ago.

LAWNS
🍃 Lay turf on earlier prepared ground.

🌢 Dig over any areas to be seeded in spring, and leave ground to be broken up by winter frosts.

GENERAL MAINTENANCE

🌢 Ventilate cold greenhouses and frames whenever the weather permits, to allow air to circulate and to prevent the build-up of diseases such as botrytis (grey mould).

🌢 Keep lawn and beds free of fallen leaves – which can be gathered and used on the compost heap or spread around any tender plants to protect them from frost.

🌢 Re-firm the soil around plants which may have loosened after periods of wind and rain or frost.

· EARLY WINTER ·

Now is the time for taking stock and replanning. New beds and paths can be made and garden carpentry carried out. If the weather permits, continue major digging, tidying up of beds and ground preparation. Complete any reconstruction of the rock garden, and refill window boxes with fresh soil.

TREES AND SHRUBS

🌢 Plant deciduous trees and shrubs, provided the soil is neither waterlogged nor frozen. Stake tall specimens and standards.

🌢 If new arrivals cannot be planted immediately, leave them in their wrapping in a cool, frost-free place, first making sure their roots are moist. If bad weather persists, heel them in temporarily on sheltered ground until conditions improve.

🌢 Re-firm soil that may have loosened in frost around the bases of newly planted trees and shrubs, and established plants exposed to wind.

🌢 If such creatures as rabbits and squirrels are present, protect the trunks of young trees and shrubs with plastic tree bandages or wire netting to a height of about 2ft.

🌢 Carry out any necessary pruning – such as thinning summer-flowering shrubs, cutting back invasive roots and overhanging branches and general shaping – in mild spells.

CLIMBERS

🌢 Check that all supports and ties are firm and renew any loose or damaged fastenings.

ROSES

🌢 Plant new bushes or transplant established ones when ground and weather conditions allow.

🌢 Spray with tar-oil to protect plants against pests and diseases.

HERBACEOUS PERENNIALS

🌢 Finish tidying beds and firm soil around plants to prevent frost damage to roots and crowns.

🌢 Place cloches over *Helleborus niger* to lengthen stems and keep flowers clean for indoor decoration.

ALPINES

🌢 Sow slow-germinating seeds and those that need chilling to germinate – that is, most alpine plants including *Gentiana acaulis, Viola biflora* and androsace – in cold frames.

BULBS, CORMS AND TUBERS

🌢 Check stored tender bulbs, corms and tubers for rot; cut out affected parts and dust the rest with fungicide. Destroy badly affected specimens.

ANNUALS AND BIENNIALS

🌢 Plan the summer planting schemes, select and send off seed catalogue orders.

🌢 Protect autumn-sown sweet peas in frames by covering glass with matting during hard frosts.

LAWNS

🌢 Lay new turf if ground conditions are suitable.

🌢 Avoid walking on the lawn after heavy frosts – it can damage the grass.

GENERAL MAINTENANCE

🌢 Dig empty borders, remove weeds between established plants, and apply a light, ground-covering mulch during mild spells.

· MIDWINTER ·

The shortest days are best suited to armchair gardening, to planning and ordering seeds and plants. Give some thought to last year's stock. Were all the plants successful and worthy of reordering? Make gardening catalogues your first read of the New Year.

TREES AND SHRUBS

🌢 During mild spells, prune dead or diseased branches from established deciduous trees and shrubs while they are bare.

🌢 In areas exposed to frost and chilling winds, protect early flowering rhododendron and azalea buds with sacking or plastic sheeting; this can be removed during dry spells.

🌢 Re-firm soil that may have been loosened by frost around roots of newly planted heathers and other shrubs.

CLIMBERS
🌿 Prepare ground ready for new spring plants.

ROSES
🌿 Plant during mild, dry, frost-free periods.

HERBACEOUS PERENNIALS
🌿 Take root cuttings of perennials such as *Phlox paniculata, Anchusa azurea* and *Papaver orientale*.

ALPINES
🌿 Top dress all alpines with small chippings of granite, or limestone for lime-lovers.

🌿 Protect plants from slugs and snails.

WATER AND BOG PLANTS
🌿 If the pond contains fish, float a rubber or plastic ball on the surface to create a 'breather' hole when ice forms.

🌿 Remove snow from ice surface, or plants may die from lack of light.

BULBS, CORMS AND TUBERS
🌿 When bulb foliage appears, aerate the soil by lightly pricking around the plants with a fork.

ANNUALS AND BIENNIALS
🌿 Sow sweet peas under glass for June-October flowering.

🌿 When weather permits, dig over beds and borders for spring planting of annuals.

LAWNS
🌿 Brush off leaves and worm casts, but keep off the lawn if it is very wet or frozen.

GENERAL MAINTENANCE
🌿 On warm, sunny days, make sure that frames and greenhouses are well ventilated to prevent diseases such as botrytis (grey mould).

🌿 Buy or prepare seed and potting compost, and store in a cool, frost-free place until ready to use.

· LATE WINTER ·

Though the weather is bleak, tasks accomplished now will yield benefits later. Take advantage of frost-hardened ground to transport manure and fertilisers, and when the ground is soft, aerate the lawn with a hollow-tined fork. Complete all digging.

TREES AND SHRUBS
🌿 Plant new specimens in suitable weather. Feed established plants with general fertiliser and mulch.

🌿 Complete pruning of deciduous specimens while they are still dormant.

ROSES
🌿 Continue planting whenever soil and weather conditions are suitable.

🌿 Support bushes damaged by winter gales.

CLIMBERS
🌿 Prune large, late-flowering hybrid clematis back to 9-10in from ground level. Feed and mulch with decayed manure, leaf mould or compost.

🌿 Prune flowered growths from *Campsis × tagliabuana* and remove unwanted stems from *Solanum crispum* if necessary to keep in check.

HERBACEOUS PERENNIALS
🌿 Prepare borders for spring planting – fork in well-rotted farmyard manure or garden compost and apply general base fertiliser.

🌿 Continue to take root cuttings of any perennials with thick, fleshy roots.

ALPINES
🌿 Re-firm soil around any plants loosened by ground frosts.

🌿 If not already done, lay fine chippings around plants to keep the soil cool in spring and summer and help to keep down weeds.

WATER AND BOG PLANTS
🌿 Sow seeds of moisture-loving plants, such as mimulus, in a heated greenhouse or frame.

🌿 Remove any weeds from the bog garden.

BULBS, CORMS AND TUBERS
🌿 Place dahlia tubers in a temperature of 13-16°C (55-61°F) to promote early growth for propagation by cuttings.

🌿 Check stored bulbs and tubers for signs of drying out.

🌿 Feed bulbs with general fertiliser as soon as they begin to push through the ground.

ANNUALS AND BIENNIALS
🌿 Sow slow-growing half-hardy annuals, such as begonias and lobelias, in heated greenhouse or heated frame.

LAWNS
🌿 When the ground is not frozen or waterlogged, spike to aerate, and rake over to remove debris.

🌿 Apply moss killer if required.

🌿 Firm, level and rake over sites ready for sowing seed in April.

GENERAL MAINTENANCE
🌿 Take advantage of frost-hardened ground (when a wheelbarrow will not get stuck in the mud), to apply manure and other dressings to beds and borders throughout the garden.

🌿 Check and overhaul garden machinery, clean and disinfect soiled pots and seed trays, and make any necessary replacements.

PREPARATION

THERE'S MORE TO preparing the ground than just clearing out the builders' rubble or the previous owner's carefully nurtured specimens if you want to get your own plants off to a good start. Much can be done to improve the soil's balance and quality.

WHAT TYPE OF SOIL?

Before choosing your plants, you need to know what type of soil you have, and how it may be improved. Look at its colour, and feel the texture. It may be a heavy clay that sticks to boots, a pale, chalky soil, or gritty sand. The ideal is loam, a mixture of sand, silt, clay and humus that clings loosely together when crumbled. And the more closely you can persuade your soil to resemble the ideal, the happier your plants will be.

Heavy clay with poor drainage can be lightened by adding grit or coarse, sharp sand and organic matter, such as garden compost. If the soil is sandy or chalky and dries out quickly, dig in plenty of humus-forming materials such as well-rotted farmyard manure to encourage moisture retention.

THE ACID TEST Soil may veer towards the acid or alkaline, whatever its structure, and while most plants can grow in either condition, some have a preference or need for one or the other. To determine which type you have, test the soil with a simple chemical kit or meter and probe, both of which can be obtained from a garden centre.

The level of acidity or alkalinity is measured on a 0-14 scale known as the pH scale; 7.0 is neutral and numbers below that indicate an acid soil, while numbers above indicate an alkaline soil. Most garden plants prefer a soil which is slightly acid, 6.5 on the pH scale. You can raise the alkalinity by adding lime, or increase the acidity by adding moss peat or animal manure to the soil. As a general rule, sandy and clay soils are usually acid, though common boulder clay and some sands are alkaline, as are chalky soils.

VITAL INGREDIENTS There are kits available which determine what nutrients are present in the soil, such as nitrogen, phosphorus and potassium. Humus is necessary in all soils and decomposed organic material (such as compost) needs to be added regularly to improve the soil structure. This can be done every other year or even every third year. Either spread the organic material thickly over the surface, and allow worms and other creatures to pull it down, or incorporate it while digging.

DIGGING AND FORKING

DIGGING TO BREAK UP THE SOIL Digging improves soil drainage and helps the roots of plants to penetrate more deeply. If possible, dig in autumn so that winter frosts can break the soil down further. If your soil is very heavy, avoid digging when it is wet, as treading on it will compress it and affect drainage.

STRAIGHTFORWARD SINGLE DIGGING Digging to just one spade's depth, or single digging, is adequate for most purposes; it does not disturb the subsoil, and can be done on ground which has been previously cultivated to a greater depth.

First dig a trench about 10in wide and take the soil to the far end of the bed; this will be used later to fill in the last trench you dig. Skim off any surface weeds as you go, and place them upside-down in the bottom of the trenches, but remove the roots of any perennial weeds. Add a layer of manure or garden compost to the sloping face of the soil you have just dug out. Dig out the next trench, placing the soil, upside-down, in the initial trench, and add the compost or manure.

1. Use pegs and string to mark out the area to be tackled. Dig out a spade's depth of soil, piling the loose earth beside the site of the final trench to be dug.

2. Dig out a second trench, placing the loose soil in the first trench. Add compost or manure to the sloping surface of the freshly turned soil as you go.

3. Dig and fill further trenches in the same way. Fill the final trench with the pile of soil from the first. If the plot is large, dig over half of it at a time.

Continue digging and filling in trenches in the same way until you have dug over the entire plot.

DO YOU NEED TO DOUBLE DIG? Double digging is time and labour-consuming, and only worth considering if you are starting a new border for long-term planting from scratch, and the soil is deep to begin with. The principles are much the same as for single digging, but the trench cut is twice as deep and wide.

WHEN TO FORK If your ground is heavy or stony, dig with a trench fork – with wide, flat prongs and a strong, reinforced shaft – instead of a spade. In spring, when the soil starts to dry and clods break down easily, use a border fork for soil which was dug in autumn, removing any remaining perennial weeds.

RAKING AND HOEING

If you are going to sow seed outdoors, either in a seedbed or in an annual border, the soil needs to be broken down into a fine tilth. This is done at the time of sowing and is only effective on ground which has been previously dug. Choose a fine day, preferably with a drying wind. Fork over the soil, levelling as you go, and let the surface start to dry. Tread evenly all over the surface to break down any lumps and firm the soil without compacting it. Rake over the ground backwards and forwards until the top inch of soil is fine and clear of any large stones. Repeat until you are satisfied with the result, each time raking in the opposite direction.

REMOVING THE WEEDS Beds that have been cultivated and left for any length of time will soon become covered with weeds. Clear them with a Dutch hoe. Disturbing the surface of the soil will uproot young weeds and, once exposed to the sun or wind, they will quickly die. If possible, hoe the beds weekly, whether they are empty or planted.

Some perennial weeds may be so deep-rooted that hoeing has little effect – bindweed, horsetail and couch grass are examples. Your best answer is to brush the leaves or dip the stems in glyphosate – take care not to get it on any cultivated plants.

IMPROVING THE SOIL

No matter what type of soil you have, it will benefit from the addition of substantial amounts of organic matter such as well-rotted farmyard manure, garden compost, mushroom compost, seaweed, shoddy (shredded rags), and waste hops from a brewery. Pulverised bark, which has been treated with ammonium sulphate, so that it does not rob the soil of nitrogen in the breaking-down process, is often a perfectly good mulching and conditioning substitute for peat, which is a non-renewable resource. By adding organic substances such as these you can improve the structure of the soil and, in some cases, also provide a certain amount of nutrients.

BUILDING A COMPOST HEAP Use strong wire or plastic mesh to enclose a compost heap of no less than 9sq ft. Build the heap in 12in thick layers. Soak each layer with water, add an organic activator such as manure, and cover with 2in of soil. Use soft material such as lawn clippings and vegetable trimmings from the kitchen, but avoid woody material, diseased plants, the roots of perennial weeds such as couch grass, and anything containing grease.

WHAT TYPE OF FERTILISER?

If plants are to grow well, you must add nutrients – nitrogen, phosphorus and potassium in particular – to replace those they draw from the soil. Such nutrients can be provided to some extent by organic matter, such as manure or compost, or in the concentrated form of dry or liquid fertilisers, which can be either organic or inorganic chemical compounds. Organic fertilisers come from the decay of living organisms – as in manure, compost, or blood, fish and bone – and 'feed' the soil, which, in turn, feeds the plants. Inorganic compounds, which occur naturally in mineral deposits or are produced synthetically in the form of chemical fertilisers, are not derived from living organisms, and feed the plants directly. They do not replace organic matter in the soil; unless used in moderation and with organic matter, the organisms within the soil die, the structure of the soil breaks down, and the ground becomes impoverished.

HOW TO USE FERTILISERS Nitrogen encourages leaf growth, phosphorus helps plants to form good root systems

NUTRIENTS FOR PLANT GROWTH

Potassium, nitrogen and phosphorus are key plant nutrients – potassium for flowers, nitrogen for leaves, and phosphorus for roots.

and potassium will benefit flowers. Fertiliser containers are marked with the letters N for nitrogen, P for phosphorus and K for potassium, and each is followed by a number indicating the percentage of the nutrient in the fertiliser. Fertilisers are available with the emphasis on the relevant nutrient needed for the specific encouragement of foliage, roots or flowers and fruit. For example, N-6%, P-6%, K-10% indicates a high potassium content and is used for flowering or berried plants.

Base fertilisers are high in phosphorus and potassium, and are added to the soil before planting to encourage root formation and sturdy growth. General fertilisers used as a top dressing are applied around growing plants and lightly forked into the surface as a stimulant during the growing season. One of the most popular fertiliser formulas, Growmore, containing equal percentages (7% by weight) of nitrogen, phosphorus and potassium, will encourage balanced growth.

Liquid fertilisers can be applied to the soil, or sprayed on the leaves of plants. They have varying amounts of nitrogen, phosphorus and potassium, and are absorbed more quickly than dry fertilisers. They are useful during rainless periods, as dry fertilisers need moisture in the soil to dissolve.

To fertilise ornamental borders organically, mulch annually with well-rotted manure or compost, top dress with blood, fish or bone fertiliser in early spring, and apply a dressing of composted seaweed every three years.

MULCHING – THE FINAL TOUCH Mulching adds a top dressing of organic material to conserve moisture and condition the soil. Pulverised and composted bark, fully decomposed garden compost or any other organic material can be used. Spread a layer 2-3in deep for the best results. Apply mulches only when the ground is moist, otherwise the soil beneath will stay dry unless there are long periods of heavy rain. Don't mulch too early in the year or you will prevent the soil from warming up.

PLANTING

WHEN BUYING, take your time and choose with care. Make sure that the plants are clearly labelled, not only with the specific name but also the variety, and check thoroughly for any signs of pests and diseases. Examine leaves and stems for rust, die-back, and any other kind of damage. The branches on trees and shrubs should be well spaced and the main ones unbroken. If they have been grafted or budded, check that all buds show signs of growth.

CHOOSING A HEALTHY PLANT

HOW LONG HAS IT BEEN IN THE POT? If you are buying a containerised plant, the container should be filled with roots. This will show that the plant has grown in the container and has not been lifted and containerised recently. A sure sign of this is if the compost and plant are loose in the container. Beware, too, of plants that have been in the same container for a long time, recognised by well-established perennial weeds in the soil, strong roots growing through the drainage holes, and thin, weak growth. Ageing herbaceous plants can often be recognised by bare patches of soil in the centre of the pot where the original shoots have died out.

Alpines are usually sold in pots, and older ones may have moss and algae covering the compost, whereas young, healthy ones should be surrounded by small, clean chippings.

TELLTALE SIGNS When buying bulbs, choose the largest, and check they are firm and free of any mould. Any sign of growth on top indicates that they have been stored too long. In the case of lilies avoid any with shrivelled outside scales.

If you are buying trays of annuals

instead of growing them from seed, choose plants that are sturdy, bushy and with no yellow leaves and no flowers. Avoid plants that are overcrowded in their containers, that are spindly, look undernourished or have bent stems. Buy plants in divided trays, one plant to each division. Don't assume that plants have been hardened off when you buy them – play safe and acclimatise them to outdoor conditions for a week or so in a cold frame or other suitable place. Alternatively, postpone buying plants until all chance of frost has gone.

Biennials may be sold in divided trays or bare-rooted – lifted from the open ground. In both cases they should be bushy, well-branched and with plenty of healthy, well-nourished leaves.

HOW TO PLANT TREES, SHRUBS AND CLIMBERS

Whether you buy trees and shrubs in a container or with their roots bare doesn't matter, as long as the plant is healthy.

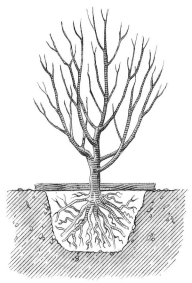

Lay a plank across the planting hole to ensure the soil mark on the trunk of the tree or shrub is level with the surface.

The advantage of containerised plants is that they can be planted at any time of the year, provided weather conditions are fair, and the soil is not frozen, covered with snow or waterlogged.

PREPARING FOR PLANTING Before planting, make sure that the root ball is moist right through. If not, stand the plant in water for several hours with the roots completely submerged.

Plant bare-rooted plants as soon as possible, preferably in autumn while the soil is still warm, or during spring in cold, exposed parts of the country. However, you can't go far wrong if you plant evergreens in early to mid-autumn or mid to late spring, and deciduous trees and shrubs between mid-autumn and early spring when soil and weather conditions are favourable. If planting is delayed for some time, heel the plants into a piece of spare ground or place them in a cold greenhouse. Packaged bare-rooted plants can be left in their wrappings for 2-3 weeks (provided they are not dry at their roots) in a cool but frost-free place. When transporting bare-rooted plants from a garden centre, protect the roots with sacking or a strong plastic bag to prevent them drying out. If the soil is very dry, water copiously during the first season after planting.

HOW DEEP A HOLE? The hole for planting must be deep enough and wide enough to accommodate the roots comfortably. Check the depth by placing the plant, still in its container, in the hole. When set in the ground, it should be at the same depth as it was in its container. Plant bare-rooted specimens up to the soil mark left from its nursery container on the main stem. To get the depth exactly right, place a piece of wood across the hole and line up the soil mark against it. Scatter a handful of bone meal in the bottom of the hole, and lightly fork another handful into the soil to be replaced. Spread manure or garden

Position the stake before planting. Place it on the windward side of the young tree to reach the lowest branches.

compost under and around the root area and, if the ground is dry, soak the planting area thoroughly.

THE IMPORTANCE OF STAKING All trees need the support of a stake in the early years of growth. Drive the stake firmly into the bottom of the planting hole on the side of the tree that is exposed to the prevailing wind. Leave about 2-3ft above ground, so as to anchor the roots and allow the top to move slightly.

Carefully remove the plant from its container, loosen a few roots and then lower the plant into the hole close to the stake. Fill with the soil you removed, using your fingers to make sure that no space is left between the root ball and the sides of the hole. When the hole is full, firm the plant in with your feet. Secure the plant to the stake with a tree tie tacked to the stake to keep it in position. Finally, apply a mulch such as pulverised

bark or well-rotted garden compost. Deal with bare-rooted trees and shrubs in much the same way, but cut off any badly damaged roots cleanly with sharp secateurs and spread the remaining ones evenly in the hole. When planting bare-rooted roses, cut back the thickest roots to encourage fibrous growth. After planting, prune the top back to a healthy bud.

SPECIAL SOIL REQUIREMENTS If you have an alkaline soil you can still grow acid-loving plants, such as rhododendrons and azaleas, by making a raised bed and adding peat to the soil at a ratio of two parts peat to one part non-chalky soil. However, enthusiasts for these plants excepted, many gardeners may find it simpler to choose plants that suit the existing soil.

Prepare the ground well for climbing plants, as the soil at the bottom of a fence, wall or trellis may be dry and impoverished. Where possible, give each plant a hole 2ft square and 2ft deep. Put in plenty of well-rotted organic matter and grit or coarse, sharp sand if the soil is heavy. Position any climbing supports before planting. Plant clematis 3-4in deeper than other climbers, so that if clematis wilt should occur there will be enough healthy buds below ground to grow after the plant has been cut down.

HERBACEOUS PLANTS

If starting from scratch, plan a herbaceous border on paper well before planting, taking into consideration heights, colours, leaf textures, habit and time of flowering. Then mark the positions in the border with pegs and labels. Generally do your planting during autumn or spring, although containerised plants can go in at any time provided the ground is not frozen or waterlogged. Make sure that the root balls are thoroughly soaked, especially if they have been in peat pots or pre-packed. Dig the planting hole of a shape and size to allow the roots to spread comfortably, and at a depth to the level of the crown – the point where the stems and roots join. Firm the plant in and water thoroughly if the soil is dry.

WATER GARDEN TECHNIQUES Aquatic plants should be set in planting baskets lined with hessian and filled with a good quality heavy loam. Avoid using such organic material as manure which encourages algae and could kill the fish. Plant firmly and top off with a layer of gravel. Containerised deep-water plants can be planted at any time of the year, but it is preferable to plant in spring when the water has begun to warm up.

Group the marginal water plants in twos and threes around the pool edge for the best effect. Marginals prefer no more than 2-3in of water over their roots, so you will need a ledge at the correct depth or bricks to support the containers. Deep water plants should be placed at a depth of 2-3ft (see page 270).

ALPINES

Water pot-grown alpines before planting, and give them enough space to spread. Don't plant them too deep as the lower leaves or the crown may rot. Spread a layer of gravel around them to allow air to circulate beneath the foliage.

BULBS, CORMS AND TUBERS

Plant spring-flowering specimens in autumn, summer-flowering ones in spring and autumn-flowering specimens in mid or late summer. If you obtain any before you are ready to plant, spread them out in a single layer and keep them in a cool, dry and airy place.

A rule of thumb for the planting depth of most bulbs is two-and-a-half to three times the height of the bulb. For example, a bulb 2in high should go in a hole 5-6in deep. They will look more natural if they are grown in irregularly shaped groups of different sizes and planted in odd numbers of say, between five and fifteen. Each group of bulbs can go into a hole large enough to hold them comfortably – that is, they can be placed close together but not touching. Spread a layer of coarse sand on the bottom of the planting hole if the soil is not a well-draining one.

To plant bulbs, such as crocuses and snowdrops, in a grassed area, it is not necessary to go through the rigmarole of stripping a section of turf and preparing the soil; it is far easier to use a bulb planter, which involves minimal disturbance to the turf.

When introducing bulbs into a spot already planted with other bulbs, you may have trouble locating the exact

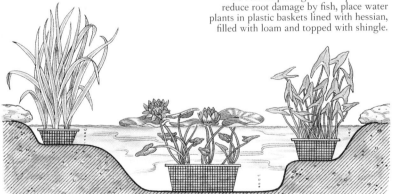

To restrict plant growth in ponds and reduce root damage by fish, place water plants in plastic baskets lined with hessian, filled with loam and topped with shingle.

position of the earlier planting. So plant groups of the new bulbs in large pots. Bury them up to their rims in a spare bit of ground. When the established bulbs begin to show above the surface, you can lift the pots, carefully tap out soil and bulbs as one, and fill any gaps on the selected site.

ANNUALS AND BIENNIALS

Annuals can be planted mid-spring to early summer, depending on the location and the type of plant. Begin with the hardier ones, such as antirrhinums and pansies, and finish with the more tender types such as salvias, asters and ageratums. Before planting, water the containers and allow the plants to absorb

the moisture before moving them. During dry periods, puddle them in – fill the planting hole with water and allow it to soak in. Then set the plant in place and fill the hole with soil.

Create a more natural effect by planting in irregular patches. Space the plants close enough to leave no gaps when they reach maturity. This will help them support themselves and keep weeds to the minimum.

Biennials that have been in a nursery bed during summer go into their final position in early autumn. Before lifting them prepare the plant hole and water well. If you intend to integrate the plants with bulbs, plant the biennials first and the bulbs afterwards.

PLANTING DEPTHS FOR BULBS	
The bulbs and corms listed below are all described in the seasonal plant guide section of the book. Depths, given in inches, are measured from the surface to the top of the bulb.	

SPRING-FLOWERING BULBS	
Anemone	2-3
Chionodoxa	2-3
Crocus vernus	2-3
Endymion hispanicus	4-6
Erythronium	5-6
Fritillaria imperialis	6-8
Fritillaria meleagris	4-6
Hyacinthus orientalis	5-6
Ipheion uniflorum	2-3
Leucojum vernum	3-4
Muscari armeniacum	3
Narcissus	4-6
Puschkinia scilloides	2-3
Scilla bifolia	2-3
Tulipa	6-8

SUMMER-FLOWERING BULBS	
Allium moly	3-4
Allium christophii	4-6
Alstroemeria	4-6
Crinum × powellii	10-12
Crocosmia	2-3
Cyclamen purpurascens	2-3
Galtonia candicans	4-6

Gladiolus byzantinus	4-6
Iris xiphioides	4-6
Lilium	4-8
Lilium candidum	Just below surface

AUTUMN-FLOWERING BULBS	
Amaryllis belladonna	4-6
Colchicum	3-4
Crocus	2-3
Cyclamen hederifolium	2-3
Dierama pulcherrimum	4-6
Galanthus reginae-olgae	2-3
Gladiolus callianthus	4-6
Leucojum autumnale	2-3
Nerine bowdenii	3-4
Sternbergia lutea	3-4
Zephyranthes candida	3-4

WINTER-FLOWERING BULBS	
Cyclamen coum	2-3
Eranthis hyemalis	3-4
Galanthus caucasicus	3-4
Iris	3-4
Narcissus	4-6
Scilla mischtschenkoana	2-3

391

MAINTENANCE

ESIDES PROVIDING the right situation and sustaining balanced soil conditions, you can encourage your plants to grow with more vigour and provide a more rewarding display by a little additional care. Some plants, such as certain annuals, will flourish naturally and need little or no attention, but others respond, depending on their growth characteristics, to being supported or guided, lightly trimmed or regularly and judiciously pruned.

KEEPING PLANTS IN TRIM

Annuals, biennials and perennials are less demanding than trees and shrubs. Alyssum and lobelia, for example, grow side shoots naturally and flourish without any help, as do plants which grow only one stem with a terminal flower.

Plants such as antirrhinums, sweet peas and wallflowers, however, benefit from having their growing tips removed (called 'stopping') when they are 3-4in high. This will promote side shoots and produce a bushier growth.

To encourage larger blooms on each side shoot, disbud plants such as chrysanthemums, dahlias, pinks and roses. Break off all flower buds from a cluster except the top, or crown, bud.

Remove any weak and stunted plants, leaving enough space between the remainder for them to develop fully. To extend the flowering season, remove the blooms as they fade (called deadheading) so that the plant's energy is concentrated on producing new blooms rather than seeds – unless you wish to harvest the seeds. Deadhead either by nipping off the flower, or for plants with single, bare flower stems such as red-hot pokers, as close as possible to the base. Remove heads of small flowers when the whole cluster has died.

Place twigs around tall, bushy perennials like asters at an early stage of growth to provide unobtrusive support as the plant grows.

Canes supporting plants such as delphiniums should eventually end just below the flower spikes; secure ties as the plant grows.

PROVIDING SUPPORT

Tall-growing plants often need some kind of support, especially if they are in an exposed position. Twigs at about half a plant's eventual height can be placed around or between plants, or you can use metal or plastic supports obtained from a garden shop. Place supports at an early stage of the plant's development so that they will be hidden as the plant grows.

Support young trees and shrubs with wooden stakes and tree ties. A stake firmly driven into the ground with about 2-3ft exposed will keep the roots and lower trunk stable, but leave the top free so that the tree can cope on its own when the stake is removed. Use longer stakes for trees trained as standards, as these tend to be top-heavy.

Most climbers need help to attach themselves to their support, such as wood, metal or plastic trellis, plastic mesh stretched between wooden battens, or horizontal wires attached to hooks. If there is no suitable framework,

some climbers will grow through trees, or up a vertical pole in the open garden.

Other climbers need no help. For example, many ivies produce aerial roots to climb with, while Virginia creepers support themselves with suckers.

THE ART OF PRUNING

There are several reasons for pruning – to keep plants within bounds, to promote fewer but stronger stems, to

remove diseased or damaged branches, to encourage flowers and to train plants to a desired shape. The right tools are essential: a pair of sharp secateurs, a pair of long-handled loppers, a narrow-bladed pruning saw and strong gloves if thorny branches are to be tackled.

First cut out any branches that are diseased or damaged, cutting right back to healthy or undamaged wood. If two branches are crossing, cut the most

BASIC PRUNING CUTS FOR TREE OR SHRUB

If the buds are positioned opposite each other on the stem, make a clean horizontal cut about ¼in above them.

With alternately placed buds, angle the cut upwards from the opposite side of the stem and finish about ¼in above the bud.

awkwardly placed one back to the main stem. Take out weak branches altogether, right down to the base.

Pruning to preserve the shape of a tree or shrub, or to promote growth, is done between the buds on the stems. Generally, buds grow either opposite each other or alternately along the stem. Where the buds are opposite, choose a suitable pair and make a straight cut just above them. If the buds alternate, make the cut slightly angled, starting on the opposite side of the stem and slanting upwards so that the top of the cut is about ¼in above the bud.

Remember that whichever way the bud you prune back to is facing, that is the direction the next branch will grow. If you prune back to two or more buds, growth will be in two or more directions. This is how you can determine the shape of the tree or shrub. For example, if the plant is encroaching over a path, prune to a bud that will encourage it to grow away from the path while, if possible, not spoiling the overall shape of the plant. To stimulate growth on a tree or shrub that is growing more vigorously on one side than the other, prune back hard on the weaker side.

WHEN TO PRUNE WHICH PLANT? Shrubs such as *Buddleia davidii* flower on the current year's growth, and are pruned in early spring for further growth and flowering later in the season. Shrubs such as weigela and deutzia, that bloom on one-year-old wood and flower early in the year, are cut back as soon as the flowers have faded to ensure flowering the following season. In early spring, too, severely prune shrubs that are grown for their coloured winter stems.

In late spring, when flowering has finished, do any necessary trimming of shrubs that produce their flowers on short growths extending from the main branch. Cut back the current season's growth to three buds – chaenomeles are prominent in this group.

WHEN TO PRUNE TREES AND SHRUBS

Prune shrubs that flower on the previous year's growth after flowering. Cut to a bud near the junction with a main stem.

Shrubs like chaenomeles need no pruning, but to train, cut lateral shoots to about five leaves from the older wood after flowering.

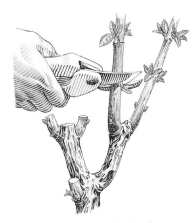

In early spring, prune shrubs that flower on the current year's growth to the first two or three buds on the previous season's stems.

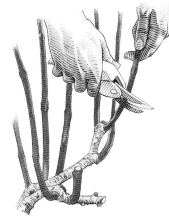

Shrubs grown for their winter stems, like *Cornus alba*, are cut back hard to a few inches above the ground in late spring.

Keep an eye on shrubs with variegated leaves. Occasionally, they may produce a stem carrying plain green leaves, which must be cut right back. These shoots are more vigorous than those with variegated leaves, and will take over the plant if not pruned out.

CUTTING BACK CLIMBERS Pruning of climbing plants is governed by their flowering times. Some flower on the current year's shoots from midsummer onwards, others flower between early spring and early summer on growth made the previous summer. Cut back the late-flowering group into older wood, just above a dormant bud. Clematis that flower late, such as *C. × jackmanii*, should be cut back to 8-9in above ground level in late winter or early spring. Lightly trim early flowering varieties, such as 'Nellie Moser', cutting

off any dead shoots at the start of the season. Cut them hard back only when they have outgrown their allotted space. This also applies to self-supporting climbers, which should be pruned back by several feet in late summer if they start to obstruct gutters and windows or to overwhelm a host plant.

BASIC RULES FOR ROSES Certain basic rules of pruning apply to all groups of roses. The aim is generally to cut out all diseased and dead stems and to remove any weak shoots.

On bush and shrub roses, completely remove all tangled and crossing branches to open up the centre of the rose. On climbing cultivars, separate any tangled branches by training them apart rather than by cutting them.

Always cut back to a dormant bud (which will eventually grow into a new shoot), preferably an outward-facing one so that the rose will develop with an open centre.

Make all pruning cuts just above a bud and slanting down, away from it.

The first time roses are pruned (after the pre-planting trim) they should be cut back fairly drastically. The idea is to encourage a good framework of strong shoots from the base of the plant. It will also reduce the strain on the root system, which will not have had much time to become strongly established.

The first step is to remove any damaged, dead and weak shoots right back to the junction with the main stems or the rootstock. Then prune large-flowered (hybrid tea) types back to an outward-facing bud about 4in above the ground. Cut back new cluster-flowered (floribunda) roses to around 5-6in, and miniatures to 2-3in.

THE FIRST CUT Prune roses that have come straight from the nursery before planting, but once planted do not prune shrub roses in the first year, apart from removing dead or damaged shoots, as

THE MAIN, SPRING PRUNING OF BUSH ROSES

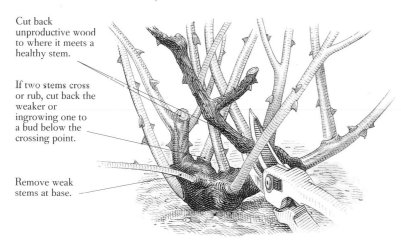

Cut back unproductive wood to where it meets a healthy stem.

If two stems cross or rub, cut back the weaker or ingrowing one to a bud below the crossing point.

Remove weak stems at base.

they flower on wood produced in the previous season. For the same reason, climbers, ramblers and species roses should not be pruned in the first year after planting, apart from removing any weak or damaged shoots and about 3in from the tips of the stems.

In subsequent years, in spring, prune large-flowered cultivars to four or five buds from the base, and cluster-flowered to six or seven buds. Do not cut back cultivars grown as standards as hard: leave 10-12in extending from where the bushy part joins the top of the main stem.

Miniature roses require little pruning. Simply cut off the thin ends of branches, and cut back diseased or damaged branches to sound wood. Similarly, shrub roses need only the occasional removal of old, dead or damaged shoots.

To prune climbers, first trim back the flowered shoots to two or three buds immediately after flowering. In winter, remove dead, diseased and spindly wood, and cut back the leading stems to strong new shoots. This ensures the regular replacement of old wood by young, healthy wood. If no strong shoots have grown from a leader, prune it and its laterals by about a half. When

an old stem ceases to throw out new shoots, remove it to promote new growth from the base of the climber.

Prune ramblers, whose new growth springs liberally from the base of the plant, by cutting flower-bearing stems to near ground level immediately after flowering. Tie in new stems to replace them in the following year. If new stems are usually produced from a point halfway or lower on the old stems, cut back the old stems to that point.

Most large-flowered and cluster-flowered bush roses need shortening and tidying up in late autumn so that they are not damaged by strong winds; do not prune completely as frosts can damage developing shoots. Remove all dead flower heads and cut back all strong shoots by a third. Carry out the main pruning, outlined above, in spring. In summer, deadhead regularly to promote continuity of bloom. Lightly prune to an outward-facing bud after all the flowers in a cluster on a stem have died.

TRIMMING HEDGES

Hedges may be clipped to a precise shape or left in a natural shape. Formal hedges need clipping during the summer months, and sometimes three or four times a year. To retain a dense hedge, do not allow more than 6in of growth between clippings, otherwise it will become straggly and open at the base. Trim a young hedge at an early stage, and continue trimming up to its desired height. A hedge shaped so that it is wider at the bottom than at the top will be more densely clothed with leaves at the base.

Let an informal hedge – of roses or heather for example – grow naturally, and cut it over completely with secateurs once a year after flowering, removing any straggling stems.

SHAPING TREES

Young trees usually need pruning only to develop or retain their shape. If any shoots appear from the trunk, cut them off cleanly. If necessary, remove any crossed branches, and any that will cause congestion in the centre of the tree. Prune deciduous trees in winter, when they are dormant. Evergreens seldom need pruning, but if they do, mid to late spring is the best time. Once a good framework of branches is built up, pruning is not necessary.

POLLARDING is a method of pruning trees hard back to the main trunk each year or every few years to encourage central, bushy growth.

COPPICING is the cutting back of old branches to ground level to encourage a bushy growth of young stems, and is particularly useful for trees and shrubs with vividly coloured young branches.

ALL-SEASON LAWN CARE

The lawn needs little attention in winter, but walking on it in hard frost or snow could damage the grass. Keep it clear of fallen leaves and other debris, otherwise the grass will yellow. For the first spring cut, set the mower blades ¾-1in high. As the season advances, mow regularly and lower the blades to ½in; trim and tidy the edges after each cut. Brush off worm casts before every cut. Apply moss killer, if necessary, and rake out dead moss. Late in mid-spring apply the first feed of a liquid or granular, general-purpose fertiliser, with or without a weedkiller, as required. If weeds persist, treat with a selective weedkiller.

Towards the end of early summer apply another feed. Mow regularly, but in autumn, raise the blades to ¾-1in.

In early autumn, spike the lawn at 3-4in intervals, and about the same depth, then top dress with sand, peat and soil. Apply another feed early in mid-autumn. If the grass is still growing in late autumn, continue to mow but set the blades to 1½in.

AERATING THE LAWN

A garden fork can be used to aerate the lawn in autumn; spike the ground at intervals of 3-4in with holes 3-4in deep.

PROPAGATION

Plants can be increased in a number of ways. For example, they can be reproduced from seeds, from cuttings, by division of the roots, by separation and replanting of bulb and corm offsets, and by layering. Many of these techniques are quite simple and more often than not successful. The more difficult ones – such as grafting and budding – are more of a technical challenge, and are not dealt with in this section.

HOW TO SOW SEEDS

Growing plants from seeds is perhaps the most interesting and satisfying way of increasing your stock, but for the best results the conditions must be correct. Moisture, oxygen and a suitable temperature are essentials, and while most seeds germinate in the dark, some prefer the light. The sowing instructions on the seed packet will usually list the plant's requirements, but generally speaking it is the fine seeds, such as those of begonias, which need light.

GERMINATION UNDER GLASS Before you start, thoroughly clean containers and propagators with a proprietary garden disinfectant. Treat wooden seed boxes with a wood preservative. The compost must be free of pests, diseases and weed seeds, so use a proprietary brand of a soil-based John Innes seed compost, or a soil-less compost containing peat or pulverised bark with possibly vermiculite, perlite or sand. Sow the seeds of acid-loving plants, such as heathers, in an ericaceous, or acid, seed compost.

Some seeds need special treatment before they are sown. Those from trees, shrubs and some alpine plants need stratifying – exposing to low temperatures – before they will germinate.

When pricking out seedlings, hold them by their leaves rather than by their stems and take care not to damage the roots.

Whatever the size of the eventual plant, most seeds from these plant groups should be sown in trays in autumn, and the trays overwintered outside or in a mouse-proof cold frame. Some small alpine seeds can be stratified in a fridge. Mix the seeds with a little moist peat and sand (50/50 by volume) in a plastic bag and place in a cool drawer of a fridge for 4-8 weeks. This will break the dormancy, so that the seeds will germinate once they are placed in the warmth. Sow the lot — seeds, peat and sand.

Soak hard-coated seeds such as sweet peas, cyclamen and lupins for about 24 hours in water, or between layers of damp tissue, until they swell. Any that don't can be encouraged by removing a small amount of seed coat on the opposite side to the eye. Some fine seeds are best sown immediately after harvesting, for example, primulas, gentians and meconopsis, none of which should be covered with soil. Protect all seeds placed outside from vermin and birds with small-mesh wire netting or gauze.

DEALING WITH HALF-HARDIES Sow half-hardy annuals and half-hardy perennials between midwinter and early spring,

under cover, in temperatures of 13-24°C (55-75°F), preferably in a heated propagator. Start with those that take a long time to germinate and to develop flowers, like *Begonia semperflorens* and lobelias, followed by mid-term plants like French marigolds and ageratum, and finishing with later-flowering plants like China asters. Choose a container of the correct size – you can get 100 or more seeds in a seed tray, and 20-30 in 3½in pots. Do not sow more than one variety in each container. If they germinate at different times there will be problems when the time comes to harden off the seedlings – that is, to acclimatise them to lower temperatures.

SOWING AND PRICKING OUT Use fresh seed compost, taken indoors a few days previously to warm, and fill the pots and trays loosely to the brim. Firm it down evenly, paying special attention to the corners, with a tamper, or light block of wood – a small, round one for pots and a rectangular one for boxes. Soak the compost thoroughly and let it drain before sowing. Sow the seeds sparingly, spacing them as evenly as possible, and cover them with a thin layer of compost,

about as deep as the seeds themselves. After sowing, water with a fine spray. Sow fine seeds on the surface – they must have no soil cover or further watering.

Do not let the seeds dry out. If they need watering again while still in the propagator, stand the containers in ½in of water to soak until the compost is wet on top. Allow them to drain before replacing them in the propagator.

Cover the seed containers with brown paper or newspaper and a sheet of glass to help to retain the moisture and exclude the light. For seeds that require light, cover with a sheet of glass only. When the seedlings begin to emerge, uncover and transfer them in their containers to a cold propagator to acclimatise them to lower temperatures. They can then be left on a greenhouse bench or an indoor windowsill.

Within a few weeks of the seedlings appearing they will need more space. Transplant them, called pricking out, 40 to a standard size tray (8in × 14in), and 20 to a half-size tray, in John Innes No 2 or a multi-purpose peat-based compost. For even better results, use divided trays or pots, and plant singly. This will allow less root disturbance when the plants are finally planted outside.

To prick out, prise the seedlings carefully from the compost with a seed label or dinner fork. Take care not to break the roots. Handle the seedlings by the leaves, not the stem, and plant them to the previous depth. Keep the compost moist. When the plants are well established and a few inches high, transfer them to a cold frame for hardening off before planting them outdoors.

SOWING SEEDS OUTDOORS

Hardy annuals and some biennials and perennials can be sown directly outdoors during warm spring weather. Sow hardy annuals where they are to flower. Prepare the seedbed and mark it out in irregular blocks for each variety of plant

SOFTWOOD CUTTINGS

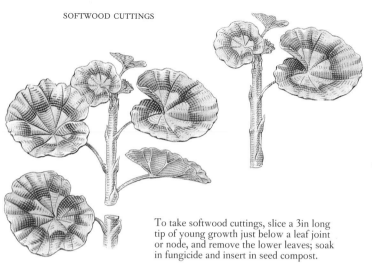

To take softwood cuttings, slice a 3in long tip of young growth just below a leaf joint or node, and remove the lower leaves; soak in fungicide and insert in seed compost.

SEMI-HARDWOOD AND HARDWOOD CUTTINGS

Take semi-hardwood cuttings, from slightly more mature stems, in mid to late summer; cut a 3-4in tip just below a leaf joint and remove the lower leaves.

Take hardwood cuttings in late autumn or early winter, and plant directly into the ground; cut an 8-9in stem just below a bud at the base and just above a bud at the top.

with the point of a stick, taking into account their height, form and colour. Draw shallow drills (furrows) no more than ½in deep, 4-6in apart across each patch, using the blade of a hoe or a pointed stick. Sow the seed sparingly, cover it lightly and firm down the soil with the back of a rake or the palm of your hand.

Sow biennials and perennials in shallow drills and move them to a nursery bed when they are large enough to handle. Plant them in their flowering positions in autumn.

INCREASING PLANTS BY CUTTINGS

Many plants can be increased from stem cuttings, which can be of softwood, semi-hardwood or hardwood. Softwood cuttings are immature shoot tips, and used for pelargoniums, chrysanthemums and many perennials. Semi-hardwood cuttings are firmer than those of softwood and less mature than hardwood cuttings and are suitable for most evergreens, heathers and conifers. As the name suggests, hardwood cuttings are hard, woody sections of vigorous stems that have just completed

their first season's growth, and are generally used to increase deciduous trees and shrubs.

Take SOFTWOOD CUTTINGS early in the year while growth is still young and soft. Take 2-3in long sections from the tips of the stems of shrubs and alpines, or young growth from the base of perennials. Carefully remove any lower leaves which would be buried and rot, and then cut cleanly across the stem, just below a leaf joint, with a sharp knife. Soak the cuttings in benomyl, a chemical fungicide, before inserting them in pots or boxes of seed compost (equal parts by volume of sand and peat). Firm them in and water gently. Keep at a temperature of about 13°C (55°F) and shade them from direct sunlight. If you use a heated propagator keep the top on and the ventilators closed. Stand the pots on a shady windowsill, cover with a plastic bag, but make sure that the bag is not in contact with the cuttings. Keep the compost and foliage moist, but not wet.

Take SEMI-HARDWOOD CUTTINGS in mid to late summer. Cut them 3-4in long, just below a node – a stem joint from where leaves, buds and side shoots arise. Cuttings of heathers need to be only

1-2in long. Root them in a mixture of half peat and half sand in a cold frame.

HARDWOOD CUTTINGS are taken in late autumn or early winter. Select shoots from the current year's growth, which should feel woody to the touch and are about the thickness of a pencil. Cut pieces 8-9in long, straight across just above a bud at the top, and at an angle just below a bud at the bottom. By this means you can distinguish top and bottom of the cutting and also have a leading bud when growth begins. Dig a V-shaped trench about 5in deep in a well-drained, sheltered position in the garden and put a layer of sand in the bottom. Stand the cuttings on the sand so that the lower half or two-thirds is below ground, and they lie about 2-3in apart. Replace the soil and firm with your feet. The cuttings will be ready for lifting and replanting in about a year's time.

LEAF-BUD CUTTINGS consist of a leaf and a short section of stem with a healthy bud in the angle between the leaf and the stem. They are particularly suitable for propagating camellias and some clematis. In late summer, take cuttings from semi-hardwood stems. Make one cut just above a bud in a leaf axil and the other

about ¾-1½in below the bud. Dip the lower end of the cuttings in hormone rooting powder and insert them in a pot filled with gritty compost. Each bud should just make contact with the compost. Keep the cuttings at 16-18°C (61-64°F) and protect from the sun.

The following types of cutting are planted in the same way:
HEEL CUTTING A hardwood or semi-hardwood cutting which retains a small part of the main stem or bark.

LEAF-BUD CUTTINGS

For a leaf-bud cutting, cut just above and below a bud in a leaf axil, and plant so that the bud just touches the compost. This pot could take three or four cuttings.

NODAL CUTTING A stem cutting taken immediately below a node (bud point).
INTERNODAL CUTTING A stem cutting severed between two nodes or buds.
BASAL CUTTING A non-flowering shoot taken from the base of the plant or at just below ground level.
ROOT CUTTINGS Plants which have thick, fleshy or wiry roots, such as dicentras, oriental poppies, romneyas, phloxes, verbascums and hollyhocks, can be propagated by root cuttings, from autumn to early spring. You can either lift the plants and take off some of the roots, or dig down and remove a length of root.

Take pieces about the thickness of a pencil and cut them into 2-3in lengths, making a straight cut at the top and a slanted one at the bottom (to distinguish which end is which). Insert the cuttings, slant cut first, into pots of John Innes seed compost with the tops level with the compost. For thinner roots, take slightly longer lengths – about 3in. Lay them flat on the compost. Cover both types of cuttings with ¼-½in of sand and overwinter in a cold frame. When the cuttings have rooted and show three to four pairs of leaves, pot them up singly, then plant out in autumn.

LAYERING – SIMPLE SHRUB PROPAGATION

This is possibly the simplest method of propagating shrubs. Deciduous species are best layered in autumn or winter; evergreens in autumn or spring. Select a non-flowering branch from the current season's growth which is flexible enough to touch the ground when bent. Where the underside touches the soil, make a cut halfway through to form a tongue. Bury this section 2-3in in the soil, peg down firmly with a U-shaped pin, and cover the split section with compost. Leave the growing tip exposed and, if possible, stake it upright. A flat stone placed over the buried section will help to hold it in position, keep it cool

and preserve moisture. In about a year's time, the wounded section should have taken root, and it can then be severed from the parent plant and replanted.

DIVIDING ROOTS AND RHIZOMES

Most herbaceous perennial plants, such as lupins, delphiniums or rudbeckias, can be propagated by division, either in spring or late autumn. Lift clumps and divide into sections. If the root clump is large and overgrown, divide it after lifting by thrusting two digging forks back to back into the centre and levering them apart. Plants with tough woody crowns may have to be split with a sharp, strong-bladed knife. Dust the cut surfaces with sulphur to prevent fungal growth. Select pieces with healthy roots and strong growth buds. Replant immediately in well-prepared ground.

Some plants, such as irises, produce swollen, horizontal stems called rhizomes. Lift clumps when they become overcrowded, and use a sharp knife to cut them apart. Select young, healthy rhizomes with a fan of leaves attached. Plant them with the rhizomes facing south – they thrive in sun – and just visible on the surface of the soil.

Water lilies have thick rhizomes; in spring, lift overcrowded clumps out of the water, clean, and divide with a sharp knife, selecting the younger growths for replanting. Each one must have several strong buds and roots.

INCREASING BULBOUS PLANTS

Both bulbs and corms reproduce by means of small offsets – known as bulbils and cormlets – which form around the sides of the parent bulb or corm during the growing season. Propagate bulbs before they become overcrowded and flower poorly. Lift the bulbs after their leaves have died back and they are dormant. Remove the bulbils and grow them for 2-3 years in a nursery bed until they reach flowering

Layering: a flexible, non-flowering stem is sliced longitudinally to form a 1-2in tongue and pegged down firmly into the soil.

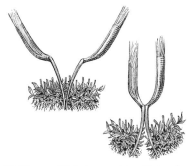

Dividing established perennials with tough crowns is easier if you use two garden forks back to back to prise clumps apart.

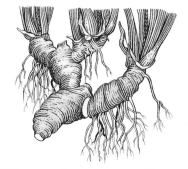

Rhizomatous plants are propagated by slicing off 2-3in long outer sections with healthy new growth and replanting them.

Cormlets form at the base of corms, bulbils at the side of bulbs; both can be separated and grown on in nursery beds.

size. Then plant them in their permanent position. Snowdrops are lifted and divided immediately after flowering, when the foliage is still green.

Lilies produce bulbils but can also be propagated by using the fleshy scales of the bulb. When the bulbs are dormant, pull off a few outer scales and place them in a moist, peat-based compost in a polythene bag. Shake the bag to ensure the scales are fully covered, secure it, and place in an airing cupboard or a propagator. When tiny bulbils have formed, plant in pots or trays for planting out in 1-3 years. Some lilies form bulbils in the axils of the leaves. Collect these in late summer and sow immediately, in pots or boxes in a cold frame or in nursery rows outside. Plant out in their final positions in 3-4 years.
CORMS AND CORMLETS Gladioli and crocuses develop new corms at the bottom of the flowering stems. These are retained and the old ones discarded when the corms are lifted after flowering. The old corms also develop cormlets which can be stored in a cool, dry place until spring (gladioli) or autumn (crocuses) and then planted in potting compost. Grow on the cormlets until autumn (or late spring for crocuses), then lift and store them for planting the following spring (or autumn for crocuses). They reach flowering size in 1-3 years.

TROUBLESHOOTING

Pests and diseases are the gardener's curse, but with care they can be controlled and their effects minimised. Sound cultivation and good feeding will provide strong, healthy plants that will be more resistant to pests and diseases.

USING CHEMICALS WITH CARE

Although, in the case of plant diseases, prevention is better than cure, blanket-spraying with chemicals is environmentally unsound. Use chemicals only when absolutely necessary, and then sparingly. If you use a chemical treatment that might also be harmful to beneficial insects, such as bees, spray very early in the morning or in very late evening when the insects are not active. Choose a time when the foliage is dry and the air still. Systemic insecticides are applied to foliage and become absorbed into the plant's system. Use them as directed on the package. It is fatal only to those insects that feed on the plant's leaves, stems, or sap and does not affect pollinating insects except at the time of application. Contact sprays, however, are non-selective, and kill both pests and beneficial insects they come into contact with. Both contact sprays and non-systemic fungicides are short-lived. Again, use them as directed.

Make sure you use the right chemical product for the specific pest, disease, and plant type. Read the container label carefully, and follow the instructions to the letter. Spray the undersides of leaves as well as the tops thoroughly, unless the manufacturer states otherwise.

Wash the sprayer before and after use, and don't store any unused diluted liquids, except those obtained ready for use as a spray. Keep all chemicals in their original containers, with the top well secured, and store them out of reach of children and pets, preferably under lock and key. Buy fresh chemicals as necessary each year, and dispose of the previous year's stock safely.

SPRING TROUBLE SPOTS

APHIDS emerge from their overwintered eggs at this time. Spray at the first real signs of infestation. Use a systemic insecticide or insecticidal soap. Also at this time protect young plants against cats. There are commercial preparations for discouraging them, and ordinary curry powder sprinkled around plants is also quite effective.

BLACK SPOT Roses, particularly those that require heavy pruning – for instance, modern roses – are prone to this fungal disease, which appears as black spots on the leaves. Regular weekly sprays of ferbam or benomyl from the time the leaves first open and expand will protect them.

CABBAGE ROOT FLIES These pests are not confined to vegetables; they will also attack stocks and wallflowers. The tiny white maggots eat the roots, causing leaves to wilt and turn a bluish colour. Before planting, dust the holes with a soil insecticide or, if plants are already in, apply it to the soil immediately around the plants before mid-spring.

CRANE FLIES The larvae, popularly known as daddy longlegs, eat roots and the base of stems of many plants. They are 2in long, grey-brown, plump, and tough-skinned. Keep them in check by dusting the soil with diazinon.

FIREBLIGHT Many woody members of the rosaceous family, such as cotoneaster and pyracantha, are prone to this bacterial disease. Leaves and flowers die and turn dark brown, as if they have been scorched by fire. There is no cure for it, and as it is very infectious, affected plants must be dug up and destroyed.

FLEA BEETLES When the leaves of wallflowers, stocks, and alyssum become pitted with small holes, these striped beetles, about ⅛in long, are the likely culprits. Keep them at bay by dusting young plants with rotenone (a natural plant extract) or sevin.

GREY MOULD If stems and flowers go mouldy, especially in damp weather, they could have this disease, also known as botrytis. Apply a systemic fungicide, repeating as necessary.

JAPANESE BEETLE GRUBS An inch long, and greyish-white with brown heads, these grubs feed on grass roots, chewing through so many that often patches of turf can be rolled back like a carpet. Inoculating the lawn with milky spore, a natural disease of the beetle, provides long-lasting control.

LEAF MINERS The grubs of this pest will tunnel inside the leaves of chrysanthemums, rhododendrons, and lilacs, leaving unsightly white tracks. Spray with chlorpyrifos, diazinon, sevin or malathion.

SCAB Pyracantha and ornamental malus are attacked by scab, which shows as brown spots on leaves and rough lesions on twigs. Spray from early spring onwards with a systemic fungicide.

SILVER LEAF This fungal infection gives the leaves of trees a silvery sheen, and they will split and turn brown. Affected branches turn brown and die back. Cut them out and burn them.

SLUGS AND SNAILS Perhaps the most common of garden pests, these gastropods cause great damage to flowers and foliage. There are slug pellets that are non-injurious to other wildlife, and liquid slug killers on the market.

SOWBUGS These grey, flat, oval-bodied creatures may feed on stems, leaves, and roots, but rarely do real damage. Regular cultivation and keeping the garden clear of plant debris will keep them at bay since they hate disturbance and light.

SPITTLEBUGS The white froth commonly known as frog spit covers the immature spittlebugs while they feed on young growth. Apply a strong water jet from a hand sprayer to dislodge them, but if they persist, spray with malathion or a systemic insecticide.

WIREWORMS These aptly named creatures – they look like pieces of wire and are almost as tough – damage the roots of most flowering plants, particularly carnations and chrysanthemums. They can be controlled by dusting the soil with diazinon, but perhaps the best and most natural way is to dig over the soil and expose them for birds to eat.

WOOLLY APHIDS Cotoneaster, pyracantha and ornamental crab apples are among the shrubs and trees at risk from these aphids, easily recognised by their small white woolly tufts. They puncture the stems and suck the sap, and also damage the bark. Get rid of them by painting the colonies with denatured alcohol.

SUMMER TROUBLE SPOTS

Among the many pests that bother the gardener during the summer months are ants which build nests in garden soil and around plant roots. Get rid of them with a proprietary ant killer.

CABBAGE WHITE CATERPILLARS The leaves of nasturtiums, wallflowers, stocks and ornamental brassicas are eaten by this green, brown or grey caterpillar. The caterpillars and egg-clusters can be picked off by hand; alternatively, spray with permethrin and dimethoate or dust with derris powder, paying particular attention to the undersides of leaves.

CAPSID BUGS These tiny creatures are ¼in long and may be green, brown or yellow. They attack herbaceous plants, leaving ragged holes and distorted tissue in young growth, and punctured buds, so that when the flowers open they are malformed. Spray with a systemic insecticide or malathion in spring if these pests attack regularly. Spraying after the damage is done is too late.

CLEMATIS DIE-BACK The cause of this disease, commonly called clematis wilt, when whole plants wilt and die for no apparent reason, is imperfectly understood. If it occurs, cut the plant back to ground level and water with a systemic fungicide. Initial planting of the clematis several inches deeper than normal allows for the development of healthy shoots beneath the surface as replacements.

CUTWORMS Plants that topple over because the stems have been eaten at soil level may have been attacked by cutworms. They are flat, soft, greeny-brown caterpillars with dark marks on each side of their 2in long bodies. Regular hoeing which will expose the creatures to frosts and birds, and keeping weeds down are preventive measures; HCH dust or bromophos can be raked into the soil around established plants that are infested.

DOWNY MILDEW There are several types of downy mildew, which is most prevalent in wet periods. Different types attack different plants, but can generally be identified by a grey mould on the undersurfaces of leaves. This can be controlled by spraying with mancozeb or copper fungicide. Systemic fungicides are of little use against downy mildews.

EARWIGS These familiar pests, with their glossy brown bodies and pincers at the tail, damage many young leaves and flowers. HCH dust or hexyl will get rid of them, or they can be enticed into upturned pots of straw placed on top of stakes and trapped. Remove and burn the infested straw every few days.

LEAFHOPPERS There are two species of this sap-sucking insect to watch out for, the pale yellow rose leafhopper and the green, red-striped rhododendron leafhopper. The insects feed on the undersurfaces of leaves, causing white flecks or mottling on the surface. Both species can be controlled by treating the plant with malathion, HCH or derris.

LEAF SPOT Disfiguring, brown, round fungal blotches appear on leaves affected by leaf spot, and as they spread invade plant tissues and destroy the cells. If not controlled quickly, leaves will shrivel and plants may die. Spray with a systemic fungicide or Bordeaux mixture.

LUPIN APHIDS These pests that appear on lupin stems are like large greenfly, but are covered with a wax coat which makes control difficult. The best way to get rid of them is to dislodge them with a strong jet of water or spray with heptenophos.

POWDERY MILDEW The fungus appears as a powdery coating on the stems and leaves of many plants during hot weather. Spray with systemic fungicide.

RED SPIDER MITES You may need a powerful hand lens to detect these tiny creatures on the underside of foliage, but their presence is indicated by the discoloration of leaves, which drop off prematurely. Treat them with malathion or douse the plants daily with cold water.

RUSTS Many types of plants are affected, especially roses, hollyhocks, hypericums, pelargoniums and sweet williams. Orange-red pustules which eventually turn black appear on the undersides of leaves, and yellow spots appear on the upper surfaces. Infected leaves should be removed and burned. Treat with propicanizole or copper fungicide.

SAWFLIES When rose leaves roll up tightly, spray them immediately with a systemic insecticide and burn infested leaves, for this is a sure sign that the larvae of the sawfly are feeding in them.

SOOTY MOULD Sap-sucking insects such as aphids and whiteflies excrete sticky honeydew which encourages the growth of this blackish fungus. Eliminate the problem by using methods described under aphids and whiteflies.

THRIPS It is the larvae of these minute brown or black insects, sometimes called thunder flies, that attack gladioli, roses and carnations and cause silver streaking on leaves and flowers. Use a systemic insecticide against them, and treat gladioli corms with HCH dust while they are in store.

VERTICILLIUM WILT This fungal disease requires drastic action. Callistephus, perennial asters and dianthus, as well as some rhus, cotinus and acers may look as if they are short of water, which gives the disease its other name of sleepy disease, but they will never recover. Dig up infected plants and destroy them, and do not put the same or any related plants in that piece of ground for several years, as the spores can survive in the soil.

WHITEFLIES The adult whitefly is a tiny, moth-like insect commonly found in greenhouses, but also known to infest outdoor plants such as rhododendrons, honeysuckles and viburnums. The young insects feed on sap and foul the leaves with a sticky excretion called honeydew, which encourages sooty mould. Control is difficult, but spraying with permethrin-based insecticides or malathion will help.

WHITE RUST Chrysanthemums may be hit by this fungal disease, which appears as round, yellowish-white pustules on the undersides of the leaves, and eventually causes premature death of the foliage. Spraying with propicanizole will prevent the disease occurring, but if it appears, destroy all affected plants.

AUTUMN TROUBLE SPOTS
As winter approaches, protect trees and shrubs, especially those newly planted, against strong winds with a windbreak material attached to strong stakes. Protect tender plants against frost with small-mesh plastic net, hessian, straw or bracken. A mulch of peat, pulverised bark or garden compost will protect roots and tubers below ground.

Heavy soil which remains wet for long periods can be detrimental to plant growth, so improve drainage before any planting is done. One answer is to add large amounts of gritty sand and organic matter to open up the soil.

There are still some pests and diseases to watch out for, especially when digging – this is the best time too for removing and burning perennial weeds.

CLUB ROOT Once this disease is in the ground it is difficult to clear. Identified by irregular swellings on the roots of wallflowers, stocks and related plants, it should not occur if you buy healthy plants. The disease is most common on wet, poorly drained soil, so improving the drainage can help. Dip the plants' roots in a systemic fungicide solution at planting time.

HONEY FUNGUS Identified by yellowish-brown toadstools or strands like boot laces in the soil around the base of a tree or shrub, this fungus can attack any plant and is very damaging. Affected plants should be lifted and burned, but get the diagnosis confirmed by an expert before destroying valuable trees and shrubs. The ground must be sterilised with an agent such as dephenolated creosote or the soil replaced before growing anything on the site again.

STEM AND BULB EELWORMS Herbaceous perennials and the bulbs of tulips, scillas and narcissi are attacked by these minute, wormlike creatures which are invisible to the naked eye. Infested bulbs feel soft around the neck and the foliage is stunted and sometimes splits. Always buy firm, dry bulbs. Destroy affected bulbs and plants, though root cuttings taken from perennials such as phloxes will be healthy. Do not, however, put any susceptible plants in infected ground for several years.

SWIFT MOTH CATERPILLARS These 1-2in long white caterpillars live underground and feed on fleshy roots and bulbs. They are often found when herbaceous borders are dug in the autumn. Dust the soil with HCH or bromophos and suppress weeds to make the border less attractive to egg-laying females.

WINTER TROUBLE SPOTS
Keep the garden tidy during winter. Decaying plant material will harbour pests such as slugs and sowbugs, and contribute to the spread of diseases.

Many pests are dormant at this time. It makes better use of your horticultural chemicals to wait and see what pests appear in spring than to spray indiscriminately with a toxic cocktail at the egg stage, which would wipe out beneficial creatures too.

Heavy snowfall on evergreens can cause them to become misshapen and their branches to break under the weight, so dislodge snow as soon as possible.

CORAL SPOT This fungal disease appears on dead or dying twigs of trees and shrubs as tiny, salmon-pink spots. It can move down into living wood, causing dieback, and will attack acers, beeches, cercis, elaeagnus, and magnolias. Remove and burn the infected wood.

DAMPING OFF This may affect seedlings that have recently germinated or have been overwintered, particularly if they were sown in unsterilised compost. Always sow in sterile compost and water all seed trays with thiram or captan after sowing and again just as seedlings appear.

DIEBACK Badly pruned and insect- or frost-damaged branches on roses and other woody plants may develop dieback. Remove and destroy the affected parts and treat the cut areas with a systemic fungicide.

MICE Young shoots, seeds, and seedlings in a cold frame or greenhouse, and bulbs in the garden, are a favourite diet of mice. Lay traps or keep a cat.

PEACH LEAF CURL Ornamental prunus are attacked by this disease. When the buds burst, the young leaves distort and eventually turn red, then thicken and later turn brown and drop off. To protect your plants, spray with Bordeaux mixture or copper fungicide in early February, and again in autumn. Collect and burn the leaves as they fall.

ENVIRONMENT-FRIENDLY CONTROL

A HEALTHY GARDEN with a wide range of plants will attract many forms of wildlife, including natural predators such as birds, ladybugs, frogs and toads. The environmental balance they bring about will keep the need for artificial pest control to the minimum. Regular hoeing between plants will not only control annual weeds but bring many pests to the surface, where birds can deal with them.

There are products available whose effect is specifically directed to a single problem or plant, or that are non-persistent – they remain active only for a short period. Many of these are derived from plants, and have a less damaging effect on the environment as a whole than all-embracing chemical fertilisers, pesticides, and fungicides.

ANTHOCORIS BUGS are 1/6in long and black-brown. They often gather on willow catkins, and eat scale insects, capsid bugs, caterpillars, and midges.

BIRDS may reduce your crop of autumn berries, but they will help to control grubs, snails, slugs, caterpillars, aphids and other pests.

CENTIPEDES sometimes shelter beneath ground cover during the day, but at night will come out to prey upon many small insects and slugs.

COPPER FUNGICIDES, including Bordeaux and Burgundy mixtures, remain effective for several weeks as a control against mildews and blights, but appear to be harmless to many beneficial insects.

FLIES can be a useful ally in the fight against insect pests. Small greyish aphid flies prey on aphids, scale insects and mealybugs; wasp-like flowerflies hover near open blossoms, searching out and

devouring aphids and other harmful insects.

FROGS AND TOADS will keep the slug population at bay, and also eat woodlice. A garden pond will provide breeding facilities for them.

GROUND BEETLES like damp, sheltered conditions during the day, but emerge at night to hunt out eelworms, larvae, and eggs of such insects as the gypsy moth.

HEDGEHOGS are partial to bread and milk, but will also leave their shelter beneath hedges or a pile of logs at night to forage for slugs, cutworms, wireworms, woodlice and millipedes.

INSECTICIDAL SOAP is a potassium-based product that is effective for only one day, but a direct hit will kill aphids, whiteflies, red spider mites, scale insects and mealybugs.

LACEWINGS produce larvae which suck the body fluids from aphids. If all the larvae produced from just one female survived, they could consume 20 million aphids in a season.

LADYBUGS, in both adult and larval stages, feed on aphids, scale insects, mealybugs, thrips, and mites.

PYRETHRUM is a non-persistent plant extract used to fight a variety of insects, including caterpillars and aphids. Also toxic to ladybugs and bees, it should be used discriminately.

DIOTOMACEOUS EARTH, the tiny, silica skeletons of ancient algae, when dusted over plants and soil, kills insects through abrasion, yet is harmless to earthworms, birds and mammals. It also has the added benefit of supplying 14 trace minerals essential to healthy plant growth.

Plant Selector

A QUICK GUIDE TO FINDING THE RIGHT PLANTS FOR YOUR GARDEN

THIS CHART PROVIDES a useful starting point for finding plants that will suit a particular situation or purpose – for example, you may be looking for a shrub that flowers in spring and will grow in a shady spot with acid soil. For easy access to the chart, the plants are listed alphabetically according to plant type – shrubs, trees, climbers, and so on. The coloured bands denote the season in which each plant is at its best – whether because of its spring blossom, autumn fruits, or coloured winter stems. By glancing along the line for each entry, you can hone down your choice even further by matching the plants' requirements to the soil and situation in your garden. Most plants tolerate a wide range of conditions; but the quality of their fruiting or flowering may tail off on either side of average conditions. For your final selection of the right plant, page numbers guide you to the illustrated main entries which contain more detailed information on each plant, companion plants, and cultivation.

For a complete index of all plants described or illustrated in the book, as well as their common names and methods of cultivation, see page 420.

KEY TO THE SYMBOLS USED IN THE CHART

SEASONS
- All seasons plants
- Spring plants
- Summer plants
- Autumn plants
- Winter plants

SOIL
- 0 Grows in ordinary soil
- D Tolerates dry soil
- M Does best in moisture-retentive to wet soil
- L Tolerates chalky or alkaline soil
- A Needs acid soil

SITUATION
- ☼ Does best in full sun
- ● Does best in shade or dappled shade
- ☼● Grows well in either sun or light shade
- ☐ Tolerates exposed, windy sites
- ■ Does best on a sheltered site

FLOWERS
1-12 equates to Jan-Dec

FRUIT
1-12 equates to Jan-Dec

LEAVES
- Aut Good autumn leaf colour
- E Evergreen
- SE Semi-evergreen

HEIGHT
Measurements are the approximate limits that can be expected in ideal conditions; tree height, for example, is the maximum in ideal conditions after 20 years. Where height is very variable according to aspect, as with camellias, the figures are omitted.

SPREAD OR PLANTING DISTANCE
Measurements are the approximate limits that can be expected in ideal conditions. Where spread varies because of habit or pruning taste (climbers and roses), figures are omitted. For non-spreading plants, such as bulbs, planting distance is given.

SHRUBS

	Soil	Situation	Flowers	Fruit	Leaves	Height	Spread or planting distance
Abelia × grandiflora 274	0	☼■	7-9		SE	5ft	5ft
schumannii 168	0	☼■	6-9			6-8ft	6-7ft
Abeliophyllum distichum 338	0	☼■	1-2			4-6ft	4-6ft
Aesculus parviflora 274	0	☼	7-8		Aut	8-10ft	10-15ft
Aronia arbutifolia 274	MA	☼●	5	9-12	Aut	6-8ft	4-6ft
melanocarpa 'Brilliant' 274	MA	☼●	5	9-12	Aut	5ft	4ft
Berberis darwinii 86	0	☼●	4-5	7-8	E	10ft	8ft
linearifolia 86	0	☼●	4-5	7-8	E	5ft	3-4ft

	Soil	Situation	Flowers	Fruit	Leaves	Height	Spread or planting distance
× rubrostilla 275	0	☼	6-7	9-12	Aut	4-5ft	4-5ft
× stenophylla 86	0	☼●	4-5		E	8ft	8ft
thunbergii 'Atropurpurea' 275	0	☼●	4-5	9-2	Aut	6ft	5ft
Buddleia alternifolia 168	0	☼	6			12ft	12ft
davidii 168	0	☼	7-8			6-8ft	6-8ft
globosa 87	0	☼●	5-6		SE	10ft	8-10ft
Callicarpa bodinieri giraldii 276	0	☼■	7	9-12	Aut	6ft	5ft
Calluna vulgaris 169	A	☼	7-10		E	1½ft	1½ft

401

SHRUBS (cont)	Soil	Situation	Flowers	Fruit	Leaves	Height	Spread or planting distance
Calluna (cont) *vulgaris* 'H.E. Beale' 276	A	☼	9-11		E	2ft	15-18in
Camellia japonica 'C.M. Hovey' 20	A	●■	3-4		E		
japonica 'Commander Mulroy' 21	A	●■	3-4		E		
japonica 'Primavera' 21	A	●■	4-5		E		
japonica 'Ruddigore' 21	A	●■	4-5		E		
japonica 'Victor Emmanuel' 21	A	●■	3-4		E		
× *williamsii* 'Anticipation' 21	A	●■	4-5		E		
× *williamsii* 'Bow Bells' 20	A	●■	2-3		E		
× *williamsii* 'Bridal Gown' 21	A	●■	4-5		E		
× *williamsii* 'Donation' 21	A	●■	3-5		E		
× *williamsii* 'Freedom Bell' 20	A	●■	3-4		E		
× *williamsii* 'Freestyle' 20	A	●■	3-4		E		
× *williamsii* 'Inspiration' 21	A	●■	3-5		E		
× *williamsii* 'Joan Trehane' 20	MA	●■	4-6		E		
× *williamsii* 'Jury's Yellow' 20	MA	●■	4-5		E		
Caryopteris × *clandonensis* 276	OL	☼	9-10			2-3ft	2-3ft
Ceanothus 'Autumnal Blue' 277	O	☼■	7-10		E	6ft	6ft
× *burkwoodii* 169	O	☼■	7-10		E	6-10ft	6-8ft

	Soil	Situation	Flowers	Fruit	Leaves	Height	Spread or planting distance
Deciduous cultivars 170	O	☼	7-9			6-8ft	5ft
'Delight' 88	O	☼■	5		E	10ft	8ft
impressus 88	O	☼■	4-5		E	8-12ft	6-10ft
thyrsiflorus 'Repens' 88	O	☼■	5-6		E	2-4ft	6-8ft
Ceratostigma willmottianum 278	OL	☼■	8-10		Aut	3ft	3ft
Chaenomeles superba 'Knap Hill Scarlet' 89	OL	☼	3-5	9-12		5-8ft	5-8ft
Chimonanthus praecox 338	OL	☼■	12			8-10ft	8-10ft
Choisya ternata 22	OL	☼■	4-5, 9		E	6ft	6-8ft
Cistus ladanifer 170	DOL	☼■	6-7		E	6ft	5ft
'Peggy Sammons' 170	OL	☼■	6-7		E	4-6ft	3-4ft
× *purpureus* 171	OL	☼■	6-7		E	3-4ft	3-4ft
Clerodendrum trichotomum fargesii 278	O	☼■	8-9	9-10		8-10ft	9ft
Clethra alnifolia 171	MA	☼	8		Aut	7ft	7ft
Cornus alba 'Elegantissima' 22	M	◐	5-6	10	Aut	8-10ft	10ft
alba 'Spaethii' 23	O	◐	5-6	10	Aut	7ft	7ft
kousa chinensis 172	O	◐	6	9-10	Aut	10-15ft	8-12ft
mas 338	O	◐	2-3	8-9		15ft	10ft
Corylopsis pauciflora 89	O	◐	3			5-8ft	4-6ft
Cotinus coggygria 'Notcutt's Variety' 278	OL	☼	7-8		Aut	8ft	8ft
Cotoneaster franchetii 279	OL	☼	6	10-12	Aut, E	5ft	5ft
lacteus 339	OL	◐	6-7	11-3	E	10ft	10-12ft
Crinodendron hookerianum 174	A	◐■	5-6		E	8-12ft	6-10ft
Cytisus battandieri 174	O	☼■	7		SE	10ft	8-10ft

KEY: SEASONS ☐ All seasons plants ☐ Spring plants ☐ Summer plants ☐ Autumn plants ☐ Winter plants

SOIL O Grows in ordinary soil D Tolerates dry soil M Does best in moisture-retentive to wet soil L Tolerates chalky or alkaline soil A Needs acid soil

SITUATION ☼ Does best in full sun ● Does best in shade or dappled shade ◐ Grows well in either sun or light shade ☐ Tolerates exposed or windy sites ■ Does best on a sheltered site

FLOWERS 1-12 equates to Jan-Dec FRUIT 1-12 equates to Jan-Dec LEAVES Aut Good autumn leaf colour E Evergreen SE Semi-evergreen

HEIGHT Eventual limits in ideal conditions after 20 years SPREAD OR PLANTING DISTANCE Approximate limits in ideal conditions

	Soil	Situation	Flowers	Fruit	Leaves	Height	Spread or planting distance
× *kewensis* 90	0	☀	5			2ft	5ft
× *praecox* 90	0	☀	4-5			4-6ft	3-5ft
Daboecia cantabrica 279	A	☀	6-11		E	15-24in	15-24in
Daphne laureola 339	0	●	2-3		E	4ft	3-4ft
mezereum 90	OL	☽	2-3	6		2-4ft	2-3ft
odora 'Aureomarginata' 340	0	☽■	2-4		E	3-5ft	3-5ft
Deutzia hybrids 174	OL	☽	6			5ft	5ft
Disanthus cercidifolius 280	MA	☽■	10		Aut	8-10ft	6-8ft
Enkianthus campanulatus 91	MA	☽	5	10-2	Aut	8-12ft	6-8ft
Erica arborea 'Alpina' 91	A	☀	3-5		E	10ft	6-8ft
australis 92	A	☀■	4-6		E	3-4ft	2-3ft
carnea 340	OL	☀	11-4		E	6-12in	1-1½ft
ciliaris 175	MA	☀	7-10		E	1ft	1½ft
cinerea 176	DA	☀	6-9		E	6-12in	1ft
× *darleyensis* 340	OL	☀	12-4		E	1½ft	2ft
erigena (syn *E. mediterranea*) 'Brightness' 92	OL	☀	3-5		E	2-4ft	2ft
tetralix 'Alba Mollis' 176	MA	☀	6-8		E	6-12in	9-15in
vagans 177	A	☀	8-11		E	1-1½ft	1½-2ft
Escallonia Donard cultivars 177	0	☀	7-8		E, SE	5-7ft	5-7ft
Euonymus alatus 281	0	☽		10	Aut	6ft	8ft
europaeus 'Red Cascade' 281	OL	☽		10-12	Aut	10ft	8ft
fortunei 'Silver Queen' 24	OL	☽	5-6		E	2-3ft	3-4ft
japonicus 'Ovatus Aureus' 25	OL	☽			E	8-10ft	6-8ft
Exochorda × *macrantha* 93	0	☀	5			8-12ft	8-12ft
Fatsia japonica 25	OL	☽	10	2-4	E	8ft	8ft
Forsythia 'Karl Sax' 93	OL	☽	3-4			8ft	8ft
suspensa 94	OL	☽	3-4			8-10ft	8-10ft

	Soil	Situation	Flowers	Fruit	Leaves	Height	Spread or planting distance
Fothergilla gardenii 281	0	☽	4-5		Aut	3ft	3ft
major 282	0	☽	4-5		Aut	6-8ft	5-6ft
Fremontodendron californicum 178	OL	☀■	5-10		E	15-25ft	8-15ft
Fuchsia 'Abbé Farges' 180	0	☽■	6-10			2-3ft	1½-2ft
'Alice Hoffman' 180	0	☽■	6-10			1½-2ft	1½-2ft
'Connie' 180	0	☽■	6-10			3-4ft	2-3ft
'Dollar Princess' 181	0	☽■	6-10			3-4ft	3-4ft
'Hawkshead' 180	0	☽■	6-10			3-4ft	3ft
magellanica gracilis 'Versicolor' 182	0	☀■	7-10			4ft	3ft
'Mission Bells' 181	0	☽■	6-10			3-4ft	2-3ft
'Navy Blue' 181	0	☽■	6-10			1½-2ft	1½-2ft
'Papoose' 181	0	☽■	6-10			1½-2ft	1½-2ft
'Santa Cruz' 180	0	☽■	6-10			3-4ft	2-3ft
'Tennessee Waltz' 181	0	☽■	6-10			3-4ft	2-3ft
'Whiteknight's Blush' 181	0	☽■	6-10			2-3ft	3ft
Garrya elliptica 341	OL	☽■	1-2	8-12	E	12ft	12ft
Gaultheria procumbens 282	A	☽	7-8	9-10	E	4-6in	2-3ft
Hamamelis × *intermedia* 'Jelena' 342	A	☽	12-3		Aut	8-10ft	8-10ft
japonica 'Zuccariniana' 94	A	☽	2-3		Aut	8-10ft	8-10ft
mollis 'Pallida' 342	A	☽	12-3		Aut	8-10ft	7-10ft
Hebe 'Autumn Glory' 282	OL	☀	8-9		E	2ft	2ft
'Marjorie' 283	OL	☀	7-9		E	3ft	4ft
pinguifolia 'Pagei' 25	OL	☀	5-6		E	3-6in	2-3ft
speciosa hybrids 182	OL	☀	7-8		E	4-5ft	4ft
Hibiscus syriacus 284	OL	☀■	8-10			6-8ft	4-6ft
Hydrangea macrophylla 'Ayesha' 287	0	●■	7-11			6ft	6ft

SHRUBS (cont)	Soil	Situation	Flowers	Fruit	Leaves	Height	Spread or planting distance
Hydrangea (cont) *macrophylla* 'Blue Wave' 287	O	●■	7-11			6ft	8ft
macrophylla 'Générale Vicomtesse de Vibraye' 286	O	●■	7-11			4ft	5ft
macrophylla 'Lanarth White' 286	O	●■	7-11			6ft	5ft
macrophylla 'Madame Emile Mouillière' 287	O	●■	7-11			4½ft	5ft
macrophylla 'Mariesii' 286	O	●■	7-11			6ft	6ft
macrophylla 'Pia' 286	O	●■	7-11			2ft	2ft
macrophylla 'Quadricolor' 287	O	●■	7-11			5½ft	5ft
paniculata 'Grandiflora' 286	O	☼■	7-11			8ft	8ft
serrata 'Preziosa' 287	O	●■	7-11			5ft	5ft
Hypericum 'Hidcote' 288	OL	☀	8-9		SE	4ft	4ft
× *inodorum* 'Elstead' 288	OL	☀	6-9	8-10	Aut	4-5ft	3-4ft
Ilex × *altaclarensis* 'Golden King' 26	OL	☀		10-3	E	12ft	8ft
Itea ilicifolia 183	OL	☀■	8-9		E	8-12ft	6-10ft
Jasminum nudiflorum 344	OL	☀□	11-3			8-10ft	6-8ft
Kalmia latifolia 26	A	☀	6		E	6-8ft	6-8ft
Kerria japonica 96	OL	☀	4-5			4-6ft	4-6ft
Kolkwitzia amabilis 183	O	☼	5-6			7-10ft	6-8ft
Lavandula angustifolia 27	OL	☼	7-8		E	2ft	2ft
Lavatera thuringiaca 'Rosea' (syn *L. olbia* 'Rosea') 184	O	☼■	7-9			6-8ft	5-7ft
Ledum groenlandicum 96	A	☼	4-6		E	2-3ft	2-3ft

	Soil	Situation	Flowers	Fruit	Leaves	Height	Spread or planting distance
Lespedeza thunbergii 288	O	☼	9-10			6ft	5-6ft
Leucothoe fontanesiana (syn *L. catesbaei*) 96	MA	●	5		Aut, E	4ft	4ft
Lonicera × *purpusii* 344	OL	☀	1-3			5-7ft	5-8ft
Magnolia grandiflora 185	OL	☼■	7-10		E	15-25ft	10-15ft
stellata 97	OL	☼■	4			6-10ft	7-12ft
Mahonia japonica 28	DO	☀	11-3		E	6-8ft	6-8ft
× *media* 29	O	☀	11-12		E	7-10ft	5-8ft
Osmanthus × *burkwoodii* (syn × *Osmarea burkwoodii*) 98	O	☀	4-5		E	7-10ft	5-8ft
delavayi 98	O	☀	4-5		E	6-10ft	6-10ft
Paeonia lutea ludlowii 98	OL	☀	5	8-10		6ft	6ft
suffruticosa (syn *P. moutan*) 99	O	●	5			4-6ft	4-6ft
Pernettya mucronata 29	A	☀	5-6	9-4	E	3ft	3ft
Philadelphus coronarius 'Aureus' 186	DOL	☀	6-7			6-10ft	5-8ft
Hybrids 186	OL	☀	6-7			3-6ft	4-6ft
Photinia × *fraseri* 'Red Robin' 30	OL	☀	5		E	8-10ft	8ft
Pieris formosa forrestii 'Forest Flame' 100	A	●■	5		E	6-8ft	6-8ft
Potentilla shrubby cultivars 187	OL	☼	5-9			1-4ft	2-4ft
Pyracantha hybrids 30	OL	☀	6	9-12	E	12ft	12ft
Rhamnus alaternus 'Argenteo-variegata' 31	OL	☼■	4	9-11	E	10ft	8ft

KEY: SEASONS ▭ All seasons plants ▭ Spring plants ▭ Summer plants ▭ Autumn plants ▭ Winter plants
SOIL O Grows in ordinary soil D Tolerates dry soil M Does best in moisture-retentive to wet soil L Tolerates chalky or alkaline soil A Needs acid soil
SITUATION ☼ Does best in full sun ● Does best in shade or dappled shade ☀ Grows well in either sun or light shade □ Tolerates exposed or windy sites ■ Does best on a sheltered site
FLOWERS 1-12 equates to Jan-Dec FRUIT 1-12 equates to Jan-Dec LEAVES Aut Good autumn leaf colour E Evergreen SE Semi-evergreen
HEIGHT Eventual limits in ideal conditions after 20 years SPREAD OR PLANTING DISTANCE Approximate limits in ideal conditions

	Soil	Situation	Flowers	Fruit	Leaves	Height	Spread or planting distance
Rhododendron 'Brocade' 34	A	●	5		E	6½ft	5ft
concatenans 35	A	●	4		E	5ft	5ft
Deciduous azaleas 100	A	●	5-6		Aut	6ft	5ft
Evergreen and semi-evergreen azaleas 101	A	●	4-5		E, SE	2-4ft	2-4ft
'Fabia' 35	A	●	5		E	6½ft	6½ft
'Hydon Dawn' 35	A	●	5		E	5ft	5ft
'Loder's White' 34	A	●	5		E	10ft	8ft
'Pink Pebble' 35	A	●	4		E	5ft	5ft
'Sennocke' 34	A	●	4-5		E	6½ft	6½ft
'St Tudy' 34	A	●	4		E	6½ft	6½ft
'Vanessa Pastel' 34	A	●	5		E	6½ft	6½ft
yakushimanum 35	A	●	5		E	5ft	5ft
Rhus typhina 288	OL	☼		10-4	Aut	8-10ft	8-10ft
Robinia hispida 188	DO	☼	5-6			6-10ft	6-8ft
Rosmarinus officinalis 36	OL	☼	4-6		E	3-4ft	3-4ft
Rubus biflorus 344	OL	◐	5-6	7-8		6-8ft	6-8ft
Ruta graveolens 'Jackman's Blue' 36	OL	☼			E	2-3ft	2-3ft
Salix gracilistyla 'Melanostachys' 345	OL	◐	2-4			6-8ft	6ft
irrorata 345	OL	◐	2-3			8ft	8ft
lanata 102	OL	◐	3-4			2-4ft	2-4ft
Salvia officinalis 36	OL	☼	6-7		E	2ft	3-4ft
Sambucus racemosa 289	OL	◐□	4	6-8		10ft	10ft
Santolina chamaecyparissus (syn S. incana) 37	OL	☼	7		E	1½-2ft	1½-2ft
Sarcococca confusa 346	0	●	1-2	2-3	E	3ft	2ft
Skimmia × 'Foremanii' 38	OL	◐	4-5	10-3	E	3-4ft	4-5ft
japonica reevesiana 38	0	◐	4-5	10-3	E	3ft	3ft

	Soil	Situation	Flowers	Fruit	Leaves	Height	Spread or planting distance
japonica 'Rubella' 38	OL	◐	4-5		E	3-4ft	4-5ft
Spiraea × arguta 103	OL	◐	5			5-6ft	5-6ft
thunbergii 103	OL	◐	3-4			4-5ft	4-6ft
Stachyurus praecox 103	0	◐	2-4			6-8ft	6-8ft
Symphoricarpos × doorenbosii 'Mother of Pearl' 289	OL	●	6-8	9-12	Aut	4-6ft	4-6ft
Symplocos paniculata 290	A	◐■	5-6	10		7-10ft	6-8ft
Syringa × josiflexa 'Bellicent' 104	OL	☼	5-6			10ft	8ft
vulgaris 104	OL	☼	5-6			10ft	10ft
Viburnum × bodnantense 'Dawn' 346	OL	◐	10-2		Aut	8-10ft	6-8ft
× burkwoodii 104	OL	◐	2-5		Aut, SE	6-8ft	6-8ft
farreri 347	OL	◐	11-3			8-10ft	7-10ft
plicatum tomentosum 105	OL	●	5-6	9	Aut	8ft	8ft
tinus 347	OL	☼□	10-3		E	6-10ft	6-8ft
Vinca major 38	OL	◐	4-6, 9		E	1-2ft	
minor 39	OL	◐	4-6		E	4-6in	
Weigela florida 188	0	☼	6			5-7ft	4-6ft

TREES

	Soil	Situation	Flowers	Fruit	Leaves	Height	Spread or planting distance
Abies balsamea 'Nana' 44	0	◐			E		
Acer capillipes 292	0	●■	5-6		Aut	15-20ft	10ft
cappadocicum 'Aureum' 293	OL	●■	5		Aut	30-40ft	15-25ft
ginnala 293	0	●■	5		Aut	10-15ft	8-10ft
grosseri hersii 293	OL	●■	4-5		Aut	10-15ft	8-12ft
japonicum 'Aconitifolium' 292	0	●■	4		Aut	8-10ft	6-8ft
japonicum 'Vitifolium' 292	0	●■	4		Aut	15-25ft	8-10ft
palmatum 292	0	●■	6		Aut	15ft	8-10ft

TREES (cont)	Soil	Situation	Flowers	Fruit	Leaves	Height	Spread or planting distance
Acer (cont)							
palmatum 'Dissectum' 292	O	●■	6		Aut	4-6ft	5-8ft
palmatum 'Osakazuki' 293	O	●■	6		Aut	10-15ft	8-10ft
palmatum 'Senkaki' (syn 'Sango Kaku') 292	O	●■	6		Aut	15ft	8-10ft
pensylvanicum 292	O	●■	5		Aut	15-20ft	10ft
rubrum 'Schlesingeri' 293	A	●■	3-4	6	Aut	25ft	10-15ft
Alnus incana 'Aurea' 347	ML	☽	2-3	11-3		15-30ft	10-15ft
Amelanchier lamarckii 40	O	☀	4-5	6-7	Aut	10-15ft	10-15ft
Arbutus × *andrachnoides* 41	OL	☀■	10-3	10-3	E	15-30ft	10-15ft
unedo 42	OL	☀■	10-12	10-1	E	10-20ft	10-20ft
Betula albo-sinensis septentrionalis 348	O	☀	4-5		Aut	18-30ft	8-15ft
utilis jacquemontii 348	M	☀	4-5		Aut	30-40ft	15-20ft
Catalpa bignonioides 'Aurea' 189	OL	☀■	7-8	9-12		15-25ft	15-25ft
Cercidiphyllum japonicum 294	M	☀■	4		Aut	40-60ft	15-20ft
Chamaecyparis lawsoniana 'Ellwood's Pillar' 44	OL	☽			E		
lawsoniana 'Minima Aurea' 45	OL	☀			E		
lawsoniana 'Pygmaea Argentea' 44	OL	☀			E		
lawsoniana 'Snow White' 44	OL	☽			E		
lawsoniana 'Treasure' 45	OL	☀			E		
pisifera 'Filifera Golden Mop' 45	OL	☀			E		

	Soil	Situation	Flowers	Fruit	Leaves	Height	Spread or planting distance
thyoides 'Ericoides' 44	OL	☽	3-4		E		
Cornus controversa 'Variegata' 190	O	☀■	6-7		Aut	8-15ft	6-10ft
florida 106	MA	☀■	5		Aut	10-15ft	8-15ft
Corylus avellana 'Contorta' 349	O	☽	1-2	10		8-10ft	6-8ft
Crataegus prunifolia 294	O	☀	5-6	10-12	Aut	12-20ft	10-18ft
Cryptomeria japonica 'Elegans' 46	ML	☀			E	8-10ft	7-10ft
Cupressus macrocarpa 'Goldcrest' 350	OL	☀			E	25-35ft	8-15ft
Davidia involucrata 190	ML	☀■	5-6			20-30ft	10-15ft
Eucalyptus gunnii 46	OL	☀■	7-10		E	45ft	20ft
pauciflora 46	OL	☀■	6-8		E	30ft	20ft
Eucryphia × *nymansensis* 'Nymansay' 191	MA	☀■	8-9		E	15-20ft	6-10ft
Gleditsia triacanthos 'Sunburst' 191	OL	☀	6-7			15-25ft	10-15ft
Juniperus communis 'Compressa' 45	OL	☽			E		
communis 'Green Carpet' 45	OL	☀			E		
communis 'Sentinel' 45	OL	☽			E		
squamata 'Blue Star' 45	OL	☽			E		
Koelreuteria paniculata 192	O	☀■	7-8	9-11	Aut	25-35ft	10-15ft
Liquidambar styraciflua 294	M	☀	5	8-12	Aut	30-60ft	15-30ft
Magnolia denudata 107	MA	☀■	4	9-10		10-15ft	8-12ft

KEY: SEASONS ☐ All seasons plants ☐ Spring plants ☐ Summer plants ☐ Autumn plants ☐ Winter plants
SOIL **O** Grows in ordinary soil **D** Tolerates dry soil **M** Does best in moisture-retentive to wet soil **L** Tolerates chalky or alkaline soil **A** Needs acid soil
SITUATION ☼ Does best in full sun ● Does best in shade or dappled shade ☽ Grows well in either sun or light shade ☐ Tolerates exposed or windy sites ■ Does best on a sheltered site
FLOWERS 1-12 equates to Jan-Dec FRUIT 1-12 equates to Jan-Dec LEAVES **Aut** Good autumn leaf colour **E** Evergreen **SE** Semi-evergreen
HEIGHT Eventual limits in ideal conditions after 20 years SPREAD OR PLANTING DISTANCE Approximate limits in ideal conditions

	Soil	Situation	Flowers	Fruit	Leaves	Height	Spread or planting distance
sieboldii 192	A	●■	5-8	9-10		6-7ft	6-7ft
sinensis 192	O	●■	5-6	9-10		8-12ft	6-8ft
× *soulangiana* 107	OL	☀■	4-5			15-25ft	10-15ft
'Wada's Memory' 108	O	☀■	4-5			10-15ft	6-10ft
wilsonii 192	O	●■	5-6	9-10		7-9ft	5-7ft
Malus 'Almey' 350	OL	☀	4-5	10-12		12-18ft	8-10ft
baccata mandschurica 108	OL	☀	4-5	9-10		15-25ft	15-20ft
'Golden Hornet' 350	OL	☀	5	9-12		10-20ft	15ft
'Red Sentinel' 350	OL	☀	5	9-3		10-20ft	10-12ft
tschonoskii 295	OL	☀	5		Aut	15-25ft	5-10ft
Nyssa sylvatica 295	MA	☀■	6	8-9	Aut	15-25ft	10-15ft
Picea glauca albertiana 'Conica' 44	O	◐			E		
pungens 'Globosa' 44	O	◐			E		
Pinus leucodermis 'Schmidtii' 45	O	◐			E		
Prunus dulcis (syn *P. amygdalus*) 108	OL	☀	2-4			15-20ft	10-15ft
'Kiku-shidare Zakura' 110	O	☀■	4			15-20ft	15-20ft
maackii 351	OL	◐■	4		Aut	18-25ft	10-15ft
mume 'Beni-shidon' 109	O	◐■	2-4			10-15ft	8-12ft
sargentii 109	OL	☀■	4		Aut	25-35ft	20-30ft
serrula 351	OL	◐■	4-5			12-18ft	12-18ft
'Shimidsu Zakura' 110	OL	☀■	5			10-15ft	10-15ft
'Shirotae' (syn *P.* 'Mount Fuji') 110	OL	☀■	4-5			18-25ft	20ft
subhirtella 'Autumnalis' 352	ML	☀■	11-4		Aut	10-15ft	8-10ft
'Tai Haku' 110	ML	☀■	4-5			20-25ft	15-25ft
'Ukon' 110	ML	☀■	4-5		Aut	15-20ft	10-20ft
× *yedoensis* 112	OL	☀■	4		Aut	20-30ft	15-25ft

	Soil	Situation	Flowers	Fruit	Leaves	Height	Spread or planting distance
Pyrus calleryana 'Chanticleer' 112	O	☀■	4		Aut	25-35ft	10-20ft
salicifolia 'Pendula' 47	OL	☀	4		Aut	8-14ft	6-10ft
Salix alba 'Britzensis' 352	ML	☀				8-10ft	6-10ft
caprea 'Kilmarnock' 47	ML	☀	2-4			4-8ft	3-6ft
daphnoides acutifolia (syn *S. acutifolia*) 353	ML	☀	2-3			10ft	6ft
matsudana 'Tortuosa' 354	ML	☀	4			15-25ft	10-15ft
Sorbus commixta 296	OL	◐	5-6	9-11	Aut	25-35ft	8-15ft
'Joseph Rock' 48	OL	☀	5	9-11	Aut	20-30ft	10-15ft
scalaris 48	OL	☀	5-6	9-11	Aut	15-20ft	10-20ft
thibetica 'John Mitchell' (syn *S. mitchellii*) 193	OL	☀□	5		Aut	20-30ft	10-20ft
vilmorinii 296	OL	◐	5-6	8-11	Aut	7-15ft	5-10ft
Stuartia pseudocamellia 48	A	◐	7-8		Aut	15-25ft	8-15ft
Styrax japonica 193	MA	◐	6		Aut	10-15ft	8-10ft
Thuja occidentalis 'Rheingold' 354	OL	☀			E	3½-5ft	2½-4ft
Trachycarpus fortunei (syn *T. excelsa*) 49	OL	◐■	5-6	10-12	E	5-12ft	4-8ft
Xanthoceras sorbifolium 113	OL	☀	5			10-15ft	5-8ft

CLIMBERS

	Soil	Situation	Flowers	Fruit	Leaves	Height	Spread or planting distance
Campsis × *tagliabuana* 'Madame Galen' 194	O	☀	7-9			20ft	
Celastrus orbiculatus 296	O	◐		9-11	Aut	40ft	
Clematis alpina 113	O	◐□	4-5	6-8		6-8ft	
armandii 114	O	☀■	3-5		E	20ft	
'Bee's Jubilee' 197	O	●	5-6, 8			10ft	
cirrhosa balearica 356	O	☀■	12-3		E	10-15ft	

CLIMBERS (cont)	Soil	Situation	Flowers	Fruit	Leaves	Height	Spread or planting distance
Clematis (cont)							
'Dawn' 197	0	☼	5-6, 8			8ft	
'Duchess of Edinburgh' 197	0	◐	6-8			8ft	
'Elsa Spath' (syn 'Xerxes') 197	0	◐	5-6, 8-9			10ft	
'Ernest Markham' 297	0	☼	6-9			10ft	
flammula 198	0	☼	8-10	9-11		10-15ft	
'Gravetye Beauty' 298	0	☼	7-9			6-8ft	
'Hagley Hybrid' 298	0	☼	7-9			8ft	
'Horn of Plenty' 196	0	☼	5-6			10ft	
× *jackmanii* 298	0	☼	7-10			10-12ft	
'Lincoln Star' 196	0	●	5-6, 9			10ft	
'Madame Baron-Veillard' 300	0	☼	8-10			15ft	
'Marie Boisselot' (syn 'Madame le Coultre') 196	0	◐	6-9			10ft	
montana 114	0	◐	4-6			30ft	
'Mrs George Jackman' 196	0	◐	5-6, 8			10ft	
'Mrs N. Thompson' 197	0	◐	6-8			12ft	
'Niobe' 197	0	◐	6-7			10ft	
rehderiana 300	0	◐	8-10			25ft	
'Richard Pennell' 196	0	◐	6-9			12ft	
'Royalty' 197	0	☼	8			8ft	
tangutica 300	0	☼	8-10	9-11		25-30ft	
'Ville de Lyon' 301	0	☼	6, 7-10			10ft	
viticella 198	0	☼	7-9			12ft	
'Vyvyan Pennell' 196	0	☼	5-6, 8			10ft	

	Soil	Situation	Flowers	Fruit	Leaves	Height	Spread or planting distance
Hedera canariensis 'Gloire de Marengo' 359	0	●			E		
colchica 'Dentata' 359	0	◐			E		
colchica 'Dentata Variegata' 359	0	☼			E		
colchica 'Sulphur Heart' 358	0	☼			E		
helix 'Atropurpurea' 358	0	◐ □			E		
helix 'Buttercup' 359	0	☼			E		
helix 'Deltoidea' 358	0	◐			E		
helix 'Glacier' 359	0	◐			E		
helix 'Goldheart' 358	0	◐			E		
helix 'Ivalace' 359	0	◐			E		
helix 'Königer's Auslese' 358	0	◐			E		
helix 'Palmata' 359	0	◐			E		
Holboellia coriacea 115	0	☼	4-5	7-9	E	15-20ft	
Jasminum officinale 199	0	◐ ■	6-9			20-30ft	
Lonicera caprifolium 199	0	◐	6-7			15-20ft	
periclymenum 200	0	◐	6-9			20ft	
periclymenum 'Serotina' 200	0	◐	7-10			20ft	
sempervirens 200	0	☼	7-9		SE	20ft	
Parthenocissus quinquefolia 302	0	◐			Aut	60ft	
Passiflora caerulea 201	0	◐ ■	7-10			20ft	
Pileostegia viburnoides 302	M	◐	8-10		E	10-15ft	
Solanum crispum 'Glasnevin' (syn *S. c. autumnale*) 201	OL	☼	6-10		SE	10-15ft	
Tropaeolum speciosum 202	MA	●	7-9	8-10		8-12ft	

KEY: SEASONS ☐ All seasons plants ☐ Spring plants ☐ Summer plants ☐ Autumn plants ☐ Winter plants
SOIL **0** Grows in ordinary soil **D** Tolerates dry soil **M** Does best in moisture-retentive to wet soil **L** Tolerates chalky or alkaline soil **A** Needs acid soil
SITUATION ☼ Does best in full sun ● Does best in shade or dappled shade ◐ Grows well in either sun or light shade □ Tolerates exposed or windy sites ■ Does best on a sheltered site
FLOWERS 1-12 equates to Jan-Dec FRUIT 1-12 equates to Jan-Dec LEAVES **Aut** Good autumn leaf colour **E** Evergreen **SE** Semi-evergreen
HEIGHT Eventual limits in ideal conditions after 20 years SPREAD OR PLANTING DISTANCE Approximate limits in ideal conditions

	Soil	Situation	Flowers	Fruit	Leaves	Height	Spread or planting distance
Vitis coignetiae 303	0	☼			Aut	50ft	
Wisteria floribunda 115	0	☼	5-6			20-30ft	
sinensis 116	0	☼	5-6			40-60ft	

ROSES

	Soil	Situation	Flowers	Fruit	Leaves	Height	Spread or planting distance
Rosa 'Albéric Barbier' 208	0	☽□	6-7, 10		SE	12-15ft	
'Aloha' 212	0	☼	6-9			6ft	
'Amber Queen' 205	0	☽	6-9			2½ft	
'Angelina' 212	0	☼	6-9			5ft	
'Ballerina' 304	0	☽	7-10			3-4ft	3-4ft
banksiae lutea 117	0	☼	5			15-25ft	
'Bonica' 213	0	☼	6-9			3ft	
'Canary Bird' 117	0	☼	5			5-7ft	5-7ft
'Champagne Cocktail' 205	0	☽	6-9			3½ft	
'Charles Austin' 213	0	☼	6-9			4-6ft	
chinensis 'Old Blush' 304	0	☼	6-12			4ft	4ft
'Climbing Arthur Bell' 208	0	☽	6-9			8ft	
'Climbing Ena Harkness' 208	0	☼	5-11			7ft	
'Climbing Iceberg' 208	0	☽	6-9			8ft	
'Compassion' 209	0	☽	6-9			8-10ft	
'Dortmund' 208	0	☽	6-10			10-12ft	
'Felicia' 212	0	☼	6-9			5ft	
'Fountain' 213	0	☽	6-9			5ft	
'Fragrant Delight' 204	0	☽	6-9			3ft	
'Frühlingsgold' 118	0	☼	5			6-8ft	6-8ft
'Frühlingsmorgen' 118	0	☼	5			5-6ft	5-6ft
glauca (syn *R. rubrifolia*) 305	0	☽	6	9-10		6-8ft	4-6ft
'Golden Showers' 208	0	☽	6-11			8ft	
'Golden Wings' 213	0	☼	6-9			6ft	
'Graham Thomas' 212	0	☼	6-9			5ft	
'Handel' 209	0	☽	6-9			8-10ft	
'Harry Edland' 205	0	☽	6-9			2½ft	
'Invincible' 205	0	☽	6-9			3ft	
'Just Joey' 204	0	☽	6-9			2½ft	
'Maigold' 118	0	☽□	5			8-12ft	
'Margaret Merril' 205	0	☽	6-9			3ft	
'Marjorie Fair' 213	0	☼	6-8			3ft	
'Mary Rose' 213	0	☼	6-9			5ft	
'Matangi' 205	0	☽	6-9			2½ft	
'Memento' 204	0	☽	6-9			2½ft	
'Mme Alfred Carrière' 208	0	☽	5-12			15ft	
'Mme Grégoire Staechelin' 306	0	☽	5-6	10		20ft	
moyesii 'Geranium' 307	0	☽	6-7	9		8-10ft	6-8ft
'New Dawn' 209	0	☽	6-10			10-12ft	
'News' 204	0	☽	6-9			2½ft	
'Paul Sherville' 204	0	☽	6-9			3ft	
'Peaudouce' 205	0	☽	6-9			4ft	
'Pink Bells' 212	0	☼	6-8			2½ft	
'Pink Perpétue' 209	0	☽	6-11			8-10ft	
'Pristine' 204	0	☽	6-9			4ft	
'Red Bells' 212	0	☼	6-8			2½ft	
'Robusta' 212	0	☼	6-9			5ft	
rugosa 307	0	☼	7-8	8-10	Aut	4-5ft	4-5ft
'Silver Jubilee' 205	0	☽	6-9			4ft	
'Summer Wine' 209	0	☽	6-9			7ft	
'Sympathie' 208	0	☽	6-9			8-10ft	

ROSES (cont)	Soil	Situation	Flowers	Fruit	Leaves	Height	Spread or planting distance
Rosa (cont)							
'The Times' 204	0	☼◐	6-9			2½ft	
virginiana 307	0	☼	7-8	9-11	Aut	3-5ft	5-7ft
'White Bells' 212	0	☼	6-8			2½ft	
'Zéphirine Drouhin' 209	0	☼	6-9			10ft	

PERENNIALS

	Soil	Situation	Flowers	Fruit	Leaves	Height	Spread or planting distance
Acanthus spinosus 214	OL	☼◐	7-9			3-4ft	3-4ft
Achillea Galaxy hybrids 214	OL	☼	6-8			2-3ft	2ft
Aconitum carmichaelii 'Arendsii' 308	ML	☼◐	9-10			4ft	2ft
napellus 215	OL	☼◐	6-8			3-5ft	2-3ft
septentrionale 'Ivorine' 215	OL	☼◐	7-8			2½-4½ft	2-3ft
Agapanthus Headbourne hybrids 215	OL	☼ ■	8	9-12		2-3ft	2ft
Ajuga reptans 49	OL	☼◐	5-7		SE	8-12in	1-1½ft
Alchemilla mollis 51	OL	☼◐	6-8			1-1½ft	2ft
Anaphalis cinnamomea 215	OL	☼	8-9			2-2½ft	3ft
Anchusa azurea 216	OL	☼	6-8			3-5ft	1½-2ft
Anemone × *hybrida* 308	OL	☼◐	8-10			2½-3½ft	2-3ft
narcissiflora 119	0	☼◐	5-6			1½ft	1½ft
Aquilegia Long-spurred hybrids 216	OL	☼◐	5-6			2-3ft	1-1½ft
vulgaris 119	OL	☼◐	5-6			2-3ft	1½-2ft
Arum italicum 'Pictum' 51	OL	☼◐	4-5	7-9		1-1½ft	1-1½ft

	Soil	Situation	Flowers	Fruit	Leaves	Height	Spread or planting distance
Asplenium scolopendrium (syn *Phyllitis scolopendrium*) 53	OL	☼◐			E	1-2ft	2ft
Aster amellus 'Violet Queen' 310	OL	☼	9-10			1½-2ft	1½-2ft
cordifolius 'Golden Spray' 311	OL	☼	9-10			2½ft	2-3ft
dumosus 'Chatterbox' 310	OL	☼	9-10			1½ft	2ft
dumosus 'Rosenwichtel' 310	OL	☼	9-10			10in	2ft
ericoides 'Pink Cloud' 311	OL	☼	9-10			2¾ft	2-3ft
ericoides 'Ringdove' 310	OL	☼	9-10			3ft	2-3ft
× *frikartii* 'Mönch' 310	OL	☼	7-10			3ft	1½-2ft
lateriflorus 'Horizontalis' 310	OL	☼	9-10			2ft	2-3ft
novae-angliae 'Alma Pötschke' 310	OL	☼	9-10			3ft	1½-2ft
novae-angliae 'Harrington's Pink' 311	OL	☼	9-10			4ft	1½-2ft
novae-angliae 'Herbstschnee' 311	OL	☼	9-10			4ft	1½-2ft
novae-angliae 'Lye End Beauty' 311	OL	☼	9-10			4½ft	1½-2ft
novi-belgii 'Chequers' 310	OL	☼	9-10			20in	1½-2ft
novi-belgii 'Fellowship' 311	OL	☼	9-10			3¼ft	1½-2ft
novi-belgii 'Royal Ruby' 310	OL	☼	9-10			1½ft	1½-2ft
turbinellus 311	OL	☼	9-10			4ft	2ft
Astilbe × *arendsii* 217	ML	●	6-8			2-4ft	1½-2ft
Astrantia major 217	OL	●	6-11			2-3ft	1½ft
Bellis perennis 120	OL	☼◐	4-6			4-6in	6-8in
Bergenia 53	OL	☼◐	3-6		E	1-1½ft	1-2ft

KEY: SEASONS ☐ All seasons plants ☐ Spring plants ☐ Summer plants ☐ Autumn plants ☐ Winter plants
SOIL **0** Grows in ordinary soil **D** Tolerates dry soil **M** Does best in moisture-retentive to wet soil **L** Tolerates chalky or alkaline soil **A** Needs acid soil
SITUATION ☼ Does best in full sun ● Does best in shade or dappled shade ☼◐ Grows well in either sun or light shade ☐ Tolerates exposed or windy sites ■ Does best on a sheltered site
FLOWERS 1-12 equates to Jan-Dec FRUIT 1-12 equates to Jan-Dec LEAVES **Aut** Good autumn leaf colour **E** Evergreen **SE** Semi-evergreen
HEIGHT Eventual limits in ideal conditions after 20 years SPREAD OR PLANTING DISTANCE Approximate limits in ideal conditions

	Soil	Situation	Flowers	Fruit	Leaves	Height	Spread or planting distance
Blechnum penna-marina 54	O	◐			E	4-10in	1-3ft
Brunnera macrophylla 121	OL	●	4-7			2ft	3ft
Campanula lactiflora 218	OL	◐	6-8			5ft	2ft
lactiflora 'Pouffe' 218	OL	◐	6-8			1½ft	1½ft
persicifolia 218	OL	◐	6		E	2-3ft	1½-2ft
Carex elata 'Aurea' (syn C. stricta 'Aurea') 56	M	☼			E	1½-2ft	1½-2ft
Centaurea hypoleuca 'John Coutts' 312	OL	☼	6-7	7-11		2ft	1½ft
Centranthus ruber 219	OL	☼	6-11			2-3ft	1½ft
Chrysanthemum indicum Pompon hybrids 312	OL	☼	10-11			2-3ft	3ft
Korean hybrids 312	OL	☼	10-11			3-4ft	2ft
maximum 219	OL	◐ □	6-9			2-3ft	2ft
Rubellum hybrids 313	O	☼	9-10			1½-2½ft	1½ft
Cimicifuga racemosa 220	M	◐	7-8			4-5ft	2-3ft
simplex 'Elstead' 313	M	●	9-10			5ft	2ft
Clematis × durandii 220	OL	◐	6-8			6-8ft	3ft
integrifolia 220	OL	◐	6-8			2-3ft	2ft
Cortaderia selloana 56	OL	☼	8-10		E	8ft	6ft
selloana 'Pumila' 56	OL	☼	8-10		E	5-6ft	4-5ft
Corydalis lutea 313	OL	◐	5-10		SE	8-12in	
ochroleuca 122	OL	◐	4-6		SE	8-12in	1-1½ft
Cynoglossum nervosum 220	OL	☼	6-7			2ft	1½-2ft
Delphinium Belladonna hybrids 314	OL	◐	6-10			5ft	2ft
Large-flowered hybrids 222	OL	☼ ■	7-8			4-7ft	2½-3ft
Dianthus 'Becka Falls' 224	OL	☼	6-7		E	9in	9-12in
'Bovey Belle' 225	OL	☼	6-7		E	12-15in	9-12in
'Cranmere Pool' 225	OL	☼	6-7		E	9in	9-12in

	Soil	Situation	Flowers	Fruit	Leaves	Height	Spread or planting distance
'Diane' 224	OL	☼	6-7		E	12-15in	9-12in
'Doris' 224	OL	☼	6-7		E	12-15in	9-12in
'Haytor' 224	OL	☼	6-7		E	12-15in	9-12in
'Houndspool Ruby' 225	OL	☼	6-7		E	12-15in	9-12in
'Joy' 225	OL	☼	6-7		E	12-15in	9-12in
'Letitia Wyatt' 224	OL	☼	6-7		E	12-15in	9-12in
'Monica Wyatt' 225	OL	☼	6-7		E	12-15in	9-12in
'Valda Wyatt' 225	OL	☼	6-7		E	12-15in	9-12in
Dicentra formosa 122	O	◐	4-7			1-1½ft	1-1½ft
spectabilis 124	O	◐	5-6			1½-2ft	3ft
Doronicum orientale 124	OL	◐	3-5			1½-2ft	1½ft
Dryopteris affinis (syn D. borreri) 56	O	●				2-4ft	3ft
Echinops ritro 226	O	☼	7-8	9-12		3-4ft	2-3ft
Epimedium × cantabrigiense 125	O	●	4		SE	1ft	1½ft
pinnatum colchicum 125	O	●	4		Aut, SE	1ft	1½-2ft
× rubrum 125	O	●	4		Aut, SE	1ft	1½ft
youngianum 'Niveum' 125	M	●	4		SE	10in	1ft
Eryngium variifolium 226	DOL	☼	7-9		E	1½ft	1ft
Euphorbia characias 57	DOL	☼	2-6			4ft	4ft
griffithii 125	OL	◐	5-6		Aut	2-3ft	3ft
polychroma (syn E. epithymoides) 126	DOL	◐	3-5			15in	2ft
Festuca glauca 59	DOL	☼	6-7		E	9-12in	9in
Foeniculum vulgare 226	DOL	☼	7-8			5-6ft	3ft
Geranium endressii 227	OL	☼	7-10			1-1½ft	1½-2ft
'Johnson's Blue' 227	OL	☼	6-7		Aut	1ft	1½ft
macrorrhizum 126	OL	◐	5-7		Aut, SE	1ft	2ft
sylvaticum 127	OL	◐	5-6			1½-2½ft	2ft

PERENNIALS (cont)	Soil	Situation	Flowers	Fruit	Leaves	Height	Spread or planting distance
Geranium (cont) *wallichianum* 'Buxton's Blue' 228	ML	◑	8-10			6-12in	2ft
Geum chiloense 228	OL	◑	6-7			1½-2ft	1½-2ft
Gypsophila paniculata 228	OL	☼	7-9			2-3ft	2ft
Hakonechloa macra 'Aureola' 59	M	◑	8-10			1ft	1-1½ft
Helenium autumnale 314	OL	☼	9-10			2-4ft	2ft
Helictotrichon sempervirens 60	OL	☼	6-7		E	3-4ft	3ft
Helleborus argutifolius (syn *H. lividus corsicus*) 60	OL	●	12-3		E	2ft	3ft
atrorubens 60	OL	●	1-7			1ft	3ft
foetidus 61	OL	●	2-4		E	1½-2ft	2ft
lividus 61	OL	●■	2-4		E	1½ft	2ft
niger 62	OL	●	1-3		E	1ft	1½ft
orientalis hybrids 62	OL	●	12-4		E	1½ft	2ft
Hemerocallis garden hybrids 229	OL	◑	7-9			1½-4ft	2-3ft
Heuchera 229	OL	◑	5-7		E	1½ft	1½-2ft
Hosta 'August Moon' 233	0	◑ ■	7			2ft	3ft
crispula 230	0	◑ ■	7			2-2½ft	2-3ft
fortunei 232	0	◑ ■	7			2-3ft	2-3ft
'Francee' 233	0	◑ ■	8-9			2ft	2-3ft
'Gold Edger' 233	0	◑ ■	7			6in	9-12in
'Golden Prayers' 233	0	◑ ■	7			9in	12-15in
lancifolia 232	0	◑ ■	6-8			1½ft	2½ft

	Soil	Situation	Flowers	Fruit	Leaves	Height	Spread or planting distance
plantaginea 315	0	◑	8-9			2ft	3ft
'Royal Standard' 233	0	◑ ■	8-9			2-3ft	3ft
sieboldiana 232	0	◑ ■	7			2ft	3-4ft
tardiflora 233	0	◑ ■	10			1½-2ft	2ft
'Thomas Hogg' 230	0	◑ ■	7-8			2-2½ft	2-3ft
undulata 230	0	◑ ■	7-8			2-2½ft	2-3ft
'Zounds' 233	0	◑ ■	6			1½-2ft	2ft
Iris foetidissima 315	OL	◑	6	11-3	E	1½ft	1½ft
pallida dalmatica 233	OL	☼	6-8			3ft	2ft
sibirica 234	ML	◑	6	8-11		3-4ft	2ft
unguicularis 63	OL	☼	11-5		E	9-12in	1½-2ft
Kirengeshoma palmata 315	MA	◑	9			4ft	2½ft
Kniphofia caulescens 316	OL	☼	9-10		E	3-5ft	3-4ft
galpinii 316	OL	☼	9-10		SE	2ft	1-1½ft
Hybrids 234	OL	☼	7-9		SE	1½-4ft	1½-3ft
'Maid of Orleans' 316	OL	☼	7-9		SE	2ft	1-1½ft
'Underway' 316	OL	☼	9-10		SE	3-4ft	3-4ft
Ligularia dentata 'Desdemona' 235	ML	◑	8			3-4ft	3-4ft
Liriope muscari 318	0	◑	9-11		E	1½ft	1-1½ft
Lobelia fulgens 318	M	◑	7-10		SE	2-3ft	1-1½ft
Lupinus × regalis 'Russell strain' 235	0	◑	6			3ft	2-3ft
Meconopsis cambrica 127	DOL	◑	5-10			1½ft	1ft
Species 236	0	●	5-7			2-3ft	2-3ft

KEY: SEASONS ☐ All seasons plants ☐ Spring plants ☐ Summer plants ☐ Autumn plants ☐ Winter plants

SOIL **0** Grows in ordinary soil **D** Tolerates dry soil **M** Does best in moisture-retentive to wet soil **L** Tolerates chalky or alkaline soil **A** Needs acid soil

SITUATION ☼ Does best in full sun ● Does best in shade or dappled shade ◑ Grows well in either sun or light shade ☐ Tolerates exposed or windy sites ■ Does best on a sheltered site

FLOWERS 1-12 equates to Jan-Dec FRUIT 1-12 equates to Jan-Dec LEAVES **Aut** Good autumn leaf colour **E** Evergreen **SE** Semi-evergreen

HEIGHT Eventual limits in ideal conditions after 20 years SPREAD OR PLANTING DISTANCE Approximate limits in ideal conditions

	Soil	Situation	Flowers	Fruit	Leaves	Height	Spread or planting distance
Miscanthus sinensis 236	ML	☼				5-8ft	3ft
Monarda hybrids 236	OL	◐	7-9			2-3ft	2ft
Nepeta × *faassenii* 237	OL	◐	6-9			1-2ft	1½ft
Oenothera tetragona 237	OL	☼	6-9			1-2ft	1-1½ft
Paeonia lactiflora 238	OL	☼	5-7		Aut	2-3ft	2-3ft
mlokosewitschii 129	OL	◑	5-6	8-9	Aut	1½-2ft	3ft
officinalis 239	OL	☼	5-6			2ft	2-3ft
Papaver orientale 239	OL	☼	6-7	7-12		2-3ft	2ft
Peltiphyllum peltatum 129	ML	◐	3-4		Aut	3-5ft	3-5ft
Penstemon hybrids 240	OL	☼■	7-10			2ft	1-2ft
Phalaris arundinacea 'Picta' 63	OL	☼	6-7			2-4ft	2-4ft
Phlox paniculata 240	OL	◐	7-9			2-4ft	1½-2ft
Phormium cookianum 63	O	☼	7-9	9-11	E	3-5ft	3-4ft
tenax 63	O	☼	7-9	9-11	E	6-10ft	6ft
Physalis alkekengi franchetii 318	OL	◐		9-11		2ft	2ft
Physostegia virginiana 319	OL	◐	8-9			1½-2½ft	1½ft
Pleioblastus viridistriatus (syn *Arundinaria viridistriata*) 64	O	◐■			E	3-5ft	3-5ft
Polemonium caeruleum 240	OL	◐	4-7			2-3ft	1½-2ft
Polygonatum × *hybridum* 130	OL	●	5-6			2-3ft	1½-2ft
Polygonum amplexicaule 241	ML	◐	7-10			4ft	3-4ft
bistorta 'Superbum' 241	OL	◐	6-7			3ft	1½-2ft
vacciniifolium 319	M	◐	8-10		Aut	3-6in	1½-2ft
Polystichum setiferum 64	OL	●			E	1-2ft	3ft
Potentilla hybrids 241	OL	☼	6-8			1½ft	1-1½ft
Primula auricula 'Old Irish Blue' 133	OL	◐	5			6-8in	6in
auricula 'Old Yellow Dusty Miller' 133	OL	◐	4-5			6-8in	6in

	Soil	Situation	Flowers	Fruit	Leaves	Height	Spread or planting distance
bulleyana 242	ML	◐	6			1½-2ft	1½ft
'Cowichan' 132	OL	◐	4-5			8-12in	10-15in
'Dawn Ansell' 133	OL	◐	3-4			6in	1ft
denticulata 132	ML	◐	3-5			6-10in	10-15in
florindae 242	ML	◐	6-7			2-3ft	2-3ft
'Garryarde Guinevere' 132	OL	◐	4-5		SE	6-10in	8-12in
'Gold Lace' 132	ML	◐	3-5		SE	6-8in	9in
helodoxa 242	ML	◐	6-7			2-3ft	1-1½ft
japonica 242	ML	◐	6			1½-2ft	1½ft
'Lady Greer' 132	OL	◐	3-5		SE	4-5in	9in
pulverulenta 242	ML	◐	6-7			2ft	1½ft
rosea 'Grandiflora' 133	ML	◐	3-4			4-8in	6-9in
sieboldii 'Snowflake' 133	O	◐	4-5			6-9in	8-12in
sikkimensis 242	ML	◐	6			1½-2ft	1½ft
vulgaris 'Miss Indigo' 132	OL	◐	3-4		SE	6in	10in
'Wanda' 133	OL	◐	3-5		SE	3-4in	9-12in
Pulmonaria angustifolia 65	OL	◐	3-7			9in	1½ft
saccharata 65	OL	◐	2-4		SE	1ft	1½ft
Ranunculus aconitifolius 134	M	●	4-5			1½-2ft	1½ft
Rheum palmatum 242	M	◐	6-8			5-6ft	4ft
Rodgersia pinnata 243	M	◐	7		Aut	3-4ft	3ft
Romneya coulteri 243	OL	☼■	7-10			4-6ft	3ft
Rudbeckia fulgida 319	OL	◐	9-10			2-3ft	1½ft
laciniata 244	OL	◐	8-9			5-7ft	2-3ft
Saxifraga fortunei 320	A	●	10-11		Aut	15in	1ft
Scabiosa caucasica 320	OL	◐	6-11			2-3ft	1½ft
Schizostylis coccinea 320	OL	☼	9-10			2-3ft	1½-2ft
Sedum 'Autumn Joy' 321	O	◐	9-12			1-1½ft	1½ft
spectabile 244	D	☼	7-10			1ft	1ft

PERENNIALS (cont)

	Soil	Situation	Flowers	Fruit	Leaves	Height	Spread or planting distance
Sidalcea malviflora 244	OL	☽	7-8			3-4ft	2ft
Smilacina racemosa 134	A	●	5-6	8-10		2-3ft	2-3ft
Solidago hybrids 245	OL	☼	8-10			3-6ft	1½-2ft
Stachys byzantina 245	DOL	☼	6-7			1-1½ft	1½ft
Symphytum grandiflorum 135	OL	☽	4-7		SE	9-12in	1½-2ft
Thalictrum aquilegifolium 246	OL	☽	5-7			2-3ft	1½-2ft
delavayi 246	O	☽	7-9			3½-5ft	2-3ft
Thermopsis montana 135	OL	☼	5-6			2ft	1½ft
Tiarella cordifolia 67	ML	●	5-6		Aut, E	6-10in	1-1½ft
Tovara virginiana 246	M	☽				2-2½ft	1½-2ft
Tradescantia × *andersoniana* 322	ML	☽	6-10			2ft	1½ft
Tricyrtis formosana 322	M	☽	9-10			2-3ft	3ft
Trillium 135	M	●	4-5			1-2ft	1-2ft
Trollius × *cultorum* 136	ML	☽	5-6			2-3ft	1½-2ft
Veronica austriaca teucrium 247	OL	☽	7			1-2ft	1-1½ft
Viola cornuta 247	OL	☽	5-11		SE	6in	1ft
Yucca filamentosa 67	OL	☼■	7-9		E	4ft	3-4ft
recurvifolia 67	OL	☼■	8-10		E	6-8ft	6ft
Zantedeschia aethiopica 248	ML	☽■	6-7			3ft	2ft

ALPINES

	Soil	Situation	Flowers	Fruit	Leaves	Height	Spread or planting distance
Acaena 'Blue Haze' 68	OL	☽		7-10	E	3-4in	1½-2ft
microphylla 68	OL	☽ □		7-10	E	1-2in	1½-2ft
Achillea tomentosa 68	OL	☽	6-8		E	6in	10in

	Soil	Situation	Flowers	Fruit	Leaves	Height	Spread or planting distance
Adonis amurensis 360	O	☽	2			10-12in	15in
Aethionema grandiflorum 69	DOL	☼	5-7		E	9-12in	1-1½ft
Androsace sarmentosa 137	O	☼	5-6		SE	3-4in	9in
Arabis caucasica (syn *A. albida*) 137	DO	☼□	2-5		E	6-9in	1-1½ft
ferdinandi-coburgii 'Variegata' 360	DO	☽	4-6		E	6-9in	9-12in
Armeria juniperifolia 69	DOL	☼	5-6		E	2-3in	6-9in
maritima 69	DOL	☼□	5-6		E	6-12in	1ft
Aubrieta deltoidea 'Variegata' 70	DOL	☼	5-6		E	4-6in	1½-2ft
Hybrids 138	O	☼	4-5		E	3-6in	1ft
Campanula cochleariifolia 249	DO	☼	6-8			3-4in	9in
garganica 249	DO	☼	7-8		E	3-4in	1ft
× *haylodgensis* 250	O	☼	7-8			6in	1ft
Daphne blagayana 138	O	☽	3-4		E	6-9in	2ft
cneorum 138	O	☼	5-6		E	6-10in	2ft
Dianthus alpinus 250	OL	☼	6-8		E	2in	9in
Hybrids 250	OL	☼	6-7		E	3-4in	9-12in
pavonius (syn *D. neglectus*) 251	OL	☼	6-7		E	3-4in	6in
Dryas × *suendermannii* 70	OL	☼	5-7		E	4-8in	1½-2ft
Erinus alpinus 139	DOL	☼	5-6		E	3-6in	6-10in
Euryops acraeus 70	O	☼	6-7		E	10-12in	15-18in
Gentiana acaulis 139	OL	☼	4-7		E	4-6in	9-12in
farreri 322	O	☽	9			4-5in	9in

KEY: SEASONS ☐ All seasons plants ☐ Spring plants ☐ Summer plants ☐ Autumn plants ☐ Winter plants
SOIL **O** Grows in ordinary soil **D** Tolerates dry soil **M** Does best in moisture-retentive to wet soil **L** Tolerates chalky or alkaline soil **A** Needs acid soil
SITUATION ☼ Does best in full sun ● Does best in shade or dappled shade ☽ Grows well in either sun or light shade □ Tolerates exposed or windy sites ■ Does best on a sheltered site
FLOWERS 1-12 equates to Jan-Dec FRUIT 1-12 equates to Jan-Dec LEAVES **Aut** Good autumn leaf colour **E** Evergreen **SE** Semi-evergreen
HEIGHT Eventual limits in ideal conditions after 20 years SPREAD OR PLANTING DISTANCE Approximate limits in ideal conditions

	Soil	Situation	Flowers	Fruit	Leaves	Height	Spread or planting distance
sino-ornata 322	A	☼	9-10		E	6in	9-12in
verna 139	O	☼	4-5		E	3in	6-8in
Geranium cinereum 'Ballerina' 251	O	◐	6-9			6-8in	12-15in
× riversleaianum 'Russell Prichard' 252	O	◐	6-9			9-12in	1-1½ft
Globularia cordifolia 71	DO	☼	6-7		E	2-4in	10in
Helianthemum nummularium 252	DO	☼	6-8		E	4-8in	1½-2ft
Hepatica transsilvanica (syn H. angulosa) 140	O	●	2-4		SE	4-5in	1ft
Hypericum olympicum 71	DOL	☼■	7-8			10-12in	1ft
Iberis sempervirens 'Snowflake' 73	O	☼	5-7		E	6-9in	1½-2ft
Lewisia cotyledon hybrids 140	DO	☼	5-7		E	8-12in	12-15in
Linum 'Gemmel's Hybrid' 253	O	☼	6-7		E	6-9in	1ft
Lithodora diffusa 253	A	☼	6-10		E	4in	2-2½ft
Oenothera missouriensis 254	O	☼	7-9			9in	1½ft
Phlox douglasii 140	DO	☼	5-6		E	2-4in	1ft
subulata 141	DO	☼	5-6		E	4-6in	15-20in
Primula frondosa 141	OL	◐	4-5			3-4in	6-8in
marginata 142	O	◐	4-5			4-6in	8-10in
× pubescens 142	O	◐	4-5		SE	4-6in	8-10in
Pulsatilla vulgaris 142	DO	☼	4-5	5-7		10in	1ft
Ranunculus gramineus 254	O	◐	5-6		SE	12-15in	9in
Saxifraga Cushion or Kabschia group 73	O	◐	2-4		E	4-6in	9-15in
Mossy group 74	O	●■	4-5		Aut, E	2-3in	8in
Silver-leaved group 74	OL	◐	6-7		E	1ft	1ft
Scabiosa columbaria 'Alpina Nana' 254	DO	☼	7-10		E	5-8in	9in

	Soil	Situation	Flowers	Fruit	Leaves	Height	Spread or planting distance
Sedum spathulifolium 75	DO	◐	6-7		E	3in	1½ft
spurium 75	DO	☼	8-9		E	4in	2ft
Sempervivum tectorum 76	DO	☼	6-7		E	6-8in	1ft
Silene schafta 324	O	◐	7-10			6in	1ft
Sisyrinchium californicum (syn S. brachypus) 324	O	◐	8-10		SE	6in	6-8in
Thymus praecox arcticus 76	DO	☼	6-7		E	2in	1ft
Viola biflora 143	O	●	4-5			4-6in	8-10in
labradorica 'Purpurea' 77	O	●	5-6		E	4-5in	6in
odorata 143	M	●	3-4		E	4-6in	1ft
Waldsteinia ternata 77	O	●	5-6		E	4in	1-1½ft
Zauschneria californica 324	DO	☼■	9-10			1ft	1½-2ft

BULBS, CORMS AND TUBERS

	Soil	Situation	Flowers	Fruit	Leaves	Height	Spread or planting distance
Allium christophii 254	O	◐	6	9-12		1-1½ft	1ft
moly 255	DO	◐	6			6-10in	4-6in
Alstroemeria aurantiaca 255	O	☼	6-7			2-3ft	1-1½ft
Amaryllis belladonna 325	O	☼■	9-10			2-2½ft	1½-2ft
Anemone blanda 144	O	◐	3			6in	6in
coronaria De Caen group 145	O	☼■	3-4			8in	6in
nemorosa 146	O	●	3-4			6-8in	6in
Chionodoxa luciliae 148	O	◐□	3-4			6in	2-4in
Colchicum agrippinum 325	O	◐	9-10			4-6in	6in
speciosum 325	O	◐	9-10			9in	8-12in
Convallaria majalis 148	O	◐	4-5	8-10		5-8in	6in
Crinum × powellii 256	O	☼■	8-9		SE	2-3ft	2-3ft
Crocosmia × crocosmiiflora 256	O	◐	8-9			1½-2ft	1ft
Crocus ancyrensis 363	O	☼	2			2-3in	2-3in

BULBS, CORMS AND TUBERS (cont)	Soil	Situation	Flowers	Fruit	Leaves	Height	Spread or planting distance
Crocus (cont)							
angustifolius 363	0	☼	2			2-3in	2-3in
chrysanthus 'Blue Pearl' 362	0	☼	2			3in	2-3in
chrysanthus 'Cream Beauty' 363	0	☼	2			3in	2-3in
chrysanthus 'Gipsy Girl' 362	0	☼	2			3in	2-3in
chrysanthus 'Ladykiller' 363	0	☼	2			3in	2-3in
chrysanthus 'Skyline' 362	0	☼	2			3in	2-3in
flavus 362	0	☼	2			4-5in	2-3in
imperati 362	0	☼	1			3-4in	2-3in
kotschyanus (syn *C. zonatus*) 326	0	☼	9-10			3-4in	2-3in
medius 326	0	☼	10-11			4-5in	2-3in
sieberi atticus 363	0	☼	2			3in	2-3in
sieberi 'Bowles White' 363	0	☼	2			3in	2-3in
sieberi 'Firefly' 363	0	☼	2			3in	2-3in
speciosus 327	0	☽	9-10			5-7in	3in
tommasinianus 'Ruby Giant' 363	0	☼	2			3-4in	2-3in
tommasinianus 'Whitewell Purple' 362	0	☼	1			3-4in	2-3in
vernus varieties 149	0	☼	3			4-5in	3in
Cyclamen cilicium 327	0	☼■	10-11			3-4in	6in
coum 364	0	●■	12-2			3in	6in
hederifolium (syn *C. neapolitanum*) 327	0	☼	9-10		SE	4-6in	8-10in
purpurascens 257	0	●	7-9		SE	4in	8-10in

	Soil	Situation	Flowers	Fruit	Leaves	Height	Spread or planting distance
Dahlia 'Alva's Doris' 330	0	☼	9			4ft	
'Biddenham Fairy' 331	0	☼	9			3½ft	
'Bishop of Llandaff' 331	0	☼	9			3½ft	
'Clair de Lune' 331	0	☼	9			3½ft	
'Daddy's Choice' 330	0	☼	9			4ft	
'David Howard' 330	0	☼	9			3½ft	
'Lady Kerkrade' 331	0	☼	9			3½ft	
'Mariner's Light' 330	0	☼	9			4ft	
'Mistill Delight' 331	0	☼	9			4½ft	
'Pearl of Heemstede' 331	0	☼	9			3½ft	
'Red Alert' 331	0	☼	9			3½ft	
'Salmon Keene' 330	0	☼	9			4½ft	
Dierama pulcherrimum 332	0	☼	9			4-6ft	1½-2ft
Endymion hispanicus 149	M	●	4-5			12-15in	6in
Eranthis hyemalis 364	0	●	1-2			4in	3-4in
Erythronium revolutum 150	M	●	4-5			1ft	4-6in
Fritillaria imperialis 150	0	☼	4			2-3ft	1-1½ft
meleagris 151	M	☼	4			8-12in	4-6in
Galanthus caucasicus 366	0	☽	1-2			6in	4-6in
elwesii 366	0	☽	1-2			6-10in	4-6in
ikariae 366	0	●	3			6-8in	4-6in
nivalis 367	M	☽	1-2			4-6in	3-4in
nivalis reginae-olgae 332	0	☼	10-11			4-6in	3-4in
Galtonia candicans 257	0	☼	8			2-3ft	9-12in
Gladiolus byzantinus 258	0	☼	6			2-3ft	6-9in

KEY: SEASONS ☐ All seasons plants ☐ Spring plants ☐ Summer plants ☐ Autumn plants ☐ Winter plants
SOIL **0** Grows in ordinary soil **D** Tolerates dry soil **M** Does best in moisture-retentive to wet soil **L** Tolerates chalky or alkaline soil **A** Needs acid soil
SITUATION ☼ Does best in full sun ● Does best in shade or dappled shade ☽ Grows well in either sun or light shade ☐ Tolerates exposed or windy sites ■ Does best on a sheltered site
FLOWERS 1-12 equates to Jan-Dec FRUIT 1-12 equates to Jan-Dec LEAVES **Aut** Good autumn leaf colour **E** Evergreen **SE** Semi-evergreen
HEIGHT Eventual limits in ideal conditions after 20 years SPREAD OR PLANTING DISTANCE Approximate limits in ideal conditions

	Soil	Situation	Flowers	Fruit	Leaves	Height	Spread or planting distance
callianthus (syn *Acidanthera bicolor murielae*) 332	O	☼	9-10			3ft	9in
Hyacinthus orientalis cultivars 151	O	☼	4			8-12in	9-12in
Ipheion uniflorum 151	DO	☼■	4-5			5-8in	3-4in
Iris danfordiae 369	O	☼	2-3			3-4in	3-4in
histrioides 'Major' 369	O	☼	1-2			3-4in	3-4in
reticulata hybrids 370	O	☼	2-3			4-6in	3-4in
xiphioides 258	O	◑	6-7			1½-2ft	6in
Leucojum autumnale 332	DO	☼	9			6-8in	3in
vernum 152	M	◑	3			6-10in	6in
Lilium 'African Queen' 261	O	◑	7-8			4-5ft	10in
'Enchantment' 261	O	◑	7			3ft	9in
'Festival' 261	O	◑	7			4ft	10in
'Golden Splendour' 260	O	◑	7			4-5ft	1ft
'Journey's End' 260	O	◑	8			3ft	12-15in
'Marilyn Monroe' 260	O	◑	7			3½-4ft	9in
'Mont Blanc' 260	O	◑	6-7			2-3ft	9in
'Pink Perfection' 261	O	◑	7			5ft	10in
regale 260	O	◑	7			4ft	1ft
'Stargazer' 261	O	◑	7-8			3-4ft	12-15in
'Sterling Star' 261	O	◑	7			3ft	1ft
tigrinum 'Splendens' 260	O	◑	8-9			4ft	1-1½ft
Muscari armeniacum 152	O	◑	4			8-10in	3-4in
Narcissus 'Actaea' 154	O	◑	4			16in	6-8in
asturiensis (syn *N. minimus*) 370	O	☼	2			3in	2-3in
'Barrett Browning' 154	O	◑	4			16in	6-8in
bulbocodium 371	O	☼	2-3			3-6in	3-4in
'Cheerfulness' 155	O	◑	4			14in	6-8in

	Soil	Situation	Flowers	Fruit	Leaves	Height	Spread or planting distance
cyclamineus 371	M	◑	2-3			6-10in	4in
'Dutch Master' 154	O	◑	3			1½ft	6-8in
'February Gold' 154	O	◑	3			14in	6-8in
'Golden Ducat' 154	O	◑	3			20in	6-8in
'Ice Follies' 154	O	◑	3			16in	6-8in
'Jack Snipe' 155	O	◑	3			9in	4-8in
'Jenny' 154	O	◑	3-4			9in	4-8in
'Minnow' 154	O	◑	4			7in	4-8in
'Passionale' 155	O	◑	4			16in	4-8in
'Professor Einstein' 155	O	◑	4			1ft	8in
'St Keverne' 155	O	◑	3			1½ft	8in
'Suzy' 155	O	◑	4			1½ft	8in
'Tete-a-Tete' 154	O	◑	4			9in	4-8in
'Thalia' 155	O	◑	4			1ft	8in
Nerine bowdenii 333	O	☼■	10			1½ft	8-10in
Puschkinia scilloides 156	O	☼	3-4			4-6in	3in
Scilla bifolia 156	O	☼	3			4-6in	3in
mischtschenkoana (syn *S. tubergeniana*) 372	O	◑	2-3			3-6in	3-4in
Sternbergia lutea 333	DO	☼■	9-10			4-6in	4-6in
Tulipa 'Aladdin' 161	O	☼	5			20in	6in
'Amulet' 160	O	☼	4			22in	6-8in
'Apricot Beauty' 160	O	☼	4			16in	6in
'Charles' 160	O	☼	4			15in	6in
clusiana 156	O	☼	4			9-12in	3in
'Dutch Princess' 160	O	☼	4			22in	6-8in
'Esperanto' 160	O	☼	4			9in	6-8in
'Estella Rijnveld' 161	O	☼	5			2ft	6-8in
'Flaming Parrot' 161	O	☼	5			26in	6-8in

BULBS, CORMS AND TUBERS (cont)	Soil	Situation	Flowers	Fruit	Leaves	Height	Spread or planting distance
Tulipa (cont)							
'Golden Artist' 160	0	☼	5			10in	6-8in
Greigii hybrids 157	0	☼□	4			9-12in	6in
'Gudoshnik' 161	0	☼	4			26in	6-8in
'Hermione' 161	0	☼	4			20in	6in
kaufmanniana 157	0	☼	3			6-10in	6in
'Keizerskroon' 160	0	☼	4			1ft	4-6in
'Marilyn' 161	0	☼	5			22in	6in
'Monte Carlo' 160	0	☼	4			16in	6in
'Pax' 161	0	☼	4			22in	6-8in
'Prominence' 161	0	☼	4			1½ft	6-8in
'Queen of the Night' 161	0	☼	5			2ft	6-8in
'Red Parrot' 161	0	☼	5			22in	6-8in
'Snow Queen' 160	0	☼	4			11in	6in
tarda 157	0	☼	4			4-6in	3in
Zephyranthes candida 333	0	☼■	9-10			6-8in	4-6in

ANNUALS AND BIENNIALS

	Soil	Situation	Flowers	Fruit	Leaves	Height	Spread or planting distance
Ageratum houstonianum 265	OL	☼	6-9			6-12in	6-12in
Agrostemma githago 'Milas' 263	OL	☼	6-9			2-3ft	9in
Amaranthus caudatus 265	OL	☼	7-10			3-4ft	1½ft
Antirrhinum 263	OL	☼	6-9			8-36in	9-12in
Bartonia aurea 263	DOL	☼	6-9			1½ft	9in
Begonia semperflorens 265	OL	☽	6-10			6-12in	6-9in

	Soil	Situation	Flowers	Fruit	Leaves	Height	Spread or planting distance
Brassica oleracea 263	OL	☽				1½-2ft	1½ft
Callistephus chinensis 265	OL	☼	7-10			8-30in	6-18in
Campanula medium 263	OL	☼	6			2-3ft	1½ft
Cheiranthus cheiri 162	OL	☼	4-5			9-18in	9-12in
Chrysanthemum parthenium 'Aureum' 263	OL	☼	7-10			1½-2ft	1ft
Clarkia 263	OL	☼	7-8			1½-2ft	9in
Coreopsis 263	OL	☼	7-10			1¼-2ft	9-12in
Cosmos bipinnatus 265	OL	☽	7-9			2-3ft	1-1½ft
sulphureus 265	OL	☽	7-9			2-3ft	1-1½ft
Dahlia 265	OL	☼	7-9			1-2ft	1-1½ft
Dianthus barbatus 263	OL	☼	6			1½-2ft	10-12in
chinensis 265	OL	☼	7-10			9-12in	6-9in
Digitalis purpurea 263	OL	☽	6			3-5ft	1½-2ft
Eschscholzia californica 264	DOL	☼	7-8			12-15in	6in
Gazania 265	DOL	☼	6-10			9in	12in
Godetia 264	OL	☼	7-8			1-2ft	6in
Helichrysum petiolare 265	DOL	☼	6-10			9-12in	2ft
Heliotrope 266	OL	☼	6-10			1½ft	12-15in
Impatiens walleriana 266	0	☽	6-9			10-24in	9-15in
Ionopsidium acaule 264	0	☽	7-8			2-3in	4in
Lathyrus odoratus 266	OL	☽	6-8			1-6ft	6-10in
Lavatera trimestris 264	OL	☼	7-8			2-2½ft	1ft
Layia platyglossa 264	OL	☼	7-9			1-1½ft	10in
Lobelia erinus 266	OL	●	6-9			4-5in	4in

KEY: SEASONS ▭ All seasons plants ▭ Spring plants ▭ Summer plants ▭ Autumn plants ▭ Winter plants
SOIL O Grows in ordinary soil D Tolerates dry soil M Does best in moisture-retentive to wet soil L Tolerates chalky or alkaline soil A Needs acid soil
SITUATION ☼ Does best in full sun ● Does best in shade or dappled shade ☽ Grows well in either sun or light shade □ Tolerates exposed or windy sites ■ Does best on a sheltered site
FLOWERS 1-12 equates to Jan-Dec FRUIT 1-12 equates to Jan-Dec LEAVES Aut Good autumn leaf colour E Evergreen SE Semi-evergreen
HEIGHT Eventual limits in ideal conditions after 20 years SPREAD OR PLANTING DISTANCE Approximate limits in ideal conditions

	Soil	Situation	Flowers	Fruit	Leaves	Height	Spread or planting distance
Lunaria annua 372	OL	●	4-6	10-1		2-3ft	1ft
Lupinus 'Pixie Delight' 264	O	☼	7-9			1ft	6in
Matthiola bicornis 264	OL	◐	6-8			1ft	4in
Mimulus 266	ML	◐	6-8			6-12in	6-9in
Moluccella laevis 266	OL	☼	7-9			3ft	9-12in
Myosotis 162	OL	◐	4-5			1ft	9in
Nicotiana 266	OL	◐	7-9			2ft	1ft
Nigella damascena 'Miss Jekyll' 264	OL	☼	6-9	7-9		1½-2ft	6in
Ocimum basilicum 'Dark Opal' 266	OL	☼	7-9			1½-2ft	9-12in
Papaver nudicaule 264	OL	☼	6-8			1½-2ft	1ft
Pelargonium 'Blandfordianum' 268	OL	☼	6-10			1½ft	2ft
crispum 'Variegatum' 269	OL	☼	6-10			1½ft	10in
× *domesticum* 'Miss Australia' 269	OL	☼	6-10			2½ft	2½ft
× *domesticum* 'South American Bronze' 269	OL	☼	6-10			2ft	2ft
× *hortorum* 'Alba' 269	OL	☼	6-10			1ft	1ft
× *hortorum* 'Alcyone' 269	OL	☼	6-10			8in	8in
× *hortorum* 'Bridesmaid' 268	OL	☼	6-10			9in	9in
× *hortorum* 'Double Skies of Italy' 268	OL	☼	6-10			1½ft	1ft
× *hortorum* 'Golden Ears' 269	OL	☼	6-10			8in	8in
× *hortorum* 'Rio' 268	OL	☼	6-10			10in	10in
peltatum 'Duke of Edinburgh' 269	OL	☼	6-10			2ft	
peltatum 'Mini-cascades' 268	OL	☼	6-10			1½ft	
Petunia 266	OL	☼	6-9			9-15in	1ft
Phacelia campanularia 264	OL	☼	6-9			9in	6in
Reseda odorata 264	OL	◐	6-8			1-2½ft	6-9in
Tropaeolum majus 264	OL	☼	6-9			1¼-6ft	10-15in
Verbena 266	OL	☼	6-9			6-12in	9in
Viola × *wittrockiana* 'Clear Crystal Mixed' 375	OL	●	11-5			6in	6-9in
× *wittrockiana* 'Crystal Azure Blue' 375	OL	●	11-5			6in	6-9in
× *wittrockiana* 'Imperial Pink Shades' 374	OL	●	11-5			6in	6-9in
× *wittrockiana* 'Imperial Silver Princess' 375	OL	●	11-5			6in	6-9in
× *wittrockiana* 'Joker Light Blue' 374	OL	●	11-5			6in	6-9in
× *wittrockiana* 'Majestic Giants Mixed' 375	OL	●	11-5			6in	6-9in
× *wittrockiana* 'Supremo Early' 375	OL	●	11-5			6in	6-9in
× *wittrockiana* 'Universal Purple' 374	OL	●	11-5			6in	6-9in
× *wittrockiana* 'Universal Red' 374	OL	●	11-5			6in	6-9in
× *wittrockiana* 'Universal White' 374	OL	●	11-5			6in	6-9in
× *wittrockiana* 'Universal Yellow' 375	OL	●	11-5			6in	6-9in

PICTURE CREDITS

The pictures in *A Garden for all Seasons* were supplied by the people listed below. Names given in italics refer to illustrations that are Reader's Digest copyright. The owners of gardens featured in the photographs are credited in brackets.

T top; *C* centre; *B* bottom; *L* left; *R* right.

COVER *artist Gill Tomblin.* 11 *artist Roy Knipe.* 12, 13 *Line On Line.* 14, 15 *artist Roy Knipe.* 16-17 S & O Mathews. 18 *artist Ann Winterbotham*, *TC* Neil Holmes, *TR* Tania Midgley. 19 *TL* Tania Midgley *TR* Eric Crichton. 20-21 *Laurie Evans.* 22 *artist Gill Tomblin*, *TL* John Glover, *TR* Tania Midgley. 23 *TL* Andrew Lawson, *TR* S & O Mathews. 24 *TL* Biofotos, *TC* Eric Crichton, *TR* Tania Midgley. 25 *artist Gill Tomblin*, *TC* Andrew Lawson, *TR* Eric Crichton. 26 *artist Ann Winterbotham*, *TL* Photos Horticultural Picture Library, *TC* Bruce Coleman/Eric Crichton. 27 *TL* Georges Lévêque, *TR* Andrew Lawson. 28 *artist Sarah Fox-Davies*, *TL* Harry Smith Collection, *TR* Georges Lévêque. 29 *artist Sarah Fox-Davies*, *TC* Eric Crichton, *TR* John Glover. 30 *artist Leonora Box*, *TL* Beckett Picture Library, *TC,TR* Andrew Lawson. 31 *artist Leonora Box*, *TC,BC* Andrew Lawson. 32 *artist Gill Tomblin*, *TL* Tania Midgley, *TR Margaret Turner.* 33 *artist Gill Tomblin*, *TL* S & O Mathews (Yew Tree Cottage, W Sussex), *TR* S & O Mathews. 34-35 *artist Leonora Box.* 36 *artist Helen Haywood*, *TL* Eric Crichton (Lord & Lady Carrington), *TC,TR* Photos Horticultural Picture Library. 37 *TL* Georges Lévêque, *TC,TR* Harry Smith Collection. 38 *artist Helen Haywood*, *TL* Tania Midgley, *TC* Andrew Lawson, *TR Margaret Turner.* 39 *artist Ann Winterbotham*, *TR* S & O Mathews (Yew Tree Cottage, W Sussex). 40 *artist Julie Banyard*, *TL Jerry Harpur*, *TC* Harry Smith Collection, *TR* Tania Midgley. 41 *artist Ann Winterbotham*, *TL* Andrew Lawson, *TR* Derek Gould. 42 *artist Gill Tomblin*, *TL* Harry Smith Collection. 43 *TR,BL* Elizabeth Whiting, *CL* Elizabeth Whiting/Jerry Harpur. 44-45 *Laurie Evans.* 46 *artist Leonora Box*, *TL* Harry Smith Collection, *TR* Tania Midgley. 47 *artist Leonora Box*, *TL* Tania Midgley, *BR* Photos Horticultural Picture Library. 48 *artist Leonora Box*, *TL* Andrew Lawson, *TR* Derek Gould, *CR* Tania Midgley. 49 *TL artist Leonora Box*, *CR artist Gill Tomblin*, *TC* Eric Crichton, *TR* Beckett Picture Library. 50 *artist Gill Tomblin*, *C* Eric Crichton. 51 *TL* Georges Lévêque, *TC,TR* Harry Smith Collection. 52 *artist Gill Tomblin*, *TC* Eric Crichton. 53 *artist Ann Winterbotham*, *TL* Beckett Picture Library, *TR* Biofotos, *C,CR* Eric Crichton. 54 *TL* Photos Horticultural Picture Library, *TC* Beckett Picture Library, *BR* Andrew Lawson. 55 *TL,TR* Andrew Lawson. 56 *artist Ann Winterbotham*, *TL* Georges Lévêque, *TC* Photos Horticultural Picture Library. 57 *TL,TR* Andrew Lawson. 58 *artist Gill Tomblin*, *TR* The Garden Picture Library/Marijke Heuff (Branklyn, Perth). 59 *artist Gill Tomblin*, *TL* John Glover, *TR* Georges Lévêque, *BC* Andrew Lawson. 60 *artist Helen Haywood*, *TL,C* Tania Midgley, *TC* Margaret Turner. 61 *TL* Photos Horticultural Picture Library, *TR S & O Mathews.* 62 *artist Helen Haywood*, *TR,BR* Andrew Lawson. 63 *artist Helen Haywood*, *CL* Natural Image, *TC* The Garden Picture Library/Brian Carter, *TR* The Garden Picture Library/Ron Sutherland. 64 *artist Helen Haywood*, *TL,CL* Andrew Lawson, *TR* Eric Crichton, *CR* Margaret Turner (Dr & Mrs N Millward). 65 *artist Julie Banyard*, *TL* Bruce Coleman/Eric Crichton, *TC* Eric Crichton, *TR artist Gill Tomblin.* 66 *artist Gill Tomblin*, *TL* Georges Lévêque. 67 *artist Brenda Katté*, *TL,TR* Tania Midgley. 68 *artist Gill Tomblin*, *TC* Andrew Lawson, *TR* Photos Horticultural Picture Library, *CL* Beckett Picture Library. 69 *artist Gill Tomblin*, *TL,CR* Beckett Picture Library. 70 *artist Brenda Katté*, *TL* Bruce Coleman/Eric Crichton, *TC,C* Eric Crichton, *TR* Beckett Picture Library. 71 *artist Brenda Katté*, *TL* Natural Image, *TC* Harry Smith Collection, *TR* Eric Crichton. 72 *artist Wendy Bramall*, *TC* Eric Crichton (Mrs M E Pinto). 73 *artist Ann Winterbotham*, *TL Tania Midgley*, *TC Eric Crichton*, *CS* & O Mathews. 74 *artist Julie Banyard*, *TL* Eric Crichton, *TR* Duncan Lowe. 75 *artist Julie Banyard*, *TL* Georges Lévêque, *TR* Eric Crichton. 76 *artist Julie Banyard*, *TL* The Garden Picture Library/Brian Carter, *TR* Beckett Picture Library, *C* Tania Midgley. 77 *artist Brenda Katté*, *TL* Harry Smith Collection, *TR* Beckett Picture Library. 78 *C* Andrew Lawson. 79 *C* Andrew Lawson. 80 *TL,TR* Elizabeth Whiting/Jerry Harpur. 81 *TL,BR* Christine Ternynck. 82 *TL* Andrew Lawson. 82-83 *C* Andrew Lawson. 83 *TR* Andrew Lawson. 84-85 Elizabeth Whiting/Jerry Harpur. 86 *artist Wendy Bramall*, *TC Eric Crichton.* 87 *TL* Georges Lévêque, *TR* Pat Brindley. 88 *artist Ann Winterbotham*, *TL* Bruce Coleman/Eric Crichton, *C* Photos Horticultural Picture Library. 89 *artist Ann Winterbotham*, *TL* Eric Crichton, *TR* Impact/Pamla Toler. 90 *TL* Tania Midgley, *TR* Andrew Lawson. 91 *artist Kevin Dean*, *TL,C* Tania Midgley, *TC* S & O Mathews, *TR* Bruce Coleman. 92 *TL* Tania Midgley, *TR* Harry Smith Collection. 93 *artist Kevin Dean*, *TL* Harry Smith Collection. 94 *artist Shirley Felts*, *TL* Harry Smith Collection, *TC* John Glover. 95 *artist Gill Tomblin*, *TL* Eric Crichton (Mrs R R Merton). 96 *artist Helen Haywood*, *TL* Bruce Coleman/Eric Crichton, *TC* Georges Lévêque, *TR* Photos Horticultural Picture Library. 97 *artist Helen Haywood*, *TL* Eric Crichton. 98 *artist Shirley Felts*, *TC* Beckett Picture Library, *TR* Harry Smith Collection. 99 *artist Shirley Felts*, *TL* Tania Midgley, *CR* Eric Crichton. 100 *artist Ann Winterbotham*, *TC,C* Pat Brindley, *TR* Tania Midgley. 101 *artist Ann Winterbotham*, *TR* Eric Crichton (Mrs C Hardy), *CL* Elizabeth Whiting. 102 *artist Wendy Bramall*, *TL* Tania Midgley, *CR* Georges Lévêque. 103 *TL* Bruce Coleman/Eric Crichton, *TR* Derek Gould, *C* Harry Smith Collection. 104 *artist Nicki Kemball*, *TC* Tania Midgley, *TR* Andrew Lawson. 105 *TL* Georges Lévêque, *TR* Harry Smith Collection, *BL* Beckett Picture Library. 106 *artist Wendy Bramall*, *TR* Harry Smith Collection, *BR* Biofotos. 107 *TL,BL* Beckett Picture Library, *TR* Tania Midgley. 108 *artist Wendy Bramall*, *TL,TR* Tania Midgley, *CR* Eric Crichton. 109 *artist Wendy Bramall*, *TL* Harry Smith Collection, *TR* Neil Holmes, *BR* Tania Midgley. 110 *TL* S & O Mathews, *TC* Tania Midgley. 111 *artist Wendy Bramall*, *TL* Andrew Lawson. 112 *artist Helen Haywood*, *TL* Andrew Lawson, *TR* John Glover. 113 *TL* Georges Lévêque, *TR* Eric Crichton. 114 *artist Helen Haywood*, *TL* Margaret Turner (Savill Gardens), *TC* Andrew Lawson. 115 *artist Helen Haywood*, *TL* S & O Mathews, *TR* Bruce Coleman, *CL* Tania Midgley. 116 *TL* Harry Smith Collection, *TR* Neil Holmes. 117 *artist Sally Smith*, *TC* Georges Lévêque, *TR* Tania Midgley. 118 *TL* Tania Midgley, *TR* Derek Gould, *BC* Tania Midgley. 119 *TL artist Sally Smith*, *TC artist Helen Haywood*, *TR* Margaret Turner. 120 *TL* Eric Crichton, *BR* Andrew Lawson. 121 *artist Gill Tomblin*, *TR* The Garden Picture Library/Didier Willery. 122 *artist Wendy Bramall*, *TL* Bruce Coleman/Eric Crichton, *TC* Natural Image, *TR* Harry Smith Collection. 123 *artist Wendy Bramall*, *TC* The Garden Picture Library. 124 *artist Kevin Dean*, *TL* Photos Horticultural Picture Library, *TR Margaret Turner.* 125 *artist Kevin Dean*, *TC* Pat Brindley, *TR* Biofotos, *C* The Garden Picture Library/Brian Carter. 126 *artist Gill Tomblin*, *TL* Biofotos, *CR* Andrew Lawson. 127 *artist Gill Tomblin*, *TL* Eric Crichton, *TC* S & O Mathews. 128 *artist Gill Tomblin*, *TL* Pat Brindley. 129 *artist Helen Haywood*, *C* Elizabeth Whiting/Jerry Harpur. 130 *artist Ann Winterbotham*, *TL* Biofotos, *TC* Andrew Lawson. 131 *artist Ann Winterbotham*, *TL* Tania Midgley, *TR* Beckett Picture Library, *CR* Biofotos. 132-3 *artist Ann Winterbotham.* 134 *artist Kevin Dean*, *TL* Photos Horticultural Picture Library, *TR* The Garden Picture Library/Ron Sutherland (Beth Chatto Gardens). 135 *TL* Bruce Coleman/Eric Crichton, *TC* Pat Brindley, *TR* Margaret Turner (Savill Gardens). 136 *artist Kevin Dean*, *TL* Eric Crichton, *CR* Elizabeth Whiting/Jerry Harpur. 137 *artist Gill Tomblin*, *TL* Andrew Lawson, *TC* Eric Crichton, *BR* Harry Smith Collection. 138 *artist Nicki Kemball*, *TL* Andrew Lawson, *TR* Eric Crichton. 139 *artist Nicki Kemball*, *TL* Eric Crichton, *TC* Pat Brindley. 140 *artist Nicki Kemball*, *TC* Photos Horticultural Picture Library, *TR* Biofotos. 141 *artist Nicki Kemball*, *TL,TC* Eric Crichton, *TR* Photos Horticultural Picture Library. 142 *artist Ann Winterbotham*, *TR* Elizabeth Whiting, *CL* Beckett Picture Library. 143 *artist Ann Winterbotham*, *TL* Tania Midgley, *TR* The Garden Picture Library/Vaughan Fleming, *CL* Andrew Lawson. 144 *TC* Georges Lévêque, *BR* Andrew Lawson. 145 *artist Wendy Bramall*, *TR* Photos Horticultural Picture Library. 146 *artist Ann Winterbotham*, *TL* Tania Midgley, *TR Tania Midgley.* 147 *artist Ann Winterbotham*, *TC,BC Eric Crichton.* 148 *TL,TR* Eric Crichton, *C* John Glover. 149 *artist Barbara Walker*, *TR* Beckett Picture Library, *C* Eric Crichton. 150 *artist Helen Haywood*, *TC* Tania Midgley, *TR Margaret Turner.* 151 *artist Helen Haywood*, *TC* The Garden Picture Library/Brigitte Thomas, *TR Margaret Turner.* 152 *TL artist Nicki Kemball*, *BR artist Gill Tomblin*, *TC Tania Midgley.* 153 *artist Gill Tomblin*, *CR* Tania Midgley, *CL* Elizabeth Whiting/Jerry Harpur, *BR* S & O Mathews. 154-5 *Laurie Evans.* 156 *artist Nicki Kemball*, *TL* Photos Horticultural Picture Library, *TC* Eric Crichton, *TR* Andrew Lawson. 157 *artist Nicki Kemball*, *TC* Photos Horticultural Picture Library, *TR,CL* Eric Crichton. 158 *TL* S & O Mathews. 158-9 *C* Christine Ternynck. 159 *artist Nicki Kemball*, *TR* Andrew Lawson, *BR* Lady Skelmersdale. 160-1 *Laurie Evans.* 162 *artist Gill Tomblin*, *TC* Eric Crichton, *C* Andrew Lawson. 163 *artist Gill Tomblin*, *TL* Andrew Lawson, *TR* Eric Crichton. 164 *C* Eric Crichton (Mrs M Fuller). 165 *TR* Elizabeth Whiting/Jerry Harpur. 166-7 Margaret Turner (Mrs M Mann). 168 *artist Wendy Bramall*, *TR* Tania Midgley, *C* Bruce Coleman/Eric Crichton. 169 *artist Wendy Bramall*, *TL* Derek Gould, *TR* Andrew Lawson. 170 *artist Wendy Bramall*, *TC* Tania Midgley, *TR* Derek Gould. 171 *artist Wendy Bramall*, *TL* Georges Lévêque. 172 *TL* Pat Brindley, *TR* Photos Horticultural Picture Library. 173 *TL artist Wendy Bramall.* 174 *artist Kevin Dean*, *TL,TC* Georges Lévêque. 175 *TL* Eric Crichton, *TR* Beckett Picture Library. 176 *artist Kevin Dean*, *TL* Pat Brindley, *TC* Eric Crichton. 177 *artist Kevin Dean*, *TL* Eric Crichton, *TC* Tania Midgley, *TR* Harry Smith Collection. 178 *TL* Tania Midgley, *TR* Andrew Lawson. 179 *artist Leonora Box*, *TL* Eric Crichton, *TR* Tania Midgley. 180-1 *artist Helen Haywood.* 182 *artist Leonora Box*, *TL* Tania Midgley, *TC* Photos Horticultural Picture Library. 182-3 *TR* Beckett Picture Library. 183 *TC* Natural Image/Robin Fletcher, *TR* Georges Lévêque. 184 *artist Sarah Fox-Davies*, *TR* S & O Mathews (Barnsley House, Glos). 185 *artist Sarah Fox-Davies*, *TR* Georges Lévêque. 186 *TL* Bruce Coleman/Eric Crichton, *TR* Georges Lévêque. 187 *artist Leonora Box*, *TL* Tania Midgley, *TC* S & O Mathews. 188 *artist Wendy Bramall*, *TL* John Glover. 188-9 *TR* Eric Crichton. 189 *TR* Tania Midgley, *BC* Harry Smith Collection. 190 *artist Helen Haywood*, *TL* John Glover, *TC* Photos Horticultural Picture Library. 191 *artist Helen Haywood*, *TR* Georges Lévêque. 192 *artist Wendy Bramall*, *TL* Derek Gould, *TR* Pat Brindley. 193 *TL* Beckett Picture Library, *TR* Tania Midgley, *CR* Andrew Lawson. 194 *artist Wendy Bramall*, *TR* Andrew Lawson. 195 *artist Wendy Bramall*, *TL* Tania Midgley, *TR* Eric Crichton (Mrs A E Pedder). 196-7 *Laurie Evans.* 198 *TL* Beckett Picture Library, *TR* Photos Horticultural Picture Library. 199 *artist Nicki Kemball*, *TC* Georges Lévêque, *TR* Photos Horticultural Picture Library. 200 *artist Helen Haywood*, *TL* Tania Midgley, *TR* Eric Crichton. 201 *artist Helen Haywood*, *TL* Tania Midgley, *TR* Eric Crichton. 202 *artist TL,C Julie Banyard*, *TC* Georges Lévêque, *artist TR Gill Tomblin*, 203 *artist Gill Tomblin*, *TL*, *TR* Photos Horticultural Picture Library. 204-5 *Laurie Evans.* 206 *artist Gill Tomblin*, *TR* Tania Midgley. 207 *C* Andrew Lawson. 208-9 *Jacqui Hurst.* 210 *artist Gill Tomblin*, 210-11 *C* Elizabeth Whiting/Jerry Harpur, *TR* Elizabeth Whiting/Jerry Harpur, *BR* The Garden Picture Library/Roger Hyam. 212-13 *Jacqui Hurst.* 214 *artist Kevin Dean*, *TC* Tania Midgley. 215 *artist Kevin Dean*, *TC*

Andrew Lawson, *TR* Photos Horticultural Picture Library. 216 *artist* *Nicki Kemball*, *TL* The Garden Picture Library/Brian Carter, *TC* Natural Image/Liz Gibbons. 217 *artist* *Leonora Box*, *TR* Eric Crichton. 218 *artist* *Nicki Kemball*, *TR* Eric Crichton (Barnsley House, Glos). 219 *artist* *Nicki Kemball*, *TL* Georges Lévêque, *TR* The Garden Picture Library/Karin Craddock. 220 *artist* *Leonora Box*, *TR* Photos Horticultural Picture Library, *TC* Tania Midgley. 221 *artist* *Gill Tomblin*, *TL* Eric Crichton (Barnsley House, Glos). 222 *artist* *Gill Tomblin*, *TL* Andrew Lawson, *TR* Harry Smith Collection. 223 *artist* *Gill Tomblin*, *TR* Harry Smith Collection, *CL* Photos Horticultural Picture Library. 224-5 *artist* *Sarah Fox-Davies*. 226 *artist* *Ann Winterbotham*, *TC* Photos Horticultural Picture Library. 226-7 *TR* The Garden Picture Library/Marijke Heuff. 227 *artist* *Ann Winterbotham*, *TR* Tania Midgley. 228 *artist* *Nicki Kemball*, *TC* Margaret Turner, *TR* Georges Lévêque. 229 *artist* *Nicki Kemball*, *TL* Georges Lévêque, *TR artist* *Leonora Box*. 230 *TL* Beckett Picture Library, *TR* The Garden Picture Library/Ron Sutherland. 231 *artist* *Leonora Box*. 232 *artist* *Gill Tomblin*, *TL* Andrew Lawson, *CR* Eric Crichton (Mrs A Stevens). 233 *artist* *Sarah Fox-Davies*, *TR artist* *Nicki Kemball*, *TL* Eric Crichton (Mr & Mrs W McWilliam), *TC* Photos Horticultural Picture Library. 234 *artist* *Gill Tomblin*, *TC* Andrew Lawson, *TR* The Garden Picture Library/Brian Carter. 235 *artist* *Gill Tomblin*, *TL* Eric Crichton, *C* Photos Horticultural Picture Library. 236 *artist* *Wendy Bramall*, *TL* Photos Horticultural Picture Library, *CR* Andrew Lawson. 237 *artist* *Wendy Bramall*, *TL* Photos Horticultural Picture Library. 238 *artist* *Gill Tomblin*, *TL* Elizabeth Whiting. 239 *TL* Tania Midgley, *TR* S & O Mathews. 240 *artist* *Nicki Kemball*, *TL* Photos Horticultural Picture Library, *TC* Eric Crichton. 241 *TL* The Garden Picture Library/Marijke Heuff (Royal Botanic Gardens, Edinburgh), *TR* Beckett Picture Library. 242 *artist* *Nicki Kemball*, *TL* Elizabeth Whiting. 242-3 *TR* Eric Crichton (Mrs A Stevens). 243 *artist* *Barbara Walker*, *TR* Eric Crichton. 244 *artist* *Gill Tomblin*, *TC* The Garden Picture Library/David Russell. 245 *TL* Eric Crichton, *TR* S & O Mathews. 246 *artist* *Wendy Bramall*, *TL* Pat Brindley, *TC* The Garden Picture Library/Marijke Heuff. 247 *TL* Photos Horticultural Picture Library, *TR* Natural Image/Bob Gibbons. 248 *artist* *Gill Tomblin*, *TR* Elizabeth Whiting/Jerry Harpur. 249 *artist* *Leonora Box*, *TC* Eric Crichton. 250 *artist* *Nicki Kemball*, *TC* Beckett Picture Library, *TR* Eric Crichton. 251 *artist* *Barbara Walker*, *TR* Eric Crichton, *C* Beckett Picture Library. 252 *artist* *Wendy Bramall*, *TL* Eric Crichton, *TR* S & O Mathews. 253 *artist* *Wendy Bramall*, *TL* S & O Mathews, *TR* Andrew Lawson. 254 *artist* *Ann Winterbotham*, *TC* Eric Crichton. 255 *artist* *Ann Winterbotham*, *TL* Eric Crichton (Mrs R R Merton), *TR* Andrew Lawson. 256 *artist* *Ann Winterbotham*, *TL* S & O Mathews (Cobblers, E Sussex), *TR* S & O Mathews. 257 *artist* *Ann Winterbotham*, *TL* Neil Holmes, *TR* Georges Lévêque. 258 *artist* *Ann Winterbotham*, *TC* Tania Midgley. 259 *artist* *Ann Winterbotham*, *TR* Georges Lévêque, *C* Tania Midgley. 260-1 *Martin Langfield*. 262 *TR* Eaglemoss Publications/Eaglemoss/Eric Crichton. 263 *artist* *Wendy Bramall*, *TC 1st left* Tania Midgley, *TC 2nd left* Bruce Coleman/Eric Crichton, *C 1st left* Eric Crichton, *C 2nd left* Georges Lévêque, *Agrostemma* Pat Brindley, *Brassica* Georges Lévêque, *Clarkia* Eric Crichton, *Coreopsis* Beckett Picture Library, *Digitalis* The Garden Picture Library/Marijke Heuff (Royal Botanic Gardens, Edinburgh). 264 *Eschscholzia* Tania Midgley, *Lavatera* Georges Lévêque, *Matthiola* Pat Brindley, *Phacelia* Pat Brindley, *Reseda* Photos Horticultural Picture Library, *Godetia* Andrew Lawson, *Layia* Photos Horticultural Picture Library, *Nigella* Eric Crichton, *Ionopsidium* Beckett Picture Library, *Lupinus* Tania Midgley, *Papaver* The Garden Picture Library/Brian Carter, *Tropaeolum* Andrew Lawson. 265 *artist* *Ann Winterbotham*, *Amaranthus* Derek Gould, *Dianthus* Beckett Picture Library, *Begonia* Eric Crichton (Fitz House), *Gazania* Andrew Lawson, *Ageratum* Tania Midgley, *Callistephus* Eric Crichton, *Cosmos*

Andrew Lawson, *Dahlia* Elizabeth Whiting, *Helichrysum* Beckett Picture Library. 266 *artist* *Gill Tomblin*, *Heliotrope* Georges Lévêque, *Lobelia* Pat Brindley, *Impatiens* Eric Crichton, *Mimulus* Andrew Lawson, *Lathyrus* Eric Crichton, *Moluccella* Andrew Lawson, *Ocimum* Tania Midgley, *Petunia* Andrew Lawson, *Verbena* Margaret Turner (The Priory, Kemerton). 267 *TR* S & O Mathews. 268-9 *Jacqui Hurst*. 270 *C* Eric Crichton (RHS, Wisley), *BL* Michael Boys/Jacqui Hurst. 271 *TR* Eric Crichton (RHS, Chelsea). 272-3 The Garden Picture Library/Brian Carter. 274 *artist* *Ann Winterbotham*, *TC* Andrew Lawson. 274-5 Tania Midgley. 275 *artist* *Ann Winterbotham*, *TR* Andrew Lawson, *BR* John Glover. 276 *artist* *Sarah Fox-Davies*, *TL* John Glover, *TC* Harry Smith Collection. 277 *artist* *Sarah Fox-Davies*, *TL* Beckett Picture Library, *TR* John Glover. 278 *artist* *Jane Reynolds*, *TL* Photos Horticultural Picture Library, *TC* Eric Crichton. 278-9 Andrew Lawson. 279 *artist* *Ann Winterbotham*, *TR* Natural Image/Bob Gibbons, *BL* Andrew Lawson. 280 *artist* *Jane Reynolds*. 280-1 *C* Christine Ternynck (Princess Sturdza's Garden, Le Vasterival), *artist* *Jane Reynolds*, *TC* Biofotos, *TC* S & O Mathews. 282 *artist* *Ann Winterbotham*, *TL* Tania Midgley, *TR* Georges Lévêque, *CL* John Glover. 283 *artist* *Ann Winterbotham*, *TR* Biofotos. 284 *artist* *Sarah Fox-Davies*, *TR* S & O Mathews. 285 *TR* Harry Smith Collection, *BL* Eric Crichton (Mrs A E Pedder). 286-7 *artist* *Barbara Walker*. 288 *artist* *Ann Winterbotham*, *TL* Tania Midgley, *TC* Harry Smith Collection. 289 *artist* *Ann Winterbotham*, *TL* Andrew Lawson, *TR* S & O Mathews. 290 *artist* *Ann Winterbotham*, *CL* Photos Horticultural Picture Library. 290-1 *C* Tania Midgley. 291 *artist* *Leonora Box*, *TR* Tania Midgley, *C* Georges Lévêque. 292-3 *Jacqui Hurst*. 294 *artist* *Leonora Box*, *TL* Harry Smith Collection, *TR* Andrew Lawson. 295 *artist* *Leonora Box*, *TL* Tania Midgley, *TR* Andrew Lawson. 296 *artist* *Leonora Box*, *TL* John Glover. 297 *artist* *Leonora Box*, *TL* Photos Horticultural Picture Library, *TR* The Garden Picture Library/Didier Willery. 298 *artist* *Leonora Box*, *TR* Tania Midgley. 299 *C* Jerry Harpur. 300 *artist* *Gill Tomblin*, *TL* Guernsey Clematis Nursery, *TC* Andrew Lawson, *TR* Pat Brindley. 301 *TL* Andrew Lawson, *TR* Eric Crichton. 302 *artist* *Gill Tomblin*, *TL* Tania Midgley. 303 *TC,BC* S & O Mathews (Barnsley House, Glos), *TR* Biofotos. 304 *TR* Beckett Picture Library, *C* Eric Crichton. 305 *artist* *Gill Tomblin*, *TL* Jerry Harpur. 306 *artist* *Gill Tomblin*, *TL* Andrew Lawson, *TR* Harry Smith Collection. 307 *artist* *Gill Tomblin*, *TL* Georges Lévêque, *TC* Impact/Pamla Toler. 308 *artist* *Catherine Slade*, *TC* Tania Midgley, *TR* Georges Lévêque. 309 *TR* Harry Smith Collection, *BC* Andrew Lawson. 310-11 *Jacqui Hurst*. 312 *artist* *Sophie Allington*, *TL* Harry Smith Collection, *TC* Derek Gould, *TR* Eric Crichton. 313 *artist* *Ann Winterbotham*, *TL* Georges Lévêque, *TR* Derek Gould, *TR* Beckett Picture Library. 314 *artist* *Sophie Allington*, *TR* Eric Crichton, *C* Pat Brindley. 315 *artist* *Ann Winterbotham*, *TL* Photos Horticultural Picture Library, *TR* Harry Smith Collection. 316 *artist* *Gill Tomblin*, *TL,TC* Harry Smith Collection. 317 *artist* *Gill Tomblin*, *TR* Eric Crichton (Mrs R R Merton). 318 *artist* *Leonora Box*, *TL* John Glover, *TR* Biofotos. 319 *artist* *Leonora Box*, *TC* The Garden Picture Library/Brian Carter, *TR* Andrew Lawson, *C* The Garden Picture Library. 320 *artist* *Leonora Box*, *TL* Harry Smith Collection, *TR* Tania Midgley, *CL* Photos Horticultural Picture Library. 321 *TL* Andrew Lawson, *TR* S & O Mathews. 322 *artist* *Leonora Box*, *TL* Pat Brindley, *TC* Georges Lévêque, *CR* Tania Midgley. 323 *artist* *Leonora Box*, *TR* Harry Smith Collection. 324 *artist* *Leonora Box*, *TL* Beckett Picture Library, *TR* Tania Midgley. 325 *artist* *Barbara Walker*, *TC* Tania Midgley, *TR,CR* Beckett Picture Library. 326 *TL* Eric Crichton, *CL* Andrew Lawson, *BR* Eric Crichton. 326-7 *artist* *Barbara Walker*. 327 *TC* Lady Skelmersdale, *TR* Biofotos, *C* Beckett Picture Library. 328 *artist* *Sarah Fox-Davies*, *TR* John Glover. 329 *TR* Tania Midgley, *BC* The Garden Picture Library/Marianne Majerus. 330-1 Jacqui Hurst. 332 *artist* *Ann Winterbotham*, *TL* Photos Horticultural Picture

Library, *TC* Harry Smith Collection, *TR* Andrew Lawson. 333 *artist* *Barbara Walker*, *TL* Elizabeth Whiting, *TR* Harry Smith Collection. 334 *C* Natural Image/Liz Gibbons. 335 *TR* Eric Crichton/(B J Honeysett Esq). 336-7 The Garden Picture Library/Roger Hyam. 338 *artist* *Gill Tomblin*, *TR,C* Harry Smith Collection. 339 *artist* *Gill Tomblin*, *TL* Eric Crichton. 340 *artist* *Gill Tomblin*, *TL* Eric Crichton, *TR* S & O Mathews, *C* Harry Smith Collection. 341 *artist* *Gill Tomblin*, *TR* Elizabeth Whiting/Jerry Harpur, *C* Harry Smith Collection. 342 *artist* *Gill Tomblin*, *TL* Georges Lévêque, *TC* Biofotos, *TR* S & O Mathews. 343 *artist* *Gill Tomblin*, *TC* John Glover. 344 *artist* *Helen Haywood*, *TL* Andrew Lawson, *TC* Natural Image/Liz Gibbons. 345 *artist* *Ann Winterbotham*, *TL* John Glover, *TC* Photos Horticultural Picture Library. 346 *artist* *Ann Winterbotham*, *TC* Tania Midgley. 347 *artist* *Ann Winterbotham*, *TL* Tania Midgley, *TC* Georges Lévêque, *C* Photos Horticultural Picture Library. 348 *artist* *Ann Winterbotham*, *TR* The Garden Picture Library/Didier Willery. 349 *TL* Derek Gould, *TR* Harry Smith Collection, *CR* S & O Mathews. 350 *artist* *Ann Winterbotham*, *TC* Georges Lévêque, *TR* Andrew Lawson, *BC* Derek Gould. 351 *artist* *Ann Winterbotham*, *TL* Tania Midgley, *TR* Eric Crichton. 352 *artist* *Ann Winterbotham*, *TL,BL* Andrew Lawson, *TR* Eric Crichton (Ness Botanic Gardens). 353 *TL* Harry Smith Collection, *TR* Photos Horticultural Picture Library. 354 *artist* *Sarah Fox-Davies*, *TL,TC* Harry Smith Collection. 355 *artist* *Sarah Fox-Davies*, *TL* John Glover. 356 *TC* Beckett Picture Library, *C* Andrew Lawson. 357 *artist* *Gill Tomblin*, *TL* Margaret Turner, *TR* Beckett Picture Library. 358-9 *Laurie Evans*. 360 *artist* *Ann Winterbotham*, *TL* Biofotos, *TR* Eric Crichton. 361 *TL* Photos Horticultural Picture Library, *TR* S & O Mathews (RHS, Wisley). 362-3 *artist* *Shirley Felts*. 364 *artist* *Barbara Walker*, *TL* Eric Crichton (Mrs R R Merton), *TC* Natural Image. 365 *artist* *Barbara Walker*, *TL* Eric Crichton (Mrs R R Merton). 366 *artist* *Julie Banyard*, all Photos Horticultural Picture Library. 367 *artist* *Brenda Katté*, *TL* Michael Boys/Jacqui Hurst, *TC* Impact/Pamla Toler, *TR* Beckett Picture Library. 368 *artist* *Sarah Fox-Davies*, *TR* Andrew Lawson. 369 *artist* *Sarah Fox-Davies*, *TL* Pat Brindley, *TR* Andrew Lawson. 370 *TL* Andrew Lawson, *TC* Photos Horticultural Picture Library, *TR artist* *Sophie Allington*, *C artist* *Ann Winterbotham*. 371 *artist* *Ann Winterbotham*, *TL* Tania Midgley, *TR* Bruce Coleman/Eric Crichton, *CL* Jerry Harpur (Beth Chatto). 372 *artist* *Brenda Katté*, *TR* Andrew Lawson. 373 *artist* *Sarah Fox-Davies*, *TL* Georges Lévêque, *TR* Harry Smith Collection. 374-5 *Jacqui Hurst*. 376 *C* Harry Smith Collection, *BR* Michael Boys. 377 *TR* Beckett Picture Library. 378-400 *artist* *Roy Knipe*.

TYPESETTING Apex Computersetting, London
SEPARATIONS J Film Process Limited, Bangkok, Thailand; Studio One Origination Limited, London
PAPER Townsend Hook Limited, Snodland
PRINTING AND BINDING Fabrieken Brepols NV, Turnhout, Belgium

40-199-1